CRITICAL INSIGHTS

The Canterbury Tales

by Geoffrey Chaucer

CRITICAL INSIGHTS

The Canterbury Tales

by Geoffrey Chaucer

Editor
Jack Lynch
Rutgers University

Salem Press
Pasadena, California   Hackensack, New Jersey

Cover photo: The Granger Collection, New York

Published by Salem Press

© 2011 by EBSCO Publishing
Editor's text © 2011 by Jack Lynch
"The *Paris Review* Perspective" © 2011 by Benjamin Lytal for *The Paris Review*

∞ The paper used in these volumes conforms to the American National
Standard for Permanence of Paper for Printed Library Materials, Z39.48-1992
(R1997).

Library of Congress Cataloging-in-Publication Data
The Canterbury tales, by Geoffrey Chaucer / editor, Jack Lynch.
    p. cm. — (Critical insights)
Includes bibliographical references and index.
ISBN 978-1-58765-723-8 (vol. 1 : alk. paper)
    1. Chaucer, Geoffrey, d. 1400. Canterbury tales. 2. Christian pilgrims and
pilgrimages in literature. 3. Tales, Medieval—History and criticism. I.
Lynch, Jack (John T.)
    PR1874.C35 2010
    821'.1—dc22
                                                                    2010030223

PRINTED IN CANADA

Contents_____

The Book and Author_____

Critical Contexts_____

Critical Readings_____

Resources

About This Volume

Jack Lynch

Geoffrey Chaucer has been at the heart of the English canon of literary masterpieces for as long as there has been a canon, ever since critics and publishers began sorting through the English literary heritage in the seventeenth century. The British Library holds more than two thousand books by or about Chaucer, and another two dozen or so are added every year—to say nothing of about eighty journal articles, forty book chapters, and eight or nine doctoral dissertations each year. Only a small handful of English works have generated more learned commentary; the volume of the scholia is staggering.

Much of this scholarship, to be fair, is written for specialists and approachable only by professional academics. Many of the books and essays written on Chaucer require a knowledge of languages, history, and theology that few modern readers have. But even if we exclude the specialized and technical scholarship, there is still abundant material for the reader of *The Canterbury Tales*, subjecting Chaucer to every conceivable variety of criticism. This volume does not have room for even a single essay on each tale, let alone multiple essays that would allow us to see the *Tales* from multiple points of view. It does, however, offer a sampling of essays that are both incisive and accessible to those who are not professional medievalists.

A series of wide-ranging overviews of Chaucer's works and career open the volume. After my own introduction, Judith Laird provides a biographical sketch of the historical Geoffrey Chaucer and Benjamin Lytal, writing on behalf of *The Paris Review*, offers a perspective on Chaucer's popularity. Next, a section titled "Critical Contexts" presents several introductory essays. Dominick Grace surveys the popular and critical reception of *The Canterbury Tales*, and Matthew J. Bolton's essay, "Chaucer's Inferno," shows some of Chaucer's characteristic techniques of reworking his source materials, in this case from Dante and Giovanni Boccaccio: what we expect to be conventional turns out to be original. Rosemary M. Canfield Reisman serves up a useful overview of the kinds of topics that feminist readers have turned up in the *Tales* in the past three decades, and Lewis Walker describes how Chaucer translated the history and culture of fourteenth-century England into the *Tales*.

A longer section, "Critical Readings," which contains samples of critical close readings from a number of schools of thought, follows and opens with several essays about Chaucer's poetic persona. The General Prologue of the *Tales* is recounted by a character named Geoffrey Chaucer, who accompanies the other tale-tellers on their pilgrimage and who tells *The Tale of Sir Thopas* and *The Tale of Melibee*. It is tempting to treat the real-world Chaucer and the poem's Chaucer as one and the same, but it turns out there are any number of points of divergence between them. Figuring out the relationship between the two has been one of the most urgent tasks of Chaucer scholarship.

The earliest essay reprinted in this volume is also one of the most influential in twentieth-century Chaucer studies. E. Talbot Donaldson was for decades one of the world's leading medievalists; he combined the rigors of traditional philological scholarship with the interpretive techniques of the New Criticism. In "Chaucer the Pilgrim," first published in 1954, he turns his attention to the narrative voice that structures the *Tales* as a whole. Donaldson reminds us that "Chaucer the pilgrim" is a *fictional* character, one created by the historical Geoffrey Chaucer in his capacity as the poet Chaucer, and he insists that we keep the three distinct. Chaucer the character, Donaldson argues, writes in the tradition of "the fallible first person singular"—a narrator whose words we cannot always take at face value.

Donald R. Howard clearly had Donaldson's title in mind when he called his own essay "Chaucer the Man." Howard is interested in the connections among the three figures that Donaldson seeks to separate: Chaucer the pilgrim, Chaucer the man, and Chaucer the poet. For Howard, the historical Geoffrey Chaucer—"this man, whom we feel that we know . . . a real and living presence in his works"—is the reason the pilgrim persona is so compelling. He offers a brief history of our culture's interest in the personality of authors from the Middle Ages to the present, and in the process invites questions about the nature of authorship itself. He concludes that "the Chaucer we know is a creation of our own response to his works," arguing that this imagined Chaucer "is no less the *real* Chaucer."

Just as Howard begins with a glance back to Donaldson, H. Marshall Leicester, Jr., opens his essay by citing Howard, though he qualifies some of that critic's claims in the light of poststructural theory. Leicester considers Howard's discussion of the narrator's "unimpersonated artistry"—the sense he gives that a tale is "not memorized but told impromptu," as if the characters speak spontaneously in verse—and uses this notion to open a discussion of "the conviction, often unspoken, that at some point it becomes necessary to move beyond or away from the pilgrim narrators of the *Canterbury Tales* and to identify the poet himself as the source of meaning." But where Howard finds the real, historical Chaucer, Leicester finds "incompleteness," "indeterminacy," and "the resistance to classification." And where Howard is confident that the Chaucer he finds is real, Leicester considers the speaker of the *Tales* to be "as fictional as the pilgrims."

Barbara Nolan too revisits some of the territory of Donaldson's and Howard's essays in an essay first published in 1986. Her attention is, like Donaldson's, on Chaucer's poetic persona; she pays particular attention to the General Prologue. Poetic prologues had a long tradition in the fourteenth century, but Chaucer's take on the familiar genre is "entirely unexpected"; in his prologue, Nolan states, we encounter "not one voice of the poet but three major attempts at authorial voicing," and she works to make sense of these voices by contextualizing them in medieval arguments about the nature of poetry. By reading the General Prologue and being attentive to the different voices, we come to understand what it meant to be a poet in fourteenth-century England.

Glending Olson approaches the framing device from a different angle—instead of investigating the nature of the narrator, he reminds us that the pilgrims tell their tales as part of a contest, and the whole narration is therefore a kind of game. "Considering medieval views of play and game," he argues, "will give us a more comprehensive and nuanced understanding of the inner Canterbury frame than we presently have." By tracing conceptions of play from Aristotle through Thomas Aquinas to Boccaccio, he argues that the collection as a whole presents "an image of social and secular conviviality that establishes itself as a norm for most of the pilgrimage but ultimately degenerates."

Interpretations of the individual tales prove just as complex as investigations of the poet's persona. Douglas Brooks and Alastair Fowler together take up the first of the pilgrims' narratives, *The Knight's Tale*, and open with the simplest possible question: "What is the tale about?" After surveying a few answers offered by other critics, they are still left with the question, "Can a literary work whose intention is so doubtful" be called "a good, perhaps a great, poem"? They advance their own argument in two parts, one having to do with the tale's organization, the other with its techniques of characterization.

Martin Stevens, in "'And Venus Laugheth,'" begins by considering the history of critical disagreement regarding *The Merchant's Tale*. Readers have clashed over how to interpret this tale for decades. As Stevens writes, some "find it an embittered, poisonous, mordant revelation of an ill-humored narrator," while others "see it as a spirited, extravagantly ironic satire in which the traditional *senex amans* [old man in love] is the subject of biting, yet gladsome ridicule." By asking a few questions about how we are to make sense of Chaucerian irony—Which passages are we to read ironically, and when are we to take Chaucer at his word?—Stevens attempts to navigate a path through the previous commentaries. His essay reminds us that to read Chaucer well—as much as to read Jonathan Swift or Jane Austen well—one needs to be exceptionally sensitive to ironies of many sorts, and irony is a recurring concern of many of the essays collected here.

Much of the groundbreaking feminist scholarship of the 1970s was concerned with the rediscovery of women authors; for as long as this was the case, Chaucer—the archetypal dead white European male—seemed to offer little to a feminist critic. In the 1980s, however, critics began realizing just how much material *The Canterbury Tales* offers for feminist readings. Katharina M. Wilson, for instance, in "*Figmenta* vs. *Veritas*," begins with the once-commonplace belief that "medieval literature is notoriously misogynistic" but then goes on to question the usefulness of this generalization. Chaucer's Wife of Bath, Alisoun, wonders what would happen "if wommen hadde writen stories"; Wilson takes the question seriously. She offers an answer to the question by turning to two actual writing women of the Middle Ages, comparing and contrasting Chaucer's portrait of a sharp-tongued woman with a tenth-century German nun, Hrotsvit of Gandersheim, and a fourteenth-century Venetian poet, Christine de Pizan. Wilson's title alludes to the lies—*figmenta*—about women, which can be countered only by the truth, or *veritas*.

Susan Crane, in an essay written two years after Wilson's, offers another feminist reading of the Wife of Bath, focusing particularly on the relationship between the character's prologue and her tale. Crane, convinced that "the history of cultural beliefs can contribute to an understanding" of fictions, works to understand the place of antifeminist ideology in fourteenth-century England. Chaucer's fiction, she writes, may not tell us much about "the daily working and living conditions of women" in his day, but it does help us to understand "the ways men and women conceived their situations."

While the Wife of Bath has prompted most of the feminist criticism of Chaucer, other tales have also been the subjects of feminist readings. Cathy Hume reads *The Franklin's Tale*, with its unusual departure from some of the conventions of courtly love, as "a story of a loving marriage struggling to survive in a world of changing social relations." In this reading, Chaucer himself is a proponent of "an egalitarian marriage ideal," one that, despite the exotic setting and magical atmosphere of the tale, he tests against "real world circumstances."

While many modern readers are inspirited by the Wife of Bath's seeming anticipation of many feminist principles, not all of Chaucer's tales are so easy to embrace today—some are positively unsavory. *The Prioress's Tale*, for instance, presents the modern reader with any number of ethical difficulties. On one hand, it is a beautifully crafted work of literature; on the other, it is an expression of "a particularly troubling form of medieval anti-Semitism." Greg Wilsbacher confronts this difficulty head-on, approaching *The Canterbury Tales* through a "translation" by R. M. Lumiansky that was published for a mass market in 1948. Acutely aware of this version's origins—it appeared just a few years after the end of World War II, when the world had come to realize the horrors of the Holocaust, and it was written by a Jewish scholar who had served in the French military—Wilsbacher argues that it "illustrates that ethical conflicts do exist for modern readers of medieval texts," and he invites us to consider a modern Chaucerian's responsibility to competing interests.

Lumiansky explained that "the present day reader has modern reactions in literature," and, as a result, *The Prioress's Tale* "possesses an unpleasantness which overshadows its other qualities"—the tale is "ruined" by its similarity to "the anti-Semitic propaganda which was current in Nazi Germany."

Steven F. Kruger also reads *The Prioress's Tale* for its attitudes toward Jews, but instead of contextualizing it in the twentieth century, he seeks to understand it in a medieval context—specifically, the conceptions of the physical body that were circulating in the fourteenth century. Christianity's complicated relationship to the body—a relationship often marked by deep discomfort—informs Kruger's reading of the depiction of the wicked Jews in the tale.

A different relation to the body shows up in Mark Miller's reading of the bawdy *Miller's Tale*. The famous naughty joke at the center of Chaucer's fabliau, in which Alisoun presents "hir hole" for Absolon to kiss, leads Miller to note that "there are after all several holes conflated here," which raises questions about "gender identity and erotic desire." The tale challenges our notions about "natural" eroticism, and the "masculine, antifeminist, and heteronormative bias" that the narrator brings to the story. Rita Copeland, too, takes the body as her subject in her study of *The Pardoner's Tale*. Taking the linkage of "sexuality, disciplining of the body, and the discipline of rhetoric" through "the political text of rhetoric's institutional history" as her starting point, she argues that the Pardoner's indeterminate sexuality makes him a product "of the metaphorical tradition of rhetoric as unregulated sexuality."

Christianity was at the center of Chaucer's mental life, and a number of essays in this collection explore the religious meanings and contexts of the *Tales*. In his learned meditation on *aventure*, Lawrence Warner explores the relation of Christian thought to exploration of the wider world. "Adventure" was taking on new meanings in Chaucer's day—the questing knights of romance were giving way to merchants seeking new trade routes. By examining the connections between the military and the mercantile, all the while remembering that all of this adventuring took place against a Christian background, Warner offers a new reading of *The Man of Law's Tale*, one thoroughly contextualized in the intellectual, economic, and cultural life of its time.

David Wallace takes a different approach to historical contextualization, focusing not on what is in the text but on what is excluded. Chaucer was born in London, and modern London is proud to claim its native son. But, as Wallace points out, *The Canterbury Tales* does *not* begin in London—it begins in Southwark, which was in the fourteenth century "an independent parliamentary borough" with its own complicated political system. It would have been easy to begin the *Tales* in London—Boccaccio had begun his *Decameron* in a city, and London was becoming increasingly central to English life—but the only glimpse we get of the city in *The Canterbury Tales* is in the fragmentary *Cook's Tale*, which breaks off after just a few dozen lines. "The City of London," writes Wallace, "is chiefly remarkable for its absence," and he goes on "to read that absence." In the process, he reveals "the absence of a single, unified discourse that could be taken to represent the city as an organic and knowable entity," and where earlier critics had seen Chaucer's worldview as coherent and consistent, Wallace sees "only conflicts of associational, hierarchical, and antiassociational discourses."

The volume's final essay addresses Chaucer's reception. Alice Miskimin comes at Chaucer not through the Ellesmere and Hengwrt manuscripts but through the illustrated editions of *The Canterbury Tales* that began to appear in the eighteenth century. By using Chaucer to extend the tradition of Romantic medievalism back into the eighteenth century, she provides both a valuable prehistory of English Gothic enthusiasm and a new angle from which to see Chaucer's works.

The volume is rounded out by a chronology of the important events in Chaucer's life, a list of his works, and a bibliography that provides suggestions for further reading.

THE BOOK
AND
AUTHOR

On *The Canterbury Tales*_____

Jack Lynch

"*Here is God's plenty*"—so wrote the greatest poet of the late seventeenth century, John Dryden, on reading Geoffrey Chaucer's *Canterbury Tales*. It is typical of many readers' responses to the greatest work of the English Middle Ages. Yet Chaucer has not always been a readers' or a critics' favorite; as both Benjamin Lytal and Dominick Grace point out in their contributions to this volume, Chaucer's popularity has waxed and waned over the centuries. The poets, however, have never forgotten him: Chaucer has always been a poet's poet. Some of the biggest names in the English poetic tradition have acknowledged his brilliance. Not long after Chaucer's death, his friend Thomas Hoccleve praised him as his "maister deere and fadir reuerent,/ Mi maister Chaucer, flour [flower] of eloquence." For Edmund Spenser, the most important epic poet of the sixteenth century, he was "Dan Chaucer, well of English undefiled." Michael Drayton, Shakespeare's younger contemporary, found Chaucer "the first of ours that ever brake/ Into the Muses' treasure." The most proficient poet of the eighteenth century, Alexander Pope, announced, "I read Chaucer still with as much pleasure as almost any of our poets. He is a master of manners, of description, and the first tale-teller in the true enlivened natural way." And the nineteenth-century poets admired him as much as did the poets of the sixteenth, seventeenth, and eighteenth centuries. William Wordsworth listed Chaucer, Shakespeare, Spenser, and Milton as the "four English poets whom I must have continually before me," and Alfred, Lord Tennyson called him

> Dan Chaucer, the first warbler, whose sweet breath
> Precluded those melodious bursts, that fill
> The spacious times of great Elizabeth
> With sounds that echo still.

Some of the most perceptive and enthusiastic comments on Chaucer have come from those writers who were equally comfortable as poets and as critics. Samuel Johnson, for instance, was the eighteenth century's greatest poet-critic. When he surveyed the history of English poetry, he called Chaucer "the first of our versifiers who wrote poetically." The Romantic poet Samuel Taylor Coleridge, who agreed with Johnson on little else, agreed with him on this, praising Chaucer's "great powers of invention" and his "love of nature," adding, "I take unceasing delight in Chaucer. . . . How exquisitely tender he is, and yet how perfectly free from the least touch of sickly melancholy or morbid drooping!" Matthew Arnold, who rivaled Johnson's stature as both poet and critic in the Victorian era, was just as enthusiastic: "He is a genuine source of joy and strength, which is flowing still for us and will flow always," adding that, as we turn from the other poets of his day to Chaucer, "we suddenly feel ourselves in another world."

Scholars eventually learned what the poets and poet-critics had known all along and have spent decades trying to map that other world. But the critics often find themselves disoriented when they arrive there. There are parts of the *Tales* that seem familiar on first reading, because Chaucer had plenty of precedents. One of the central tasks of medieval scholarship has been to track down the "sources and analogues," the works from which Chaucer borrowed his plots and themes. Chaucer's means of collecting many short tales into one framing narrative, for instance, was not original with him; it shows up in dozens of earlier works of literature. Chaucer might have been inspired by classical works such as Ovid's *Metamorphoses*, by Continental works such as Giovanni Boccaccio's *Decameron*, or by contemporary English works such as John Gower's *Confessio Amantis*. And virtually every individual tale has been shown to derive structures, images, and metaphors from earlier works. It should feel familiar when we arrive in Chaucer's literary world.

The seeming familiarity of that world soon evaporates, however, because Chaucer, a master of taking commonplaces and turning them inside out, transmuted his materials into something wholly new. The Wife of Bath's prologue, for instance, recycles dozens of clichés from a misogynist literary tradition that thrived from late antiquity through the Middle Ages—and yet Chaucer turns that tradition on its head by putting them in the mouth of a singularly headstrong woman.

It is this remarkable ability to reinvigorate commonplaces and tired conventions that gives *The Canterbury Tales* its appeal—even now, more than six centuries after Chaucer's death. Those centuries do sometimes get in the way of readers' appreciation: Middle English can be difficult for beginners, and the work's many allusions to unfamiliar books and alien cultural practices can be off-putting for those who are not immersed in fourteenth-century English history. But once readers make the effort to understand Chaucer's language and take the time to situate themselves in his historical moment, they discover a degree of depth and complexity found in few other authors.

Readers have always been amazed at Chaucer's ability to get inside the minds of his characters—a talent in which his only English rival is Shakespeare. That richness, however, for all its rewards, can also be baffling: it is notoriously difficult to pin Chaucer down. This probably accounts for the volume of criticism devoted to *The Canterbury Tales*. Lesser medieval works have been read, interpreted, and more or less dispensed with, but the *Tales* continues to inspire critical disagreement. "Chaucer" is always at the center of discussions of his poem, but critics are not always sure which Chaucer they are talking about, and many of his tales have been subject to vastly different interpretations—perhaps even more diverse than the interpretations of any comparable collection of narratives. We realize after a while that we know precious little about the mind behind the poem. Is Chaucer a misogynist or a protofeminist? Is he hopeful about the human condition or bitter? Is he an upholder of traditional class hierarchies or a closet revolutionary? Does he share the anti-Semitism and xenophobia of some of his narrators, or does he critique it? Nevertheless, the sheer variety of styles and tones Chaucer mastered, ranging from the elevated diction of the courtly romance to the earthy bawdry of the fabliau, from homely folktales to sophisticated philosophizing, may be without compare, and they certainly make him one of literature's most compelling poets.

Biography of Geoffrey Chaucer_____

Judith Laird

Geoffrey Chaucer, one of the greatest of English writers, made his living as a civil servant and composed poetry as an avocation. His career, however, contributed to his literary growth. He was born into a prosperous family and reared in London. His father, a wine importer, was able to find him a position (in 1357 or earlier) as a page boy in the household of King Edward III's daughter-in-law, Elizabeth of Ulster. From this period on, despite the political uncertainties of the age, Chaucer enjoyed the uninterrupted favor of the members of the courts of, successively, Edward, Richard II, and Henry IV, both as a man of business and as a poet.

Chaucer served as a soldier in France in the campaigns of the Hundred Years' War in 1359 to 1360. Between 1368 and 1387 he was sent abroad on diplomatic missions to France and Italy on at least seven occasions. He acquired the training necessary for business, probably at the law school known as the Inner Temple. He was a controller of customs in London from 1374 to 1385, became a justice of the peace in Kent in 1385 and a member of Parliament for the county in 1386, served in London again from 1389 to 1391 as a clerk of the works, and was thereafter awarded a less active royal appointment as subforester.

About 1366 he married Philippa Roet of Flanders, who was lady-in-waiting to Queen Philippa and later to John of Gaunt's second wife, Constance. (Chaucer's wife's sister became Gaunt's third wife.) Records suggest that he had two sons and a daughter and that his wife died in 1387. He died in 1400 in a house that he had rented on the grounds of Westminster Abbey, and he was buried in that section of the Abbey later to become known as the Poets' Corner.

The maturation of Chaucer's genius can be illustrated by four works. In the *Book of the Duchess* the narrator dreams that he shares the grief of a lonely young knight, who proves to be John of Gaunt mourning his newly lost first wife. The conception is original, and the expression of sympathy is gracefully tender, but the framework of the dream vision and the knight's description of his love are strongly influenced by French models.

In the uncompleted *House of Fame*, another dream vision, the narrator is carried off by an eagle to learn whether those who are in the service of love are happy. The self-confident and domineering eagle was suggested to Chaucer by his reading of Dante's *Paradise*, but it here plays a novel comic role in a work that parodies the artificiality of medieval courtly love conventions.

Troilus and Criseyde, Chaucer's first major poem, amplifies Giovanni Boccaccio's pseudoclassical romance *Il filostrato* (c. 1335), giving depth to the sorrowful Troilus, elusiveness to the timid Criseyde, robust comicality to the officious Pandarus, immediacy to the setting, and a new significance to the tragedy of the two lovers separated by the Trojan War.

In *The Canterbury Tales*, a masterpiece though uncompleted, Chaucer turns to the English scene, as do his contemporaries William Langland and John Gower, and focuses on the men, women, children, and animals familiar to him in life. An assorted group of pilgrims entertain themselves by telling stories on the way from London to Canterbury. Through his descriptions in the General Prologue and dramatizations in the links connecting the tales, he portrays in detail seven members of the feudal order, thirteen people associated with religious life, and fourteen townspeople—the chivalrous Knight, the aristocratic Prioress, the fraudulent Pardoner, the impoverished Canon's Yeoman, the amorous Wife of Bath, the reticent narrator, and the rest who have gained an independent identity. The tales that Chaucer supplies match the tellers in their rich variety—the Knight's courtly romance, the Miller's racy fabliau, the Second Nun's pious saint's life, the Nun's Priest's mock-heroic fable, the Pardoner's hypocritical sermon, and the Parson's sincere one.

Like most medieval craftspeople, Chaucer, whether as young apprentice or as mature master, followed the pattern of established models. His success can therefore be partially explained by the vast extent of his reading of "old approved stories." The sources for most of his works influenced his style. His comic tone, for example, is often reminiscent of that of Ovid, his favorite Latin poet, and his philosophical ideas are usually those of Boethius. He appears to have culled materials in turn from the French—notably Guillaume de Machaut and Jean Froissart—then from the Italians—Dante, Petrarch, and Boccaccio—and finally, perhaps, from his fellow countryman Langland. His ultimate achievements, however, were profoundly original. Chaucer's skill as a raconteur, his deftness of characterization and description, his perfection in metrical technique, his understanding of human religious, moral, and philosophical instincts, his knowledge of life and acceptance of its mingled tragedy and comedy, and his transcendent sense of humor are, in combination, unique.

Bibliography

Blamires, Alcuin. *Chaucer, Ethics, and Gender*. New York: Oxford University Press, 2006. Examines not only Chaucer's treatment of women but also how gender affects the moral tone of his works. Offers a new perspective on Chaucer's writing, using philosophical questions of ethics and morality to view the traditionally fixed notions of gender in Chaucer's works. Lucid writing style makes the difficult subject matter easy to fathom and puts a new spin on issues of gender in Chaucerian studies.

Borroff, Marie. *Traditions and Renewals: Chaucer, the Gawain-Poet, and Beyond.* New Haven, Conn.: Yale University Press, 2003. Collection of essays provides a fresh and different analysis of Chaucer's work.

Bowden, Muriel. *A Commentary on the General Prologue to "The Canterbury Tales."* 2d ed. New York: Macmillan, 1967. Restricted in scope to the General Prologue, the most widely read (and taught) of Chaucer's writings. Provides a detailed explication that explores the prologue virtually line by line, collecting and arranging all significant discussions of the text. A valuable reference for the specialist, while remaining clear enough to be accessible to the general reader.

Brewer, Derek. *Chaucer.* 3d ed. London: Longman, 1977. Relatively short biography for the general reader by a respected Chaucerian scholar judiciously interprets the somewhat sparse and sometimes puzzling facts of the poet's life.

_____. *The World of Chaucer.* Rochester, N.Y.: D. S. Brewer, 2000. An illustrated look at Chaucer's work and the intellectual life of his time. Includes bibliography and index.

_____, ed. *Chaucer: The Critical Heritage.* 2 vols. Boston: Routledge & Kegan Paul, 1978. Volume 1 (1385-1837) contains contributions ranging from Eustache Deschamps to Samuel Taylor Coleridge; volume 2 (1837-1933) includes criticism by Virginia Woolf, among others. In the vast resources on Chaucer, this volume edited by an eminent Chaucerian stands as an excellent source for reviewing Chaucer scholarship and criticism.

Brown, Peter, ed. *A Companion to Chaucer.* Malden, Mass.: Blackwell, 2000. Part of the Blackwell Companions to Literature and Culture series, offers broad and detailed essays by scholars of Chaucer and his era.

Chute, Marchette Gaylord. *Geoffrey Chaucer of England.* Rev. ed. New York: E. P. Dutton, 1962. General reader's life of Chaucer, first issued in 1946, remains the best of its type. The style is clear and unpretentious, and the facts are set forth in the context of needed background information. The author discusses the poet's literary achievement but is more successful at conveying the flow of his life.

Coghill, Nevill. *The Poet Chaucer.* 2d ed. New York: Oxford University Press, 1967. Interweaves three biographical chapters with discussions of Chaucer's poetry, emphasizing matters that influenced his writing and omitting details of his official life.

Condren, Edward I. *Chaucer and the Energy of Creation: The Design and the Organization of "The Canterbury Tales."* Gainesville: University Press of Florida, 1999. Examines the motives behind Chaucer's layout of the stories.

Crow, Martin M., and Virginia E. Leland. "Chaucer's Life." In *The Riverside Chaucer*, edited by Larry D. Benson. 3d ed. Boston: Houghton Mifflin, 1987. Biographical essay briefly but authoritatively presents the principal known facts of Chaucer's life.

Gittes, Katharine S. *Framing "The Canterbury Tales": Chaucer and the Medieval Frame Narrative Tradition.* Westport, Conn.: Greenwood Press, 1991. Analyzes the influence of the Asian frame narrative tradition on *The Canterbury Tales*; argues that what was once taken for incompleteness is the result of the influence of Eastern modes of narrative structure.

Hirsh, John C. *Chaucer and "The Canterbury Tales": A Short Introduction*. Malden, Mass.: Blackwell, 2003. An introduction to *The Canterbury Tales* for the general reader.

Horobin, Simon. *The Language of the Chaucer Tradition*. Rochester, N.Y.: D. S. Brewer, 2003. A discussion of the development of Middle English during Chaucer's time.

Howard, Donald R. *Chaucer: His Life, His Works, His World*. New York: Fawcett Columbine, 1989. Comprehensive and authoritative biography, by a renowned critic, valuable for both the novice and the advanced student. Combines biographical and historical material with insightful commentary on the poetry.

_____. *The Idea of "The Canterbury Tales."* Berkeley: University of California Press, 1976. Addresses the idea of the poem in a historical perspective. Looks at language, customs, institutions, values, and myths, as well as the use of visual models such as rose windows and pavement labyrinths to understand the sprawling form. Pays special attention to the darker side of Chaucer, the concept of pilgrimage and medieval aesthetics, and elucidates the implied meanings behind the juxtapositions of some of the tales.

Kittredge, G. L. *Chaucer and His Poetry*. Cambridge, Mass.: Harvard University Press, 1915. Classic work of Chaucerian scholarship includes a critical appraisal of the chief works based on lectures given by the author in 1914. The first chapter is a short discussion of the man and his times, but the meat of the criticism develops around the poems, with two chapters devoted to *The Canterbury Tales*.

Narkiss, Doron. "The Fox, the Cock, and the Priest: Chaucer's Escape from Fable." *The Chaucer Review* 32 (1997): 46-63. Examines Chaucer's reworking of Aesop's fable in "The Nun's Priest's Tale." Argues that Chaucer moves the fable away from the realm of learning and wisdom to mockery and a way of reading that in "The Nun's Priest's Tale" fable is extended by characterization and action. Asserts that Chaucer's use of the fable suggests doubling, repetition, and substitutions.

Payne, Robert O. *Geoffrey Chaucer*. 2d ed. Boston: Twayne, 1986. A concise introduction to Chaucer and his period for the beginning student by one of the leading scholars in the field. Addressed to readers who have no previous background in medieval literature or cultural studies.

Pearsall, Derek. *The Life of Geoffrey Chaucer: A Critical Biography*. Cambridge, Mass.: Blackwell, 1992. Comprehensive biographical work.

Percival, Florence. *Chaucer's Legendary Good Women*. New York: Cambridge University Press, 1998. Suitable for introductory students yet containing challenging insights for scholars. Attempts to provide a comprehensive interpretation of the puzzling *Legend of Good Women* without ignoring any of the contradictory views that it contains about women.

Robertson, D. W., Jr. *A Preface to Chaucer: Studies in Medieval Perspectives*. Princeton, N.J.: Princeton University Press, 1962. Classic of Chaucerian new historicism, developed by Robertson partly in reaction to G. L. Kittredge and the New Criticism, which downplay the religious and cultural influences on Chaucer. Clearly presents the principles of medieval aesthetics through which Chaucer's work can be processed and given richer meaning. Focuses on the prevalent ideas of Chaucer's time, the importance of allegory in medieval theories of literature and religion in medieval life. Amplified with more than one hundred illustrations.

Rossignol, Rosalyn. *Chaucer A to Z: The Essential Reference to His Life and Works*. New York: Facts On File, 1999. An indispensable guide for the student of Chaucer.

Rowland, Beryl, ed. *Companion to Chaucer Studies*. Rev. ed. New York: Oxford University Press, 1979. Contains twenty-two essays, each followed by an extensive bibliography, by major authorities in the field. Surveys the history of Chaucer criticism in a wide range of topics, beginning with Chaucer's biography and influences. Contains six chapters on *The Canterbury Tales* and individual chapters on the more important minor poems.

Schoeck, Richard, and Jerome Taylor, eds. *Chaucer Criticism*. 2 vols. Notre Dame, Ind.: University of Notre Dame Press, 1960-1961. Volume 1, *The Canterbury Tales*, assembles some of the most important early studies of Chaucer's masterpiece, including John Matthews Manly's "Chaucer and the Rhetoricians" and George Lyman Kittredge's seminal "Chaucer's Discussion of Marriage." A valuable introduction to major critics and approaches. Volume 2 contains an introduction to "The System of Courtly Love" by William George Dodd, followed by twelve essays on *Troilus and Criseyde*.

Storm, Mel. "Speech, Circumspection, and Orthodontics in the Manciple's Prologue and Tale and the Wife of Bath's Portrait." *Studies in Philology* 96 (Spring, 1999): 109-126. Asserts that Chaucer's "The Manciple's Tale" is his apologia for his life as a poet. Suggests that "The Wife of Bath's Tale" is balanced both thematically and dramatically in "The Manciple's Tale."

Taavitsainen, Irma. "Narrative Patterns of Affect in Four Genres of *The Canterbury Tales*." *The Chaucer Review* 30 (1995): 191-210. Discusses four genres: sermons, saints' lives, courtly romances, and fabliaux. Argues that an assessment of inherent linguistic patterns of genres reveals new ways of seeing how the audience is manipulated, how their emotions are provoked, and how narrative suspense is sustained.

West, Richard. *Chaucer, 1340-1400: The Life and Times of the First English Poet*. New York: Carroll & Graf, 2000. A discussion of the history surrounding Chaucer's achievements and the events of his life. Chapters take up such matters as the Black Death's impact on the anti-Semitism evident in "The Prioress's Tale" and the impact of the great English Peasants' Revolt of 1381 on Chaucer's worldview.

The *Paris Review* Perspective

Benjamin Lytal for *The Paris Review*

Winter looked bleak. It was October 1386; Geoffrey Chaucer was about to lose his position as customs comptroller of the London docks, and so he was moving house, quitting Greenwich, which was suburban and expensive. We do not know precisely what his house was like, but like most fourteenth-century homes it was probably drafty, with small windows and a cold flagstone floor. Chaucer must have liked it, though: he had recently planted an arbor outside and returfed the lawn. But, thanks to royal machinations, his prosperity was temporarily at an end. And his poetry, too, was in bad shape.

By day a civil servant, Chaucer had by night already written some of the best poetry in all of English history. Even his contemporaries must have realized how much better Chaucer was than his nearest living rival, John Gower, who mainly wrote in French, except when the king demanded otherwise. At this time poetry was not published, since type had not been invented. Instead, it was read aloud, often as a kind of verbal concert for an audience at court— and was therefore often less dense, less psychologically satisfying than our own poetry. But Chaucer had taken steps forward: he had finished a very long poem, *Troilus and Criseyde*, that unfolds like a novel, carefully plotting the personalities and changing motives of two lovers.

Chaucer's most recent effort, however, had been a fiasco. He had not even wanted to write it, but he was moved by a sense of guilt: afraid that he had said too many bad things about women in his previous work, he attempted to make up for it by writing *The Legend of Good Women*. He grew bored and began to insert jokes at solemn moments, eventually breaking off the manuscript, never to finish it.

And a new type of literature was beginning to interest him. The fabliaux of France were racier than any poetry that had been written down in English. Most of what Chaucer had written before was visionary, allegorical, inspired by the polite traditions of court. Now, in his late middle age, he wanted to do something different. But he was nervous—he did not want to be accused of vulgarity.

As he packed and prepared to leave the house at Greenwich, Chaucer would have had to go through all his orphaned manuscripts. These were poems of varying length, each of them lovingly worked, but with no clear destiny. How to organize them? They had nothing to do with one another: the story of Palamon and Arcite, two jousting knights who fight over a woman neither has met; the moral fable of Griselda, translated from the Italian of Petrarch but made more physical with bodily details and earthy metaphors; the pious life of Saint Cecilia; a collection of miniature tragedies concerning figures such as Hercules and Julius Caesar. Perhaps Chaucer simply put all of these into one pile, one bundle, when he moved out of his house.

Was this how he conceived *The Canterbury Tales*? A band of pilgrims, from all walks of life, brought together by convenience, with their horses at a walk, telling stories. A collection of tales within a frame story, like others from the Middle Ages but with this crucial difference: each tale matches its teller, opening up a world of overtone and connotation and making possible the diversity of styles that Chaucer, for the last outing in his creative life, must have deeply desired. He would find homes for his orphans. He would get away with his dirty fabliaux, putting vulgar tales in the mouths of vulgar characters. He would get to do whatever he needed to do.

A little chaos suited Chaucer. He had spent his life staked between two classes, always a London citizen serving the nobility, and now he would finally get to show some of his salt. As a teenager doing military service in France, he had been taken prisoner and ransomed. He traveled to Genoa and set up a port for English traders. He worked in London collecting duties for wools, skins, and hides. He sat in Parliament. He was made responsible for maintaining the riverbanks of the Thames. He was robbed of public money by bandits. He oversaw the construction of royal bleachers for a jousting match in Smithfield.

All this gave Chaucer an encyclopedic of knowledge of real life, and for his *Canterbury Tales* he was able to sketch millers, monks, knights, ship captains, landowners, and others. But he did not set out their tales according to rank; he scrambled them, having the drunken miller interrupt as soon as the stately knight has finished. Thus, with the second tale, begins the tumult that Chaucer so desired—one tale offered up as a rebuke to that which preceded it, all ears straining to see if one character or another will take offense. Chaucer expanded his lines, using the first pentameter in English, giving warmth and personality to dirty French ditties, lacing Aesop's fables with grandeur, bringing order and snap to rambling stories from other medieval sources.

The chivalric adventures on which Chaucer had trained himself were disorganized and uncertain. Decorum called for learned allusions and windy digressions. Chaucer preferred now to be indecorous—he had always been funny. He liked the things that we like: the perfect detail, the ominous setup, the punch line.

We still read Chaucer, and most readers probably think we always have. Not so. He died in 1400, but in 1700, the poet John Dryden had to go out on a limb to praise Chaucer. He was not in fashion for long periods of history, but since the early twentieth century Chaucer has seemed indispensable. His worth has always been obvious in his verse: in the original, if readers take the time to make it out, Chaucer writes the most natural and convincing heroic couplets in English. What has made him especially interesting in the past century has been his personality—his ribaldry and his willpower. We are still just learning to look over Chaucer's shoulder, and to see how eagerly the aged storyteller finally set to work.

Works Consulted

Chaucer, Geoffrey. *The Canterbury Tales*. Norton Critical Edition. 2nd ed. New York: W. W. Norton, 2005.

Coghill, Nevill. *The Poet Chaucer*. New York: Oxford UP, 1960.

Kittredge, George Lyman. *Chaucer and His Poetry*. Cambridge, MA: Harvard UP, 1915.

Lawrence, William Witherle. *Chaucer and the Canterbury Tales*. New York: Columbia UP, 1959.

Schmidt, Michael. *Lives of the Poets*. New York: Vintage, 2000.

Speirs, John. *Chaucer the Maker*. London: Faber, 1951.

CRITICAL
CONTEXTS

The Canterbury Tales:
Critical Reception

Dominick Grace

Though a case could be made for *Troilus and Criseyde*, *The Canterbury Tales* is arguably Chaucer's masterwork. Ever since Chaucer's own day, the *Tales* has easily been his most popular work. While it is dangerous to judge a book's popularity by how many copies of it survive from a period in which books were expensive, rare, and copied by hand, the sheer number of surviving *Canterbury Tales* manuscripts suggests that the work was widely read (only one medieval text—*The Ayenbite of Inwit*—survives in more manuscripts, but, unlike *The Canterbury Tales*, it has not remained popular for centuries). The *Tales* survives, at least in part, in more than eighty manuscripts, more than twice the number of *Troilus* manuscripts to survive in whole or in part, and this popularity is all the more remarkable given that many of the tales are tales of "solaas," or entertainment. Designed to provide pleasure to an audience, these tales were copied and preserved much less frequently than were tales of "sentence," or moral doctrine, which were designed to edify an audience. Chaucer himself includes an apology for "thilke [of the tales] that sownen into synne" (X.1086) ["those (of the tales) that tend towards sin"][1] in the retraction that ends the work. Further evidence of the early and continued popularity of the *Tales* is the fact that other hands took very quickly to writing Chaucerian pastiches (since *The Canterbury Tales* is incomplete, it was relatively easy for writers to insert their own tales into the Chaucerian framework—an early example of fan fiction in practice, perhaps).[2] William Caxton, the first printer to work in England, issued two editions of *The Canterbury Tales*, around 1476 and 1483, among his early publications, and numerous editions of Chaucer's works have been printed consistently through the subsequent centuries.

One of the most basic issues that editors, scholars, and students of the *Tales* have had to face is the unfinished nature of the work. Chaucer comes nowhere near to realizing the ambitious agenda he lays out in the General Prologue,[3] and even the most complete surviving manuscripts reflect the fragmentary nature of what Chaucer did complete. It was not until the nineteenth-century emergence of editorial practices akin to those used today that the sequencing and grouping of the *Tales* became somewhat standardized. In 1868, F. J. Furnivall became the first editor to attempt to reconstruct the order in which Chaucer might have intended to place the individual tales, at least insofar as can be determined from the fragments. Furnivall grouped and sequenced the tales according to indicators he found within them, such as geographical references, labeled each group with a letter and then, if he believed that two distinct segments belonged together even though they were not sequenced in all of the manuscripts, gave each segment within a group a number (Group A, Group, B, and so on, with B_1 and B_2 designations for separate segments that likely belong together). W. W. Skeat followed Furnivall in his 1894 edition, which is still in some respects the text underlying modern editions, some of which continue to follow its readjusted order.[4] However, many twentieth-century editions—including the Riverside edition, which is widely regarded as the most authoritative—return to the manuscripts themselves and follow the order in which the chunks appear in the Ellesmere manuscript, arguably the best surviving manuscript, and number each chunk as a discrete fragment (I, II, and so on). Despite extensive debate about order, scholars remain divided about which sequence to adopt; whichever sequence a particular edition adopts, it generally also employs the designation methods of other systems so that readers construct these alternate sequences for themselves.

This structural complexity oddly reflects the analytic complexities raised by *The Canterbury Tales*. Chaucer, like Shakespeare, Milton, and a handful of other writers, is central to the canon and, as a result, attracts an enormous amount of critical attention, not only because his work is sufficiently complex and elusive to merit ongoing study but also because applying a critical approach to such work grants that approach a degree of reflected glory. Consequently, swimming in the depths of Chaucerian scholarship is challenging even for professional Chaucerians. The title of Anne Rooney's 1989 guide to Chaucerian scholarship is amusingly accurate: *Geoffrey Chaucer: A Guide Through the Critical Maze*. And it is only one of the many books offering insights into the complexities of Chaucerian scholarship; in another such book, Helen Cooper has noted that "there are as many interpretations of Chaucer as there are readers" (Oxford Guides 2). The problem of structure is reflected in the frequency with which questions of form govern the titles of studies.[5] Nevertheless, several trends and subjects recur in the ongoing debates and reconsiderations of this most diverse and complex work.

Perhaps the first significant contributor to modern considerations of Chaucer is George Lyman Kittredge, who in 1893 first proposed that the tales should be read dramatically, as reflections of the characters and natures of the pilgrims themselves, not merely as stories conveniently gathered together under the device of tale-telling. That is, Kittredge proposed that the tales are not just stories but also reflections of the personalities of their tellers as they reveal themselves and use their narratives as covert (or overt) critiques of one another. There is little doubt that Chaucer did indeed frequently think of the relationship between teller and tale and of how the pilgrims could self-consciously use their tales, as Kittredge suggested. Both the Pardoner and the Wife of Bath, for instance, preface their tales with lengthy biographies, and both clearly see some degree of connection between their narratives and their natures. The Pardoner even explicitly comments on this relationship, albeit to suggest a disjunction between his nature and his tale, when he asserts that "though myself be a ful vicious man,/ A moral tale yet I yow telle Kan" (VI.459-60) ["though I am a wholly vicious man/ Don't think I can't tell moral tales. I can!"].

Numerous subsequent studies have focused on Kittredge's notion, from R. M. Lumiansky's *Of Sondry Folk: The Dramatic Principle in "The Canterbury Tales"* through Bertrand H. Bronson's *In Search of Chaucer* to such recent studies as the essay collection edited by Wendy Harding, *Drama, Narrative, and Poetry in "The Canterbury Tales,"* which debates the continued applicability of Kittredge's roadside drama idea. So compelling is Chaucer's characterization that some scholars have even sought for historical figures lurking behind some of the pilgrims. There was a real innkeeper named Harry Bailly, scholars have found, but other attempts to find specific historical models are unconvincing, and, indeed, Chaucer's methods of characterization are clearly indebted to conventional character types. Nevertheless, Kittredge's dramatic theory continues to influence criticism of the *Tales*, as the ongoing interest in the pilgrims as characters attests.

Kittredge also first articulated the idea that marriage serves as a recurrent theme, at least within several tales. Explaining that "the Marriage Group of Tales begins with the Wife of Bath's Prologue and ends with the Franklin's Tale," he associated the debate on marriage—the Marriage Group, as it is usually called—with the sequence of Fragments III-V ("Chaucer's Discussion" 467). Kittredge's 1912 article is an early and influential attempt to find subgroupings of tales that deal with specific thematic or ideological issues, and numerous comparable attempts to find thematic patterns have followed this one. Even the idea of the Marriage Group itself continues to hold currency, though more recent scholars have extended the parameters of the debate, recognizing that other tales also deal to some extent with marriage. Fragment VII, for instance, is a popular addition, but tales from other later fragments (e.g., "The Nun's Priest's Tale," "The Tale of Melibee," "The Shipman's Tale," "The Physician's Tale," even "The Second Nun's Tale")[6] have also been grafted onto Kittredge's original grouping. References to the Marriage Group continue to appear in current scholarship—one discussion folds even the beginning of the poem into the marriage debate, arguing that "Chaucer's discussion of marriage is not so much the pilgrims' debate on 'auctoritee' in Fragments III-V, as an extended discussion beginning from Fragments I-II" (Cai 93)—yet other scholars have moved away from Kittredge's focus on marriage, though the ongoing interest in Chaucer's sexual politics has at least some of its roots in Kittredge's pioneering study.

In the years following Kittredge, literary criticism in general was transformed by the development of literary theories as tools to apply to literary texts. New Criticism, which emerged in the 1930s and dominated critical discourse for the next few decades, in general terms brought a formalist approach to texts. Text-driven and focusing on the specific details of the primary work under discussion, it often favored the close reading of a text over the examination of authorial intent, historical context, or other factors external to the text itself. Charles Muscatine, in his *Chaucer and the French Tradition: A Study in Style and Meaning* (1957), provides a good example of the New Critical approach to Chaucer. Though his title might suggest an interest in historical context and tradition (and historicist readings of Chaucer were and are important), Muscatine's primary focus is the text itself as he seeks to give "form and style their due attention as essential, inseparable concomitants of meaning" (1). Muscatine historicizes his approach by applying the principles of gothic construction to Chaucer's work (an idea also explored extensively by Robert M. Jordan), but his actual readings focus closely on the details of the work itself; he describes Chaucer as "supremely an artist of his own age" (247), but his focus on Chaucer's characteristic stylistic and poetic devices does not depend heavily on this historicity.

Also important as a New Critical reader is E. Talbot Donaldson, whose chief contribution, perhaps, is his focus, in his essay "Chaucer the Pilgrim" (1954), on the persona Chaucer creates for the narrator of *The Canterbury Tales*. Donaldson points out what might seem obvious now: that readers of the poem need to be careful not to conflate the author of the poem with the "I" who narrates within the poem, and that Chaucer the pilgrim is himself a character subject to the same ironic and critical view applied to the other pilgrims. Donaldson notes that there is certainly some overlap between these characters and Chaucer but that "Chaucer the poet" "operates in a realm which is above and subsumes those in which Chaucer the man and Chaucer the pilgrim have their being" (936). Donaldson makes the narrator a character in the roadside drama, so his study lies at the root of subsequent studies of authorial persona in *The Canterbury Tales*. As Geoffrey W. Gust asserts, in an article that first appeared in a 2007 special issue of *The Chaucer Review* devoted to a reevaluation of New Critical approaches to Chaucer and to Donaldson specifically, "The fact that we now unflinchingly refer to the first-person narrator of *The Canterbury Tales* as 'Chaucer the Pilgrim' attests to the significance of Donaldson's well-known essay" (314).

Readings of the *Tales* rooted in New Critical sensibilities continue to this day, though as early as the 1950s they were being challenged by alternate approaches. It is not difficult to recognize why New Criticism was vulnerable. The New Critical focus on the specifics of a text encourages close reading, and its scepticism about such concepts as the intentional fallacy (or granting primacy to what one thinks the author might have *meant* rather than to what the text actually *says*) is very useful, especially when one is dealing with a narrative voice as seductive as Chaucer's, but it also fails to acknowledge sufficiently that meaning does not reside merely in a text but also in a context. As dangerous as is the intentional fallacy, equally dangerous is the tendency to read a text through the lens of one's own time, thereby forcing it to conform to values and ideologies that may not have even existed at the time the work was written.

Two trends in mid-twentieth-century Chaucerian criticism addressed such limitations. One of these is the exegetical, or patristic, approach adopted by figures such as D. W. Robertson beginning in the 1960s. "Exegesis" refers to the method of reading a text allegorically as an expression of Christian values; "patristic" refers to the major early Christian theologians—the fathers (or, in Latin, the *patria*) of the Church—so patristic readings interpret medieval literature in light of the strategies of biblical interpretation adopted by early Christian theologians such as Augustine. Robertson was one of the more vocal proponents of the view that, in order to understand medieval art properly, "we must first determine some of the chief differences between those attitudes which underlie modern aesthetic judgments and the corresponding attitudes which underlie medieval theory and practice" (4). For Robertson, these medieval attitudes were informed by a belief in the moral function of literature. Certainly, Chaucer's text at times might seem to encourage such a view—the Nuns' Priest, for instance, asserts that "al that writen is,/ To oure doctrine it is ywrite, ywis;/ Taketh the fruyt, and lat the chaf be stille" (VII.3441-43) ["all things are written for our learning;/ So take the grain and let the chaff be still"], a statement that could be seen as encouraging allegorical reading as readers look for the fruit concealed within the husk of the literal narrative. And perhaps it is not surprising then that, although the Nun's Priest himself asserts that his tale is merely a tale of a rooster, Robertson reads it as an allegory about a priest and a friar, and other scholars have attempted even more surprising allegoreses of the tale, such as Richard Neuse's assertion that it "shows Chauntecleer in a twofold 'imitation of Christ,' suffering a kind of crucifixion in the Fox's mouth and achieving a triumphant resurrection with his flight up the tree" (93). Many of the tales, notably "The Tale of Melibee" and "The Parson's Tale," have clear moral agendas, but many others can be read usefully in relation to medieval religious ideologies despite their apparent secularity. In recent years, scholarship has tended to veer away from the Robertsonian approach, however, to problematize and complicate the relationship between Chaucer's text and his moral purpose, rather than attempting, as does Robertson, to find in the work merely a reflection of dominant theological discourse in Chaucer's day.

Still, useful as the exegetical approach can be, it addresses only one aspect of the context in which Chaucer wrote *The Canterbury Tales*. On the other hand, historicist readings attempt to situate the tales in broader historical contexts, stressing the correlations between the tales (or at least some of them) and contemporary events and controversies. For instance, Chaucer was a contemporary of John Wycliffe, a controversial religious reformer whose movement was known as lollardy,[7] and Chaucer makes passing reference to lollardy in *The Canterbury Tales*. As early as the 1920s, scholars began to explore the extent to which lollard sympathies can be detected in *The Canterbury Tales*, and the subject is still occasionally debated today.[8]

Though medieval science is not a major element in *The Canterbury Tales*, knowledge of some aspects of it, especially in relation to medieval ideas that differ profoundly from twenty-first-century ones, can be helpful, and historicist scholars have also pursued this line of inquiry. Walter Clyde Curry established the groundwork for considerations of how medieval science is reflected in Chaucer's work, and many subsequent scholars have followed in his footsteps. Examples include numerous discussions of alchemy (the medieval antecedent to the science of chemistry), especially in "The Canon's Yeoman's Tale." Peggy A. Knapp published a good article in 2000 that explains alchemy and provides some insights into its relevance to *The Canterbury Tales*, and students interested in this subject may also wish to consult Corinne E. Kauffman, who shows that the herbs Pertelote prescribes for Chauntecleer in "The Nun's Priest's Tale" would be more likely to kill than heal him; C. David Benson, who demonstrates that Chaucer's Physician, who might seem less than reliable to modern readers for his use of astronomy as a diagnostic tool, is in fact behaving according to accepted medieval medical practice ("Astrological Medicine"); or, on an earthier level, Robert Hasenfratz and Timothy D. O'Brien, who read the flatulence joke of "The Summoner's Tale" in light of medieval mechanics and meteorology.

Other scholars see Chaucer engaging, at least obliquely, with contemporary politics, providing commentary on contemporary issues. Gardiner Stillwell, for instance, sees in "The Tale of Melibee" (despite the fact that is it a close translation of a French text) a commentary on King Richard II's desire for peace with France; in an essay published forty-two years after Stillwell's article appeared in 1944, William Askins relates this same tale to the parliamentary crisis of 1387. Numerous other readings of various tales link them with contemporary events or issues, such as the Peasant's Revolt of 1381, though it remains to be seen the extent to which one ought to agree with a critic such as Lee Patterson, who argues that "Chaucer's meditations on history remain . . . for the most part divorced from the specificity of local events" (*Chaucer* 24), or with critics such as David Aers, who sees Chaucer as actively, and critically, engaged in the political issues of his day.

One of the most important historically engaged readings of Chaucer is Jill Mann's. If Robertson reads Chaucer in relation to medieval theology, Mann reads him in relation to medieval social theory as well as medieval satirical practice. In approaching the work, she asks, "What does it tell us about the society it represents?" (1), and her answer is guided by the social roles into which class casts Chaucer's pilgrims. Her sociohistorical reading of the General Prologue to *The Canterbury Tales* provides valuable insights into the medieval estates, or social classes, into which all people were divided; the conventions associated with the depictions of those estates; and the tradition of satirizing abuses within those estates, especially those of the clerical estate. While Mann's focus on how work defines individuals does not perhaps quite amount to a Marxist reading of Chaucer, it shares much with the extensive theoretical engagements with Chaucer—such as Marxism, psychoanalytic theory, feminism, gender and queer theory, postmodern approaches such as deconstruction, and more recently ecocriticism and fecopoetics—that began to predominate during the 1980s.

Along with Stephen Knight, David Aers is arguably the most influential Marxist reader of Chaucer. Marxist theory is rooted in the belief that art is inevitably influenced by the economic climate in which it is created and that it reflects the economic and social determinants of its culture. Aers and Knight see Chaucer as essentially progressive in Marxist terms, in that they read him as critiquing the dominant class and religious structures of his time. Aers, for instance, reads the Pardoner in a way very different from the dominant approach to the character, which is still rooted in Kittredge's view of the Pardoner as a "thorough-paced scoundrel" ("Chaucer's Pardoner" 830) and a "lost soul" (832), the one irredeemable pilgrim whose frank acknowledgment of his viciousness has led to considerable scholarly debate. Aers argues that Chaucer creates in the character a conscious and deliberate critique that "unmask[s] the dominant practices and values of the orthodox institution which claimed a monopoly on the means of grace and correct doctrine" (163). Knight is similar in his analysis, arguing, for instance, that the Wife of Bath offers a "potentially revolutionary" critique of the social order and is herself a "courageous, self-conscious, domestic, and mercantile person" (100). Not all Marxist-influenced readings agree, however. Alcuin Blamires, for instance, diplomatically suggests that "Chaucer is committed to the 'dominant' social view and categorically does not sympathize with political dissent" ("Chaucer the Reactionary" 524). David R. Carlson is rather more blunt: "Chaucer was the police" (1).

If the Wife of Bath and the Pardoner can be read in light of Marxist theory, they can equally be read in the light of other theoretical approaches. Though psychoanalytic critics have been relatively few in Chaucer studies, these two characters have especially benefited from psychoanalytic readings. Literary theory rooted in psychoanalysis is itself a complex field and difficult to explain briefly, but, to oversimplify, it applies the techniques of psychoanalysis to literary texts, looking for repressed or latent meaning beneath their surfaces. Sigmund Freud and Jacques Lacan are the most influential figures in the development of psychoanalytic literary theory. The Wife of Bath is handily treated by Louise O. Fradenburg, who applies psychoanalytic theories about mourning to explain the character. The Pardoner, however, has arguably invited more psychoanalytic reading than any other character in the *Tales*, though whether he is, as Paul G. Ruggiers suggests, "the ultimate example of Chaucer's subtle handling of human psychology" (123) or simply the most psychoanalyzed of Chaucer's characters is open to debate. Regardless, a range of psychological explanations for his behavior have been offered, from a simple need for approval (Condren) to alcoholism (Bowers). The Pardoner's sexuality, however, has been of the greatest critical interest.

Chaucer's sexual politics have been the subject of discussion since Kittredge identified marriage as a central theme in *The Canterbury Tales*, yet one of the most significant developments in Chaucer studies in the past few decades has been the application of feminist theory to the *Tales*. Feminist theory is also difficult to boil down to a sentence or two, but, in a nutshell, it is centrally concerned with the representation of women and the ways in which female identity has traditionally been defined. The Wife of Bath, traditionally one of the most criticized Canterbury pilgrims (though she has always had her admirers), has been an exceptional beneficiary of feminist rehabilitation. Her advocacy of women and her recognition that the antifeminist tradition (which Chaucer in fact invokes extensively in his depiction of her) imposes a male perspective on women (just as a painting of a man defeating a lion represents a particular bias—"Who peyntede the leon, tell me who?" [III.692] ["Who called the lion savage? Do you know?"] she pointedly asks) make her an obvious candidate for such recuperation. Mary Carruthers's important essay on her, "The Wife of Bath and the Painting of Lions," in fact invokes this very question of representation in its title. Carolyn Dinshaw's *Chaucer's Sexual Poetics* explores in considerable detail and across several tales and characters the problems that masculine representations of the female and feminine experience raise, noting especially the extent to which female voices are silenced. Readers must remember that even when a female character speaks in the text, her voice is in fact coming from the male author behind the character, yet Dinshaw nevertheless attempts to argue that Chaucer's female characters assert themselves by appropriating the imposed model, enabling them to "convert a form of subordination into an affirmation" (115).

Elaine Tuttle Hansen's *Chaucer and the Fictions of Gender* offers an extension to feminist criticism. Close cousins to feminist theory are gender theory and queer theory, approaches that ask further questions of sexual politics. Gender theory interrogates the idea that sexual identity is biologically determined, and it differentiates between "sex" (as a matter of biology) and "gender" (as the constellation of associations society attaches to sex). That is, gender theory questions the extent to which masculinity and femininity are inherent qualities and to what extent they are culturally determined. In this way, it problematizes the notion that there is a clear divide between the sexes. Queer theory extends this exploration by focusing especially on questions of sexual orientation and identity by noting the array of orientations beyond the heteronormative, such as homosexuality, bisexuality, and asexuality, and the array of gender identities, such as male, female, transgendered, and intersex. Hansen, who focuses on gender as a social construction and especially on the blurring of distinction between masculine and feminine, raises the question of whether a female voice, like that of the Wife of Bath, can exist in a male-authored text such as *The Canterbury Tales*. She notes that, despite apparently having a voice, the Wife of Bath is really absent, merely a construction of masculine voice.

Hansen's discussion of "The Miller's Tale" offers her most trenchant commentary on the anxieties of sexual identity and the "humiliating and frightening lack of difference between male and female bodies" (228). Hansen explores "the instability of gender boundaries" (Ashton 176) in her discussion of the notorious misdirected kiss of "The Miller's Tale," concluding that male and female genitalia are ultimately indistinguishable in the episode. Following such an argument, it was perhaps inevitable that a subsequent critic would extend the implications of Hansen's essay to claim that Alisoun, the young wife of the tale, is really a man in drag, as Linda Lomperis has averred.

Numerous other scholars have applied gender or queer theory to Chaucer, notably to discussions of the Pardoner, whose sexuality has long been recognized as problematic, as the narrator says of him in the General Prologue, "I trowe he were a gelding or a mare" (I.691) ["I judge he was a gelding, or a mare"]. Whether this means he is homosexual, castrated, or something else has been much debated. Robert S. Sturges's *Chaucer's Pardoner and Gender Theory* offers a comprehensive but far from final discussion of the matter, and Glenn Burger's *Chaucer's Queer Nation* redefines the marriage debate by raising the question of why marriage needs to be so insistently harped on in the first place. What anxieties lurk beneath this socially imposed insistence on heteronormative relations?

Such explorations of the constructedness—the fictionality—of identity are also inherently postmodern in nature. Indeed, Burger remarks that "my reading of Chaucer's Queer nation is postmodern" (xvii). Put briefly, postmodernist literary theories are marked by stress on such factors as the unreliability of any interpretive frame, the play of possible meanings rather than the fixity of meaning, the relationships among discourses, and the self-conscious and metafictive aspects of literature. In short, the postmodern is self-reflexive, self-aware, recursive, and playful. It is not difficult to see how at least some elements of postmodernism are reflected in *The Canterbury Tales*, with its ironic and self-aware narrator, deliberate play with literary conventions, and metafictive elements. C. David Benson's book *Chaucer's Drama of Style* offers an intriguing reading of *The Canterbury Tales*, claiming that the tales make fiction itself their subject. Benson sees the work as a self-conscious exploration of the nature and limitations of various narrative modes, though his approach is perhaps no more truly postmodern than Jill Mann's is Marxist. H. Marshall Leicester, Jr.'s *The Disenchanted Self*, on the other hand, is a good candidate for the most substantial deconstructive reading of Chaucer to date. Leicester touches on many strands of postmodern analysis as he reads several of the key tales in relation to the representation and construction of self and subject and the interpenetration of text and context.

Scholars aligned with new theoretical schools inevitably apply their theories to Chaucer and *The Canterbury Tales* to prove the theories' legitimacy and standing. Two interesting recent ones are ecocritism and fecopoetics. Ecocriticism is an interdisciplinary approach driven, as its name no doubt makes clear, by environmental concerns. It approaches literary texts with an eye toward understanding how they treat the concept of "nature" and operates on the assumption that the environment ought to be granted the same ethical consideration as such humancentric subjects as race, sex, and class. There is not as yet an abundance of ecocritical Chaucerian analysis, but Sarah Stanbury has recently offered "Ecochaucer: Green Ethics and Medieval Nature," in which she concludes, "In his representations of nature as an active force shaping a human subject, Chaucer takes a critical eye, inviting our examination of her effects on social institutions and human drives" (13). Fecopoetics is the very recent (and controversial) approach developed by Susan Signe Morrison, whose research led her to uncover a "network linking excrement to all aspects of medieval culture" (3). She is hardly the first scholar to address scatological issues in Chaucer, but she is the first to turn them into a book developing a theory of Chaucerian fecopoetics and analyzing such subjects as "urban excrement in *The Canterbury Tales*," "sacred filth," and "the excremental human God and redemptive filth." Whether such approaches will ultimately illuminate the *Tales* and enlighten readers or merely offer ingenious and inventive diversions remains to be seen. Certainly, even today there are many Chaucerians who would agree with Paul A. Olson's caustic suggestion that theorizing Chaucer makes him "the Narcissus image of our own historical or semiological fantasies" (18).

Regardless, as new literary theories emerge, they continue to be applied to Chaucer and *The Canterbury Tales*. Whether all those applied so far (and this overview has not addressed all the theoretical approaches, let alone all the possibilities for interpretation) have been equally useful is open to debate. Unquestionably, however, we have a deeper and more diverse understanding of *The Canterbury Tales* than we did a generation ago, and we will have a still deeper and more diverse understanding a generation from now, when the work of the past few decades is as distant as Kittredge's, Donaldson's, or Robertson's is now. Just as earlier insights remain useful today, so will at least some of today's scholarship remain useful in thirty years. Chaucer's work is sufficiently complex and variegated to accommodate a plurality of approaches. As John Dryden observed of *The Canterbury Tales* more than three hundred years ago, "'Tis sufficient to say according to the Proverb, that here is God's Plenty."

Notes

1. I have used Nevill Coghill's modernization throughout, to render Chaucer's meanings more clear. However, in attempting to preserve Chaucer's rhyme and meter, Coghill occasionally modifies or rewrites Chaucer, capturing the basic meaning but not necessarily in the same way or with the same examples. The translations are a guide to meaning but are not a substitute for the original Middle English text for the purposes of interpretation or analysis.

2. See *The Canterbury Tales: Fifteenth-Century Continuations and Additions*, edited by John M. Bowers, for such texts and an analysis of the phenomenon.

3. The General Prologue promises four tales from each pilgrim, although, in fact, no pilgrim tells more than one (unless one counts the interrupted "Tale of Sir Thopas" and "Tale of Melibee" as two from the narrator) and not even all of the pilgrims identified in the Prologue tell tales.

4. Among these are Albert C. Baugh's edition of Chaucer's works and Nevill Coghill's translation.

5. See, for instance, Judson Boyce Allen and Theresa Anne Moritz's *A Distinction of Stories*, Ralph Baldwin's *The Unity of "The Canterbury Tales,"* Helen Cooper's *The Structure of "The Canterbury Tales,"* Lee Patterson's *Temporal Circumstances*, and William E. Rogers's *Upon the Ways*.

6. See, for instance, the articles by William Witherle Lawrence, Albert N. Silverman, Germaine Dempster, and Donald R. Howard in the list that follows.

7. Wycliffe's dissidence caused him to be branded as a heretic and led to the exhumation and cremation of his body after his death. He later came to be known as the morning star of the reformation, a kind of proto-Protestant.

8. See, for instance, Ezra Kempton Maxfield's "Chaucer and Religious Reform" for an early contextualization of Chaucer in relation to lollardy, or such recent studies as those by Blamires ("Wife of Bath") and Craig T. Fehrman.

Works Cited

Aers, David. *Chaucer*. Brighton: Harvester Press, 1986.

Allen, Judson Boyce, and Theresa Anne Moritz. *A Distinction of Stories: The Medieval Unity of Chaucer's Fair Chain of Narratives for Canterbury*. Columbus: Ohio State UP, 1981.

Ashton, Gail. *Chaucer: "The Canterbury Tales."* New York: St. Martin's Press, 1998.

Askins, William. "The Tale of Melibee and the Crisis at Westminster, November 1387." *Studies in the Age of Chaucer* 2 (1986): 103-12.

Baldwin, Ralph. *The Unity of "The Canterbury Tales."* Copenhagen: Rosenkilde and Bagger, 1955.

Benson, C. David. "The Astrological Medicine of Chaucer's Physician and Nicholas of Lynn's Kalendarium." *American Notes and Queries* 22 (1984): 62-66.

_____. *Chaucer's Drama of Style: Poetic Variety and Contrast in "The Canterbury Tales."* Chapel Hill: U of North Carolina P, 1986.

Blamires, Alcuin. "Chaucer the Reactionary: Ideology and the General Prologue to *The Canterbury Tales*." *Review of English Studies* 51.204 (2000): 523-39.

_____. "The Wife of Bath and Lollardy." *Medium Ævum* 58.2 (1989): 224-42.

Bowers, John M. "'Dronkenesse Is Ful of Stryvyng': Alcoholism and Ritual Violence in Chaucer's Pardoner's Tale." *ELH* 57.4 (1990): 757-84.

Bronson, Bertrand H. *In Search of Chaucer*. Toronto: U of Toronto P, 1960.

Burger, Glenn. *Chaucer's Queer Nation*. Minneapolis: U of Minnesota P, 2003.

Cai, Zong-qi. "Fragments I-II and III-V in *The Canterbury Tales*: A Re-examination of the Idea of the 'Marriage Group.'" *Comitatus* 19 (1988): 80-98.

Carlson, David R. *Chaucer's Jobs*. New York: Palgrave Macmillan, 2004.

Carruthers, Mary. "The Wife of Bath and the Painting of Lions." *PMLA* 94.2 (1979): 209-22.

Chaucer, Geoffrey. *The Canterbury Tales*. Ed. Larry D. Benson. Boston: Houghton Mifflin, 2000.

_____. *The Canterbury Tales*. Trans. Nevill Coghill. 1951. London: Century, 1992.

_____. *The Canterbury Tales: Fifteenth-Century Continuations and Additions*. Ed. John M. Bowers. Kalamazoo, MI: Medieval Institute Publications, 1992.

_____. *Chaucer's Major Poetry*. Ed. Albert C. Baugh. New York: Routledge & Kegan Paul, 1963.

Condren, Edward I. "The Pardoner's Bid for Existence." *Viator: Medieval and Renaissance Studies* 4 (1973): 177-205.

Cooper, Helen. *The Canterbury Tales*. Oxford Guides to Chaucer. 2nd ed. New York: Oxford UP, 1996.

_____. *The Structure of "The Canterbury Tales."* London: Duckworth, 1983.

Curry, Walter Clyde. *Chaucer and the Mediæval Sciences*. 2nd ed. New York: Barnes & Noble, 1960.

Dempster, Germaine. "A Period in the Development of the *Canterbury Tales* Marriage Group and of Blocks B2 and C." *PMLA* 68 (1953): 1142-59.

Dinshaw, Carolyn. *Chaucer's Sexual Poetics*. Madison: U of Wisconsin P, 1989.

Donaldson, E. Talbot. "Chaucer the Pilgrim." *PMLA* 69.4 (1954): 928-36.

Dryden, John. "Preface to *The Fables*." 1700. The Geoffrey Chaucer Page. Harvard Univer-

sity. 29 Apr. 2010. http://www.courses.fas.harvard.edu/~chaucer/special/authors/dryden/
dry-intr.html.

Fehrman, Craig T. "Did Chaucer Read the Wycliffite Bible?" *The Chaucer Review* 42.2
(2007): 111-38.

Fradenburg, Louise O. "The Wife of Bath's Passing Fancy." *Studies in the Age of Chaucer* 8
(1986): 31-58.

Gust, Geoffrey W. "Reevaluating 'Chaucer the Pilgrim' and Donaldson's Enduring Persona."
The Chaucer Review 41.3 (2007): 311-22.

Hansen, Elaine Tuttle. *Chaucer and the Fictions of Gender.* Berkeley: U of California P,
1992.

Harding, Wendy, ed. *Drama, Narrative, and Poetry in "The Canterbury Tales."* Toulouse:
Presses Universitaires du Mirail, 2003.

Hasenfratz, Robert. "The Science of Flatulence: Possible Sources for the *Summoner's Tale.*"
The Chaucer Review 30.3 (1996): 241-61.

Howard, Donald R. "The Conclusion of the Marriage Group." *Modern Philology* 57.4 (1960):
223-32.

Jordan, Robert M. *Chaucer and the Shape of Creation: The Aesthetic Possibilities of Inorganic Structure.* Cambridge, MA: Harvard UP, 1967.

Kauffman, Corinne E. "Dame Pertelote's Parlous Parle." *The Chaucer Review* 4.1 (Summer
1969): 41-48.

Kittredge, George Lyman. "Chaucer's Discussion of Marriage." *Modern Philology* 9.4
(1912): 435-67.

_____. "Chaucer's Pardoner." *Atlantic Monthly* 72 (1893): 829-33. The Geoffrey
Chaucer Page. Harvard University. 29 Apr. 2010. http://www.courses.fas.harvard.edu/
~chaucer/canttales/pardt/kitt-par.html.

Knapp, Peggy A. "The Work of Alchemy." *Journal of Medieval and Early Modern Studies*
30.3 (2000): 575-99.

Knight, Stephen. *Geoffrey Chaucer.* New York: Blackwell, 1986.

Lawrence, William Witherle. "The Marriage Group in the *Canterbury Tales.*" *Modern Philology* 11.2 (1913): 247-58.

Leicester, H. Marshall, Jr. *The Disenchanted Self: Representing the Subject in "The Canterbury Tales."* Berkeley: U of California P, 1990.

Lomperis, Linda. "Bodies That Matter in the Court of Late Medieval England and in Chaucer's 'Miller's Tale.'" *Romanic Review* 86.2 (1995): 243-64.

Lumiansky, R. M. *Of Sondry Folk: The Dramatic Principle in "The Canterbury Tales."* Austin: U of Texas P, 1955.

Mann, Jill. *Chaucer and Medieval Estates Satire: The Literature of Social Classes and the
General Prologue to "The Canterbury Tales."* New York: Cambridge UP, 1973.

Maxfield, Ezra Kempton. "Chaucer and Religious Reform." *PMLA* 39.1 (1924): 67-74.

Morrison, Susan Signe. *Excrement in the Late Middle Ages: Sacred Filth and Chaucer's
Fecopoetics.* New York: Palgrave, 2008.

Muscatine, Charles. *Chaucer and the French Tradition: A Study in Style and Meaning.* Berkeley: U of California P, 1957.

Neuse, Richard. *Chaucer's Dante: Allegory and Epic Theater in the Canterbury Tales.*
Berkeley: U of California P, 1991.

O'Brien, Timothy D. "'Ars-Metrik': Science, Satire, and Chaucer's Summoner." *Mosaic* 23 (1990): 1-22.

Olson, Paul A. *"The Canterbury Tales" and the Good Society*. Princeton, NJ: Princeton UP, 1986.

Patterson, Lee. *Chaucer and the Subject of History*. Madison: U of Wisconsin P, 1991.

_____. *Temporal Circumstances: Form and History in "The Canterbury Tales."* New York: Palgrave Macmillan, 2006.

Robertson, D. W. *A Preface to Chaucer: Studies in Medieval Perspectives*. Princeton, NJ: Princeton UP, 1962.

Rogers, William E. *Upon the Ways: The Structure of the Canterbury Tales*. Victoria, BC: University of Victoria, 1986.

Rooney, Anne. *Geoffrey Chaucer: A Guide Through the Critical Maze*. Bristol: Bristol Press, 1989.

Ruggiers, Paul G. *The Art of "The Canterbury Tales."* Madison: U of Wisconsin P, 1965.

Silverman, Albert N. "Sex and Money in Chaucer's *Shipman's Tale*." *Philological Quarterly* 32 (1953): 329-36.

Stanbury, Sarah. "Ecochaucer: Green Ethics and Medieval Literature." *The Chaucer Review* 39.1 (2004): 1-16.

Stillwell, Gardiner. "The Political Meaning of Chaucer's *Tale of Melibee*." *Speculum* 19 (1944): 433-44.

Sturges, Robert S. *Chaucer's Pardoner and Gender Theory: Bodies of Discourse*. New York: St. Martin's Press, 1999.

Chaucer's Inferno:
Dantean Burlesques in *The Canterbury Tales*_____

Matthew J. Bolton

After telling the story of Count Ugolino, the unfortunate lord who, along with his young sons, was locked in a tower to starve to death, Chaucer's monk cites his sources. For those who would like to know more about Ugolino, the monk has a recommendation:

> Whoso wol here it in a lenger wise,
> Redeth the grete poete of Ytaille
> That highte Dant, for he kan al devyse
> Fro point to point, nat o word wol he faille.
> (VII.2459-62)

> Those who wish more, and on a nobler scale,
> Should turn and read the great Italian poet
> Dante by name; they will not find him fail
> In any point or syllable, I know it.
> (203)[1]

The monk is speaking for Chaucer himself, who knew Dante's *Commedia* well enough to appropriate it here and elsewhere in *The Canterbury Tales*. The Monk's Tale, for example, draws quite explicitly from Canto XXXIII of the *Inferno*, while the prologues to both The Prioress's Tale and The Second Nun's Tale are adaptations of a prayer in the *Paradiso* (Fisher 242, 311). While these may be two of the more obvious of Chaucer's adaptations of Dante, the English poet is indebted to his Italian counterpart in several other and more subtle respects. Like Dante, Chaucer composed in the vernacular rather than in Latin, organized his work by means of the frame story of a guided pilgrimage, and included himself as a character in the journey that he describes. Yet Chaucer gives each of these elements a carnivalesque turn, so that the serious matter of Dante's *Commedia* becomes, in *The Canterbury Tales*, the stuff of comedy. In particular, the two poets' contrasting depictions of Satan illustrate the difference between their solemn and comic sensibilities, and may also write large two modes of medieval thought and imagination.

As a courtier, a bureaucrat, and a diplomat, Chaucer knew several European languages and bodies of literature. He spoke the English of the street and the French of the court, read and wrote Latin, which was the language of record keeping and the Church, and read Italian. He traveled to France as a young man and to Italy in middle age, and therefore would have been exposed to European vernacular verse. In his earlier work he was heavily influenced by French literature; the *Romaunt of the Rose* is the best example of Chaucer recasting a French work into English. By the 1370s, however, Chaucer's primary influences seem to have been the Italian poets and writers. He began to compose *The Canterbury Tales* under the sway of Boccaccio and Dante, close contemporaries who were creating a new vernacular literature in Italy. Like these two, Chaucer eschewed Latin in favor of composing verse in the language he actually spoke. Much as Boccaccio and Dante would establish the dialect of Tuscany as the standard Italian language, so Chaucer would establish the London dialect as the standard for written English. The Italian poets also served as a font of stories, myths, and characters on which Chaucer drew. The Knight's Tale, for example, is an adaptation of Boccaccio's *Il Teseida* (Fisher 8).

As Boccaccio had in *The Decameron*, Chaucer used a frame story to allow for many speakers to trade tales in a range of voices, genres, and forms. The frame story of *The Decameron*, however, is a static one in which a group of young aristocrats trade tales after they have fled from a plague-ridden Florence to a country villa. In choosing the motif of the pilgrimage, and in making himself one of the pilgrims, Chaucer echoes the overall framework not of Boccaccio's *Decameron* but of Dante's *Commedia*. Dante's work begins, of course, with the narrator discovering that he is lost in a dark wood:

> Nel mezzo del cammin di nostra vita
> mi ritrovai per una selva oscura
> chè la dirrita via era smarrita.
> (I.1-3)

> Midway along the journey of our life
> I woke to find myself in some dark woods
> for I had wandered off from the straight path.[2]

The shade of the poet Virgil comes to Dante's aid, offering to lead him through Hell so that he may eventually ascend the Mount of Purgatory to Paradise. Virgil is a wholly dependable guide; commissioned by the angelic Beatrice, he has only Dante's best interests in mind. Moreover, as the author of the *Aeneid*, which Dante considered the greatest poem of antiquity, Virgil is a uniquely appropriate guide for a poet. Dante says,

> Tu sé lo mio maestro e 'l mio autore;
> tu sé solo colui da cu' io tolsi
> lo bello stilo che m'ha fatto onore.
> (I.87-89)

Critical Insights

> You are my teacher, the first of all my authors
> and you alone the one from whom I took
> the beautiful style that was to bring me honor.

Later he refers to Virgil as "tu duca, tu segnore, tu maestro" (II.140) ["You are my guide, you are my lord and teacher"]. Virgil describes his own role this way: "tu mi segue, e io sarò tua guida" (I.113) ["you follow me . . ./ and I shall be your guide"]. Dante will refer to Virgil as his guide ["guida"], teacher or master ["maestro"], and leader ["duca"] throughout the *Inferno*.

Whereas Dante is led by the shade of the poet Virgil, Chaucer's guide has a far less noble character and motives. At the start of *The Canterbury Tales*, a group of pilgrims have gathered to eat at the Tabard Inn in Southwark. Harry Bailey, the inn's owner, proposes that the pilgrims travel together and engage in a story contest. Bailey outlines the rules for the contest, as well as the reward for the winner:

> And which of yow that bereth hym best of alle,
> That is to seyn, that telleth in this caas
> Tales of best sentence and moost solaas,
> Shall have a soper at oure aller cost
> Heere in this place, sittynge by this post,
> Whan that we come agayn fro Caunterbury.
> And for to make yow the moore mury,
> I wol myselven goodly with yow ryde,
> Right at myn owene cost, and youre gyde.
> And whoso wole my juggement withseye
> Shal paye al that we spenden by the weye.
>   (I.796-806)

> And then the man whose story is best told
> That is to say who gives the fullest measure
> Of good morality and general pleasure,
> He shall be given a supper, paid by all,
> Here in this tavern, in this very hall,
> When we come back from Canterbury.
> And in the hope to keep you bright and merry
> I'll go along with you myself and ride
> All at my own expense and serve as guide.
> I'll be the judge, and those who won't obey
> Shall pay for what we spend along the way.
>   (24)

Harry Bailey has a clear ulterior motive for proposing to be the party's "gyde." By keeping the twenty-nine pilgrims together, he can assure that they will all be repeat customers at the Tabard Inn. Note that the feast that will honor the winner is to be paid for not by Bailey himself but rather "at aller cost." The group of pilgrims will return to the inn and will again pay for a meal and lodgings. Moreover, while Bailey says he will travel "at myn owene cost," he intimates a moment later that he will have a say over which pilgrims pay the group's expenses during the journey, for "whoso wole my juggement withseye/ Shal paye al that we spenden by the weye." Bailey has a pecuniary interest in the pilgrimage, and he accompanies Chaucer and his fellow travelers because he hopes to profit from the experience. He might sympathize with Shakespeare's Iago, who says, "Thus do I ever make my fool my purse" (1.3.383). Virgil and Harry Bailey therefore represent two ends of a spectrum, with one guide appointed by divine mandate and the other self-appointed in the hope of turning a profit.

It is not only the guides but also the pilgrims themselves who make the *Inferno* and *The Canterbury Tales* a study in contrasts. One of the most fascinating dynamics in the *Inferno* (and in the *Commedia* as a whole) lies in the dual role that Dante himself plays in the work. He is both pilgrim and poet: one Dante traverses Hell, Purgatory, and Heaven, while another, later incarnation of the poet writes about the journey. Putting himself into his narrative is an audacious act, for as humble as Dante the pilgrim may be on his journey, Dante the poet has elected himself worthy to be shown all the mysteries of the cosmos. At the beginning of the poem, Dante the pilgrim is an unworthy figure, wandering in the *selva oscura* of sin and despair. But as Virgil leads him onward, Dante's nobility and worthiness are gradually revealed. When Dante meets the great poets of the classical world in Limbo, for example, he is welcomed among them not merely as a guest but as a coequal:

> Da ch'ebber ragionato insieme alquanto,
> volsersi a me con salutevol cenno;
> e 'l mio maestro sorrise di tanto:
> e più d'onore ancora assai mi fenno,
> ch'e' sì mi fecer de la loro schiera,
> sì ch'io fui sesto tra cotanto senno.
> (IV.97-102)

> After they talked awhile together,
> they turned and with a gesture welcomed me,
> and at that sign I saw my master smile.

> Greater honor still they deigned to grant me:
> they welcomed me as one of their own group,
> so that I numbered sixth among such minds.

Dante the pilgrim seems appropriately humbled by his reception. But, of course, the *Commedia* is not a memoir, and Dante the poet has invented out of his own imagination and his own sense of self-worth a scenario in which Homer, Virgil, and the other poets of antiquity acknowledge him as one of their own.

Whereas Dante aggrandizes his own status as a poet, Chaucer casts himself in a very different light. When Harry Bailey asks him to tell a tale, Chaucer the pilgrim launches into The Tale of Sir Thopas, a story that gives such attention to its hero's armor, dress, horse, and manners, and in which after some two hundred lines nothing has yet happened. Harry Bailey interrupts Chaucer:

> "Namoore of this, for Goddes dignitee,"
> Quod oure Hooste, "for thou makest me
> So wery of thy verray lewednesse
> That, also wisly God my soule blesse,
> Myne eres aken of thy drasty speche.
> Now swich a rym the devel I biteche!
> This may wel be rym doggerel," quod he.
> (VII.919-25)

> "No more of this for God's dear dignity!"
> Our Host said suddenly. "You're wearying me
> To death, I say, with your illiterate stuff.
> God bless my soul! I've had about enough.
> My ears are aching from your frowsty story!
> The devil take such rhymes! They're purgatory!
> That must be what's called doggerel-rhyme," said he.
> (183)

According to Harry Bailey, Chaucer's speech is "drasty," or full of dregs (Fisher 252). The innkeeper has passed judgment on the poet using a term drawn from his own tapster profession: Chaucer's words are the worthless remains of the language.

The hapless Chaucer protests, arguing that he is doing the best he can, at which Bailey again firmly passes judgment:

Dantean Burlesques in *The Canterbury Tales*   **35**

"Why so," quod I, "why wiltow lette me
Moore of my tale than another man,
Syn that it is the beste rym I kan?"
    "By God," quod he, "for pleynly, at o word,
Thy drasty rymyng is nat worth a toord!
Thou doost noght ells but despendest tyme.
Sire, at o word, thou shalt no lenger ryme."
                                    (VII.926-32)

"Why so," said I, "Why should you hinder me
In telling of my tale more than another man,
Since I am giving it the best I can?"
    "By God," he said, "put plainly in a word
Your dreary rhyming isn't worth a turd!
You're doing nothing else but wasting time.
Sir, in a word, you shall no longer rhyme."
                                    (183-84)

Harry Bailey wins the argument, and Chaucer the pilgrim tells a new tale in prose rather than in poetry. Ironically, the man who composed *The Canterbury Tales* itself is forced to speak in prose, for his "rymyng is nat worth a toord!" Chaucer's self-deprecating portrayal of himself is tremendously effective and funny. He ascribes to himself none of the wit or insight that he clearly possesses, lending it instead to the innkeeper and other characters. In doing so, Chaucer grants his characters authenticity and autonomy, for they overshadow the author himself.

While Dante and Chaucer both include themselves in their stories, they do so to opposite ends. If Dante elevates himself to the status of the poets of antiquity, assuming the mantle of his guide and master Virgil, Chaucer makes himself the butt of his other characters' jokes. An innkeeper passes judgment on Chaucer's verse and deigns him the only pilgrim unfit to speak in rhyme. In their self-representations, Dante and Chaucer illustrate the range of the medieval sensibility and imagination. Dante presents himself as a poet worthy not only to stand among Homer, Virgil, and the other great classical poets but also to ascend to Heaven itself and look upon the face of God. Chaucer's pilgrim, on the other hand, moves toward the base and the scatological; indeed, Bailey compares his rhyming to "a toord" and forbids him to speak in verse. Midway through his own poem, Chaucer finds that his rhyming is no longer welcome.

A pair of scenes in the *Inferno* and *The Canterbury Tales* illustrate clearly the two different modes in which Dante and Chaucer composed: the two poets' depictions of Satan. At the climax of the *Inferno*, Virgil and Dante come to the dead center of Hell, where they find Satan frozen in a lake of his own tears. It is good to read Dante in the original here, since Chaucer himself did so and may well have had this scene in mind when he wrote the Summoner's prologue.

> Lo 'mperador del doloroso regno
> da mezzo il petto uscia fuor de la ghiaccia;
> e più con un gigante io mi convegno,
>
> che giganti no fan le sue braccia
> (XXXIV.28-31)

> The king of the vast kingdom of all grief
> stuck out with half his chest above the ice;
> my height is closer to the height of giants
>
> Than theirs is to the length of his great arms

The fallen angel is built on an entirely different scale than a man, for his ruined wings are larger than sails:

> Sotto ciascuna uscivan due grand'ali,
> quanto si convenia a tanto Uccello:
> vele di mar non vid'io mai cotali
> (XXXIV.46-48)

> Beneath each face two mighty wings stretched out,
> the size you might expect of this huge bird
> (I never saw a ship with larger sails)

Satan has three heads, each a different color, and in each mouth he gnaws at a man:

> Da ogne bocca dirompea co' denti
> un peccatore, a guise di maciulla,
> sì che tre ne facea così dolente.
> (XXXIV.55-57)

In each of his three mouths he crunched a sinner
with teeth like those that rake the hemp and flax,
keeping three sinners constantly in pain.

This is the punishment reserved for the three great betrayers of the classical and biblical worlds: Satan holds in his three sets of jaws Brutus and Cassius, who betrayed Julius Caesar, and Judas Iscariot, who betrayed Jesus Christ. Dante's image of Satan is a powerful and terrifying one, as is the eternal punishment he reserves for these three arch-sinners.

Chaucer, too, describes Satan, in the words exchanged between the Summoner and the Friar. These two pilgrims are at odds with each other, and each man tells a tale that denigrates the other's profession or religious order. The Friar speaks first, telling the story of a summoner who falls into the company of a devil. The summoner goes about his regular practice of threatening to summon a peasant to appear in ecclesiastical court if she does not offer him a bribe. The peasant woman damns the summoner to Hell, and the devil gladly follows through on the woman's threat. On hearing the Friar's tale, the actual Summoner is incensed. In revenge, he launches into the story of a friar who dreams of visiting Hell. After touring the infernal kingdom, the friar is surprised and pleased to find that there are no friars to be found there. He asks his guide whether it is the case that the friars are all in heaven. By way of an answer, the angel who is leading the friar through Hell takes him to see Satan:

> "And now hath Sathanas," seith he, "a tayl
> Brodder than of a carryk is the sayl.
> Hold up thy tayl, thou Sathanas" quod he,
> "Shewe forth thyn ers, a lat the frere se
> Where is the nest of freres in this place!"
> And er that half a furlong wey of space
> Right so as bees out swarmen from an hyve,
> Out of the develes ers ther gonne dryne
> Out of the develes ers ther gonne dryve
> Twenty thousand freres in a route,
> And thurghout helle swarmeden aboute,
> And comen agayn, as faste as they may gon,
> And in his ers they crepten everychon.
> He clapte his tayl again and lay ful stille.
>   (III.1686-99)

"Satan," the angel said, "has got a tail
As broad or broader than a barge's sail.
Hold up thy tail, thou Satan!" then said he,
"Show forth thine arse and let the friar see
The nest ordained for friars in this place!"
Ere the tail rose a furlong into space
From underneath it there began to drive,
Much as if bees were swarming from a hive,
Some twenty thousand friars in a rout
And swarmed all over Hell and round about,
And then came back as fast as they could run
And crept into his arse again, each one.
He clapped his tail on them and they lay still.
(304)

Chaucer's Satan is on the same scale as Dante's Satan; the former has "a tayl/ Brodder than of a carryk is the sayl," while Dante says of the latter "I never saw a ship with larger sails." And both use their massive bodies to punish the tiny bodies of sinning men. But Chaucer inverts Dante's image in a grotesque and comic way: whereas the Satan of the *Inferno* holds sinners in his mouth, his counterpart in *The Canterbury Tales* holds them in his "ers."

This inversion of bodily orifices is a reductio ad absurdum illustration of two different mind-sets in medieval thought. Critic Mikhail Bakhtin describes these two modes this way:

> It could be said (with certain reservations, of course) that a person of the Middle Ages lived, as it were, two lives: one that was the official life, monolithically serious and gloomy. . . . the other was the life of the carnival square, free and unrestricted, full of ambivalent laughter, blasphemy, the profanation of everything sacred. (*Problems* 129-30)

In his portrayal of Satan, Chaucer transports the "serious" matter of Dante's poem into the "free and unrestricted" space of the carnival. Whereas the devil gnashing his teeth on the bodies of sinners is a frightful image, the image of friars nesting in the devil's anus is a ridiculous one. The Summoner's description makes not only the friars but also Hell and Satan objects of laughter and ridicule. In shifting his attention from the devil's head to his tail—to say nothing of the "unmentionable" body parts that the tail hides—Chaucer produces a comic and carnivalesque parody of the *Inferno*.

In fact, this process of substitution and inversion is at work throughout *The Canterbury Tales*. The Miller's Tale, for example, functions according to much the same logic. The "joly" and "amorous" Absolon (I.3371, 3657), who subscribes to a courtly vision of love and romance, pines for the married Alison. One night, he asks Alison to lean out her window and kiss him. The trick Alison plays on Absolon is one of the tale's punch lines:

> Dirk was the nyght as pich, or as the cole,
> And at the wyndow out she putte hir hole,
> And Absolon, hym fil no bet ne wers,
> But with his mouth he kiste hir naked ers
> Ful savourly, er he were war of this.
>
> (I.3731-35)

> Dark was the night as pitch, and black as cole,
> And at the window out she put her hole,
> And Absalon, so fortune framed the farce,
> Put up his mouth and kissed her naked arse
> Most savourly before he knew of this.
>
> (103)

In a maneuver that is reminiscent of Chaucer's parody of Dante, Alison presents Absolon not with her face but with her backside. In so doing, she effectively upends his whole conception of romance. Absolon is a Petrarchan lover who earlier in the story was struck physically ill by his lovesick devotion to Alison; in this respect, he might be read as belonging to the same tradition as the lovesick gentlemen Palamon and Arcite in The Knight's Tale. This sort of courtly devotion is predicated on distance and separation. In kissing Alison's backside, Absolon comes into contact with a physical and bodily reality that banishes forever his romantic conceptions:

> His hoote love was coold and al yqueynt
> For fro that tyme that he hadde kist hir ers
> Of paramours he sette nat a kers,
> For he was heeled of his malaide
> Ful ofte paramours he gan deffie
>
> (I.3754-58)

> The fiery heat of love by now had cooled,
> For from the time he kissed her hinder parts
> He didn't give a tinker's curse for tarts;
> His malady was cured by this endeavor
> And he defied all paramours whatever.
>
> (103)

Absolon's worldview is not broad enough to allow for both the courtly and the corporeal, and after falling victim to Alison's trick he swears off the amorous pursuits that had once been his obsession.

Bakhtin's work on medieval notions of the body and of laughter can help shed light on both The Miller's Tale and the Summoner's prologue. According to Bakhtin, the spirit of the medieval carnival or marketplace feast involved bringing the ideal and unchanging order back down to the level of the earthly and the bodily. He writes, "The essential principle of grotesque realism is degradation, that is, the lowering of all that is high, spiritual, ideal, abstract; it is a transfer to the material level, to the sphere of earth and body in their indissoluble unity" (*Rabelais* 19-20). The grotesque involves the body's assertion of itself; it is the revelation and predominance of those parts of the anatomy that are normally clothed and concealed: "To degrade also means to concern oneself with the lower stratum of the body, the life of the belly and the reproductive organs; it therefore relates to acts of defecation and copulation, conception, pregnancy, and birth" (21). Alison's treatment of Absolon enacts this process of degradation, for she foists upon him the lower strata of her body. The Summoner—and, by extension, Chaucer himself—engages in a similar process of degradation by describing not Satan's face and mouth but his lower strata. The Satan of the Summoner's prologue cannot be fearsome, for the ridiculous portrayal of his "ers" brings him out of the realm of the infernal or the cosmic and back to that of the earthly.

In the *Inferno*, Dante and Virgil actually must climb the length of Satan's body to escape from Hell, and it is fascinating to note what parts of the devil's anatomy Dante omits from his narrative. Satan is positioned at the very center of Hell, and, with Dante clinging to his neck, Virgil uses the devil as a ladder to pass through the realm's center:

> appigliò sé a le vellute coste;
> di vello in vello giù discese poscia
> tra 'l folto pelo e le gelate croste.
>
> Quando noi fummo là dove la coscia
> si volge, a punto in sul grosso de l'anche,
> lo duca, con fatica e con angoscia,
>
> volse la testa ov'elli avea le zanche,
> e aggrappossi al pel com'om che sale,
> sì che 'n inferno i' credea tornar anche.
> (XXXIV.73-81)

he grabbed on to the shaggy sides of Satan;
    then downward, tuft by tuft, he made his way
    between the tangled hair and frozen crust.

When we had reached the point exactly where
    the thigh begins, right at the haunch's curve,
    my guide with strain and force of every muscle,

turned his head toward the shaggy shanks of Dis
    and grabbed the hair as if about to climb—
    I thought that we were heading back to Hell.

Virgil has inverted himself, so that where a moment before he was climbing down Satan's torso, he will now climb up his legs and into the world's other hemisphere. He will later explain to Dante that in climbing down and then up Satan, the two men passed through the center of the world and the center of gravity: "quand'io mi volsi, tu passasti 'l punto/ al qual si traggon d'ogni parte I pesi" (XXXIV.109-10) ["When I turned myself, you passed the point/ to which all weight from every part is drawn"]. Hell and earth alike are centered on Satan's nether regions. Elsewhere in the *Inferno*, Dante is quite explicit about the sufferings and torments visited on the bodies of the shades in Hell. Yet here, in describing Satan, he becomes suddenly euphemistic, alluding to Satan's genitals and buttocks as "the point at which the thigh begins" ["là dove la coscia/ si volge, a punto in sul grosso de l'anche"]. Does Satan lack genitals and the buttocks that figure so prominently in the Summoner's prologue, or does Dante assume that he possesses them but shy away from describing them? The question, of course, is a semantic one: in either case, Satan's lower stratum cannot be represented in the text of the *Inferno* without moving Dante's vision of the cosmos into the realm of the medieval carnival.

In fact, Dante comes perilously close to this carnivalesque mode in describing what he saw on looking back down at Satan. Because Virgil and Dante have crossed through the center of the world and begun to climb up into the Southern Hemisphere, their perspective on Satan is now reversed:

Io levai li occhi, e credetti vedere
    Lucifero com'io l'avea lasciato;
    e vidili le gambe in sù tenere;
        (XXXIV.88-90)

I raised my eyes expecting I would see
the half of Lucifer I saw before.
Instead I saw his two legs stretching upward.

(245)

The image is hard to take seriously. After the terror and drama of Satan's head and torso, the sight of his legs sticking up in the air is rather silly (from this vantage point, incidentally, Dante could say whether there were indeed any friars in "the develes ers"). But the devil's nether regions are concealed; the text clothes them with silence and omission as readily as would a garment. In fact, this kind of silence about the body's lower half is a commonplace in many bodies of literature, particularly those dealing with other worlds. Consider works of science fiction such as the *Star Wars* and *Star Trek* films and television series, where spaceships the size of cities hurtle across the galaxy without seeming to possess any bathrooms. J. R. R. Tolkien's *Lord of the Rings* trilogy is another example of a meticulously detailed fantasy world that is rich in myths and songs but entirely devoid of sex, money, and other commonplace concerns. To create a setting that is not of the earth, science-fiction and fantasy writers tend to ignore the earthly. Dante, too, ignores or elides those elements of human nature and the human body that tend toward the comic. The pilgrim's last view of Satan's legs sticking up in the air might be read as one of the few instances in which Dante fails to contain the subversive nature of the body's lower half. For a moment, his portrayal of the terrors of Hell is compromised by Satan's body reasserting itself in the most earthly of ways.

It is valuable to identify the ways in which Chaucer parodies Dante, because doing so illustrates the range of medieval modes of thought and representation. Yet it would be a mistake to conclude that Dante's work is wholly serious and Chaucer's wholly comic. In point of fact, both *The Canterbury Tales* and the *Inferno* are animated by a tension between the serious and the comic and the high and the low. Because their work draws on a great many genres and traditions, both Dante and Chaucer should be seen as representing the full spectrum of medieval life and sensibilities that Bakhtin describes. The remarkable architectonics and deep structure of Dante's *Commedia* can keep the reader from seeing how disparate and wide-ranging is the poet's source material. In the three books of the *Commedia*, Dante fuses classical literature, the Bible, folktales, and local politics into a single, manifold text. Chaucer's work likewise involves the synthesis and interplay of a great many genres and traditions. As characters from different social strata tell their tales, each new episode challenges and illuminates the tales that have preceded it. The Knight's Tale and The Miller's Tale are the first of many such contrasts; the courtly sentiments of the one and the ribald bawdiness of the other do not exist on the same plane of reality, and yet neither invalidates the other. Chaucer's accomplishment in *The Canterbury Tales* lies not merely in his having synthesized so many literary and popular traditions and forms but also in his having put into dialogue the opposing sensibilities of these traditions. One should therefore see in Dante and Chaucer two poles of this medieval range of thought, but having established this range, one should look for it within the work of each poet.

Notes

1. Quotations from *The Canterbury Tales* appear first from the edition of Chaucer's works edited by John H. Fisher and then in Nevill Coghill's translation.

2. Quotations from the *Inferno* appear first in the original Italian and then in Mark Musa's translation.

Works Cited

Bakhtin, Mikhail. *Problems of Dostoevsky's Poetics*. Minneapolis: U of Minnesota P, 1984.
_____. *Rabelais and His World*. Bloomington: Indiana UP, 1984.
Chaucer, Geoffrey. *The Canterbury Tales*. Trans. Nevill Coghill. New York: Penguin, 1951.
_____. *The Canterbury Tales. The Complete Poetry and Prose of Geoffrey Chaucer*. Ed. John H. Fisher. New York: Harcourt Brace, 1989.
Dante. *Dante's Inferno: The Indiana Critical Edition*. Ed. and trans. Mark Musa. Bloomington: Indiana UP, 1995.
_____. *La divina commedia: Testo critico della Societa Dantesca Italiana. Rifatto da Giuseppe Vandelli*. Milan: Ulrico Hoepli, 1987.
Shakespeare, William. *Othello. The Riverside Shakespeare*. New York: Houghton Mifflin, 1997.

A Feminist Perspective on *The Canterbury Tales*_____
Rosemary M. Canfield Reisman

In looking at *The Canterbury Tales* from a feminist perspective, it is important to remember the caveats expressed by critics Ruth Evans and Lesley
Johnson: that one cannot ignore the differences between the medieval past and
the present day; that, in the poststructuralist period, no character in a literary
work can or should be reduced to a single interpretation; that most of the stories in *The Canterbury Tales* are told by males; and that both Chaucer the pilgrim and Chaucer the author are also males (1-2). Moreover, since the work
was not finished, we cannot know whether it would have been structured
around the Seven Deadly Sins, as some scholars believe, or around the theme
of marriage, as others have claimed. Feminist critics differ among themselves
as much as do their male predecessors about the implications of individual
tales, as well as about Chaucer's views of women. Certainly Chaucer was
more sympathetic to the plight of women than most other male medieval writers; however, it is evident that the relations between his men and women are
rarely, if ever, harmonious. Chaucer's women are imbued with a variety of
traits—courage and cunning, purity and duplicity—yet, reflecting the society that Chaucer knew, they are nearly all dependent upon male protectors,
whether ruler, father, brother, husband, or lover.

It is perhaps not surprising that many feminist critics have looked toward
the colorful Wife of Bath as a feminist model. Her life story is a blueprint for
success in the rapidly changing society in which she lives. She is a successful
cloth maker, a skill she may have acquired as a child or perhaps after she married her first husband at the age of twelve. She confides to the company that
she married three elderly husbands, won them to her will, and acquired their
goods and land; her fifth, scholarly husband was more difficult to handle, but
she was intelligent enough to hold her own with him in argument and, after he
struck her, clever enough to use his sense of guilt to subdue him. Now she answers to no one. Her wealth and her self-confidence allow her to travel wherever she likes. Meanwhile, when she is at home on the Sabbath, she continues
to remind her community of her high social status by leading the parade "to
the offringe" (450) ["Toward the altar steps" (15)].[1]

Though the Wife of Bath does not mention her parents, it can be assumed
that her first marriage was arranged, likely by her father, for she lived in a patriarchal society. Chaucer's tales reflect the feudal tradition: an inferior expects protection from a superior, and the superior, in turn, is assured of the
inferior's obedience. Where a female is concerned, the protector is a male—
a father, a husband, a brother, or a ruler. Thus "The Knight's Tale" begins with
appeals to Theseus, the king of Athens, from a group of highborn Theban la-

dies whose protectors, their husbands, have been killed in the Theban civil war and are being denied burial. Theseus promptly disposes of the tyrannical ruler, Creon, and permits the burials. Then he makes two young knights who have survived the battle his prisoners, transports them to Athens, and places them in a tower keep.

At this point, the romance begins. From their prison, the two Theban princes, Arcite and Palamon, can see Theseus's young sister-in-law, Emily, wandering in the garden, and soon they are both in love with her. The young men have always been as close as brothers; they had thought that the bond between them would be unbreakable. Now, however, their love for Emily makes them enemies. Eventually, it is Theseus who must decide between them; in fact, an even higher authority takes a hand, for after Arcite, the votary of Mars, has won Emily's hand in a tournament, Saturn, the grandfather of the gods, takes the side of Venus, whose help has been enlisted by Palamon, and Arcite is eliminated after a fatal fall from his horse.

However, a feminist reader cannot help noticing that, unlike most of Chaucer's heroines, Emily is so passive as to appear spiritless. Even during the year or so that Arcite spent in her household, first as her page and then as a favorite squire of Theseus, Emily seems to have been immune to his charms. In fact, in a prayer to Diana, she reminds the goddess of chastity that she, too, would like to remain a "maiden all my lif" (2305) ["a virgin all my life" (65)] and "noght to been a wife and be with childe" (2310) ["not to be a wife or be with child" (65)] or ever to "knowe compaignye of man" (2311) ["to know the company of man" (65)]. Diana informs Emily that she cannot grant her wish: Emily will marry one of the men, but the goddess cannot tell her which one.

When Arcite is on his deathbed, Emily is by his side, and after his death, she mourns appropriately, though she would hardly qualify for the rather smug comment the knight makes about widows who die of grief. After the funeral and a suitable period of mourning, Theseus sends for Emily and suggests that she accept Arcite's death as reflecting the will of Jupiter; it would be wise, he continues, "To maken vertu of necessitee" (3042) ["To make a virtue of necessity" (84)]. Theseus bestows Emily's hand in marriage upon Palamon, and their union is a happy one. According to the pilgrim who is telling the story, a man, "Emelye him loveth so tendrely,/ And he hir serveth so gentilly/ That nevere was ther no word hem bitwene /Of jalousye, or any oother tene" (3103-6) ["He's tenderly beloved of Emily/ And serves her with a gentle constancy,/ And never a jealous word between them spoken/ Or other sorrow in a love unbroken" (86)]. It is unusual for what began as courtly love to end up in a happy marriage, for, as Barbara Feichtinger points out, "a skeptical attitude toward marriage is an integral part of the code of courtly love, which idealizes extramarital love" (202). Indeed, the glorification of extramarital relationships, which presented such obvious temptations, was the primary reason the Church so strongly opposed the courtly love movement.

Though Emily's story is set in the ancient world, her initial desire to remain a virgin would not have been improbable in a medieval setting. As Jocelyn Wogan-Browne explains, for the women who read them, the lives of saints became "an important critique of courtly love" (181), with its erotic implications, and even, by extension, of marriage, which involved sexual relations, childbearing, and, too often, death in childbed. Moreover, young girls like Emily, who was never given the opportunity to express an opinion about her own destiny, might have seen that saintly virgins were given choices. In "The Physician's Tale," for example, Virginius gives his daughter Virginia a choice, "deeth or shame" (446) ["death or shame" (237)], and, at her request, he allows her some time to consider her decision. The outcome is not surprising, given her training in virtue: rather than surrender her virginity to a corrupt judge, she chooses to have her father strike off her head. Nevertheless, she is given more freedom than Emily. Moreover, if her power is limited, she is equal to men in at least one respect—she has the kind of courage that Chaucer apparently believes is as valuable in a woman as in a man.

Virginity is also presented as an ideal in "The Second Nun's Tale," which appropriately is preceded by Chaucer's invocation to the Virgin Mary, who, he reminds his audience, was the undefiled mother of Jesus Christ. Then the Second Nun begins retelling a saint's story she has read. Cecilia, the heroine, is a young Roman woman of noble birth who has long prayed to God, "Biseking him to kepe hir maidenhede" (617) ["Beseeching Him to guard her maidenhead" (437)]. Even at her wedding, she continues to pray for virginity. That night, she explains to her young husband, Valerian, that if he touches her, her guardian angel will kill him. Understandably, Valerian insists on seeing this angel, and Cecilia says that he must first profess his faith in Christ and be baptized. Valerian does so, and when he returns home, he does indeed meet Cecilia's angel. As a result of these events, Valerian's brother Tiburce, too, is converted. In due course, the two men are sentenced to be executed, but before they die, they are responsible for the conversions of the Roman officer and of the torturers assigned to kill them.

Brought before the prefect, Almachius, Cecilia not only proclaims her faith but also argues with him as if she were his equal, infuriating him, and when he offers her a choice between abjuring her faith and dying, she compounds the insult by laughing at him. When Almachius tries to burn her alive, her body remains cool. Though an executioner finally succeeds in wounding her mortally, Cecilia continues to preach and teach for the three days before she dies and ascends to Heaven. As Wogan-Browne puts it, in the lives of such saints it was evident that such courageous "virgin heroines can both gaze and answer back and are shown as much cleverer than their tormenters" (181). At least in martyrdom, a female can attain equality.

One of the most difficult of Chaucer's stories for feminists to deal with is "The Clerk's Tale." It is true that the medieval Church emphasized the subordination of the individual will to that of a higher power as a means of attaining grace, pointing out that such an act was indeed an imitation of Christ. What feminists find disturbing is that in his story of Patient Griselda, Chaucer's Clerk applies this principle to marriage. It is interesting to note that the Clerk begins his tale by describing Walter, the marquis of Saluzzo, as a man who, though he is generally benevolent and courteous, lives in the moment, with no thought for the future. Walter's subjects' chief concern then is that the marquis has made no provisions for succession. When they finally confront him with the problem and urge him to take a wife, they present marriage in the most favorable terms: it is a "blissful yok/ Of sovereinetee, noght of servise" (113-114) ["blessed yoke!/ It is a kingdom, not a slavery" (323)]. Yet Walter is not so sanguine about matrimony: "I me rejoised of my libertee,/ That selde time is founde in marriage" (146-146) ["I go rejoicing in my liberty,/ And that and marriage seldom go together" (324)]. Still, he agrees to place himself in what he insists on calling servitude, but on two conditions: that the choice of a wife will be left up to him and that his subjects will accept the woman he selects. Walter decides on a poor girl called Griselda, who is both beautiful and virtuous. He asks her father, Janicula, for her hand in marriage, and when the old man consents, Walter proposes to the maiden herself. Before she accepts, however, he makes one stipulation: she must promise to obey him unconditionally and cheerfully, no matter what he asks of her. She agrees.

The marriage begins well. Griselda proves to be a good mediator in disputes that arise among Walter's subjects, and, after she bears Walter a daughter, it is evident that she is not barren and the realm can hope for a male heir. However, while their child is still at her mother's breast, Walter decides to test his wife. Telling her that their subjects are objecting to the child because of her mother's lowly birth, he has the baby taken away, supposedly to be killed. Griselda does not protest the loss of her child, nor does she ever mention the subject to Walter, to whom she continues to be an affectionate and considerate wife. Four years later, Walter and Griselda have a son, and this time Walter waits until the child is two years old before having him seized. Again, Griselda does not let her husband see how grievously he has wounded her.

However, Walter is still in the grips of his obsession. He devises a third test of his wife's promise, and again he lies to her. Although their subjects have come to love Griselda, Walter insists that they are unhappy with her because of her low birth, and therefore he feels it is his duty to replace her with someone more suitable. He pretends to obtain a divorce, sends for the girl who is supposedly his new bride, and watches as Griselda leaves for her father's house, dressed only in a smock like that in which she first came to Walter. At this point, Walter does feel some pity, but nevertheless he has one final test for Griselda. He sends for her and when she appears before him, he asks her to supervise the decorating of his house so that all will be in order for the reception of his new wife. Again Griselda makes no objection. At last, Walter is satisfied. He declares, "'This is inogh, Griselde min'" (1051) ["It is enough, Griselda mine" (351)] and takes Griselda into his arms. He now proceeds to introduce Griselda to her long-lost daughter, who is identified as the supposed bride, and to their seven-year-old son, explaining that both children have been reared by his sister, the countess of Bologna. As for what motivated his behavior toward Griselda, Walter tells her that it was not "malice" or "crueltee" (1074) ["cruelty" (351)] but "t'assaye in thee thy wommanhede" (1075) ["for the trial of your womanhood" (351)].

The Clerk ends by saying that the purpose of his story is not to suggest that women imitate Griselda's humility—for even if they wished to, they would be incapable of withstanding such trials—but instead to present a model of constancy in adversity when it is God, not a human being like Walter, who is testing us. This explanation addresses one of the persistent critical issues plaguing "The Clerk's Tale": what are we to make of Walter?

Jill Mann asserts, "There is no shred of support for Walter's behavior in the narrative; on the contrary, Chaucer carefully adds to it explicit condemnations of his obsessive desire to test Griselda" (117), and she points out a specific passage in the text. Just before Walter informs Griselda that their daughter is to be taken from her, Chaucer has the Clerk comment, "ivele it sit/ T'assaye a wif whan that it is no need,/ And putten hire in angwyssh and in drede" (460-62) ["what was the need/ Of heaping trial on her, more and more?/ . . ./For my part, I should say it could succeed/ Only in evil; what could be the gain/ In putting her to needless fear and pain?" (333-34)]. Thus, despite his later protestations, Walter is branded as having behaved in an "evil" manner. One can hardly argue with that. By choosing a woman from such a humble social position for his wife, Walter guaranteed that the communication in his marriage would run in only one direction. He would speak; Griselda would listen. The implication is that her feelings are unimportant. Again, when he takes away the two children, Walter expects Griselda to smother her maternal instincts. She cannot even protest. Afterward, she continues to express her love for the man she believes is the murderer of her children.

Walter's final tricks are less surprising—he is hardly the first man to trade in the mother of his children for a new wife—though his demand that his former wife prepare his house for his new one is unusual. It should also be pointed out that Walter further fails as a husband in that, while testing his wife, he has no compunction about lying to her. Not only does he lie to her about what will happen to their children, about the validity of the divorce, and about his plans for a remarriage, but he also lies about how his subjects feel about Griselda. By pretending that they resent her because of her lowly birth, Walter isolates her from a populace that in fact has come to love her and has lost respect for him.

As Mann points out (118), there are serious flaws in Bernard Levy's theory that Walter tests Griselda to prove her worthy of joining the ruling class (403). Aside from the fact that Chaucer explicitly remarks that it was unnecessary to test Griselda, critics have noted that so elitist an attitude is not consistent with *The Canterbury Tales* or with the poet's other works (Brewer 89-109). Chaucer makes it clear that gentilesse is not a matter of rank but of values. Marquis or not, Walter's disregard for the truth and his discourteous treatment of his wife both bar him from possessing gentilesse.

"The Clerk's Tale" has sometimes been interpreted as a religious parable. Certainly Griselda's patience under adversity has much in common with the behavior of Virginia and Cecilia. However, if one equates Walter with God, serious issues must be confronted. For example, as Mann notes, Walter is motivated not by love—as the biblical God is—but by a selfish obsession (123). On the other hand, the biblical God is often shown testing human beings, as he does when he demands that Abraham sacrifice his son, Isaac, or when he casts his faithful servant Job upon an ash heap to see whether or not Job will curse his Maker. The most profound significance of "The Clerk's Tale," according to Mann, is the presentation of Griselda as "the divine in woman's form" (123). Thus she should not be viewed as a model for wives to emulate but as a Christlike suffering servant. Feminists who are wary about a story that seems to advocate relinquishing sovereignty to human males may find this religious view of "The Clerk's Tale" more acceptable than other interpretations. As Mann puts it, "If Walter's tyranny caricatures God's 'governance', Griselda's patience *truly* reflects God's suffering. Her 'vertuous suffraunce' is not opposed to God's 'governaunce'; it is one with it" (128).

Any feminist interpretation of "The Clerk's Tale" should focus on Chaucer's ironic "Envoy" to the story, in which Chaucer warns husbands not to expect to find women like Griselda and even encourages wives to seize control of their marriages through verbal aggression and by making their husbands jealous. The male pilgrims apply the story of Griselda to their own lives. The Host wishes his wife could have heard the tale; the Merchant describes his own wife of two months as a cruel and malicious shrew. January, who is the elderly hero of "The Merchant's Tale," entered into marriage expecting it to be a "paradis" (1265) ["paradise on earth" (357)]. Bitterly the Merchant outlines January's expectations of marriage, his reasons for abandoning a long life of libertinism, his decision to marry a young, beautiful virgin, whom he can mold into an ideal wife. January dismisses the warnings of his friend Justinus and instead listens to Placebo, who characteristically voices his support of the decision January has already made. January makes his choice, a lovely creature named May, and the two are united.

Throughout the wedding feast, January anticipates the bliss of their first sexual encounter. He is not disappointed. However, May is put off by his person and his performance. As Chaucer puts it, "Whan she him saw sitting in his sherte,/ In his night-cappe, and with his nekke lene; She preiseth nat his pleying worth a bene" (1852-54) ["Seeing him sit there in his shirt apart, Wearing his night-cap, with his scrawny throat./ She didn't think his games were worth a groat" (373)]. Meanwhile, January's lusty young squire, Damien, is so overcome with desire for May that he has taken to his bed. When January sends May to visit his ailing retainer, Damien manages to slip her a love letter, and the two begin corresponding. In time, January goes blind, and he becomes so possessed by jealousy that "He nolde suffre hire for to ride or go/ But if that he hadde hond on her alway " (2090-91) ["nor anywhere/ Would he allow his wife to take the air/ Unless his hand were on her, day and night" (379)]. By now, May is so desperate with desire for Damien that "she moot outher dien sodeinly,/ Or ellis she moot han him as hir leste;/ She waiteth when hir herte wolde breaste!" (2094-20) ["sudden death was her design/ Unless she could enjoy him; so at first/ She wept and waited for her heart to burst" (379)]. Finally, she hits upon a plan. Knowing that January likes to make love in a walled garden, she waits until the garden's pear trees bear fruit and then entices her husband inside. Damien is hidden in one of the trees and, saying that she'd like a pear, May has January support her while she climbs into the tree. While they are perched there, Damien satisfies her. Pluto spies them, however, and, siding with the old man, restores his sight to him. Yet the quick-witted May convinces January that because his eyesight was restored so suddenly, he is mistaken about what he saw, and January accepts her answer.

One of the questions that this story raises is whether Chaucer means to portray May as sexually passive or as equal to any man in her desire for sexual pleasure. Susan K. Hagen points out that if indeed May is so desperate that she feels she will die without Damien's love, it can be argued that her primary motivation for arranging the pear-tree episode is not her desire to make her lover happy but her need to attain sexual satisfaction for herself (139). In contrast, Alcuin Blamires insists that though May is "less inhibited and less passive than many Chaucerian women," the language used in the description of the act in the pear tree is more applicable to a female's passive role in sex than to the posture of an aggressor (96).

"The Miller's Tale" involves some of the same issues. Again, the husband in the story is an old man, newly married to a young and beautiful wife, and, again, he has a young man living with him. Yet for some reason, though he is extremely jealous, the elderly carpenter, John, does not suspect that his poor young lodger, the clerk Nicholas, is determined to have his way with Alison, John's young wife. Alison is initially described as "yong and wilde" (3225) ["wild and young" (89)], and, in a later passage, the Miller says, "Winsing she was, as is a joly colt" ["Skittish she was, and jolly as a colt" (90)]. One cannot miss the implication: she is equal to anyone in her sexual impulses and undoubtedly superior to her elderly husband. Though she coyly dodges away when, in the absence of her husband, Nicholas "caught hire by the queinte" (1376) ["caught her by the quim" (91)], in time she promises the clerk her love, and the two hatch a plan to get John out of the way. They convince him that a biblical flood is coming and that they will survive it only if they suspend themselves in three separate tubs. With John hanging in a tub, Alison and Nicholas have the run of the house. Alison is as eager as Nicholas for their rendezvous: "ful softe adoun she spedde./ . . / And thus lith Alison and Nicholas/ In bisinesse of mirthe and of solas,/ Till that the belle of laudes gan to ringe" (3649, 3653-55) ["Came Nicholas and Alison, and sped/ Softly downstairs, without a word, to bed,/. . . / And thus lay Nicholas and Alison/ Busy in solace and the quest of fun,/ Until the bell for lauds had started ringing" (101)].

The situation in "The Reeve's Tale" is somewhat different. Because Symkin, the miller in the story, has stolen flour from them, the clerks feel justified in stealing his young daughter's virginity as well as romancing his wife. It must be admitted that the wife is surprised and pleased with the new vigor of the man she thinks is her husband and that, before they part, the daughter calls her clerk her "deere lemman" (4240) ["my sweet" (116)] and tells him where to find the cake made from the flour the miller had stolen from the clerks. The fact that the loss of her virginity reduces her value in the marriage market does not seem to occur to her at the time. However, as Blamires notes, in a patriarchal society, women belong to the male head of the household, and, therefore, what might be regarded as offenses against the women are considered thefts of property—in this case, the property of the miller—and thus constitute an appropriate revenge for the miller's theft of the clerks' flour (98-101). Again, in this situation Chaucer seems sympathetic to the women while at the same time he recognizes that in his society women are owned by men.

Whatever the Church and her society might say, the Wife of Bath does not consider herself the property of any male. However, unlike many of her male companions on the pilgrimage, she likes being married—likes it so much, in fact, that she has defied Church doctrine by taking not just one husband but five. Virginity and marital continence may be all right for some, she admits, but her vocation is different. If sex is wrong, she argues, why would God have equipped human beings with the appropriate instruments? Moreover, "Why sholde men ellis in hir bokes sette/ That man shal yelde to his wif her dette?" (129-130) ["Why else the proverb written down and set/ In books: 'A man must yield his wife her debt'?" (262)]. Clearly, the Wife believes that women enjoy sex and that men are obligated to pleasure them. This idea may well explain why Chaucer allows some of the female adulterers in his fabliaux to emerge unscathed from their escapades, like the young wives in "The Merchant's Tale" and "The Miller's Tale," whose families were too poor to give them dowries and who were therefore effectually sold as sex slaves to well-to-do elderly men. It seems only just that such a girl would be allowed at least one fling with a young man who can give her pleasure. Since the Wife of Bath was married at twelve to a rich, elderly husband, we can assume that her situation was no different from that of the young wives in the other stories.

However, both in her prologue and in her Arthurian fairy tale, the Wife of Bath defines a happy marriage as one in which the woman rules. She did not find it difficult to gain sovereignty over her first three husbands, all of whom were old, she tells us. First, she charmed them into giving her control of their property and then she wore them out sexually; whenever they became suspicious of her extramarital activities, she flattered them by accusing them of adultery, then refused to have sex with them until they bought her off. Her fourth husband was younger, and though she could not force him to abandon his paramour, the Wife of Bath did make his life miserable by pretending to have affairs of her own. Her fifth husband, a student half her age who was steeped in antifeminism, was more difficult to control. However, after he deafened her with a hard blow to the head, she was able to prey upon his sense of guilt and win sovereignty over him.

"The Franklin's Tale" has traditionally been seen as the cornerstone of Chaucer's "Marriage Group," a mean between the extremes represented by "The Clerk's Tale" and "The Wife of Bath's Tale." Before Arveragus and Dorigen are married, Arveragus seems to have solved the problem of sovereignty: he promises Dorigen that he will continue to obey her as he has during their courtship, though he must appear to be her ruler "for shame of his degree" (752) ["lest it should shame his honour" (409)]. Thus courtly love merges with knightly ideals. As Blamires points out, there is a widespread assumption that the theme of "The Franklin's Tale" is generosity (149-51). This knightly virtue is displayed by Arveragus, when he tells his wife that she must keep her promise and sleep with the squire Aurelius; then by the squire, when he refuses to take advantage of her; and finally by the magician, who refuses payment for aiding the squire and thus shows that a clerk, too, can "doon a gentil dede" (1611) ["come as near to nobleness/ as any" (432)]. However, in Dorigen, Chaucer presents a woman who is not preoccupied merely with the honor of chastity but with what was viewed as a more masculine ideal of honor—keeping one's word. As she broods about her dilemma, Dorigen focuses on the loss of her chastity and seriously considers escaping by committing suicide. However, after Arveragus returns and is told of her situation, he insists that she honor her promise to Aurelius, for, as he puts it, "'Trouthe is the hyeste thing that man may kepe'" (1479) ["Truth is the highest thing in a man's keeping" (429)].

By endowing Dorigen with a knightly virtue, Arveragus—and Chaucer—places her on a higher level than that of the passive ladies of courtly romance; by showing her communicating with her husband rather than simply outwitting him, the Franklin—and Chaucer—removes her from the company of the shrews and scolds with whom a number of the married male pilgrims complain they are afflicted. However, Dorigen is not the independent heroine one might like to find in *The Canterbury Tales*, for, after making a foolish promise, she does not solve the problem herself; rather, when her husband returns, she turns the problem over to him. Though one can sympathize with her decision, it cannot be denied that she thus relinquishes any pretense of equality. Certainly Chaucer was more sympathetic to the plight of women than were most other male medieval writers; however, it is evident that he did not actually envision a relationship in which men and women would be truly equal.

Admittedly, a feminist reading of Chaucer is, as Elaine Tuttle Hansen puts it, both "biased and partisan." However, it is valuable in that it may "make masterworks more available and interesting," particularly to "those [such as women] whom they have hitherto helped to silence and exclude from the game" (291-92).

Note

1. Quotations from *The Canterbury Tales* are first cited by line number from the edition edited by Jill Mann and then cited by page number from the edition translated by Nevill Coghill.

Works Cited

Blamires, Alcuin. *Chaucer, Ethics, and Gender*. New York: Oxford UP, 2006.

Brewer, Derek S. *Tradition and Innovation in Chaucer*. New York: Macmillan, 1982.

Chaucer, Geoffrey. *The Canterbury Tales*. Ed. Jill Mann. London: Penguin, 2005.

_____. *The Canterbury Tales*. Trans. Nevill Coghill. Rev. ed. London: Penguin Classics, 2003.

Evans, Ruth, and Lesley Johnson. "Introduction." *Feminist Readings in Middle English Literature: The Wife of Bath and All Her Sect*. Ed. Ruth Evans and Lesley Johnson. New York: Routledge, 1994. 1-21.

Feichtinger, Barbara. "Change and Continuity in Pagan and Christian (Invective) Thought on

Women and Marriage from Antiquity to the Middle Ages." *Satiric Advice on Women and Marriage: From Plautus to Chaucer.* Ed. Warren S. Smith. Ann Arbor: U of Michigan P, 2005. 182-209.

Hagen, Susan K. "Chaucer's May, Standup Comics, and Critics." *Chaucer's Humor: Critical Essays.* New York: Garland, 1994. 127-43.

Hansen, Elaine Tuttle. *Chaucer and the Fictions of Gender.* Berkeley: U of California P, 1992.

Levy, B. S. "The Meanings of *The Clerk's Tale.*" *Chaucer and the Craft of Fiction.* Ed. Leigh A. Arrathoon. Rochester, MI: Solaris Press, 1986. 385-409.

Mann, Jill. *Feminizing Chaucer.* Rochester, NY: D. S. Brewer, 2002.

Wogan-Browne, Jocelyn. "The Virgin's Tale." *Feminist Readings in Middle English Literature: The Wife of Bath and All Her Sect.* Ed. Ruth Evans and Lesley Johnson. New York: Routledge, 1994. 165-94.

Chaucer's Translation of the Fourteenth Century_____
Lewis Walker

Geoffrey Chaucer lived in and through a period of great change in English history that was nevertheless characterized by the persistence of a multitude of traditional ways of acting, thinking, and writing. An example of this paradoxical state of affairs was the emphasis placed on chivalric education (Chaucer himself experienced such an education) in the households of the king and other members of the royal family when feudalism was in decline and "the old ideals lay in tatters" (Howard 3). As the Middle Ages waned, an enormous number of conventions relating to virtually every area of life jostled against each other. Very few were discarded; instead, they were frequently allowed to exist side by side, even if they were not wholly compatible. An important instance can be seen in the traditional medieval view of society as divided into the three estates of clerics, knights, and peasants. This was still an important model in the fourteenth century, and it forms the basis of Chaucer's conception for his little society of pilgrims on the way to Canterbury. In a strict sense, however, *The Canterbury Tales* includes only one pilgrim from each estate: the Parson, the Knight, and the Plowman. And these three characters, being largely positive, do not by themselves permit Chaucer to engage in much satire.

While retaining the traditional idea, Chaucer seemed also to have in mind a more organic notion of social structure, like the one suggested by Bishop Thomas Brinton in a sermon delivered in the 1370s. As Paul Strohm explains:

> We are all, [Brinton] says, the mystical members of a single body, of which the head (or heads) are kings, princes, and prelates; the eyes are judges, wise men, and true counsellors; the ears are clergy; the tongue is good doctors. Then, within the midsection of the body, the right hand is composed of strenuous knights; the left hand is composed of merchants and craftsmen; the heart is citizens and burgesses. Finally, peasants and workers are the feet which support the whole. (2)

In this more inclusive, less hierarchical rendition of society, there is greater recognition for the middle class, especially prosperous urban figures such as Chaucer's Merchant and tradesmen (Strohm 3). Such a revised and enlarged version of the social paradigm seems to inform Chaucer's General Prologue; it allows him to include more characters of the middling sort, including many that he could subject to the kind of satiric treatment often given to the traditional estates.

Chaucer's adaptation of the estates model is a good example of what may, in a broad sense, be called translation. Of course, he was also a skillful and prolific translator in the narrow sense—he translated a variety of texts such as Boethius's *The Consolation of Philosophy* (Latin, sixth century C.E.) and substantial parts of the *Romaunt of the Rose* (French, thirteenth century) into English. But the act of taking a text—an inherited idea, an entire work in whatever "discipline" modern readers might place it, a single line, a word, even a current event or personal experience—and placing it in a new situation, where it does not lose its meaning entirely but is modified and in turn modifies other texts—this is the kind of translation at which Chaucer excelled. He shared the medieval habit of eschewing intellectual specialization, aspiring instead to "an encyclopaedic grasp of the universe" (Kittredge 7).

Even the two translations mentioned above did not remain "narrow" in Chaucer's hands. At the end of *The Knight's Tale*, itself a translation from the Italian of Boccaccio's *Teseida*, Chaucer uses passages from Boethius as the basis for the speech of Duke Theseus, who is attempting to reconcile those around him to the death of Arcite. Arcite had won the right to marry Emily, Theseus's sister-in-law, by defeating his cousin Palamon in a tournament, but he was then killed in a riding accident.

Theseus, addressing the seeming capriciousness of Arcite's death, explains that the First Mover of the universe, who holds all together by the "faire cheyne of love"[1] ["shining chain of love"],[2] does not allow anything on earth to live forever:

> And therfore, of his wise purveiaunce,
> He hath so wel biset his ordinaunce
> That speces of thynges and progressiouns
> Shullen enduren by successiouns,
> And nat eterne, withouten any lye.
>
> (1.3011-15)

> [And so our God, from wisdom and foresight divine,
> Has carefully established every line,
> Allowing different species living on earth
> To endure by succession only; first comes birth,
> Then death. Life on earth is never eternal.]
>
> (2140-44)

This passage is a reworking in verse—a translation in a broader sense—of what Chaucer had already put into English prose in his translation of Boethius's *Consolation*, which he called *Boece*. It is also a translation in the sense that Chaucer took it from the speeches of Lady Philosophy in the *Consolation*, who tries to reconcile the Christian Boethius to his misfortune, and gave it to a pagan ruler who is urging his small circle of intimates to accept an inexplicable death and get on with their lives.

Chaucer's assimilation of Boethius is testimony to his engagement with certain central issues in Christian thought of the Middle Ages. First of all, if God is good, why is there so much suffering and evil in the world? Second, if God is omniscient, he must know what is to come, and if he knows the future, it is there anything we can do to change it? And if we are *predestined* to enact what is divinely known, how can we have free will? Boethius answers the first question by saying that evil and pain in the world are real to us only because we seek happiness in the wrong forms, that is, in worldly things such as goods, fame, and family. If we seek happiness rightly, in God alone, then we can transcend earthly hardships. To the question about God's foreknowledge and man's free will, Boethius responds that, since God is outside of time, his knowledge is not truly about the future. The past, present, and future of human beings are all one to God, who thus does not "foresee" or predetermine human actions. Furthermore, man's passions are what make him subject to the chain of inevitable cause and effect. Once a man rises above his passions by loving God, his will is free. Although Boethius seems to endorse a dualistic view that despises worldly things in favor of the divine, at times he suggests the possibility of reconciling the two realms, as in the joy he takes in "the fayre chaine of love" (quoted above in Chaucer's adaptation for *The Knight's Tale*) that orders all earthly things. Chaucer was heavily influenced by Boethius's dualism, but he was sometimes attracted by the possibility of synthesizing the two extremes (Brewer 92-93).

Two other Canterbury tales make heavy use of Boethius, in particular his image of Fortune, the Roman goddess of chance, and her wheel. In Book 2 of the *Consolation*, Fortune is described as being constant only in her mutability, and she is allowed to describe in her own words how she turns her wheel, changing the lowest to the highest and the highest to the lowest. This, she says, is the basis of tragedy. Boethius, of course, believes that Fortune should be disregarded, for she is a symbol of reliance on earthly prosperity, which will inevitably fail. And his Lady Philosophy says the same. In the prologue to *The Monk's Tale*, the Monk proposes to tell tragedies, and he gives a definition of the genre:

> Tragedie is to seyn a certeyn storie,
> As olde bookes maken us memorie,
> Of hym that stood in greet prosperitee,
> And is yfallen out of heigh degree
> Into myserie, and endeth wrecchedly.
> (7.1973-77)

[Tragedies are fixed, historical stories
Which ancient books restore to memory,
Tales of those who lived in prosperity,
Then tumbled down to wretched misery,
Fallen from what was once great height.]
(83-87)

This definition, standard if oversimplified, is closely modeled on what Boethius's Fortune says about her workings. The Monk then recaps the definition at the beginning of his tale proper, naming Fortune, and his tale consists of a series of sketches, all of them following rather mechanically his outline of tragedy. The first two, of Lucifer and Adam, respectively, suggest that Chaucer might have been thinking of letting the Monk organize his tragedies according to the standard medieval scheme of salvation history, beginning with the fall of Lucifer and ending with the Last Judgment. After the first two portraits, however, the Monk veers off to recount the stories of Samson and Hercules, Queen Zenobia of Palmyra, and, interestingly, three contemporary figures. The most up-to-date of these, Bernabò Visconti, lord of Milan—and someone Chaucer had met—fell from power and died in prison late in 1385. Chaucer's account of him must have been written almost immediately after his death (Benson ed. 933n). On one hand, all of the stories are forced into the narrow straitjacket of the fall from prosperity: "This work is strikingly unmodern," one commentator notes (Brewer 196). On the other hand, Chaucer, through the Monk, seems to be experimenting with different ways of sequencing serious stories and with pushing the traditional definition of tragedy to the limits of its applicability.

Another tale that refers to Boethius and his philosophy—and places them in the context of a multitude of contemporary concerns—is the one told by the Nun's Priest. This tale purports to be a moral one. After its teller has finished his account of how the cock Chauntecleer ignores the warning of his own dream to engage in sex with his wife (the hen Pertelote) and is captured by a fox and later escapes, he invites interpretation from the other pilgrims: "Taketh the moralite, goode men" (7.3440) ["At least approve the story's moral, good men" (601)]. The problem is that there is so much moralizing, combined with "literary allusions and verbal extravagances," that it is difficult to figure out whether there is a message. If there is one, modern scholars cannot agree on its nature (Benson ed. 936n). The Nun's Priest mentions Boethius in company with two other illustrious intellectuals as he describes the fox lying in wait to ambush Chauntecleer and as he considers whether Chauntecleer's capture is predestined because God has foreknowledge of it:

But I ne kan nat bulte it to the bren
As kan the hooly doctour Augustyn,
Or Boece, or the Bisshop Bradwardyn,
Wheither that Goddes worthy forwityng
Streyneth me nedely for to doon a thing.
(7.3240-44)

[But I can't possibly sift the chaff from the bran,
After the style of Doctor Augustine,
Or Boethius, or Bishop Bradwardine,
Or even determine if God, with his future knowledge,
Obliges me to go where his knowledge knows.]
(404-8)

Here is a trio of authorities on the subject of predestination and free will: St. Augustine (354-430), one of the most important of the early Christian theologians; Boethius (c. 480-524); and Thomas Bradwardine (c. 1290-1349) (Benson ed. 939n), who was nearly contemporary with Chaucer. As with the tragedies in *The Monk's Tale*, traditional examples are brought together with modern instances. In most cases, the modern instances are made to fit a received pattern, but the fact that Chaucer uses them at all leaves open the possibility that the pattern may be altered by something new.

The Nun's Priest's Tale is loaded with different bits of fourteenth-century culture. In addition to the updated version of the predestination debate, Chaucer has Chauntecleer and Pertelote engage in an extended discussion of medieval dream theory (Benson ed. 937n), and he (or the Nun's Priest) parodies part of the standard medieval text on rhetoric in lamenting the capture of the cock by the fox (Benson ed. 940n). The tale is also a parody of the tragedy formula espoused by the Monk. Like the Monk's tragic figures, Chauntecleer holds a high position; he falls both by flying down from his perch to dally with Pertelote and by allowing the fox to abduct him. But then miraculously he tricks the fox into letting him escape, and he flies back to a high position, out of harm's way.

Although Chaucer did not usually discuss contemporary events directly (Rigby 15), this tale may offer a glimpse of history breaking through into his fictional world. The setting is described in part as follows: "A povre wydwe, somdeel stape in age,/ Was whilom dwellyng in a narwe cotage,/ Biside a grove, stondynge in a dale" (7.2821-23). ["A widow, poor and somewhat advanced in age,/ Was living, some time ago, in a tiny cottage,/ Close to a cluster of trees deep down in a valley" (1-3)]. The argument can be made that this description and further details that follow it contain "moments of realism that recall the sometimes brutal inequities of fourteenth-century English society" (Fehrenbacher 138). The rhetorical extravagance of the Nun's Priest's description of Chauntecleer and his actions serves partly "to draw the reader's attention from the pathetic world of the poor widow, from the realm of the historical to the realm of the rhetorical" (Fehrenbacher 140). However, toward the end of the tale, "the repressed historicity" returns: the fox makes off with Chauntecleer, and the widow and her daughters attempt a rescue, in which they are joined by other members of their village community (Fehrenbacher 142). All of this is attended by harsh sounds that undermine the fine rhetoric that has gone before. As the pursuit of the fox continues, we hear "the berkying of the dogges/ And shoutyng of the men and wommen eeke" (7.3386-87) ["the furious barking of dogs/ And the shouts and yells of men, and also the shrieking/ Of women" (548-50)] who "yolleden as feendes doon in helle" (7.3389) [who "sounded much like fiends in hell" (551)]. This can be seen as the intrusion of realistic detail about peasant life into the rhetorical world created by the elaborate description of Chauntecleer. Of particular interest is the Nun's Priest's comparison of this hubbub with the uproar made during the Peasants' Rebellion of 1381 by Jack Straw and his followers:

> Certes, he Jakke Straw and his meynee
> Ne made nevere shoutes half so shrille
> Whan that they wolden any Flemyng kille,
> As thilke day was maad upon the fox.
> (7.3394-97)

> [even Jack Straw and all his breakers of peace
> Could never muster shouting half so shrill
> When they were hunting up a Fleming to kill,
> As the waves of sound that followed the fox.]
> (556-59)

Such a reference to the very recent destruction wrought in London by groups of aggrieved peasants pulls the tale in the direction of contemporary social commentary. The rebels, reacting to a variety of injustices, including excessive taxation and the arrogant behavior of John of Gaunt, duke of Lancaster, engaged in widespread acts of violence in London in June of 1381. They occupied buildings associated with official repression (and burned many); destroyed Gaunt's great palace, the Savoy; and dragged many officials to summary execution (McKisack 384-410). Resentful of foreigners for taking English wages, they slaughtered a group of Flemings who had sought refuge in what had been Chaucer's childhood parish church (Howard 323). Jack

Straw was one of their leaders (McKisack 411). The four lines devoted to the Peasants' Revolt here, with their evocation of the horrors it unleashed and their emphasis on sound, can be viewed as part of a critique by Chaucer of his own tale's "failure to take seriously the peasant voice," which "mirrors aristocratic English society's own failure to attend to the voices of the third estate" (Fehrenbacher 145).

Having looked at a work that may reveal something like a modern social awareness, we can now examine some of the more traditional ways in which Chaucer translated the features of his culture in *The Canterbury Tales*. For example, he made great use of contemporary scientific theory in describing his pilgrims. According to this theory,

> all matter was comprised of four basic elements: earth, water, fire and air, invisible essences or spirits which imparted attributes such as heat, weight and moistness to specific material substances. Within the human body, four humours correspond to the attributes of these four basic elements: 'black bile' or 'melancholy,' corresponding to the coldness and dryness of the earth; phlegm, corresponding to the moistness and coldness of water; choler, corresponding to the dryness and heat of fire; and blood, corresponding to the warmth and moistness of the air. Each of these humours had its seat in a particular organ, giving rise to a particular 'complexion': the melancholic, phlegmatic, choleric and sanguine respectively. (Rigby 7)

In describing the pilgrims in the General Prologue, the narrator makes liberal use of these physiological types. The Reeve, for example, is described as a "colerik man" (1.587) ["choleric man" (587)], which makes him "sharp-witted, cunning, crafty, vengeful and lecherous" (Rigby 8). These qualities come into play when the Miller tells a tale in which a carpenter is a fool and the butt of a joke. The Reeve, angered because carpentry is his trade, retaliates by telling a tale in which a dishonest miller is beguiled. The Summoner is also choleric, as is seen when he reacts angrily to the tale told by the Friar about a summoner who is carried off to Hell by a devil (Rigby 9). The Franklin's complexion is of another type: "Of his complexioun he was sangwyn" (1.333) ["his face was clearly/ Sanguine" (332-33)]. As a consequence, he is red-faced, "healthy, vigorous and confident" (Rigby 8). These qualities seem to be reflected in the tale he tells, which shows a marriage undergoing a crisis that is resolved with goodwill on all sides.

To return to scientific theory, "the balance of humours within the individual was held to be determined astrologically by the position of the seven 'planets' (the Moon, Mercury, Venus, the Sun, Mars, Jupiter and Saturn) as they moved around the earth through the twelve houses of the zodiac." For example, Venus, the planet of love, "was associated with blood and those of sanguine complexion" (Rigby 7). Each of the planets had a particular house or houses of the zodiac as its home, which it ruled. Extremely important for a person's character and fortunes was the "position of the stars and planets" at his or her birth, especially the zodiacal sign that was "'ascendant' (just rising over the eastern horizon) and the planet within it" (Rigby 8). Probably the most well-known astrological characterization in *The Canterbury Tales* is the Wife of Bath's self-portrait (Rigby 9) in the prologue to her tale:

> For certes, I am al Venerien
> In feelynge, and myn herte is Marcien.
> Venus me yaf my lust, my likerousnesse,
> And Mars yaf me my sturdy hardynesse;
> Myn ascendent was Taur, and Mars therinne.
> Allas, allas! That evere love was synne!
>   (3.609-14)

> [I'm truly born of Venus, most certainly,
> In all my feelings, but my heart belongs to Mars.
> Venus gave me desire, and all the parts
> I needed, but it was Mars that made me daring.
> My astral ascendant was Taurus, with Mars sharing
> The sky. Alas, alas! That love should be sinful.]
>   (609-14)

We know from this that the Wife's ascendant sign was Taurus and that Mars was in Taurus. The significance is clear: "When Mars is in either of the houses of Venus [Taurus being one of the houses] in the nativities of women, they will be unchaste" (Wood 175). The Wife's sexual career would seem to bear this out: her five husbands, her "oother compaignye in youthe" (1.461) ["other men she'd known in youth" (461)], mentioned in the General Prologue, and her strong hints in her prologue that she was unfaithful while married. Toward the end of her own prologue, she returns to the subject of astrology to provide an amusing explanation of why clerks do not praise women. Identifying clerks as children of Mercury and women as children of Venus, she notes:

> Mercurie loveth wysdam and science,
> And Venus loveth ryot and dispence.
> And, for hire diverse disposicioun,
> Ech falleth in otheres exaltacioun.
>   (3.699-702)

[For Mercury favors wisdom, and loves all science,
While Venus loves good parties and huge expenses.
And simply because their marks are wholly opposed,
One being down will drive the other up.]

(699-702)

She thus sets up her account of her conflict with, and eventual conquest of, her fifth husband, a clerk who read "lessons" to her from his book of wicked wives. She also seems to motivate the Clerk, who is her fellow pilgrim and who is devoted to books and learning, to answer her tale of an exceptionally compliant husband with one of his own about a patient wife whose obedience is cruelly tested. There is much use of astrology throughout the other tales. Other pilgrims, like the Miller and the Franklin, tell about astrologers and "give horoscopes or other astrological data about the characters in their tales—such as the Man of Law about Custance" (Wood 174). It is only the Wife, however, who gives her own horoscope and later provides a kind of comparative group horoscope for women (wives) and clerks to explain their opposition (Wood 174).

The Wife's prologue, in addition to its astrological concerns, brings together a large number of other kinds of materials, thus partaking in the culture's encyclopedic habit of mind. The Wife's character is derived from La Vieille in the *Romaunt of the Rose*, who is a kind of philosophical bawd, "an ex-prostitute, with a talent for gain and an organic weakness for sex" (Muscatine 74). Chaucer also used a cluster of medieval antifeminist writings as the source for the arguments the Wife attacks (Benson ed. 864n), as well as giving her the attributes of a master of the art of love as described by the classical Roman poet Ovid (Calabrese 81). And in the Wife's explorations of the conflict between experience and authority—which she mentions in the first line of her prologue—Chaucer makes liberal use of proverbs. These anonymous expressions of folk wisdom carry with them a kind of double-edged power: they are both experience and authority, far enough down in the hierarchy of learning to be identified with experience, with a common oral culture, but formulaic enough to be considered in some way authoritative. After discussing Saint Paul's preference for virginity over marriage, the Wife notes that "The dart is set up for virginitee;/ Cacche whoso may, who renneth best lat see" (3.75-76) ["Announce a contest, and a prize for virginity;/ All women can run, but who runs best? We'll see" (75-76)].The proverb in line 76 (Whiting 92) undercuts the privileged place of virginity in the foregoing discussion. And when the Wife talks about her three old husbands, a proverb—"With empty hand men may none haukes lure" (3.415) ["No one catches hawks with an empty hand" (415)]—expresses the attitude with which she subverted their authority (Whiting 93). In keeping with her privileging of experience over authority, the Wife employs more proverbs than does any other pilgrim (Whiting 92).

The Wife's prologue, along with several other tales, provides an intriguing look at Chaucer's interest in the ideas of John Wycliffe, the Oxford scholar and radical church reformer who was condemned as a heretic and executed in 1384. Wycliffe, for example, was interested in "discernment of authorities," the Wife's special topic. He attacked not only monks and friars but also "the ideals they stood for." Chaucer does not go that far, but much of his criticism of such figures as the Monk, the Friar, the Summoner, the Pardoner, and the Prioress parallels that of Wycliffe. Predestination, another one of Wycliffe's central subjects, is dealt with, as we have seen, in *The Nun's Priest's Tale* (Daniell 97). Near the beginning of *The Pardoner's Tale*, there is a passage about cooks preparing food: "Thise cookes, how they stampe, and streyne, and grynde,/ And turnen substaunce into accident" (6.538-9) ["See cooks and how they stamp, and strain, and grind,/ Turning reality into mere appearance" (76-77)]. In giving the Pardoner these lines, which he uses to preach against gluttony, Chaucer also comes close to mocking (or having the Pardoner mock) the Christian doctrine of transubstantiation, the belief that, during the Mass, the bread and wine, when consecrated by the priest, actually become the body and blood of Christ. In these lines he shows his sympathy for Wycliffe, who attacked transubstantiation (Daniell 98).

Chaucer's Parson can also be viewed as having Wycliffite tendencies: he is praised in the General Prologue for his careful performance of pastoral duties, but he is *not* praised for saying Mass or hearing confessions, things that were problematic for Wycliffe. When, in the epilogue to *The Man of Law's Tale*, the Parson rebukes the Host for swearing, the Host mockingly comments, "I smelle a Lollere in the wynd" (2.1173) ["I smell the scent of Reforming blown in the air!" (11)]; "Lollard" was a term used for followers of Wycliffe, who were often identified as heretics (Daniell 97). Later, in the Parson's prologue, the Host orders the Parson to "Telle us a fable anon, for cokkes bones!" (10.29) ["Tell us a fable please, by the cock's own bones!" (29)]. We can see that Chaucer has given the Parson further Wycliffite qualities when he tells the Host that he will not tell "fables and swich wrecchednesse" (10.34) ["fables and other tales that hurt you" (34)]. Instead, the Parson plans to tell the pilgrims "Moralitee and vertuous mateere" (10.38) ["Morality and virtuous, holy matter" (38)]. His serious temperament is in accord with what is known of Wycliffe himself, who had a "narrowly theological outlook" and a "distaste for music, art, romance . . . and for all secular learning" (McKisack 516).

Chaucer, then, seems to have been attentive to the chief ideas of the

Lollards and aware also of the ways in which their straitlaced attitudes could be mocked. His sympathy for them can be seen in the fact that he allows his Parson to tell the last tale, a lengthy disquisition on penance that includes a section describing and offering remedies for the Seven Deadly Sins. The Parson believes that this tale will lift the company from their current journey to a contemplation "Of thilke parfit glorious pilgrymage/ That highte Jerusalem celestial" (10.50-51) [of "The road to that perfect, glorious pilgrimage/ We call Jerusalem, but high in heaven" (50-51)]. And Chaucer seems, at least at one point when he was thinking about his legacy, to have agreed in part with his Lollard-leaning Parson. After *The Parson's Tale*, Chaucer added a short "Retraction," renouncing "my translacions and enditynges of worldy vanitees" (10.1085) ["my translations and other writings, which deal only with worldly vanities" (597)]. This is the category into which he places *The Canterbury Tales*, or at least those tales "that sownen into synne" (10.1086) ["which tend to be sinful" (597)]. He follows the list of sinful works with thanksgiving to God for his translations of Boethius and other moral works. On one hand, Chaucer is here following the pattern of a typical medieval Christian, preparing himself for death by denouncing all in his life that is worldly and vain. The transience of earthly life had recently been brought home to him and his contemporaries by several episodes of the plague, or Black Death. On the other hand, he did not allow his otherworldliness to win out entirely: by naming his works, even the sinful ones that he professed to retract, he made sure to establish his canon and thus to ensure some measure of fame (Howard 500-502).

Perhaps the most interesting connection of *The Canterbury Tales* with Wycliffe and the Lollards has to do with the English translation of the Bible. During the 1380s, a number of English Bibles, some of them complete, were in circulation; they were associated with Wycliffe, though not by name (Daniell 66). Chaucer could hardly have avoided contact with these, and he might have used passages from them, though he was perfectly capable of translating scriptures for himself. As in so many other cases, his biblical "translations" are more than simple renderings from the Latin of the Vulgate Bible. Scriptural passages are translated into English and then resituated in *The Canterbury Tales* to form new entities. The Wife of Bath, for example, cites Saint Paul frequently, usually to undermine or willfully misunderstand what he says in order to advance her marital agenda. And the Pardoner, within the first hundred lines of his tale, quotes or refers to a dizzying array of scriptural passages in giving the pilgrims a sample of his preaching (Daniell 98). In tales like these, Chaucer seems to be sharing in and making assumptions about his audience's knowledge of the Bible in English.

Chaucer's participation in the Englishing of the Bible is part of his involvement in a larger cultural movement in the fourteenth century: the development of the English language into an important medium of communication at court and in literature. Up until the middle of the century, the question of what *was* the language of England would have been hard to determine. The royal family and the nobles spoke mostly French, though they did admit some English for practical purposes (Howard 22). Chaucer's early and (at court) continued immersion in French gave him access to the courtly literature that he translated and made a part of *The Canterbury Tales*. In the last quarter of the century, Latin was still "the language of ecclesiastical and theological discourse," and French was "the language of statecraft and civil record-keeping, as well as a literary language in some circles" (Strohm 6). Things were beginning to change, however. National pride was boosted "as a result of famous victories [in the Hundred Years' War] at Crecy (1346) and Poitiers (1356)," and the Black Death caused a depopulation that "made the English-speaking working class more important in the economy" (Howard 23). Later, John of Gaunt, Chaucer's and Wycliffe's patron, supported a bill (in 1362-63) "that made English the official language of the law courts" (Howard 86). The poet John Gower, Chaucer's contemporary, wrote major works in Latin, French, and English (Strohm 8), thereby exemplifying the many linguistic choices available to authors of the time. Although Chaucer could have spread himself around linguistically in this manner, he instead always chose to write in English. In this, he may have been inspired by Dante, who had written *The Divine Comedy* in his native Italian (Acocella 142).

Chaucer also provided English poetry with something new: the ten-syllable, five-stress line—iambic pentameter—which he used in couplets for the first time in *The Canterbury Tales*. He thus created—or helped to create—the basis for the blank verse of Shakespeare and Milton and the heroic couplets of Dryden and Pope. The rhyme royal stanza, with its seven rhyming lines of *ababbcc*, is credited to Chaucer as well. It was considered to be more elegant than couplets, and a few of the Canterbury pilgrims who aspire to elegance—the Man of Law, the Clerk, the Prioress, the Second Nun—use it to tell their tales (Howard 263-66).

Like most of the tales discussed above, *The Pardoner's Tale*, one of Chaucer's most powerful stories, derives a great deal of its strength from its combination of diverse traditional elements. Its spectacular display of biblical knowledge has already been mentioned; it is also generically varied. For one thing, it shows strong resemblances to the medieval sermon in its easy assumption that one sin metamorphoses into another (in this case, the drunkenness of the three young tavern rioters leads inevitably into gluttony, and both of these sins are linked to blasphemy) (Owst 425-49). But it also includes an exemplum, or anecdote with a moral, about how the sins of the rioters lead to death. Finally, it is framed in a way that links it to the fabliau (Benson ed. 905n), a short comic tale: the three rioters, drunk and cursing, seek to slay Death as a personified abstraction, ironically failing to recognize that the impulse for death is within themselves. Despite the tale's indebtedness to a variety of cultural traditions, one cannot help but sense that its beginning with the death of the rioters' friend from the plague, and especially its harrowing demonstration that death comes from within, owes something to Chaucer's observation of the workings of the Black Death, which visited England at least four times during his life (McKisack 331).

Another aspect of Chaucer's encyclopedic frame of mind and his role as a translator in the broader sense is the great range of genres we find in *The Canterbury Tales*. *The Knight's Tale*, with its dignified style and serious investigation of love and worldly transience, is a romance; the tales of the Miller, the Reeve, the Cook, and the Friar are fabliaux; *The Clerk's Tale* of Griselda is about an excruciatingly cruel test of wifely patience; *The Second Nun's Tale* is a saint's legend about the martyrdom of Saint Cecilia. In many of these works, as in *The Pardoner's Tale*, Chaucer includes elements of other genres in addition to the predominant one, often to great artistic effect. For example, in *The Miller's Tale*, which "may be the dirtiest story ever told by a first-rank writer in English" (Acocella 142), Nicholas, a lusty clerk, conceives a passion for a carpenter's young wife, "And prively he caughte hire by the queynte,/ And seyde, 'Ywis, but if ich have my wille,/ For deerne love of thee, lemman, I spille'" (1.3276-78) ["And suddenly he caught her by the crotch/ And said: 'By God, unless I take you to bed,/ Sweetheart, I want you so badly I'll end up dead'" (86-88)]. The words "deerne" (secret), "lemman" (sweetheart), and "spille" (die) come from the courtly love tradition, in which the gallant knight woos the highborn lady with exalted respect, but here they are hilariously debased by Nicholas's actions. Chaucer's penchant for playing ironically with traditional materials is further illustrated when Alison, the carpenter's wife, and Nicholas have deceived her husband and are in bed together. Absolon, the parish clerk, who also loves Alison, stands at her window and mournfully calls for her in absurdly inappropriate courtly language. To get rid of him, she says, "Go forth thy wey, or I wol caste a ston" (1.3712) ["Take yourself off, or I'll say goodbye with a stone" (513)]. This might seem a small, naturalistic detail, but it is also the key to a huge spiritual joke: in the biblical story of the woman taken in adultery, Jesus deals with those who would stone her by saying, "He that is without sin among you, let him first cast a stone at her" (John 8:7). Amusingly, in this case, the adulteress threatens to cast a stone at a would-be lover.

A question that is continually being revisited among readers of Chaucer is the extent to which *The Canterbury Tales* reflects "real life." A great deal of evidence exists to support the view that "what often appear to the modern reader to be individual traits or naturalistic details in portraits of the pilgrims . . . are, in fact, often traditional or stereotypical characteristics of their estates" (Rigby 13). The details of Friar Huberd's behavior in the General Prologue, for example—including his merry songs, his lisping, his intimate acquaintance with barmaids and with "worthy wommen of the toun" (1.217) ["proper matrons of the town" (217)], and his ingenious use of scriptural passages to squeeze money out of poor widows—are derived from a tradition of satire against friars that dates back to more than a century before Chaucer's time (Rigby 13-14). As a general rule, instead of viewing *The Canterbury Tales* "as an immediate or passive reflection of contemporary society, the pilgrims and the characters within their tales are best seen as active reinterpretations of reality in terms of the literary conventions, scientific doctrines and stock social satires of the day" (Rigby 15).

This does not mean that we should abandon the attempt to find history in Chaucer; in many cases, we just need to change our focus and seek it in indirect ways. The Knight, for example, is not simply described in abstract terms; we have a lengthy list of his battles. The point is not that an actual knight might have done all this. What Chaucer does is "refer the reader to specific policy issues and discussions at the court of Richard II" (Rigby 16). The portrait of the Clerk in the General Prologue is not of a specific scholar in a given year, but it does provide a glimpse into the way that students progressed through the university curriculum in the fourteenth century. The information that he "unto logyk hadde longe ygo" (1.286) [was "steeped in philosophy's depths" (286)] is a likely hint that he has "persisted in his study of logic rather than moving on to the higher study of theology." This would not have been surprising in the Oxford of Chaucer's day, given the university's eminence in the field of logic (Dillon 109).

These portraits, and many of the others in the General Prologue and in the pilgrims' tales, show that Chaucer had absorbed enormous amounts of information about the institutions and practices of his society. Somewhat more difficult to pin down, but of great interest, is the extent to which his own character in the *Tales*—that of the pilgrim Chaucer, who is the narrator—is shaped by his culture. Donald Howard has speculated that Chaucer's long service as a diplomat might have fostered in him "concision of speech," which would have combined with "a certain defensive reticence" that came naturally to him (196). This probably has something to do with Chaucer the reticent pilgrim, who is addressed by the Host in the following terms: "Thou lookest as thou woldest fynde an hare,/ For evere upon the ground I se thee stare" (7.696-97) ["You seem as if you're always hunting a hare./ You never look up. The ground is all you stare at" (6-7)]. A few lines further on, he comments to the other pilgrims on Chaucer's unsociability: "He semeth elvyssh by his conten-aunce,/ For unto no wight dooth he daliaunce" (7.703-4) ["His face resembles, I think, a dwarf or an elf:/ Like them he lingers out of sight, by himself" (13-14)]. Chaucer's response is to confess a poverty of material: apologetically, he says that all he knows is "a rym I lerned longe agoon" (7.709) ["an ancient rhyme/ I learned long ago" (19-20)].

Chaucer's *Tale of Sir Thopas*, which follows, is an artfully wretched piece, a "parody of vernacular romance" that relies on "formula, cliché, and filler lines" (Cooper 305). It is so bad that the Host, who does not recognize how brilliant the parody is, interrupts and tells Chaucer the pilgrim that "Thy drasty ryming is nat worth a toord!" (7.930) ["Your awful rhyming isn't worth a turd!" (12)]. Here we enjoy the irony of the great poet who assigns a deliber-ately bad piece of verse to his surrogate. And we may suspect that Chaucer's experience as a diplomat inspired this tale, which is in part about being reti-cent and then, when called upon to speak, about not having the right verbal formulas to respond to the situation. In his official capacity as royal emissary, Chaucer must have witnessed this sort of awkwardness; perhaps he experi-enced it himself. And so here he makes fun of it. That Chaucer was influenced by considerations such as these is supported by what his surrogate does next. To compensate for his initial failure, the pilgrim Chaucer tells the prose *Tale of Melibee*. This partly allegorical work is devoted almost wholly to the attempts of Melibee's wife, Dame Prudence, to persuade her husband not to take ven-geance on his enemies. In the end, he agrees. What we have, then, is a success-ful verbal performance by Prudence, the kind of thing that a diplomat, or a no-bleman's or king's adviser, would admire.

Despite Chaucer's tendency to deal indirectly with contemporary events and culture, and despite his affinity for the typical and the traditional, there is a quality of freshness about his writing that makes it seem realistic. Joan Acocella bears eloquent testimony to this when she admires "the variety and high color of his pilgrims—the Miller with a hairy wart on his nose, the lisping Prioress, the gap-toothed Wife of Bath" (141). We need to keep an open mind about details in *The Canterbury Tales* that *could* stem from accurate observa-tion and thus mean that Chaucer was being more direct than conventional. The famous opening of the General Prologue, which refers to "the droghte of March" (1.2) ["dried up roots [of March]" (2)], was once thought to be "a purely rhetorical fiction," because England is not dry in March. But then scholars discovered that "March in England may be dry in *some places*," "that weather may have changed since Chaucer's day," and "that the word 'drought' in Middle English meant not total lack of rain but only dryness" (Howard xiii). Thus what had been thought of as only a literary convention could now be seen as a more direct representation of reality.

Critical Insights

In the 1380s, the French poet Eustache Deschamps wrote an admiring verse letter to Chaucer in which the latter is compared to Socrates, Seneca, and Ovid. Each stanza ends with the phrase "grand translateur, noble Geffroy Chaucier" ["great translator, noble Geoffrey Chaucer"] (40). It is clear that by "translator" Deschamps means "one who turns writings from one language to another," but he also means "one who transmits values and poetic traditions from one culture to another and from one age to another." This is related to the broader sense of "translate" with which this essay began, and it is an appropriate way to describe what Chaucer did in and with his age.

Notes

1. Geoffrey Chaucer, "The Knight's Tale," in the edition of *The Canterbury Tales* edited by Larry D. Benson, 1.2988. Middle English quotations from *The Canterbury Tales* are from this edition and are included in the text by reference to the manuscript fragments and line numbers in which they occur.

2. Geoffrey Chaucer, "The Knight's Tale," in the Modern Library translation by Burton Raffel, 2120. Modern English quotations from *The Canterbury Tales* are from this edition, are marked off by square brackets, and are indicated in the text by reference to line numbers, except in the case of prose passages, which are referred to by page numbers.

Works Cited

Acocella, Joan. "All England." *The New Yorker* 21 Dec. 2009: 140-45.

Brewer, Derek. *An Introduction to Chaucer.* London: Longman, 1984.

Calabrese, Michael A. *Chaucer's Ovidian Arts of Love.* Gainesville: UP of Florida, 1994.

Chaucer, Geoffrey. *The Canterbury Tales. The Riverside Chaucer.* Ed. Larry D. Benson. Boston: Houghton Mifflin, 1987.

_____. *The Canterbury Tales.* Trans. Burton Raffel. New York: Modern Library, 2009.

Cooper, Helen. *The Canterbury Tales.* Oxford Guides to Chaucer. Oxford: Clarendon Press, 1989.

Daniell, David. *The Bible in English: Its History and Influence.* New Haven, CT: Yale UP, 2003.

Deschamps, Eustache. "Autre Balade." *Chaucer: The Critical Heritage.* Vol. 1. Ed. Derek Brewer. London: Routledge, 1978. 40.

Dillon, Bert. "'A Clerk Ther Was of Oxenford Also.'" *Chaucer's Pilgrims: An Historical Guide to the Pilgrims in "The Canterbury Tales."* Ed. Laura C. Lambdin and Robert T. Lambdin. Westport, CT: Greenwood Press, 1996. 108-15.

Fehrenbacher, Richard W. "'A Yeerd Enclosed Al Aboute': Literature and History in *The Nun's Priest's Tale.*" *The Chaucer Review* 29 (1994): 134-48.

Howard, Donald R. *Chaucer: His Life, His Works, His World.* New York: Dutton, 1987.

Kittredge, George Lyman. *Chaucer and His Poetry.* Cambridge, MA: Harvard UP, 1915.

McKisack, May. *The Fourteenth Century: 1307-1399.* Oxford: Clarendon Press, 1959.

Muscatine, Charles. *Chaucer and the French Tradition.* Berkeley: U of California P, 1957.

Owst, G. R. *Literature and Pulpit in Medieval England.* 2nd rev. ed. Oxford: Blackwell, 1966.

Rigby, S. H. *Chaucer in Context: Society, Allegory, and Gender.* Manchester: Manchester UP, 1996.

Strohm, Paul. "The Social and Literary Scene in England." *The Cambridge Companion to Chaucer.* 2nd ed. Ed. Piero Boitani and Jill Mann. New York: Cambridge UP, 2003. 1-19.

Whiting, Bartlett Jere. *Chaucer's Use of Proverbs.* 1933. New York: AMS Press, 1973.

Wood, Chauncey. *Chaucer and the Country of the Stars: Poetic Uses of Astrological Imagery.* Princeton, NJ: Princeton UP, 1970.

CRITICAL READINGS

Chaucer the Pilgrim

E. Talbot Donaldson

Verisimilitude in a work of fiction is not without its attendant dangers, the chief of which is that the responses it stimulates in the reader may be those appropriate not so much to an imaginative production as to an historical one or to a piece of reporting. History and reporting are, of course, honorable in themselves, but if we react to a poet as though he were an historian or a reporter, we do him somewhat less than justice. I am under the impression that many readers, too much influenced by Chaucer's brilliant verisimilitude, tend to regard his famous pilgrimage to Canterbury as significant not because it is a great fiction, but because it seems to be a remarkable record of a fourteenth-century pilgrimage. A remarkable record it may be, but if we treat it too narrowly as such there are going to be certain casualties among the elements that make up the fiction. Perhaps first among these elements is the fictional reporter, Chaucer the pilgrim, and the role he plays in the Prologue to the *Canterbury Tales* and in the links between them. I think it time that he was rescued from the comparatively dull record of history and put back into his poem. He is not really Chaucer the poet—nor, for that matter, is either the poet, or the poem's protagonist, that Geoffrey Chaucer frequently mentioned in contemporary historical records as a distinguished civil servant, but never as a poet. The fact that these are three separate entities does not, naturally, exclude the probability—or rather the certainty—that they bore a close resemblance to one another, and that, indeed, they frequently got together in the same body. But that does not excuse us from keeping them distinct from one another, difficult as their close resemblance makes our task.

The natural tendency to confuse one thing with its like is perhaps best represented by a school of Chaucerian criticism, now outmoded, that pictured a single Chaucer under the guise of a wide-eyed, jolly, rolypoly little man who, on fine Spring mornings, used to get up early, while the dew was still on the grass, and go look at daisies. A charming portrait, this, so charming, indeed, that it was sometimes able to maintain itself to the exclusion of any Chaucerian other side. It has every reason to be charming, since it was lifted almost *in toto* from the version Chaucer gives of himself in the Prologue to the *Legend of Good Women*, though I imagine it owes some of its popularity to a rough analogy with Wordsworth—a sort of *Legend of Good Poets*. It was this version of Chaucer that Kittredge, in a page of great importance to Chaucer criticism, demolished with his assertion that "a naïf Collector of Customs would be a paradoxical monster." He might well have added that a naïve creator of old January would be even more monstrous.

Kittredge's pronouncement cleared the air, and most of us now accept the proposition that Chaucer was sophisticated as readily as we do the proposition that the whale is a mammal. But unhappily, now that we've got rid of the naïve fiction, it is easy to fall into the opposite sort of mistake. This is to envision, in the *Canterbury Tales*, a highly urbane, literal-historical Chaucer setting out from Southwark on a specific day of a specific year (we even argue somewhat acrimoniously about dates and routes), in company with a group of persons who existed in real life and whom Chaucer, his reporter's eye peeled for every idiosyncrasy, determined to get down on paper—down, that is, to the last wart—so that books might be written identifying them. Whenever this accurate reporter says something especially fatuous—which is not infrequently—it is either ascribed to an opinion peculiar to the Middle Ages (sometimes very peculiar), or else Chaucer's tongue is said to be in his cheek.

Now a Chaucer with tongue-in-cheek is a vast improvement over a simple-minded Chaucer when one is trying to define the whole man, but it must lead to a loss of critical perception, and in particular to a confused notion of Chaucerian irony, to see in the Prologue a reporter who is acutely aware of the significance of what he sees but who sometimes, for ironic emphasis, interprets the evidence presented by his observation in a fashion directly contrary to what we expect. The proposition ought to be expressed in reverse: the reporter is, usually, acutely unaware of the significance of what he sees, no matter how sharply he sees it. He is, to be sure, permitted his lucid intervals, but in general he is the victim of the poet's pervasive—not merely sporadic—irony. And as such he is also the chief agent by which the poet achieves his wonderfully complex, ironic, comic, serious vision of a world which is but a devious and confused, infinitely various pilgrimage to a certain shrine. It is, as I hope to make clear, a good deal more than merely fitting that our guide on such a pilgrimage should be a man of such naïveté as the Chaucer who tells the tale of *Sir Thopas*. Let us accompany him a little distance.

* * *

It is often remarked that Chaucer really liked the Prioress very much, even though he satirized her gently—very gently. But this is an understatement: Chaucer the pilgrim may not be said merely to have liked the Prioress very much—he thought she was utterly charming. In the first twenty-odd lines of her portrait (A118 ff.) he employs, among other superlatives, the adverb *ful* seven times. Middle English uses *ful* where we use *very*, and if one translates the beginning of the portrait into a kind of basic English (which is what, in a way, it really is), one gets something like this: "There was also a Nun, a Prioress, who was very sincere and modest in the way she smiled; her biggest oath was only 'By saint Loy'; and she was called Madame Eglantine. She sang the divine service very well, intoning it in her nose very prettily, and she spoke French very nicely and elegantly"—and so on, down to the last gasp of sentimental appreciation. Indeed, the Prioress may be said to have transformed the rhetoric into something not unlike that of a very bright kindergarten child's descriptive theme. In his reaction to the Prioress Chaucer the pilgrim resembles another—if less—simple-hearted enthusiast: the Host, whose summons to her to tell a tale must be one of the politest speeches in the language. Not "My lady prioresse, a tale now!" but, "as curteisly as it had been a mayde,"

> My lady Prioresse, by youre leve,
> So that I wiste I sholde yow nat greve,
> I wolde demen that ye tellen sholde
> A tale next, if so were that ye wolde.
> Now wol ye vouche sauf, my lady deere?
> (B1636-41)

Where the Prioress reduced Chaucer to superlatives, she reduces the Host to subjunctives.

There is no need here to go deeply into the Prioress. Eileen Power's illustrations from contemporary episcopal records show with what extraordinary economy the portrait has been packed with abuses typical of fourteenth-century nuns. The abuses, to be sure, are mostly petty, but it is clear enough that the Prioress, while a perfect lady, is anything but a perfect nun; and attempts to whitewash her, of which there have been many, can only proceed from an innocence of heart equal to Chaucer the pilgrim's and undoubtedly directly influenced by it. For he, of course, is quite swept away by her irrelevant *sensibilité*, and as a result misses much of the point of what he sees. No doubt he feels that he has come a long way, socially speaking, since his encounter with the Black Knight in the forest, and he knows, or thinks he knows, a little more of what it's all about: in this case it seems to be mostly about good manners, kindness to animals, and female charm. Thus it has been argued that Chaucer's appreciation for the Prioress as a sort of heroine of courtly romance *manquée* actually reflects the sophistication of the living Chaucer, an urbane man who cared little whether amiable nuns were good nuns. But it seems a curious form of sophistication that permits itself to babble superlatives; and indeed, if this is sophistication, it is the kind generally seen in the least experienced people—one that reflects a wide-eyed wonder at the glamor of the great world. It is just what one might expect of a bourgeois exposed to the splendors of high society, whose values, such as they are, he eagerly accepts. And that is precisely what Chaucer the pilgrim is, and what he does.

If the Prioress's appeal to him is through elegant femininity, the Monk's is through imposing virility. Of this formidable and important prelate the pilgrim does not say, with Placebo,

> I woot wel that my lord kan moore than I:
> What that he seith, I holde it ferme and stable,
> (E1498-9)

but he acts Placebo's part to perfection. He is as impressed with the Monk as the Monk is, and accepts him on his own terms and at face value, never sensing that those terms imply complete condemnation of Monk *qua* Monk. The Host is also impressed by the Monk's virility, but having no sense of Placebonian propriety (he is himself a most virile man) he makes indecent jokes about it. This, naturally, offends the pilgrim's sense of decorum: there is a note of deferential commiseration in his comment, "This worthy Monk took al in pacience" (B3155). Inevitably when the Monk establishes hunting as the highest activity of which religious man is capable, "I seyde his opinion was good" (A183). As one of the pilgrim's spiritual heirs was later to say, Very like a whale; but not, of course, like a fish out of water.

Wholehearted approval for the values that important persons subscribe to is seen again in the portrait of the Friar. This amounts to a prolonged gratulation for the efficiency the deplorable Hubert shows in undermining the fabric of the Church by turning St. Francis' ideal inside out:

> Ful swetely herde he confessioun,
> And plesaunt was his absolucioun.
>
> For unto swich a worthy man as he
> Acorded nat, as by his facultee,
> To have with sike lazars aqueyntaunce.
> (A221-222, 243-245)

It is sometimes said that Chaucer did not like the Friar. Whether Chaucer the man would have liked such a Friar is, for our present purposes, irrelevant. But if the pilgrim does not unequivocally express his liking for him, it is only because in his humility he does not feel that, with important people, his own likes and dislikes are material: such importance is its own reward, and can gain no lustre from Geoffrey, who, when the Friar is attacked by the Summoner, is ready to show him the same sympathy he shows the Monk (see D1265-67).

Once he has finished describing the really important people on the pilgrimage the pilgrim's tone changes, for he can now concern himself with the bourgeoisie, members of his own class for whom he does not have to show such profound respect. Indeed, he can even afford to be a little patronizing at times, and to have his little joke at the expense of the too-busy lawyer. But such indirect assertions of his own superiority do not prevent him from giving substance to the old cynicism that the only motive recognized by the middle class is the profit motive, for his interest and admiration for the bourgeois pilgrims is centered mainly in their material prosperity and their ability to increase it. He starts, properly enough, with the out-and-out money-grubber, the Merchant, and after turning aside for that *lusus naturae*, the non-profit-motivated Clerk, proceeds to the Lawyer, who, despite the pilgrim's little joke, is the best and best-paid ever; the Franklin, twenty-one admiring lines on appetite, so expensively catered to; the Gildsmen, cheered up the social ladder, "For catel hadde they ynogh and rente" (A373); and the Physician, again the best and richest. In this series the portrait of the Clerk is generally held to be an ideal one, containing no irony; but while it is ideal, it seems to reflect the pilgrim's sense of values in his joke about the Clerk's failure to make money: is not this still typical of the half-patronizing, half-admiring *un*understanding that practical men of business display towards academics? But in any case the portrait is a fine companion-piece for those in which material prosperity is the main interest both of the characters described and of the describer.

Of course, this is not the sole interest of so gregarious—if shy—a person as Chaucer the pilgrim. Many of the characters have the additional advantage of being good companions, a faculty that receives a high valuation in the Prologue. To be good company might, indeed, atone for certain serious defects of character. Thus the Shipman, whose callous cruelty is duly noted, seems fairly well redeemed in the assertion, "And certeinly he was a good felawe" (A395). At this point an uneasy sensation that even tongue-in-cheek irony will not compensate for the lengths to which Chaucer is going in his approbation of this sinister seafarer sometimes causes editors to note that *a good felawe* means "a rascal." But I can find no evidence that it ever meant a rascal. Of course, all tritely approbative expressions enter easily into ironic connotation, but the phrase *means* a good companion, which is just what Chaucer means. And if, as he says of the Shipman, "Of nyce conscience took he no keep" (A398), Chaucer the pilgrim was doing the same with respect to him.

Nothing that has been said has been meant to imply that the pilgrim was unable to recognize, and deplore, a rascal when he saw one. He could, provided the rascality was situated in a member of the lower classes and provided it was, in any case, somewhat wider than a barn door: Miller, Manciple, Reeve, Summoner, and Pardoner are all acknowledged to be rascals. But rascality generally has, after all, the laudable object of making money, which gives it a kind of validity, if not dignity. These portraits, while in them the pilgrim, prioress-like conscious of the finer aspects of life, does deplore such matters as the Miller's indelicacy of language, contain a note of ungrudging admiration for efficient thievery. It is perhaps fortunate for the pilgrim's reputation as a judge of men that he sees through the Pardoner, since it is the Pardoner's particular tragedy that, except in Church, every one can see through him at a glance; but in Church he remains to the pilgrim "a noble ecclesiaste" (A708). The equally repellent Summoner, a practicing bawd, is partially redeemed by his also being a good fellow, "a gentil harlot and a kynde" (A647), and by the fact that for a moderate bribe he will neglect to summon: the pilgrim apparently subscribes to the popular definition of the best policeman as the one who acts the least policely.

Therefore Chaucer is tolerant, and has his little joke about the Summoner's small Latin—a very small joke, though one of the most amusing aspects of the pilgrim's character is the pleasure he takes in his own jokes, however small. But the Summoner goes too far when he cynically suggests that purse is the Archdeacon's hell, causing Chaucer to respond with a fine show of righteous respect for the instruments of spiritual punishment. The only trouble is that his enthusiastic defense of them carries *him* too far, so that after having warned us that excommunication will indeed damn our souls—

> But wel I woot he lyed right in dede:
> Of cursyng oghte ech gilty man him drede,
> For curs wol slee right as assoillyng savith—
> (A659-661)

he goes on to remind us that it will also cause considerable inconvenience to our bodies: "And also war hym of a *Significavit*" (A662). Since a *Significavit* is the writ accomplishing the imprisonment of the excommunicate, the line provides perhaps the neatest—and most misunderstood—Chaucerian anticlimax in the Prologue.

I have avoided mentioning, hitherto, the pilgrim's reactions to the really good people on the journey—the Knight, the Parson, the Plowman. One might reasonably ask how his uncertain sense of values may be reconciled with the enthusiasm he shows for their rigorous integrity. The question could, of course, be shrugged off with a remark on the irrelevance to art of exact consistency, even to art distinguished by its verisimilitude. But I am not sure that there is any basic inconsistency. It is the nature of the pilgrim to admire all kinds of superlatives, and the fact that he often admires superlatives devoid of—or opposed to—genuine virtue does not inhibit his equal admiration for virtue incarnate. He is not, after all, a bad man; he is, to place him in his literary tradition, merely an average man, or mankind: *homo*, not very *sapiens* to be sure, but with the very best intentions, making his pilgrimage through the world in search of what is good, and showing himself, too frequently, able to recognize the good only when it is spectacularly so. Spenser's Una glows with a kind of spontaneous incandescence, so that the Red Cross Knight, mankind in search of holiness, knows her as good; but he thinks that Duessa is good, too. Virtue concretely embodied in Una or the Parson presents no problems to the well-intentioned observer, but in a world consisting mostly of imperfections, accurate evaluations are difficult for a pilgrim who, like mankind, is naïve. The pilgrim's ready appreciation for the virtuous characters is perhaps the greatest tribute that could be paid to their virtue, and their spiritual simplicity is, I think, enhanced by the intellectual simplicity of the reporter.

The pilgrim belongs, of course, to a very old—and very new—tradition of the fallible first person singular. His most exact modern counterpart is perhaps Lemuel Gulliver, who, in his search for the good, failed dismally to perceive the difference between the pursuit of reason and the pursuit of reasonable horses: one may be sure that the pilgrim would have whinnied with the best of them. In his own century he is related to Long Will of *Piers Plowman*, a more explicit seeker after the good, but just as unswerving in his inability correctly to evaluate what he sees. Another kinsman is the protagonist of the *Pearl*, mankind whose heart is set on a transitory good that has been lost—who, for very natural reasons, confuses earthly with spiritual values. Not entirely unrelated is the protagonist of Gower's *Confessio Amantis*, an old man seeking for an impossible earthly love that seems to him the only good. And in more subtle fashion there is the teller of Chaucer's story of *Troilus and Cressida*, who, while not a true protagonist, performs some of the same functions. For this unloved "servant of the servants of love" falls in love with Cressida so persuasively that almost every male reader of the poem imitates him, so that we all share the heartbreak of Troilus and sometimes, in the intensity of our heartbreak, fail to learn what Troilus did. Finally, of course, there is Dante of the *Divine Comedy*, the most exalted member of the family and perhaps the immediate original of these other first-person pilgrims.

Artistically the device of the *persona* has many functions, so integrated with one another that to try to sort them out produces both oversimplification and distortion. The most obvious, with which this paper has been dealing—distortedly, is to present a vision of the social world imposed on one of the moral world. Despite their verisimilitude most, if not all, of the characters described in the Prologue are taken directly from stock and recur again and again in medieval literature. Langland in his own Prologue and elsewhere depicts many of them: the hunting monk, the avaricious friar, the thieving miller, the hypocritical pardoner, the unjust stewards, even, in little, the all-too-human nun. But while Langland uses the device of the *persona* with considerable skill in the conduct of his allegory, he uses it hardly at all in portraying the inhabitants of the social world: these are described directly, with the poet's own voice. It was left to Chaucer to turn the ancient stock satirical characters into real people assembled for a pilgrimage, and to have them described, with all their traditional faults upon them, by another pilgrim who records faithfully each fault without, for the most part, recognizing that it is a fault and frequently felicitating its possessor for possessing it. One result—though not the only result—is a moral realism much more significant than the literary realism which is a part of it and for which it is sometimes mistaken; this moral realism discloses a world in which humanity is prevented by its own myopia, the myopia of the describer, from seeing what the dazzlingly attractive externals of life really represent. In most of the analogues mentioned above the fallible first person receives, at the end of the book, the education he has needed: the pilgrim arrives somewhere. Chaucer never completed the *Canterbury Tales*, but in the Prologue to the *Parson's Tale* he seems to have been doing, rather hastily, what his contemporaries had done: when, with the sun nine-and-twenty degrees from the horizon, the twenty-nine pilgrims come to a certain—unnamed—*thropes ende* (I12), then the pilgrimage seems no longer to have Canterbury as its destination, but rather, I suspect, the Celestial City of which the Parson speaks.

If one insists that Chaucer was not a moralist but a comic writer (a distinction without a difference), then the device of the *persona* may be taken primarily as serving comedy. It has been said earlier that the several Chaucers must have inhabited one body, and in that sense the fictional first person is no fiction at all. In an oral tradition of literature the first person probably always shared the personality of his creator: thus Dante of the *Divine Comedy* was physically Dante the Florentine; the John Gower of the *Confessio* was also Chaucer's friend John Gower; and Long Will was, I am sure, someone named William Langland, who was both long and wilful. And it is equally certain that Chaucer the pilgrim, "a popet in an arm t'enbrace" (B1891), was in every physical respect Chaucer the man, whom one can imagine reading his work to a courtly audience, as in the portrait appearing in one of the MSS. of *Troilus*. One can imagine also the delight of the audience which heard the Prologue read in this way, and which was aware of the similarities and dissimilarities between Chaucer, the man before them, and Chaucer the pilgrim, both of whom they could see with simultaneous vision. The Chaucer they knew was physically, one gathers, a little ludicrous; a bourgeois, but one who was known as a practical and successful man of the court; possessed perhaps of a certain diffidence of manner, reserved, deferential to the socially imposing persons with whom he was associated; a bit absent-minded, but affable and, one supposes, very good company—a good fellow; sagacious and highly perceptive. This Chaucer was telling them of another who, lacking some of his chief qualities, nevertheless possessed many of his characteristics, though in a different state of balance, and each one probably distorted just enough to become laughable without becoming unrecognizable: deference into a kind of snobbishness, affability into an over-readiness to please, practicality into Babbittry, perception into inspection, absence of mind into dimness of wit; a Chaucer acting in some respects just as Chaucer himself might have acted but unlike his creator the kind of man, withal, who could mistake a group of stock satirical types for living persons endowed with all sorts of superlative qualities. The constant interplay of these two Chaucers must have produced an exquisite and most ingratiating humor—as, to be sure, it still does. This comedy reaches its superb climax when Chaucer the pilgrim, resembling in so many ways Chaucer the poet, can answer the Host's demand for a story only with a rhyme he "lerned longe agoon" (B1899)—*Sir Thopas*, which bears the same complex relation to the kind of romance it satirizes and to Chaucer's own poetry as Chaucer the pilgrim does to the pilgrims he describes and to Chaucer the poet.

* * *

Earlier in this paper I proved myself no gentleman (though I hope a scholar) by being rude to the Prioress, and hence to the many who like her and think that Chaucer liked her too. It is now necessary to retract. Undoubtedly Chaucer the man would, like his fictional representative, have found her charming and looked on her with affection. To have got on so well in so changeable a world Chaucer must have got on well with the people in it, and it is doubtful that one may get on with people merely by pretending to like them: one's heart has to be in it. But the third entity, Chaucer the poet, operates in a realm which is above and subsumes those in which Chaucer the man and Chaucer the pilgrim have their being. In this realm prioresses may be simultaneously evaluated as marvelously amiable ladies and as prioresses. In his poem the poet arranges for the moralist to define austerely what ought to be and for his fictional representative—who, as the representative of all mankind, is no mere fiction—to go on affirming affectionately what is. The two points of view, in strict moral logic diametrically opposed, are somehow made harmonious in Chaucer's wonderfully comic attitude, that double vision that is his ironical essence. The mere critic performs his etymological function by taking the Prioress apart and clumsily separating her good parts from her bad; but the poet's function is to build her incongruous and inharmonious parts into an inseparable whole which is infinitely greater than its parts. In this complex structure both the latent moralist and the naive reporter have important positions, but I am not persuaded that in every case it is possible to determine which of them has the last word.[1]

Note

1. Quotations from Chaucer in this paper are made from F. N. Robinson's text (Cambridge, Mass., n.d.). Books referred to or cited are G. L. Kittredge, *Chaucer and His Poetry* (Cambridge, Mass., 1915), p. 45; Eileen Power, *Medieval People* (London, 1924), pp. 59-84. Robinson's note to A650 records the opinion that *a good felawe* means a 'rascal.' The medieval reader's expectation that the first person in a work of fiction would represent mankind generally and at the same time would physically resemble the author is commented on by Leo Spitzer in an interesting note in *Traditio*, iv (1946), 414-422.

Chaucer the Man

Donald R. Howard

So much study has gone into the rhetorical workings of Chaucer's satire that almost anyone who reads Chaucer is now acutely aware of the persona or narrator in each poem. The fact of a disparity between the narrator and Chaucer himself has become a kind of premise or dogma of Chaucer criticism; we have become accustomed to phrases like "the fictional Chaucer," "the postures of the narrator," or "the finiteness of the narrator-role." And yet because his major poems confer upon him the status of a major figure, we continue to be interested in Chaucer the man despite the prevailing formalism of Chaucer criticism. We read minor works by him for which, were they anonymous, we should not take the trouble to turn a page. We talk about his education, thought, "development," "mind." And in his best poems we *feel* him as a "man speaking to men." As for the man himself, we have a few records, though none of these really proves that civil servant and poet were the same person. Mostly, we believe in him. Of course it is entirely possible that someone will come along and argue that the *Canterbury Tales* were an instance of group authorship, or were really written by John of Gaunt; but if someone did, we should all pooh-pooh him and ostracize him and direct plenty of irony at him.

My theme is that this man, whom we feel that we know, is a real and living presence in his works, and that his presence in them is what makes them interesting and good. I present this not as a corollary of any humanistic or existential principles, but as a fact. I say that we are interested in the fictive narrator, the rhetorical workings of the irony, the method of creating illusion and reality—all the "devices" of his high art—not because they are devices, but because everywhere *in* and *behind* them lies Chaucer the man. I will even go a step further: I say that this is the point which various analyses of "narrator" and "persona" have really proved.

It was, to begin with, the point of Professor Donaldson's famous article: he was attempting to show how Chaucer the poet masks himself behind the comic figure of Chaucer the pilgrim in order more effectively to say what he has to say.[1] Professor Bronson's objection is that this is not a matter of the rhetoric of fiction, but a result of oral delivery—that it is a perfectly natural manner of ironic conversation.[2] The disagreement, it seems to me, is a kind of pseudo-problem.[3] Any such device, conversational or literary, is a matter of rhetoric and can be analyzed by distinguishing between the author and his projected persona. That the persona is wholly a fictive character—a "puppet"— with no element of the author's own character in it, is something which I think few would maintain. Is it not, after all, a matter of degree? Does not the writer project some element of himself into any character? Do we not all present ourselves in various roles to various people—even to ourselves? And can anyone know his "real" self well enough to present *or* conceal it? To borrow a phrase from Patrick Cruttwell,[4] the writer is by necessity an exhibitionist, and so presents something of himself in everything he writes. He may choose to do so by fragmenting himself behind various masks, but he does not, and cannot, make himself disappear. However we analyze his presence in his works, we are therefore all of us—myself, Professor Bronson, Professor Donaldson, and many another—"in search of Chaucer."

* * *

This search for an author on the part of his readers is a cultural phenomenon of some interest. We could say that the reader's curiosity is piqued by the self-projection of the author, and the more so if the author attempts a masked presentation of himself. But this is not quite the whole story, since authors would perhaps avoid more than a very elementary, or naive, self-presentation if they were not able to anticipate curiosity on the part of readers. Readers have, that is, a "sense of the author." Authors may encourage it, but they did not necessarily invent it. Simple and natural as it seems, it has not always been so important as it is in modern times. Indeed, our curiosity about the *private* life of the author—our desire to read his letters and know hidden facts about him—does not appear to have come into being until the eighteenth century; it begins, probably, with Boswell.[5] Before the eighteenth century, except perhaps in vituperative public controversies, the reader's curiosity was satisfied by what the writer *said* about himself. No one seems to have wondered, until quite recent times, whether or not (for example) Sir Philip Sidney really *did* look into his heart and write, just as no one tried to shed any light on the Dark Lady.

In the earlier Middle Ages, the sense of the author, the mention of his name, and the expression of his pride in his achievement were not entirely absent. But they were counterbalanced by frequent anonymity and by warnings against pride and worldly vanity. Moreover, the poet's name was sometimes mentioned only to ask forgiveness for shortcomings and request the prayers of readers;[6] Chaucer's "Retraction" would be an instance of the latter convention. It is only in the twelfth century that we begin to find open pride in authorship. Poets begin then to argue that true nobility springs from the individual intellect, and that letters are equal to arms as a means of conferring nobility.[7] By the time of the Italian Renaissance, the argument is carried further: poets begin to claim not merely a kind of nobility from what they write, but the power to confer fame upon others and the expectation of an earthly immortality through reputation.[8] In Chaucer we can find something like this Renaissance interest in fame, but it is very much more sparing than the extravagant claims of the humanists. *The House of Fame* shows Chaucer, quite early in his career, thinking about the problem of fame. Still, what does *The House of Fame* teach but the old medieval lesson that good or bad fame is often conferred unjustly in this transitory world? The envoy of the *Troilus* is a better place to look for Chaucer's hope of an earthly immortality:

> Go, litel bok, go, litel myn tragedye,
> Ther God thi makere yet, er that he dye,
> So sende myght to make in som comedye!
> But litel book, no makyng thow n'envie,
> But subgit be to alle poesye;
> And kis the steppes, where as thow seest pace
> Virgile, Ovide, Omer, Lucan, and Stace.
>   (v.1786-92)

Still, while the poet puts himself in very noble company, the passage is, in form at least, a conventional protestation of humility:[9] the poet's book is to be "subgit to alle poesye" and to kiss the steps where it sees these great poets go. One might quote the sentiment of the *Knight's Tale*, "Thanne is it best, as for a worthy fame,/ To dyen when that he is best of name" (A.3055-56), as evidence of Chaucer's interest in a just reputation as a reward for good labors; still of course the labors are not poetical ones and Chaucer is not speaking of himself. On the whole it does not appear to me that Chaucer put more stock in lasting fame than did any late medieval author; he does not claim to confer fame on others, and his hopes of fame for himself are suggested only with the utmost modesty. In the Man of Law's Prologue, the lawyer mentions Chaucer by name and reels off an impressive bibliography of his works, but he takes a rather condescending tone toward the poet, who he says "kan but lewedly/ On metres and on rymyng craftily" (B.47-48), and prefers him to Gower only because he is more moral. Again, the passage gives a hint of Chaucer's hope of fame, but it is sardonic indeed to make one's critics talk like J. Donald Adams.

Another aspect of the changing sense of the author in the late Middle Ages comes about as the result of technological progress. In the earlier Middle Ages a manuscript was read by few and copied seldom, but with the rise of professional scriptoria in the fourteenth century and the invention of printing in the fifteenth, the writer could begin to imagine an audience going unpredictably beyond his immediate milieu. People could then conceive of the writer as having the power to address and influence an ever increasing body of readers—a "public."[10] The writer could imagine himself no longer a scribe, a maker of books or a transmitter of authorities, but the originator of an irreversible process. Here again Chaucer is in the transitional stage of an important cultural

---

change. Certainly in the *Troilus* he takes the position of a scribe or pedant transmitting from an "authority" matters of which he claims no personal experience. This was, as Professor Bethurum has shown,[11] generally his pose in his earlier poems. On the other hand, it is distinctly a pose. Chaucer might not have made extravagant claims for the originality of the *Troilus*, but it is clear that he felt he had created something. Seeing himself as the originator rather than the transmitter in a process of publication through copying, he even expresses anxiety over the accuracy of the process:

> And for ther is so gret diversite
> In Englissh and in writyng of oure tonge,
> So prey I God that non myswrite the,
> Ne the mysmetre for defaute of tonge.
> And red wherso thow be, or elles songe,
> That thow be understonde, God I biseche!
>
> (v.1793-98)

Again, in the *Canterbury Tales*, we get a sense of his hope that he will be received well by an unseen audience of readers. In the General Prologue he warns us,

> But first I pray yow, of youre curteisye,
> That ye n'arette it nat my vileynye,
> Thogh that I pleynly speke in this mateere,
> To telle yow hir wordes and hir cheere,
> Ne thogh I speke hir wordes proprely.
>
> (A.725-729)

There is the same kind of anxious apology just before the Miller's Tale, and here Chaucer suggests,

> whoso list it nat yheere,
> Turne over the leef and chese another tale.
>
> (A.3176-77)

To be sure he wrote with oral delivery in mind, and in many ways the expectation of oral delivery colored his style. But it is evident that he expected also to be copied by unseen hands and read by unseen readers. To some extent this was true throughout the Middle Ages; the formula "readers and hearers" is enough to suggest it.[12] Chaucer conceives of his function as we should expect a writer of the fourteenth century to do—with an increased sense of an unpredictable and irreversible process of communication going beyond his milieu and beyond his time, but with nothing like the feeling which the printing press was to encourage.

These changes in the idea of authorship—this steadily increasing expectation of being read and admired—created a corresponding change in the idea of anonymity. In the earlier Middle Ages anonymity was a mark of the scribe's or writer's humility: it showed his deference to the "authorities" he transmitted. He viewed himself as a mere agent in a process of transmission and preservation. Writers who mention their own labors often deprecate them—one thinks of Einhard, who tells us that although his powers are almost nil he is willing to risk the opinion of the world in order to preserve the deeds of Charlemagne. By the twelfth century we can find a writer like Bernard of Morval, in the prose dedication of his *De contemptu mundi*, asking for criticism and defending his use of rime on the ground that it commends moral precepts more readily to the mind. Bernard argues, too, that the Bible contains lyrics and quotes Horace that writing should instruct and delight. He claims to have been inspired to his work by a vision, and boasts of his ability to sustain the metrical pattern at such length. All of this sounds very modern for a twelfth-century monk writing at Cluny, and Bernard injects much of his own strong personality into his indignant denunciation of the evils of his time. Yet he does absolutely nothing to preserve his name: it is mentioned only in the salutation to his abbot. Scribes did no more, for it is not certain that he wrote "Bernardus Morvalensis" rather than "Morlanensis" or "Morlacensis." Nor has anyone discovered what Morval might have been.[13]

By Chaucer's time, of course, writers are much less reserved about mentioning their own names. A fashion has taken shape. The new interest in names of writers is reflected by the appearance, in the early fifteenth century, of the *De scriptoribus ecclesiasticis* by Johannis Trithemius, a biographical dictionary which contains chiefly dates, lists of works, and stereotyped praise of each man's piety and learning. Chaucer himself likes to name authors and praise them. At the same time, anyone who has worked with fifteenth-century manuscripts will know that while the names of authors may be more frequently recorded than in previous times, there are still many manuscripts which omit altogether the writers' names. It would be interesting to have some statistics about the decline of anonymity after the fourteenth century. What is important, however, is the increasing sense of the author: when curiosity about the author could be assumed as a normal attitude among readers, it permitted the author to use anonymity not merely to avoid criticism or persecution, but to whet the interest of his public. *Gulliver's Travels* is the classic example: the reader is purposely led to seek out in the text the true views of the anonymous author which lie behind the literal statement of the pseudonymous one. It is the sense of the author, considered as a cultural phenomenon, which makes possible a tension between the persona or narrator and the understood or felt personality of the author. And Chaucer is the first English poet to use the full artistic possibilities of this masked presentation of self.

* * *

Chaucer saw himself, then, as an originator of literary works who could hope for a continuing audience and reputation. He speaks of himself with modesty and, usually, with self-deprecating humor; but he does not seek anonymity—indeed, he provides us, in the prologue to the *Legend of Good Women*, in the Retraction of the *Canterbury Tales*, and in the Man of Law's Prologue, with lists of his writings. He did, however, mask his personality. This seems like a kind of anonymity, but it is not anything like the simple, unintentional anonymity of, say, the Gawain-poet. We should do better to call it masquerade.[14]

What is distinctive in this element of Chaucer's style begins, perhaps, with *The House of Fame*. Here the narrator is actually called "Geffrey"; he is a plump, bookish fellow with little experience in the high courtly practices of love. The portrait is humorously autobiographical—for our author is a bourgeois, a customs-clerk; and his audience is composed of knights and ladies, or of people like himself who are knowledgeable about court fashions. What is out of character, of course, is the narrator's obtuseness and insensitivity. This, I suspect, was a humorous development of the half-comprehending, naive reactions which one finds in the conventional "dreamer."[15] Such a narrator serves the artistic function of throwing attention on the subject matter: the audience perceives the *meaning* of the facts, while the narrator does not. And of course it is high comedy for the writer to adopt the mask of a fool when his artistry shows him to be anything but.

The device is essentially the same in the *Troilus*, but there are refinements. The narrator is a devotee of books, and a "servant of the servants of love." He himself is unsuccessful as a lover, on account of his "unliklynesse," yet he stands in wide-eyed and somewhat envious admiration of the affair as he transmits it from his "author." He is no longer the conventional dreamer of the earlier poems—he is a *reader*. What Professor Bloomfield has brilliantly described in his article on "distance and predestination" in the *Troilus*[16] is, after all, the common experience of those who read: the alternation between emotional involvement in the illusion and aesthetic distance from it. The "narrator" of the *Troilus*, this reader with his old book in hand, is therefore like ourselves: we are, as the English say, "reading Lollius with him." He is closer to the events than we are (for he has already read the book from which he draws his tale), but he is willing at times to remove himself from our attention and let us look on directly with him as the story unfolds.

Pandarus is a kind of mirror image of this narrator. He, too, is an unsuccessful lover, taking a vicarious enjoyment in place of a real one. He reacts to the story quite as the narrator does—fearful for Troilus, eager over the progress of the affair, exercised in the consummation scene, helpless and dejected by the way things turn out. And, as the narrator manipulates the events of his story, Pandarus manipulates the events themselves. But the similarities between Pandarus and the narrator all merely emphasize one enormous difference between them. Pandarus is a pagan who believes in a pagan philosophy of *carpe diem* ("cache it anon," he says at one point), whereas the narrator is a Christian. Pandarus is of their time, the narrator of ours. Hence Pandarus is of no use when things go wrong. His morality, which consists chiefly of the notion that one should take advantage of Fortune while one may, can provide no better consolation to Troilus than another affair. He "stant, astoned of thise causes tweye,/ As stille as ston; a word ne kowde he seye" (v.1728-29). At the end, the narrator, like any reader, sees a lesson in the story shaped by his own age and culture: he is a Christian, and he learns from his story the error of "payens corsed olde rites," though he had been carried away at first by enthusiasm for them.

Now this narrator, this reader and learner, *is Chaucer.* We learn this from the epilogue, where he speaks in his own person—"Go, litel bok, go, litel myn tragedye." To say that the narrator goes off stage at the end and Chaucer steps on to speak the envoy *in propria persona* is simply to misread the text: At the end of the envoy, after expressing his worries over the diversity of English, Chaucer says "But yet to purpos of my rather speche," and then, going back to what he had been saying, "The wrath, as I bigan row for to seye . . . ." What is this if not an explicit statement that the "I" of the epilogue is identical with the "I" who has told the story? We could, of course, say with Professor Jordan that the narrator *becomes* Chaucer at the end.[17] But what would be the point? Do we not rather discover here, if we had any doubt before, that it was Chaucer speaking all along? It was Chaucer the enthusiast of courtly love, who is now convinced that Christian love is best. And why is this so different from the real live Chaucer of the fourteenth century? We know that he *was* a lover of books. And he *did* have a certain "unliklynesse" as concerns courtly love, because it was aristocratic behavior and he was not an aristocrat. At least for a time he did take the poetry of courtly love seriously. But also, quite early in his career, he began to search for other materials and other styles. And he wrote Christian poems throughout his life. One cannot really find anything in the *Troilus* (except "Lollius") which makes the narrator *factually* different from Chaucer the man. The difference is simply a matter of tone. It is the humorous exaggeration of his bookishness and "unliklynesse" that makes him seem different from the presumably "real" Chaucer of the epilogue—the Chaucer we *think* we know.

This element of humorous and exaggerated self-presentation is carried a step further in the narrator of the *Canterbury Tales*. In the *Troilus* Chaucer unmasks himself at the end, but in the *Canterbury Tales* he avoids any direct self-revelation, except in the Retraction. Rather than unmask himself, he unmasks the pilgrims. And his knowledge of them is based upon direct observation.[18] He is not a "dreamer" here, nor a "reader" either; he is a returned traveller. Now returned travellers always have a certain air of omniscience. When the narrator says, as he does of the Merchant, "Ther wiste no wight that he was in dette," we do not have to think it out of character or charge it up to an omniscient author: returned travellers report gossip and surmises along with facts. It is the most natural kind of storytelling in the world, utterly realistic and utterly convincing. As a dreamer in the earlier dream-poems, Chaucer had been reporting what was an illusion to begin with; as a reader in the *Troilus*, he claimed only to be translating and adapting an old story. But in the *Canterbury Tales* he claims to be reporting real events in which he has been a participant, things he can remember. And yet, while he claims this, we enter into the most improbable illusion in the world: that each of thirty people can tell tales in rimed verse as they ride horseback in a group—through open country.

What this means is that the "fictive illusion" of the *Canterbury Tales* is less real and less convincing, despite its contemporaneity, than the intense events of the ancient, doomed city in the *Troilus*. All that was far and strange in Troy was made to seem near and real; but on the way to Canterbury, something in the author himself endues the familiar world of his audience with a strangeness. As we read the General Prologue we perceive that the author does not think what the narrator says. Our curiosity about the author is brought into play; we wonder about his real opinions. Chaucer even throws dust in our eyes by telling (as pilgrim) a dull tale like *Sir Thopas*, which we know he intends (as poet) to be a spoof, then following it with the quite serious *Melibee*. Again, he titillates our sense of the author by having the Man of Law drop his name and discourse on his works. Indeed, he conceals himself so skillfully that we continue, almost six centuries later, to argue about what he really thought. For just as soon as Chaucer the returned traveller is removed from the fictive illusion, just as soon as we are listening directly to one of the pilgrims, we think we detect Chaucer the man in the pilgrim's words. For example, when we read the Miller's Tale we are delighted by all the echoes of the Knight's Tale in it. Is the Miller poking fun at the Knight's Tale? or is Chaucer poking fun at it? Or is Chaucer poking fun at the Miller for not understanding the Knight's high seriousness? or is it all three at once? And even in the Knight's Tale, for all its high style, we are faced with lines like these on Palamon's imprisonment:

And eek therto he is a prisoner
Perpetuelly, noght oonly for a yer.
   Who koude ryme in Englyssh proprely
His martirdom? for sothe it am nat I;
Therfore I passe as lightly as I may.
   It fel that in the seventhe yer, of May
The thridde nyght, (as olde bookes seyn,
That al this storie tellen moore pleyn)

(A.1457-64)

Is the Knight merely being humble? If so, why the reference to riming? or is the Knight being ironic, making fun of his own tale? Or is it Chaucer himself speaking? and if so, is he making fun of the Knight, or of himself? We want to say to Chaucer, as the Host does, "What man artow?" But it is an essential part of the style of the *Canterbury Tales* that no real answer to the question is ever given. And it is probably time we stopped trying to decide who is speaking where.

What I am arguing is that Chaucer the man is present in the *Canterbury Tales* not "objectively" through any explicit representation, but dynamically—through an implied relationship between himself and his audience. And his role is precisely what it must have been in reality—that of a bourgeois addressing his social betters. From all the biographical facts which we know about Chaucer, exactly two major ones emerge: that Chaucer was a bourgeois who successfully established himself as a civil servant, and that he was a poet who wrote for the court. His aristocratic audience, which certainly admired him, would still have looked upon him as a social inferior. In such a milieu a man of wit is on guard not to show any bourgeois vices—literal-mindedness, uncritical gregariousness, pedantry, naiveté, inexperience, or pretentiousness. It is the perennial problem of the bourgeois: he does not want to appear bourgeois in the eyes of the upper class, but he knows that the most bourgeois thing he can do is to show discomfort about his status or, worse, attempt to deny it. I can think of only two ways to get out of the dilemma. One is good-natured clowning with an edge of modest self-deprecation; the other is to be a sober, useful fellow and let your betters like you for what you are, not what you say you are. In the *Canterbury Tales*, and to an extent in the earlier poems, Chaucer adopts both these attitudes. He presents himself in the General Prologue as an exaggerated bourgeois type—uncritical, affable, admiring the rich and powerful, even impressed with successful thievery. He presents with humor exactly those bourgeois qualities which the average bourgeois would conceal from aristocrats, makes them into an elaborate joke, and parades it before the court. In doing so he tactfully conceals his wit, his intelligence, his learning, his philosophical depth, his wisdom—traits which could hardly have escaped any member of his audience. To make it easier, he pokes gentle fun at other bourgeois—the sober Man of Law, for example, or the genial Franklyn. His own tale of Sir Thopas illustrates the method perfectly. He presents himself as a bourgeois dunderhead attempting to tell an aristocratic tale of knightly deeds. And in the tale itself the joke revolves around the notion of a Flemish bourgeois ineptly playing knight. The real and necessary implication is that Chaucer himself really sees it all not from any bourgeois point of view but from that of true knights and ladies. He leaves his audience to assume that he is indeed *au courant* with their aristocratic attitudes. In a word, he leaves the audience *to create him in their own image*. In the *Troilus*, as Professor Payne has lately shown,[19] the narrator carries on a kind of running dialogue with us the audience—implies what kind of an audience we are and draws us into the poem so that we become a part of its reality. But in the *Canterbury Tales* Chaucer does something different: he draws the audience into the work not by engaging in a dialogue with us but by expecting us to intuit what he thinks, to project ourselves into the role of the implied author, to overreach ourselves and become one with him.

I will venture a step further and suggest that in one fundamental respect the naive narrator is wiser, has a truer vision, than this "implied author" with whom we align ourselves—that in the narrator Chaucer has isolated and presented one important trait of his own personality, his interest in people and his tolerant humanity.[20] Everyone is accustomed to say that through the narrator Chaucer presents the surface appearance and lets the pilgrims themselves show the underlying reality. But is it not equally true that the wide-eyed narrator, blind as he may be to the vices of his companions, sees the good side of them with a strange clarity? This—if you care to be allegorical—is quite consistent with medieval theology. Chaucer had it from St. Augustine that all created things are fundamentally good—that evil is parasitic, a deprivation of goodness rather than an entity; that one should on this account "hate the vice but love the man." So, in the masquerade of the literal-minded, gregarious pilgrim, Chaucer plays a kind of Holy Fool who stumbles into Christian charity unawares. We, with the implied author, perceive his intellectual errors, but his foolish generosity infects us all the same. Through it we are made to see—in the Monk, say, or the Pardoner—the created man beneath the canker evil.

If I am right in this, then Chaucer's fragmented self-presentation leads us to grasp two things at once—that evil lurks beneath good appearances, but that good lies beneath evil. The pilgrimage begins with the narrator's doubtful notion that everything and everyone is good. It ends with a sermon whose point is that we should look to our *own* sins—and, in the Retraction, Chaucer makes his own act of penance. For Chaucer's own audience I should not be surprised if this had finally the effect of making them look within themselves and examine their own lives as Christians. To a degree Chaucer's audience might also have wondered about the elusive Master Chaucer himself—which pilgrims he liked, or thought absurd, or condemned. Since Boswell's time it is much more our tendency to wonder of the author "What man artow?" and to go in search of him. It would be *nice* to know more facts about him, but finally the most relevant information we can have comes from the style of his works. The Chaucer of biographical documents, the Chaucer of the customs-house, might for all we know have *been* literal-minded, uncritical, bookish, and fat—what might we not say, if we cared to collect anecdotes, about the Wallace Stevens of the insurance company or the T. S. Eliot of the publishing house? The Chaucer we know is a creation of our own response to his works. For that he is no less the *real* Chaucer. This is true for a reason which, as exegetes, we sometimes set aside, but which as humanists we always assume: that for every man who creates great poems there is an infinite truth, of grandeur and terror, in the adage *style is the man himself*—that there must be in him, and in those who would read him, all of the human possibilities which can be realized in his works.

Notes

This article was presented in a shorter form to the Chaucer section of the Modern Language Association, 1963.

1. E. Talbot Donaldson, "Chaucer the Pilgrim," *PMLA*, LXIX (1954), 928-936.

2. Bertrand H. Bronson, *In Search of Chaucer* (Toronto, 1960), pp. 25-32.

3. Cf. Robert M. Jordan, "Chaucer's Sense of Illusion: Roadside Drama Reconsidered," *ELH*, XXIX (1962), 19-33.

4. "Makers and Persons," *Hudson Review*, XII (1959-60), 487-507. The idea is developed by Wayne C. Booth, *The Rhetoric of Fiction* (Chicago, 1961), esp. pp. 16-20, 67-77, 396-398.

5. Cruttwell, pp. 497-500

6. See Ernst Robert Curtius, *European Literature and the Latin Middle Ages*, trans. Willard R. Trask, Bollingen Series XXXVI (New York, 1953), pp. 515-518. Leo Spitzer, "Note on the Poetic and the Empirical 'I' in Medieval Authors," *Traditio*, IV (1946), 414-422, argues that medieval readers had little interest in the empirical person behind the "I," and tended to regard him as representative, though the autobiographical touch might add poignancy. R. W. Chambers, on the other hand, argues against the idea of "personas" in medieval poetry, showing with many examples that the dreamer or narrator in a medieval poem *is* the author; see "Robert or William Longland?" *London Mediæval Studies*, I, 3 (1948 for 1939), 442-451.

7. Curtius, pp. 476-477, 485-486.

8. Jacob Burckhardt, in *The Civilisation of the Renaissance in Italy*, trans. S. G. C.

Middlemore (London and New York, 1928), pp. 139-153, dealt with the idea of fame. Owing in part to Burckhardt's influence, many would say that the sense of the author was shaped largely by the rise of humanistic individualism and by the imitation of ancient writers like Horace who boasted that their works would outlast their own times; hence they might say that Chaucer's awareness of himself as a writer is a harbinger of the Renaissance. But in fact the sense of the author antedates the revival of the classics and the rise of humanism; it is quite as possible to regard it as a cause, rather than a result, of the "revival of learning."

9. See *The Works of Geoffrey Chaucer*, ed. F. N. Robinson, 2nd ed. (Cambridge, Mass., 1957), p. 837. All quotations are from this edition.

10. The *OED* reports the earliest uses of the word in the fifteenth century, and in this sense only in the sixteenth century.

11. Dorothy Bethurum, "Chaucer's Point of View as Narrator in the Love Poems," *PMLA*, LXXIV (1959), 511-520.

12. On the tradition of oral delivery and its influence on Chaucer, see Ruth Crosby, "Oral Delivery in the Middle Ages," *Speculum*, XI (1936), 88-110; "Chaucer and the Custom of Oral Delivery," *Speculum*, XIII (1938), 413-432; and Bertrand H. Bronson, "Chaucer's Art in Relation to his Audience," *Five Studies in Literature* (Berkeley, Calif., 1940), pp. 1-53. For an excellent analysis of Chaucer's estimate of himself with relation to his audience, see Rosemary Woolf, "Chaucer as a Satirist in the General Prologue to the *Canterbury Tales*," *Critical Quarterly*, I (1959), 150-157. It is not necessary to suppose that the printing press and silent rapid reading caused modern writers to stop thinking in terms of oral delivery. Writers still read orally, if only to their wives, and they may well imagine themselves speaking aloud as they compose. We write "I should like to say" and similar expressions without implying oral delivery. Language is by nature spoken, and a writer who writes with any degree of fluency is bound to "hear" spoken discourse as he writes. The difference between medieval and modern in this respect, as in others, is a matter of degree. Cf. Jordan, "Chaucer's Sense of Illusion," p. 21, n. 3. On the oral-aural component in western culture, see Marshall McLuhan, *The Gutenberg Galaxy: The Making of Typographic Man* (Toronto, 1962); Walter J. Ong, *Ramus: Method, and the Decay of Dialogue* (Cambridge, Mass., 1958), and *The Barbarian Within* (New York, 1962), esp. pp. 68-87, 220-229.

13. See Bernard of Morval, *De contemptu mundi: A Bitter Satirical Poem of 3000 Lines upon the Morals of the XIIth Century*, ed. H. C. Hoskier (London, 1929), pp. XV, XXII, XXXV-XXXIX.

14. See Ruth Nevo, "Chaucer: Motive and Mask in the 'General Prologue'," *Modern Language Review*, LVIII (1963), 1-9.

15. On the early development of the device, see Bethurum, esp. pp. 511-516; Alfred L. Kellogg, "Chaucer's Self-Portrait and Dante's," *Medium Ævum*, XXIX (1960), 119-120; David M. Bevington, "The Obtuse Narrator in Chaucer's *House of Fame*," *Speculum*, XXXVI (1961), 288-298; and Charles A. Owen, Jr., "The Role of the Narrator in the 'Parlement of Foules'," *College English*, XIV (1953), 264-269.

16. Morton W. Bloomfield, "Distance and Predestination in *Troilus and Criseyde*," *PMLA*, LXXII (1957), 14-26. Cf. E. Talbot Donaldson, *Chaucer's Poetry* (New York, 1958), p. 966.

17. Robert M. Jordan, "The Narrator in Chaucer's *Troilus*," *ELH*, XXV (1958), 255.

18. On the narrator's stance in the General Prologue, see Ralph Baldwin, *The Unity of the Canterbury Tales* (Copenhagen, 1955), pp. 55-57, and Edgar Hill Duncan, "Narrator's Points of View in the Portrait-sketches, Prologue to the *Canterbury Tales*," *Essays in Honor of Walter Clyde Curry* (Nashville, Tenn., 1954), 77-101.

19. Robert O. Payne, *The Key of Remembrance: A Study of Chaucer's Poetics* (New Haven and London, 1963), pp. 227-232.

20. The point is anticipated by Donaldson, "Chaucer the Pilgrim," p. 936.

Critical Insights

The Art of Impersonation:
A General Prologue to *The Canterbury Tales*_____
H. Marshall Leicester, Jr.

Nec illud minus attendendum esse arbitror, utrum . . . magis secundum aliorum opinionem quam secundum propriam dixerint sententiam, sicut in plerisque Ecclesiastes dissonas diversorum inducit sententias, imo ut tumultuator interpretatur, beato in quarto dialogorum attestante Gregorio.

In my judgment it is no less necessary to decide whether sayings found [in the sacred writings and the Fathers] are quotations from the opinions of others rather than the writers' own authoritative pronouncements. On many topics the author of Ecclesiastes brings in so many conflicting proverbs that we have to take him as impersonating the tumult of the mob, as Gregory points out in his fourth *Dialogue*.

Abelard

In his much praised book *The Idea of the* Canterbury Tales, Donald R. Howard has isolated a perennial strand in the Chaucer criticism of the last thirty years or more—isolated it, defined it clearly, and given it a name. Discussing the Knight's Tale, he remarks:

Chaucer . . . introduced a jocular and exaggerated element that seems to call the Knight's convictions into question. For example, while the two heroes are fighting he says "in this wise I let hem fighting dwelle" and turns his attention to Theseus:

> The destinee, ministre general,
> That executeth in the world over all
> The purveiaunce that God hath seen biforn,
> So strong it is that, though the world had sworn
> The contrary of a thing by ye or nay,
> Yet sometime it shall fallen on a day
> That falleth nat eft within a thousand yeer.
> For certainly, our appetites here,
> Be it of wer, or pees, or hate, or love,
> All is this ruled by the sight above.
> This mene I now by mighty Theseus,
> That for to hunten is so desirous,
> And namely at the grete hert in May,
> That in his bed there daweth him no day
> That he nis clad, and redy for to ride

With hunt and horn and houndes him beside.
For in his hunting hath he swich delit
That it is all his joy and appetit
To been himself the grete hertes bane.
For after Mars he serveth now Diane.
                                        (1663-1682)

All this machinery is intended to let us know that on a certain day Theseus took it in
mind to go hunting. It is impossible not to see a mock-epic quality in such a passage, and hard not to conclude that its purpose is ironic, that it is meant to put us at a
distance from the Knight's grandiose ideas of destiny and make us think about
them. This humorous element in the Knight's Tale is the most controversial aspect
of the tale: where one critic writes it off as an "antidote" to tragedy another puts it at
the center of things, but no one denies it is there. It introduces a feature which we
will experience in many a tale: we read the tale as a dramatic monologue spoken by
its teller but understand that some of Chaucer's attitudes spill into it. This feature
gives the tale an artistry which we cannot realistically attribute to the teller: I am
going to call this *unimpersonated artistry*. In its simplest form it is the contingency
that a tale not memorized but told impromptu is in verse. The artistry is the author's, though selected features of the pilgrim's dialect, argot, or manner may still
be impersonated. In its more subtle uses it allows a gross or "low" character to use
language, rhetoric, or wit above his capabilities. (Sometimes it is coupled with an
impersonated *lack* of art, an artlessness or gaucherie which causes a character to tell
a bad tale, as in *Sir Thopas*, or to violate literary conventions or proprieties, as in the
Knight's Tale.) The effect is that of irony or parody, but this effect is Chaucer's accomplishment, not an impersonated skill for which the pilgrim who tells the tale deserves any compliments.[1]

Having generated this principle, Howard goes on to apply it, at various
points in the book, to the tales of the Miller, the Summoner, the Merchant, the
Squire, and the Manciple. He is in good and numerous company. One thinks
of Charles Muscatine's characterization of certain central monologues in
Troilus: "the speeches must be taken as impersonal comments on the action,
Chaucer's formulation, not his characters'"; of Robert M. Jordan, who, having presented an impressive array of evidence for a complicated Merchant in
the Merchant's Tale, argues from it, like Dryden's Panther, "that he's not there
at all"; of Anne Middleton's exemption of selected passages of the Physician's
Tale from the pilgrim's voicing; of Robert B. Burlin's praise of the Summoner's Tale despite its being "beyond the genius of the Summoner"; and of
many other commentators on the Knight's Tale, some of whom I mention
later.[2]

Now in my view this "unimpersonated artistry" is a problem, and a useful one. Howard's formulation—an attempt to describe an aspect of Chaucer's general practice—is valuable because it brings into the sharp relief of a critical and theoretical principle something that is more diffusely present in the practical criticism of a great many Chaucerians: the conviction, often unspoken, that at some point it becomes necessary to move beyond or away from the pilgrim narrators of the *Canterbury Tales* and to identify the poet himself as the source of meaning. If the assumption is stated this generally, I probably agree with it myself, but Howard's way of putting it does seem to me to reflect a tendency, common among Chaucer critics, to invoke the poet's authority much too quickly. Howard helps me to focus my own discontent, not with his criticism (much of which I admire), but with a more general situation in the profession at large. If we consider "unimpersonated artistry" as a theoretical proposition, it seems open to question on both general and specific grounds; that is, it seems both to imply a rather peculiar set of assumptions to bring to the reading of any text and, at least to me, to be an inaccurate reflection of the experience of reading Chaucer in particular.

"Unimpersonated artistry" implies a technique, or perhaps an experience, of reading something like this: we assume that the Canterbury tales are, as they say, "fitted to their tellers," that they are potentially dramatic monologues or, to adopt what I hope is a less loaded term, that they are instances of *impersonated* artistry, the utterances of particular pilgrims. After all, we like to read Chaucer this way, to point out the suitability of the tales to their fictional tellers, and most of us, even Robert Jordan, would agree that at least some of the tales, and certainly the Canterbury frame, encourage this sort of interpretation.[3] We read along, then, with this assumption in mind, until it seems to break down, until we come across a passage that we have difficulty reconciling with the sensibility—the temperament or the training or the intelligence—of the pilgrim in question. At that point, alas, I think we too often give up. "This passage," we say, "must be the work of Chaucer the poet, speaking over the head or from behind the mask of the Knight or the Miller or the Physician, creating ironies, setting us straight on doctrine, pointing us 'the righte weye.'" Unfortunately, these occasions are seldom as unequivocal as the one case of genuine broken impersonation I know of in the *Tales*, the general narrator's "quod she" in the middle of a stanza of the Prioress' Tale (VII.1771). Different critics find the poet in different passages of the same tale and often have great difficulty in deciphering his message once they *have* found him—a difficulty that seems odd if Chaucer thought the message worth a disruption of the fiction.

Thus, Howard, whose observations on the critical disagreement over the humorous element in the Knight's Tale are well taken, offers an interpretation

---

of "The destinee, ministre general . . ." that is in fact uncommon. His account of the ironic tone of these lines in context is at least more attentive to the effect of the language than are the numerous readings that take the passage relatively straight. Even within this group, however, the range of proposed answers to the question "Who's talking here?" is sufficiently various to raise the issue I am interested in. To mention only those who discuss this particular passage, Frost, Ruggiers, and Kean are representative of the large body of criticism that remains relatively inattentive to the whole question of voicing in the tale.[4] They share a view of the passage as a piece of "the poem's" doctrine, to be taken seriously as part of an argument about man's place in the cosmos. Of those who, like Howard, find something odd about the passage, Burlin suggests that the speaker is Chaucer, who intends to suggest by it that Theseus is a man superior to Fortune but unaware of Providence (p. 108), while Neuse, the only critic to attribute the speech unequivocally to the Knight, maintains that it differentiates the latter's implicitly Christian view of the story from Theseus' more limited vision.[5] Who *is* talking here, and to what end? One might ask what the consequences for interpretation are if one concedes both that the passage makes gentle fun of the machinery of destiny, at least as applied to so trivial an event, and that it is the Knight himself who is interested in obtaining this effect. Howard's suggestion to the contrary, the passage is not really directed at Theseus' hunting but at the improbably fortuitous meeting in the glade of Theseus, Palamon, and Arcite, described in the lines that immediately follow (I.1683-713). This encounter is one of many features in the first half of the tale that show that most of the plot, far from being the product of portentous cosmic forces (Palamon and Arcite are consistently made to look silly for taking this view), is generated by human actions and choices, not least by those of the narrating Knight in conspicuously rigging events and manipulating coincidences. The Knight, as Neuse points out (p. 300), is adapting an "olde storie" for the present occasion, and the irony here reflects his opinion of the style of those "olde bookes." To him that style embodies a dangerous evasion of human responsibility for maintaining order in self and society by unconsciously projecting the responsibility onto gods and destinies.

The point is that a notion like "unimpersonated artistry," by dividing speakers into parts and denying them the full import of their speaking, puts us in the difficult position of trying to decide which parts of a single narrative are to be assigned to the pilgrim teller and which to the "author," and in these circumstances it is not surprising that different critics make the cut in different places. All such formulations involve finding or creating two speakers (or even more)[6] in a narrative situation where it would appear simpler to deal with only one. The procedure seems to me theoretically questionable because it is unparsimonious or inelegant logically: it creates extra work, and it also tends to lead to distraction. Narrative entities arc multiplied to the point where they become subjects of concern in their own right and require some sort of systematic or historical justification such as "unimpersonated artistry" or the deficiency of medieval ideas of personality,[7] and before long we are so busy trying to save the appearances of the epicyclic constructs we ourselves have created that we are no longer attending to the poems that the constructs were originally intended to explain. Therefore, I would like to preface my more detailed opposition to "unimpersonated artistry" with a general caveat. I call it Leicester's razor: *narratores non multiplicands sunt praeter absolutum necessitatem.*

Naturally I do not intend to let the matter rest with this general and essentially negative formula, though I think its application would clear up a lot of difficulties. I want to use the space my principle gives me to argue that the Canterbury tales are individually voiced, and radically so—that each of the tales is primarily an expression of its teller's personality and outlook as embodied in the unfolding "now" of the telling. I am aware that something like this idea is all too familiar. Going back, in modern times, at least as far as Kittredge's characterization of the *Canterbury Tales* as a "Human Comedy," with the pilgrims as dramatis personae, it reaches its high point in Lumiansky's *Of Sondry Folk*[8] (and apparently its dead end as well, since no one since has attempted to apply the concept systematically to the entire poem). Moreover, as I said before, we are all given to this sort of reading now and then. I think one reason the idea has never been pushed so hard or so far as I would like to take it is that the voicing of individual tales has almost always been interpreted on the basis of something external to them, usually either some aspect of the historical background of the poems (e.g., what we know from other sources about knights, millers, lawyers, nuns, etc.) or the descriptions of the speakers given in the Canterbury frame, especially in the General Prologue. Such materials are combined in various ways to construct an image of a given pilgrim outside his or her tale, and each tale is then read as a product of the figure who tells it, a product whose interpretation is constrained by the limitations we conceive the pilgrim to have. The specific problem of historical presuppositions, the feeling that medieval men *could not* have thought or spoken in certain ways, I would like to postpone until later, because the assumptions involved are often relatively tacit and well hidden and the problems they present are easier to handle in specific instances. It is clear, I hope, how such assumptions can lead to the kind of constraint on interpretation I have just outlined and how such a constraint puts us in danger of arguing from inference back to evidence, in Robert O. Payne's useful phrase,[9] when what is desired is an understanding of the evidence—the text—in front of us.

It is the specific problem of the Canterbury frame, however, that has been the more stubborn obstacle to reading the tales as examples of impersonated artistry. Since I do not mean by this phrase what either the critics or the defenders of similar notions appear to have meant in the past, the topic is worth pausing over. The issue is generally joined over the question of verisimilitude, the consistency with which the fiction of the *Tales* can be felt to sustain a dramatic illusion of real people taking part in real and present interaction with one another. The critic who has most consistently taken this dramatic view of the poem is Lumiansky, who locates both the "reality" of the pilgrims and the "drama" of their relations with one another outside the tales themselves, preeminently in the frame. He ordinarily begins his discussion of a given tale and its dramatic context with a character sketch of the pilgrim drawn from the General Prologue (and from any relevant links) and then treats the tale itself as an exemplification and extension of the traits and situations in the frame. He is attentive to such details as direct addresses to the pilgrim audience within a tale (such as the Knight's "lat se now who shal the soper wynne") and to a degree to the ways tales respond to one another, as in Fragment III, or the Marriage Group. This approach leads to an account of the poem as a whole that doubles the overt narrative of the frame and, in effect, allows the frame to tyrannize the individual tales: what does not fit the model of actual, preexisting pilgrims really present to one another is not relevant to the enterprise and is variously ignored or dismissed. Other critics have not been slow to point out that this procedure neglects a great deal.[10]

The objection to this "dramatic" model that I would particularly like to single out is its disregard for the poem's insistent, though perhaps intermittent, *textuality*, for the way the work repeatedly breaks the fiction of spoken discourse and the illusion of the frame to call attention to itself as a written thing. The injunction in the Miller's Prologue to "turne over the leef and chese another tale" (I.3177), the more interesting moment in the Knight's Tale when the supposedly oral narrator remarks, "But of that storie list me nat to write" (I.1201)[11]—such interruptions not only destroy "verisimilitude" but call attention to what Howard has named the "bookness" of the poem (*Idea*, pp. 63-67), as do, less vibrantly, incipits and explicits, the patently incomplete state of the text, or "the contingency that a tale not memorized but told impromptu is in verse." Now this conspicuous textuality (by which I mean that Chaucer not only produces written texts but does so self-consciously and calls attention to his writing) certainly militates strongly against the illusion of drama as living presence. It is no doubt this realization, coupled with the counterperception that some tales do seem "fitted to the teller," that has led Howard and others to adopt formulations like "unimpersonated artistry" in order to stay responsive to the apparent range of the poem's effects. Such a notion allows the critic to hover between "bookness," which the French have taught us always implies *absence*, and what Howard calls "voiceness": the *presence* we feel when "the author addresses us directly and himself rehearses tales told aloud by others: we seem to hear his and the pilgrim's voices, we presume oral delivery" (*Idea*, p. 66). If we cannot have presence fully, we can at least have it partly. But when and where exactly and, above all, *whose*? As I have tried to suggest, a phenomenon like "unimpersonated artistry"—which is, remember, an *intermittent* phenomenon—tries to save the feeling that someone is present at the cost of rendering us permanently uncertain about who is speaking at any given moment in (or of) the text: the pilgrim, the poet, or that interesting mediate entity Chaucer the pilgrim.

It seems to me that the "roadside-drama" approach, the critiques of this approach, *and* compromise positions (whether explicitly worked out like Howard's or more intuitive) have in common a central confusion: the confusion of *voice* with *presence*.[12] All these views demand that the voice in a text be traceable to a person, a subject, *behind* the language, an individual controlling and limiting, and thereby guaranteeing, the meaning of what is expressed. The language of a given tale, or indeed of a given moment in a tale, is thus the end point of the speaker's activity, the point at which the speaker delivers a self that existed prior to the text. For this reason all these approaches keep circling back to the ambiguous traces of such an external subject—in the frame, in the poet, in the facts of history, or in the "medieval mind." But what I mean by "impersonated artistry" does not involve an external subject.

In maintaining that the *Canterbury Tales* is a collection of individually voiced texts, I want rather to *begin* with the fact of their textuality, to insist that there is nobody there, that there is only the text. But if a written text implies and enforces the absence of the subject, the real living person outside the text who may or may not have "expressed himself" in producing it, the same absence is emphatically *not* true of the voice *in* the text, the voice *of* the text. In writing, voice is first of all a function not of persons but of language, of the linguistic codes and conventions that make it *possible* for an "I" to appear.[13] But this possibility means that we can assign an "I" to any statement. Language is positional. It always states or implies a first person in potential dramatic relation to the other grammatical persons, and it does so structurally—qua language—and regardless of the presence or absence of any actual speaking person. Thus, by its nature as a linguistic phenomenon, any text generates what it is conventional to call its speaker. The speaker is created by the text itself as a structure of linguistic relationships, and the character of the speaker is a function of the specific deployment of those relationships in a particular case to produce the voice of the text.

This kind of "voiceness" is a property of any text, and it is therefore theoretically possible to read any text in a way that elicits its particular voice, its individual first person. Such a reading would, for example, try to attend consistently to the "I" of the text, expressed or implied, and would make the referential aspects of the discourse functions of the "I." To put it another way, a voice-oriented reading would treat the second and third persons of a discourse (respectively, the audience and the world), expressed or implied, primarily as indications of what the speaker *maintains* about audience and world and would examine the way these elements are reflexively constituted as evidence of the speaker's character. We would ask what sort of person notices these particular details rather than others, what sort of person conceives of an audience in such a way that he or she addresses it in this particular tone, and so forth.

One might conceive of a study that undertook to work out a poetics of the speaker in literature. It would be a classic structuralist enterprise, moving from linguistic structures to a systematic demonstration of how it is possible for literary speakers to have the meanings they do. But since I do not believe, for reasons I will not go into here,[14] that such an enterprise would succeed, and since in any case it is not where my interests lie, I would like to move back to Chaucer by way of a further distinction. While any text can be read in a way that elicits its voice, some texts actively engage the phenomenon of voice, exploit it, make it the center of their discourse—make it their content. A text of this sort can be said to be *about* its speaker, and this is the sort of text I contend that the *Canterbury Tales* is and especially the sort that the individual tales are. The tales are examples of impersonated artistry because they concentrate not on the way preexisting people create language but on the way language creates people.[15] They detail how what someone says "im-personates" him or her, that is, turns the speaker into a person, or better, a personality (I prefer this word to "person" because "personality" suggests something that acts like, rather than "is," a person). What this implies for the concrete interpretation of the poem is that the relation that I have been questioning between the tales and the frame, or between the tales and their historical or social background, needs to be reversed. The voicing of any tale, the personality of any pilgrim, is not *given* in advance by the prologue portrait or the facts of history, nor is it dependent on them. The personality has to be worked out by analyzing and defining the voice created by each tale. It is this personality in the foreground, in his or her intensive and detailed textual life, that supplies a guide to the weighting of details and emphasis, the *interpretation*, of the background, whether portrait or history. To say, for example, that the Miller's Tale is not "fitted to its teller" because it is "too good" for him, because a miller or the Miller would not be educated enough or intelligent enough to produce it, is to move in exactly the wrong direction. In fact, it is just this sort of social typing that irritates and troubles the Miller himself, especially since both the Host and the general narrator social-typed him long before any Chaucer critic did (I.3128-31, 3167-69, 3182). The characters in his tale repeatedly indulge in social typing, and the Miller types several of them in this way.[16] The Miller's handling of this practice makes it an issue in the tale, something he has opinions and feelings about. The end of the tale makes it quite clear how the maimed, uncomfortably sympathetic carpenter is sacrificed to the mirth of the townsfolk and the pilgrims; he is shouted down by the class solidarity of Nicholas' brethren: "For every clerk anonright heeld with oother" (I.3847). One could go on to show how the Miller's sensibility in the tale retrospectively and decisively inflects the portrait of him in the General Prologue, making it something quite different from what it appears to be in prospect, but the same point can be suggested more economically with the Physician. When we read in the Prologue that "His studie was but litel on the Bible" (I.438), the line sounds condemnatory in an absolute, moral way. Reconsidered from the perspective of the tale, however, the detail takes on a new and more intensive individual life in the light of the Physician's singularly inept use of the exemplum of Jephthah's daughter (VI.238-50). Retrospectively the poet's comment characterizes a man of irreproachable if conventional morality whose profession channels his reading into medical texts rather than sacred ones and who uses such biblical knowledge as he has for pathetic effect at the expense of narrative consistency: he forgets, or at any rate suppresses, that Jephthah's daughter asked for time to bewail her virginity, whereas Virginia is being killed to preserve hers. The situation in the tale is a good deal more complex than this, but I think the general point is clear enough: it is the tale that specifies the portrait, not the other way around.

The technique of impersonation as I am considering it here has no necessary connection whatever with the question of the integration of a given tale in the Canterbury frame. The Knight's mention of writing in his tale is indeed an anomalous detail in the context of the pilgrimage. It is often regarded as a sign of the incomplete revision of the (hypothetical) "Palamon and Arcite," supposedly written before Chaucer had the idea of the *Tales* and afterward inserted in its present position in Fragment I. The reference to writing is taken as evidence that the Knight was not the "original" speaker and, in a reading like Howard's, that he is still not always the speaker.[17] As far as it goes, the argument about the chronology of composition is doubtless valid, but it has nothing to do with the question of whether or not the tale is impersonated, a question that can, and ought to, be separated, at least initially, from the fiction of the pilgrimage. Details like the Knight's "write" are not immediately relevant because they do not affect the intention to create a speaker (they may become relevant at a different level of analysis later). Impersonation, the controlled use of voicing to direct us to what a narrative tells us about its narrator, *precedes dramatization of the Canterbury sort* in Chaucer, analytically and no doubt sometimes chronologically. The proper method is to ascribe the entire narration in all its details to a *single* speaker (on the authority of Leicester's razor) and to use it as evidence in constructing that speaker's consciousness, keeping the question of the speaker's "identity" open until the analysis is complete. It is convenient and harmless to accept the frame's statement that the *Knight's Tale* is "the tale the Knight tells" as long as we recognize that it merely gives us something to call the speaker and tells us nothing reliable about him in advance.

I want to conclude an already perverse argument with a further perversity. I have argued that we ought to reverse the ordinary commonsense approach to the relations between foreground and background in the poem and see the pilgrims as the products rather than as the producers of their tales. I have suggested further that Chaucer's fiction may explain, rather than be explained by, the facts of fourteenth-century social history. I now want to maintain that the poet is the creation rather than the creator of his poem. More perversely still, I want to put a nick in my own razor and reintroduce a version of the double narrator in Chaucer. I do this in order to question a notion more widespread and apparently more durable than the various versions of "unimpersonated artistry," the notion of Chaucer the pilgrim. I must admit to being less sure of my ground here. For one thing, I am challenging an idea first put forward by E. Talbot Donaldson,[18] who has for years been producing the best line-by-line interpretations of Chaucer that I know, using what amounts to the very technique of reading I have been urging here.

Nevertheless, it seems clear on the face of it that issues of the sort I have been discussing are raised by the notion of Chaucer the pilgrim, the naïve narrator of the General Prologue and the links, who so often misses the point of the complex phenomena he describes in order that Chaucer the satirist or the poet or the man can make sure *we* see how very complex they are. The idea leads to a multiplication of speakers of the same text, not serially (though some critics have considered this possibility too),[19] but simultaneously. It requires that in any given passage we first decide what Chaucer the pilgrim means by what he says and then what Chaucer the poet means by what the pilgrim means. Here, too, there is often confusion about the distinction between the voice of the text and a presence behind and beyond it who somehow guarantees the meaning we find there.[20] Descriptions of Chaucer the poet sometimes take on a distinctly metaphysical cast, as in this passage from Donaldson's *Speaking of Chaucer*:

Undoubtedly Chaucer the man would, like his fictional representative, have found [the Prioress] charming and looked on her with affection. To have got on so well in so changeable a world Chaucer must have got on well with the people in it, and it is doubtful that one may get on with people merely by pretending to like them: one's heart has to be in it. But the third entity, Chaucer the poet, operates in a realm which is above and subsumes those in which Chaucer the man and Chaucer the pilgrim have their being. In this realm prioresses may be simultaneously evaluated as marvellously amiable ladies and as prioresses. (p. 11)

But the "higher realm" Donaldson is talking about is and can only be the *poem*, the text—as he himself knows perfectly well—and Chaucer the poet can only be what I have been calling the voice of the text. Donaldson is, as always, attentive to what the text *says* here, in particular to the tensions among social, human, and moral elements that the General Prologue undeniably displays. The division of the speaker into pilgrim, man, and poet is a way of registering these tensions and their complexity, of suggesting "a vision of the social world imposed on one of the moral world" (p. 9), and I can have no objection to this aim. I do not see the need, however, to reify these tensions into separate personalities of the same speaker, and I think this way of talking about the narrator of the General Prologue is misleading because it encourages us to treat him *as if we knew who he was* apart from his utterances. The general personality traits of Chaucer the pilgrim have themselves become reified in the Chaucer criticism of the last twenty years, and this frozen concept of the character has fostered a carelessness in reading that Donaldson himself rarely commits.

If I were going to try to characterize the speaker of the General Prologue myself, I would follow the lead of John M. Major in calling him, not naïve, but extraordinarily sophisticated.[21] I doubt, however, that this characterization, even if accepted, would go very far toward solving the problems of the poem, because it still does not tell us much about who the speaker is, and that is what we want to know. The notion of Chaucer the pilgrim at least offers us an *homme moyen sensuel* with whom we can feel we know where we are, but I think that it is just this sense of knowing where we are, with whom we are dealing, that the General Prologue deliberately and calculatedly denies us. For a brief suggestion of this intention—which is all I can offer here—consider these lines from the Monk's portrait, a notorious locus for the naïveté of the narrator:

> He yaf nat of that text a pulled hen,
> That seith that hunters ben nat hooly men,
> Ne that a monk, whan he is recchelees,
> Is likned til a fissh that is waterlees,—
> This is to seyn, a monk out of his cloystre.
> But thilke texte heeld he nat worth an oystre;
> And I seyde his opinion was good.
> What sholde he studie and make hymselven wood,
> Upon a book in cloystre alwey to poure,
> Or swynken with his handes, and laboure,
> As Austyn bit? How shal the world be served?
> Lat Austyn have his swynk to hym reserved!
> Therfore he was a prikasour aright . . .
>
> (I.177-89)

The Monk's own bluff manner is present in these lines. I agree with most commentators that he is being half-quoted, that we hear his style, for example, in the turn of a phrase like "nat worth an oystre!" Present too are the standards of his calling, against which, if we will, he may be measured. The social and moral worlds do indeed display their tension here, but who brought these issues up? Who is responsible for the slightly suspended enjambment that turns "As Austyn bit?" into a small firecracker? For the wicked specificity with which, at the beginning of the portrait, the Monk's bridle is said to jingle "as dooth the *chapel* belle"? Who goes to such pains to explain the precise application of the proverb about the fish, "This is to seyn . . ."? Who if not the speaker? But these observations do not permit us to say that he is only making a moral judgment or only making fun of the Monk (the two are not quite the same, and both are going on). A sense of the positive claims made by the pilgrim's vitality, his "manliness," is also registered by the portrait.[22] The speaker's amused enjoyment of the Monk's forthright humanity is too patent to let us see him as just a moralist. The way his voice evokes complex possibilities of attitude is neatly caught by "And I seyde his opinion was good": that's what he said when he and the Monk had their conversation, but is he saying the same thing now in this portrait? Did he really mean it at the time? Does he now? In what sense?

The point of this exercise is not merely to show that the speaker's attitude is complex and sophisticated but also to stress how obliquely expressed it is, all in ironic juxtapositions and loaded words whose precise heft is hard to weigh. What we have, in fact, is a speaker who is not giving too much of himself away, who is not telling us, any more than he told the Monk, his whole mind in plain terms. The tensions among social, moral, and existential worlds are embodied in a single voice here, and they are embodied precisely *as tensions*, not as a resolution or a synthesis, for we cannot tell exactly what the speaker thinks either of the Monk or of conventional morality. What we *can* tell is that we are dealing with a speaker who withholds himself from us, with the traces of a presence that asserts its simultaneous absence. The speaker is present as uncomprehended, as not to be seized all at once in his totality. He *displays his difference* from his externalizations, his speaking, in the very act of externalizing himself. It is this effect, I think, that creates the feeling of "reality" in the text, the sense that there is somebody there. In literature (as in life) the reality of characters is a function of their mystery, of the extent to which we are made to feel that there is more going on in regard to them than we know or can predict. Criseyde is a well-known and well-analyzed example in Chaucer,[23] and I suggest that the general narrator of the *Canterbury Tales* is another. His lack of definition may also explain why he can be taken for Chaucer the pilgrim. Because his identity is a function of what he leaves unspoken—because it is derived from implication, irony, innuendo, the potentialities of meaning and intention that occur in the gaps between observations drawn from radically different realms of discourse[24]—there is a temptation to reduce his uncomfortable indeterminacy by forcing the gaps shut, by spelling out the connections. But suppressing the indeterminacy in this way involves reducing complex meanings to simpler ones. One infers "Chaucer the pilgrim" by ignoring the things the speaker "does not say" (since, after all, he does not *say* them—only suggests) and by insisting that he "means" his statements in only the plainest, most literal sense. Such an interpretation does not fail to recognize that the complexities of meaning are there; it simply assigns them to "the poem" or to "Chaucer the poet," thus producing what I am arguing is a contradiction: the simple and naïve narrator of a complex and sophisticated narration.

In fact, however, not only the General Prologue but the whole of the *Canterbury Tales* works against a quick or easy comprehension of the speaker. It is to suggest how it does so that I am going to reintroduce a sort of double narration. First of all, though, it should be clear that there is only one speaker of the entire poem and that he is also the poem's maker. The conspicuous textuality of the work makes this fact inescapable. It may be that Chaucer would have "corrected" anomalies like the Knight's "But of that storie list me nat to write" and that he would have supplied a complete and self-consistent set of links between the present fragments to round out the Canterbury fiction. It seems much less likely that he would have revised the Man of Law's promise to tell his rime-royal tale in prose or the "quod she" in the middle of the Prioress' Tale or the "turne over the leef" passage in the Miller's Prologue or the inordinate and undramatic length of the Melibee. And I am quite certain that he would not have altered the fundamental "contingency that a tale not memorized but told impromptu is in verse." What is at issue here is not simply a neutral medium that we are entitled to ignore. If pentameter couplets are the *koiné* of the poem, stanzaic verse (especially rime royal but also the Monk's stanza and even Sir Thopas' tail rhyme) functions as a formal equivalent, a translation into writing, of a different level of diction: it identifies a speaker with pretensions to an elevated style, in life as well as in storytelling. If it is functional in the poem that one kind of verse be sensed as verse, why not other kinds, and prose as well? The poem's insistence on these distinctions has interesting implications for the problem of oral delivery. The *Canterbury Tales* is not written to be spoken as if it were a play. It is written to be read, but read *as if* it were spoken. The poem is a literary imitation of oral performance.[25]

One effect of this fundamental textuality is to keep us constantly aware that the frame, the reportage, is a patent fiction. There is no pilgrimage, there are no pilgrims. Whether or not Chaucer ever went to Canterbury, whether or not the characters in the poem are drawn from "real life," what we have in front of us is the activity of a poet, a maker, giving his own rhythm and pattern, his own shape and voice, his own complex interpretation to the materials of the poem. And that maker *is the speaker of the poem*, the voice of the text. There is no one there but that voice, that text. The narrator of the *Canterbury Tales* is the speaker we call Chaucer the poet, though it would be more accurate—I cannot resist, this once—to call him Chaucer the poem.

This being said, it is also true that one of the first discoveries we make when we try to characterize this maker and speaker on the evidence of his discourse, to begin to specify the voice of the text, is that he is an impersonator in the conventional sense: he puts fictional others between himself and us. This is the sense in which the tales are double-voiced: each of them is Chaucer impersonating a pilgrim, the narrator speaking in the voice of the Knight or the Reeve or the Second Nun. They are his creatures, voices that he assumes; he gives them his life.

But it would be as accurate, from another perspective, to say that he takes his life from them, and the amount of time and effort spent on making the pilgrims independent, the sheer labor of consistent, unbroken impersonation to which the poem testifies, suggests that this is the more compelling perspective, for Chaucer as for us. The enterprise of the poem involves the continual attempt, continually repeated, to see from another's point of view, to stretch and extend the self by learning to speak in the voices of others; and the poem itself is, among other things, the record of that attempt.

I have tried to evoke, however briefly, the incompleteness—the indeterminacy and the resistance to classification—of the voice that speaks in the General Prologue. One corollary of this quality is the cognate incompleteness of the Prologue itself, one of whose principal themes is the insufficiency of traditional social and moral classifying schemes—estates, hierarchies, and the like—to deal with the complexity of individuals and their relations. The speaker not only embodies this insufficiency, he recognizes it and feels it: "Also I prey yow to foryeve it me,/ Al have I nat set folk in hir degree/ Heere in this tale, as that they sholde stonde" (I.743-45). From this insufficiency he turns to the pilgrims. He sets them free to speak in part to free himself from the constraints and uncertainties generated by his own attempt to classify them—an attempt that, however universal and impersonal it may look at the beginning of the Prologue, is always only his view and one too complex for him to speak by himself. The Prologue does not do justice to the pilgrims. By the same token and for the same reasons it does not do justice to the narrator and his understanding of his world. In the tales, therefore, he slows us down, keeps us from grasping him too quickly and easily, by directing our attention to the variety and complexity of the roles he plays, the voices he assumes. He is, we know, each of the pilgrims and all of them, but he seems to insist that we can only discover him by discovering for ourselves who the Knight is, who the Parson, who the Pardoner and the Wife of Bath.

We may be impatient to know the speaker of the General Prologue, but as the voice of the poem as a whole, he is the last of the pilgrims we may hope to comprehend, and then only by grasping each of the others individually and in turn and in all the complexity of their relationships to one another. The relation of the voice that speaks in the General Prologue to the personality of the poet is like that of an individual portrait to its tale and that of the Prologue itself to all the tales. It is a prologal voice, a voice that is only beginning to speak. Chaucer's Prologue, like this prologue of mine, needs the tales to fulfill itself in the gradual and measured but always contingent and uncertain activity of impersonation, in both senses. The speaker of the *Canterbury Tales*—Chaucer—is indeed as fictional as the pilgrims, in the sense that like them he is a self-constructing voice. He practices what I have called the art of impersonation, finally, to impersonate himself, to create himself as fully as he can in his work.[26]

Notes

1. Howard, *The Idea of the Canterbury Tales* (Berkeley: Univ. of California Press, 1976), pp. 230-31.

2. Muscatine, *Chaucer and the French Tradition* (Berkeley: Univ. of California Press, 1957), pp. 264-65. In a more general statement on the *Canterbury Tales*, on pp. 171-72, Muscatine observes: "No medieval poet would have sacrificed all the rich technical means at his disposal merely to make a story sound as if such and such a character were actually telling it. The *Miller's Tale*, to name but one of many, would have been thus impossible." See also John Lawlor, *Chaucer* (New York: Harper, 1968), Ch. v. Jordan, *Chaucer and the Shape of Creation* (Cambridge: Harvard Univ. Press, 1967), Ch. vi. Jordan is, on theoretical and historical grounds, the most thoroughgoing and principled opponent of the notion of consistent impersonation in Chaucer's work. In this connection the book just cited deserves to be read in its entirety, as does Jordan's "Chaucer's Sense of Illusion: Roadside Drama Reconsidered," *Journal of English and Germanic Philology*, 29 (1962), 19-33. Middleton, "The *Physician's Tale* and Love's Martyrs: 'Ensamples Mo than Ten' in the *Canterbury Tales*," *Chaucer Review*, 8 (1973), 9-32. Burlin, *Chaucerian Fiction* (Princeton: Princeton Univ. Press, 1977), p. 165, Elizabeth Salter's reading of the Knight's Tale, in *Chaucer: The Knight's Tale and the Clerk's Tale* (London: Edward Arnold, 1962), pp. 7-36, is perhaps the most consistently developed in terms of the "two voices" of the poet. See also Paul T. Thurston, *Artistic Ambivalence in Chaucer's Knight's Tale* (Gainesville: Univ. of Florida Press, 1968).

3. Howard states the position admirably (pp. 123-24). I suppose no one would question that the Wife of Bath's and Pardoner's tales virtually demand this approach.

4. William Frost, "An Interpretation of Chaucer's Knight's Tale," *Review of English Studies*, 25 (1949), 290-304; Paul Ruggiers, "Some Philosophical Aspects of *The Knight's Tale*," *College English*, 14 (1958), 296-302; P. M. Kean, "The *Knight's Tale*," in her *Chaucer and the Making of English Poesy* (London: Routledge and Kegan Paul, 1972), II, 1-52.

5. Richard Neuse, "The Knight: The First Mover in Chaucer's Human Comedy," *University of Toronto Quarterly*, 31 (1962), 312-13.

6. See, e.g., Jordan, *Shape of Creation*, p. 181, where what is apparently envisioned is Chaucer the poet projecting Chaucer the pilgrim as the (intermittent?) narrator of the Knight's story. For an instance of how far this sort of thing can go, see A. P. Campbell, "Chaucer's 'Retraction': Who Retracted What?" *Humanities Association Bulletin*, 16, No. 1 (1965), 75-87.

7. Jordan once again provides the clearest example of this historicist form of argument, but D. W. Robertson also uses it, e.g., in the Introduction to his *Chaucer's London* (New York: Wiley, 1968), pp. 1-11, where he both specifies and generalizes such statements in his *A Preface to Chaucer* (Princeton: Princeton Univ. Press, 1962) as the following: "The actions of Duke Theseus in the Knight's Tale are thus, like the actions of the figures we see in the visual arts of the fourteenth century, symbolic actions. They are directed toward the establishment and maintenance of those traditional hierarchies which were dear to the medieval mind. They have nothing to do with 'psychology' or with 'character' in the modern sense, but are instead functions of attributes which are, in this instance, inherited from the traditions of medieval humanistic culture" (pp. 265-66; see also the discussion of the Friar's Tale that immediately follows). This whole line of argument probably originated with Leo Spitzer's "A Note on the Poetic and the Empirical 'I' in Medieval Authors," *Traditio*, 4 (1946), 414-22. Spitzer's argument is drawn from particular textual investigations and is relatively tentative about its conclusions. Judging from his remarks on Boccaccio, I am not at all sure that Spitzer would see Chaucer as a representative user of the "poetic 'I,'" but in any case I think his successors, unlike him, are arguing from "history" to texts, not the other way around. Spitzer's formulation has become fossilized in these Chaucerians.

8. G. L. Kittredge, *Chaucer and His Poetry* (Cambridge: Harvard Univ. Press, 1915), Ch. v; the famous phrases are on pp. 154-55. R. M. Lumiansky, *Of Sondry Folk: The Dramatic Principle in the* Canterbury Tales (Austin: Univ. of Texas Press, 1955).

9. Payne, *The Key of Remembrance: A Study of Chaucer's Poetics* (New Haven: Yale Univ. Press, 1963), p. 3.

10. Jordan is particularly good at evoking the element of "the girlhood of Shakespeare's heroines" that often finds its way into this sort of interpretation; see "Roadside Drama," esp. pp. 24-26.

11. Quotations from Chaucer are from F. N. Robinson, ed., *The Works of Geoffrey Chaucer*, 2nd ed. (Boston: Houghton, 1957).

12. In what follows I ought to acknowledge a general obligation to the work of Jacques Derrida, perhaps more to its spirit than to any specific essay or formulation. For a representative discussion of the problem of presence and a typical critique of "logocentric metaphysics" see "Writing before the Letter," Pt. 1 of *Of Grammatology*, trans. Gayatri Chakravorty Spivak (Baltimore: Johns Hopkins Univ. Press, 1976), pp. 1-93.

13. See Emile Benveniste, *Problems in General Linguistics*, trans. Mary Elizabeth Meek, Miami Linguistics Series, No. 8 (Coral Gables, Fla.: Univ. of Miami Press, 1971). Chapters xviii and xx are especially helpful, but the whole section (Chs. xviii-xxiii, pp. 195-248) is of value.

14. One might observe in passing that many "structuralist" discussions of voice in literature seem plagued by the same confusions as Chaucerian ones. See, e.g., Roland Barthes, "To Write: An Intransitive Verb?" in Richard Macksey and Eugenio Donato, eds., *The Structuralist Controversy: The Languages of Criticism and the Sciences of Man* (Baltimore: Johns Hopkins Univ. Press, 1970), where he remarks of the discourse of the traditional novel that it "alternates the personal and the impersonal very rapidly, often even in the course of the same sentence, so as to produce, if we can speak thus, a proprietary consciousness which retains the mastery of what it states without participating in it" (p. 140). There is not space here to deal with this extraordinary idea, but see Jonathan Culler's sympathetic and skeptical discussion of this notion and related ideas in *Structuralist Poetics* (Ithaca: Cornell Univ. Press, 1975), pp. 189-205.

15. There are a number of tales—the Prioress' is one and the Shipman's another—that suggest how this happens whether the speaker intends it or not.

16. E.g., "A clerk hadde litherly biset his whyle,/ But if he koude a carpenter bigyle"; "What! thynk on God, as we doon, men that swynke"; "She was a prymerole, a piggesnye,/ For any lord to leggen in his bedde,/ Or yet for any good yeman to wedde" (I.3299-300, 3491, 3268-70).

17. See Alfred David, *The Strumpet Muse* (Bloomington: Indiana Univ. Press, 1976), pp. 77-89.

18. Donaldson, "Chaucer the Pilgrim," *PMLA*, 69 (1954), 928-36; rpt. in his *Speaking of Chaucer* (London: Athlone, 1970). Howard discusses the topic in his "Chaucer the Man," *PMLA*, 80 (1965), 337-43.

19. See Rosemary Woolf, "Chaucer as a Satirist in the General Prologue to the *Canterbury Tales*," *Critical Quarterly*, 1 (1959), 150-57.

20. I suspect that this confusion has to do with a natural desire on the part of critics to evade the feelings of contingency and responsibility that haunt the act of interpretation. If the voice of the text is assumed to be that of an external subject, one justifies what one reads out of the text on the authority of a poet who must have "meant" to put it in. See Donaldson's brilliant and humane critique of stemma editing on similar grounds in "The Psychology of Editors of Middle English Texts," *Speaking of Chaucer*, pp. 102-18.

21. See Major's valuable and neglected article "The Personality of Chaucer the Pilgrim," *PMLA*, 75 (1960), 160-62.

22. See Jill Mann's excellent discussion in *Chaucer and Medieval Estates Satire* (Cambridge: Cambridge Univ. Press, 1973), pp. 17-37, esp. p. 20.

23. See Arthur Mizener, "Character and Action in the Case of Criseyde," *PMLA*, 54 (1939), 65-81, and Robert P. apRoberts, "The Central Episode in Chaucer's *Troilus*," *PMLA*, 77 (1962), 373-85.

24. This observation suggests that a paratactic style is particularly conducive to producing the kind of effect I am describing, because the information (syntax) that would *specify* the connection between statements is left out. See Erich Auerbach, "Roland against Ganelon," in his *Mimesis:*

The Representation of Reality in Western Literature (Garden City, N.Y.: Anchor-Doubleday, 1953), pp. 83-107. Parataxis is one of the main descriptive techniques of the General Prologue, particularly noticeable in the three central portraits of the Shipman, the Physician, and the Wife of Bath, but widely employed throughout. Further, the structure of the Prologue itself is paratactic (composed of juxtaposed independent portraits), and so is that of the poem as a whole (composed of juxtaposed independent tales).

25. I have neglected B. H. Bronson's criticisms of Chaucer the pilgrim and related matters (see esp. his *In Search of Chaucer* [Toronto: Univ. of Toronto Press, 1960], pp. 25-33), because my assumptions about the relations between literary and oral cultures in Chaucer's poetry start from a position very nearly opposite to his. I agree with him, however, that the problem of performance in Chaucer is worth further study; in fact, I think it is a central theme throughout the poet's career. In the *Canterbury Tales*, the frame exists precisely to provide a literary representation of the ordinarily extratextual and tacit dimensions of storytelling in writing. The poem presents not merely stories but stories told to an audience that is part of the fiction, and this circumstance allows Chaucer to register the effects of a range of conditions of performance.

26. In preparing this article, I was assisted by a grant from the Research Committee of the Academic Senate of the University of California, Santa Cruz; I am grateful for this support.

"A Poet Ther Was":
Chaucer's Voices in the General Prologue to *The Canterbury Tales*

Barbara Nolan

Chaucer gives us no explicit portrait headed "A Poet ther was" in the General Prologue to *The Canterbury Tales*. Yet the entire Prologue, like so many vernacular invitations to narrative from the twelfth century on, is designed to introduce the poet, describe his task, and gain the goodwill of the audience. Scholars generally agree that the later medieval practice of composing prologues depended on the grammar school study of rhetorical handbooks and classical poetry. By the fourteenth century a self-reflexive prologue conforming to handbook definitions had become more or less de rigueur for aristocratic narrative, both secular and religious.[1] Chaucer's Prologue, though longer and more complex than most, is no exception. It raises expectations in just the areas the handbooks propose, promising to take up important matters of natural and social order, moral character, and religion and outlining the organization the work will follow. Above all, the poet *presents himself*, as the handbooks direct, to ingratiate himself with his listeners or readers and render them receptive to his argument.

Chaucer's Prologue, however, meets these generic expectations in entirely unexpected ways. Most recent critics have recognized that it does not provide a neat, straightforward portrait of the poet. Chaucer's authority remains elusive, exceeding the requirements of the humility topos. Furthermore, whatever potential there may be for coherence in his self-presentation tends to be undermined by the several abrupt changes of style and subject. In fact, the parts of the General Prologue seem to function as several attacks on a beginning, each of them probing from a different angle a problem that traditionally belonged to prologues, "How shall I begin and to what purpose?" At first the various styles and subjects juxtaposed in the Prologue appear to suggest no clear answer. Moreover, the parts, or attempts at beginning, are governed not by a single, cumulatively enriched and deepened figure of the poet but, as I argue, by a series of impersonations. None of these taken alone reveals the poet's presence fully. Nor, taken together, do they reveal the poet literary tradition might have led readers to expect.

The General Prologue, I suggest, contains not one voice of the poet but three major attempts at authorial voicing. Each constitutes part of a complex argument about the nature of the poet and poetry in terms authorized by well-known medieval theory and practice. The first of these voices declaims the April opening with the learned assurance and scientific attention of a clerk deliberating in venerable literary formulas on the causes of things. The last is a tavern keeper's, urging good cheer and play for material profit. In between we hear the modest, devout "I" of Chaucer the pilgrim, intent on giving systematic order to his experience. But the voices of the other pilgrims so intrude on his own that he is left at last simply with genial apologies for failing to do what he had promised. All the voices are finally Chaucer's, of course, all of them impersonations. And all participate in the poet's complex, unexpected argument concerning his character(s) and purpose.[2]

For the most part, only the voice of the pilgrim has been related to Chaucer's self-presentation. In his well-known and brilliantly persuasive essay, E. Talbot Donaldson urges a separation of the pilgrim from the poet. He argues that the pilgrim persona is a comic device that the poet manipulates as an ironic foil for his own incisive wit. The poet, he says, "operates in a realm which is above and subsumes those in which Chaucer the man and Chaucer the pilgrim have their being" (936).

Few critics have questioned the isolation of the pilgrim persona as Chaucer's principal foil in the Prologue, though several have challenged Donaldson's way of explaining the relationship between the persona and the poet or the man. In an important article and in his book, Donald Howard argues for a more complex and mysterious relationship between the pilgrim and the poet than Donaldson proposes. The pilgrim, he suggests, gives a tantalizingly partial sense of the man behind the work; the limitations invite us to create Chaucer finally in our own image ("Chaucer the Man").[3]

More recently, Marshall Leicester has objected to all interpretations that separate the pilgrim from the poet, contending that the poet's presence is to be discovered not beyond the work but in the voicing of the text. Positing a separation, he argues, gives us the comfortable (and false) sense that we can know who is speaking at any given moment and what position each speaker holds on the matter presented. In his view, it is "just this sense of knowing where we are, with whom we are dealing, that the General Prologue deliberately and calculatedly denies us" (219). Instead of a pilgrim persona juxtaposed with an unimpersonated poet, Leicester proposes the model of a "prologal voice" that belongs to an impersonator preparing to take on the character of each pilgrim in turn. This thesis is provocative, important because it insists that we listen to the text's voicings of character rather than read from preconceived character to text.

But Leicester assumes that such attention to voices should aim at discovering the "personality" of the poet and his pilgrims. This concern for "personality," as also for the presence of the "man," misses the essentially rhetorical, ideologically oriented character of the poet's self-presentation. Heeding Leicester's warning against positing more speakers than necessary and casting Howard's concern for the man in different terms, I argue that Chaucer as a single author projects three major "authorial" voices in his Prologue to examine several possibilities for poetry, all of them empowered by well-known medieval theory and all of them useful for his tales. The three voices lead us not to the poet's "personality" or to Chaucer the man in a general sense but rather to the problem of being a poet in the late fourteenth century. Instead of giving us a single image of the poet and a single definition of the poet's authority, Chaucer juxtaposes images of himself as three possible kinds of poet. The pilgrim is only one of these, though he holds a privileged position among the rest. He is the "I" from whom the others take their being, and he provides a moral center from which to judge the other voices. But an impersonal voice pronounces the opening third-person narration, and Harry's "boold" voice finally replaces the pilgrim's to announce the literary theory and design of the fictive order that follows.

Poetry and poets occupy an uncertain position in medieval theory. Some writers—among them the twelfth-century Platonists, Dante, Petrarch, and Boccaccio—contend that the poet can express truth under the veil of "beautiful lies." In this well-known argument, the reader is to take the fruit, or sentence, and discard the rhetorical chaff of the poet's fictive covering. Another, less generous position—put forward by the Parson in *The Canterbury Tales*—refuses to traffic in "fables" at all. In this view, poetry is frivolity, diversion, false consolation; poets, the perpetrators of falsehood. Chaucer's three voices in the General Prologue form dramatic images of several theories, carrying us from a notion of poetry as philosophy to Harry's view of poetry as distracting merriment.

The argument Chaucer makes about the poet and poetry is neither mechanical nor detached. In the Prologue and in the tales, he explores the whole range of medieval positions regarding poetry, not so much to establish a "true" position as to emphasize his sense of the ambiguities and contradictions surrounding fiction's valuation, and also to turn these difficulties to his advantage. The pilgrim-poet deliberately places himself in the midst of the questions he poses—and he has his pilgrims take up the problem again and again in their prologues and tales. In his many voices, he invites readers to share intimately his quest for a radically new, personal (and ultimately comic, provisional) poetic, one true to his sense of the ironies and limitations inherent in his art of fiction.

I. Multiple Voicing in Medieval Theory and Practice

Multiple voicing as a mode of argument was essential to later medieval narrative, whether in allegorical debate or exemplary private conversation or interior monologue framed by first- or third-person narration. Indeed, romance and allegory, the two dominant narrative forms of the later Middle Ages, positively required multiple voicing. These essentially dialectical forms typically pose challenging social or moral or spiritual questions to be solved by means of the narrative process. Nearly always, the subjectivity of such texts—their grounding in the poet's authority—is presented through two or more voices. Beatrice, Vergil, Raison, Gracedieu, a hermit, a grotesque maiden may serve in the poet's place as a guide to wisdom at various moments in the narrative. By putting on a number of voices, the poet can mask his position and thus draw the audience into an exacting, unpredictable process of discovery.

When we listen to Chaucer's several voices in the General Prologue (and in the tales), therefore, we hear the master of an art cultivated by generations of French and Italian writers. To be sure, in Chaucer the art of playing voice against voice assumes a decisive new direction predictive of the novel's complexities. Yet his invention depended absolutely on the prior discoveries of those major poets who had most influenced him—among them, Benoit de Sainte-Maure, Guillaume de Lorris, Jean de Meung, Boccaccio, Dante, and Machaut.

To find the main theoretical bases for multiple voicing in the Middle Ages, we must turn to the rhetorical handbooks universally used in the grammar schools and to schoolroom exegesis of the curriculum authors. Handbook discussions give primary attention to calculated voicing and impersonation in the orator's self-presentation and in the acting out of the client's attitudes, feelings, and experiences in order to build a convincing case.

When Quintilian describes the orator's self-presentation in the exordium, or prologue, he recommends an artful management of voice, style, and manner:

> [W]e should . . . give no hint of elaboration in the *exordium.* . . . But to avoid all display of art in itself requires consummate art. . . . The style of the *exordium* . . . should . . . seem simple and unpremeditated, while neither our words nor our looks should promise too much. For a method of pleading which conceals its art . . . will often be best adapted to insinuate its way into the minds of our hearers. (4.1.56-60; 2: 36-39)

If artifice and adjustments of voice are to be used even in the defense of honorable cases, they become all the more important for doubtful or discreditable ones.

In this regard, the rhetorical handbooks distinguish between a direct prologue (*principium*) for good causes and a subtle approach (*insinuatio*) for doubtful ones. The *Ad Herennium*, for example, a popular rhetoric attributed to Cicero, defines the difference as follows:

> The direct opening should be such that by . . . straightforward methods . . . we immediately make the hearer well-disposed or attentive or receptive; whereas the Subtle Approach should be such that we effect all these results covertly, through dissimulation, and so can arrive at the same vantage-point in the task of speaking. (1.7; 20-21)

As the classroom handbooks suggest, the assumption of a persona to mask intentions and win favor in the exordium has to do with pragmatic manipulation and strategic dissimulation quite separate from issues of truth and falsehood.

There was also, however, another, larger theory of multiple voicing, propounded in well-known scriptural and literary exegesis. This theory supports the indirect pursuit of true understanding in and through narrative discourse that dramatically represents several opinions, including the author's. Commentators on a variety of texts describe the ways in which a writer can use personae or characters to represent various positions on a given subject. These discussions are rich with suggestion for understanding Chaucer and other vernacular poets. Servius, for example, explaining Vergil's first eclogue, writes:[4]

> A certain shepherd is introduced lying safe and at leisure under a tree in order to make a musical composition; another, indeed, has been expelled from his homelands with his flock, who, when he has seen Tityrus reclining, speaks. And in this place we must understand Vergil under the character [persona] of Tityrus; however, not everywhere, but wherever the argument demands it. (1: 4)

Here, according to Servius, the author presents himself through his characters, not to reveal his personality, but to serve his argument. Tityrus does not always represent Vergil, but speaks for him only when the argument requires it. In this dispensation the author is present not as a distinctive personality but, rather, as a writer strictly speaking, arranging characters and voices in relation to the large argument being made.

In terms still more suggestive for medieval poetry, commentators regularly identify dialogical self-dramatization as a formal feature of some of the most important and influential works of the period, including Augustine's *Soliloquies* and Boethius's *De consolatione*. Of these two texts Peter Abelard says:

> [It is] as if someone, speaking with himself, set up his argument as if two [were speaking], just as Boethius in his book, the *Consolation of Philosophy*, or Augustine in his *Book of Soliloquies*. (760)[5]

And Conrad of Hirsau writes of the *Consolation*:

> Three characters [personae] are brought forward by Boethius: miserable Boethius seeking to be consoled; Philosophia who consoles; Boethius the author who speaks about both of them. (Huygens 108)[6]

There can be no doubt that such dialogical forms as the *Consolation* and the *Soliloquies*, together with the commentaries surrounding them, provided powerful models for multiple voicing in many kinds of texts throughout the medieval period, but particularly from the twelfth century on.

Gregory the Great's comments on Ecclesiastes offer us yet another full and well-known discussion of the writer's manipulative use of personae and voices in philosophical argument. His description of Solomon's authorial strategies might well have served as a headnote for many a medieval text, including *The Canterbury Tales*. Emphasizing the orator's role in bringing together and reconciling the opinions of a contentious audience, Gregory explains how Solomon impersonates the characters and views of many people as if to pacify a cantankerous crowd:

> This book is called "The Orator" because Solomon takes up there the thinking of a crowd which is in disagreement: under the form of questions he expresses what the man on the street is tempted to think. All the ideas that he takes up in his inquiry correspond to the various characters he impersonates. (4.1; 3: 26-27)[7]

According to Gregory, Solomon ends his multivoiced discourse by addressing his listeners in his own voice and drawing them into unity. After he has assumed the many characters and positions leading away from salvation, he argues for the necessity of fearing God and understanding the world's vanity.[8]

Hugh of St. Victor's homily on Ecclesiastes improves on Gregory's description of impersonation and sheds further light on Chaucer's art of multiple voicing:

> [A] many-sided disputation is signified, and [one that has] elicited diverse opinions. For since, in this book, the moral conduct, aspirations, and achievements of many are described, it is necessary for the speaker to assume the voices of many speakers, to express the opinions of many in his discourse, so that he has the power to present the characters of many in his own person, when he who speaks is nonetheless only one. For at the end of the book, having spoken in many [voices], he himself testifies that he has been many [characters] in himself, saying: Let us all equally hear the end of the speaking: "Fear God, and obey his commandments. This is every man." For this is why he wanted to be called "Ecclesiastes" in his work,

namely, because his discourse is directed here not to a certain person particularly but to the whole Church—that is, the assembly or multitude of people—and the argument in this book serves at once to portray the conduct of many and to form an image of it. (115)[9]

Of course, Chaucer's art of voicing is far more complex than the kind described by Gregory and Hugh. Among other things it involves a detailed dramatic action so compelling that some eminent critics have assumed that the drama itself was Chaucer's principal concern.

But medieval theorizing about multiple voicing, both the rhetoricians' and the exegetes', suggests a different emphasis, and one well suited to the intricate play of Chaucer's Prologue and tales. While the exegetical comments I have quoted do not explain precisely how multiple voicing works in medieval poetry or in Chaucer, they do provide a rationale for its use and encourage us to examine Chaucer's complex management of voicing with a closer scrutiny than it has generally been given. As I have already suggested, critics propose a false problem when they try to determine who is speaking in a Chaucerian passage—whether, for example, we are to hear the poet or the pilgrim or the man at a particular moment in the General Prologue (see also Christianson). The real question is not autobiographical but rhetorical and dialectical.[10] For what rhetorical purpose does the poet assume the pilgrim's voice? How and why is this voice juxtaposed with others in the Prologue and in the tales?

In the General Prologue, we must listen closely to all the voices—the impersonal voice of the opening lines, the pilgrim's, the Host's—as aspects of an argument in which the poet himself participates through his juxtaposition of tonally and stylistically different voices. The poet's presence and his self-definition inhere in his acts of manipulation and his multiple impersonation. Seen in this light, Chaucer emerges from the Prologue, as from the tales, a quick-change artist, a shape shifter, a prestidigitator, a player with voices.

Chaucer's play, however, is more like Solomon's than like Harry Bailly's. It takes the form of an exacting dialectic that dramatically articulates various positions on the human condition. If one attends only to the linear, temporal, narrative process of the Prologue and tales, the play is a source of rich comedy. But for those who assume the poet's perspective as master player and look to the form, the many voices also offer a way to philosophical clarification. By experiencing the voices as parts in a complex argument, the reader, like the poet, may avoid commitment to the misplaced seriousness, the ego attachments, and the foolishness that govern most of the characters. Chaucer's deft juxtapositions of one position with another point in a wise, deep way to the absurdities, the pain, the poignancy, the pretensions, the limited perspectives of the human condition. The poet's own fully conscious play, expressed through his multivoiced dialectic, allows him to acknowledge his fiction making, and that of his characters, for what it is. In this way, he can vindicate the muses of poetry as Boethius could not. Chaucer's play with voices does not issue in a resolution as clear or univocal as Solomon's in Ecclesiastes. Yet the Parson's Tale and the Retraction offer images of finality and closure that *may* bring the Canterbury fictions to an end by an appeal to an order of being beyond the tales.

II. Chaucer's Voices in the General Prologue

As I have suggested, three voices and three attitudes toward poetic authority vie for control in the Prologue—the "clerk's," the pilgrim's, and the Host's.[11] While the first and last are diametrically opposed, the important central voice of the pilgrim mediates between them and explains the unavoidable "fall" from the first to the last in the deliberate absence of a truth-telling allegorical guide. Harry Bailly becomes the necessary muse for *The Canterbury Tales* because no Philosophia or Raison or Gracedieu or Holichurche provides a graceful alternative. But Harry's worldly theory of poetry does not prevail entirely. The other two major prologal voices encourage the possibility of higher poetic aspirations. "Authors" in search of philosophical or spiritual wisdom—like the Knight, the Oxford Clerk, the Second Nun, and the Parson—imitate the clerkly or pilgrim voice in one way or another. In this respect they counter the fictions of others—like the Miller, the Reeve, the Merchant, and the Pardoner—who in one way or another follow the Host in his purely secular play. In addition, the higher voices remain available as alternative models of authority and purpose for readers who will "rewrite" the tales in their private quests for a saving doctrine.

III. The Clerk's Voice

The first of the Chaucerian voices we hear—the first impersonation—gives us the learned poet of the schools. Versed in the literary topoi of the Latin tradition and skilled in rhetorical composition, he is also a scientist of sorts who knows precisely how plants grow and a philosopher who looks into the nature of things.

The rhetorical description of spring spoken in Chaucer's clerkly voice occurs over and over in classical and medieval poets, philosophers, and encyclopedists alike. It belongs to no particular genre or poetic form but appears in a wide variety of contexts—in Lucretius, in Vergil and Boethius, in Carolingian and Goliardic poetry, in encyclopedias like the one by Bartholomeus Anglicus, in scientific manuals like the *Secreta secretorum*, in vernacular lyric and narrative poetry.[12] Whether philosophic or lyrical, the spring topos usually serves as a synecdoche, pointing to the whole order of creation. In medieval lore, spring, as the first of the four seasons, signals the regularity of nature and implies the causal presence of the Creator. In love poetry the arrival of spring may explain the beginnings of erotic feeling and the lover's joyful discovery of his beloved. Or the regularity of spring's appearance may be shown to be at odds with a lover's unseasonal dejection at the loss of his lady.

Like his predecessors, Chaucer in his clerkly guise uses the synecdoche of spring to imply a hierarchy in the universe, one that points inevitably to God as the source of love and order. Within this cosmic scheme Chaucer emphasizes the erotic movement of all creation, imperfect and incomplete, inherently synecdochic, toward completion and the fulfillment of longing. The "when . . . then" construction of the long opening monologue, full of "gret and high sentence," underscores the poet's philosophical urge to explain the causes and laws of things (including human behavior). Within this tight syntactic construction the speaker's facile descent from pilgrimages in general to the Canterbury pilgrimage—from genus to species—exemplifies schoolroom habits of logical thought. Furthermore, the highly literary beginning exactly coincides with its subject, the cosmic beginnings of things, whether in lower nature or in human life. The outer garb of poetry in the high style suits its philosophical subject perfectly, as if the poet could explore and explain the deep matter of natural and human and divine causality.

This sort of beginning sums up a dominant medieval tradition of narrative authority. Just such a voice might well have initiated an allegorical vision of the kind written by Raoul de Houdenc or Dante or Deguileville. Or it might have generated a rewriting of the *Roman de la rose*, exploring the philosophical distinctions between secular and religious love. Allegories like these presuppose the poet's (and humanity's) power to know causes, to give cosmic explications of the kind the first Chaucerian "beginning" seems to promise.[13] The heightened, philosophizing voice is the voice of authoritative literary tradition. It articulates a general longing—shared by poet and readers alike—for a wise, full vision of the human condition and even for entrance into the recesses of divine privity. Yet Chaucer's clerkly articulation of the poet's task is abruptly truncated. It remains a fragment, a possibility unexploited. In the very next section of the Prologue a second voice definitively denies access to the high mysterious realm of causes—a realm that had been confidently explored by medieval poets of the greatest importance, including Bernard Silvestris, Alain de Lille, and Dante.

IV. The Pilgrim's Voice

The poet's startling shift from a clerk's voice to a pilgrim's turns on the important word *bifil*. It is a word that, together with *bifalle, falle,* and *fil* in the same sense, occurs often in the course of *The Canterbury Tales*. It typically signifies chance happenings, unexpected events occurring at random. The order of time governed by *bifil* and *fil* is radically different from the mythic, cyclic time of the spring topos. It is, in fact, the "order" of the fallen historical world, in which chance, change, unpredictability hold sway. Nor is this time synecdochic; unlike the springtime imagery, it does not point beyond itself. By its nature it does not lend itself to allegory and the wise explication of causes but, rather, supports the more modest claims of chronicle, storytelling, and confession.

The abrupt break in Chaucer's introductory monologue, initiated by the word *bifil* and dominated by a personal "I," constitutes just the sort of "semantic reversal" that the Czech critic Jan Mukarovsky has singled out as a sign of "dialogic discourse."[14] We are unexpectedly jolted from the monologic structure of the clerkly discourse, largely free of involvement in specific time or space, to the pilgrim's direct dialogic address to the other pilgrims and to the readers. Mukarovsky's description of this kind of discourse precisely suits the complex interplay in the pilgrim's speech as the "I" introduces himself and the other pilgrims: "by a sleight of hand the listener becomes the speaker, and the function of the carrier of the utterance constantly jumps from participant to participant" (113).

We observe immediately that the character into which the poet has "fallen" defines him as essentially imperfect, incomplete, on the way: "I lay/ Redy to wenden on my pilgrymage/ To Caunterbury with ful devout corage" (1.20-22). Through his pilgrim "I" as the central voice in the Prologue, Chaucer exploits to the full the humility topos the rhetorical handbooks recommend for the exordium. He genially claims incompetence in the art of making arguments, and he speaks directly and personally to his audience with the same ingratiating deference he had evidently used in insinuating himself into the fellowship of pilgrims. As we follow Chaucer's development of the pilgrim's character, however, we discover that the device is no mere device. The pilgrim persona is not just a mask but a central fact of this and every poet's existence. Chaucer's genius here, as elsewhere, lies in his ability to transform a familiar topos into a precise metaphor.

The image of the pilgrim is heavy with meaning, though critics have had a tendency to pass lightly over it, settling for its function as a comically ironic front for the poet. In fact, this assumption leaves us with an incomplete understanding of Chaucer's point in having his central persona and voice develop as they do. Chaucer gives us not a poet assuming the guise of a pilgrim but a pilgrim attempting the poet's task. His "I" persona identifies the speaker as *first* a pilgrim. The priority thus defined is an important one because it establishes an ontological perspective from which to measure all the rhetorical play recorded in the portraits.

How are we to interpret this voice, this image, if we take it seriously as a necessary replacement for the clerkly voice? As pilgrim, the poet participates in "corrumpable" nature, acknowledging by his pilgrimage that his nature takes its beginning from a being greater than himself and finds its end beyond himself in a "thyng that parfit is and stable" (1.3009). The pilgrim, like Everyman, proceeds at least to some extent "dronke . . . as is a mous" who "noot which the righte wey is thider" (1.1261, 1263). Of course the pilgrim Chaucer is not the lovesick Arcite or the drunken Miller or any of the other "sondry folk" in and out of the tales. But he claims fellowship with them. His identity and his voice are intimately bound up with theirs, and he discovers his own powers and limits by investigating theirs.[15]

The pilgrim insists that his investigation be made not from the superior vantage point assumed by the clerkly voice but from within: "I was of hir felaweshipe anon,/ And made forward erly for to ryse,/ To take *oure* wey ther as I yow devyse" (1.32-34). Chaucer the pilgrim submits himself explicitly to the demands and limits of the occasion "in *that* seson on *a* day" (19). And he makes an immediate accord with the motley crowd of travelers who have come together at the Tabard "by aventure" (25). Accepting their chance fellowship as a matter of course, he assumes the responsibility of telling us about them and their plans. Instead of casting about in old books and authorities for material, as his clerkly and courtly predecessors had typically done, Chaucer simply "finds" the matter that has fallen in his way—the flesh and blood (and words) of his fellows at the Tabard. Instead of remaining apart from this matter to infuse it with wise meaning, the pilgrim joins the group, becomes a part of the matter he proposes to investigate and invest with form.

Now from the point of view of literary history such involvement is not unprecedented. Dante had, after all, admitted his own participation in the sins of his purgatorial ascent—particularly lust and pride. Yet he had also styled himself a visionary, blessed with a higher understanding of his matter, able to transcend his mortal blindness by intellect and grace. Chaucer the pilgrim, by contrast, eschews the perspective of the allegorist and the comforts of enlightenment. The relationship he establishes with his pilgrim characters and their stories is rather the historian's than the visionary's.

Indeed, in his self-defining art of portraiture in the General Prologue and in the imitation he proposes to undertake, the pilgrim as *auctor* probably owes his greatest debt to the literary example of Dares, the self-styled eyewitness chronicler of the Trojan War. Dares, perhaps chiefly through his medieval "translators," had profoundly influenced Chaucer in writing the *Troilus*. In the General Prologue, the influence of Dares and his progeny appears once again, this time as part of the poet's complex defense of his art. Chaucer the pilgrim, like Dares, claims direct, personal observation as the basis for his "true" writing.[16] But in the Prologue, the historian's voice is absorbed into the character of the pilgrim-poet and linked to a game of storytelling.

The connection Chaucer makes in linking the pilgrim persona, historiographic mimesis, and the Canterbury fictions is deep and important, for it crystallizes one of the most painful lessons of medieval Christianity: that human beings in their condition of exile must depend for their knowledge on limited powers of observation, an imperfect understanding of events, and a language essentially different from, and inadequate to, the truths it seeks to express.

The pilgrim-poet acknowledges his metaphysical condition most directly at the end of his "historiographic" portrait gallery in the well-known declaration "My wit is short, ye may wel understonde" (1.746). This disclaimer is most often interpreted as a tongue-in-cheek gesture, the calculated stance of a brilliant bourgeois before his social betters. And it probably is an opportune rhetorical strategy. But, as is often true in Chaucer, the surface significance may be shown to belie a deeper, or even opposite, sense. If we consider the apology not only a ploy but also a straightforward, nonironic statement of fact—and the language, as well as medieval theology, allows us to do so— then Chaucer's self-definition as poet assumes a new direction in this central voice. The pilgrim seeks to authorize himself not by his brilliance or learning or moral perspicuity but by his common humanity. If we read *wit* in its central medieval acceptation as "power of knowing and understanding" rather than as "ingenuity" only, the clause "My wit is short" assumes a philosophical sense.[17] Absolute shortness of wit supplies a principle of organization whereby the poet may bypass high cultural literary order in favor of a larger, ironic inquiry into the sorry but also comic plight of the human spirit in this world's exile.[18]

V. The Pilgrim's Portrait Gallery

In every aspect of his self-presentation, Chaucer's pilgrim persona practices a comically incomplete power of "devysyng," one that reveals the *humana fragilitas* in the historian's stance. He begins his portrait series with the confident formula "A Knyght ther was" (1.43), as if he intends to uncover the nature of each social type by giving a full, precise, ordered example. The formula proposes rhetorical and philosophical plenitude by way of synecdoche; yet the text fails to deliver fullness or completeness. Individual characters systematically escape from or evade the expected formulas, leaving us with a sense not only of the social "obsolescence" Donald Howard has suggested but also of an essential partiality and eccentricity (*Idea* 94-106).

Through his voice as pilgrim-historian, Chaucer structures the portraits so as to deny us a clear, total representation of the individuals as types related to transcendent ideals. The portraits fail to arrange themselves in a recognizable hierarchical order, an order that would call our attention to the expected, or "proper," order of society. Nor, for the most part, do the eccentric characters who claim nominal participation in the various estates fully clarify their preordained roles, either negatively or positively. The ideal knight, the ideal monk and friar, the ideal wife (or their systematically developed opposites) remain notions partly beyond the horizon of the text.

What is important in the fictions of the portrait gallery is that the pilgrim participates in them, allowing his "exemplary" figures to overtake his own voice dialogically through indirect discourse. As rhetor and historian, Chaucer, delights in his pilgrims as dramatis personae. He observes, often with admiration, the details of their self-dramatization—the fictions they project to fool themselves or to impress, cajole, or exploit others.

Yet, if the pilgrim-poet were *homo rhetoricus* and secular historian only, there would be no moral center against which to measure the wanderings and eccentricities of those he describes.[19] And the portraits would lack just the tension that gives them their lasting power and point. In fact, the amorality of the historian's rhetorical stance is pervasively countered by reminders of a nonrhetorical, suprahistorical mode of existence. Not only the "ful devout corage" of the pilgrim himself but also the figure of the Parson provides a point of reference for this alternative mode. The Parson's "pose"—or, more properly, "role"—as a shepherd conscientiously caring for his flock approximates his central identity. He imitates Christ the Good Shepherd in every detail of his life and thereby identifies himself exclusively as a son of God. Indeed, our *only* image of the Parson's physical presence is that of a Christian shepherd of souls with staff in hand. What Chaucer emphasizes in the Parson's portrait is the coincidence of word and deed, of Christian teaching and high moral conduct. There is in the Parson's life little matter for "troping," little rhetorical distance between his soul's self and his outward presentation.

From the perspective of Christian pilgrimage, the social or religious roles of most of the other characters appear to be added onto them, like their costumes, often accompanied by distorting or falsifying elaborations. The Knight's remarkable achievements in battle, the Pardoner's fashionable cape, the Friar's girlfriends, the Wife of Bath's old and young husbands—all distract the pilgrims more or less from their single proper concern, the destiny of their souls. In rhetorical terms, the lives and speech of most of the pilgrims are "troped," turned in one way or another away from transcendent truth in the direction of Harry Bailly's kind of worldly fiction making.

Both the Parson's life and the poet's brilliant juxtapositions of detail call attention to the artifices the pilgrims practice. The obvious contradictions between pretension and fact encourage us to recognize the fictions for what they are. Yet we do not hear in the pilgrim's portraits the voice of the strict moralist anatomizing human folly with clerical rigor. In his rendering, the fictions of daily life in the temporal world of "bifil" coincide with the fictions of art, and the poet exploits, even as he delights in, the coincidence.

For an anagogically "true" reading of the poem's matter we must wait for the Parson. It is he who will insist on a definitive separation of fact and truth from fiction:

> Thou getest fable noon ytoold for me;
> For Paul, that writeth unto Thymothee,
> Repreveth hem that weyven soothfastnesse,
> And tellen fables and swich
> wrecchednesse.
>
> (10.31-34)

Chaucer might have given the Parson's voice to himself as "I" from the beginning. Had he done so, however, he would have had to reject all the "pley," all the voices, of *The Canterbury Tales*. Boethius's Lady Philosophy, it will be remembered, had rejected the muses of falsifying, consolatory poetry at the start of his *Consolation*. In pointed (and I think calculated) contrast, Chaucer's Retraction comes only at the end of his work. The very existence of the tales depends on his deliberately *not* beginning as Boethius had, not rejecting the sweet venom of fiction until its pleasures and possibilities have been fully explored as well as exposed.

VI. The Pilgrim Voice and the Question of Truth

The pilgrim broaches the question of truth, and broaches it explicitly, in the General Prologue. Yet when he invokes a Platonic theory to support his tale-telling, he misapplies the theory and thereby brilliantly defers the question of a transcendent truth beyond the truth of historical reportage:

Critical Insights

Whoso shal telle a tale after a man,
He moot reherce as ny as evere he kan
Everich a word, if it be in his charge,
Al speke he never so rudeliche and large,
Or ellis he moot telle his tale untrewe,
Or feyne thyng, or fynde wordes newe.

. . . .

Eek Plato seith, whoso that kan hym rede,
The wordes moote be cosyn to the dede.

(1.731-36; 741-42)

Here, in a flagrant misreading, the pilgrim comically conflates his own "historiographic" notion of truth as the imitation of passing life with Plato's theory relating words to the transcendent truth of things. We may pass lightly over the conflation and assume that the poet is simply pleading for a new kind of artistic freedom. But Chaucer seems to intend something deeper by deliberately juxtaposing the pilgrim's and Plato's ideas of imitation. In placing his theory cheek by jowl with Plato's, he aims, I think, to provide a mortal correction for what he considers an impossible dream.

The pilgrim's description of his language is straightforwardly *anti*allegorical in an age that generally revered allegorical poetry: his words will not, at least easily or directly, point to things (or truth or doctrine) as words were said to do in allegorical poems like the *Roman de la rose*. They will simply imitate the words and "chiere" of the other pilgrims, which are neither Platonic "things" nor stable ideas, but transient phenomena. The text as a collection of unstable, ambiguous signs will mark the beginning rather than the completion of speculation about the nature of things. The poet in his pilgrim voice will not be a philosopher or a repository of high wisdom, at least not in a traditional sense. Instead he will simply be an earthly maker and historian, putting idiosyncratic words and actions together according to his limited powers of observation and invention and the unpredictable demands of the matter.[20] Chaucer the pilgrim, like Dares the historian, thus turns the text over to the audience, who will have to interpret or translate the signs into meaning, discerning the "true" inner structure informing the ensemble of outward manifestations. While this management of the poet's and the audience's roles may appear modern, or even postmodern, it is in fact thoroughly explicable as a logical (though also brilliantly original) development from dominant medieval theories concerning fiction and the limits of human knowledge.

The Platonic theory Chaucer's pilgrim invokes originated in the *Timaeus* (29B), and versions of it appear in many a medieval text, including Boethius's *Consolation* (3, pr. 12) and Jean de Meung's *Roman de la rose* (Guillaume, lines 6943-78 and 15159-94). Underlying all the arguments from Plato to Jean is a confidence that words describe objective, knowable, nameable reality, whether that reality is the motions of the will (Plato) or ideas in the mind (Chalcidius) or God (Boethius) or testicles (Jean de Meung). For writers of fictions, the theory provided some assurance that poetic narratives—"beautiful lies" according to the dominant learned tradition—could legitimately explore the causes of things and teach truth. In Boethius and Jean, voices of authority—Philosophia, Raison, the Poet—speak the theory. Their authority is in a certain sense absolute. They grant the poet and therefore the reader power to cut through the artifices of allegorical fabrication to touch the secrets of philosophy.

What distinguishes Chaucer from earlier poets is that he refuses to give the Platonic doctrine to an authority figure. Instead of speaking it through Philosophia or Raison or Gracedieu, he presents it through his pilgrim voice. The pilgrim as historian proposes to use words not to represent things or truth or doctrine or ideas, as a clerk would have done, but to mimic the transient words and gestures of others. These acts belong to the sundry folk of the fallen world, who are not likely, by and large, to speak or behave philosophically. Some of them are counterfeiters. Some are professional (lying) rhetoricians. Others are professional cheaters or tricksters or swindlers. Of course all of them are finally given voice by Chaucer. All are part of his grand masquerade, and all represent aspects of his self-presentation as pilgrim-poet.

Paradoxically, the pilgrim's very act of mimicry bespeaks an oblique recognition of the truth about his poetry. On one side of his equation are the stories he and his subjects offer—the fictions they construct about themselves as well as those they construct for the game's sake. On the other is his own *humana fragilitas*, yearning for, needing transcendent truth, the explanation of causes, but bound by the necessities of limited wit, imperfect observation, ambiguous language, and inevitable mortality. The pilgrim-poet can do no more than endeavor to record and illustrate these limitations, using trope and omission at every turn to acknowledge his distance from truth and wholeness. As a sort of magician, an illusion maker, he—like the Orleans clerk of the Franklin's Tale, or the Fiend of the Friar's Tale—can only make free with necessities. His tellers, in presenting themselves as "characters" and telling their tales, will propose causal explanations for themselves and try to elucidate the events of their stories. But the explanations will be limited finally by their fictiveness. Only the Parson's Tale will probe the true causes of things directly, but his "tale" is not a fiction. The language of the tales is deliberately and designedly the language of error, as judged by an unrealized, extratextual language of transcendent truth.

In the pilgrim's argument, fiction, like history, is a necessity imposed by the Fall. Chaucer's pilgrim voice as it mingles with the voices of the other Canterbury pilgrims proclaims the delights of tale-telling. The poet willingly, even willfully, engages the fallen world's illusions, opinions, and beliefs, questioning by his play their relations to truth.

Is there, then, any "truth" to be found in the pilgrim's report of the Canterbury adventure? And, if so, where and how? As the orchestrator of all the artifices, all the falsifications, all the voices of the *Tales*, the pilgrim Chaucer unashamedly encourages his fictive surrogates in their mendacious enterprises. A shapeshifter and a trickster, he himself thrives on lying. Yet because he styles himself a pilgrim, his lying, like that of the Fiend of the Friar's Tale, may be read as part of God's service. The Fiend, as he tells the summoner, lies partly because human "wit is al to bare" to understand the truth (3.1480). Even when he tells the summoner the transcendent truth about himself—recessed within the fiction of his bailiff disguise and voice—the summoner fails to grasp it. In a parallel way, Chaucer gives his tellers matters of truth in their stories, but the truth more often than not remains unobserved by the tellers and their characters within the fictive frames.

Of course, as the Fiend says, some withstand "oure temptacioun"—see through the disguises—and this act is "cause of [their] savacioun" (3.1497-98). Multiple (and wrong) interpretation must be the rule in reading the "divers art and . . . diverse figures" of the Fiend and the pilgrim-poet alike (3.1486). Yet Chaucer, like the Fiend, holds out the possibility of "right" interpretation. Such interpretation, however, will depend more on the reader's intention than on the fiction itself—the individual's personal concern for truth and salvation.

Chaucer provides this saving extraliterary definition of fiction and interpretation not through his pilgrim but through his final voice and final image in *The Canterbury Tales*. In his Retraction after the Parson's Tale, he says, "'Al that is writen is writen for oure doctrine,' and that is myn entente" (10.1083). The poet in this last voice also begs pardon for any of his tales that "sownen into synne" and apologizes for his "enditynges of worldly vanitees" (10.1085, 1084). Yet, while he, like the Fiend, warns of the dangers of fiction, he knows that his audience may not heed the warning. In fact, he himself has succumbed to temptation in allowing his many fictive voices to enjoy the delights of Harry's game.

VII. The Host's Voice

Harry Bailly's voice, which dominates the final movement of the General Prologue, follows directly from the pilgrim's declaration "My wit is short." From that point on, another "I," another character, empowered by the pilgrim voice, assumes control over the design of the tales. Like most Chaucerian transitions, the juxtaposition of the apologetic voice with Harry's portrait and his "boold" speech requires more than cursory attention. It is as if Harry were born of the pilgrim-poet's essential limitation.

Yet, as a child of insufficiency, Harry lacks the self-critical awareness of his parent. Like the pilgrim, he espouses a theory of fiction. But while his notion of "making"—the third in Chaucer's series in the General Prologue—coincides with the pilgrim's in fundamental ways, it lacks the pilgrim's acknowledgment of partiality, limitation, and absence. Despite Harry's pious bow to "sentence" in the General Prologue, his fiction is essentially fiction for the sake of play and mirth and also for financial profit. As such, it is a fiction unmoored in ideas about truth or the quest for truth.[21]

Harry, the fourteenth-century bourgeois innkeeper, has often been regarded as an "original," having no clear literary antecedents. Manly even identifies him with a historical Henry Bailly, thus establishing his credentials as a "realistic" character (78-79). Like so many other Chaucerian characters, however, Harry owes his originality not only to his apparently idiosyncratic, realistic "condicioun" and "chiere" but also to the poet's complex manipulation of well-established literary and theoretical formulations. Understood as the latter-day spokesman for an ancient tradition, Harry assumes a climactic place in Chaucer's dialectical argument concerning the character of the poet and the functions of poetry.

We first meet Harry Bailly in the dining room of his inn after he has served supper to his guests and collected their bills. For this third major voice in Chaucer's complex introductory defense of his fiction, the context has narrowed significantly. The vast panorama of the external, seasonal world served as locus for the clerkly voice. An entire inn treated *as* an inn—a place on the way—framed the pilgrim. By contrast, a single public room designed for drinking and eating encloses Harry's authority and poetic theory. And Harry is at home in the Tabard. As the scene narrows, so too do the possibilities for poetry as an art of wise interpretation. In the dining room of a tavern we listen to the host's limited and limiting notions about the poet and poetry.

As the innkeeper "reads" poetry, it fully deserves the notoriety assigned to it by the stricter antique and medieval theorists, from Paul, Augustine, and Boethius to Chaucer's Parson. Harry sponsors fiction for reasons very like those of Boethius's muses—the "scaenicas meretriculas" 'theatrical whores'—at the beginning of the *Consolation*. The Muses that Lady Philosophy dismisses from Boethius's chamber are those Plato and Cicero had also condemned, those who inspire laments over bad fortune and celebrate pleasure as the proper goal of poetry (and life). Some medieval commentators widened Philosophia's condemnation to include all secular poetry. As one exegete puts it, Boethius's "theatrical whores" are the "Musas quas inuocant illi qui saeculariter scribunt Horatius Virgilius et alii qui nouem Musas nouem deas fingunt et inuocant" 'The Muses whom those invoke who write in a worldly way: Horace, Vergil, and others who depict the nine Muses as nine goddesses and invoke them' (Silk 7).[22] In the environment of philosophy, so the medieval commentator's argument goes, all worldly poetry is to be recognized as falsifying fiction. Later theorists—among them Petrarch and Boccaccio—fully aware of such religiously based opposition to secular poetry, took pains to redress the criticisms.[23] They insisted with humanist zeal on the correctness of ancient definitions that allow poetry both its fictive covering and its truth. Chaucer, by contrast, turns over the direction of his poetry making to Harry Bailly and thereby gives a hearing to a notion of poetic fiction divorced from the philosophical search for truth.

Despite his brief, perfunctory bow to Horatian "sentence," Harry prefers poetry as mirthful distraction from the hard realities and pain of the human condition. His interest in tale-telling coincides with his pleasure in drinking and, covertly, his desire for money. This last use of fiction for profit aligns him particularly with Boethius's theatrical strumpets. As Nicholas Trivet puts it in his commentary on the *Consolation*, "the poetic muses are called theatrical whores—[because] just as a whore copulates with those [lovers] for love not of procreation but of lucre, so poets were writing about those [things]—for the love not of wisdom but of praise, that is to say, of money" (fol. 6v).[24] Harry's ultimate goal in generating the fictions of the Canterbury journey is to collect the price of twenty-nine suppers, minus his own small contribution to the winner's meal at the end of the trip.

As a master of mirth, Harry is also kin to the all-important figure of Déduit in Guillaume de Lorris's *Roman de la rose*.[25] This character, whom Chaucer called "Sir Mirth" in his translation of the *Roman*, is the courtly proprietor of the garden into which the poet enters as a young lover (about to be trapped by erotic desire). In this garden Déduit acts as choragus for a troop of jongleurs, jugglers, musicians, singers, and dancers. In a parallel way, Harry in his dining room proposes himself as the leader of a band of fiction makers. As Déduit's followers are distracted by the garden's "siren" birds and the music of his players, Harry's pilgrims succumb without demur to the innkeeper's strong wine and promises of mirth through storytelling.

Above all, both Déduit and Harry traffic in "divertissement." In Chaucer's translation of the *Roman*, Sir Mirth in the garden "walketh to solace . . . for sweeter place/ to pleyen ynne he may not find" (lines 621-23). Like Guillaume's allegorical figure, Harry, who seeks play for the sake of solace, is essentially mirthful. The words *mirth*, *myrie*, *pley*, *disport*, and *comfort* appear twelve times in twenty-six lines as Chaucer gives us Harry's portrait and has him explain his game. The very name Déduit suits both characters exactly, containing as it does the two senses "having a good time" and "turning away from a [right] course" (Dahlberg 361, line 590n). To be sure, Harry and his followers leave the Tabard and walk out into the world engaged to play a diversionary game, whereas Déduit remains at home in his symbolic garden. Yet Harry sees to it that his pilgrim subjects never forget that they have contracted to remain within the bounds of his play and his notions of solace. The fictions themselves, together with Harry's framing commentary, become the pilgrims' "pleasure garden" for the duration of the Canterbury journey. At the same time, however, the inescapable fact of the pilgrimage serves as an ever-present critique of the game, reminding us that there is another, "right" course.

While Harry, in framing his game, shares Déduit's concern for mirth and solace, his image of diversionary art is richer and more philosophically complex than his French counterpart's. In his avowed antipathy for silence and his intended use of fiction for financial profit, he sums up Boethius's whole argument concerning the conflict between distracting fictions and the search for philosophical truth. Harry's kind of fiction explicitly opposes the silence of spiritual introspection proper to the life of true pilgrimage. Poetry is, for him, a pleasant noise that keeps the mind conveniently distracted from any pilgrim sense of the need for truth or meditation on the *lacrimae rerum*. "And wel I woot," he says,

> as ye goon by the weye,
> Ye shapen yow to talen and to pleye;
> For trewely, confort ne myrthe is noon
> To ride by the weye doumb as a stoon;
> And therfore wol I maken yow disport,
> As I seyde erst, and doon yow som confort.
> (1.771-76)

Harry's interest in distraction coincides with his pervasive urge to rush from one tale to another. Gaps in diversionary discourse, like the absence of mirth, may allow introspection to enter, and this Harry cannot bear.[26]

Why, we must ask, does Chaucer turn over the important last place in his prologal argument to so disreputable a voice and position? He does so at least in part, I believe, to give a full, unabridged account of all aspects of the fiction he proposes to write. Like Dante in the *Commedia*, he intends to include—and even praise—the impure, infernal element in his poetry as well as its potential for philosophical vision. Indeed, poetry as rhetorical bedazzlement may have seemed to him the most evident, accessible, attractive aspect of his art, the one most likely to charm his audience into paying attention. By way of Harry's voice, Chaucer, unlike many of his critics, defends (though with the substantial reservations imposed by the other prologal voices) the delights of puzzlement, diversion, and absorption in the illusions wrought by rhetorical coloring.

Through Harry, Chaucer also calls attention to the common tendency, in which the tavern keeper's notion of fiction making participates, to miss or set aside contemplation of the providential design of the universe and humanity's place within it. Storytelling, at least at one level, affords a pleasure not unlike the Wife's putative joy in wealthy and virile husbands, the Friar's enjoyment of rich patrons and comfortable taverns, the Monk's pleasure in hunting, January's delight in his love garden, and the myriad other diversions by which the Canterbury characters live. Chaucer the poet does not exempt himself or his writing from this pleasurable, spiritually subversive function of fiction. But he admits his involvement in so disreputable a cause only indirectly, as a good orator should, using Harry's voice and character to mask his own. In his last voice, Chaucer slyly celebrates poetry in just the terms that the strictest theorists had used to condemn it.

In doing so, however, Chaucer is not giving Harry's ideas about poetry precedence over other, higher notions. Like the opening formulations of the clerkly voice, the Host's game provides a framing contrast for the central, dynamic notion of the poetic enterprise in the General Prologue—the one articulated by the pilgrim's voice. The voices of the clerk and the innkeeper offer relatively fixed, static images of poetry: one is concerned with causality, hierarchy, and order, the other with the disorders, sexual exploits, and trivialities of quotidian life. Both positions are curiously abstracted, though in opposite ways, from the complex central subject of poetry as the pilgrim voice proposes it—human consciousness of a universe that emanates from God but also participates in entropy, mortality, disintegration.

Neither the first nor the last notion of poetry entertained in the General Prologue allows for the rich, active, tentative, dialogic exploration of that difficult subject as the pilgrim voice engages it. The pilgrim Chaucer may reach upward toward the clerk's philosophical formulations or downward to Harry's bourgeois laughter. He is bound by neither, though he may play with both. His deeply human engagement with his flawed, mortal subject and art precludes direct statements of transcendent truth in his fiction. By the same token, his storytelling will rise above the category of fictions made simply for the sake of rhetorical play and distracting frivolity. What remains—the poetry at the center—is fictive, certainly. But it is as richly various and morally dense and stubbornly inconclusive as its total subject. Its self-conscious fictionality will press well-disposed readers toward a new awareness of the nature of illusion and self-deception, whether in literature or in life. The truths the tales uncover have to do mainly with human ways of knowing (and not knowing) the self and the mortal world.

To find the truths of Christian doctrine, however, one must set the tales aside. Transcendent truth remains largely absent from the Chaucerian narratives, and it must. In Chaucer's argument, this is just the kind of truth that makes all secular fiction untenable. Nonetheless, Chaucer the poet in his several voices points directions, marks boundaries, poses questions and puzzles that bear heavily on the truths beyond his fictions.

From *PMLA: Publications of the Modern Language Association of America* 101, no. 2 (March 1986): 154-169. Copyright © 1986 by the Modern Language Association of America. Reprinted by permission of the Modern Language Association of America.

Notes

1. Hunt provides a useful history of this medieval genre, including an outline of its characteristics. See also Arbusow 97-103; Curtius 83-89; Porqueras Mayo; Cunningham; and Baldwin 32-35.

2. For a valuable discussion of Chaucer's creative engagement with classical notions of the orator, see Payne.

3. Other helpful studies on this issue include Malone; Duncan; Hoffman; Woolf; Bronson; Major; Nevo; Jordan, "Chaucer's Sense" and *Chaucer* 111-31.

4. All translations from works not cited in translation are my own.

5. "Quasi ergo aliquis secum loquens se et rationem suam quasi duo constituit . . . , sicut Boetius in libro 'De consolatione Philosophiae' vel Augustinus in libro 'Soliloquorum.'"

6. "Tres autem a Boetio inducuntur personae, Boetius miser querens ut consoletur, Philosophia quae consolatur, Boetius auctor qui de utrisque loquitur."

7. "Hic igitur liber idcirco concionator dicitur, quia Salomon in eo quasi tumultuantis turbae suscepit sensum, ut ea per inquisitionem dicat, quae fortasse per temptationem imperita mens sentiat. Nam quot sententias quasi per inquisitionem mouit, quasi tot in se personas diuersorum suscepit."

8. Gregory's description of Ecclesiastes was well-known and popular in the later Middle Ages. It appears, for example, in a truncated form in Wyclif's English commentary on Ecclesiastes. I am indebted to Eric Eliason for this reference to Wyclif.

9. "Multiplex disputatio signatur, et ad diversas deducta sententias. Quia enim in hoc libro multorum mores, studia, et opera describuntur: propterea necesse est loquentem multorum voces assumere, multorum opiniones in suo sermone exprimere, ut valeat multorum personas (cum ipse tamen nonnisi unus sit, qui loquitur) in sua persona presentare. Nam circa finem libri multis locutum se, et in se multos fuisse testatur, dicens: Finem loquendi omnis pariter audiamus. *Deum time, et mandata ejus observa hoc est omnis homo.* Hoc est etiam cur se in hoc opere Ecclesiasten nominari voluit; quia videlicet sermo ejus hic non ad unum aliquem specialiter, sed ad totam Ecclesiam, id est concionem, sive multitudinem populi dirigitur, et multorum moribus exprimendis simul, et informandis ejus in hoc libro oratio famulatur."

10. For useful discussions of the medieval rhetorical "I," see Spitzer; Bethurum; Kellogg; Bevington; and Kane. See also Anne Middleton's excellent description of the public voice (and public "I") developed by certain English poets, including Langland and Gower, during Richard II's reign. Derek Brewer offers important observations about Chaucer's dramatized tellers.

11. These three voices coincide interestingly with T. S. Eliot's description of the poet's three voices. Chaucer's articulation of the theory, however, grows out of rhetorical tradition and serves a philosophical argument, while Eliot is describing his own writing experience (4).

12. Numerous studies trace the history of the spring topos. Among the most important for Chaucer are Cook; Hankins; Tuve, *Seasons* and "Spring"; and Baldwin 19-28. See also Curtius 185-202 and Ross. For a discussion of the *Secreta secretorum* and Chaucer's spring opening, see esp. Tuve, *Seasons* 52-58.

13. For a suggestive discussion of the relations between allegory, explorations of causality, and the language of truth, see Quilligan, esp. 156-223. See also Brewer 222-23.

14. See ch. 3, "Two Studies of Dialogue" (81-115). I am grateful to Ralph Cohen for directing me to Mukarovsky and other modern theorists who deal with the question of voicing in fiction.

15. For discussions of Chaucer's involvement with his pilgrims, see Malone 40-45; Green; and Mandel.

16. R. M. Lumiansky and Jill Mann have rightly observed a connection between the portrait gallery in Benoit de Sainte-Maure's *Roman de Troie*, based on Dares, and Chaucer's portraits in the General Prologue. Even more important is Chaucer's borrowing of the authorial perspective of the eyewitness historian that supports the portraits in Dares and Benoit. See Lumiansky, "Benoit's"; Mann 179-81.

17. In Middle English the word *wit* has several more or less related meanings: "mind," "faculty or power of thinking and reasoning," "bodily and spiritual powers of perception," "sanity," "genius, talent, or cleverness." When the pilgrim says, "My wit is short," he is usually thought to be referring to his ingenuity or power of invention. In the immediate context, he is speaking about his inability to set the rest of the pilgrims in their proper order. Because this task is, technically speaking, an act of rhetorical invention, the reading "my ingenuity is short" is not improbable. Then we have only the simple irony of the brilliant poet's "humility." If, however, the deeper meaning, "my power to know is limited," is the central one, then Chaucer is affirming the metaphysical irony of absolute human limitation and acknowledging his necessary participation in this condition.

18. Two centuries later Cervantes would choose a similar ploy to explore similar questions. His *Don Quixote*, he tells us, emanated from a shriveled brain. From this comic vantage point he can reveal high literary romances as elegant (falsifying) fabrications designed, consciously or unconsciously, to obscure the sad, sordid reality of quotidian life. For Cervantes and Chaucer alike a self-critical posture coincides with an ironic critique of all linguistic efforts—particularly efforts by courtly poets—to express truth or to describe reality accurately.

19. For a thought-provoking discussion of *homo rhetoricus* in Western tradition, see Lanham, esp. ch. 1, "The Rhetorical Ideal of Life" (1-35).

20. See Olson for a useful discussion of the poet as maker.

21. Alan Gaylord offers one of the fullest, most helpful discussions of Harry Bailly's involvement in the theory of story-telling. He rightly observes that Harry's principal concern in the tales proper is solace and not the "sentence" he piously invokes in the General Prologue. For other discussions of Harry's theoretical commitments and significance, see Lumiansky, *Of Sondry Folk* 85-95; Ruggiers 6; David 75-76; Richardson; Scheps; and Bloomfield 49.

22. For the attribution of this commentary, see Courcelle 304.

23. See Petrarch's coronation speech in Godi; also, his *Invective contra medicum* in Petrarch 648-93.

24. "Scenicas meretriculas muse poetice dicuntur, meretricule sic enim meretrix conmiscetur cuibus non amore prolis sed lucri, sic poete scribebant de quobus non amore sapientie sed laudis videlicet lucri."

25. Alan Gaylord points out the connections between Harry's interest in mirth and its impor-

tance in the *Roman de la rose* (230), but he does not observe the direct relation between Déduit and Chaucer's innkeeper.

26. Harry's notions of tale-telling as a source of mirth align his poetry with the sphere of "curiositas"—"a fastidious, excessive, morally diverting interest in things and people" (Zacher 20). Zacher's discussion of "curiositas" is full and illuminating.

Works Cited

Abelard, Peter. *Expositio in hexameron*. Migne 178: 731-84.

Arbusow, Leonid. *Colores rhetorici*. 1948. Geneva: Slatkin, 1974.

Baldwin, Ralph. *The Unity of The Canterbury Tales*. Copenhagen: Rosenkilde, 1955.

Benoit de Sainte-Maure. *Roman de Troie*. Ed. L. Constans. 6 vols. Paris: Firmin-Didot, 1904 12.

Bethurum, Dorothy. "Chaucer's Point of View as Narrator in the Love Poems." *PMLA* 74 (1959): 511-20.

Bevington, D. M. "The Obtuse Narrator in Chaucer's *House of Fame*." *Speculum* 36 (1961): 288-98.

Bloomfield, Morton W. "*The Canterbury Tales* as Framed Narratives." *Leeds Studies in English* ns 14 (1983): 44-56.

Boccaccio, Giovanni. *Genealogie deorum gentilium libri*. Ed. V. Romano. Bari: Laterza, 1951.

Boethius, Anicius Manlius Severinus. *Philosophiae consolationis in libri quinque*. Leipzig, 1871.

Brewer, Derek S. "Towards a Chaucerian Poetic." *Proceedings of the British Academy* 60 (1974): 219-52.

Bronson, B. H. *In Search of Chaucer*. Toronto: U of Toronto P, 1960.

Chaucer, Geoffrey. *Works*. Ed. F. N. Robinson. 2nd ed. Boston: Houghton, 1957.

Christianson, Paul. "Chaucer's Literacy." *Chaucer Review* 11 (1976): 112-27.

[Cicero]. *Ad C. Herennium. De ratione dicendi*. Ed. and trans. Harry Caplan. Cambridge: Harvard UP; London: Heinemann, 1964.

Cicero. *De oratore*. Ed. and trans. E. W. Sutton and H. Rackham. Cambridge: Cambridge UP; London: Heinemann, 1967.

Cook, A. S. "Chaucerian Papers: I." *Transactions of the Connecticut Academy of Arts and Sciences* 23 (1919): 5-10.

Courcelle, P. *La consolation de philosophie dans la tradition littéraire*. Paris: Studies Augustiniennes, 1967.

Cunningham, J. V. "The Literary Form of the Prologue to *The Canterbury Tales*." *Modern Philology* 49 (1951-52): 172-81.

Curtius, E. R. *European Literature and the Latin Middle Ages*. Trans. R. W. Trask. New York: Pantheon, 1953.

Dahlberg, Charles, ed. and trans. *Le roman de la rose*. By Guillaume de Lorris and Jean de Meun. Princeton: Princeton UP, 1971.

Dares Phrygius. *De excidio Troiae historia*. Ed. F. O. Meister. Leipzig, 1873.

David, Alfred. *The Strumpet Muse*. Bloomington: Indiana UP, 1976.

Donaldson, E. Talbot. "Chaucer the Pilgrim." *PMLA* 69 (1954): 928-36.

Duncan, E. H. "The Narrator's Point of View in the Portrait-Sketches, Prologue to *The Canterbury Tales.*" *Essays in Honor of Walter Clyde Curry.* Nashville: Vanderbilt UP, 1954. 77-101.

Eliot, T. S. *The Three Voices of Poetry.* Cambridge: Cambridge UP, 1953.

Gaylord, Alan. "Sentence and *Solaas* in Fragment VII of *The Canterbury Tales*: Harry Bailly as Horseback Editor." *PMLA* 82 (1967): 226-33.

Godi, Carlo. "La 'Collatio laureationis' del Petrarca." *Italia medievale e umanistica* 13 (1970): 1-27.

Green, Eugene. "The Voices of the Pilgrims in the General Prologue to *The Canterbury Tales.*" *Style* 9 (1975): 55-81.

Gregory the Great. *Dialogues.* Ed. A. de Vogüé. Trans. into French P. Antin. 3 vols. Paris: Cerf, 1980.

Guillaume de Lorris and Jean de Meun. *Le roman de la rose.* Ed. Ernest Langlois. 5 vols. Paris: Firmin-Didot, 1914-24.

Hankins, John E. "Chaucer and the *Per Virgilium veneris.*" *Modern Language Notes* 44 (1934): 80-83.

Hoffman, A. "Chaucer's Prologue to Pilgrimage: The Two Voices." *ELH* 21 (1954): 1-16.

Howard, Donald. "Chaucer the Man." *PMLA* 80 (1965): 337-43.

_____. *The Idea of the Canterbury Tales.* Berkeley: U of California P, 1976.

Hugh of St. Victor. "Homilia prima." *In Salomonis Ecclesiasten. Homiliae XIX.* Migne 175: 115-33.

Hunt, Tony. "The Rhetorical Background to the Arthurian Prologue: Tradition and the Old French Vernacular Prologues." *Forum for Modern Language Studies* 6 (1970): 1-23.

Huygens, R. B. C., ed. *Accessus ad auctores. Bernard d'Utrecht. Conrad d' Hirsau.* Leiden: Brill, 1970.

Jordan, R. M. *Chaucer and the Shape of Creation.* Cambridge: Harvard UP, 1967.

_____. "Chaucer's Sense of Illusion: Roadside Drama Reconsidered." *Journal of English and Germanic Philology* 29 (1962): 19-33.

Kane, George. *The Autobiographical Fallacy in Chaucer and Langland Studies.* London: Lewis, 1965.

Kellogg, A. L. "Chaucer's Self-Portrait and Dante's." *Medium aevum* 29 (1960): 119-20.

Lanham, Richard. *The Motives of Eloquence.* New Haven: Yale UP, 1976.

Leicester, Marshall. "A General Prologue to the *Canterbury Tales.*" *PMLA* 95 (1980): 213-24.

Lumiansky, R. M. "Benoit's Portraits and Chaucer's General Prologue." *Journal of English and Germanic Philology* 55 (1956): 431-38.

_____. *Of Sondry Folk.* Austin: U of Texas P, 1955.

Major, John. "The Personality of Chaucer the Pilgrim." *PMLA* 75 (1960): 160-62.

Malone, Kemp. "Style and Structure in the Prologue to the *Canterbury Tales.*" *ELH* 13 (1946): 38-45.

Mandel, Jerome. "Other Voices in the *Canterbury Tales.*" *Criticism* 19 (1977): 338-49.

Manly, John. *Some New Light on Chaucer.* New York: Holt, 1926.

Mann, Jill. *Chaucer and Medieval Estates Satire.* Cambridge: Cambridge UP, 1973.

Middleton, Anne. "The Idea of Public Poetry in the Reign of Richard II." *Speculum* 53 (1978): 94-114.

Migne, J. P., ed. *Patrologia Latina.* 221 vols. Paris, 1844-64.

Mukarovsky, Jan. *The Word and Verbal Art*. New Haven: Yale UP, 1977.

Nevo, Ruth. "Chaucer: Motive and Mask in the General Prologue." *Modern Language Review* 58 (1963): 1-9.

Olson, Glending. "Making and Poetry in the Age of Chaucer." *Comparative Literature* 31 (1979): 714-23.

Payne, R. O. "Chaucer's Realization of Himself as Rhetor." *Medieval Eloquence*. Ed. J. J. Murphy. Berkeley: U of California P, 1978. 270-87.

Petrarch. *Prose*. Ed. G. Martellotti et al. Milano: Ricciardi, 1955.

Plato. *The Timaeus*. Trans. F. M. Cornford. Indianapolis: Bobbs, 1959.

Porqueras Mayo, A. *El prólogo como genero literario*. Madrid: Consejo Superior de Investigaciones Científicas, 1957.

Quilligan, Maureen. *The Language of Allegory*. Ithaca: Cornell UP, 1979.

Quintilian. *Institutio oratoria*. Ed. and trans. H. E. Butler. 4 vols. London: Heinemann; New York: Putnam, 1921.

Richardson, Cynthia. "The Function of the Host in the *Canterbury Tales*." *Texas Studies in Literature and Language* 12 (1970): 325-44.

Ross, Werner. "Über den Sogennanten Natureingang der Trobadors." *Romanische Forschungen* 65 (1953): 49-68.

Ruggiers, Paul. *The Art of the* Canterbury Tales. Madison: U of Wisconsin P, 1965.

Scheps, Walter. "'Up Roos Oure Hoost, and Was Oure Aller Cok': Harry Bailly's Tale Telling Competition." *Chaucer Review* 10 (1975-76): 113-28.

Servius. *In Vergilii carmina commentarii*. Ed. G. Thilo and H. Hagen. 3 vols. Leipzig, 1897.

Silk, Edmund T., ed. *Saeculi noni auctores in Boetii* Consolationem philosophiae *commentarius*. Rome: American Acad. in Rome, 1935.

Spitzer, Leo. "A Note on the Poetic and the Empirical 'I' in Medieval Authors." *Traditio* 4 (1946): 414-22.

Trivet, Nicholas. Commentary on Boethius's *Consolation of Philosophy*. Latin ms. 18424. Bibliothéque Nationale.

Tuve, Rosamond. *Seasons and Months*. Paris: Librairie Universitaire, 1933.

_____. "Spring in Chaucer and before Him." *Modern Language Notes* 52 (1937): 9-16.

Virgil. *The Eclogues and Georgics*. Ed. Robert D. Williams. New York: St. Martin's, 1979.

Woolf, Rosemary. "Chaucer as a Satirist in the General Prologue to the *Canterbury Tales*." *Critical Quarterly* 1 (1959): 150-57.

Zacher, Christian. *Curiosity and Pilgrimage*. Baltimore: Johns Hopkins UP, 1976.

Chaucer's Idea of a Canterbury Game_____

Glending Olson

The *Canterbury Tales* is a collection of narratives bound together in a frame that has two central features—a pilgrimage and a game. The pilgrimage is the outer framing device, the occasion for the gathering together of the company of storytellers; the game is a second, inner, framing device, the organizing principle that brings the stories into being. Chaucer did not have to have his pilgrims play a game in order to have them tell stories. Their prologues and tales could have emerged as part of conversation or debate or advice. Chaucer knew how the *Roman de la rose* incorporated lengthy discourses representing distinct points of view within a narrative structure. He knew the familiar didactic model of Gower's *Confessio amantis* and other story collections in which narratives function more or less as exemplary illustrations of general precepts. But he took the option Boccaccio took in the *Decameron*—he made the storytelling the playing of a game. And we need to think about the implications of that choice.

There are signs that the role of play and game in the *Canterbury Tales* is beginning to garner some overdue critical attention. For decades the dominant approaches rather ignored this central structural feature of the *Tales*, and the reasons are not far to seek. The kind of psychological, tale-teller inquiry we associate with Kittredge and Lumiansky wants to read the fictions as expressions of their narrators' personalities; it would naturally not emphasize the greater mediation between pilgrim-self and performance implicit in Chaucer's choice of a game structure. The allegorical approach associated with Robertson and Huppé fixes on the larger framing device of pilgrimage and finds it convenient to neglect the more obviously sportive and secular (though as I will show, far from amoral) game frame. And I suspect that for many critics of whatever persuasion the idea of game has seemed somehow essentially trivializing, conceding too much to the ghost of Matthew Arnold.

With some newer theory has come a more playful spirit, or at least a recognition that the game itself occupies a role in the *Tales* every bit as important as the pilgrimage. In two articles, Richard A. Lanham and Gabriel Josipovici established what should have been clear all along—that the framing narrative is permeated with references to play and game (the linking passages give us no such persistent foregrounding of pilgrimage). The critical conclusions they drew were based more on modern than on medieval views of play. Recently Carl Lindahl has explored the *Tales* in light of medieval festivity and Laura Kendrick in light of Bakhtin's idea of carnival and Freudian views of humor. Such ideas came to seem important to Donald Howard, as his discussion of the *Tales* in his biography of Chaucer attests.[1]

To this interest in the Canterbury game I add my own. It is an extension of some ideas I have presented elsewhere, and I refer readers to that book for documentation of certain basic points simply assumed here.[2] Chaucer's relationship to medieval notions of literary entertainment and recreation is so rich and complicated that it needs separate treatment beyond the few pages I gave it earlier solely in order to establish its continuity with a tradition. Toward that fuller treatment I aim now—first in this essay and subsequently in longer form, with more extensive documentation and critical discussion. My orientation is historical—I think that considering medieval views of play and game will give us a more comprehensive and nuanced understanding of the inner Canterbury frame than we presently have. Not that Huizinga, say, or Bakhtin is irrelevant; but there are medieval theories of play, too, and if we are going to think about the role of game in the *Canterbury Tales* we ought not exclude some ideas demonstrably a part of Chaucer's intellectual environment.

When Harry Bailly proposes, and the pilgrims accept, the playing of a game in order to provide comfort and mirth, the *Canterbury Tales* draws on a medieval understanding of the legitimacy and benefits of recreational play. That understanding, and its role in medieval thinking about literature conceived as a form of entertainment, was the subject of my earlier book. Here I want to explore in much more detail one aspect of that understanding and its relevance to Chaucer's collection. For the beginning of the *Canterbury Tales*, what we call Fragment I, is a sequence of storytelling that parallels directly a sequence of thoughts about play and players that was commonplace in the later Middle Ages. Chaucer's idea of the Canterbury game, though it ends in something very different, begins as an enactment of some Aristotelian distinctions.

* * *

The *Nicomachean Ethics* discusses a number of virtues, one of which is a virtue in regard to play or entertainment—*ludus* in Robert Grosseteste's translation, which was standard for the later Middle Ages. Chaucer (at least according to one interpretation of *LGW* F 165-66) knew the principle by which Aristotle defined his virtues and their corresponding vices: "vertu is the mene,/ As Etik seith."[3] Aristotle treats the virtues as means between extremes, one of excess, one of defect. Courage, for example, is the virtue in regard to fear—the mean between cowardice, excessive fear, and recklessness, the lack of fear even in situations where it would be appropriate. Liberality, the virtue in regard to the use of wealth, is the mean between the excess of prodigality and the defect of avarice, both of which sins Dante punishes in the fourth circle of *Inferno* and mentions again in connection with Statius in *Purgatorio* XXII. The mean in regard to play is *eutrapelia*, the excess *bomolochia*, the defect *agroica*—"wittiness," "buffoonery," and "boorishness" are the usual modern English translations, but the first of these is particularly inadequate to convey the resonance of the concept in medieval discussion, and I will keep the transliterated Greek as a key term.

Briefly, we can chart the late medieval dissemination of Aristotle's approach to play as follows. Grosseteste's complete Latin translation of the *Ethics* was made in 1246-47, supplemented by his translation of some early Greek scholia and some notes of his own. Shortly thereafter Albert the Great wrote a long commentary on it and later wrote a second. His student Thomas Aquinas, relying heavily on Albert's work, also wrote a commentary on the *Ethics* and subsequently incorporated Aristotelian ideas into his discussion of play in the *Summa theologica* (2-2, q.168). The texts of Albert and Aquinas contain nearly all of the thinking about the mean and extremes in regard to play that appeared in later treatises; their analyses and conclusions were variously abridged and combined by subsequent commentators. Material in the *Summa theologica*, particularly, influenced not only academic thinking but a host of later medieval works on morality intended for a less specialized audience.[4] Chaucer would not have had to go to scholastic commentaries in order to learn that eutrapelia was a mean between extremes; he could have found the idea in such places as Giles of Rome's *De regimine principium*, John of Freiburg's influential *Summa confessorum*, Dante's *Convivio*, and Robert Holcot's popular commentary on the book of Wisdom. We know he read at least portions of the latter two.

Listen to Aquinas discussing the *eutrapelus*, the man who plays virtuously:

[Aristotle says] that men who devote themselves to amusement in moderation are called witty (*eutrapeli*), as it were, good at turning because they becomingly give an amusing turn to what is said and done. . . . It is proper to men of this sort to narrate and listen to such amusing incidents as become a decent and liberal man who possesses a soul free from slavish passions. . . . it pertains to the mean habit of virtue to speak and listen to what is becoming in jesting.[5]

Moderation, propriety, decency in language—these are the features of one whose play is morally upright. Like Aristotle, Aquinas allows for some kinds of humorous insult or reproach, but it too must be "pleasing and polite" (1370). In the *Summa* Aquinas also calls the virtue *jucunditas*, as does Giles of Rome, thereby implicitly extending the range of the virtue beyond the narrow limits of jesting. *Eutrapelia* is not simply the ability to engage in witty repartee but a properly cheerful disposing of one's words and actions in the context of social conviviality and entertainment. An alphabetical summary of the ideas of the *Nicomachean Ethics* suggests this wider implication: "*Eutrapeli* are merry people, who act appropriately and pleasantly in social play and conversation."[6] There is even the possibility of instruction via amusement: Aquinas allows that some kinds of reproach may aim at "a man's correction" (1:370), and a later commentator, Petrus de Corveheda, claims that true *eutrapeli* intend their playing to have good, perhaps even morally beneficial, effects.[7]

The person who errs by excessive play is a *bomolochus* or buffoon. "These people lie in wait," says Aquinas,

> so they can pounce upon something to turn into a laugh. On this account persons of this kind are a nuisance because they want to make laughter out of everything. They make more effort to do this than to engage in becoming or polite conversation and avoid disturbing the man they heap with playful reproach. They would rather tell scandalous stories, even at the risk of offending others, than (not) cause men to laugh. (1:368)

Later Aquinas adds two important points concerning this vice: the buffoon "spares neither himself nor others in attempting to create laughter," and his speech goes beyond what a virtuous person would say (1:370). Brunetto Latini, working in this case not from Aristotle directly but from a Latin translation of an Arabic abridgment of the *Ethics*, calls the person who plays excessively a "jangler" and says that for the sake of laughter and play he derides himself, his wife, his sons, and everyone else.[8]

Many medieval commentators stress that the excess of the buffoon lies not just in the quantity of his playing, in his failure to observe the necessary subordination of entertainment to seriousness, but also in the nature of his play, particularly the use of foul language. Nicole Oresme's French translation of the *Ethics* gives an interesting contemporary example of such excess. In his discussion of proper and improper language in play Aristotle had alluded briefly to old and new Greek comedy, contrasting the greater obscenity of the former with the more refined innuendo of the latter. His meaning was not totally clear to medieval commentators, but most recognized a moral judgment being made in regard to the decency of language in some kind of performance or composition. In a gloss on this passage Oresme explains that Aristotle's use of the term "comedies" refers to "plays such as those where one person represents St. Paul, another Judas, another a hermit," and that such plays sometimes include vulgar language, improper and distasteful.[9] I take Oresme's present tense here to encompass contemporary as well as classical habits; his explication is telling not just for what it says about religious drama in his day but for its implicit conceptualization of performance within Aristotle's moral perspective on play; other such publicly presented narrative, whether enacted drama or recited tale, would logically fall in the same category due to the context of social entertainment. This passage supplements other evidence assembled in *Literature as Recreation* that shows the discussion of play in *Nicomachean Ethics* 4.8 to have been a central point of reference for making judgments about forms of public entertainment, some of which we now call literature.

And what of the vice that is defect? Aquinas explains:

> . . . men who never want to say anything funny and are disagreeable to the people who do . . . seem to be uncultured or boorish and coarse, like those who are not mellowed by amusing recreation. . . . [Such a person] is useless at these witty conversations. He contributes nothing to them but is disagreeable to everyone. He is vicious in that he completely abhors jest, which is necessary for human living as a kind of recreation. (I. 368-70)

Latini describes the boor as one who "always appears stern, with a pained expression, and does not enjoy himself with others, nor speak or associate with people having a good time" (204). The vice entails not merely lacking a sense of humor but lacking a capacity to participate in humanly necessary social pleasures. Albert the Great cites a line from Gregory's *Moralia* to help define the boor: anyone who cannot participate in social entertainment remains alone, living "bestialiter."[10] Social conviviality here seems to be an image of human community, as I think it is in the *Canterbury Tales*. The nature of one's play can be a measure of the nature of one's ability to participate in and contribute to the common good. It is significant that John Buridan discusses eutrapelia not only in his questions on the *Ethics* but in his questions on Aristotle's *Politics* as well, concluding that *eutrapeli* do have a place in a well-ordered community because of their usefulness in providing necessary recreation.[11]

The treatment of play I have been delineating is certainly not the only medieval thinking on the subject. But it is, I believe, the dominant learned *secular* tradition, and its very secularity is perhaps as significant for understanding its importance to the *Canterbury Tales* as are the more detailed parallels I discuss shortly. The fact is that most medieval thinking about play (granting the bias of the surviving texts) is fundamentally moral rather than psychological or anthropological. That does not mean that such thinking need always be intended moralistically, or that it does not include insights into play compatible with other approaches; but it does suggest the likelihood that medieval reflections on play would at least work out of a conceptual framework that concerns itself less with the nature of play than with its ethical or social propriety. In this regard Aristotle's mean and extremes fit compatibly with medieval *distinctiones* on play based on biblical usage, which generally recognized that some playing was spiritual, some was evil or diabolical, and some more neutrally human or recreational. The Aristotelian analysis could enter in to such thinking as a means for further discrimination within that third category.

Thus Robert Holcot, after a long discussion of the conditions that must obtain in order for recreational play to the virtuous, offers a typology of play based on Aquinas's *Sentences* commentary: there is a "ludus turpis et inhonestus" (such as the gentiles played in theaters and temples before their gods), a "ludus gaudii spiritualis" (such as David's dancing before the ark and Christian playing on Corpus Christi day), and a "ludus humane consolationis" whose mean is "eutropolia" [*sic*], exemplified in the Bible in Zacharias 8.5.[12] This passage is deservedly well-known because it suggests the possibility of an early date for some form of Corpus Christi drama, as Siegfried Wenzel has argued most forcefully. It is also interesting theoretically: first for its possible inclusion of the drama as a form of play judged by moral or spiritual rather than aesthetic criteria; second for the way its Christian perspective manages both to include and to delimit Aristotle's secular approach to play. Play that promotes human solace is the sphere in which the Aristotelian mean and extremes constitute a basis for judgment; beyond that sort of play lie other kinds conceived in a framework of Christian understanding. Chaucer's framing structure, the playing of a game while on a pilgrimage, establishes much the same dual focus: an arena of secular activity with its own conceptual criteria bounded by a more inclusive perspective that is spiritual rather than ethical.

The Canterbury storytelling begins as a game to provide "comfort" and "mirthe." That fact alone serves to establish an initial secular delimitation, though one with its own claims to integrity. And despite the drama of spontaneity—the Knight wins by luck, the Miller interrupts, the Reeve takes offense at the Miller's story—an ordering principle appears among the first three tales, which reveal three distinct responses to the game that correspond to the Aristotelian analysis of the mean and the extremes in playing.

Particularly when read retrospectively, the portraits in the General Prologue suggest a triangulation of Knight-Miller-Reeve in regard to their social speech. The Knight, described first, "nevere yet no vileynye ne sayde/ In all his lyf unto no maner wight" (I.70-71). The spectacular quadruple negative suggests possibly some prudishness but more probably the kind of decency in social behavior that was the subject of many regimens of princes and courtesy books in the fourteenth and fifteenth centuries. That social decency will be reflected in his tale, which for all its stylistic range never lapses into the "vileynye" of speech or action that abounds in the fabliaux. The Miller and Reeve appear near the very end of the portraits, in that closing collection of moral dwarfs among whom Chaucer disconcertingly puts himself. On the Miller's use of language: "His mouth as greet was as a greet forneys./ He was

a janglere and a goliardeys,/ And that was moost of synne and harlotries"
(I.559-61). We can see now some of the resonance of that word "janglere." In
Middle English it usually means someone who talks too much, often with implications of mischievous intent—gossiping, backbiting. But in Latini's
Tresor the French *jangleor*, from which the ME word is derived, refers specifically to the person excessive in play; and to further complicate the issue
jangleor and *jogleor* (entertainer), though etymologically distinct, are associated in Latini and in other texts.[13] In Middle English too "janglere" can refer
not just to excessive talkers but to more or less professional storytellers.
"Goliardeys," with its origins back to the legendary bishop Golias, patron of
all those tavern-haunting renegade clerics popularized in some of the
Carmina Burana, also has associations with publicly performed entertainment. The Miller likes to tell dirty stories, one of which we will be hearing,
and if "janglere" carries any of the resonance that it has in Brunetto Latini,
then Chaucer is not only describing Robin's inclinations as a speaker but giving us a particular conceptual framework for thinking about them.

Concerning the Reeve's speech the narrator says nothing. Oswald's medium of expression is the account book, the financial reckoning. His tight-
lipped manipulation inspires dread. To compare with the Knight's verbal propriety and the Miller's indecent verbal extravagance we have only, appropriately, negative evidence. The Reeve's social engagement restricts itself to
matters of business. He lives apparently alone, apart from others in the shad-
ows of the trees on the heath. He rides at the back of the pilgrimage "evere"
(I.622)—an emblem not only of his opposition to the Miller, who is leading
the company out of town with his noisy bagpipes, but of his alienation from
the group itself and their conviviality.

These characteristics delineated in the General Prologue manifest themselves in the speech-acts that make up the bulk of the first fragment. Particularly interesting is the Knight's reaction when he discovers that he is to tell the
first tale:

> And whan this goode man saugh that it was so,
> As he that wys was and obedient
> To kepe his foreward by his free assent,
> He seyde, "Syn I shal bigynne the game,
> What, welcome be the cut, a Goddes name!
> Now lat us ryde, and herkneth what I seye."
> And with that word we ryden forth oure weye,
> And he bigan with right a myrie cheere
> His tale anon, and seyde as ye may heere.
>
> (I.850-58)

The Knight is first of all a good man who has agreed to play a game, and he honors that agreement. The logic of his thinking in lines 853-54 merits notice: his welcoming of the cut follows upon his selection as the one to play first. I think the most probable interpretation of these lines is that the Knight is not necessarily eager to tell the first story, but having won the cut he *then* conducts himself in a manner suitable to the sense of "disport" that is appropriate to the purposes of the game. He has agreed to play, has found himself scheduled to lead off, and thus speaks according to the proper demands of recreational play. In other words, he is eutrapelic. He takes on a "myrie cheere," becomes *jucundus*. His geniality is in fact an aspect of his moral goodness, the observation of the mean in regard to the social play that the company has committed itself to. And as we know, the Knight continues to support the game and its recreational goals subsequently—in his reconciliation of Pardoner and Host and in his cutting off of the Monk's depressing tragedies. He is as loyal in the company's play as in his lords' wars.

The Aristotelian analysis of play describes human behavior, not stories, and I certainly do not claim that the game-structure of Fragment I in any way "accounts for" all that is in the tales themselves. I do think, though, that it can and should be enrolled as a factor in interpretation, and that in the case of the Knight's Tale it suggests a rationale for some features of the story that have been found problematic. One is the pervasive amount of *occupatio*, which works to keep us aware of the Knight's solicitous concern for proper behavior as he plays the game: "I wol nat letten eek noon of this route;/ Lat every felawe telle his tale aboute" (I.889-90). Places where his tone seems overly clinical or even flip may reflect a kind of detachment necessary to give this story, riddled with chaos and tragedy, a tone suitable to its final focus on the joy that can follow woe. This is not to say that the Knight's attitude is Chaucer's or is not subject to irony: it is to say that the tale, considered as the earnest effort at a morally beneficial, "cheerfully turned" contribution to the game, may not be the uncontrolled stylistic hodgepodge some revisionist criticism contends it is.

Even Harry Bailly, whose literary tastes are hardly aristocratic, appreciates that with the Knight's Tale "the game is wel bigonne" (I.3117). He turns to the Monk but gets instead the Miller, the drunken buffoon who has seen his chance to turn the ideals of the first story into laughter. The tone of The Miller's Tale is one of cheerful ridicule: Alisoun turns Absolon's earnest into a "jape," says the Miller at one point (I.3390), and later the townspeople turn John the carpenter's punishment "unto a jape" (I.3842). The tale mocks everyone, all for the sake of laughter. The Miller also derides himself and his wife, as Latini says of the *bomolochus*, intimating humorously in his prologue that as long as he can find "Goddes foyson" at home he will not worry about whether others are being equally well nourished there (I.3158-66). All is grist for his jangling, and the jangling emerges in "cherles termes" (I.3917), the kind of vulgarity universally scorned in moral treatments of proper verbal play.

Following upon the Knight's noble entertainment and the Miller's churlish frivolity comes the Reeve's vicious retaliation. He is unable to let pass the swipe at carpenters that is merely a portion of the Miller's repertoire of what Aquinas calls "playful reproach." Though opinion is not unanimous, in general the pilgrims laugh at The Miller's Tale. Only Oswald grieves at it and then spews out a morbidly self-conscious discussion of his old age. It is the first example on the pilgrimage of "sermonyng" (I.3899), preaching, which throughout *The Canterbury Tales* indicates discourse opposed to the recreative tale-telling the pilgrims have agreed to engage in. The Reeve is a sermonizer, deadly serious about everything; amusement has not mellowed him, nor humor moderated his infinite acerbity. He really is not capable of play, and his tale is so obviously an attack upon the Miller that it seems outside the spirit of the game.

Thinking of the Miller and the Reeve as excess and defect restores a medieval perspective that Chaucer himself proclaims just before the two fabliaux are told: "The Miller is a cherl; ye knowe wel this./ So was the Reve eek and othere mo,/ And harlotrie they tolden bothe two" (I.3182-84). These lines group the two together because they are equidistant from the conventionally proper attitude toward the storytelling recreation. I think Chaucer makes the Miller less distasteful than the Reeve, more in keeping with the sportive circumstances of the storytelling, in contrast to many commentaries on eutrapelia that treat the buffoon as more reprehensible than the boor since seriousness is the more proper human condition than playfulness. But we should not simply rank the first three storytellers on a descending scale of decency in language or outlook, as the prevailing critical consensus on Fragment I holds. Chaucer distinguishes them first in terms of a two-part hierarchy, mean and extremes, gentil and churls, and only secondarily in terms of the differing characteristics of each extreme. I hasten to add that I do not see this conceptual pattern as allegorically reductionistic—the Reeve, for example, is not only Aristotle's boor but is also a choleric Norfolker. But the presence of details that "explain" the Reeve's temperament in terms of occupation, or physiology, or regional stereotyping need not mean that other more philosophically and ethically charged patterns are not also present. Paul A. Olson has argued that the Knight-Miller-Reeve sequence reenacts the triangulation of Theseus-Palamon-Arcite in The Knight's Tale, which is itself an exemplification of familiar medieval moral/psychological categories: reason, concupiscibility, irascibility.[14] I think those categories probably lie behind the rather more particular pattern I suggest, which seems most germane because it operates at that precise nexus of character and storytelling that is such an important feature of the *Canterbury Tales*.

The organizing principle of virtue and vices in regard to play can help illuminate logic and motive within the first fragment. It can also help us see how the action at the beginning of the *Tales* functions as a natural introduction to the entire work. Having decided to tell stories en route to Canterbury, the pilgrims begin in a way that we can recognize as staking out, so to speak, the directions that the game can take. It would have been as natural for Chaucer to think of mean and extremes as a starting point for the Canterbury stories as it was for Dante to think of mean and extremes when he came to the subject of avarice. The first three tales open up the collection and foreshadow, broadly, the range of responses to follow. There will be those pilgrims like the Knight who play the game as decently as they can, alert to their social obligation and to the kind of pleasure it is proper for a liberal person to offer. The Clerk is one such, certainly, as are the Franklin and Man of Law—these three among Anne Middleton's "new men," self-conscious about the ways in which stories can claim to please and profit.[15] The Miller's exuberant irreverence portends the Shipman's fabliau and, more significantly, the outrageous yet compelling Wife of Bath, who as Lee Patterson has argued occupies an analogous structural position of subversive play following upon a tale of authority.[16] The Reeve's performance anticipates that of those like the Friar and Summoner, who would turn an opportunity for communal recreation into a vehicle for their own personal, private hatreds. I am certainly not trying to pigeonhole all the storytellers into these three classes, for Chaucer goes far beyond them. But they are a convenient and suggestive structure to begin with.

Nor does Chaucer's exploration of how people play end with The Reeve's Tale. Both The Cook's Prologue and his fragmentary story deal principally with questions of play and truth in a way that is intellectually related to the game structure of the first fragment. Grosseteste's Latin translation of the *Ethics* introduces a fourth type of player into its chapter on eutrapelia, even though there is no mention of such a type in Aristotle: "Bomolochus autem minor est derisore"—the buffoon, the excessive player, is less wicked than the mocker.[17] Aquinas explains: "the mocker tries to put another to shame while the buffoon does not aim at this but only at getting a laugh" (1:370).

Mockery lies just at the borderline between game and earnest. On the one hand its appearance (by mistake) in the *Ethics* seems to make it a species of excessive play. On the other, its intentions are injurious rather than playful—it uses play for (earnestly) malicious purposes. Robert Holcot links *bomolochi* and *derisores* together as improper players when he discusses play, but when he examines sins of speech he mentions *derisio* only, ignoring Aristotle's defect and excess in regard to play.[18] The interest of the commentators in the relationship between play and mockery receives dramatic illustration when the Cook and Host exchange words. And of course, as Carl Lindahl has shown, that interest is not simply an academic and theoretical one; insult, defamation, was an important legal and social issue in Chaucer's day, and it is hard to imagine anyone in a court circle not sensitive to the power of language to cast suspicion, to affect reputation, even—or perhaps especially—when it appears in the guise of playfulness.

When the Cook proposes to continue the storytelling game with a "litel jape that fil in oure citee" (I.4343), it is quite clear that he wishes to continue in the same vein as the two previous speakers of "harlotrye." At this point, though, his speech appears no more degenerate or unrefined than the Miller's or Reeve's, and in fact his request to tell the next tale is rather more polite and respectful of the rules of the game than either Robin's interruption or Oswald's grouching. It is the Host who surprises us, by telling the Cook that his tale needs to be good because his cuisine hasn't been. After sundry claims about the culinary and sanitary defects of the Cook's operation, Harry Bailly ends his gibing as abruptly as he started: "But yet I pray thee, be nat wroth for game;/ A man may seye ful sooth in game and pley" (I.4354-55). To which the Cook responds with another proverb, "Sooth pley, quaad pley," and tells the Host not to be "wrooth" if he subsequently should tell a story of an innkeeper. V. A. Kolve, in an important revaluation of the Cook's performance, reads this exchange as "bantering," intended by both participants "to amuse the company, not to defame each other's person," and his interpretation is a valuable corrective to the easy identification of Chaucer's point of view with the Host's.[19] I think there is an edge to the banter that he neglects. Harry's accusations come out of thin air—nothing prepares us for them except perhaps the detail of the Cook's mormal in the General Prologue, yet that defect, unlike the Miller's garrulousness and the Reeve's irascibility, has not been emphasized in the behavior of the pilgrim himself in the framing story.

The banter is public, and it ends in the Cook's laughter. But it introduces the problem of where joking stops and insult starts, the problem that concerned commentators on Aristotle's discussion of the morality of playful speech. At this point Harry Bailly becomes, perhaps, a *derisor*, a mocker, who, as Aquinas says, under cover of play seeks to embarrass someone else; because of the privileged status of speech made in play, his victims will not actually lose their reputation (a fact the mocker understands), but they will fear such a loss since the charges have been made public and could well be reasserted outside the special context of "game" which allows them to be at once both entertained and dismissed.

Or perhaps the Host's intentions remain purely playful, and his insults meant solely for amusement. Even if this were the case, he has approached the boundary at which it becomes difficult to know whether his raillery aims at *contemptus* or *ludus*, and the Cook's response is intended to alert Harry Bailly that he is in danger of stepping over into territory where claims of play can no longer provide moral protection. The proverb he cites may tacitly acknowledge that the Host's mockery has some truthful basis, but its chief purpose is to make him understand that his own verbal play at this point is on the verge of becoming the "quaad pley," the *malus ludus*, of the *derisor*; and his threatened retaliation is a reminder of the practical consequences of turning play into insult.

The Cook's Prologue, then, tells us as much about the Host as about the Cook, and while there is no developed equation of either character with any traditional type of player of games, the issue raised in the exchange is a logical extension of the game given medieval thinking about playful speech. We have seen the mean and the extremes in regard to play, and now Chaucer brings to the fore one important aspect of excessive play not yet considered, the problem of drawing the line between game and earnest when playful language impugns someone else. The exchange occurs in a prologue that promises the telling of a "jape" in an atmosphere of "joye" and coarse hilarity, which is Chaucer's dramatic equivalent of the commentary treatment of mockery in the context of excessive play, whose chief representative in the first fragment is the Miller. The Miller has insulted the Reeve only as part of a desire to reduce everything to laughter. The Host's more pointed attack on the Cook claims similar status as "game and pley" yet is of a different order; it is what scholastic commentators, I think, would have defined as *derisio* rather than *bomolochia*.

What remains of The Cook's Tale explores in a different way the tension between play and seriousness established in the Prologue. We meet Perkyn Revelour, who at least initially seems to evoke the atmosphere of The Miller's Tale: he has something of Alisoun's coltish manner and of Absolon's tastes in entertainment—he is always singing, hopping, leaping, dancing, playing (I.4375-84). But as the story develops, Perkyn's play begins to appear both more insistent and more insidious. It usurps his work time rather than supporting it with recreational refreshment; it includes dicing, the classic evil game of medieval moral treatises, which in turn leads to the serious crime of theft. His playing becomes "revel," "riot," and finally the master victualer releases the unreliable apprentice from his service.

In only fifty-eight lines The Cook's Tale presents a view of play that is quite complex—the fragment, as Kolve has argued, is certainly not the unremitting portrait of debased life that many critics have taken it to be. A variety of terms ("pleyen," "disport," "revel," "riot") and a variety of kinds of play (dancing, singing, public merrymaking, tavern-haunting, dicing, and by implication activities "paramour") appear in a rapid sequence that in general turns progressively more disreputable but that retains a certain ambiguity throughout. The fragment's antepenultimate line says that Perkyn's friend "lovede dys, and revel, and disport" (I.4420), a strangely ameliorative sequence of nouns given the context—"disport," after all, is the term Harry Bailly uses to define the legitimate benefits of the Canterbury game, and elsewhere in Chaucer it has quite positive associations. The effect is meant to be deliberately disquieting, I think, and its implications extend beyond the tale itself to reflect on the previous fabliaux and their framing action, in which the Miller's play and the Reeve's earnest were so readily distinguishable. The Cook's Tale complicates such distinctions by presenting play action that is sometimes buoyant and recreative and other times anti-social and destructive and by making it difficult to say exactly when one sort becomes the other, when "disport" turns into "revel" or "revel" into "riot." The tale reenacts the problem that The Cook's Prologue presented in terms of playful speaking rather than playful actions. In either case, whether the playing is in words or deeds (*dicta vel facta*, in the language of the commentaries), the moral issue concerned medieval thinkers and writers because like Freud they knew that jokes express more than themselves, like Natalie Zemon Davis they knew that forms of play, even when serving overtly only to recreate or let off steam, have serious social implications.[20]

The appearance of the Cook at the end of the first fragment, then, follows logically upon the previous sequence of tale-telling if we see it in light of medieval discussions of the morality of play: after presenting the mean and the extremes, Chaucer takes up the question of distinguishing between excessive play and mockery, the point at which distinctions between play and seriousness become most difficult and yet most necessary to make. This pattern, I would stress, works more descriptively than normatively. The first fragment is proleptic: it introduces us to a range of attitudes toward the game that will become ever more complicated as the *Canterbury Tales* progresses. In this regard The Cook's Prologue and Tale in particular point toward some of the most problematic and fascinating of the Canterbury performances, as some of Chaucer's richest characters, notably the Wife and the Pardoner, force us to look very closely at the ways in which their playing and their truthtelling are related.

Throughout the *Tales* the game is usually the norm. In places Chaucer reminds us, in one way or another, that beyond the game lies the pilgrimage—perhaps most obviously in the Pardoner's performance and exchange with the Host, where the breakdown of social agreeableness occurs in a context of phony promises of what should be a goal of the pilgrimage itself, spiritual absolution. But such episodes are the exception rather than the rule, though perhaps all the more telling for their infrequency; for the most part of the linking passages are filled with the language of game and obligation, and with Harry Bailly's energetic and often overbearing presence as director of entertainment.[21] But toward the end of the work—and here I evade a variety of questions concerning order and closure—something happens to the game. At its fullest this development encompasses the last three fragments.[22] I want to mention, rather briefly, some aspects of Fragment IX only, which present a deliberately disturbing recapitulation of some of the central features of the framing action in Fragment I. Part of Chaucer's idea of the Canterbury game is its degeneration; The Manciple's Prologue enacts such debasement of social conviviality and playful speech as to make us uneasy with the game as a sufficient ordering principle, and correspondingly his tale ends in admonitions not to tell stories of any sort.

The contrasts with the first fragment are quite specific. Although drunkenness appears throughout the pilgrimage and tales, drunkenness as it relates to storytelling is foregrounded most extensively in Fragments I and IX. The Miller's interruption is clearly due in part to his inebriation, yet whatever loss of control and decorum it implies in his case, he at least remains articulate, a participant in the game. The Cook's drunkenness in Fragment IX results in silence, sleep, nonparticipation. It is a more extreme version of the loss of reason that inebriation causes. Both Miller and Cook are "pale" because of drink (I.3120, IX.20), but the physical symptoms in the Cook's case are developed further to include glazed eyes and foul breath. A single line informs us that the Miller can scarcely keep his balance on horseback (I.3121). The Cook's transportation problems get substantially more attention: first Harry's notice that he is about to fall off his horse, then the Manciple's allusion to his jousting at the quintain, and finally his response to the Manciple's insults, a wordless angry twisting of the head that sends him off his horse into the mire.

Whatever the reasons for the incompleteness of his tale at the start of the game, whatever the order in which Chaucer actually composed the scenes, the contrast between the Cook of Fragment I and the Cook of Fragment IX is striking and indicative of the substantially different view of Canterbury conviviality in the later fragments. The Cook now becomes the featured nonspeaker among the pilgrims, excused by the Host from participation in the game on the grounds of inebriation. His fall from his horse is the most potent image in The Manciple's Prologue of the social behavior of the company having gone awry. In the muck lies the "hevy dronken cots" of a Canterbury pilgrim. Images of death, judgment, and hell flicker throughout the Prologue— the thief who might come upon the Cook, the association of his open mouth with hellmouth.[23] Whereas the Miller's drunkenness leads to a story that prompts laughter, the Cook's leads only to "lakke of speche" and reminders of mortality. Whereas the Host speaks disdainfully of Robin's condition in Fragment I, in Fragment IX he laughs "wonder loude" at the situation and offers a paean to alcohol: good drink will turn rancor into "accord and love"; Bacchus can "turnen ernest into game" (IX.95-100). The language here echoes, disconcertingly, what had earlier been the province of the storytelling. In Fragment I the narrator had warned us not to "maken ernest of game" (I.3186) in regard to the Miller's and Reeve's fabliaux; the pilgrims had "been acorded" (I.818) to the Host's proposal for a game of stories to provide pleasure. In Fragment IX alcohol replaces storytelling as the source of recreation and harmony, and the master of revels who scorned the Miller's drunkenness now worships at the altar of Bacchus.

In the first fragment the Cook had warned the Host about the dangers of play that comes too close to the truth and in so doing had exposed a problem in the social uses of language well known to medieval commentators and moralists. In the ninth fragment too the Cook is a victim of insult, but here with no such teasing ambiguity as in his exchange with Harry Bailly. The Manciple "openly," to use the Host's own terminology (IX.70), reproves the Cook for his drunkenness and hurls the kind of invective at him that Carl Lindahl has shown is extreme in the rhetoric of Chaucer's churls, not to mention dangerous in real life (93-96), and that the Parson condemns as fostering disaccord and anger (X.621-30). Only when the Host reminds the Manciple that the Cook might similarly defame him does he reverse himself, suddenly announce "I seyde it in my bourde," and offer more wine to the Cook to placate him. What in the first fragment is a comic but subtle exploration of the problem of determining a borderline between play and insult, in which Harry self-consciously advertises his mockery as play, becomes in the ninth an instance of insult that, only in response to someone else's warning, attempts cynically and transparently to cover itself as jest. The secular norms of play no longer function as a governing communal standard but appear now as merely a convenient excuse for verbal attack, a self-interested afterthought.

Aristotelian, recreational justifications of play are by definition self-limiting. When play becomes excessive or offensive it can no longer claim the moral or social legitimacy extended to it via the *Nichomachean Ethics*. The context for thinking about such speech and action might well then shift to a different and more familiar kind of moral perspective, one we see emerging in the course of Fragment IX—first in the degeneration and thus the delegitimizing of the secular conviviality epitomized by the playing of a game, then in the fate of the crow punished for speaking imprudently, and finally in the Manciple's concluding moralizing, a harangue on the theme of "keep wel thy tonge" (IX.319, 333, 362). The language at the end of Fragment IX is not the language of Aristotelian commentary on play, not the language of game and social contract that has been dominant throughout the *Tales*—it is rather the language of Christian commentary on the sins of the tongue and on the virtues of *custodia linguae*.[24] The Manciple's Prologue begins with an image of the Cook's yawning open mouth that the Manciple asks him to "Hoold cloos"

(IX.37), and his tale ends with an image of teeth and lips "wall[ing] a tonge" (IX.323); in a sense the whole fragment enacts the closing of a mouth, the shutting down of speech in and for "compaignye."

As we have seen, the Aristotelian framework is a view of speech that accommodates literature as a social phenomenon. Without the category of eutrapelic play, whatever Aristotle's original notions about its range of applicability, medieval thinkers found room for those kinds of lyric and narrative that give public pleasure. The Christian tradition of the sins of the tongue has no such comparable category. Playful speech, words and deeds that provide pleasure and recreation, are subsumed without a strict logic that forces all language either into words of morality and devotion or words of worldly vanity. Yet in a sense that difference, though it is thrust upon as almost brutally in Fragment IX, has been implicitly a factor all along in understanding the *Canterbury Tales* insofar as the double frame of a game played on a pilgrimage has always allowed for, and sometimes actively encouraged, reflection on the relationship of the one to the other.

This is where Chaucer, though he followed the *Decameron* in choosing to incorporate his stories into the playing of a game, parts company from Boccaccio; and Donald Howard has written acutely about this difference:

> The frame [of the *Decameron*] puts a parenthesis around the world of story: the stories are told in an aura of moral neutrality. The frame (the escape from the plague) is static, and as an image pessimistic. But in the *Canterbury Tales* the frame of the pilgrimage to Canterbury (and the Heavenly Jerusalem) is dynamic, as an image optimistic: and the inner form, the storytelling game, is not an escape—it is what reveals the darker side of human nature. . . .[25]

The *Decameron* begins and ends with the author's voice explaining the conditions under which his collection of fictions claims value. The stories are for idle ladies; they will provide pleasure and profit *if* they are read in the appropriate circumstances; and so on. The *Canterbury Tales* in effect makes Boccaccio's authorial commentary a part of the drama. The very efforts at isolation of a particular arena for fiction that Howard, and earlier Singleton, argued as central to the *Decameron* become themselves subject to scrutiny in Chaucer's collection. He is not content to let Aristotelian and scholastic ideas about permissible play and legitimate recreation suffice.

What he creates instead, his idea of the Canterbury game, is an image of social and secular conviviality that establishes itself as a norm for most of the pilgrimage but ultimately degenerates in a way that calls into question its adequacy as a means of communication. What he creates is an image not just of how fictions function within society but how social discourse operates within and moves between the secular and the sacred. There is no simple formula to explain how the *Canterbury Tales* enacts that movement, particularly at the end. The game as initially established provides a set of respectable social norms, though easily subject to abuse or disruption. Occasionally a passage reminds us of what lies beyond the game. In Fragment IX the behavior of the company turns cynical and offensive, and in Fragment X the Parson speaks with hostility toward the telling of fables. He seems to reject the game, to point to another kind of discourse. But his speaking too is a *tale*, and for all his self-separation from what has preceded, the pilgrims agree that he should end the storytelling; they see his particular kind of wisdom as appropriate, not discontinuous. The Parson's Tale is both somehow within and beyond the game, and in spite of what happens in Fragment IX the structure implies that there is at least some common ground between the earlier fictions and his own "meditacioun." We know that Boccaccio's brigata takes time out from storytelling to pray and reflect on religious matters, but we do not hear the prayers and meditations because they are not part of the game. The final complexity of Chaucer's Canterbury game is the difficult of knowing when it's over, of knowing, even in the face of his Retraction, how sharply to distinguish the worldly vanity from the devotion.

From *The Idea of Medieval Literature: New Essays on Chaucer and Medieval Culture in Honor of Donald R. Howard*, edited by James M. Dean and Christian K. Zacher (1992), pp. 72-90. Copyright © 1992 by Associated University Presses. Reprinted by permission of Associated University Presses.

Notes

1. Lanham, "Game, Play, and High Seriousness in Chaucer's Poetry," *English Studies* 48 (1967): 1-24; Josipovici, "Fiction and Game in the *Canterbury Tales*," *Critical Quarterly* 7 (1965): 185-97; Lindahl, *Earnest Games: Folkloric Patterns in the Canterbury Tales* (Bloomington: Indiana Univ. Press, 1987); Kendrick, *Chaucerian Play: Comedy and Control in the Canterbury Tales* (Berkeley and Los Angeles: Univ. of California Press, 1988); Howard, *Chaucer: His Life, His Works, His World* (New York: Dutton, 1987), pp. 421-26.

2. Olson, *Literature as Recreation in the Later Middle Ages* (Ithaca: Cornell Univ. Press, 1982).

3. All Chaucer quotations are from *The Riverside Chaucer*, 3rd ed., gen. ed. Larry D. Benson (Boston: Houghton Mifflin; 1987).

4. For the history of the Latin text of the *Ethics* and the medieval commentary tradition, see the introduction to Aristotle, *L'Ethique à Nicomaque*, trans. R. A. Gauthier and J. Y. Jolif, 2 vols. in 4 (Louvain: Publications Universitaires, 1970), 1.1.111-46, and Georg Wieland, "The Reception and Interpretation of Aristotle's *Ethics*," *The Cambridge History of Later Medieval Philosophy*, edited by N. Kretzmann et al. (Cambridge: Cambridge Univ. Press, 1982), pp. 657-72. On the influence of Aquinas's *Summa* see Martin Grabmann, "Das Weiterleben und Weiterwirken des moraltheologischen Schrifttums des hl. Thomas von Aquin im Mittelalter," *Divus Thomas* 25 (1947): 3-28.

5. *Commentary on the Nicomachean Ethics*, trans. C. I. Litzinger, 2 vols. (Chicago: Regnery, 1964), 1:368-69.

6. "Iocundi uocantur eutrapeli, qui conuenienter et delectabiliter se habent in ludis et conuersacionibus hominum." *Tabula super decem libros ethicorum.* Cambridge: Gonville and Caius College MS 462/735, f. 29v.

7. "Eutrapeli ueri sunt homines intendentes ludum ad bonum et ad bonos mores." *Sententia declarata super librum Ethicorum.* Vatican City: Vatican Library MS Urbin. lat. 222, f. 251r.

8. "Gengleour est celui ki gengle entre les gens a ris et a gieu, et moke soi et sa feme et ses fiz et tous autres." *Li Livres dou Tresor,* ed. Francis J. Carmody, Univ. of California Publications in Modern Philology, vol. 22 (Berkeley and Los Angeles: Univ. of California Press, 1948), p. 204.

9. "Il entent ici par comedies aucuns gieux comme sont ceulz ou. i. homme represente Saint Pol, l'autre Judas, l'autre un hermite, et dit chascun son personnage. . . . Et aucunes fois en telz giex l'en dit de laides paroles, ordes injurieuses et deshonestes." *Le Livre de Ethiques,* ed. A. D. Menut (New York: Stechert, 1940), p. 271.

10. Albertus Magnus, *Super ethica commentum et quaestiones,* ed. W. Kübel, *Opera omnia 14/1,* fasc. 1 (Münster: Aschendorff, 1968), p. 297.

11. Johannes Buridanus, *Quaestiones super octo libros Politicorum Aristotelis* (Paris, 1513; reprint, Frankfurt: Minerva, 1969), ff. 89r-v.

12. Robert Holkott, *Super libros sapientiae* (Hagenau, 1494; reprint, Frankfurt: Minerva, 1974), lectio 172D. For a better text see Siegfried Wenzel, "An Early Reference to a Corpus Christi Play," *Modern Philology* 74 (1977): 390. I discuss *distinctiones* on play in more detail in a forthcoming article, "Plays as Play."

13. Raleigh Morgan, Jr., "Old French *jogleor* and Kindred Terms. Studies in Mediæval Romance Lexicology," *Romance Philology* 7 (1953-54): 290-91, 304-5.

14. Olson, *The Canterbury Tales and the Good Society* (Princeton: Princeton Univ. Press, 1986), pp. 70-71.

15. Middleton, "Chaucer's 'New Men' and the Good of Literature in the *Canterbury Tales,*" in *Literature and Society,* ed. Edward W. Said (Baltimore: The Johns Hopkins Univ. Press, 1980), pp. 15-56.

16. Patterson, "'No man his reson herde': Peasant Consciousness, Chaucer's Miller, and the Structure of the *Canterbury Tales,*" *South Atlantic Quarterly* 86 (1987): 457-95.

17. The Latin text of Aristotle is in Albertus Magnus, 297.

18. Holkott, *Super libros sapientiae,* lectiones 172D and 27A.

19. Kolve, *Chaucer and the Imagery of Narrative: The First Five Canterbury Tales* (Stanford, Calif.: Stanford Univ. Press, 1984), p. 267.

20. Davis, "The Reasons of Misrule," *Society and Culture in Early Modern France* (Stanford, Calif.: Stanford Univ. Press, 1975), pp. 97-123.

21. See Kendrick, *Chaucerian Play,* 102-15, for discussion of the Host as a master of revels and Lord of Misrule.

22. See James M. Dean, "Dismantling the Canterbury Book," *PMLA* 100 (1985): 746-62, who cites previous work on the question of closure in Fragments VIII-X.

23. Rodney Delasanta, "Penance and Poetry in the *Canterbury Tales,*" *PMLA* 93 (1978): 245; Roy J. Pearcy, "Does the Manciple's Prologue Contain a Reference to Hell's Mouth?" *English Language Notes* 11 (1974): 167-75.

24. V. J. Scattergood, "The Manciple's Manner of Speaking," *Essays in Criticism* 24 (1974): 124-46.

25. Howard, "Fiction and Religion in Boccaccio and Chaucer," *Journal of the American Academy of Religion* 47 (1979), Supplement: 320. Cf. Charles S. Singleton, "On *Meaning* in the *Decameron,*" *Italica* 21 (1944): 117-24.

The Meaning of Chaucer's *Knight's Tale*_____

Douglas Brooks and Alastair Fowler

I

The critical problem presented by *The Knight's Tale* is still the simple primary one of interpretation. What is the tale about? Most readers and critics agree that it cannot be regarded as a simple external narrative, after the manner of much of Boccaccio's *Teseida*. Its psychology seems too debatable for that, its descriptive passages too powerful and richly symbolic. Yet the difficulties of deciding what forms of organization Chaucer has added—whether philosophical, moral, or psychological—have proved formidable. Indeed, one of the best of the poem's critics, Charles Muscatine, has been provoked into cutting the gordian knot by asking the more radical question, Is the tale about anything? And he gives the answer that 'the *Knight's Tale* is essentially neither a story, nor a static picture, but a poetic pageant, and that all its materials are organized and contributory to a complex design expressing the nature of the noble life'.[1] While admiring Muscatine's sure sense of the tale's ceremonial gravity and nobility, we cannot rest content with a description that would apply equally well to so many other literary works. The description is hard to quarrel with, but only because it is too broad to have a disprovable content. Every romance expresses the nature of the noble life. Besides, the detachment of texture from subject postulated by Muscatine is altogether too Mannerist to be possible at this date. We may reasonably expect an early Renaissance narrative work, and specifically a work of Chaucer's, to have subject, theme and story, and a poetic impact closely related to these elements. This is so with the other *Canterbury Tales* and it is so with *The Knight's Tale*.

The primary problem of interpretation presents itself in practice as three specific difficulties in reading the poem. First, seeing the meaning and full relevance to the human action of the mythological episodes (2438-78, 2663-70). The problem here is not rendered any the less acute by our knowledge that these passages are largely original with Chaucer. Secondly, seeing the relevance of the elaborate description of the champion kings Lygurge and Emetreus, who support Palamon and Arcite in the tournament. True, W. C. Curry has shown that the champion kings have pronounced physiognomical characteristics, such as would be produced by the influence of the two maleficent planetary deities.[2] But to say that Lygurge is Saturnian and Emetreus Martian does not apparently help our understanding of the tale as a whole. And, indeed, Muscatine, in desperation, falls back on a simpler consensus view: for him the 'contribution to the surface narrative' of the portraits of Emetreus and Lygurge is 'slight'—'the imagery is organized around no central conception of personality, but rather connotes the magnificence that befits nobility'.[3]

Thirdly, and most crucially, there is the difficulty of distinguishing between Palamon and Arcite, who seem so alike in terms of ordinary moral and psychological characterization. H. N. Fairchild's schematic contrast between a contemplative Palamon and an active Arcite has not met with much acceptance. In fact some critics, taking advantage of the slenderness of naturalistic characterization, have actually stood Fairchild's evaluation on its head and defended Arcite.[4] J. R. Hulbert, however, finds the poem defective in character altogether: he sees it as posing a courtly *demande d'amour* such as no modern reader can take seriously. Who cares which hero wins Emelye? Subsequent criticism, though taking the tale more seriously, has in different ways minimized its heroes' moral and psychological differences. Muscatine goes so far as to hail 'the equalization of Palamon and Arcite' as Chaucer's 'crowning modification' of the *Teseida*, allowing a formal symmetry that he regards as the English poem's principal source of satisfaction.[5] Even D. W. Robertson's *A Preface to Chaucer*, generally eager to restore the moral and theological significances of which previous criticism emptied Chaucer's poetry, makes no distinction between Palamon and Arcite, except a little in the extent of their corruption: Arcite suffers from the disease of love and its consequent 'manye', while 'Palamon's condition differs only in degree', so that the tale offers no subject for dramatic identification.[6] But we may suppose that, if Palamon and Arcite were always indistinguishable, the tale must have been unsatisfactory and puzzling to its first readers too.

Yet *The Knight's Tale* remains a good, perhaps a great, poem. Can a literary work whose intention is so doubtful deserve such an estimate? Only if the import and meaning were formerly clearer—potentially, at least—than they have since become. It need not follow that the clearer meaning is recoverable. *Volat irrevocabile.* But in this case, fortunately, Chaucer's consistency, unity, even clarity, can be vindicated. From an examination of descriptive details (more often significant than not, in his work) underlying schemes of thought once taken for granted but now obscure can be reconstructed. In relation to these reconstructed schemes the particular problems mentioned above are resolved and the different parts of the poem seen to be meaningfully articulated. We propose a new interpretation starting from two assumptions: first, that Chaucer's poem is organized in the early Renaissance manner, with details belonging harmoniously to an overall simple unity of meaning and form; secondly, that Curry's work on the champion kings carries an ineluctable implication—the tale's psychological content must be expressed through emblematic symbolism rather than naturalistic characterization.

II

The bearing of the mythological episode depends on a system of corre-spondences between the tale's planetary deities and human characters. Chau-cer's point is that these deities do not merely influence human affairs sporadi-cally or at random: they have each constant protégés under their special patronage. The decorative programmes of the three temples at the lists draw attention to this in a very direct way, in fact, for in each Chaucer has made use of the familiar convention whereby a planetary deity's influence was shown by portraying a group of his 'children'—that is, those carrying on the trades, professions and activities under his patronage.[7] And when, in the same tem-ples, the two lovers and their lady make their critical intercessions on the morning of the tournament, each displays a devotion too intimate to be a mat-ter of casual whim.

The correspondence most obvious in its main lines, yet also the most com-plex, is that between Jupiter and Theseus. Theseus, 'lord and governour' of Athens,[8] throughout the tale dominates the political order, manifesting in turn the qualities of a just ruler and a wise king, as the Knight conceives them. Thus he displays the imperial virtue *Clementia* when he is moved to take pity on the wronged widows who waylay him at the 'temple of the goddesse Clemence' (928), and when he revenges them he displays the complementary virtue of *Iustitia*. Later, in parting Palamon and Arcite, and again at the tourna-ment, Theseus assumes the role of arbiter: 'I wol be thwe juge' (2657). In all these respects he shows himself the child of Jupiter:

> In his magisterial capacity Jupiter possesses adequate knowledge pertaining to law, delivers just decisions, and judges with integrity. When he beholds men engaged in altercations and litigations, he has the happy faculty of restoring peace and estab-lishing concord among them.[9]

For Jupiter is governor of the gods, *necessitas*, the ultimate power—as indeed Theseus himself pronounces at the climax of the poem: 'What maketh this but Juppiter, the kyng,/ That is prince and cause of alle thyng . . . ?' (3035 f.).

Nevertheless, additional planetary influences are clearly at work in Theseus' character. The activity of the moment might adequately account for the Knight's statement that 'after Mars he serveth now Dyane' (1682). But he rode against Creon under a banner specifically charged with the image of Mars (975-7). And an emotional disposition is unambiguously indicated when Theseus interrupts the forest duel of Palamon and Arcite, trembling with rage and threatening them with death, in speeches that begin and end with invocations of Mars (1708, 1747):

'By myghty Mars, he shal anon be deed.'
'Ye shal be deed, by myghty Mars the rede!'

Again he is moved to pity, however, by a company of weeping ladies. Mars is tempered by Venus, so that Theseus not only spares the two lovers but exclaims at the power of love:

'The god of love, a, *benedicite*!
How myghty and how greet a lord is he!'
(1785 f.)

Appreciation of this incident partly depends on a knowledge of the mediating function of Jupiter. Like Luna, Jupiter was a temperate deity, who held extremes in concord. In particular, he was supposed to mediate judiciously between rough Mars and soft Venus.[10] The acknowledgment of love's power quoted above, coming so soon after oaths by Mars, may be seen as Theseus' binding of Mars by Cupid. Earlier, the same child of Jupiter, who knew by experience 'of loves peyne' (1815) united Mars and Venus—though as martially as possible—in his marriage with the Amazonian queen Ypolita.

Considered in this light, Theseus might appear the ideal arbiter between Palamon and Arcite. And so, for a time, until the tournament itself, things seem to work out. But—and this is one of the tale's difficulties—it is ultimately not Theseus who resolves the conflict between Palamon and Arcite, just as in the heavens it is not Jupiter who resolves the conflict 'Bitwixe Venus, the goddesse of love,/ And Mars, the stierne god armypotente' (2440 f.). Jupiter is 'bisy' to stop that strife, but ineffectually: somewhat surprisingly it is 'pale Saturnus the colde' who, against his nature (2451) 'gan remedie fynde'—a remedy capable of answering everyone's prayer. And on earth as in heaven Jupiter's authority is again undercut by Saturn: Theseus may declare, 'I wol be trewe juge, and no partie./ Arcite of Thebes shal have Emelie' (2657 f.). But he awards victory only to see it snatched away by the god whose course has more power than any man knows (2455): Arcite is thrown from his horse through the agency of a fury 'sent at request of Saturne' (2685).

Saturn, like Jupiter, has his earthly counterpart, this time in Egeus.[11] Egeus is Theseus' 'olde fader' (2838), just as Saturn is mythologically father of Jupiter. And it is he whose counsel brings the human action to a resolution, corresponding to the heavenly accord reached by following the advice of Saturn. The main basis of correspondence lies in the fact that Saturn is the god of old age, the age of wisdom. Thus the line in the mythological episode, describing Saturn, 'In elde is bothe wysdom and usage' (2448), is complemented by the description of Egeus exhorting the people 'ful wisely' (2851). Indeed, Egeus' sole function seems to be to instruct Theseus when he is at a loss, helplessly grieving over the death of the victorious Arcite. Egeus' qualification for this role of comforter is his knowledge of 'this worldes transmutacioun': 'he hadde seyn it chaunge bothe up and doun' (2839 f.). The child of Saturn, god of time, is naturally an expert on mutability.

Emelye's mythological connections are in some ways the most instructive of all from the point of view of the present enquiry. Primarily, she is a child of Diana-Luna. For this correspondence we have the explicit evidence of her devotions before the tournament. It is to Diana's temple that she goes, to pray to the goddess of 'thre formes' (2313), Luna-Diana-Proserpina. There Emelye prays that the Martian Arcite and the Venerean Palamon may be reconciled: 'sende love and pees bitwixe hem two' (2317). She hopes that this may be achieved through her own virginity—that is, through the mediating influence of Luna as she understands it. Consequently she prays that Palamon's and Arcite's love may be quenched or turned from her (2318-21):

> 'Syn thou art mayde and kepere of us alle,
> My maydenhede thou kepe and wel conserve,
> And whil I lyve, a mayde I wol thee serve.'
> (2328-30)

At the same time, there are also hints of Venus in the portrayal of Emelye. Indeed, when she is first introduced, Palamon actually takes her for the goddess, or at least her transfigured appearance: 'I noot wher she be womman or goddesse,/ But Venus is it soothly, as I gesse' (1101 f.). More obliquely, one of Emelye's characteristic actions conceals an astronomical symbolism that carries the same implication. It was her habit to rise with the sun, or even 'er it were day' (1040 f., cf. 2273): an allusion, clearly, to the astronomical Venus, the morning star. The mingling of these two contrasting deities in Emelye should not, however, surprise us, for the tale is moving here towards the familiar Renaissance composite figure Venus—Diana, symbolic of the moral ideal of virtuous love. (Significantly, Emelye's 'yelow heer'—a colour of Venus'— was carefully 'broyded in a tresse'.[12]) These features of Emelye are only present, of course, *in potentia*; but they help us to understand her experience at the temple of Diana, when she discovers the three-fold goddess to be more mysterious that she had realized.

Already in the description of Diana's temple, the goddess has been depicted not only as chaste huntress but also as Proserpina, wife of Pluto, and as Lucina, patroness of women in childbirth (2081-7): now, in the incident of Emelye's prayer, virginity is again shown to be only one of the stages of female life over which the goddess presides. The incident, in fact, is best approached as psychological allegory. Emelye is afraid to enter on the next stage of life, marriage, with all that that signifies, so that her first prayer is an outright expression of her desire to remain virgin: 'Chaste goddesse, wel wostow that I/ Desire to ben a mayden al my lyf' (2304 f.). At the same time she recognizes the possible inappropriateness of this attitude—'if my destynee be shapen so/ That I shal nedes have oon of hem two' (2323 f.)—and is drawn forward by a natural interest in the opposite sex. Amusingly enough (and in this we can hear the Knight's irony) Emelye finds herself praying to Diana of all goddesses to 'sende me hym that moost desireth me' (2325). The answering omen of the quenched altar fire is decisive. For the blazing brand is an attribute of Venus and Hymen, while the blood dripping from it represents the blood shed in menstruation, defloration and childbirth.[13] At first Emelye is terrified, not knowing what the omen signifies (2343) But then she learns that it means marriage: 'Thou shalt ben wedded' (2351). In other words, to put it in paler and more prosaic terms, Emelye must grow up and accept the onset of the next stage of her maturity. She has to pass from the patronage of Diana to that of Venus, and learn Venus' ways, just as Theseus has to be instructed in the ways of Saturn. The point is neatly, if unobtrusively, expressed in ll. 2486 f. ('al that Monday justen they and daunce,/ And spenden it in Venus heigh servyse') for, in the planetary week, Monday is dedicated to Luna, so that here Luna has surrendered her day to Venus.

The correspondences with Palamon and Arcite at first sight seem simpler, in that they are more broadly and explicitly drawn. In the strife among the gods Venus takes Palamon's part and Mars Arcite's, in response, obviously, to the mortals' prayers. And these prayers may be expected to be in decorum with the nature of the worshippers. Arcite prays to Mars because he is a child of Mars, Palamon to Venus because he is a child of Venus—her 'owene knyght' (2471), in fact, to use Saturn's words. This has still to be demonstrated in terms of moral character, but it is already clear that all the actions of the lovers, at the time of the tournament that sums up their opposition, are performed in accordance with the appropriate planetary influence. Thus, as W. C. Curry has shown, each lover (and also Emelye) goes to pray at the hour of the astrological week presided over by the deity addressed.[14] Moreover, the tournament that gives Arcite victory significantly takes place on the Tuesday, *dies Martis*—though the victor will be thrown from his horse at one of the hours of that day presided over by Saturn.[15]

To these decorums may be added a further harmony, which expresses even more fully the interrelation of planetary influences and human actions. For it appears that the architectural design of the lists, even the physical arrangement of the characters at the beginning of the tournament, is subject to a formal organization that has its astrological meaning. Everyone who reads *The*

Knight's Tale is struck by the elaborate extensiveness of the descriptions of the lists and of the oratories prepared by Theseus during the year (1850) that elapses between Palamon's and Arcite's first duel and their second. Much of the tale's Third Part, indeed, is occupied by these descriptions. Yet their relevance is no longer understood. The account of the design of the lists—'Round was the shap, in manners of compas,/ Ful of degrees' (1880 f.)—leaves no doubt that a mathematical construction is intended. In one sense, of course, the *degrees* are simply the graduated levels on which spectators will be set (1891); but we are also told that the design occupied the attention of every available 'crafty man/ That geometrie or ars-metrike kan' (1897 f.). What can this round construction be, with its carefully calculated positions for domiciles of planetary deities? Only a zodiac.[16] The Knight's statement that 'swich a place/ Was noon in erthe' (1895 f.) has a special sense for the reader that it did not have for the pilgrims. It hints that the lists are a cosmic model. In confirmation of this is the vast size of the lists—a mile in circumference.

The siting of all the domiciles or temples to Mars, Venus and Diana, moreover, is in accordance with an actual state of the heavens. It will be recalled that Palamon and Arcite fought their first duel on Saturday 5 May[17] and that Theseus instructed them to return a year later for the tournament.[18] This instruction they obeyed to the letter, arriving at Athens on Sunday 5 May of the following year (2188). Sunday night and early Monday morning were given over to the devotions of Palamon, Emelye and Arcite, and Monday 6 May was a feast day, spent in Venus' service (2189), so that the tournament itself took place on Tuesday 7 May. On that day, before the sun had fully risen—'It nas nat of the day yet fully pryme' (2576)—Theseus and the spectators took their places 'in degrees about' and Arcite entered 'westward, thurgh the gates under Marte' (2581), that is, under the house of Mars situated above the western gate:[19]

> And in that selve moment Palamon
> Is under Venus, estward in the place.
>
> (2584 f.)

Now at sunrise on 7 May in the late fourteenth century the sign on the eastern horizon was Taurus, a domicile of Venus, while the sign on the western horizon was Scorpio, a domicile of Mars. Cancer, the only domicile of Luna, lay on the north-drawn meridian—where the oratory of Diana was situated, in fact, 'northward, in a touret on the wal'.[20] As for Theseus, 'set . . . ful riche and hye' (2577), his position seems to correspond to mid-heaven, where indeed we should expect to find one 'arrayed right as he were a god in trone', in the seat of cosmic judgment.[21] Here, however, there is a subtlety. For on 7 May there culminated, not the domicile of Jupiter we expect, but Capricorn, a domicile of Saturn:

Medium coeli

CAPRICORN:
domicile
of Saturn

E.	TAURUS: domicile of Venus: Palamon		SCORPIO: domicile of Mars: Arcite	W.
		CANCER: domicile of Luna		

Imum Coeli

N.

Yet again, it seems, the authority of Theseus and Jupiter has been undercut by Saturn.

Our examination of the correspondence between the planetary deities and their protégés has, then, served to integrate the mythological digression with the rest of the tale, and to show that the mythological and human actions are closely interrelated. But we are left more curious than ever as to what the import of all these planetary influences may be. And our difficulty with respect to the assistant kings has if anything been increased.

III

To support Palamon in the tournament comes Lygurge, King of Thrace; to support Arcite, Emetreus, King of India. The arrivals of the assistant kings are elaborately described in two immediately succeeding passages in Part iii, which are obviously carefully balanced against one another (2128-54, 2155-86). But the problem is to see how the kings are related to their respective knights. Curry, the only critic to attempt a solution, has analysed the descriptions of the kings from a physiognomic point of view. He finds that 'Emetreus, who comes to support Arcite the protégé of Mars, is a typical Martian figure; and Lycurgus, who aids Palamon, now under the protection of Saturn, is Saturnalian in form.'[22] Some of the details of Curry's argument are convincing, but his general conclusion creates far more problems than it solves. In particular, his offhand description of Palamon as 'now under the protection of Saturn' begs a large question. Why is not Lygurge Venerean, as the simple symmetry of the tournament seems to require? Why is the contest not the direct 'strif' between Mars and Venus that it appears to be in heaven? Alternatively, if we accept the association of Lygurge with Saturn, why should that planetary deity contend with Mars, when he means to give him the interim victory in any case? What can it possibly mean that the two unfortunate planets should contend? Such a conflict seems, indeed, to make astrological nonsense.

Answers to these questions can be given—but only after the iconology of the descriptions of Lygurge and Emetreus has been analysed more closely. We begin by adducing further evidence to confirm the surprising identification of Lygurge, Palamon's ally, as a child of Saturn. As Curry has shown, Lygurge's physical appearance marks him out physiognomically as Saturnian. The black beard (2130), the 'kempe heeris' (2134), the 'lymes grete' (2135): all these details carry the same implication.[23] Going beyond physiognomy, we note that Lygurge, 'grete kyng of Trace' (2129), is modelled on the Thracian king Lycurgus of ancient myth, who fought against Bacchus-Dionysus on his return from India: that Dionysus' Thracian war was against Saturn would be sufficient authority for making Lygurge Saturnian.[24] In addition, the associations of all the animals in the description, both those mentioned as present and those appearing only as images, have a similar parameter. Thus Saturn's chariot, like Lygurge's (2139), was drawn by bulls, in accordance with the extreme slowness of his orbit.[25] Obviously, Lygurge could not simultaneously have his chariot drawn by the alternative griffins, but he could himself be described as looking 'like a grifphon'.[26] Similarly, his hair (2144) is as black as the raven, a bird often associated with *Tristitia* or Melancholy.[27] And the huge dogs that surround his chariot (2148) were familiar symbols of the same temperament.[28]

Other particulars of the description seem to have a moral rather than a psychological meaning. It is noteworthy, for example, that whereas Emetreus rides on a horse, Lygurge stands on 'a chaar of gold' (2138). The primary reference here is of course to the Saturnian *aurea aetas*; but there may also be an allusion to Saturn's gift of Prudence, the 'charioteer of the virtues'. In schemes associating the seven gifts of the Holy Spirit with the seven planets, the supreme gift—Prudence or Wisdom—was most often allotted to Saturn, the planet of outermost orbit.[29] Equally striking is the prominence of gold in the equipment of Lygurge's entourage. His chariot is of gold, his dogs' muzzles are 'colored of gold' (2152) and the nails of his bearskin are 'yelewe and brighte as any gold' (2141). Gold was sometimes in itself attributed to Saturn, because of its weight.[30] But gold *muzzles* suggests more specifically the gold of restraint,[31] and the gold nails of the bear confirm this connection, since the bear could apparently be an emblem of 'Perfection with age and discipline'.[32]

A similar but more obvious train of thought emphasizes instead the fact that the bear has been skinned and therefore killed: traditionally the bear was associated with anger and the choleric temperament,[33] so that the details seem to mean that Lygurge has overcome the bear of anger. A closely related implication is probably to be seen in the 'wrethe of gold, arm-greet, of huge wighte . . . set ful of stones brighte,/ Of fyne rubyes and of dyamauntz' (2145-7), since the gold wreath in itself was a symbol of reward for virtue.[34] But the diamond and ruby are Martian-Solar,[35] and hence associated with the choleric temperament, so that the appropriation of the jewels parallels exactly the killing of the bear. At the same time, there may also be a suggestion that Saturn's course is 'so wyde for to turne' (2454) that it contains in its circle the powers of the lower planets.

Emetreus responds equally well to iconological analysis, though in this case the result does not altogether bear out Curry's conclusion. Emetreus' Martian qualities, it is true, are immediately apparent. On a bay steed with steel trappings he 'Cam ridynge lyk the god of armes, Mars' (2159). As Curry points out, the 'even bright citryn' (2167), the 'sangwyn' colour and the 'frakenes' or freckles (2169) were all Martian attributes.[36] To complement Lygurge's Saturnian menagerie, moreover, Emetreus has one that, in part at least, is Martian. He carries a Martian eagle,[37] is accompanied by Martian leopards[38] and rides a Martian horse of Martian colour.[39] He himself speaks with a martial voice like 'a trompe thonderynge' (2174). Even his age, twenty-five, alludes to a number dedicated to Mars.[40]

Nevertheless Emetreus is not to be explained simply as a child of Mars. Indeed, Solar attributes and Solar imagery are almost equally prominent in his description. Physiognomically, this is made quite explicit: 'His crispe heer lyk rynges was yronne,/ And that was yelow, and glytered as the sonne' (2165 f.). We need not try, as Curry does, to force this detail into the Martian mould. Chaucer says sun and means it.[41] As for the description of Emetreus' facial complexion—

> his colour was sangwyn;[42]
> A fewe frakenes in his face yspreynd,
> Bitwixen yelow and somdel blak ymeynd
> (2168-70)

—it seems to apply equally well to Solar and Martian subjects. Thus Agrippa of Nettesheim tells us that 'the *Sun* makes a man of a tauny colour, betwixt yellow and black, dasht with red'.[43]

Other details of the description are either exclusively Solar, or ambiguous in their associations between Solar and Martian. The lions that surrounded

Emetreus (2185 f.) and that he himself is compared to (2171) are in terms of planetary associations obstinately Solar—though they might indicate wrath and the choleric temperament.[44] The leopards, which, as we have seen, were Martian, may also have been known to Chaucer as attributes of Dionysus, the winter sun.[45] The eagle, as a primate, was often associated with Sol the sovereign planet.[46] Even the horse has to be distinguished as Martian by its colour, because the horse in itself was often a Solar attribute.[47] In the same way, the 'laurer grene . . . gerland' (2175 f.) worn by Emetreus is a Martian crown of victory, but made from a Solar plant.[48] The gold of his saddle and trappings, however, like the rubies sparkling on his mantle, are in this context simply Solar;[49] while the 'perles white and rounde and grete' (2161) with which his coat-armour is couched are an association with India, the place Emetreus and Dionysus alike left for their wars with Lycurgus and Saturn.[50]

It should be stressed that Emetreus' Martian and Solar qualities are in no way antithetic. On the contrary, they complement each other, since the two planets were regarded as being very similar in character. Mars was 'hot and dry, cholerick and fiery': Sol was 'Hot, Dry' and had 'dominion of fire and cleere shining flames . . .'.[51] Throughout the description of Emetreus, indeed—as was the case, we now see, with Lygurge too—the emphasis is more on the nature and attributes of a complexion than on those of a planetary influence. The introduction of the second planetary deity Sol, otherwise confusing, puts this beyond doubt. There will be no confusion if the details, both Martian and Solar, are regarded as symbols of the choleric complexion. Thus the rubies of Emetreus' mantlet are 'rede as fyr' (2164), the corresponding element. His lions were attributes of Mars because they were first choleric animals.[52] And in an engraving by Virgil Solis the choleric complexion is represented, as here, by lion and eagle together.[53] It goes without saying that Emetreus' lions are tame because they are in accord with his complexion, while Lygurge, by contrast, hunts lions with his huge dogs, just as he hunted the bear to acquire the skin he wears.[54] Choleric bears and lions are to him not tame attributes, but wild animals to be conquered in the hunt, symbol of life's arduous moral pursuit.

Although this enquiry has clarified the function of many descriptive details, it does not at first seem to have taken us very far beyond Curry's position. We know that the opposition of Lygurge and Emetreus is not an opposition of Saturnian and Martian influences, but of Saturnian and Martian-Solar influences; or, rather, of melancholic and choleric complexions. But we are still faced with the question what such an opposition can mean. We believe that the answer lies in the indications of age that are included in both descriptions—Lygurge's face 'manly' (2130) and bearded, his bearskin black 'for old' (2142), Emetreus' appearance of being 'of fyve and twenty yeer' (2172) with a beard 'wel bigonne for to sprynge' (2173). For these details, taken together with the attributes of planetary deities and complexions, would bring to the mind of any mediæval reader the familiar scheme of the Four Ages of Man. In that scheme, planetary influences, complexions and ages were correlated as in the accompanying Table:[55]

	AGE	PLANET	ELEMENT	COMPLEXION
I	Youth (0-20)	Jupiter (and Venus)	Air	Sanguinic
II	Prime (20-40)	Mars	Fire	Choleric
III	Middle Age (40-60)	Saturn	Earth	Melancholic
IV	Old Age (60-)	Moon (and Venus)	Water	Phlegmatic

Lygurge is clearly a representative of the Third Age, just as Emetreus is of the Second. Moreover, as the Ages are portrayed in the tale (though this was by no means generally the case) the sequence from Age II to Age III is a moral sequence.[56] Lygurge, that is to say, is in the fullest sense more mature than Emetreus. He hunts choleric animals, he can assimilate the choleric virtues symbolized in his diamond-and-ruby wreath, because he had left behind the fiery impetuosity of youth. Through the temperance and restraint appropriate to his age and manifested, as we have seen, in his emblematic accoutrements, he has matured to a stage of experience beyond that of Arcite's Dionysiac ally. The Lycurgus of ancient legend, we recall, was a lawgiver. It is in keeping with this polarity that Lygurge should wear the jewelled wreath that symbolized the rewards of virtue, and Emetreus merely the laurel wreath of victory.

We would not be thought to imply that the assistant kings' poetic function and meaning can be exhausted solely in terms of the theme of the Ages of Man. They have a part also in the narrative and emotional movement of the Third Part of the tale. Thus, they arrive between the static descriptions of the temples of the planetary deities, decorated with murals showing their fixed influence on human activities (1893-2088), and the narrative of prayers to living and responding gods (2209-2437). Their advent is, in fact, Palamon's and Arcite's summoning up of their deepest psychological resources. The terms of life's contest have already been fixed in imagery strange and dark enough, but the arrival of the kings is told in a passage even stranger: an appropriate bridge to the religious experiences to follow. Indeed, the kings' entourages are among the most mysterious images in the whole of mediæval English poetry. The planetary deities of Henryson, Douglas and Lydgate hardly compare. For figures as mysterious as Lygurge and Emetreus, uniting imagery of so many different kinds (astrological, physiognomic, psychological, emblematic, moral and sensuous) in so original and exploratory a manner, we have to turn to Elizabethan poetry, or to sixteenth-century engraved Temperament series—to Spenser, or to the Dürer of *Melencolia I*. The mysteriousness of Lygurge and Emetreus, however, is clearly enough of the kind that results from psychological depth. It may well be that they are not to be fully understood. But if we are to try to understand them, it must be as powers at work in Palamon and Arcite, and not as instances of nobility.

IV

That Palamon and Arcite ally themselves with Lygurge and Emetreus for the tournament can only mean that at this stage they have assimilated and can call upon the psychological qualities represented by the two kings. Arcite's choleric complexion under Martian-Solar influence is abundantly in evidence throughout the tale. His devotion to Mars, shown in his prayer at that god's temple and in his entry at the tournament under Scorpio, has already been noticed. We can now see, however, that Arcite is devoted, more precisely, to Mars in aspect with Sol. The temple murals show several activities characteristic of that particular influence (notably, 'The cook yscalded, for al his longe ladel'[57]), and when Arcite returns from his prayer he is 'as fayn as fowel is of the brighte sonne' (2437). Moreover, some of Emetreus' choleric attributes reappear associated with Arcite—notably, the horse. Arcite's steed as he went to do his May observance was 'a courser, startlynge as the fir'.[58] Significantly, his choleric complexion was then extreme enough to distort his view of the real powers at work in his nature: at a time when he might be expected to have thoughts only for love, and when the narrator explicitly states—at some length, indeed—that the lover's heart has been overcast by 'geery Venus' to make his mood as changeable as her day Friday (1530-9), it was not to Venus but to jealous Juno and 'felle Mars' (1559) that Arcite prayed. True, he acknowledged that Love had struck his heart through with his 'firy dart so brennyngly' (1564); but with no suggestion that he thought of love as a divine power. Just as on the occasion of his first falling in love he described the event as merely human, so now he apostrophized Emelye, not Venus; 'Ye sleen me with youre eyen, Emelye!/ Ye been the cause wherfore that I dye' (1567 f.).

Earlier, when he was sent into exile, Arcite suffered, the narrator tells us, from a lover's melancholy. It was not, however, the ordinary love-sickness called Hereos,

> but rather lyk manye,
> Engendred of humour malencolik,
> Biforen, in his celle fantastik.
> (1374-6)

The specific, even technical, character of the language of this passage encourages us to see an equally specific psychological implication. Mania was the term used in medicine for one particular form of melancholy, the choleric—'si ex colera [melancholia], tunc vocatur proprie mania'.[59] Thus Arcite's malady, which demonstrates like his death the unrecognized power of Saturn,[60] is a malady possible only in one of extreme choleric complexion. As D. W. Robertson remarks, it was a dreaded affliction involving radical disorder of the patient's imagination and even, perhaps, of his moral judgment; so that it is hard to think that the pilgrims were invited to identify with Arcite, however much they might pity him.

Palamon, by contrast, shows no symptoms of excessive choler. From the outset he is devoted to Venus, whose power he rightly sees at work in his love for Emelye. (When he first falls in love with Emelye he even takes her for a form of the goddess.) In accordance with this Venerean influence, he enjoys a sanguinic complexion—the morally superior one, according to the commonest mediæval belief.[61] In prison, Palamon suffers under the contrary influence, that of Saturn, god of prisons.[62] Unlike Arcite, however, he can recognize the gods into whose power he has fallen

> 'I moot been in prisoun thurgh Saturne,
> And eek thurgh Juno, jalous and eek wood,
>
> .   .   .   .
>
> And Venus sleeth me on that oother syde.'
>   (1328-32)

This passage occurs in a long complaint, which shows that Saturn's influence has taught Palamon to philosophize, at least to the point of adopting a *contemptus mundi* attitude. There is also something like a submission of Saturn in Palamon's calm acknowledgment that his destiny may be as a prisoner: 'And if so be my destynee be shapen/ By eterne word to dyen in prisoun' (1108 f.). In other words, whereas Arcite acknowledges only his own ruling deity, Palamon learns to temper his devotion to Venus with submission to reality's other powers. His cruel seven-year imprisonment in darkness—described by the narrator as a 'martirdom'—eventually drives Palamon mad too. But in his case the temporary madness is a simple love-melancholy.[63]

The resulting moral distinction between Palamon and Arcite is complete, and is manifested at almost every stage of the tale. It is not, however, a crude moral contrast: the Knight is too experienced and too well-bred for that. Consequently readers and even critics have been able to misunderstand his intention. We confine ourselves to three salient points of differentiation between the two lovers.

First, the confusion of Arcite's moral values is displayed in his betrayal of Palamon when he first falls in love. Palamon not only saw Emelye before Arcite did, but also confided his love (1093-1111). Arcite's duty as sworn friend and confidant, therefore, is to help Palamon. Instead, he claims freedom to love Emelye on his own account. In reply to reminders of his oath and accusations of treachery, he jeers at the exalted character of Palamon's love (1153-9); openly asserts a readiness to break 'positif lawe' for the sake of the love he himself pursues (1162-71); and concludes with the amoral declaration, 'Ech man for hymself, ther is noon oother' (1182). Later this argument is repeated for emphasis, when Palamon, escaped from prison, overhears Arcite's soliloquy of love and addresses him as 'false traytour wikke' (1580). Again Arcite does not deny the charge, but fierce as the choleric lion (1598) replies in amoral terms: 'thynk wel that love is free' (1606). The full wrong that he is doing to Palamon is not understood unless one recalls that in the Middle Ages promises were really supposed to be kept, and that in any case the value of love was inferior to that of friendship. But the tale reminds us of this ideal of friendship by introducing the legend of Pirithous and Theseus, an ancient exemplum of *felix concordia*.[64] The relation of the true friends Perotheus and Theseus may at first appear to be in simple contrast with that of Arcite and Palamon. Theseus was prepared to descend into hell's prison for Perotheus' sake (1200); unlike Arcite, who let Palamon languish in prison until another unnamed friend (1468) helped him escape. But closer examination shows a more complex analogy. Pirithous and Theseus, like Arcite and Palamon, were friends whose love grew out of conflict. And the fact that it is Arcite whom Chaucer's Perotheus assists, rather than Palamon, may well allude to the legendary Pirithous' denial of a brother's claim.[65]

Secondly, the prayers before the tournament show Palamon's moral superiority no less decisively. Arcite prays primarily for personal success in battle: 'Yif me victorie, I aske thee namoore' (2420). When he mentions love and Venus, it is significantly to her adultery that he refers, and to the dominating power of Mars' lustful victory over her. The licentiousness of the diction is unmistakable, and in context shocking:

> thow usedest the beautee
> Of faire, yonge, fresshe Venus free,
> And haddest hire in armes at thy wille[66]

Palamon, on the contrary, explicitly renounces victory—'Ne I ne axe nat tomorwe to have victorie' (2239)—praying instead that he may 'have fully possessioun/ Of Emelye' (2242 f.). And though he refers to Venus' love for Adonis (2224), he omits any allusion to her adultery, addressing her rather as 'spouse of Vulcanus' (2222). The contrast here is sharp. Arcite's prayer for victory shows his short-sightedness: he cannot see beyond the glory of battle to the deeper implications of union with Emelye. Palamon, however, can see that union as more than a victory, and knows that Venus' power is greater than Mars' (2248-50). He has learned, as Arcite obviously has not, that Mars must be bound by Venus.[67] Moreover, in looking to the 'end' of his desire rather than to any immediate event, he shows that he has learned from Saturn the virtue of perseverance. In addition, his more submissive and thoughtful prayer manifests a readiness for that perfection and completion of experience which is the province of the god of time.

Finally, there is a direct contrast between Palamon and Arcite in what was, to a mediæval audience, the critical matter of pride. The humility of Palamon's prayer has already been remarked. He has no interest in 'renoun in this cas, ne veyne glorie/ Of pris of armes blowen up and doun' (2240 f.). Arcite's contrary prayer for glory—a rather insolent one in tone—is in keeping with his behaviour outside the temple of Mars. Thus, to Palamon's first accusation of betrayal, Arcite replies 'ful proudly' (1152). And he loses his life after the tournament while parading his victory, enacting what would have been recognized by the Knight's audience as an emblem of *Superbia*.[68] Lacking the discipline and prudence of Palamon, Arcite, who inclines too much to the impetuous rigour of the choleric, has fallen into vainglory.

In short, it is as far as possible from the truth to say, as Robertson does,[69] that Palamon's condition differs from Arcite's 'only in degree'. The difference is qualitative, both morally and psychologically, and it is so extreme that Palamon's eventual winning of Emelye should be felt as poetic justice.

Nevertheless, Arcite's supersession is not felt quite in this way. For it is also true that from the beginning the two lovers have been very closely twinned. We can even sympathize, to some extent, with the casual reader who finds it hard to distinguish them. Thus, Palamon and Arcite are closely related members of one family; at the sack of Thebes they are found, both insensible, in the same heap of wounded 'Bothe in oon armes, wroght ful richely' (1012); at the tournament they appear at the 'selve moment' (2584); and the exact evenness of their forces 'withouten variacioun' is the theme of a long and emphatic passage (2587-94). Besides, the moral contrast between Palamon and Arcite is by no means schematic or unrelieved. A defence of Arcite's character, though it would be misguided, would not be a ridiculous or hopelessly perverse undertaking. On occasion he is by no means lacking in magnanimity and honour—as witness his succour of the weakened Palamon at 1608-19, or the true nobility of his dying words. After Arcite's death, moreover, Palamon thinks him worth mourning. Indeed, his grief is prolonged and almost inconsolable.

All these apparently conflicting features of the tale can be reconciled, however, if it is seen as a symbolic representation of character-development. Palamon's grief is so extreme because he has, as it were, witnessed the passing of a part of himself—the Martian, choleric part—his early youth. He may recognize the discipline maturity demanded: he may ally himself with the lawgiver Lygurge: but that does not diminish a chivalric knight's regret for the passing of youth's freedom and glory. Arcite's moving speech at the point of death confirms this interpretation, for he comes at the end to see the vanity of his desires ('what asketh men to have'), to confess his own choleric 'strif and rancour . . . and . . . jalousye' and to recognize Palamon as 'the gentil man' (2777, 2784 f., 2797). At that point, when he acknowledges the superiority of Palamon's values, he is reunited with him and at the same time ceases to exist. His separate existence, indeed, is now superfluous: the conflict over, his better qualities are incorporated in the lover who survives, the more mature stage of the super-character Palamon-Arcite-Emetreus-Lygurge. In Daniel Richter's words,

> If you want to be a man
> You must kill a boy.

It may be asked why, in that case, the gods should permit Arcite to be the winner of the tournament, however briefly. Why should Palamon ever have been bound by Arcite and his supporters, when it was Venus who ought to have bound Mars? The answer can again be given in terms of character-formation and the sequence of ages. In schemes of the Ages of Man—both in four-age and in seven-age schemes—the choleric Martian and Solar phase intervened between the earlier Venerean (sanguinic) and the later Saturnian (melancholic). Thus we may think of the tale's supercharacter as passing out of sanguinic youth, through an all-too-brief sunny prime or 'flour' of martial success, into the Third or Middle Age.[70] In terms of generated characters, the Venerean Palamon—Palamon as supported in heaven by Venus—is inevitably defeated by the representative of the next phase, the Martian Arcite. But time (Saturn) has a further surprise in store. The Martian Arcite is himself in turn overthrown through Saturn's agency, i.e. by a further lapse of time ('by processe and by lengthe of certeyn yeres'),—being superseded by a changed Palamon who has become very much the child of Saturn. Significantly, the tale's last description of Palamon is of a Tristitia or *Melancholia* figure:

> Tho cam this woful Theban Palamoun,
> With flotery berd and ruggy, asshy heeres,
> In clothes blake, ydropped al with teeres . . .[71]

Only in the last resort, with Saturn's help, is Venus stronger than Mars. Only with the long passage of time (repeatedly dwelt on throughout the tale[72]) can love grow out of passion and wilful freedom, or come to the maturity of lawful stable marital relation.

V

Fitting Emelye and Theseus into the above theory of *The Knight's Tale* is a matter of greater delicacy. Both characters show subtly conflicting tendencies in respect of their maturity. This does not seem to reflect any indecision, however, on the part of the poet, but is rather designed to betray an ambivalence in the narrator.

Emelye most obviously represents the phlegmatic complexion (the complexion in a sense of all women, regardless of age), associated usually with Luna though sometimes also with Venus.[73] Palamon's final attainment of union with Emelye is in accordance with this identification, since the phlegmatic was commonly the complexion of the last age of man. That age of man was of course rheumy and unpleasant—a time 'whan his name apalled is for age,/ For al forgoten is his vasselage' (3053 f.). Yet none the less its equanimity[74] might also be seen as a not unworthy goal of moral effort. As we have said, Emelye's uniting elements of Diana and of Venus constituted an ideal of moderation. And her family relation with the Jovian Theseus further supports such an interpretation, since Jupiter and Luna were the two mediating planets in the astrology of the time.

On the other hand, what we have seen of Emelye's movement to maturity suggests a somewhat different interpretation. Her marriage to Palamon is from her own point of view a union with the knight of Venus. It completes a transference from Diana's patronage to Venus' that began in her prayer before the tournament, and allowed the generative goddess to fulfil her purpose through the temporal means of Saturn. This interpretation also has a basis in scheme. For Venus was more often associated with the sanguinic complexion than with the phlegmatic, and a common arrangement of the Ages ran:[75]

Phlegmatic	Sanguinic	Choleric	Melancholic	Phlegmatic
Childhood	Youth	Prime	Middle Age	Second Childhood
Luna	Venus, Jupiter	Mars	Saturn	Luna

Moreover, in the seven-age scheme Venus again governed a later age than that of Luna:

LUNA	MERCURIUS	VENUS	SOL	MARS	JUPITER	SATURNUS
Infantia	Pueritia	Adolescentia	Iuventus	Virilis	Senilis	Senecta et decrepita

It will be noted that this interpretation of Emelye places a high evaluation on the sanguinic complexion, that associated also with Jupiter. In the Middle

Ages, as we have already remarked, the sanguinic complexion was often regarded as morally preferable.

It is Theseus' character, however, that is presented most ambivalently. To a superficial view—and for the most part the narrator's own view is in agreement—Theseus grows to maturity like the other characters. After Arcite's death, for example, Theseus has the benefit of Egeus' advice about Time the healer. He learns that the resolution that he (and Jupiter) cannot accomplish by busyness,[76] Saturn can bring about by the lapse of slow time. Theseus' consequent passage from the Jovian Sixth Age to the Saturnian Seventh appears to form the climax of the tale, in his long speech acknowledging time's function in the ultimate workings of the universe:

> He [the Prime Mover] hath so wel biset his ordinaunce,
> That speces of thynges and progressiouns
> Shullen enduren by successiouns,
> And nat eterne, withouten any lye.
>
> (3012-15)

But a deeper scrutiny suggests that Theseus remains oddly impervious to Egeus' advice, so that it can actually be said, inappropriately enough, to 'gladen' him (2837). His response to sentiments about the transitoriness of life's pilgrimage is not *contemptus mundi* but only more busyness, more plans, more practical activity: 'Duc Theseus, with al his bisy cure/ Caste now wher that the sepulture/ . . . may best ymaked be' (2853-5). Yet again officers run to execute his commands. And even his speech before the Athenian parliament, though spoken with sad visage from a breast called wise (2183), represents imperfect submission to Saturn. It is Theseus' deepest, most considered judgment, delivered with Saturnian slowness and weight. It formally acknowledges the power of mutability. Yet it nevertheless betrays an incomplete detachment, by mediæval standards, from the world and from Jupiter, to whose necessity it ascribes the real power. The 'First Moevere' may decree that the oak (Jupiter's tree!) shall endure only by succession and be 'nat eterne', but somehow this is still Jupiter's doing

> 'What maketh this but Juppiter, the kyng,
> That is prince and cause of alle thyng . . .'
>
> (3035 f.)

Incorrigibly Jovial, Theseus to the end makes 'vertu of necessitee' (3042.): his secular stoicism is saddened and deepened, not abandoned.

This is surprising, even disturbing, in face of Theseus' special role as the

---

tale's ideal character. The story is told from a point of view that Theseus alone, of all its characters, would find it possible to share. Adopting a transformational approach analogous to that of Chomsky's, we might imagine the same story related from Egeus' point of view, say, or Palamon's. In the latter—told perhaps by the Squire—love would be treated with absolute solemnity. But in the story we have, told by the Knight, even Palamon's love is subjected (1798ff.) to the same benign, tolerant, jovial irony that pervades almost all the narrative, and that, if style had been our subject, would have been a main concern of the present paper. Only Theseus has the narrator's full and evident sympathy.

Yet Theseus, though a formidable character of many strengths, is never completely satisfactory from a moral standpoint. It is not only during the final stage of the story that he falls short of the ideal: throughout he manifests an individuality faulty both in attitude and in behaviour. We notice especially a hard, angry, pitiless rigour more Martian than jovial. When he discovers Palamon and Arcite fighting Theseus 'quook and sterte' with ire (1762), and the whole company of ladies has to get down on their 'bare knees' on the ground before he will relent (175 8). Understandably enough, his long service of Mars has left him hard, though not, in the end, unyielding. It seems that we are to think of him as being in process of transition from the age of Mars to that of Jupiter: his choleric tendencies are still only with difficulty subdued. As late as the tournament, he shows himself more Martian than Saturnian. Thus, in planning the temples at the lists he conspicuously omits a temple to Saturn. (This would have been very noticeable at a time when the Four Ages and their associated complexions and deities were often portrayed as quadrants of a circle.[77]) And earlier, we recall, there were oaths by Mars and a Martian banner.

All this is intelligible if, and only if, the character of the narrator himself is taken into account. Theseus seems an ideal figure to the Knight because the Knight shares his faults and to some extent his virtues. It is natural, for example, that a knight who has been 'at many a noble armee' and fought in fifteen battles (*Gen. Prol.* 60 f.) should look to victory and to Mars. The Knight's service of Mars is often in evidence in the tale—most obviously, perhaps, when he has the dying Arcite pray almost with his last words 'Juppiter so wys my soule gye' (2786), then within a few lines comments, in his own person, 'Arcite is coold, ther Mars his soule gye!' (2815). Understandable, too, in a soldier, even a crusader, is a certain jovial secularity and stoicism of attitude. Luck is inevitably important to him: as Petrarch put it, Fortune is 'in battaglia potentissima'.[78] So it is appropriately by lot that the Knight begins the story-telling. And it is a highly appropriate stance that he should exclaim: 'welcome be the cut, a Goddes name!' (*Gen. Prol.* 854). For the Knight's God, like Theseus', is Jupiter *Fortuna maiora*. The other gods he portrays, on the whole, as tricky, dangerous and malevolent, if not quite as evil as D. W. Robertson has it. Sometimes his view is strikingly partial, as when he makes Saturn say 'I slew Sampsoun, shakynge the piler' (2466), as if the death of Samson had never been regarded as anything but a sinister catastrophe. To the Knight, the other gods are for the most part enemies of Jupiter's secular order, which has to be maintained, or even fought for, against them.

The Knight's Tale would gain much poignancy if it were regarded, in some such way as we have proposed, as an expression appropriate to a particular stage of its narrator's life. The Knight may be conscious that his own career as a soldier is far advanced, even near its end. With whatever reluctance, he must face the onset of age and the necessity of turning to a more peaceful occupation. It is perhaps no accident that he tells a story in which outgrowing the choleric Martian age bulks so largely—in which war passes in the process of time to formal combat *à l'outrance*, then to tournament, and finally to peace. For we have to think of the wise 'meeke' (*Gen. Prol.* 69) Knight as being himself in passage from the Sixth to the Seventh Age. Perhaps going on the pilgrimage has for him a more serious meaning than for some of the other pilgrims.

As we would interpret *The Knight's Tale*, its meaning is neither general expression of chivalric nobility nor portrayal of the evil of passionate involvements. It is meant to convey something of the order underlying the unpredictable changes of human destiny: of growth to wise maturity through a succession of ages and attitudes; of the soul's formation and ascent through a series of planetary stages. Within its four Parts[79] it attempts to box the whole compass of human life, aiming at a comprehensive irony that will embrace all attitudes more extreme and less mature. Yet it is also, like the other *Canterbury Tales*, told from an individual, dramatic point of view. Its schemes have the effect, not of definitive universal conventions, but of tentative exploratory essays. They seem to form the scaffolding of self-understanding at a particular stage of development, and as such to make possible new access and fresh ordering of experience. The result is a position worthy of deep respect, but also, inevitably, one partial and relative in its truth. It is noble and comprehensive enough to be surpassed in scope only by the sermon that concludes *The Canterbury Tales*. Then at last, in the Parson's call to repentance for all mortal life, with its scheme of seven sins and answering virtues, the Knight's secular vision of seven ages and planetary guardians finds its superior divine counterpart.[80]

From *Medium Ævum* 39, no. 2 (1970): 123-146. Copyright © 1970 by The Society for the Study of Mediæval Languages and Literature. Reprinted by permission of The Society for the Study of Mediæval Languages and Literature.

Notes

1. 'Form, Texture, and Meaning in Chaucer's *Knight's Tale*', in *Chaucer: Modern Essays in Criticism* ed. E. Wagenknecht (New York 1959) p. 69.

2. *Chaucer and the Mediæval Sciences* (London 1960) pp. 131-7.

3. Wagenknecht p. 70.

4. Fairchild 'Active Arcite, Contemplative Palamon' *JEGP* xxvi (1927) 285-93; see, e.g., Muscatine's comment, Wagenknecht p. 61. The most recent and the most ingenious of the briefs for Arcite is that in A. V. C. Schmidt 'The Tragedy of Arcite: a Reconsideration of the *Knight's Tale*' *EC* xix (1969) 107-17, which makes shrewd points *en passant* about Arcite's magnanimity, but has to resort to special pleading to justify his moral position and press his superiority to a spiteful Palamon.

5. Wagenknecht p. 68.

6. *A Preface to Chaucer: Studies in Medieval Perspectives* (Princeton, N.J. 1963) p. 49f.

7. On this convention, see Jean Seznec *The Survival of the Pagan Gods* tr. Barbara F. Sessions, Bollingen Series xxxviii (New York 1953) pp. 70ff.

8. 861. All Chaucer quotations are from *The Complete Works* ed. F. N. Robinson (London 1957).

9. Alcabitius, cit. Curry p. 127. For mediæval representations of Jupiter as a jurist, see Seznec pp. 156, 158f. Ptolemy lists compassion, magnanimity, justice and qualities of leadership among the attributes of Jovian subjects (*Tetrabiblos* iii 13; Loeb edn p. 347).

10. A Renaissance medal based on the idea of Jupiter's maintenance of equity between Mars and Venus is discussed in E. Wind *Pagan Mysteries in the Renaissance*, rev. edn (London 1967) pp. 95f.

11. This and the other mythological identifications in the present section were first set out, though without supporting argument, in Richard Neuse's highly perceptive paper 'The Knight: The First Mover in Chaucer's Human Comedy' *University of Toronto Quarterly* xxxi (1962) 299-315 (see especially 304, 313). Our own paper, written in ignorance of Neuse's, is in substantial agreement with many of his findings.

12. 1049. For the Renaissance ideal of the composite deity Venus-Diana, see Wind pp. 75ff.; for braided hair as a symbol of chastity, ibid. p. 103; and for yellow as a Venerean colour, Ptolemy *Tetrabiblos* ii 9. Throughout the present article, free use has been made of authors later than Chaucer. It is not suggested that these have equal literary historical value with earlier sources, but they may help to illuminate the meaning of our first Renaissance poet.

13. For the blazing brand as an emblem of Venus, see Guy de Tervarent 'Attributs et symboles dans l'art profane' *Travaux d'Humanisme et Renaissance* xxix (Geneva 1928) col. 381, s.v. *Torche*, citing *Roman de la Rose* 3424-6. As an attribute of Hymen, god of marriage, the 'nuptial torch of pine' is mentioned in Ovid *Fasti* ii 558; Loeb edn p. 97. Cesare Ripa in his *Iconologia* connects Luna's torch very closely indeed with childbirth: its function, he says, is to light the way out of the womb for the baby at birth (1603 Rome edn, pp. 49f.). Support for an internal psychological interpretation of the fires (as against the common connection of them with the suitors) is to be found in two glosses in MS. Laud 600: at l. 2334, 'Ignis Castitatis', at l. 2337, 'Ignis Virginitatis'; see *The Text of the Canterbury Tales* ed. J. M. Manly and E. Rickert (Chicago 1940) iii 485.

14. The Unequal Hours (Temporal Hours), twelve-part divisions of the periods of light or darkness, were allotted according to the Ptolemaic order of the planets. The days of the week were assigned to planetary deities (and named *dies Lunae*, etc.) according to which god presided over the first temporal hour after sunrise on the day in question. See *Chaucer and the Medieval Sciences* 124-6, following Tyrwhitt but getting the day of the week wrong—it is Monday morning, not Sunday, since its first diurnal hour is Luna's (2273). Note further that although several other

arrangements of hours presided over by the same appropriate deities could have been adopted, one is chosen that puts Emelye's prayer in a mean position between Palamon's nocturnal and Arcite's diurnal prayers:

Palamon's prayer		Emelye's prayer			Arcite's prayer
VENUS	MERCURIUS	LUNA	SATURNUS	JUPITER	MARS
23	24	1	2	3	4

The symmetry is a little less exact, however, than John North suggests in 'Kalenderes enlumyned ben they: some astronomical themes in Chaucer', Pt 1, *RES* N.S. xx (1969) 151. Some emphasis on the astrological week is justified by Chaucer's elaborate passage on Venus' day at 1530-9.

15. 2483-91, 2637; see Curry p. 138 following W. H. Browne. If the indication in the text—that Palamon was overcome 'er the sonne unto the reste wente'—is considered not precise enough to specify the Saturnian first nocturnal hour for Arcite's overthrow, Browne's point still stands. For the whole of the third quarter of the day, 3 p.m. to 9 p.m., was considered proper to melancholy and hence to Saturn: see R. Klibansky *et al.*, *Saturn and Melancholy* (London 1964) pp. 11 n. 24, 320 n. 119.

16. For compass = year's circle, see *OED* V 11 b (Douav transl. of *anni circulum*). Cf. the technical astronomical term 'mansioun' in the description of Mars' temple (1974); also 'opposit' (1894), not a common word then in non-technical contexts.

17. See Robinson's note to 1462ff., lines that date Palamon's escape from prison on the 'thridde nyght' of May. An alternative interpretation of Manly's, leading to the date 4 May for the duel, is less plausible, and in any case does not affect our argument.

18. 1909. The argument would not be much affected if 'this day fifty wykes, fer ne ner' (1850) were taken literally to mean 50 weeks and not a year. In that case Taurus would still be on the East horizon, Scorpio on the West horizon. The arrival of the combatants on a Sunday (2188), however, seems to count decisively against the 50 weeks interpretation, since the first duel was fought on a Saturday (1530-9, 1621), not a Sunday.

19. Significantly, several manuscripts gloss 2581 'vnder Marte. i. sub Marte' (see Manly and Rickert iii 485); suggesting an astrological interpretation of the lists.

20. I.e., the fixed sign *in imo coeli* was Cancer.

21. 2529. On the zenith as the place of the throne of cosmic judgment in mediæval thought, see E. Panofsky *Meaning in the Visual Arts* (New York 1955) p. 262, citing Pierre Bersuire's *Repertorium morale* on Mal. iv 1. Panofsky notes 'the equation of the astrological notion, *medium coeli*, with the theological notion, *medium coeli et terrae*, presumed to be the seat of the judge'. For the astronomical information here and in the previous paragraph, I am much indebted to Dr. John North, of the Ashmolean Museum of the History of Science, Oxford, who answered many queries. See now his 'Kalenderes enlumyned ben they' *RES* N.S. xx (1969) esp. pp. 149-54, which succeeds in assigning the tournament to the date 5 May, 1388.

22. Curry p. 131.

23. 'The cercles of his eyen in his heed' that 'gloweden bitwixen yelow and reed' (2131f.) present more of a problem; but for lack of a more convincing explanation, we may accept Curry's Saturnian one (pp. 134ff.). Cf. Alcabitius, cit. Klibansky, p. 131: under Saturn's influence a child will have 'medium eyes inclining from black to yellow'.

24. See Hyginus, *Fab.* 132, which may well have been known to Chaucer; also Lactantius Placidus' sixth-century gloss on Statius, *Theb.* vii 164. Cf. Lactantius on *Theb.* vii 180: 'Lycurgus Thracum rex fuit, qui Liberum deum esse negabat.' For a fuller account of Lycurgus, see Natale Conti *Mythologiae* v 13 (Lyons 1653) pp. 502ff. Interestingly, the Lycurgo of the *Teseida* (there

an ally, however, of Arcita), is described as *lagrimoso*. On the close connection between *Tristitia* and *Melancholia* in mediæval art, see Klibansky pp. 221ff.

25. See Tervarent col. 72, and Ripa s.v. *Carro di Saturno* p. 54. Ripa cites Sextus Pompeius, epitomizer of Verrius Flaccus' *De significatu verborum*. On the bullock as a melancholic and Saturnian animal, see also Klibansky pp. 102, 132.

26. 2133. Klibansky's pl. 144 shows Saturn's chariot drawn by griffins in an engraving by Marten van Heemskerck of *The Children of Saturn*. Saturn was more commonly associated with dragons or basilisks, however: cf., e.g., Klibansky's pl. 53, and see Cornelius Agrippa *Three Books of Occult Philosophy* tr. J.F. (1651) I xxv (p. 56), also Tervarent col. 82.

27. Klibansky p. 296 n. 55.

28. For the dog as a beast of Saturn and a symbol of melancholy, see Klibansky pp. 322f. The number of the dogs—20—was doubly appropriate. It was regularly associated with *Tristitia*, to such an extent that Pietro Bongo writes that it is found *nunquam fete in rebus laetis*; see *Numerorum mysteria* (Bergamo 1591) pp. 424ff. It is no coincidence, however, that 20 was also the number of stars in the constellation Canis, according to Hyginus' setting.

29. The description Charioteer of the Virtues had the authority of St. Bernard: see Rosemond Tuve *Allegorical Imagery* (Princeton, N.J. 1966) pp. 69, 94. On schemes associating the Seven Gifts of the Spirit with the seven planets, see Klibansky pp. 164ff. Note that in the *Fulgentius metaforalis*, which is based on a totally different system, Saturnus is again allegorized as Prudence (ed. H. Leibeschutz, p. 71).

30. Agrippa I xxv (p. 55): 'Saturnine things . . . amongst Metals [are] Lead, and Gold, by reason of [its] weight. . . .' In this connection it is significant that Lygurge's coronet is 'of huge wighte' (2145). It may also be worth noting that the griffin traditionally guarded gold (Pliny *Nat. hist.* VII x).

31. See Pierio Valeriano *Hieroglyphica* (Frankfort 1613) p. 29, 'Venus cur Aurea dicta'. As one of the noblest metals, gold was an obvious symbol of temperance and virtue, while in alchemical thought it was the only tempered metal.

32. Ibid. p. 136f., citing St. Ambrose. Black was, of course, the colour associated with Saturn and Melancholy.

33. Klibansky p. 378; Tervarent col. 292; Valeriano p. 138.

34. Tervarent col. 126, s.v. *Couronne* vii, 'Symbole des récompenses que promet la vertu'; cf. Valeriano p. 518: 'Torquem aureum solidae virtutis praemium fuisse traditum est'; also Erasmus *Praise of Folly* tr. John Wilson (Ann Arbor, Mich. 1961) p. 113: it is the function of 'a crown set with diamonds' to remind a prince 'how he ought to excel all others in heroic virtues'.

35. Agrippa I xxiii (p. 52); I xxvii (p. 58).

36. Curry pp. 132-4.

37. 2178. For the Martian association, see Agrippa I xxvii, p. 58. As we shall see, it is by no means irrelevant that the eagle was also an attribute of Jupiter, of Victory and rule (Tervarent col. 4f.) and of the Choleric complexion (Klibansky p. 378).

38. 2186. For the Martian attribution, see Agrippa I 58; William Lilly *Christian Astrology* (London 1647) I x, p. 68.

39. 2157. Both Agrippa (I 58) and Lilly (p. 68) attribute the horse to Mars, as does Du Bartas (tr. Sylvester (London 1613) p. 576). Emetreus' horse is a bay, and red was Mars' colour: cf. Pyrochles's 'bloody red' steed in *Faerie Queene* II v 2. For *bay* = red, see *OED*, s.v. *Bay* a.[1]2, citing J. Bryant (1774) 'bright red. We call such horses bays.'

40. According to the system of planetary magic squares. Klibansky reproduces an example (c. 1300) of the square of Mars at p. 326. Agrippa's identical table is set out at I 245 and its efficacy explained at I 240: Mars' numbers—of which there are 25 in all—'being engraven on an Iron plate, or sword, makes a man potent in war . . . and terrible to his enemies, and victorious against them'.

41. Curry (p. 133) has to suppose a mixed temperament for Emetreus: 'From what Mr. Richard Saunders has to say about Mars's influence in sanguine complexions I would judge Emetreus's temperament to be of that sort.' Yellow hair, however, was far more typical of the Solar subject, since yellow was a Solar colour; see Lilly I xi, p. 71; Peacham *Compleat Gentleman* (1634), ed. Gordon (London 1906) p. 156.

42. Red, ruddy; not carrying any implication of a sanguine complexion in the technical sense.

43. *Three Books of Occult Philosophy* I lii, p. 107. For the Martian interpretation of these details see Curry pp. 133f.

44. See, e.g., Valeriano p. 14; Agrippa I 53; Du Bartas p. 578; Lilly p. 71; and Klibansky pp. 102, 296, citing William of Conches, Shepherds' Calendars and Books of Hours.

45. Ovid, *Met.* iii 669, associates leopards with Bacchus. See also Tervarent col. 234, citing Philostratus *Imagines* i.15.

46. The eagle is sovereign of birds in Peacham, Sebonde and many other authors.

47. See, e.g., Valeriano p. 46. From Ovid through Boccaccio (*De genealog.* iv 3) to Ripa (p. 52) the chariot of the sun was drawn by horses.

48. For the laurel crown of victory, see Tervarent col. 233; for the laurel as Solar, ibid. 231.

49. 2158, 2162, 2164. It was elementary alchemic doctrine that gold was the metallic body corresponding to Sol. Cf. *Cannon's Yeoman's T.* 825f.: 'The bodyes sevene eek, lo! hem heere anoon:/ Sol gold is. . . .' As implied above, however, the steel is Martian. Thus steel and iron are prominent in the *décor* of Chaucer's Temple of Mars (1983, 1992, 1994). For the ruby as Solar, see Agrippa I 52.

50. The mediæval belief that the largest pearls came from India, as expressed by Marbod of Rennes, can be found in P. Studer and Joan Evans, *Anglo-Norman Lapidaries* (Paris 1924) pp. 64, 108, 316; see also *The travels of Friar Odoric* in *Cathay and the Way Thither* tr. and ed. Sir H. Yule, Hakluyt Soc. (1915) i 146. Marbod's account, like most mediæval treatments of the pearl, is derived from Pliny *Nat. hist.* IX liv 106ff. (Loeb edn iii 235). Against the present argument, it must be admitted that Emetreus' being king of India might also be taken to imply aid from a Saturnian region.

51. Lilly pp. 66, 70, 72.

52. Klibansky pp. 102, 296.

53. The engraving is discussed in Klibansky p. 378.

54. For the lion-crushing alans, see the fine passage in Pliny *Nat. hist.* VIII lxi 149f. (Loeb edn iii 105).

55. See Klibansky pp. 369 *et passim*, Seznec p. 47 and F. Boll *Neue Jahrbücher für das klassische Altertum* xvi (1913) 102. Note that Venus was sometimes regarded as presiding over Age I, sometimes over Age IV. Sol did not usually figure in mediæval versions of the four-age scheme. In the equally familiar seven-age scheme, however, with the planets in reverse Ptolemaic order, Sol's place was earlier than Saturn's, as Mars' was in both schemes:

1. Luna, infantia	2. Mercurius, pueritia	3. Venus, adolescentia	4. SOL, iuventus	5. MARS, virilis aetas	6. Iupiter, senilis aetas	7. SATURNUS, senecta et decrepita

Thus, if the inclusion of a partly Solar figure brought the seven-age scheme to mind, it would not be a contradictory suggestion.

56. Moral interpretations of the four ages were common enough, however, at a later period. Thus Bongo (p. 216) presents Age III as the age of wisdom: 'prima aetas est incrementi; secunda roboris; tertia sapientiae; quarta debilitatis'.

57. 2020. See Ptolemy *Tetrabiblos* iv 4 (Loeb edn 384f.). Mrs. M. Twycross has kindly drawn

our attention to an instance in MS. Laud Or. 133. Other Martian-Solar occupations include those of the 'barbour' (cauterizer) and the 'smyth' (2025; see *Tetrabiblos*, ibid.).

58. 1502, close to a mention of 'firy Phebus' (1493).

59. See Klibansky pp. 89f., citing Averroes, Platearius and Melanchthon.

60. Recognized, however, by Curry (pp. 147f.).

61. See Klibansky pp. 79f., 103, 105, 110f., citing William of Conches, St. Hildegard and others.

62. Cf. 2457: 'Myn is the prison'.

63. As the narrator (1455f.: 'Palamon, that love destreyneth so/ That wood out of his wit he goth for wo') and Arcite (1600: 'thou art sik and wood for love') remark. Brief outbursts of well-motivated rage were compatible with simple melancholy: see Averroes, cit. Klibansky p. 89.

64. Ovid *Metam*. viii.

65. Virgil *Aen*. vi 601ff.

66. 2383-92. Arcite's violently passionate imagery (cf. 1564) is in keeping both with his choleric complexion and his 'manye'.

67. On Plutarch's theory of Mars and Venus, see Wind pp. 86ff.

68. For Superbia as a rider, see Prudentius *Psychomachia* ll. 178ff. The iconographical tradition stemming from Prudentius is traced in Adolf Katzenellenbogen *Allegories of the Virtues and Vices in Mediæval Art* (New York 1964).

69. *A Preface to Chaucer* p. 49.

70. Alternatively, in the seven-age scheme, we have the same sequence: 1. Luna, 2. Mercurius, 3. VENUS, 4. SOL, 5. MARS, 6. Iupiter, 7. Saturnus. Theseus devotes the whole passage 3047-56 to the fact that Arcite died in his prime.

71. 2882-4; cf. Palamon's appearance at the Athenian parliament 'in his blake clothes sorwefully' (2978).

72. E.g., at 1381, 1451-62., 1850, 2967.

73. See Klibansky p. 127.

74. See ibid. p. 107; the early authority for the equanimity of the phlegmatic was Vindician.

75. Older and less common, however, than the scheme already cited above. See Klibansky pp. 10f., 122 n. 163, 292f. The order of complexions, it should be noted, was the same in both schemes.

76. An important word in the tale. For Jupiter's busyness see 2442, for Theseus', 1883. In the passage that follows we are much indebted to Mr. John Burrow for criticism and suggestions.

77. See, e.g., Klibansky pls. 75f., and cf. the Wheel of Life motif, ibid. pls. 58, 79.

78. Cit. Howard R. Patch *The Goddess Fortuna in Medieval Literature* (Cambridge, Mass. 1927) p. 108; cf. ibid. p. 85 on Fortuna's weapons.

79. The four-part division here seems inevitable in a tale so much concerned with the four complexions and the Four Ages of Man.

80. On mediæval schemes connecting the seven planetary deities with the seven gifts of the Holy Spirit and the seven sins they remedy, see Klibansky pp. 163ff. Not surprisingly, the planets receive scant mention in this parson's sermon. But the scheme of association is perhaps adumbrated, in that a sole mention of the moon—the only planet mentioned during the treatment of the seven sins, apart from figurative references to the sun's light—comes at the appropriate place, in the account of the corresponding vice *Superbia*, at X 423.

"And Venus Laugheth":
An Interpretation of the *Merchant's Tale*_____

Martin Stevens

The story of Januarie and May has proved among the more elusive of the *Canterbury Tales*. Critics, by and large, have lined up in one of two camps: those who find it an embittered, poisonous, mordant revelation of an ill-humored narrator, and those who see it as a spirited, extravagantly ironic satire in which the traditional *senex amans* is the subject of biting, yet gladsome ridicule. The argument, indeed, has run full circle: from Kittredge's early remark that the Merchant has loaded the story "with savage and cynical satire,"[1] to J. S. P. Tatlock's characterization of the Merchant as a "sour narrator" telling a "repugnant" tale,[2] to T. W. Craik's[3] and Bertrand H. Bronson's[4] separate efforts at restoring the comically satiric fabliau apart from the prologue to which it became imperfectly attached, and then to E. T. Donaldson's recent reassessment of the tale, *qua* tale, as grimly misogynistic and bitter.[5] Even more recent is Norman T. Harrington's article, "Chaucer's Merchant Tale: Another Swing of the Pendulum,"[6] which, as its title implies, takes us back very nearly full-stroke to the earlier view. Accordingly, he argues that "the tale must be read in the context of the Merchant's prologue, that [it] is satisfactorily unified by a consistent narrative point of view, and finally that [it] may impress us in any number of ways, but its final effect is not comic" (p. 26). If we are to accept Mr. Harrington's metaphor, the pendulum must now swing back, and this paper is, consequently, meant to ride with the momentum.

The problem with the *Merchant's Tale* is that it has beguiled us so thoroughly. An age that has learned to read its fiction from Henry James expects the narrative to arise out of the motivations of its characters, and thus, January becomes, however unjustifiably, a surrogate for the Merchant. There are those, in both critical camps, who have attempted to read the tale as if the prologue never happened (as, indeed, it did not in the vast majority of Chaucer manuscripts). But even these critics, and Bertrand Bronson is their most persuasive spokesman, misrepresent the Merchant when they finally put the narrative pieces together once more. Thus, in Bronson's view, "when the Merchant was first drawn Chaucer had not yet divined that his private life was a witches cauldron of marital bitterness and disillusion" (p. 585). But where, indeed, in the later prologue do we get such a hopelessly baleful view of the Merchant's life? From his complaint about his shrewish wife? Are we to take this complaint all that seriously? Might it not as well be the typical humorous exaggeration of the newly-wedded husband who bewails the loss of his erstwhile freedom? It is curious that the Merchant has been made out a bitter, churlish misogynist solely on the basis of his opening speech, while the Host, who complains as much and in the same vein, is usually dismissed as a jovial pragmatist who takes cheer from the absence of the shrewish Goodelief during the pilgrimage:

> But douteless, as trewe as any steel
> I have a wyf, though that she povre be,
> But of hir tonge, a labbyng shrewe is she,
> And yet she hath an heep of vices mo;
> Therof no fors! lat aile swiche thynges go.
> But wyte ye what? In conseil be it seyd,
> Me reweth soore I am unto hire teyd.
>
> (E 2426-32)[7]

At the very conclusion of his article, Bronson goes so far as to say that "the Merchant's misogyny impregnated the whole piece with a mordant venom, inflaming what originally had been created for the sake of mirth" (p. 596). It is clear that in Bronson's eyes the Merchant raped and infected the innocent fiction that awaited him in Chaucer's pages.

Almost all critics have allowed their reading of the tale to be influenced by the man they envision as its teller. Yet this teller, in circular fashion, is almost wholly characterized by the tale. Let us examine some instances. Muriel Bowden carefully points out that "the Merchant probably does not think of himself as a kind of January, for the Merchant is not old and decrepit." Yet, she also tells us that the Merchant of the prologue is "much older than the Squire" and that May could well be "the portrait of his own wife." This observation is followed by the statement: "Again Chaucer develops the character of the teller of the tale through the tale itself."[8] J. S. P. Tatlock speaks of "women who betray merchant-husbands" (p. 187). Maurice Hussey describes the Merchant as "a man of undetermined middle-age, and now a disillusioned one."[9] E. T. Donaldson concludes at one point that "the *Merchant's Tale* was most carefully written to present the kind of world that can come into being if a man's approach to love and marriage is wholly mercantile and selfish . . ." (p. 45). Norman Harrington comments that "the story of January and May was meant to be told by an older man still smarting from a disastrous marriage" (p. 26). Finally, Robert Lumiansky classifies the *Merchant's Tale* as one of the tales of self-revelation (in a category with the Wife of Bath, the Canon's Yeoman, and the Pardoner), although he is careful to add that "the Merchant's remarks about his unhappy married life are cautiously brief."[10] In the *General Prologue*, the Merchant, according to Lumiansky, emerges as "a pompous bore who makes and breaks laws in an unprincipled fashion." As for relationship of tale and teller, Lumiansky offers the following observation: "I am not saying that the *Merchant's Tale* is pure autobiography, or that January in the tale is the Merchant. But I am saying that because of the wide discrepancy between what the Merchant thinks is the 'moral' to be drawn from his tale, on the one hand, and the inevitable conclusion to which that tale leads, on the other, the Merchant unwittingly gives considerable grounds upon which to base speculations about the reason for his own marital situation" (p. 156). Remarks about the Merchant's age, his sexual expectations, his disillusionment, even his pompousness, are grounded not in the prologues but in the tale. And if, indeed, Chaucer wrote the tale before he found a narrator for it, as I believe to have been the case, the alleged "self-revelation" is an invention of the critics, *post hoc, ergo propter hoc*. (What a pity that the Merchant didn't tell the *Shipman's Tale* with its even more mercantile imagery and plot!)

What does Chaucer actually reveal about the Merchant? First let us look at the familiar lines of the *General Prologue*:

> A Marchant was ther with a forked berd,
> In mottelee, and hye on horse he sat;
> Upon his heed a Flaundryssh bever hat,
> His bootes clasped faire and fetisly.
> His resons he spak ful solempnely.
> Sownynge alwey th'encrees of his wynnyng.
> He wolde the see were kept for any thyng
> Bitwixe Middelburgh and Orewelle.
> Wel koude he in eschaunge sheeldes selle.
> This worthy man ful wel his wit bisette:
> Ther wiste no wight that he was in dette,
> So estatly was he of his governaunce
> With his bargaynes and with his chevyssaunce.
> For sothe he was a worthy man with alle,
> But, sooth to seyn, I noot how men hym calle.
>
> (A 270-84)

I fail to see why Professor Lumiansky considers this a "uniquely unsympathetic portrait" (pp. 156-57). My impression is much the opposite. The first four lines describe a man of fashion, dressed in the latest style. This is clearly the sense conveyed by the Ellesmere illustrator, who is entirely faithful to the details of Chaucer's portrait. As seen by this illustrator, the Merchant is dressed in a colorful red gown with white and blue flowers. A grey Flemish beaver-hat is modishly cocked over his eyebrows, and his boots are "elegantly" laced (a better gloss for *fetisly* in this context than A. C. Baugh's "neatly"[11]). The forked beard, as apparent in the illustration as in the portrait, is another sign of fashion. And to show the Merchant "hye on horse," the illustrator takes pains to provide a prancing horse, eyes uplifted and front feet in the air. Indeed, for gaiety and cheerfulness only the Ellesmere illustration of the Squire can compete with the Merchant's. Of incidental interest is the fact that the Ellesmere illustrator depicts a man in his prime, distinctly youthful and energetic (in sharp contrast with the Malcolm Thurgood illustration which accompanies Lumiansky's text). It is true, of course, that the illustrator could have mistaken Chaucer's tone, but there is nothing in the sketch of the *General Prologue* to suggest that possibility. Moreover, this illustrator, who worked in the decade after Chaucer's death, was in a better position to assess the tonal significance of contemporary fashions than we are. A man who sits "hye on horse" is not *ipso facto* vain, as Lumiansky suggests; he could be successful, perhaps a little ostentatious, or just plain erect of posture [see *MED*, s.v. Heigh, adv. lb]. Nor must we assume because the Merchant spoke earnestly about his success in business that he was a "pompous bore." Like the other representatives of the middle class—for example, the Sergeant of the Law or the Physician—the Merchant is an expert at his trade, given to shop-talk and occasionally to breaking a law or two if a profit is to be made. There is nothing "unique" about the tone of this characterization. The Merchant is a thriving, fashionable man of the world, the sort with whom Chaucer was likely to contrast the outwardly threadbare Clerk whose portrait follows immediately.

The Merchant's prologue gives no further description of physical appearance or professional stature. In fact, it consists almost entirely of a twenty-seven line speech by the Merchant concerning his unfortunate marriage. We learn that he has been married "thise monthes two" to a woman he characterizes as a "shrewe at al"—"in every respect." She is "the worste that may be"—so wicked, indeed, that if she were married to the devil, he would be no match for her (E 1218-20). Recalling the *Clerk's Tale*, he tells us,

> Ther is a long and large difference
> Bitwix Grisildis grete pacience
> And of my wfy the passyng crueltee.
> (E 1223-25)

It has been customary to read the opening speech of the Merchant's as if the whole of it were delivered in solemn high seriousness. Kittredge tells us that "excitement loosens [the Merchant's] tongue, he goes all lengths, for he is half-mad with rage and shame" (p. 202). For Paul Ruggiers the speech is a "heartfelt prayer for deliverance from the snare of marriage."[12] Robert Jordan sees it as an "outcry of conjugal grief . . . , an impulsive and direct expression of bitter personal disillusionment."[13] But is it really meant to be read so? Suppose the whole of this speech were spoken with the tongue just slightly in cheek, by a man momentarily freed from domestic confinement? The Merchant exaggerates very nearly to the point of absurdity. And he never tells us just exactly what brings on his "wepyng and waylyng, care and oother sorwe" after only two months of marriage. Notice that we know no specific details about his wife. The temptation is there to identify her, *post hoc*, with May. But there is no textual warrant for the identification. We do not know her age, and we have no details about her appearance. Indeed, all that we know specifically is that she is a shrew. Now that is exactly what Harry Baillie's wife is—a "labbyng shrewe"—and we know what her offenses are. Far from being sexually desirable, Goodelief Baillie is a scold and a nag, ever ready to supply her husband with the club to beat his "knaves" and strong enough in her own arms that her husband "dar nat hire withstonde" [B^2 3110]. Interestingly, where between the Merchant's wife and Griselda there is a "large difference" as regards the latter's "grete patience," we learn of Goodelief that "she nys no thyng of swich patience/ As was this Mehbeus wyf Prudence" (B^2 3085-86). What then if the Merchant is similarly henpecked by an overbearing nag of a wife, as the verbal parallels would indicate? Nothing in his prologue rules out this reading; to the contrary, the tone of the exaggeration begs it.

The reference to Griselda in the Merchant's prologue (much as the reference to Prudence in the Monk's) may have a good deal more significance than is commonly realized. Perhaps in writing some of his prologues, Chaucer focused on the tale that preceded rather than the one that followed. Manly and Rickert tell us that the Merchant's prologue is a relatively late accretion in the genesis of the *Canterbury Tales*.[14] Suppose then that the *Clerk's Tale* was already written but as yet unassimilated. At a certain stage of composition, Chaucer decided to add the *Merchant's Tale*, also completed but unconnected to another tale, immediately after the *Clerk's Tale*. He then decided to replace the original ending of the *Clerk's Tale* (the troublesome Host's Stanza [E 1212^{a-g}]) with the Envoy. The *Clerk's Tale* would thus end with the line, "And lat hym care, and wepe, and wrynge, and waille" (E 1212). Thereafter he wrote the Merchant's prologue, and to begin it, he picked up the words *care, wepe,* and *waille*: "Wepyng and waylyng, care and oother sorwe" (E 1213). (See "Postscript," below.) The intent, then, is for the reader to be reminded of what he has just heard—essentially to cast a glance backward, not forward. This method occurs elsewhere as well. Surely, the fact that the Franklin has a son in whom he is disappointed relates primarily to the preceding *Squire's Tale*. It has, so far as I can tell, only tangential bearing on the Franklin's own fiction. It may be thus with the Merchant's shrewish bride. Not only is there a large difference between her and Griselda, but there also seems to be an implicit likeness between her and the Wife of Bath. It is well to bear in mind that the Clerk has just referred to the "Wyves love of Bath" (E 1170), and, indeed, the whole of the Envoy, as Kittredge has remarked long ago, is a mock encomium to her.

Just how pervasively the Envoy is directed to the Wife of Bath can be attested by its puns and veiled allusions. The Clerk, who is surely the intended speaker even if the Envoy is attributed to Chaucer in the rubrics,[15] addresses his ironic remarks to the "noble wyves" (E 1183) of the present times, now that "Grisilde is deed" (E 1177). Foreshadowing the remarks of the Merchant, he tells the pilgrims that a husband must not test his "wyves pacience in trust to fynde/ Grisildis, for in certein he shal faille" (E 1181-82). Rather, he advises wives to follow "Ekko," a veiled reference to the chattering Wife of Bath:

> Folweth Ekko, that holdeth no silence,
> But evere answereth at the countretaille
> Beth nat bidaffed for youre innocence,
> But sharply taak on yow the governaille.
> (E 1189-92)

The puns in this passage are inescapable: Ekko answers "at the countretaille," an innocent idiomatic phrase meaning "in reply" (see *MED*, s.v. Countretaille, n. [b]) but also an obscene reference to the Wife's "bele chose." *Bidaffed* is a *hapax* usually glossed as "outwitted" (see *MED*, s.v. Bidaffed, ppl.), but in this context it apparently also carries the meaning of "deafen" or "make deaf" (cf. *OED*, s.v. Bedeaf, v. Obs.). The Clerk, thus, in effect advises women not to be "deafened" for their innocence but to take the upper hand—a neat and ironic inversion of the lesson taught by Alice's ultimate adventure in marriage. Later, he offers more practical advice to the liberated wives of his own times, recalling in this instance the tale of the loathly hag:

> If thou be fair, ther folk been in presence,
> Shewe thou thy visage and thyn apparaille;
> If thou be foul, be fre of thy dispence . . .
> (E 1207-09)

The Merchant's prologue seen thus as an extension of the ironic remarks made by the Clerk invites the identification of the Merchant's shrewish wife with the domineering Wife of Bath (at least as she characterized herself in relation to her first three husbands) and not with the lusty May. Most critics who represent the *Merchant's Tale* as a savagely bitter drama of self-revelation have built their argument on a hypothetical resemblance, in plot situation if not in character, between the Merchant-teller and the dotard Januarie (who, incidentally, is *not* a merchant but a "worthy knyght" [E 1246]). They have failed to focus on the two wives. Another look at the Merchant's prologue will show that his complaints center on his wife's "malice" (E 1222), her "crueltee" (E 1225), and her "cursednesse" (E 1239). Nowhere does the Merchant make an explicit, or even implicit, suggestion that his wife has cuckolded him with a Damian of her own. There is nothing seductive in the portrait he draws of her. The "faire, fresshe lady May" (E 1882) who has not passed "twenty yeer, certayn" (E 1417) stands in sharp contrast. She at all times meekly submits to the carnal demands of her lecherous old husband—"she obeyeth, be hire lief or looth" (E 1961). Compliance is her trademark, whether she sports it with Damian or succumbs to the will of her hoary husband. Even at the climactic moment of discovery, May appears the very essence of the solicitous and meek helpmate, calmly imploring her husband in polite address: "Sire, what eyleth yow?" (E 2368). This nimble and artful wench is hardly to be identified with the pugnacious and ill-tempered wife of the Merchant.

Those who read the *Merchant's Tale* as savage and mordant self-revelation would have to assume that the Merchant speaks ironically when, in response to the Host's call for a story about the art of marriage, he avows: ". . . of myn owene soore,/ for soory herte, I telle may namoore" (E 1243-44). But why necessarily ironic? Suppose that Chaucer originally wrote the tale without a particular teller in mind. And suppose, then, that he ascribed it to the Merchant when he joined it, in the fashion mentioned, to the *Clerk's Tale*. This context provides for a teller who still rankles over the Wife's bold assault on the dominance of men, who represents himself as abused by the cursed cruelty of a shrew, and who is temporarily emancipated after two months of domestic confinement in wedlock to celebrate his release, now that "smale foweles maken melodye." Much like the Host, who rejoices over the absence of Goodelief, he revels in his freedom and tells a story intending to show the deceitfulness of women—outside the earshot of his shrewish wife. The newly-wed Merchant, whose age is left unspecified but who is characterized earlier as a man in his prime, then proceeds to tell a tale of the stock comic victim in the battle of the sexes—the *senex amans*. The story, of course, in true Chaucerian fashion recoils upon the teller, for in the final analysis it is not the deceitfulness of women but the vanity and foolishness of self-beguiled old men which is held up to ridicule. Unwittingly, thus, the Merchant, too, follows "Ekko." And yet the irony recoils once more, for the Wife herself, by demonstrating in the flesh the weakness of women, is Chaucer's most ardent antifeminist.

Perhaps the most upsetting feature of the *Merchant's Tale* is Januarie's failure, at the end, to recognize his folly. For those who identify Januarie with the Merchant, there emerges in consequence a psychologically complex fiction in which the narrator acts out his own senile delusions and lecherous self-indulgence without holding himself morally accountable. According to this essentially modern interpretation, the reader is asked to trust the tale, not the teller (Januarie as the Merchant's paradigm shows that husbands, not wives, are ultimately to blame). Under such circumstances, satire must perforce curdle into cynicism. No other Chaucerian fiction works that way, not even the tales of self-revelation by the Wife of Bath, the Canon's Yeoman, and the Pardoner, for all of these narrators openly—perhaps too openly—admit their culpability.

Once we remove the person of the narrator from his fiction, we are free to regard the *Merchant's Tale* as the supreme example of its kind, the fabliau turning on the *senex amans* as its butt. The *Miller's Tale* had already made an attempt in that direction for here, too, a deluded old man jealously guarded his young wife:

> This carpenter hadde wedded newe a wyf,
> Which that he lovede moore than his lyf;
> Of eighteteene yeer she was of age.
> Jalous he was, and heeld hir narwe in cage,
> For she was wylde and yong, and he was old,
> And denied hymself been lik a cokewold.
> . . . .
> Men sholde wedden after hire estaat,
> For youthe and elde is often at debaat.
> But sith that he was fallen in the snare,
> He moste endure, as oother folk, his care.
>   (A 3221-26, 3229-32)

Here, in germ, is the situation of the *Merchant's Tale*. The essential difference is that Nicholas and Absalon, unlike Damian, take the initiative in the husband's deception. As such, they are culpable, and true to the genre, they as well as the old carpenter are made to suffer the verdict of poetic justice. Morton Bloomfield has recently argued that John, in the *Miller's Tale*, "is unjustly punished," and that the tale itself should be grouped with the *Merchant's* and the *Shipman's Tales* for its glorification of injustice and unfairness, thus demonstrating that "the universe . . . is really deeply irrational" and un-Boethian.[16] But this interpretation ignores the special code of law that governs the world of fabliau. This world is crowded with fallible mortals for whom life flows joyfully and for whom sex is a natural and healthy pleasure, enjoyed most salubriously by the young and the free. The offenders are those who threaten this natural order: the arrogant, the vain, the greedy. Ripe and willing maidens are the traditional innocents; their free-hearted sex is their liberation. Hence,

Alisoun, Malyne, May, even the "revelous" wife of the Shipman's merchant are left unpunished, and they are sated from the "bisynesse of myrthe and of solas" (A 3654). The guilty, in contrast, suffer according to their deserts. Some like John the carpenter endure pain and public ridicule; others like the "squaymous" Absalon are brought to a more private though equally uncomfortable retribution. The heaviest punishment is reserved for the most cupidinous—such moneyed patrons of sex as the Shipman's merchant and Januarie. These offenders are deceived without knowing it, and the deception will continue to afflict them even beyond the bounds of the narrative. Given the world of the fabliau (and for that matter the world at large), there is nothing unfair about such a dispensation of justice.

Amidst the derision and contempt that so many critics are wont to find in the tone of the *Merchant's Tale*, we are likely to forget that much of it is gay and laughable. The fact is that Januarie is blind, but we are not. Fortunately, we can see the "fresshe May" throughout the story in all her vernal briskness. It is her energy, subdued at first, which brings forth the climactic encounter in the pear-tree. The playful gods watch over her, and Proserpina, who herself was once ravished by old King Pluto, the god of the underworld, "whil that she gadered floures in the mede" (E 2231), ultimately prevails. Proserpina is the spirit of Spring, and May is her embodiment. Recently I saw the Martin Starkie-Nevill Coghill musical version of the *Canterbury Tales*, and in that performance the *Merchant's Tale*, perhaps more than any other, conveyed the sense of sheer exuberance as youth conquers foolish old age. It is interesting to note that the parts of the Merchant and Januarie, unlike those of the Wife of Bath and the old woman of the tale, were assumed by different actors. And, true to form, the actor playing Januarie had earlier taken the part of John the carpenter in the *Miller's Tale*. The sense of erotic fun and irreverent merriment conveyed by the performance is intrinsic to the tale. Even some of the fifteenth-century editors must have felt that spirit, as witness the following ribald elaboration of the seduction scene found in three manuscripts:

> And sodenly a-non this Damyan
> Gan pullen up the smok and yn he throng
> A gret tente he preste yn and a long
> Sche seide it was be meriest fit
> That euyr in hir lyue sche was at yit
> Me lordis tente sche seide serueþ me not þus
> He foldith twifolde bi swete Ihesus
> He maie not swyue worth a leke
> And yet he is full gentill and full meke
> This is leuyr to me than Evensong[17]

This interpolation, as well as several more in the same vein, is undoubtedly apocryphal. And while I would not claim that their creator was a poet-critic of unusual insight or talent, the very fact that he set out to add these lines in the margin says something of the spirit of bawdry and uncontained merriment with which he approached the tale.

E. T. Donaldson, in a recent essay, has attempted to argue that the *Merchant's Tale* itself, even when one detaches it from what is said by the narrator in the prologue, is "intensely bitter" (p. 34). According to Donaldson, the narrator as he intrudes in the story is exclusively given to see "the dark side of things" (p. 34). In evidence, he cites various discordances in the narrator's diction: the reference to God seeing Adam "bely-naked" (E 1326), to the priest who "croucheth" (E 1707) Januarie and May, or to the characterization of the Song of Solomon paraphrase as "swiche olde lowed wordes" (E 2149). But, as the *MED* will attest, neither *bely-naked* nor *croucheth* necessarily carry the profane connotations that Professor Donaldson finds in them (by reason of such usage elsewhere in Chaucer), and the line "swiche olde lowed wordes used he" surely does not mean "such stupid old words he used," as Professor Donaldson glosses it, but "such *unlearned* words he used" to highlight the irreverent paraphrase that Januarie has just spoken (cf. *OED*, s.v. Lewd, a.2). To find in such instances "the disgusted disillusion of the narrator" (p. 41) is to me unconvincing. In the final analysis, Professor Donaldson does not succeed in separating the tale from the context of the prologue, in which he has read it all along.[18] At one point, in the midst of his argument, the characterization of the prologue clearly intrudes: "But the Merchant's hard-earned conviction that wives are inevitably and triumphantly deceitful and unfaithful so infects his depiction of the world that the reader is made, willy-nilly, to suffer some measure of pity and terror" (p. 42). All this goes to prove that Chaucer has given us a Merchant's prologue, and no matter how we interpret it, we cannot—even for the sake of argument—forget it when we read the tale. For that reason, it is important to recall that the image projected by the Merchant in his prologue is not that of a cuckold or an old lecher, but simply of a much-abused henpecked husband.

My point has been that there is no textual reason for identifying the Merchant with January. Nothing in the prologue warrants this association, and yet that is finally the basis for the venom, the biliousness, and the cynicism that modern critics have found in the story. Perhaps what is needed is a look down from the pear-tree as well as up. If so, we might find that the "fresshe May's" parting words—on a deeper level of meaning—are a good warning to critics as well as blind husbands:

Beth war, I prey yaw; for, by hevene kyng,
Ful many a man weneth to seen a thyng,
And it is al another than it semeth.
He that mysconceyveth, he mysdemeth.

(E 2407-10)

Postscript: The Evolution of the E-F Fragments

Chaucer's method of composition is, of course, a subject wide open for speculation. I subscribe to Manly's theory, summarized by Germaine Dempster, that one MS ranging from fair copy to working draft of the individual tales was in Chaucer's possession at the time of his death, and that some earlier drafts, at various stages of composition, were in the hands of Chaucer's friends (cf. "Manly's Conception of the Early History of the *Canterbury Tales*," *PMLA*, 61 (1946), 390). Since the E-F Fragments present no stable order of tales and little agreement on headlinks and endlinks, one can only speculate what order and form Chaucer finally accepted, if any. My own hypothesis is the following: At very first, the *Merchant's Tale* followed the unfinished *Squire's Tale*, followed in turn by Group D (W-Fri-Su) and by the *Clerk's* and *Franklin's Tales*. Such is the order of the commercial MSS of the fifteenth century (Manly's Group **d**). At this point, the *Merchant's Tale* had no head or endlink. In the second stage, he moved the *Merchant's Tale* from its position before the D-group to one immediately behind it, leaving the order Sq-W-Fri-Su-Cl-Me-Fr, which is reflected in Manly's Group **c** among fifteenth-century MSS. This arrangement may have resulted from Chaucer's desire to break up the heavy sequence of Clerk-Franklin. But whatever the reason, at this stage, he cancelled the Host's stanza [E 1212$^{a\text{-}g}$] at the end of the *Clerk's Tale*, replaced it with the Envoy and wrote the Merchant's headlink. The last stage is reflected in the Ellesmere MS. and Group **a**; it involves the transfer of the *Squire's Tale* from its position preceding the Wife of Bath to one following the Merchant (i.e., W-Fri-Su-Cl-Me-Sq-Fr). This placement might have been occasioned by Chaucer's unwillingness to finish the *Squire's Tale*. He consequently moved it, inserted the Franklin's headlink and established the order now generally accepted as authentic. My assumption is that several archetypes of each stage were in circulation at Chaucer's death. This would account for the fact that spurious links appear in so many MSS, especially the commercial ones. The scribe copying a Stage One MS would have followed the order of the tales, but finding no headlinks or endlinks in the E and F Fragments, he made certain adaptations perhaps from a Stage Two or Stage Three MS in the same scriptorium. It is possible that such an occurrence happened in the Hengwrt-Ellesmere workshop. The two MSS, both early and copied by the same scribe, clearly had different exemplars, as attested by their different orders. The same scribe could have put together the archetype of the commercial manuscripts by adapting the Ellesmere head and endlinks to a Stage One MS. It is thus that the Franklin's headlink might have been used to link the *Squire's Tale* and the *Merchant's*, as found in the Group **d** MSS. To change the attribution, the scribe simply substitutes "Marchant" for "Frankeleyn," and when the latter occurs as a rhyme word, he writes "Marchant certeyn" as in Morgan MS. M249 (F.91^r). Later, when he is stuck for a Franklin's headlink, he takes the discarded Host's stanza and the customary Squire's headlink and edits them into two spurious stanzas—again a common occurrence in the **d** Group.

From *The Chaucer Review 7*, no. 2 (Fall 1972): 118-131. Copyright © 1972 by The Pennsylvania State University. Reprinted by permission of Penn State Press.

Notes

This paper was read in modified form at the Chaucer section of the 86th Annual MLA Meeting.

1. George Lyman Kittredge, *Chaucer and His Poetry* (Cambridge, Mass., 1915), p. 202.

2. "Chaucer's *Merchant's Tale*," *MP*, 33 (1936), rpt. in *Chaucer Criticism: The Canterbury Tales*, eds. Richard J. Schoeck and Jerome Taylor (Notre Dame, 1960), pp. 176, 188.

3. *The Comic Tales of Chaucer* (London, 1967), pp. 133-53.

4. "Afterthoughts on the *Merchant's Tale*," *SP*, 58 (1961), 583-96.

5. *Speaking of Chaucer* (London, 1970), pp. 30-45.

6. *PMLA*, 86 (1971), 25-31.

7. My quotations are from *The Works of Geoffrey Chaucer*, 2nd ed., ed. F. N. Robinson (Boston, 1957); hereafter cited by line number within the text. For further comments by the Host about his wife, see the Monk's headlink (B^2 3081-3113). It should be noted that Kittredge interprets E 2426 to mean "His own wife . . . is true as any steel" (p. 202), but despite the indication in the *OED* that "true as steel" applies more often to persons than to statements (s.v. Steel sb^1, 1b), it seems here to be a simple asseveration and should be set off in commas. If Kittredge is right, however, we would have further evidence that shrews, like the Merchant's wife, were not inherently regarded as unfaithful.

8. *A Reader's Guide to Chaucer* (New York, 1964), pp. 111, 130.

9. *The Merchant's Prologue and Tale* (Cambridge, 1966), p. 2.

10. *Of Sondry Folk* (Austin, 1955), pp. 248-49.

11. See *Chaucer's Major Poetry* (New York, 1963), p. 243, n. 273.

12. *The Art of the Canterbury Tales* (Madison, 1965), p. 111.

13. *Chaucer and the Shape of Creation* (Cambridge, Mass., 1967), pp. 133-34.

14. *Text of the Canterbury Tales*, II (Chicago, 1940), 266.

15. See F. N. Robinson, p. 712, n. on line 1177.

16. "The Miller—An Un-Boethian Interpretation," *Medieval Literature and Folklore Studies*, eds. Jerome Mandel and Bruce A. Rosenberg (New Brunswick, 1970), pp. 206, 210-11.

17. See Harley MS. 1758 (Ha^2),f.88^r; also cf. the Helmingham (He) and New College (Ne) MSS. I am grateful to Jeffery Kluewer for calling the passage to my attention.

18. *Chaucer's Poetry* (New York, 1958), p. 921.

Figmenta vs. *Veritas*:
Dame Alice and the Medieval Literary Depiction of Women by Women

Katharina M. Wilson

The observation that medieval literature is notoriously misogynistic has been so often reiterated that it has become axiomatic. Nor is that judgment limited to modern literary historians. The Wife of Bath, that robust and unabashedly honest creation of Chaucer's double-edged satire, explodes with contempt at the portraits of women in literature. She scoffs at books written by men depicting (or rather deprecating) women as addicted to lechery, treachery, shrewishness, and greed, depictions which clerks supply copiously and with considerable gusto from their ivory towers of ascetic studiousness. She comments:

> For trusteth wel, it is an impossible
> That any clerk well speke good of wyves,
> But it be of booty seintes lyves,
> Ne of noon oother womman, never the mo.
> Who peynted the leoun, tel me who?
> By God! if wommen hadde writen stories,
> As clerkes ban withinne hire oratories,
> They wolde ban written of men moore wikkednesse
> Than al the mark of Adam may redresse.[1]

Dame Alice is referring to Aesop's fable about a lion puzzled by a sculpture which shows a man killing a lion. The Wife emphasizes the moral of the tale (that the result of the combat would have been depicted differently by the lion), thus drawing the parallel between the fable's moral and the medieval literary view of women. She suggests—as Euripides' Medea did eighteen centuries before her—that an artist's creation (or rather, the verity of his perception) is conditioned by his personal experience, his personal sympathies, inclinations, and his sex, and that, consequently, stories told about women by the very class that knew least of them and was taught to fear them most, the clergy, could hardly be realistic.[2]

This paper deals with two of the Wife of Bath's hypotheses: first, that "if women hadde written stories," then much of literature would be misandric rather than misogynistic, and second, that men alone are responsible for upholding the one-dimensional ideal of feminine excellence. I would like to examine Dame Alice's assertions by focusing on the attitudes of two medieval women writers, Hrotsvit of Gandersheim and Christine de Pizan.

Dame Alice's assessment of the medieval literary scene regarding women and women characters is by and large true: most of medieval literature was written by men and for men; much of it was written by clerks; women in clerkly literature are traditionally depicted as self-indulgent, lustful, treacherous, domineering, greedy, shrewish, prone to sin, and, most importantly, a constant danger to man's salvation unless they are saints or chaste women in monastic orders.[3] Her suggestion that if women had been the writers, then literature would be misandric rather than misogynistic, on the other hand, is only partially true and manifests a psychologically intriguing instance of Chaucer's craftsmanship by presenting—tongue in cheek—the wishful as well as self-revealing generalization of his ironic heroine. When her generalization applies to the works of medieval women writers, it occurs either in situations of direct confrontation between men and women or is conditioned by the conventions of a given genre; if there is a victim, there must be a villain; if there is triumphant resistance, there must be an appealing tempter; if there is rejection or suffering, there must be a culprit. Since medieval women writers do tend to prefer female protagonists, a negative view of men necessarily occurs when the tale has tragic overtones or depicts a struggle between contending moral or religious principles exemplified or simply embraced by the characters. Similarly, the conventions of certain genres traditionally prescribe the negative depiction of either men or women. Ascetic propaganda, when written by men and addressed to men, contains, almost invariably, misogynistic passages; when written for women by men, it contains—though less frequently, less overtly and less violently—misandric details.[4] Clearly, if chastity is to be upheld as the pinnacle of excellence and chaste virtue (as a martyr-like total devotion to Christ and His Church) is to be emulated, then the fortitude of that virtue can only be adequately presented if the virginal hero or heroine is shown to triumph over the persistent and appealing temptations of a member of the opposite sex.[5]

The Wife is also correct in her description of the role model upheld for women in religious literature written by men—namely, the ascetic ideal—even though her assessment of the ascetic ideal as entirely one-dimensional is a self-serving overgeneralization. Her observation concerning the sexual dimorphism of the perception and depiction of the worldly or other-worldly ideals of female behavior, however, does not hold true for the bulk of medieval literature, even though the Wife is correct in suggesting that women writers would, if they had the chance, create less stereotypical women characters and would describe, like the painting lion, reality from their own perspective. That dimorphism in the Middle Ages is most pronounced between religious and lay writers: medieval monastic writers (be they women or men) tend to promote the same feminine ideal of excellence as that attributed to clerks by the Wife of Bath—namely, the ideal of chastity. (Albeit, unlike men, religious women do explore the complex potentialities of the virginal ideal.) Secular writers, both male and female, tend to diverge from the ideal, but here again, women offer less stereotyped depictions of women.[6] Among religious writers, women often offer role models and perceptions diametrically opposed to those of their male contemporaries: there are those of the assertive female *miles Christi* and the female teacher, preacher, and healer, as well as conceptions of God as a loving, nourishing mother. Among secular writers, women not only depict the secular and courtly ideals of the lady in love, but also provide at least marginally diversified role models of female excellence; often these are genuine alternatives to the ideals depicted by men.

The women writers exemplifying both the male/female and the secular/religious dimorphism of the literary view of women whom I have chosen to discuss are representatives of different chronological, social and intellectual points on the spectra of the Middle Ages: Hrotsvit of Gandersheim was a tenth-century monastic author of the Saxon Imperial abbey of Gandersheim; Christine de Pizan, fifteenth-century secular writer of Italian descent, was Dame Alice's contemporary and the first woman of the West to earn her living by the pen. Both writers were concerned with the literary depictions of women which they designate as *"figmenta"*—untrue, unwarranted, even malignant flights of the poetic imagination, the phantasmagoric products of minds not familiar with the lives of virtuous women; both attempted to supplant the calumnious literary view of women by creating alternate literary models of feminine excellence, models which they admittedly base on their own (feminine and virtuous) experience; both attempted (albeit for different reasons) to combat the demonstrably noxious effects of the negative literary depiction of women by challenging the stereotype. Both wrote works in which women characters are depicted as catalysts, not of perdition, but of salvation and betterment for their husbands, lovers, or would-be lovers.

The misogynistic male authors on whom the two women writers concentrated their attack were not their contemporaries but canonized writers of the past whose works enjoyed widespread popularity during the Middle Ages. The monastic Hrotsvit in the tenth century saw the pagan Terence as the arch-enemy; the secular Christine armed herself against the Christian clerics, Jean de Meung and Matheolus.[7] The three men's depictions of women frolicking in the pleasures of the flesh have much in common. All three created women characters imbued with the very qualities so memorably summarized by the Wife of Bath: those of lechery, treachery, domineerance, and greed.

In the prologue to her comedies Hrotsvit defines her poetic program. She says:

There are many Catholics, and we cannot entirely acquit ourselves of this charge, who prefer the vanity of pagan books on account of the elegance of their style, to the usefulness of sacred scripture. There are also others, who, devoted to sacred writings and spurning pagan works, yet read the (*figmenta*) phantastic fiction of Terence frequently, and while they delight in the sweetness of his style, they are stained by the knowledge of [exposure to] wicked events. Wherefore I, the Strong Voice of Gandersheim, did not refuse to imitate in composition him whom others are wont to read, so that in the same form of writing in which the shameless acts of lascivious women have been sung, the laudable chastity of Christian women may be celebrated according to the ability of my poor talent. (*Opera* 235)

Hrotsvit's reference to Terence's noxious *figmenta* stands in marked contrast to her own repeated attestations of useful *veritas*—or hagiographic truth—as the source and theme of her works, reflecting in this way Hrotsvit's triple purpose: first, she contrasts helpful Christian truths with dangerous pagan lies; secondly, she substitutes chaste Christian women for the pagan poet's lascivious courtesans, thus creating female characters of her own (true) experience who exemplify traits worthy of emulation; thirdly, she creates Christian alter- or antiplays intended to supplant pagan comedy, at least for her limited audience.[8] In this manner hagiographic truth is conveyed through the depiction of feminine excellence, and the glorious triumph of Christianity over paganism is achieved through the victory of faithful, determined, and chaste Christian women over amorous, weak, and evil pagan men.

According to Hrotsvit, Terence's comedy posed a grave danger to his readers because they could be mesmerized by the sweetness of his style. His sweetness, however, masked only the wickedness of his subject matter, thus corrupting readers and endangering their hopes for salvation—an assessment of the power of amatory literature not very different from Dante's account of Paolo and Francesca. To Hrotsvit this was clearly a misuse of poetic talent; that, in addition, Terence told fiction (*figmenta*), rather than truth, prompted Hrotsvit to respond and fortify herself not only with Christian ideals but also with attested truth, priding herself in putting her God-given philological talent to such good use. The glorification of God and Christianity is her poetic aim; serial vindications of virtuous women through whom God works His miracles constitute her recurring theme.

Terence's women characters are often seductresses, usually harlots, almost invariably involved in love-affairs, frequently avaricious, and, unless married, weak. The plots of his six comedies revolve around philandering husbands or love-sick young men and their stern fathers. All six of Hrotsvit's comedies are about women, often virgins, who are not only bulwarks of strength and endurance, persistent in their Christian faith, successful in resisting all temptations or glorious in their repentance, but who, as chaste wives and mothers, become catalysts of virtue and salvation for their husbands and lovers by converting them to Christianity. The canoness's male characters, on the other hand, are usually lascivious, cruel, devious, unjust, and greedy; they are often power-less, in spite of all their worldly splendor and their socially exalted positions, when confronted with the unshakable strength and moral force of frail Chris-tian maidens. Theirs is physical or socio-political strength which crumbles in the face of the religious and moral fortitude of Hrotsvit's women characters who exemplify the victory of the spirit over the flesh. The exceptions to these good/evil dichotomies along sexual lines (or, more precisely, to this literary misandry) are provided by the saintly monks in her plays who pose no moral danger to her chaste heroines.[9]

This inversion of the Terentian roles in Hrotsvit's comedies is, of course, an exact manifestation of Dame Alice's metaphor of the lion as a painter: for Terence's *fictitious* depiction of depraved or weak women and triumphant men, Hrotsvit substitutes the acclaimedly *true* picture of her own experience as a Christian canoness: the depiction of chaste and virtuous Christian women triumphing (because fortified by Christian truth and aided by God) over the temptations of the world is usually highlighted by the despicable male protag-onists of the plays. Her stated dramatic intent, to show frail Christian virgins reaping the glory of victory while strong men are routed with confusion, thus becomes the vehicle for the triumph of Christianity over paganism, and, by extension, of Hrotsvit over Terence.[10]

In spite of her insistence on the divine truth of her Christian themes and the reliability of her sources, Hrotsvit's comedies are no more realistic and no less schematized than those of Terence; neither are her female characters any less single-role and single-purpose creations than those of her male clerkly con-temporaries. In fact, Hrotsvit's heroines differ little from the ideal women of man-composed or man-compiled saints' lives and legends.[11] Dame Alice's metaphor of the lion thus applies to the works of Hrotsvit as well; so, however, does her complaint about the one-dimensional female model depicted sympa-thetically by clerks—the chaste, Christian, virginal ideal. Hrotsvit, like the medieval clerks so scorned by the Wife of Bath, wrote ascetic propaganda from her own oratory, and while Hrotsvit's male characters *are* villainous, *do* present temptations and tribulations for her heroines, and do indulge in "moore wikkednesse/ Than al the mark of Adam may redresse," her women characters triumph only because they are strengthened by the Christian ascetic ideal. The Saxon canoness made no attempt to glorify or even vindicate virtu-ous lay women and even less so women who, like the Wife, "live in the flesh." Like the man in Aesop's fable, she was depicting her own experience, inclina-tions and hierarchy of values. As such she was more concerned with the ascetic ideal and with the triumph of Christianity than with widening the narrow definition of feminine virtue supplied by clerks.[12] Where her consciousness as a woman does make itself felt is in her concentration on women as exemplary characters and in her repeated presentations of women as not only virtuous and chaste but as catalysts of men's salvation.[13]

Hrotsvit may be one of the first medieval woman poets to have attempted to come to grips with the negative literary view of women, but she is by no means the most theoretical or the most profound thinker on the subject. As a privileged noble canoness in one of the richest of the flourishing abbeys of the tenth century, Hrotsvit's proposed solution to the woman-question remains purely literary, entirely Christo-centric, and fully within the monastic-ascetic system of desirable female behavior. In addition, she never blames the male hierarchy of her society for the difficulties women experience. But even those medieval religious women writers who had more obstacles to overcome and more to suffer from their male contemporaries, avoid large-scale diatribes of the *Quid est mulier* type against masculine society.[14] There is simply no extant medieval text written by a woman comparable to the vitriolic attacks on the "weaker sex" written by men. As in Hrotsvit's comedies so in most texts written by medieval women, literary misandry is incidental, limited to particular men attempting to thwart a chaste heroine's pursuit of virtue, and secondary to the glorification of the ascetic ideal. Ascetic and mystic writers, such as Angela of Foligno, Catherine of Siena, Bridget of Sweden, Hadewijch, Margarete Porete, and even Margery Kempe invariably uphold the ascetic, virginal ideal through which (and only through which) women can rise above their subordinate position, but they do not attack men in general for placing obstacles in their way. Even the learned and very outspoken Hildegard of Bingen or the charismatic Catherine of Siena censure only particular men for their corruption or incompetence, but they rarely attack men in general.[15] For that type of general bombast, we have to wait until well after Chaucer's death, until Anna Bijns in the seventeenth century composes her scathing attacks on husbands, attacks which, like medieval ascetic propaganda written by men, see the opposite sex as embodying the evils that beset women.[16]

Thus, while Dame Alice's hypothetical projection into the past does not hold true entirely (and certainly not on the practical level), her observation, when examined in light of medieval evidence, may hold true on a more theoretical level: if her contrast between men and women writing from their oratories is taken as a comment on the power principles involved in having an almost exclusive monopoly on establishing ideological tenets and upholding thus the politics of a patriarchal system, then the inverse of that situation would involve an almost exclusively female class of *literati* possessing unlimited power and creating/perpetuating their own matriarchal system of values.

That power structure, of course, did not exist in the Middle Ages, and Dame Alice's hypothesis must remain precisely that: a theoretical speculation.

The Wife of Bath's observation concerning misandric literature by medieval women, then, holds only partially true for monastic women writers; similarly, her criticism concerning the one-dimensional role model of feminine behavior perpetuated by monastic writers finds exception in the works of the female saints and visionaries of the Middle Ages. Dame Alice, it seems, has an overly simplistic view of asceticism, being unaware of—or ignoring—the complexities of the ascetic ideal of female excellence, an ideal which provided many medieval women with an alternative to marriage and gave them a fulfilling opportunity for self-realization. In fact, the ascetic female ideal, contrary to Dame Alice's corporeal view, need not be one-dimensional. Elizabeth Petroff's book on Italian religious women, for instance, demonstrates the great variety of role models that women could embrace in their pursuit of personal fulfillment within orthodox Christianity.[17] In fact, the striking argument of Petroff's book is that the medieval saint is "no patient Griselda," for goodness and sanctity in women occupy the opposite poles of the spectrum of medieval ethics (1-13). Her assertion is amply borne out by the texts of the writers she discusses. Contrary to the ideals of passivity, obedience, and invisibility upheld by the medieval church as the desiderata of female behavior, the saint had not only to exhibit evidence of moral integrity but also give proof of heroic virtue, responsibility, signs of leadership and decisiveness in the vigorous pursuit of asceticism, a task which often entailed the direct rejection of, and active opposition to, the stereotypic qualities of womanly virtue. By insisting on their rights to preach and to teach, medieval female mystics often had to battle the Church's male hierarchies. Moreover, these women do offer theoretical models of ultimate emancipation: the seventh and final stage of the female mystic's experience often culminates in visions of cosmic order when the saint is made aware of the absolute equality of male and female in heaven. Women visionaries, such as Julian of Norwich, Ghirardesca of Pisa, Umilta of Florence, Margarita of Faenza, Aldobrandesca of Siena, Mechthild of Magdeburg, Mechthild of Hackeborn and Margery Kempe, just to mention a few, all emphasize the female, nurturing aspect of the godhead and assign a tremendously significant importance to Mary not only as genetrix but also as the Queen of Heaven.[18]

Dame Alice's observations concerning the lion as a painter are also to the point regarding secular medieval women writers. Marie de France (in the twelfth century) and the troubairitz of Occitania (in the twelfth and thirteenth centuries) writing in the vernacular tradition of *fin amour*, depict diversified role models for women and do occasionally offer mildly misandric or misogamous views.[19] Their heroines, like the saints and mystics of the thirteenth, fourteenth and fifteenth centuries, are seldom the passive, acquiescing, and obedient women or the lascivious, greedy, and cruel women of the ecclesiastical and social stereotypes. Rather, they differ greatly from the demure or cruelly resisting ladies who often people the pages of male-composed romances and troubadour poetry: they often take the initiative in acquiring lovers or in bettering their situation. More importantly, they depict the ennobling effect of love on women. Marie de France also freely interchanges the traditional romance roles of lover and beloved. While Marie's lais usually have happy endings and treat both men and women sympathetically, the troubairitz, on the other hand, often write of disappointed love from the woman's perspective, depicting thus a frequently less complimentary view of men in their versions of the cruel, perfidious male lover.

The confluence of the two alternate models of female excellence (i.e., the secular and the religious) and the emergence of a new, composite and well-rounded female ideal occurred not in the medieval monastic or courtly setting but in a late medieval/early Renaissance urban one. Christine de Pizan, Hrotsvit's "anti-pole," lived four centuries later than the Saxon canoness. Much had changed in those four centuries, and the intellectual, religious and social forces that shaped the Reformation shaped too the feminine ideal of excellence as well as the social importance of women's role within and without marriage.[20] The general emphasis on man's dignity and individuality and the importance of liberal education, as well as the relative distrust of asceticism, applied to a certain degree to women of the upper and middle classes. Indeed, women's entry into the labor market paved the way toward quasi-practical emancipation of women by making them financially independent.

Coinciding with the rise of cities and bourgeois culture, the great upsurge in women's participation in the labor market began in the thirteenth and fourteenth centuries. The bourgeois woman of the thirteenth and fourteenth centuries had considerable *de facto* equality with her male compatriots, not only as the wife and co-worker of her artisan husband, but also as a single woman practicing her own trade. As Eileen Power observes, single working women would often even undercut their male competitors' prices.[21] Manorial records show women in a variety of occupations—as glovers, girdlers, brewers, net-makers, bakers, cultivators, chandlers, iron-mongers, and weavers, and they were often plaintiffs or defendants in business matters.[22] Four percent of London taxpayers in 1319 were unmarried, independent women—some quite prosperous. Women were not only admitted to eighty of the 120 guilds, but they commanded a few guilds of their own, such as the silk guild.[23] In 1260 Etienne Boileau's *Livres des métiers* lists the exclusively female crafts: spinners of silk, weavers of silk, weavers of silken trains, milliners, and makers of alms purses.[24] In fact, some Cologne guilds admitted male members only if they were related to one of the female members.[25] A Paris ordinance of 1281 mentions that certain female workers (*tisserandes de toiles*) were in brisk competition with men, and in Philippe Verdier's study of Gothic manuscript marginalia showing women engaged in a variety of trades, the author remarks on the frequent occurrence of depictions of the topos *mundus inversus* in the pictures.[26] Women's participation in the labor force also had some legal repercussions. Some city ordinances decreed that a woman who went to the market to buy and sell would enjoy the same rights with regard to inheritance and ownership as her husband.[27]

Thus, women were very much a part of the late-medieval labor market; they brought economic benefits to their husbands by means of their substantial dowries and their production skills; the surplus of nubile women created a competitive marriage market; the relative peace (crusades by the thirteenth century were predominantly fought by mercenary armies) and a growing economy provided for a bourgeois prosperity.

Moreover, while the Church still placed chastity at the pinnacle of the hierarchy of values, it now had to uphold the value of marriage in the face of several dualist heresies preaching the evil of the married state. For laymen, marriage was recommended as the "natural way of life" and was recognized as one of the seven sacraments (one of the lesser sacraments because it did not serve salvation directly). Indeed, in spite of the efforts of rigorists, the Old Testament precept to increase and multiply was upheld throughout the centuries. As J. Gilchrist points out, a minority current of medieval theology put a special value on multiplying human souls.[28] Twelfth-century philosopher Duns Scotus, for example, seems to propose that the more offspring there are on earth, the greater the population will be in heaven. Procreation, he suggests, is the reparation of the Fall of Lucifer.[29] Moreover, population increase was recognized in several concilar decrees as a value.[30] The rise of antinomian heresies in the twelfth and thirteenth centuries required the Church to confirm repeatedly the sacred nature and divine origin of marriage and of the procreative ideal. Another twelfth-century writer, Alain de Lille, eulogizes marriage thus (*Summa de Arte Praed* Ch. 45): "It had its beginning in paradise. It removes the vice of incontinence. . . . It preserves the fidelity of the marriage bed. . . . It frees their offspring from infamy. It excuses carnal intercourse from fault." Similarly, thirteenth-century Italian Franciscan St. Bonaventura asserts (in *Four Sentences* d.31 a 1g.1): "Were it not for that remedy which is marriage, there would be disorder not only in the feelings but also in the reason and thus there would always be sin." Moreover, Peter the Chanter (*Summa de Sacramentis*) and Robert Courson (*De matrimonio*) attacked the rigorists as semi-heretics who aimed to destroy marriage by indirect means. They even went so far as to propose that lawful coitus was meritorious.

The upholding of a dual system of values by the Church—celibate ideal for clergy, marital ideal for laymen—served as a concession to social reality. Secular society, on the other hand, had always considered marriage as the fundamental social unit of society. As Georges Duby observes, marriage bestowed official recognition and society legitimized it "as a means of perpetuating itself without endangering its structural stability."[31] From the twelfth century on, Duby remarks, marriage became very important as a principle representing order in aristocratic society: a woman became a "*domina*," but "marriage came to be perceived as an event that transformed a man's life perhaps even more profoundly. To a young man, marrying meant leaving behind his unsteady existence . . . acquiring both power and wisdom," for all power was in the hands of the *conjugati* (12).

Christine de Pizan, member of the secular upper-middle-class and married, writing at the onset of the Renaissance, not only showed great concern for social, domestic and moral injustice, reflected in, and sometimes resulting from, misogynistic literature, but she also made an attempt at a self-definition and self-valuation.[32] She perceived a disconcerting dichotomy between what she herself experienced and observed of other women and what men wrote about them. Her own experience as a secular and (happily) married woman and later as a widow with two young children and a mother to support prompted a response very different from that of Hrotsvit. Around 1402 Christine became a participant in a debate now usually called the "*querelle des femmes*," a debate which commenced over the literary merits of Jean de Meung's continuation of the *Roman de la Rose* and in which Christine partook to modify (or to at least call into question) public opinion. Christine's objection to the *Roman* was chiefly based on its many misogynistic passages which she labelled as unrealistic, dangerous and untrue. In a letter to the Provost of Lille, she says:

> How can it be good and useful that he [Jean de Meung] accuses so excessively, impetuously and falsely, blames and defames women for several serious vices, claiming that their morals are full of perversity. . . . I do not see how it is suitable to the part of Genius, who recommends, and even insists that women should go to bed with men without delay for the purpose he praises so highly, and then he says so many slanderous things about them because they do it. In fact, he says: "Flee! Flee! Flee from the venomous snakes." And then he says that one should not cease to pursue them. This is certainly a great contradiction to command one to flee what he is expected to pursue and pursue what one tells him to flee.
>
> He is so insistent about not telling a secret to a woman, who is so bereft of discretion, as he recalls, and I can't imagine where in the devil he found so much nonsense and so many futile words as are hurled at them throughout that long trial, but I bet that all those who consider this quite authentic and put so much faith in it will

tell me how many men they have known to be accused, killed, hanged, or even reproached in the street because of the denunciation of their wives; I think they will find them very thinly scattered.

Moreover, the poet speaks so unnecessarily and in such an ugly way of married women who deceive their husbands, a matter he can scarcely know from experience and of which he speaks very categorically. Of what use is this, what good can come of it? I think it is only a hindrance to peace and well-being by making husbands who listen to such nonsense, if they pay attention to it, suspicious and mistrustful of their wives. . . . Indeed, as he blames women in general, I am led to believe it is because he has never known or frequented any virtuous women, but through knowing a few who are dissolute and evil, as the lecherous are in the habit of doing, he believed or pretended to know what all are like, just because he never had any experience of others. If only he had blamed the dishonest ones and suggested that this sort should be shunned it would have been good and just advice. But no! Instead he accused all women without exception. But if the author took it upon himself to accuse them or judge them falsely so entirely beyond reasonable limits, they are not the ones who should be blamed, but rather him who tells such lies that they are beyond belief, especially as the opposite can be clearly seen. For even if he and all his accomplices swear to it, let none take offense, there have nevertheless been, are now, and will always be women more valiant, honest, better bred, and even wiser, and through whom more good has come to the world, than has ever come from him. And some are even more versed in the affairs of state and have more virtuous habits, some have been responsible for reconciling their husbands with their enemies, and borne their affairs and their secrets and their passions gently and confidentially, even when their husbands have been disagreeable and unfaithful.[33]

The secular Christine thus considers the negative literary depiction of women to be libelous and dangerous, not, like Hrotsvit, because of the moral danger that illicit and sinful stories pose for their audience, but because they are blatantly untrue and pose the practical danger that married men may pay credence to them and mistrust their wives. It is a concern she shares with Dame Alice, who looked upon Jankyn's *Book of Wikked Wyves* in a similar vein. To Christine the literary denigration of women becomes a real and even dangerous threat to marital harmony and an unjust burden for virtuous wives.

Christine would seem to extend the Wife of Bath's metaphor about the painting lion by her objections to generalizations that are based on insufficient and unrepresentative data or that are presented by men who, by their very profession, are ignorant of the situations they are so indignantly condemning. Not only may a depiction offer passive evidence to the artist's lack of perception and experience, she suggests, but it also may present active evidence: a writer's malignant depiction of depraved womanhood can be thus an indication of his own depravity. Why else would he be so familiar with female depravity and so oblivious to female virtue? She observes: "In spite of the fact that my judgement tells me that Master Jean de Meung was a very learned man and eloquent and would have been capable of writing a much better work, more profitable and with more elevated sentiments if he had tried, which is a pity, but I suppose that the great lechery which obsessed him perhaps made him more prejudiced than profitable, as by our actions our inclinations commonly reveal themselves" (344-45).

While the canoness Hrotsvit wrote entirely within the framework of the monastic hierarchy of excellence and was thus limited to the exaltation of the patristic definition of the virginal ideal for women as sexual purity, Christine's conception of the virginal ideal is general and concerns a moral integrity applicable to both single and married women. As Christine Reno observes, while Christine does organize her *cité des dames* around the ideal of virginity, "the ideal of virginity she sets forth is metaphoric as well as literal. Virginity implies, in addition to sexual purity, the freedom from any sort of involvement with men that might hamper woman's pursuit of her particular goals. Moreover, Christine's (unlike Hrotsvit's) focus in the *Cité* is not the spiritual reward of more perfect state of eternal bliss that the Church held out to the celibate, but rather a triumph that could be measured primarily in terms of the standards of this world."[34]

Christine de Pizan recognized the danger of misogynistic fiction for women in all walks of life, and she created outstanding and complex female characters encompassing most social classes and many different lifestyles. Her proposed solution to the problem of literary misogyny involves a thoughtful reconsideration of the merits of misogynistic fiction which she urges the reader to compare with the truth of personal experience. Compare the women you know, she suggests, with those you read about:

> And do not think, dear sir, nor let anyone else believe, that I am saying this, or presenting this defense through favorable excuses because I am a woman, for the fact is that my motive is merely to uphold the truth as I know it be certain knowledge to be the opposite of these things I am objecting to; but as I am indeed a woman, I can bear better witness to the truth than those who have no experience of the state, but only speak through supposition or in general terms. (*Ideals for Women*, 344)

In her works Christine, like Hrotsvit, creates praiseworthy and admirable women; unlike Hrotsvit, however, Christine does not simply paint a gallery of admirable female chastity triumphing over male wickedness and lust, but rather she depicts a wide range of qualities of feminine excellence, some of which are independent of chastity and many of which depend on a moral conception of chastity. Christine's point, as Diane Bornstein points out, ". . . is not whether or not a woman has kept her maidenhead, but whether or not she practices chastity."[35] Hrotsvit's monastic/patristic ideals for female excellence are thus countered by Christine's well-rounded female characters of diverse accomplishments and diversified roles. Depicting women and exploring the feminine ideals of excellence, Christine does not limit herself to the traditional patristic ideal of chastity; neither does she simply invest her women characters with the traditional male heroic attributes of courage, valiance, strength, and courtesy, but to the universal ideals transcending sex as, for example, courage, strength, courtesy, wisdom, and learning, she adds some paradigmatically feminine virtues such as kindness, warmth, peace-making and patience.[36] In this manner it is the secular Christine and not so much the monastic Hrotsvit who acts on Dame Alice's objections to misogynistic literature.

While Hrotsvit's heroines were oblivious to literary misogyny and Chaucer's Wife of Bath exemplified as well as criticized the misogynistic stereotype of the greedy, lascivious woman, Christine de Pizan exhibits her concern with the fictional denigration of women inside her fiction and out of it. Her characters are made to seem conscious of the unrealistic, untruthful but seldom challenged misogynistic stereotype, and they seek answers and solutions to it. In the *City of Ladies* (II, IIV) Christine asks Lady Rectitude why the "many valiant women who lived before have not contradicted the books written by men which speak ill of them." Rectitude replies,

> As for the long time which has passed without their detractors and false witnesses being contradicted, I tell you that there is a proper moment for everything and each thing comes in its own time, just as God has suffered heresies against his Holy Law to exist in the world. (348)

The analogy between phantastic lies, or *figmenta*, about women and heresy, both of which can only be eradicated by confrontation with *veritas*, or truth, attests to the severity with which women were capable of reacting against the literary denigration of women. In fact, one famous literary heroine did act on the very same analogy: Chaucer's Wife of Bath not only labelled misogynistic literature heretical like Christine, but she treated Jankyn's *Book of Wikked Wyves* as such: she threw the book into the fire, condemning its heretical pages to their appropriate end.

From *Tulsa Studies in Women's Literature* 4, no. 1 (Spring 1985):17-32. Copyright © 1985 by the University of Tulsa. Reprinted by permission of the University of Tulsa.

Notes

1. *The Works of Geoffrey Chaucer*, ed. F. N. Robinson, 2nd ed. (Boston: Houghton Mifflin Co., The Riverside Press, 1961), 82. I presented a short version of the present study at the *Third Symposium on Comparative Literature and International Studies*, March, 1983.

2. On the same subject, see Eileen Power, *Medieval Women*, ed. M. M. Postan (Cambridge: Cambridge University Press, 1975), 9, and *Medieval Woman*, ed. Derek Baker (Oxford: Basil Blackwell, 1978), Introduction.

3. See for example Francis L. Utley, *The Crooked Rib* (Columbus: Ohio State University Press, 1944), especially the analytical index, and Katherine M. Rogers, *The Troublesome Helpmate* (Seattle and London: Washington University Press, 1966), 56-99.

4. Interestingly, when ascetic propaganda is written by men for women in holy orders, emphasis shifts from presenting a negative view of the opposite sex to vivid depictions of the horrors of pregnancy and childbearing. See *Hali Meidenhad*, ed. B. Millett (London, 1982), 524-43.

5. Hrotsvit, for example, says in the prologue to her dramas: "quanto blanditiae amantium ad illiciendum promptiores, tanto et supemi adiutoris gloria sublimior et triumphantium victoria probatur gloriosior, praesentim cum feminae fragilitas vinceret et virilis robur confusioni subiaceret." See *Hrotsvithae Opera*, ed. Helena Homeyer (München, Padeborn, Wien: Verlag Ferdinand Schöningh, 1972), 232. Further references to this work will be cited parenthetically in the text.

6. I assume that Dame Alice's reference to the lion projects female authorship of both religious and secular literature.

7. *Matheoli Lamentationes, Les Lamentations de Matheolus*, ed. A. G. van Hamel (Paris: 1892-1905) is a long complaint by Matheolus about his marital misfortunes; unfrocked for bigamy, he sees his wife Petra as the source of all suffering; Jean de Meung is cited by Christine de Pizan for his continuation of the *Roman de la Rose*.

8. The medieval meaning of *figmenta* is associated with fiction. See North African Christian apologist Lactantius (ca. 240-320) in 7, 22 (*figmenta poetarum* and *figmenta somniorum*). Spanish Archbishop Isidore of Seville (ca. 560-636), Etymologiarum Lib. (XVIII 46; VIII, 7, 7) defines comedy: "comoedi sunt qui privatorum hominum acta dictus aut gestu cantabant, atque stupra virginum et amores meretricum in suis fabulis exprimebant." Isidore was also a theologian and encyclopedist.

9. In *Paphnutius and Abraham*, for example, the ascetic hermits of the desert are depicted as the male versions of Hrotsvit's chaste heroines; driven by identical concerns and motivations, they are catalysts of salvation.

10. Hrotsvit's success was modest: only one of her plays, *Gallicanus* (*Opera*, 328-49) became widely distributed in the twelfth century as part of the Austrian *Passional*, and Terence continued to be read in schools and religious houses. On the Passional, see Gerhard Eis, *Prager deutsche Studien*, 6, 1932. See also Hrotsvit's plays *Paphnutius* (328-49) and *Abraham* (303-20), both in *Opera*.

11. Rather, Hrotsvit simply shifts the dramatic emphasis, the point of view; and the desired outcome by inversions of sexually dimorphic honorable/dishonorable, strong/weak, ascetic/passionate dichotomies, placing women at the center of her plots, and substituting happy martyrdom in defense of virginity, faith and ultimate union with the heavenly bridegroom for Terence's happy endings achieved by earthly marriage and economic settlement. In most of her plays women are the models of admirable excellence while men are the villains. Hrotsvit's exceptions to these stereotypes (mirroring Dame Alice's assessment of misogynistic literature) are the saintly men of the Church who pose no danger to her virginal and Christian heroines.

12. In this manner Hrotsvit is first a canoness and only secondly a woman; her depictions of virtuous womanhood are not only one-dimensional, linking virtue and strength to chastity, but

they stand fully in the monastic and hagiographic tradition of the Church. She says little in the praise of women that would not occur in clerkly legends and vitae of female saints; her self-definition is entirely derivative and couched in conventional patristic and hagiographic terms.

13. See *Hrotvithae Opera*: two plays, *Gallicanus* (244-63) and *Callimachus* (283-97), and three legends, "Agnes" (210-26), "Theophilus" (154-70), and "Basilus" (176-86).

14. See for example the selections of August Wulff, *Die Frauenfeindlichen Dichtungen in den Romanischen Literaturen des Mittelalters* (Halle: Niemeyer, 1914); Francis L. Utley, *The Crooked Rib*; Arthur More, "Study in a Medieval Prejudice: Antifeminism" (Diss. Vanderbilt 1943).

15. Hildegard of Bingen, while restating the traditional view of man's superiority over women, does counter the prevailing view that women are more lustful than men. She maintains (*Patrologia Latina* 197. 461, 594) that it is men who are lustful—women only cohabit in hope of children.

16. In her poem, "Unyoked is best, and happy the woman without a man," Anna Bijns says: "It's good to be a woman, and much better to be a man. You maidens, you wenches, remember this lesson: nobody should run too fast to get married. The saying goes: 'Where there's no spouse there's no honour'; but one who can earn her own board and clothes shouldn't hurry to suffer under a man's rod. So much for my advice, because I suspect—and I see it sadly proven every day—'t happens all the time! A woman might be very rich in goods, but if she gets married she's as good as shackled. If she stays single, however, and manages to remain pure and untainted, then she's lord as well as lady: no better life than that! I don't look down on wedlock; nevertheless: unyoked is best, and happy the woman without a man.

"Fine girls turn into ugly hags—indeed, poor sluts, poor tramps—; thank marriage for that! That's enough for me to run away from wedding bells. But, poor dears! though at first they marry the guy, thinking their love simply cannot cool, they are sorry after less than a year. Ah! the burden of marriage is far too heavy; they know it best who've carried it. A wife is so often afraid and distressed. If her husband goes out hither and thither, to ease tensions, carousing and gambling by day and by night, then no doubt she reproaches herself to ever have begun. Thus, take care before it's too late, so as not to complain later; but heed my remark, don't get involved: unyoked is best, and happy the woman without a man.

"Also, a man will come home all drunk and pissed, just when his wife has worked her fingers to the bone (the things one has to take care of if one wants to keep house decently!) and if it's she who wants to wag her tongue once in awhile, she gets to taste his fists till she can say no more; and that besotted keg she's supposed to obey! Then, all he does is scold and shout; these are his ways. Poor she who suffers all this. If he visits Venus' handmaidens, why just think of the hearty welcome that waits him at home! You maidens, you young women, make another's mistake a lesson for you—before you too are fettered like that. And if you were to contradict me: I couldn't care less who disagrees, because I firmly stick to this: unyoked is best, and happy the woman without a man." Anna Bijns, "New Varianten Bij Anna Bijns," F. Van Winckenroye, ed. *Nieuve Taalgids* 53 (1960), 264-66. For the above translation I am indebted to Kristiaan Aercke.

17. Elizabeth Petroff, *Consolation of the Blessed* (New York: Alta Gaia, 1979).

18. Dame Julian's pronouncements are representative of the topos. She says: "And so is Jesus truly our natural mother of creation, and he is our mother in grace by assuming our nature. All the fair work and the sweet kindly offices of beloved motherhood are appropriate to the second person. . . . I understand three ways of seeing motherhood in God. The first is the foundation of our natural creation, the second is taken from our nature and there begins the motherhood of grace, and the third is the activity of motherhood." Translated by Catherine Jones in her chapter, "The English Mystic: Julian of Norwich," in *Medieval Women Writers*, ed. K. M. Wilson (Athens: University of Georgia Press, 1984), 288.

19. *The Lais of Marie de France*, ed. Joan M. Ferrante and R. W. Harming (New York: Dutton, 1978) and Meg Bogin, *The Women Troubadours* (New York: Paddington, 1976).

20. See for example Edward A. Westermarck, *The History of Human Marriage*, 5th ed. (New York: The Allerton Book Company, 1922); George H. Tavard, *Women in the Christian Tradition* (South Bend: University of Notre Dame Press, 1974); and Joseph E. Kerns, *The Theology of Marriage* (New York: Sheed and Ward, 1964).

21. Eileen Power, *Medieval Women*, ed. M. Postan (Cambridge: Cambridge University Press, 1975), 60.

22. See Power, 59 ff.

23. Sue Sheridan Walker, "Widow and Ward: The Feudal Law of Child Custody," *Women in Medieval Society*, ed. Susan Mosher Stuard (Philadelphia: University of Pennsylvania Press, 1976), 127.

24. Shulamith Shahar, *Die Frau im Mittelalter* (Königstein: Atheneum, 1981), 170.

25. Frances and Joseph Gies, *Women in the Middle Ages* (New York: Thomas Crowell Company, 1978), 182.

26. See Philippe Verdier, "Women in the Marginalia of Gothic Manuscripts," in *The Role of Women in the Middle Ages*, ed. Rosemary T. Morewedge (Albany: State University of New York Press, 1975), 128-30.

27. See Power. 53 ff.

28. J. Gilchrist, *The Church and Economic Activity in the Middle Ages* (New York: Macmillan, St. Martin Press, 1967), 275.

29. See Gerhard Owst, *Literature and Pulpit in Medieval England*, 2nd ed. (New York: Barnes and Noble, 1961), 379.

30. See Gilchrist, 275 ff. Mansi 31: 1054. Scotus (ca. 1265-1308) suggests the values of procreation in *Opus Super quatuor libros Sententiarum* (*On the Sentences*), 4.28. Also Rudolf Weigand, "Die Lehre der Kanonisten des 12 und 13 Jhats im den tehzwecken," *Studia Gratiana* 12 (1967), 451, points out that the Fall of Angels is sometimes brought in contact with the procreative model.

31. Georges Duby, *Medieval Marriage*, trans. E. Forster (Baltimore and London: Johns Hopkins University Press, 1978), 10 ff.

32. By initiating the *querelle des femmes*, Christine de Pizan took a first step in the long and complex process of attempted change by creating awareness of the problem of literary misogyny; the next step, the creation of self-definition and self-valuation to supplant both the misogynistic stereotype and the one-dimensional ideal of chaste female excellence, soon followed in her fictional work. The self-definition and self-valuation offered by Christine operate on the assumption that both morally and intellectually, woman is man's equal. Consequently, it is a social injustice to justify the double standard.

33. Letter 1, translated by Charity Cannon Willard in *Medieval Women Writers*, 342-743. Further references within this text are to this translation.

34. Christine Reno, "Virginity as an Ideal in Christine de Pizan's *Cité des Dames*," in *Ideals for Women in the Works of Christine de Pizan*, ed. Diane Bornstein, Medical and Renaissance Monograph Series, I, Michigan Consortium for Medieval and Early Modern Studies, 1981, 70. On the genesis of the *Querelle*, see Charity C. Willard, "Christine de Pizan and the Order of the Rose," in *Ideals for Women*, 51-67.

35. Diane Bornstein, "Introduction," *Ideals for Women*, 7.

36. Some of the attributes have been previously associated with women, particularly that of peace-weaver in medieval epics. For an intriguing discussion of medieval female authorship, see Susan Shibanoff, "Medieval Frauenlieder," *Tulsa Studies in Women's Literature* I, 2 (1982), 189-200.

Critical Insights

Alison's Incapacity and Poetic Instability in the Wife of Bath's Tale

Susan Crane

Geoffrey Chaucer's Wife of Bath's Tale so closely illustrates the concerns of its prologue that critics agree it can only be understood in relation to its assertive, female, marriage-minded narrator. But why does Alison's tale resemble an Arthurian romance? Her prologue is based on antifeminist tracts, marital satire, biblical exegesis—a clerical mixture from which Alison draws life and departs like the Eve of amphibians leaving the sea while carrying its salt in her veins. It would seem beyond this creature's ken to speak of ladies' gracious mercy, of quests and fairy knowledge. Only the Wife's idealizing nostalgia for her happily-ever-after with Jankyn anticipates the generic character of her tale.

I argue that we can better understand the disjunction between the Wife's prologue and tale, and the peculiar generic makeup of the tale itself, by appealing to the works' historical situation. I am not referring to the recent critical trend that analyzes Alison as if she were a real, fully developed personality. So treated, she appears to be a "sociopath," homicidal, nymphomaniacal, a mass of bizarre symptoms (see, e.g., Rowland; Palomo; Sands). A second historicizing trend associates her trade and station with medieval land tenure laws, dower practices, and legal records, but these efforts, while valuable contextually, remove us from confronting Alison as she exists in her own language (see, e.g., Margulies; Colmer; Robertson, "'And'"). She is neither an individual (if she were, she would indeed be monstrous) nor a mirror for historical conditions but a fiction who tells a fiction.

Yet the history of cultural beliefs can contribute to an understanding of these fictions. Ideologies inform genres more directly than do economic and social conditions, and they can mediate for us between a literary text and its historical moment.[1] Romances, for example, shape ideals of chivalry and courtesy into narratives about how to interpret and assess those ideals. This is more fully what romances do than is representing the daily life of courts. Similarly, antifeminist satire tells us little about what actual marriages were like but much about how the clergy conceived of sexuality and femininity.

The Wife of Bath's Tale draws heavily on romance and antifeminist satire. Alison has no existence independent of her words, but her words in their generic formations allude to social and religious convictions that have extra-literary importance. Attending to those convictions can help us see why Alison draws on romance, why she draws on it imperfectly, and what the discourse on *gentillesse* has to do with the rest of her performance.

Two issues in particular—gender and sovereignty—are of concern to

Alison. Both issues have intertextual subtleties of some depth, and both also have practical influence in the world. The Wife's tale confronts the social belief that feminine power should be strictly limited, and it attempts to establish a defense of secular women's sovereignty that opposes the conventions available to Alison. She revels in the attractions of power and argues that her active desire for it is justified by the benefits she wins from it and the peace and happiness that yielding to it will bring to men. Yet her vaunted abilities as a "wys wyf" (D 231) are precisely those the satirists condemn, while her happy endings are patently illusory. The illogicalities and confusions in her narrative are commonly attributed to her error: she is a parodic or comic figure who inverts accepted morality, or a sinful one who denies Christian teaching, and therefore she cannot argue cogently. But whether or not she is comical or morally wrong, she is of substantial interest from other perspectives. Her attempt to redefine women's sovereignty is rhetorically and culturally significant, and from these perspectives Alison's apparent confusions propel her convictions beyond traditional discourses toward a realm of expression where there is as yet no language. In her narrative and logical ruptures themselves, in her destabilizations of genre, gender, *gentillesse*, and sovereignty, we can perceive something of what "wommen moost desiren" (D 905) as well as how inexpressible that desire is.

The kinds of power Alison designates as "sovereignty" vacillate contradictorily, in part because she confronts generic and ideological differences on the issue. Her tale analyzes a belief that informs both antifeminist satire and romance: that gender sets limits on personal capability and social power. Both literatures develop conventions about feminine abilities, women's special knowledge in affairs of the heart and hearth, and the ways women exercise their capacity in those affairs. Chaucer's works often venture far from generic norms, but his poetry can still illustrate the conventions of these two genres regarding feminine power.

Heroines of romance tend to be more delicate emotionally and less capable intellectually than men (Dorigen's laments, Criseyde's fear, Theseus's subjection of Femenye), but their exceptional beauty inspires love and adumbrates a fineness of character that may not quite be fulfilled (Dorigen's rash promise, Criseyde's falseness). For men they are the arbiters of love, courtesy, and high sentiment. Their excellence in these matters reproduces in the emotional sphere the hierarchy of feudal relations, leading to a sublimation and refinement of passion that are metaphorically elevating (Arveragus's and Aurelius's courtships of Dorigen, the Man in Black's courtship of fair White). But the demanding standards of noble ladies, after inspiring men to improve, are complemented by the ultimate compliance that brings courtship to fruition. From the romance tradition at large it is clear that resourcefulness, sharp wit, and magical power are located in minor female figures or dangerous ones more than in heroines (La Vieille, Lunete, Morgan le Fay, Chaucer's Cassandra). The admirable women of romance wield their emotional sovereignty in ways beneficial to men and pleasurable to audiences, deferring stasis for a time but finally yielding in harmonious accord with male desire.

In contrast, antifeminist satire is nonnarrative, organized instead by an authoritative voice that rigidifies and fragments femaleness into a set of discrete exempla and negative topoi on nagging, mercenary dependence, overbearing sexuality, and so on:

> And if that she be foul, thou seist that she
> Coveiteth every man that she may se,
> . . . .
> Thou liknest [wommenes love] also to wilde fyr;
> The moore it brenneth, the moore it hath desir
> To consume every thyng that brent wole be.
> . . . .
> "Bet is," quod he, "thyn habitacioun
> Be with a leon or a foul dragoun
> Than with a womman usynge for to chyde."
> (D 265-66, 373-75, 775-77)[2]

Seeking to discourage clerics from cohabitation and sexual relations, the satirists mount an all-out attack on feminine emotional and domestic power. Significantly, romance poets and satirists agree in according women a potential for excellence in domesticity and love, but satirists make the failure of that potential a chief argument for avoiding women: contrary to what the suitor expects, a woman will not delight or comfort him. Moreover, the qualities that in romance contribute to women's emotional excellence define their unworthiness in satire. Their greater fragility manifests itself in weeping and clinging, their capacity for love leads to torments of jealousy and sexual conflict, and their irrationality tyrannizes men like a child's or a badly trained animal's: "For as an hors I koude byte and whyne./ I koude pleyne, and yit was in the gilt,/ Or elles often tyme hadde I been spilt" (D 386-88). Antifeminists thus argue that women's emotional sovereignty is harmful, aggressive, and falsely exercised instead of imagining with the romance poets that women's sovereignty derives from native feminine virtues.

Initially, the Wife of Bath addresses the issues of gender and power as they are formulated in antifeminist satire. As readers have long noted with pleasure, her own origin in the very texts she disputes forces her to shadowbox with herself, receiving almost as many blows as she delivers. However cleverly Alison attempts to parry satiric convictions—by celebrating the less-than-perfect life rather than accepting admonishments to perfection, by claiming that the rational male should yield reasonably to the less rational female—still the notion that women's claims to sovereignty are unjustified is inextricably woven into the generic fabric of her prologue. Alison's shift to romance is thus a strategic one, challenging antifeminist versions of the issue by confronting them with a genre that celebrates women's emotive power instead of undermining it. Romance is the "profeminist" literature, it would appear, that can combat the negative formulations of Theophrastus and Jerome.

But her tactic comes as a surprise in view of her own textual origins and of conventional rebuttals of the antifeminist version of women's sovereignty. The Wife's character is drawn from the gender conceptions of estates literature as well as from satire, and neither of these points of origin prepares us for her romance.

Alison's "Venerien" (D 609) femaleness is more firmly rooted, as Jill Mann has shown, in her estate than in her horoscope (see also Shahar; Monfrin). Estates literature distinguishes not only among ways of life (workers, nobles, clergy) but also between men and women. Secular women are assigned to a separate female estate. This fourth estate is subdivided according to women's social status in their relations to men rather than according to professions or work in the world: women are maidens or spouses or widows; they tempt, bear children, and so on. This formulation of social identity obviously makes women's significance dependent on their relations to men, providing little justification for Alison's claims to supremacy. Nor does the presentation of her trade offer her any better justification. Alison's cloth making, mentioned only in her General Prologue portrait, turns out to have no importance in her life. Little more than a version of the spinning proverbially assigned to women along with deceit and weeping (D 401-02) as secondary sex characteristics, cloth making is not what gives Alison some measure of dominance during and beyond her marriages. Rather, her "sexual economics" extract wealth from her husbands in exchange for domestic peace (Delany).[3] The effacement of the Wife's trade from her prologue and tale is a disenfranchising move that underlines her functional dependence. In keeping with estates ideology, her social identity is restricted to her wifehood, while her defense of "Marcien" hardiness and dominance (D 610) inverts antifeminist condemnations of the marital estate.

What history can show us about the Wife of Bath is less the daily working and living conditions of women than the ways men and women conceived their situations. The strong presence of antifeminist and estates ideology in the Wife's portrait and prologue renders her claim to sovereignty intensely problematic, and a wider context of women's voices demonstrates her isolation even from her own fictive sex.[4] It is not only male writers who pervasively assert that women's sexuality defines their situation and that men should be sovereign over women. Heloise, who is anthologized in Jankyn's "book of wikked wyves" (D 685), portrays herself in her letters as the source and, from birth, nothing but the source of Abelard's misfortune: "What misery for me—born as I was to be the cause of such a crime! Is it the general lot of women to bring total ruin on great men? Hence the warning about women in Proverbs." Submissiveness offers her a way to minimize her sex's power to do harm, so Heloise represents her love's merits to have been the extraordinary sacrifices by which "I have carried out all your orders so implicitly that when I was powerless to oppose you in anything, I found strength at your command to destroy myself. . . . I believed that the more I humbled myself on your account, the more gratitude I should win from you" (*Letters* 130, 113).[5] Margery Kempe, who like Heloise takes uneasy refuge from marriage in celibacy and religious self-castigation, likens Mary and Joseph's wedding to her own spiritual marriage to God, praying that like a perfect wife she "myth han grace to obeyn hym, louyn & dredyn hym, worschepyn & preysyn hym, & no-thyng to louyn but þat he louyth, ne no-thyng to welyn but þat he wolde, & euyr to be redy to fulfillyn hys wil bothyn nyght & day wyth-owtyn grutchyng er heuynes" (199).[6]

That Margery speaks through two male amanuenses and that Heloise was educated in clerical orthodoxy by Abelard himself only begin to indicate the constraints on their self-presentation. Yet they concur, while Chaucer's Alison does not, that women should value submission and sacrifice and should watch vigilantly over their explosive sexuality. Christine de Pizan also chooses obedience as her touchstone when refuting the antimatrimonial satirists of Jankyn's book. Despite her argument in the *City of Ladies* that women are capable of independence, Christine counters the claims of Valerius and Theophrastus that women are domineering and unloving with examples of wives supreme in servitude—they follow their husbands to battle and exile, eat their cremated husbands' ashes or kiss the rotting corpses; they treat unfaithful husbands with love and respect; they are as constant as Griselda (117-34, 170-76).[7] From the unlettered Margery to the highly educated and original Christine, women writers defend their sex partly by accepting cultural models of female submission.

A story of Griselda, then, would be the widely expected rebuttal to the antifeminist challenge of The Wife of Bath's Prologue. But the Clerk's tale comes later (and differently); the Wife's tale is another kind of rebuttal altogether.

Initially, romance provides Alison with an argument to use against the satirists. In that her tale lacks chivalric or military adventures and features a crucially knowledgeable and capable female character, it is not a standard romance. But it does answer to the phrase Chaucer uses, according to Donald Howard (52-53n), to designate his romances, "storial thyng that toucheth gentillesse" (A 3179).[8] True to the genre are the setting in "th'olde dayes of the Kyng Arthour" (D 857) and the educative knowledge by which women direct men's emotional development. Arthur's justice is tempered by Guinevere's mercy as is Theseus's by the "verray wommanhede" of weeping ladies who plead for Palamon and Arcite (A 1748-61).[9] The old hag, like other romance heroines, has special insight in matters of love and morality that leads the knight to change for the better and to achieve happiness in love.

Alison manipulates her romance with an eye to antifeminist assertions, using her new genre to attract validity to the version of women's sovereignty condemned by antifeminist writers. For that sovereignty is not identical in romance and in satire. Wives of satire seize tangible economic and physical terrain by force and subterfuge: "I have the power durynge al my lyf/ Upon his propre body, and noght he"; "Atte ende I hadde the bettre in ech degre/ By sleighte, or force, or by som maner thyng" (D 158-59, 404-05). Ladies of romance control men's devotion not by force or even by their own volition but by reason of their excellence (Dorigen, Criseyde). The Wife's tale, in referring to romance conventions, implies an equivalence between the unjustified tyranny of satire's wives and the meritorious supremacy of romance heroines. Clearly, there is no Dorigen or Criseyde in her story. The hag is aggressive, manipulative, and sexually demanding in the best satiric vein, but her high and magical attributes—as queen of fairies, as goal of a quest for life, as moral guide, and finally as love object of the knightly hero—obscure her antifeminist connections and work to validate her active exercise of power.

But while romance dignifies the claim to women's sovereignty in this tale, frequent antifeminist touches paradoxically vitiate the romantic elevation Alison seems to desire. The answers proposed to Guinevere's question catalog feminine weaknesses, from "Somme seyde wommen loven best richesse" to "we kan no conseil hyde" (D 925, 980). The violence of sexual relations through Alison's tale and the animal metaphors for women (limed like birds, kicking like galled horses, booming like bitterns) answer to the satiric conviction that women are profoundly irrational, sensual creatures.

One explanation of this difficulty in the narration is that the Wife is incapable of sustaining the romance mode; she cannot help slipping back into the antifeminist attitudes from which she herself was drawn. For other critics, the "restrained idiom of the tale proper . . . suggests that a courtly narrator has replaced the Wife" or that Chaucer speaks directly in some passages (Winney 23).[10] These explanations place Alison's tale beyond her control and make its antifeminist elements no more than inopportune and debilitating interruptions of a standard romance. We would do better to accept that the Wife of Bath is the voice Chaucer assigns to prologue and tale alike and to hear her out. Alison is not a person constrained by plausibility but a fictional voice that knows and can perform whatever is useful to dramatizing the interests attributed to it. Her tendency to slip from the realm of satire into romance and back again is worth considering as her move, one suited to her concern with women's sovereignty.

Alison's transitions between satire and romance betray the incongruity of the two generic visions and, consequently, their shared inadequacy to her argument. The knight's trial culminates this process of recognition. Several shifts that may have seemed involuntary, from queenly power to proverbial foibles, from fairy illusion to all-too-solid flesh, are here recuperated in a full return to romantic sensibility. The hierarchical display of Guinevere's assembly of judgment evokes fictional love courts, with the "queene hirself sittynge as a justise" (D 1028), and the answer she and her ladies accept from the knight seems to tally with courtly conventions about women's superiority in matters of the heart. Yet the hag anticipates that the ladies will not gladly admit the knight's answer; even "the proudeste" will simply not "dar seye nay" (D 1017-19). Echoing her suspicion, the knight concludes his answer insistently: "This is your mooste desir, thogh ye me kille" (D 1041). The implication of resistance marks a disparity between satiric sovereignty, actively claimed and energetically wielded, and the passive, apparently unwilled sovereignty of women in romance. To force the queen's ladies into accepting that "Wommen *desiren* to have sovereynetee" (D 1038) is to confront the romance vision that has dignified women's power with Alison's fiercer vision that women consciously seek and enjoy it.

The Wife's return to a satiric conviction at this point underlines the insufficiency of either conventional discourse for dramatizing a worthy sovereignty of secular women. Satire denies their worth. Romance seems a genre in which women's excellence brings power, but the appearance proves false. A heroine's strength lasts only for the temporal and fantastic space that delays her submission and demonstrates the capabilities of her suitor. Her mercy and compliance are the necessary closure to her aloof independence and her ability to command devotion. In a historical study of marriage practices, Georges Duby concludes that the Old French poetry of adultery and love service is based on a "fundamentally mysogenous" conception of woman as merely a means to male self-advancement: "Woman was an object and, as such, contemptible" (*Medieval* 14, 108).[11] Eugene Vance corroborates Duby's historical analysis by connecting early lyrics of adultery to romances of proud ladies: throughout, love's poetic expression is typically "le combat érotique," an aesthetic of antithesis recognizing the violence that is veiled by the mystified perfection of *fine amor* (548; see also Bloch 153-56).

Poetic Instability in the Wife of Bath's Tale   **219**

These researches suggest that the violent sexual relations of the Wife of Bath's Tale do not depart from romance tradition so much as exaggerate it, while the tale's presentation from the knight's point of view, its evasion of punishment for the knight, and the queen's merely contingent authority (for which she "thanketh the kyng with al hir myght" [D 899]) offer a recognizably romantic, masculine imagining. The hag's power over her "walwing" knight is anomalous, more like the power of Morgan le Fay in *Sir Gawain and the Green Knight* than like that of a conventional heroine. But even the hag surrenders in the end. The joyful and thoroughly fanciful resolution that fulfills the knight's "worldly appetit" (D 1218) illustrates the most romance can render. Here, as in Alison's prologue, "her very verbalizations remain unavoidably dependent, feminine respeakings of a resolutely masculine idiom" (Patterson 682; see also Aers 143-51).

Heloise, Christine, and Margery Kempe similarly reiterate clerical wisdom about the failings and duties of their sex. One further female voice, taking a noble rather than a clerical perspective, demonstrates that modern critics are not the first to find misogyny and male violence in courtly conventions. Toward the end of his book of instruction for his daughters, Geoffroy de la Tour Landry writes at some length of his wife's opposition to his belief "that a lady or damoyselle myght loue peramours in certayne caas." According to Geoffroy, his wife objected that men's assertions about the value of love service "are but sport and esbatement of lordes and of felawes in a langage moche comyn." Men's conventional language (drawn from courtly tradition) has no relation to their feelings, says this wife, so their declarations of love should not be trusted. Her understanding that courtly speaking is masculine rather than feminine presages modern analyses of romance. Men use this discourse against women, to make conquests: "these wordes coste to them but lytyll to say for to gete the better and sooner the grace and good wylle of theyr peramours." Nor do they undertake tasks for love but "only for to enhaunce them self, and for to drawe vnto them the grace and vayne glory of the world" (*Book* 163, 164; *Livre* 246-48).[12] In her view, then, male power does not surrender to female excellence in courtly interaction. Consequently, her arguments on the subject support Geoffroy's instructions to their daughters to restrain their sexuality and to be humbly obedient in their relations with men.

If the elevation of women in romance was understood to be chimerical and if even noble writers concur with clerical ones on the importance of female submissiveness, how is the Wife of Bath to formulate (even fictionally) an argument in defense of women's desire for sovereignty? In many ways her tale does not manage to transcend the categories of her age, and her argument remains partial, awkward, and illogical. For example, the curtain lecture urges the knight to rise above the worldly indulgences of wealth and station, but the lecturer then fulfills his sensual desires. She rejects the social hierarchy and nobility of blood in the same speech, yet she appeals to "my sovereyn lady queene" (D 1048) for the knight's hand and promises him to become as beautiful "As any lady, emperice, or queene" (D 1246; see Haller; Murtaugh; Bolton).

There are many such confusions in the Wife's prologue and tale; perhaps most elusive is what Alison means by sovereignty in the first place. The power it signifies seems constantly to vacillate, but three major contradictions can be distinguished. Alison sometimes associates sovereignty with economic gain, "wynnyng" (D 416), yet she seems to win nothing from her fourth husband, gives up her gains to Jankyn, and makes the hag speak eloquently against the significance of wealth. At other points, coercion, including physical domination, renders Alison's metaphor "myself have been the whippe" (D 175) very nearly literal, but she moves easily from coercion to accommodation with Jankyn as does the hag with her knight. And finally, her conception of sovereignty seems to demand the trust or the high opinion of her husbands. "Thou sholdest seye, 'Wyf, go wher thee liste . . ./ I knowe yow for a trewe wyf, dame Alys'" (D 318-20), she instructs her old husbands, and Jankyn fulfills her desire in acceding, "Myn owene trewe wyf,/ Do as thee lust the terme of al thy lyf" (D 819-20). Nonetheless, the Wife cheerfully undermines her demand for trust and respect by asserting and demonstrating that women are untrustworthy: "half so boldely kan ther no man/ Swere and lyen, as a womman kan" (D 227-28).

Why does Alison constantly alter and even cancel each of her versions of sovereignty? The solution is not that women's desire for power is nothing but a desire for love. Love is a relatively simple matter for her, something she often gets from men. In contrast, sovereignty vacillates confusingly even in love's presence: with the "daungerous" Jankyn and knight (D 514, 1090), it works to perpetuate love, as if it were analogous to integrity or merit, but in her four earlier marriages it tyrannizes or substitutes for love, as if it were mere self-interest. The Wife's casual manipulation of her old husbands' devotion—"They loved me so wel, by God above,/ That I ne tolde no deyntee of hir love" (D 207-08)—suggests that the question of power precedes and subsumes the question of men's love: it is sovereignty that "worldly wommen loven best" (D 1033). The object of this fundamental love is elusive, and its elusiveness partly accounts for its desirability, in accordance with Alison's psychological principle "Forbede us thyng, and that desiren we" (D 519). Female power, in any form, is the most heretical of her desires (Howard 252; Aers 143-46), unsustained in any of the conventional discourses on which she draws. Looking beyond those discourses necessarily leaves the Wife inarticulate, even about the meaning of the sovereignty she imagines. She desires to validate the forbidden but can hardly formulate what it is.

Still, her very failures of articulation make gestures that indicate what the worth of female power might be. Alison signals the direction of her desire through a series of poetic transformations. The hag's physical metamorphosis is only the most dazzling of many mutations demonstrating that genres, genders, and words themselves are not fixed phenomena but fluid media through which new potential can be realized.

Romance is the appropriate form for confronting an unknowable desire. Its "strategy of delay" holds narrative "on the threshold before the promised end, still in the wilderness of wandering, 'error,' or 'trial'" (Parker 5, 4). This fantastic space permits traditional medieval romance to imagine, however contingently, a kind of female sovereignty that Alison manipulates, as we have seen, to justify the willed power condemned in antifeminist satire. But in that very manipulation, she recognizes the illusoriness of women's power in romance and cracks the tale's generic frame. Neither romance nor satire can answer Alison's longing, and her vacillation expresses her desire to pass beyond their limits.

Women also cross gender lines in the Wife's tale. The barber in Midas's story becomes a wife; the ladies' court of judgment replaces Arthur's; and the hag comes to speak like a cleric, while her husband submits with wifely meekness to her "wise governance" (D 1231). These substitutions make women the active movers of plot, as they are not in conventional romance, where they may inspire chivalric activity but where that activity is itself the source of change and growth. Gender displacements extend to the fairy realm, as the "elf-queene with hir joly compaignye" (D 860), who are all feminine when the knight encounters them (D 992), seem to metamorphose during Alison's introduction from "joly" dancers to potent incubi threatening women in the Arthurian countryside. The knight-rapist and the king both move from having power to surrendering it, while women throughout the tale move themselves into male purviews. Does this plot's exclusion of chivalric adventures echo and reverse the prologue's effacement of Alison's cloth-making profession, emphasizing the dependence of men on women in the tale? Even the comic victory of friars over fairies in the tale's first lines is vitiated when the fairy wife's pillow sermon demonstrates her intimate knowledge of religious texts. Reassigning women to positions of authority traces the path of their transgression in the narrative itself. The power they exercise is not always benign or even admirable, since worthy female sovereignty is a concept Alison cannot fully articulate, but the gender shifts themselves loosen the bond between maleness and power that makes female sovereignty inconceivable.

In the lecture on *gentillesse* and *poverte*, we are taught that even words are unfixed, because the categories they designate can be reconceived from changed perspectives. *Gentillesse* is not, as the knight thinks, a question of "nacioun" and "kynde" (D 1068, 1101), of merit determined by blood alone. Rather, "he is gentil that dooth gentil dedis" (D 1170). This familiar clerical topos restricts and relativizes the second estate's claim to superiority by emphasizing the disjunction between supremacy of birth and the moral supremacy over which the church has special authority (see Duby, *Three*).[13] So alien does this argument seem to Alison's views on female sovereignty that some critics treat it as a mere interruption: "it is in fact addressed to the audience. Chaucer apparently wished to include such a discourse at this point" (Jordan 89).[14] But in that it challenges fixed categories, the speech on *gentillesse* and *poverte* is of a piece with the tale's other instances of transformation and is appropriate to an old hag who can so easily redefine herself as beautiful and young.

Beginning with the words themselves, the hag's speech subverts the conventional meanings of *gentillesse* and *poverte*, using paradox and oxymoron to emphasize the process of reversal: the sinner "nys nat gentil, be he duc or erl;/ For vileyns synful dedes make a cherl" (D 1157-58); "Poverte is hateful good" (D 1195). The direction of these reversals moves away from the concept of nobility and poverty as objective states beyond individual control, asserting instead that conscious choices determine them: "Thanne am I gentil whan that I bigynne/ To lyven vertuously" (D 1175-76); "he that noght hath, ne coveiteth have,/ Is riche, although ye holde him but a knave" (D 1189-90). The two processes, the semantic destabilization and the assertion that individuals can define their situations, connect this speech to Alison's wider preoccupation with sovereignty: that is the most unstable of her terms and the one she seeks most persistently to reconceive. Without a culturally authoritative recourse for her half-imagined redefinition, Alison displaces the achievement to the hag's analogous transformations of *gentillesse* and *poverte*. Perfectly in consonance with recognized authorities, yet grounded in arguments for self-determination, the hag's definitions imply that *sovereynetee* may also be open to new and freely chosen meanings. Emphasizing the possibility, the hag's mutation into an authoritative expert enacts the claim that women can deserve power, and her husband recognizes that when he surrenders *marital* sovereignty to her on the basis of her *moral* excellence.[15] Like the elevation of romance, the morality of clerical exhortation is here appropriated (partially and not altogether fairly) to support Alison's defense of female sovereignty.

The hag's self-transformations culminate the various shifts and changes surrounding gender and power in the Wife of Bath's Tale. Perhaps we have not attended sufficiently to these instabilities because of Alison's air of tenacious assurance. She tackles her issue with such conviction that we expect her account to make sense, and so we resolve her inconsistencies by deciding that she is driven by nymphomania, or represents fallen willfulness, or conversely that she rises to philosophical wisdom through the experience of her tale.[16] Critical conclusions about what Alison "wants" proliferate, yet it is meaningful that she does not provide a consistently readable answer.[17] If I were attempting to wrest coherence from the Wife's preoccupation with women's sovereignty, I would argue that sovereignty's associations with and dissociations from financial gain, domestic control, sexual aggressiveness, and love are all informed by a conviction that women should not strive for equality in marriage but should, rather, refuse to wield power that they have securely won. This tactic appears to resolve the battle of the sexes into blissful reciprocity, but the Wife's envoy reveals a still-polarized combativeness that denies transcendence.

But when we make the Wife of Bath coherent, she becomes too easy to dismiss. She inscribes something more complex in her inconsistencies themselves, and it is important to consider how they too comment on gender and power. They stress that the Wife's justification of sovereignty is inexpressible in that it cannot be sustained by any conventional discourse. Whatever is compelling in her self-defense does not finally come from the language of satire or romance or moral philosophy, all of which she misappropriates. The inadequacy of her arguments, the mutability of *gentillesse* and *sovereynetee*, the shifting genders, and the flow of genres in her tale record the impossibility of Alison's undertaking. Her own restless metamorphoses, from antifeminist creation to romancer to clerical scholar and back to militant wife in her envoy, emphasize that each tradition on which she draws denies women sovereignty. In this context, that she and her old hag do not exercise their hard-won power intriguingly contradicts their persistent desire to win it. Is this a surrender to male fantasy? Or is Alison incapable of representing the full achievement of women's power? Or is sovereignty here again to be construed as trust, rather than as economic security or coercive domination? Can her envoy sustain any one of these explanations?

More important than Alison's failure to resolve such dilemmas is the elusive longing her many transformations betray. Her insatiable desire is more forceful and preoccupying than any of her illusory conclusions. Sovereignty's redefinitions are all provisional, each canceling another, because the most Alison can tell us about her ideal of female power is that it is not present. In her present, she can only tear the inert texts that have determined her, and wish for more.

From *PMLA: Publications of the Modern Language Association of America* 102, no. 1 (January 1987): 20-28. Copyright © 1987 by the Modern Language Association of America. Reprinted by permission of the Modern Language Association of America.

Notes

1. I use the term *ideology* not to disparage but, rather, to describe a set of interrelated beliefs that informs a particular way of life and works to validate that way of life in its attempts to win and maintain a place for itself in the world. On relations between history, ideology, and romance see Jameson; Shahar; Crane.

2. Robinson's notes list the connections between such passages and the works of Theophrastus, Jean de Meun, Matheolus, Jerome, and others. In this discussion I am claiming a "clerical" and "satiric" sensibility for these writers and their works, even for those who were not themselves clerics (e.g., Ovid) and for works that are not satires in the full generic sense, because antifeminist writing was so fully integrated into the medieval tradition of clerical satire. Some scholars prefer the term *antimatrimonial* to *antifeminist*, but the strategy of the tradition is to speak against marriage by speaking against women. On the WBP and another kind of clerical satire, the *sermon joyeux*, see Patterson.

3. Many critics have noted Alison's conflation of sex and gain in her marriages. It is also important that, in the dynamic of these marriages, Alison does not herself produce the wealth she deploys. Wealth is something inert that she wins from men by subterfuge and force, not something she generates by cloth making.

4. Her distance from models of womanhood may contribute to exegetical interpretations that her prologue and tale are not so much about femininity as about "the problem of willfulness" or "carnality": see Koban; Robertson, *Preface* 317-31. If the text has a tropological level on which the interactions of pure moral qualities can be analyzed, it nonetheless also makes literal statements with which I am concerned.

5. The ideas of Heloise anthologized in Jankyn's book are probably those against marriage that Abelard reports in the *Historia calamitatum* (*Letters* 70-74), adapted in Jean de Meun's *Roman de la rose* (vol. 2, lines 8729-58; *Romance*, pp. 177-78).

6. See also Margery's account of her own marriage to God (87).

7. For editions of Christine's French text in preparation, see Richards's introd. xxv.

8. On Chaucer's romances cf. Jordan; Ruggiers 151-246.

9. See also *The Legend of Good Women* G 317-444 (Alceste, "so charytable and trewe" [G 434], rescues Chaucer from the God of Love's punishment) and Ruggiers 208. In the following discussion I assume that Arthur's queen in WBT may be called Guinevere and that the old hag is the "elf-queene" of line 860.

10. According to Malone, "If the tale befits her, it does so by contrast, not by likeness" (489). My argument owes much to Leicester, "Art."

11. See also 12-15, 105-10. Green draws a similar conclusion on the social implications of later courtly poetry.

12. Mary Carruthers proposes that WBT opposes "courtesy-books" like Geoffroy's.

13. Some scholars relate the speech on *gentillesse* to Alison's "social class, the new rich, resentful of the claims of the old rich" (Colmer 329; see also Carruthers; Howard 105-06), but her class and professional origins are suppressed so markedly in favor of her estate and sex that the latter categories should have more to do with the speech than the former. Nor is the topos "he is gentil that dooth gentil dedis" to my knowledge ever a bourgeois one for medieval writers; rather, when it appears outside clerical contexts, its use is to sustain the nobility's separateness by adding moral criteria to those of birth: see Vale 14-32; Specht 104-08.

14. According to Koban, the speech is one of the *CT*'s "crystallizing utterances" in which Chaucer educates us in "humanizing truths" (227-28; see also Winney 24).

15. Only by accepting that the knight has listened to his wife and been changed by her words can we explain the difference between "My love? . . . nay, my dampnacioun!" (D 1067) and "My lady and my love, and wyf so deere,/ I put me in youre wise governance" (D 1230-31). Unless he

---

Poetic Instability in the Wife of Bath's Tale   **225**

is "glosing" her like Jankyn (D 509), which is unlikely in view of his thoughtful sigh (D 1228), the hag has talked him into loving and respecting her.

16. See Gallacher; see also Rowland; Palomo; Sands; and n. 4 above.

17. Chaucer's dramatization of an undecided Alison is remarkable not least in refraining from authorial judgment, a gesture Leicester attributes to Chaucer's own character: "This lack of closure in the Wife's life and personality is, finally, an aspect of Chaucer's feminism" ("Of a Fire" 175).

Works Cited

Aers, David. *Chaucer, Langland, and the Creative Imagination*. London: Routledge, 1980.

Bloch, R. Howard. *Medieval French Literature and Law*. Berkeley: U of California P, 1977.

Bolton, Whitney. "The Wife of Bath: Narrator as Victim." *Women and Literature* ns 1 (1980): 54-65.

Carruthers, Mary. "The Wife of Bath and the Painting of Lions." *PMLA* 94 (1979): 209-22.

Chaucer, Geoffrey. *The Works of Geoffrey Chaucer*. Ed. F. N. Robinson. 2nd ed. Boston: Houghton, 1957.

Christine de Pizan. *The Book of the City of Ladies*. Trans. Earl Jeffrey Richards. New York: Persea, 1982.

Colmer, Dorothy. "Character and Class in *The Wife of Bath's Tale*." *Journal of English and Germanic Philology* 72 (1973): 329-39.

Crane, Susan. *Insular Romance: Politics, Faith, and Culture in Anglo-Norman and Middle English Literature*. Berkeley: U of California P, 1986.

Delany, Sheila. "Sexual Economics: Chaucer's Wife of Bath and the Book of Margery Kempe." *Minnesota Review* ns 5 (1975): 104-15.

Duby, Georges. *Medieval Marriage: Two Models from Twelfth-Century France*. Trans. Elborg Forster. Baltimore: Johns Hopkins UP, 1978.

_____. *The Three Orders: Feudal Society Imagined*. Trans. Arthur Goldhammer. Chicago: Chicago UP, 1980.

Gallacher, Patrick J. "Dame Alice and the Nobility of Pleasure." *Viator* 13 (1982): 275-93.

Geoffroy de la Tour Landry. *The Book of the Knight of the Tower*. Trans. William Caxton. Ed. M. Y. Offord. EETS ss 2. London: Oxford UP, 1971.

_____. *Le livre du Chevalier de la Tour Landry*. Ed. Anatole de Montaiglon. Paris: Jannet, 1854.

Green, Richard Firth. "The *Familia Regis* and the *Familia Cupidinis*." *English Court Culture in the Later Middle Ages*. Ed. V. J. Scattergood and J. W. Sherbourne. New York: St. Martin's, 1983. 87-108.

Haller, Robert S. "The Wife of Bath and the Three Estates." *Annuale mediaevale* 6 (1965): 47-64.

Howard, Donald. *The Idea of the* Canterbury Tales. Berkeley: U of California P, 1976.

Jameson, Fredric. *The Political Unconscious Narrative as a Socially Symbolic Act*. Ithaca: Cornell UP, 1981.

Jean de Meun and Guillaume de Lorris. *Le roman de la rose*. Ed. Félix Lecoy. 3 vols. CFMA 92, 95, 98. Paris: Champion, 1973-76.

_____. *The Romance of the Rose*. Trans. Harry W. Robbins. New York: Dutton, 1962.

Jordan, Robert M. "The Question of Genre: Five Chaucerian Romances." *Chaucer at Albany*. Ed. R. H. Robbins. New York: Franklin, 1975. 77-103.

Kempe, Margery. *The Book of Margery Kempe*. Ed. Sanford Brown Meech. EETS os 212. London: Oxford UP, 1940.

Koban, Charles. "Hearing Chaucer Out: The Art of Persuasion in the Wife of Bath's Tale." *Chaucer Review* 5 (1970-71): 225-39.

Leicester, H. Marshall, Jr., "The Art of Impersonation: A General Prologue to the *Canterbury Tales*." *PMLA* 95 (1980): 213-24.

_____. "Of a Fire in the Dark: Public and Private Feminism in the Wife of Bath's Tale." *Women's Studies* 11 (1984): 157-78.

The Letters of Abelard and Heloise. Trans. Betty Radice. Harmondsworth: Penguin, 1974.

Malone, Kemp. "The Wife of Bath's Tale." *Modern Language Review* 57 (1962): 481-91.

Mann, Jill. *Chaucer and Medieval Estates Satire*. Cambridge: Cambridge UP, 1973.

Margulies, Cecile Stoller. "The Marriages and the Wealth of the Wife of Bath." *Mediaeval Studies* 24 (1962): 210-16.

Monfrin, J. "Poème anglo-normand sur le marriage, les vices et les vertus, par Henri (XIIIe siècle)." *Mélanges de langue et de littérature du moyen-âge et de la renaissance offerts à Jean Frappier*. 2 vols. Geneva: Droz, 1970. 2: 845-66.

Murtaugh, Daniel M. "Women and Geoffrey Chaucer." *ELH* 38 (1971): 473-92.

Palomo, Dolores. "The Fate of the Wife of Bath's 'Bad Husbands.'" *Chaucer Review* 9 (1974-75): 303-19.

Parker, Patricia A. *Inescapable Romance: Studies in the Poetics of a Mode*. Princeton: Princeton UP, 1979.

Patterson, Lee. "'For the Wyves love of Bathe': Feminine Rhetoric and Poetic Resolution in the *Roman de la rose* and the *Canterbury Tales*." *Speculum* 58 (1983): 656-95.

Robertson, D. W., Jr. "'And for My Land Thus Hastow Mordred Me?': Land Tenure, the Cloth Industry, and the Wife of Bath." *Chaucer Review* 14 (1979-80): 403-20.

_____. *A Preface to Chaucer: Studies in Medieval Perspectives*. Princeton: Princeton UP, 1962.

Rowland, Beryl. "Chaucer's Dame Alys: Critics in Blunderland?" *Neuphilologische Mitteilungen* 73 (1972): 381-95.

Ruggiers, Paul. *The Art of the Canterbury Tales*. Madison: U of Wisconsin P, 1965.

Sands, Donald B. "The Non-comic, Non-tragic Wife: Chaucer's Dame Alys as Sociopath." *Chaucer Review* 12 (1977-78): 171-82.

Shahar, Shulamith. *The Fourth Estate: A History of Women in the Middle Ages*. Trans. Chaya Galai. London: Methuen, 1983.

Specht, Henrik. *Chaucer's Franklin in the Canterbury Tales*. Copenhagen: Akademisk, 1981.

Vale, Malcolm. *War and Chivalry: Warfare and Aristocratic Culture in England, France, and Burgundy at the End of the Middle Ages*. London: Duckworth, 1981.

Vance, Eugene. "Le combat érotique chez Chrétien de Troyes." *Poétique* 12 (1972): 544-71.

Winney, James, ed. *The Wife of Bath's Prologue and Tale*. By Geoffrey Chaucer. Cambridge: Cambridge UP, 1965.

"The Name of Soveraynetee":
The Private and Public Faces of Marriage
in *The Franklin's Tale*_____

Cathy Hume

Chaucer's *Franklin's Tale* opens with a description of a marriage of apparently idyllic happiness. The marriage of Arveragus and Dorigen follows a
long courtship where Arveragus served his lady Dorigen through many acts of
chivalry and is to be quite different from the model of dominant husband and
obedient wife adopted by Walter and Grisilde in the *Clerk's Tale*. Arveragus
swears

> That nevere in al his lyf he, day ne nyght,
> Ne sholde upon hym take no maistrie
> Agayn hir wyl, ne kithe hire jalousie,
> But hire obeye, and folwe hir wyl in al,
> As any lovere to his lady shal.[1]

In return, Dorigen swears to be his "humble trewe wyf" (758). The narrator
approves this as a "humble, wys accord" (791) and goes on to explain that,
paradoxically, Arveragus is

> . . . bothe in lordshipe and servage.
> Servage? Nay, but in lordshipe above,
> Sith he hath both his lady and his love;
> His lady, certes, and his wyf also.
> (794-97)

This arrangement has been seen as utopian—most famously by G. L. Kittredge, who argued that "a better has never been devised or imagined" and
that it was Chaucer's own ideal.[2] Indeed, it leads to more than a year of marital
bliss.

However, the model contains a contradiction that is more than a mere elegant oxymoron. Although Jill Mann argues that the alternation between
"lordshipe" and "servage" represents a flexible, fluctuating relationship, the
fact is that Arveragus's public role is going to show no such flexibility.[3] While
renouncing "maistrie" in private, he will retain "the name of soveraynetee . . .
for shame of his degree" (751-52). In other words, his concern with reputation
will lead him to pay lip service to an ideal of male dominance that he does not
espouse in private.[4] At the poem's crisis, Arveragus's behavior becomes even
more contradictory. He tells Dorigen that she should fulfill her adulterous

promise to Aurelius, which implies that he respects her as an autonomous human being whose personal word should be honored rather than someone he owns and controls. But he then orders her to tell no one about what she is doing and threatens her with death if she does so. Arveragus has, then, both reneged on his vow to "take no maistrie" and deepened the fissure between the couple's private marital behavior (which now encompasses husband-sanctioned adultery) and the conventional face they present to the public.

How can we account for this? In Alfred David's view, "Arveragus' insistence on keeping up the appearance while willing to suffer the fact diminishes his nobility and raises a serious question about the depth of the Franklin's conception of 'gentilesse.'"[5] Cynthia A. Gravlee believes that Arveragus's concern for his public image outweighs his love for Dorigen and that his apparent interest in "trouthe," which suits his image of worthy knight, is undermined by his suppression of the truth from the public.[6] Should we, then, consider Arveragus a hypocrite? Was he never truly committed to an equal marriage? Or was his utopian ideal unworkably flawed from the outset; are we to believe, with Felicity Riddy and Angela Jane Weisl, that the equality he promised was never meant to be anything more than a polite fiction and that male dominance is inevitable in a medieval marriage?[7]

I want to argue in this essay that none of these conclusions is justified. Rather, as Robert R. Edwards has recognized, the *Franklin's Tale* is a story of a loving marriage struggling to survive in a world of changing social relations, "competing ambitions and mixed practices."[8] I hope to show that, having established an egalitarian marriage ideal at the beginning of the *Tale*, Chaucer goes on to explore how such an ideal would be tested by real world circumstances. Notwithstanding the *Tale*'s ostensibly pagan and Breton context, I will present parallels from late medieval letter collections and advice literature to suggest that Dorigen is tested in ways that would have seemed familiar and therefore meaningful to Chaucer's medieval readers; that the conception of honor and reputation portrayed in the *Tale* reflects the complex conception found in other contemporary sources; and that we understand Dorigen and Arveragus's divergent behavior in private and public best if we see it as related to contemporary expectations of proper behavior for married couples.

The signal that we are to read the *Tale* as a test of a particular kind of marriage ideal comes at its opening, which, as Edwards has also recognized, diverges entirely from Chaucer's presumed sources—the tale that Menedon tells as the fourth of thirteen love questions in Boccaccio's *Il Filocolo* and, perhaps, Boccaccio's other version of the same story in the *Decameron*.[9] In the *Decameron*, the marriage is not even established as loving—the implication of the comment that the wife "deserved to be loved greatly" by her illicit suitor is that her husband does not love her.[10] Chaucer, by contrast, opens with the story of the couple's romantic courtship as well as setting out in detail the kind of marriage they agree to have. This marriage ideal imports ideas from the *Roman de la Rose*—that "love wol nat been constreyned by maistrye" (764) and that "wommen, of kynde, desiren libertee" (768)—but comes to quite a different conclusion. Whereas the *Roman* sees marriage as destroying love, along with friendship and equality, here a model of marriage is proposed that sustains love through a combination of roles.[11] Each partner will serve one another, allowing each spouse to be served as lord or lady, so that Arveragus has, in Dorigen, "lady," "wyf," and "love." However, the idea that there may be a difficulty lurking within this ideal is suggested by the obtrusively complicated presentation of the "servage"/"lordshipe" paradox (quoted above)—as several critics have noted.[12] Moreover, Chaucer gives us a discursus on the need for patience in marriage that will prove to be more than mere filler:

> Lerneth to suffer, or elles, so moot I goon,
> Ye shul it lerne, wher so ye wole or noon;
> For in this world, certein, ther no wight is
> That he ne dooth or seith somtyme amys.
> Ire, siknesse, or constellacioun,
> Wyn, wo, or chaungynge of complexioun
> Causeth ful ofte to doon amys or speken.
> On every wrong a man may nat be wreken.
> (777-84)

Interestingly, this passage seems to recall the warnings given in medieval marriage sermons about the daily conflicts that marriage is likely to entail.[13] If the narrator's warning about the hypothetical problems married life throws up is drawn from Chaucer's immediate historical context, so too are the actual problems he creates for Dorigen and Arveragus. Chaucer alters the circumstances of his source story throughout, so that Dorigen's encounters with Aurelius occur quite differently and are presented as part of a complex, late medieval social world where personal and business relationships are intertwined and need careful negotiation if both public reputation and private virtue are to be maintained.

We can establish this by considering evidence of how historic married couples were expected to behave, and did behave, to preserve their reputations and maintain their social connections. As in my earlier essay on the social comedy of the *Shipman's Tale*, I will use two main kinds of evidence: advice literature for women written in the late fourteenth century and fifteenth-century letter collections.[14] The usefulness of English and French advice literature as evidence for late medieval ideologies has been well established as a

Critical Insights

general principle in studies such as Diane Bornstein's *The Lady in the Tower: Medieval Courtesy Literature for Women* and as a relevant context for Chaucer in essays such as Carolyn Collette's "Heeding the Counsel of Prudence: A Context for the Melibee" and Juliette Dor's "The Wife of Bath's 'Wandrynge by the Weye' and Conduct Literature for Women."[15] Here I will make use of Christine de Pizan's 1405 *Livre des Trois Vertus*, *The Book of the Knight of the Tower* (Caxton's fifteenth-century translation of the Chevalier de la Tour Landry's ca. 1371 original), and the *Menagier de Paris*, written by a Parisian bourgeois between 1392 and 1394—all texts that consider wives' duties in detail.[16] Letter collections have been less frequently used than advice literature to throw light on Chaucer, though there are several exceptions, such as Mary Carruthers' discussion of the Paston and Stonor letters in her classic article on the Wife of Bath.[17] No doubt this is because the surviving collections by the Paston, Stonor, Cely, and Plumpton families are of a later date—with the most interesting material dating from around the 1440s to the 1470s—than the *Canterbury Tales*. Nevertheless, since historians of marriage have found both ideology and practice largely unchanged in that period and since the letters offer such unparalleled evidence of the actual behavior of historical couples, I will make use of their contents as interestingly extending, corroborating, and complicating the evidence of ideological guides.[18]

Dorigen and Arveragus: A Portrait of a Medieval Marriage

Chaucer presents Dorigen's encounters with Aurelius in such a way as to reflect the daily life of late medieval gentlewomen. She meets him without her husband, talks with him, and makes and sets out to fulfill a contract with him in a set of circumstances that must have been intended to strike a chord with Chaucer's readers. The first similarity Dorigen and Arveragus share with real medieval married couples is their long separation, when Arveragus's need for "worship and honour" (811) takes him away to England to seek glory in arms. This makes a stark contrast from Boccaccio's narratives, where the husband is continually present. Arveragus's absence has a profound impact on Dorigen's behaviour. She misses him hugely:

> For his absence wepeth she and siketh,
> As doon thise noble wyves whan hem liketh.
> She moorneth, waketh, wayleth, fasteth, pleyneth;
> Desir of his presence hire so destreyneth
> That al this wyde world she sette at noght.
>
> (817-21)

The second line above has been read as carrying the scornful implication that Dorigen's sorrow is no more than an aristocratic indulgence, but the evidence of letter collections argues that Chaucer's implication may be more gently humorous, portraying her behavior as predictably typical of women in her situation.[19] As Kathryn Jacobs notes, the practicalities of everyday gentry (and merchant) life led to many medieval couples being separated, and it is to these frequent separations that we owe the existence of the fifteenth-century letters between husbands and wives.[20] But just because the separations were commonplace does not mean they were not painful. Margaret Paston often reports unhappiness at being left alone and worries about her husband's welfare. In Paston letter 126 she tells John I that she has been worrying ever since she heard of his sickness and that she wants him home: "myn hert is in no grete esse, ne nowth xal be tyl I wott þat ʒe ben very hol" (218). When she finds out that he will be away at Christmas, she writes in letter 153 that she will "thynke my-selfe halfe a wedowe" without him (258). In letter 169 Elizabeth Stonor is worried that her husband William will catch the pox in London and wants him to come home where he will be safe—or if that is not possible, she will go to be with him "for in good faith I thought never so longe sith I see yow" (267). A month later in letter 173, she tells him "I longe sore ffor you" even though she understands he has been occupied with "gret besynys" (272). Anne Stonor, William's third wife, also finds his absences difficult and writes in letter 306 that it seems "long sith I saw you, and if I had knowen þat I shold hav ben this long tyme from you I wold have be moche lother then I was to have comyn into this ferre Countrey," where she is staying with friends (140).

So, even when wives appreciate the reasons for their husbands' absence, they regret it, grieve, miss them, and worry about them. Dorigen's sorrow, then, may be predictable, but this does not make it self-indulgent: if gentry wives missed husbands who might be absent on business trips for five weeks at a time or fourteen weeks in a year, as John Paston I was, how much more distraught may we allow Dorigen to be, whose husband is absent for years, much of that time engaged in life-threatening feats of arms?[21]

In order to distract herself from her sorrow, Dorigen feels obliged to agree to her friends' request to spend her time in company and attends their May gathering in the garden.[22] Margaret Hallissy argues that this is inappropriate behavior: the conduct books prescribe, in her view, that Dorigen should not go out when her husband is away, and it is true that Christine de Pizan advises keeping outward show to a minimum in one's husband's absence (bk. 1, ch. 13, p. 56).[23] However, this prohibition is not repeated in the other advice literature for women, and the Knight of the Tower sees dancing and attending festivals as generally acceptable occupations for wives, so long as they are accompanied by their friends and neighbors (ch. 24, p. 45). Moreover, it is clear that medieval wives were expected to socialize in their husbands' absence: Margaret Paston reports going to dinner with her cousin Toppys and Lady Felbrygg on St Peter's Day in Paston letter 141, and although she tells John I that they would "all a be þe meryere if ye hadde ben there" (243), this has not stopped her from going.

It has been argued that Dorigen, in attending this party, is trying to play the role of a flirtatious courtly lady or that she sees it as an escape from reality and normal social expectations.[24] But Chaucer takes care to distinguish her encounter with her suitor from those of her precursors in Boccaccio. In Boccaccio's versions of the story, the suitor has already been courting the married lady for some time, and the lady—who is explicitly characterized as devious in *Il Filocolo*—fixes on the idea of requesting a magical tribute in the hope of getting rid of him. Each of Boccaccio's ladies makes a show of playing along with her suitor's courtship and being willing to satisfy him if only he can provide an adequately elaborate tribute. Chaucer, by contrast, creates a situation whereby Dorigen talks to Aurelius in complete ignorance of his love for her and speaks to him at this gathering:

> By cause that he was hire neighebour
> And was a man of worshipe and honour,
> And hadde yknowen hym of tyme yoore.
>
> (961-63)

Aurelius is a respectable neighbor whom Dorigen ought to be able to trust. As such, he is the kind of person whom a medieval wife would be expected to maintain as part of a social/business network in her husband's absence. As Jennifer C. Ward writes, for the medieval English noblewoman "social activities undoubtedly provided enjoyment, but also had deeper significance," and while husbands were away, their wives would be expected to keep friendship networks going for the practical advantages they could provide.[25] Dorigen encounters Aurelius only in public. Unlike Boccaccio's characters, who meet according to their own initiative at one another's houses, Aurelius accosts Dorigen at events that she feels obliged to attend: first at this dance, then at the temple, and lastly when she is walking in the street after he has been spying on her. Their meetings all arise as a consequence of the commitments that Dorigen, like any medieval wife who is obliged to operate independently of her absent husband, must fulfill: to maintain social bonds, to attend worship, to honor a contract. At the same time, Dorigen's rash promise to Aurelius arises out of her love for Arveragus and desire to protect him, thus implicitly reasserting her married status even as she jokingly promises to be Aurelius's "love" (990).

The obligation to honor contracts brings us to another reality for medieval wives whose husbands are away: they must carry out business, whether on their husbands' behalf or semiautonomously. This requires them, as mentioned above, to converse with their male acquaintances, as Dorigen does with Aurelius. There is plentiful evidence of this in the Paston letters: for example, in letter 624, John, Prior of Bromholm, mentions to John I that he has been speaking to Margaret about his dealings with another clergyman; in letter 636 William Lomnor explains that he has told her about the disposition of the Earl of Norfolk's men. Second, wives frequently make business arrangements and conclude agreements in a way that goes far beyond keeping the household ticking over in their husbands' absence. Margaret Paston's activities include arranging a commission to appoint a new parson to Drayton church (letter 183); speaking to the sheriff and having him send out writs (letter 192); extracting a promise from Lord Moleyns's men that they will not harm John Paston I's men (letter 131); and renting some property in the pretense that she is keeping her husband in the dark about what she is doing, securing a good deal for herself in the process (letter 147).

Although Margaret is frequently operating under John I's instructions, this does not appear to be the case in any of the above situations, and she is clearly able to do business even when she is explicitly claiming that her husband is unaware of what she is doing, as in the rental agreement. This supports Richard Firth Green's view that, on a day-to-day basis, medieval married women were able to contract independently of their husbands.[26] The expectation that a wife would honor her personal "trouthe" would have been a necessary part of daily business, so when it comes to Dorigen's promise to Aurelius, his attempt to enforce it and Arveragus's respect for her word seem more reasonable than "unrealistic."[27] Moreover, even though Dorigen makes her vow "in pley" (988), she surrounds it with a straightforward honesty about her real intentions and a matter-of-fact attitude to the bargain that may well have reflected real medieval practice. Perhaps it is not too far-fetched to see a similarity to Margaret Paston's frankness in her dealings with Lord Moleyns's men, mentioned above. Margaret has a confrontation with them when Lord Moleyns had already seized Paston properties, and Margaret reports to John I that she told Lord Moleyns's men that she did not trust their words and would not be inviting them into the house where she was staying (letter 131); Dorigen tells Aurelius to give up his "folies" (1002) and reminds him that she is the wife of another man "that hath hir body whan so that hym liketh" (1005).[28]

Finally, Dorigen has in common with these fifteenth-century wives a preference for consulting her husband when things become difficult. Dorigen waits for Arveragus to return before deciding how to deal with Aurelius, unlike Boccaccio's women whose husbands force an explanation of what is going on out of them. David Aers thinks Dorigen acts submissively and dependently by turning to Arveragus in her crisis, but if this is true, it is true of several other medieval wives.[29] Elizabeth Stonor's desire for her husband to return in Stonor letter 169, mentioned above, is partly motivated by the difficult week she has had, full of various problems: she tells him, "I wot will that ye coulde an answeryd in certayn maters better þen I" (267). Margaret Paston pleads with John I in Paston letter 188 to do something to protect his servants who are being attacked at Hellesdon: she says, "to my powere I wyl do as I can or may in yowre materys," but she leaves it to him to "seke a meen" for his servants to be at peace (310). These requests for help and advice would have been approved by the author of the *Menagier de Paris*, who recommends that wives check different courses of action with their husbands wherever possible rather than making their own decisions (bk. 1, art. 6, p. 89).

Honor and Hypocrisy

Thus far, then, Dorigen's circumstances seem to be suggestively similar to those of real medieval wives and dissimilar to those of her literary predecessors. Can the same be said of the sometimes conflicting values of public reputation, honor, truth, secrecy, and private egalitarianism that she and Arveragus hold?

Any accusation of Arveragus's hypocrisy must hinge on his determination to keep the "name of soveraynetee" in public while renouncing "maistrie" in private. However, this appears to reflect a medieval pattern of husbands expecting a show of obedience in public while adopting a far less domineering and more egalitarian mode of behavior to their wives in private. There are signs of this even in the advice literature prescribing ideal marital behavior. While Christine de Pizan's *Livre des trois vertus*, *The Book of the Knight of the Tower*, and *Le Menagier de Paris* all emphasize that a wife should obey her husband, they make exceptions to this when the couple is in private. The Knight of the Tower repeatedly condemns arguing with or contradicting a husband "shamefully to fore the peple," but he sees a wife who reprehends her husband in private as doing "her parte" (ch. 17, p. 35; ch. 75, p. 106; and chs. 95-96, pp. 128-29). A substantial section of *Le Menagier de Paris* is devoted to obedience, but the author also suggests that wives may ask for an explanation of their husband's behavior (bk. 1, art. 6, p. 79) or reprehend them in private (bk. 1, art. 9, p. 113). Christine de Pizan recommends that the wife should obey her husband in general (bk. 1, ch. 13, p. 53), but suggests that some commands should be carefully considered before they are followed (bk. 1, ch. 11, p. 44) and that a wife may need to admonish her husband (bk. 1, ch. 13, p. 55). She even suggests that a wife may wish to involve her husband's confessor and some other "bonnes gens" to help correct him. This does not, I think, imply that she will be seen to be correcting her husband by the court at large, undermining her public deference. Rather, it implies that trusted friends would happily accept the notion that a wife might play a slightly different role in private.[30]

The motivation for this split between private and public behavior is explained as follows in *Le Menagier de Paris*: a wife must "*monstrer* son obeissance" (show her obedience; my emphasis) lest people suspect the husband is under her thumb, which would be extremely shameful to her and damaging to her husband: "Ce que femme ne doit pas vouloir que l'en apparçoive; car en tel cas elles se demonstrent comme maistresses et dames, et a elles mesmes feroient grant blasme, et grant vilenie a leurs mariz" (the wife should not want this to be perceived; for in such cases they show themselves to be mistresses and ruling ladies, and cause great blame for themselves and great shame for their husbands; bk. 1, art. 6, p. 77). It does not seem to occur to this author or his contemporaries that there is anything inconsistent or shameful about behaving differently in private.

The Paston wives follow a similar pattern of greater deference in public. They normally address their husbands as "worshipful husband" or "master" at the opening of letters and on the dorse. The address written on the dorse would have been the only public-facing part of the letter, visible to the messenger carrying it and anyone else who handled it but did not break the seal.[31] The opening of the letter would have been visible only to its reader but was usually formulaic and thus formalized in a deferential mode.[32] However, the substance of the letters is often less obedient.[33] Margaret writes to John Paston I in letter 154—which, as usual, is addressed outside and at the beginning of the letter to her "ryth worchepfull husband"—that she is not going to follow his request to speak to an unnamed person about some secret matter, because "me semyth he is to yonge" and "he schall neuer loue feythfully the todyr man" on whose behalf he would be working (258-59). She has made her own judgment of the situation and decided to disobey him for their common good. She makes no apology—nor does she in letter 138 where she also disobeys him on a business matter. In letter 418, Margery uses the formal "mayster" for the dorse of her letter to her husband John III (665) but begins the letter itself with the more equal and loving "myne owyn swete hert" (though she reverts to a more respectful mode of address subsequently) and dares to make a complaint: "I mervell sore that I haue no letter from you."[34]

For their part, the Paston men are far from domineering. In letter 77 John I calls Margaret his "owne dere souereyn lady" (140), implying that he is subservient to her rather than vice versa. In more public letters—those addressed simultaneously to Margaret and their servants—he favors the respectful form "maistresse" for his wife, perhaps in order to emphasize Margaret's status relative to their servants. But if writing to her alone, he uses "cosyn," a term that implies a relationship of equality. As well as giving their wives instructions about business matters, both John I and John III ask their advice on some questions (for example, in letter 389 John III wants medical advice) and leave others to their wives' discretion (in letter 76, for example, where John I leaves his wife to decide how enquiries into the payments made to the farmers of Akthorp since Sir John Fastolf's death should be made). It is true that none of these sources contains anything as radically unmasterful as the marriage in the *Franklin's Tale*, but the hints they offer of marriage as partnership rather than hierarchy and of greater wifely deference in public suggest that Dorigen and Arveragus's marriage would have struck Chaucer's audience as a more pronounced version of something quite familiar.[35]

If Arveragus and Dorigen's decision to behave differently in public and private might have seemed perfectly normal to a medieval audience, what of their concern with worldly reputation and secrecy? Arveragus's desire to keep the nature of his marriage quiet comes after Dorigen decides "pryvely" to marry him (741), and this emphasis on keeping the details of their married life, and threats to it, private continues throughout the *Tale*.[36] Dorigen's friends are ignorant of what has passed between her and Aurelius in the garden (1014); Dorigen goes on to tell no one when Aurelius announces that he has kept to his side of the bargain (1350); then, at the story's crisis, Arveragus tells Dorigen to "make no contenance of hevynesse" (1485) that might lead anyone to suspect Dorigen, having forbidden her ever to tell what has happened "up peyne of deeth" (1481). It is true that the husband in *Il Filocolo* tells his wife to fulfil her promise in secret, but this isolated comment is quite different in force from Dorigen and Arveragus's painstaking discretion.

Chaucer's approach seems, again, to be bringing his narrative closer to late medieval practice in England and France, where discretion and secrecy formed an important part of the medieval marriage ideal. *Le Menagier de Paris* recommends that wives should keep their husbands' secrets (bk. 1, art. 8, pp. 105-6), and an extended treatment of the ideal through a series of exemplary stories about Cato and his son forms the final section of the *Book of the Knight of the Tower*. Christine de Pizan extends this ideal of discretion to unhappy marriages; if a husband is treating his wife unlovingly or is unfaithful, she is to give no indication of it and to contradict anyone who speaks ill of him (bk. 1, ch. 13, 55). Margaret Paston's letters give us a number of examples of her withholding what appears to be personal or sensitive information from letters that might fall into the wrong hands and were in any case dictated to scribes. She prefers to tell her husband about such matters in private: so, in letter 190, she promises to explain to her husband why she is at Caister when she sees him, and in letter 126 she makes a cryptic reference to a token that they have already discussed in private: "I xal sende my moder a tokyn þat sche toke me, for I sopose þe tyme is cum þat I xulde sendeth here yf I kepe þe behest þat I have made—I sopose I have tolde yow wat it was" (218). Davis's suggestion that this refers to her pregnancy seems eminently plausible, but for our purposes it is more interesting that she chooses not to write openly about whatever it is.

In both the *Franklin's Tale* and our other sources, secrecy is found alongside a preoccupation with honor, which, again, is given more weight than it was by Boccaccio. Honor has two conflicting associations in the *Franklin's Tale*. First, it is connected with "trouthe." This is brought into play when Dorigen swears her "trouthe" (998) to Aurelius in a far more formal manner (even though it is "in pley" [988]) than in the corresponding episode in *Il Filocolo*. When Arveragus comes to hear about this, he responds as follows:

> Ye shul youre trouthe holden, by my fay!
> For God so wisly have mercy upon me,
> I hadde wel levere ystiked for to be
> For verray love which that I to yow have,
> But if ye sholde youre trouthe kepe and save.
> Trouthe is the hyest thyng that man may kepe.
>
> (1474-79)

This take on the issue is quite different from that of his precursors in Boccaccio: in the *Decameron*, the husband tells his wife to try to get out of the promise, and in *Il Filocolo*, he tells her to keep the promise because Tarolfo has earned his reward reasonably. Here, Arveragus's reason for wanting his wife to keep her promise is his regard for her personal "trouthe" in both its legal and ethical senses. For Arveragus, "trouthe" appears to carry both the narrow sense of an oath and agreement and the broader sense of integrity and fidelity to one's word—essentially, the same kind of "trawþe" that proves to be at issue in *Sir Gawain and the Green Knight*.[37] In the Italian analogues the idea of a gentlewoman's word being her oath occurs only to the suitor in the *Decameron*, who hopes it will help him to get what he wants. But in the *Franklin's Tale* it becomes more than a principle that can be exploited: Arveragus's love for Dorigen means that he cannot bear to see his beloved wife fail to live up to this truth ideal.

Honor also has another aspect in this *Tale*, as a reputation for marital fidelity. Dorigen herself is attached to this ideal, which, as Derek Brewer has shown, is the more traditional basis for women's honor, telling us that she would rather die "than of my body to have a shame" (1361) and giving us a number of examples of legendary women who have made the same choice.[38] Arveragus's guidance to Dorigen prioritizes truth to her word over sexual fidelity to him, but this seems to be at least partly because he is able to release her from the latter obligation but not the former. Indeed, his earlier determination to have the public "name of soveraynetee . . . for shame of his degree" suggests that he, too, values the sexual aspect of honor and that for him that honor entails not only public knowledge of his wife's chastity but also creating a public impression that he dominates his wife more generally.[39] At the crisis of the poem, Arveragus again attempts to preserve this traditional basis of the couple's honor by maintaining their reputation for sexual fidelity. Does this make him a hypocrite? Why espouse one ideal—of spiritual, rather than bodily, fidelity—in private but refuse to admit that this is what you are doing in public? The answer must be that Arveragus is trying to sustain a social image of a successful, faithful marriage that fits with society's expectations rather than his own principles.[40] But this would probably not have struck Chaucer's original audience as hypocritical.

Advice literature and letter collections testify that medieval married couples took pains to create and preserve their reputation for honor and chastity. The *Livre des trois vertus* emphasizes the importance of a wife speaking well of her husband and preserving his honor (bk. 1, chs. 8-9, pp. 32-33) and of cultivating her own reputation for honor, chastity, and loving her husband (bk. 1, ch. 11, pp. 41-42; ch. 13, p. 56); it also warns of the dire consequences of any suspicion of infidelity for her reputation and even her life (bk. 1, ch. 27, pp. 110-19). The *Menagier de Paris* also stresses the importance of a chaste reputation: the mere suspicion that a wife is unchaste leads to her losing all good, which no other merit can restore (bk. 1, art. 4, p. 47). Interestingly for our purposes, the *Menagier* author gives several examples of husbands saving their wives' honor by concealing their infidelity in the eighth Article of his first Book. He also discusses spouses' duties to preserve one another from any public blame, whether or not it results from a real error, especially since a wife must share any blame a husband has: she "partiroit a son blasme pour ce qu'elle seroit mariee a si meschant" (will share his blame because she is married to such a wretched man; 110). Presumably the same would apply to a husband with an erring wife. Two things follow from this: that a reputation for chastity is, as in the *Franklin's Tale*, considered far more important to honor than chastity in fact; and that the *Menagier* author's conception of shared shame supports Brewer's observation that the honor of medieval married couples worked collectively—they formed an "honour group," and thus had to work together to sustain and increase their honor.[41]

Philippa Maddern has analyzed the meaning and importance of honor for the Pastons. She demonstrates that for them, rather than being associated with military prowess and men alone, honor resided in "quotidien relationships," which both men and women could maintain; that in the fifteenth century honor was becoming increasingly associated with virtue but was still importantly rooted in public renown; and that it could involve, for example, holding off from insisting on one's rights through litigation and performing business transactions faithfully.[42] Honorable behavior, she argues, could involve lying: in letter 73 John Paston I tells Margaret it is "worshep for yow to confort yowr tenantis" (133)—"worship" is the Pastons' usual term for honor—and he goes on to recommend that she lie to them that she has not heard from her husband. Margaret evidently considers reputation very important: she frequently sends John I reports of what is being said about him: for example, in letters 164 or 166 where she refers to what might be considered "wurchepful" for him (275). And she was not alone in this: writing about the Stonors, Christine Carpenter says that "a gentry family's concern for its local standing, its worship, is a constant thread running through the letters."[43] The Pastons and families like them, then, would have recognized the importance to a woman's honor of keeping to her side of a contract and, along with Dorigen and Arveragus, sometimes cultivated their honor through a lack of transparency about what was going on in their marriage.

Conclusions

If Chaucer was, then, drawing on his own social reality in creating his picture of a marriage under stress, how should this affect our reading of the *Franklin's Tale* and Arveragus's behavior in particular? First and perhaps most importantly, we should interpret Arveragus's concern for "shame" to his social rank and for people thinking "harm" of Dorigen in line with contemporary ideas of honor. Both the advice literature and the letter collections show that maintaining an honorable reputation greatly concerned medieval men and women. For women, this honorable reputation would have been linked to chastity, making it important to conceal Dorigen's sexual infidelity. But a woman's honor would also have been conceived far more broadly, as John Paston I's comments to his wife show, so that faithfulness to one's word, especially in a world where women transacted so much business on their own account, would have seemed of comparable importance. A medieval audience would not, I think, have seen Arveragus's interest in reputation as "shallow" or as having an inappropriate priority in relation to his love for his wife, as David and Gravlee argue.[44] Keeping secrets from the world and presenting a united front to others, which can involve an element of dissimulation, are recommended by the advice books and practiced by medieval husbands and wives.[45] Moreover, Arveragus is not claiming higher standards or beliefs than those he really holds—rather the reverse. His aim is to have his private behavior, which is generally admirable, reflected in an honorable reputation. This would probably not have struck a medieval audience as hypocritical.

However, Chaucer clearly had a point to make in creating a split between private and public behavior. Arveragus and Dorigen's marriage has an unavoidable social aspect, and this has the potential to threaten their private happiness. In order to function socially, both Arveragus and Dorigen feel that they must keep the public from full knowledge of their marriage relationship. By doing so, they perhaps leave the way open for individuals such as Aurelius to make mistaken assumptions about the nature of their marriage, imagining, given the conventional face they present to the public, that theirs was the kind of loveless, political union that seems to have been particularly prevalent among the upper classes of medieval society.[46] That would, of course, leave greater scope for Aurelius's adulterous suit. The existence of such assumptions might seem to argue for greater transparency, but it probably does no such thing. If Aurelius can imagine, on no basis whatsoever, that Dorigen might be favorably inclined toward a love affair, what might others assume of her if they knew that her husband showed her no "maistrie" or that she had been unfaithful to him with another man? The threat that an ignorant neighbor causes to his marriage goes a long way towards justifying Arveragus's determination to keep the world in the dark.[47]

Finally, I do not think we are intended to read Arveragus's behavior as flawless. However, neither do I believe that his failure lies in declaring that Dorigen should keep her promise (which some have seen as an order that demonstrates he has never really rejected "maistrie").[48] Unlike Boccaccio's husbands, who do command their wives at this point, Arveragus simply makes an assertion about what Dorigen should do and considers the matter closed. Dorigen, unlike Boccaccio's wives, does not argue. Arveragus, by making this assertion, has surrendered his prior claim to Dorigen's sexual fidelity, releasing her from her marriage vow so that she can keep the promise that she (not he) made to Aurelius.[49] This, as Aurelius notes, is an act of generosity and gentilesse. Arveragus is showing respect for Dorigen's word and her autonomy—at considerable personal cost—rather than treating her as his property. Once Arveragus has sanctioned Dorigen's infidelity, she has no option but to keep her promise to Aurelius if she is to act honorably. However, threatening Dorigen "up peyne of deeth" to keep what she is doing quiet must strike us as unpleasantly out of accord with what Arveragus had promised when he undertook to "take no maistrie Agayn hir wyl." But, since Arveragus's failure to live up to his ideal comes as an outburst of negative emotion, it mirrors Dorigen's own failure, where she breaks her vow to be "trewe" to Arveragus as a result of her distress about the rocks that endanger him.

Thus both partners in this marriage are imperfect, just as the narrator had foretold, but this imperfection arises from their love for one another, making it especially forgivable. Moreover, it creates an equality of imperfection between Dorigen and Arveragus, so that rather than the story ending with a superior husband correcting his erring wife, as in Boccaccio, Chaucer's couple are both at fault; both need to be forgiven, and both will try harder in the future. As Davis puts it, "their original mutuality is restored, but this time on a more mature and self-aware footing."[50] As a realistic married couple—the sort of couple that Chaucer might have encountered—neither of them has been capable of perfect adherence to their ideals. But their ideals and their love remain intact, and this is why Chaucer finally allows them to escape reality and gives them an optimistic ending that confirms his original marital ideal: Dorigen is again "trewe"; Arveragus again "cherisseth hire as though she were a queene", and they both "leden forth hir lyf" in "sovereyn blisse" for evermore (1551-55).[51]

Notes

1. *The Franklin's Tale*, in *The Riverside Chaucer*, 3rd ed., gen. ed. Larry D. Benson (Oxford: Oxford University Press, 1987), lines 746-50. Subsequent references to *The Franklin's Tale* are to this edition and will be cited parenthetically within the text by line number.

2. Kittredge, "Chaucer's Discussion of Marriage," *Modern Philology* 9 (1912): 467.

3. Mann, *Feminizing Chaucer* (Cambridge: D. S. Brewer, 2002), 90.

4. John M. Fyler and Craig R. Davis argue that we are to see this public show as a way of compensating for Arveragus's low social status ("Love and Degree in the *Franklin's Tale*," *Chaucer Review* 21 [1987]: 321-37; "A Perfect Marriage on the Rocks: Geoffrey and Philippa Chaucer, and the *Franklin's Tale*," *Chaucer Review* 37 [2002]: 129-44). However, I am not convinced that we are meant to see any serious disparity of status between the "knyght" Arveragus and Dorigen's "heigh kynrede" (735), since the latter is so briefly and vaguely mentioned and seems to be significant mainly as a manifestation of Arveragus's conventional feeling of being unworthy of his lady.

5. David, *The Strumpet Muse: Art and Morals in Chaucer's Poetry* (Bloomington: Indiana University Press, 1976), 190.

6. Gravlee, "Presence, Absence and Difference: Reception and Deception in *The Franklin's Tale*," in *Desiring Discourse: The Literature of Love, Ovid through Chaucer*, ed. James J. Paxson and Cynthia A. Gravlee (Selinsgrove, PA: Susquehanna University Press, 1998), 181.

7. Riddy argues that Arveragus never really surrenders his male powers, and merely wishes to envisage Dorigen as his lady in order to confirm his status ("Engendering Pity in the *Franklin's Tale*," in *Feminist Readings in Middle English Literature: The Wife of Bath and all her Sect*, ed. Ruth Evans and Lesley Johnson [London: Routledge, 1994], 54-71); Weisl argues that romance cannot allow a wife to be simultaneously a lady with real power and that the equality of Dorigen's marriage is an illusion (*Conquering the Reign of Femeny: Gender and Genre in Chaucer's Romance* [Cambridge: D. S. Brewer, 1995], 106).

8. Edwards, "Source, Context, and Cultural Translation in the *Franklin's Tale*," *Modern Philology* 94 (1996-97): 154-56.

9. It is not known whether Chaucer encountered Menedon's story as part of a complete text of *Il Filocolo* or as an excerpted section of the Love Questions, which circulated separately, but for the purposes of my argument either scenario could be assumed. See Edwards, "Source, Context, and Cultural Translation" for a full discussion. The question of whether Chaucer knew the *Decameron* also remains open; in light of this, I will refer to some parallels and contrasts with the *Decameron*'s version of the story.

10. See *Sources and Analogues of the Canterbury Tales*, ed. Robert M. Correale, 2 vols. (Cambridge: D. S. Brewer, 2002), 1:239.

11. As has been noted, for example, by Mark N. Taylor in "Servant and Lord/Lady and Wife: The *Franklin's Tale* and Traditions of Courtly and Conjugal Love" (*Chaucer Review* 32 [1997]: 73), this section is similar to a passage at the end of Chrétien de Troyes's *Cligés* (ed. Claude Luttrell and Stewart Gregory, Arthurian Studies 28 [Cambridge: D. S. Brewer, 1993], lines 6731-36): "De s'amie a feite sa fame, Mes il l'apele amie et dame, Et por ce ne pert ele mie Que il ne l'aint come s'amie, Et ele lui tot autresi Con l'en doit feire son ami" (He had made his beloved his wife, but he called her beloved and lady, for she lost nothing by this since he loved her as his beloved, and she also loved him in the way one should love her lover). However, in *Cligés* the contradiction is far less labored and is merely between actual wife-status and treatment as beloved and lady, not between private and public statuses. Coming at the close of the romance, it is a solution rather than, as in Chaucer, a possible problem.

12. See, for example, David Aers, *Chaucer, Langland and the Creative Imagination* (London: Routledge, 1980), 163; Weisl, *Conquering the Reign of Femeny*, 106.

13. See Rüdiger Schnell's discussion of the content of a collection of Latin marriage sermons, drawn together by a Dominican friar at the end of the thirteenth century, which survives in more than 350 manuscripts, in "The Discourse on Marriage in the Middle Ages," *Speculum* 73 (1998): 771-86. Schnell discusses the sermons' emphasis on couples living together lovingly and peacefully and making a shared contribution to the success of the marriage in the face of daily conflict (772-76).

14. See my "Domestic Opportunities: The Social Comedy of *The Shipman's Tale*," *Chaucer Review* 41, no. 2 (2006): 138-62.

15. Bornstein, *The Lady in the Tower* (Hamden, CT: Archon, 1983); Collette, "Heeding the Counsel of Prudence," *Chaucer Review* 29 (1995), 416-33; and Dor, "The Wife of Bath's 'Wandrynge by the Weye,'" in *Drama, Narrative and Poetry in the "Canterbury Tales,"* ed. Wendy Harding (Toulouse: Presses Universitaires du Mirail, 2003), 139-55.

16. All subsequent references will be to the following editions and will be cited parenthetically within the text: Christine de Pizan, *Le Livre des trois vertus*, ed. Charity Cannon Willard and Eric Hicks (Paris: Champion, 1989); *The Book of the Knight of the Tower*, trans. William Caxton, ed. M. Y. Offord, Early English Texts Society, Supplementary Series 2 (London, 1971); *Le Menagier de Paris*, ed. Georgine E. Brereton and Janet M. Ferrier (Oxford: Clarendon Press, 1981); and for the letter collections, *Paston Letters and Papers of the Fifteenth Century*, ed. Norman Davis, vol. 1 (Oxford: Clarendon Press, 1971); and *Kingsford's Stonor Letters and Papers, 1290-1483*, ed. Christine Carpenter (Cambridge: Cambridge University Press, 1996). All forms that Davis presents in italics (expanded from abbreviated forms in the Paston letters) are silently de-italicized here.

17. Carruthers, "The Wife of Bath and the Painting of Lions," *PMLA* 94 (1979): 209-22.

18. See, for example, Alan Macfarlane, *Marriage and Love in England: Means of Reproduction, 1300-1840* (Oxford: Basil Blackwell, 1986); Christopher L. Brooke, *The Medieval Idea of Marriage* (Oxford: Oxford University Press, 1989); and Peter Fleming, *Family and Household in Medieval England* (Basingstoke: Palgrave, 2001).

19. For the former view, see Elaine Tuttle Hansen, *Chaucer and the Fictions of Gender* (Berkeley: University of California Press, 1992), 272; Davis, "Perfect Marriage," 136; and Conor McCarthy, *Marriage in Medieval England: Law, Literature and Practice* (Woodbridge: Boydell, 2004), 102.

20. For Jacobs' comment, see "Rewriting the Marital Contract: Adultery in the *Canterbury Tales*," *Chaucer Review* 29 (1995): 345. Since these separations were so much a part of medieval life, it seems difficult to accept Jacobs' conclusion (345-46) that Arveragus disobeys Dorigen's will by going away and that Dorigen would therefore be justified in being unfaithful to him. Gravlee's criticism of Arveragus as being irresponsibly "absent at key moments" seems similarly anachronistic ("Presence," 180).

21. Colin Richmond calculates John Paston's absences thus in the accounting year 1457-58 in *The Paston Family in the Fifteenth Century: Fastolf's Will* (Cambridge: Cambridge University Press, 1996), 25-26.

22. In obliging her friends, Dorigen acts similarly to Troilus, who allows Pandarus to persuade him to distract himself from missing Criseyde by going to Sarpedon's party and seems to feel a similar sense of compulsion to attend and an inability to enjoy himself once he gets there (*Troilus and Criseyde*, 5.402-62).

23. Hallissy, *Clean Maids, True Wives, Steadfast Widows: Chaucer's Women and Medieval Codes of Conduct* (Westport, CT: Greenwood Press, 1993), 38.

24. See Weisl, *Conquering the Reign of Femeny*, 110, and Davis, "Perfect Marriage," 137.

25. Ward, "English Noblewomen and the Local Community in the Later Middle Ages," in *Medieval Women in their Communities*, ed. Diane Watt (Cardiff: University of Wales Press, 1997), 189. See also Christine Carpenter's description of how the Stonors and their contemporaries built and maintained their networks at casual meetings and dinners in "The Stonor Circle in the Fifteenth Century," in *Rulers and Ruled in Late Medieval England: Essays presented to Gerald Harriss*, ed. Rowena E. Archer and Simon Walker (London: Hambledon Press, 1995), 178, and my discussion in "Domestic Opportunities," 141-45.

26. Green, *A Crisis of Truth: Literature and Law in Ricardian England* (Philadelphia: University of Pennsylvania Press, 1999), 311. Further support for this view is lent by Kay E. Lacey, who observes that late medieval women seem to have had far more freedom to contract than the law officially allowed them ("Women and Work in Fourteenth and Fifteenth Century London," in *Women and Work in Pre-industrial England*, ed. Lindsey Charles and Lorna Duffin [London: Croom Helm, 1985], 57). These findings contradict McCarthy's claim (citing Gratian) that Dorigen is unable to contract as a married woman (*Marriage in Medieval England*, 105).

27. See David (*Strumpet Muse*, 190) for this view of the characters' behavior. As Jacobs notes in "The Marriage Contract of the *Franklin's Tale*: The Remaking of Society" (*Chaucer Review* 20 [1985-86]: 138), Aurelius relies on the language of law to enforce his contract.

28. I am not sure that this suggests, as Riddy argues ("Engendering pity," 62), that Dorigen really considers herself the sexual property of men; she may instead see this as a pertinent objection to the deal with Aurelius, which she knows could consist only of sexual possession and not of true love.

29. Aers, *Chaucer, Langland and the Creative Imagination*, 165.

30. This hypothesis is perhaps supported by Joel T. Rosenthal's argument that Margaret and John Paston I had no apparent concern about their sons or servants knowing their private business, despite taking pains to conceal it from outsiders (*Telling Tales: Sources and Narration in Late Medieval England* [Philadelphia: Pennsylvania State University Press, 2003], 112).

31. See Davis's introduction to the *Paston Letters*, xxxiv.

32. Ibid., xxxiv-xxxv. Davis also discusses the Pastons' use of formulae at length in "Style and Stereotype in Early English Letters," *Leeds Studies in English* 1 (1967): 7-17. Giles Constable

notes that the salutation of medieval letters was often determined by class and paid "careful attention to the respective ranks and titles of the correspondents" but that this was not an invariable rule (*Letters and Letter-Collections*, Typologie des sources du moyen âge occidental 17 [Turnhout: Brepols, 1976], 17).

33. Rosenthal notes that the form of the address does not usually bear any relation to the content of Margaret's letters, even though it is sometimes identical to the internal salutation (*Telling Tales*, 117). Alison Hanham, in *The Celys and Their World: An English Merchant Family of the Fifteenth Century* (Cambridge: University Press, 1985), suggests that the observation of formal politeness in letters "does not mean that any unnatural degree of respect coloured private attitudes" (14).

34. It is perhaps worth noting that both Arveragus and Dorigen and the Paston and Stonor spouses invariably address one another with the polite "ye" form rather than the familiar "thou," so that the use of "you" does not stand out as belonging to a heightened formal register here.

35. This idea is supported by Peter Coss, who argues that marriage relationships based on something other than male dominance "seem to have been easier to imagine from the latter part of the fourteenth century" (*The Lady in Medieval England, 1000-1500* [Stroud: Sutton, 1998], 104). Coss also connects the "distance between the public expectation and the private reality of relationships" manifested in Margaret and John Paston's correspondence to Dorigen and Arveragus's marriage agreement, arguing that relationships like the Pastons' make this equal marriage seem "at least feasible" (108).

36. Angela M. Lucas and Peter J. Lucas read "pryvely" as referring to a clandestine marriage and go on to interpret the whole of the *Franklin's Tale* on this basis, in "The Presentation of Marriage and Love in Chaucer's *Franklin's Tale*," *English Studies* 72 (1991): 501. Their reading strikes me as perverse, since they are forced simultaneously to accept that Arveragus creates an "outward show of wedded lordship," which would seem to make the secrecy of a clandestine wedding redundant.

37. See Green's discussion of the meaning of "trouthe," in *Crisis of Truth*, 9-19. Mervyn James defines faithfulness to one's freely given word as "the essence of the social dimension of honour" in *English Politics and the Concept of Honour, 1485-1642* (Oxford: Past and Present Society, 1978), 15.

38. Brewer, *Tradition and Innovation in Chaucer* (London: Macmillan, 1982), 103. See also the more general discussions in Julian Pitt-Rivers, "Honour and Social Status," in *Honour and Shame: the Values of Mediterranean Society*, ed. J. G. Peristiany (London: Weidenfeld and Nicolson, 1965), 19-77, and James, *English Politics*.

39. As Shannon McSheffrey notes, the honor that came from a woman's chastity was related to the fact that she was under proper male governance, so Arveragus's extension is logical (*Marriage, Sex, and Civic Culture in Late Medieval London* [Philadelphia: University of Pennsylvania Press, 2006], 175).

40. Pitt-Rivers discusses the potential conflict between virtue and social status that honor, which claims to be about virtue, entails ("Honour and social status," 37). Arveragus's desire for honor seems to reflect that described by Pitt-Rivers: the wish to have one's own estimation of worth reflected in society's eyes. Pitt-Rivers argues that this becomes difficult in a complex society where there is no consensus about what is honorable (21-22). This lack of consensus is what leads Arveragus to dissemble.

41. Brewer, *Tradition and Innovation*, 101.

42. Maddern, "Honour among the Pastons: Gender and Integrity in Fifteenth-Century English Provincial Society," *Journal of Medieval History* 14 (1988): 357-71.

43. Carpenter, "Stonor Circle," 192.

44. See notes 5 and 6 above.

45. The same holds true for twentieth century couples, as Erving Goffman argues persuasively in *The Presentation of Self in Everyday Life* (New York: Anchor Books, 1959; repr., London: Allen Lane, 1971), especially 68 and 91.

46. For this characterization of medieval marriage, see, for example, Aers, *Chaucer, Langland and the Creative Imagination*, 143.

47. This is the conclusion that Jill Mann reaches (*Feminizing Chaucer*, 93).

48. See David, *Strumpet Muse*, 189, and Riddy, "Engendering Pity," 63.

49. Jacobs notes this as does Mann ("Marriage Contract," 135; *Feminizing Chaucer*, 92-93).

50. Davis, "Perfect Marriage," 141.

51. I would like to thank John Burrow, Ad Putter, Robert R. Edwards, and Alcuin Blamires for their many helpful comments on earlier versions of this essay.

Critical Insights

Lumiansky's Paradox:
Ethics, Aesthetics, and Chaucer's "Prioress's Tale"

Greg Wilsbacher

Now, for the first time, twentieth-century readers can have *The Canterbury Tales* in their own modern, idiomatic language, unembarrassed by archaic expressions or by attempts to torture the free and easy rhythms of the original into rhyme and meter.

The famous stories—the wise, the witty, the racy and romantic—are given unexpurgated in a translation at once faithful to the original and in a prose as clear and modern as a freshly minted coin.

Whatever our response to this advertisement is now, Simon and Schuster thought that audiences in 1948 would respond favorably to this dust jacket blurb for R. M. Lumiansky's newly printed edition of the *Canterbury Tales*. The good folks at Simon and Schuster tried to sell the book on many levels. The *Canterbury Tales* will enlighten ("wise"), entertain ("witty"), endear ("romantic"), and even arouse ("racy"): not even Harry Bailey could ask for more. All of this, of course, is only possible if the book circulates like the newly minted coin at the close of the passage. Books must be read if they are to have any transformative effect (titillating or otherwise), something of which writers are well aware—I don't think Lumiansky is any exception. But if we consider—as Chaucer certainly did at the close of *Troilus and Criseyde*: "Go, litel bok, go, litel myn tragedye . . ." (V. 1786)—the enormity of this prospect, the fact that one loses control of one's own writing once published, then we may come face to face with a sense of responsibility for the future that will ultimately inherit our texts. I doubt most of us tend to think in these terms on a regular basis, but I believe Lumiansky did so on at least one occasion, and his recognition of the ethical consequences of his own scholarly work serves as a telling exemplum of the paradoxical bind that results when two competing senses of obligation crash together in the course of "doing one's job."

Of all of Chaucer's poems, "The Prioress's Tale" is perhaps the most prominent example of a difficult or problematic text that challenges medievalists' ability to "do our job" without conflict. Not only does the poem present a variant of a particularly troubling form of medieval anti-Semitism (the Blood Libel), but "The Prioress's Tale" also has been praised in the past (directly and indirectly) for the beauty of its verse. As aesthetics remains an important—even if often understated—reason for teaching not only Chaucer but literature in general, coming to terms with the ethical demands enjoined upon us by the tale's potent combination of anti-Semitism and art remains a legacy and a central problem for medievalists who read and teach this poem to students in an era during which religious bigotry remains very much part of our world. What might it mean to treat the Prioress's anti-Semitism with "respect"—the term is Art Spiegelman's—is the heart of this essay's concerns and at the heart of what I call Lumiansky's Paradox.[1] By exploring this paradox, I endeavor to perform one possible manifestation of that *respect*, one that places post-structuralist ethics alongside the practice of literary criticism within the context of the modern university.

Lumiansky's Paradox

Shortly after the conclusion of the Second World War, Lumiansky published a modern edition of the *Canterbury Tales*, a prose translation intended for a broad audience of non-specialists.[2] His modernization should be seen as part of a growing trend toward the translation of Chaucer's works, one that had already produced Nicholson's famous Fine Print edition illustrated by Rockwell Kent as well as F. E. Hill's illustrated edition. Indeed, as Lumiansky argued, Chaucer's work deserved such a broad contemporary audience not only because it belonged to the canon of English Literature, but also because it contained "new ideas and attitudes toward our own twentieth-century world and the people in it which can come to us from thinking about the motives and actions of these people in the *Canterbury Tales*" (1948, xvi). Clearly, Lumiansky envisioned his edition as providing a useful tool for the modern age; however, the utility of the prose translation stemmed, somewhat ironically, from Lumiansky's belief that only through prose, rather than verse, "can we approach the language and spirit of Chaucer today" (xvi). The audience envisioned for this prose edition would be at once "modern" (denizens of the twentieth-century) and "medieval" (capable of hearing the "language and spirit of Chaucer" in a way analogous to his medieval audience). Temporarily inhabiting both worlds, post-war readers would enjoy the fruits of *sentence* and *solace* in a way surpassing the one-dimensional understanding of Chaucer's poetry as an artifact from another time.

Inhabiting two vastly different historical and cultural realms is not so easy, as Lumiansky's edition itself demonstrated. The ethical imperatives of the "modern world" may come into conflict with the culture of the "medieval world." Publishing only three years after the public revelation of the full horrors of the Shoah, he found himself in just such a bind. Lumiansky chose to pass over "The Prioress's Tale," offering in its stead an explanation and a summary, both of which deserve closer attention. The summary is placed within the *Tales* as a substitute for the tale itself:

The Prioress tells a tale which belongs to a large body of religious stories called "Miracles of Our Lady." A little choirboy is murdered, but through the action of the Virgin he is enabled to speak and to make known the facts concerning his death. This miracle makes a great impression upon the people of the vicinity, who bury the little boy in holy fashion. (Lumiansky 1948, 248)

The sparseness and lack of detail make this summary, if not downright poor, at least uninteresting enough that it is unlikely to stimulate any desire to read the tale in its entirety. One cannot be sure, but I suspect that this was Lumiansky's intent. Stripped of any reference to Jews, anti-Semitism, ritual murder, or pogroms, his summary of "The Prioress's Tale" is as general as possible. For instance, he casts the murder of the chorister into the passive voice, masking the fact that in this tale Jews kill the little Christian boy. Similarly, while he mentions that the boy's death "makes a great impression upon the people of the vicinity," he does not relate the retaliatory justice meted out to an entire community. To do so would raise the question: the community comprised of whom? It seems that Lumiansky first and foremost does not want to tell the anti-Semitic tale; but, in addition, he wants to be certain that after reading his summary no one will decide to read the tale *because* it is anti-Semitic.

While the text of his prose translation makes no mention of anti-Semitism, the same cannot be said of Lumiansky's introduction to the book. That such frankness is reserved for the introduction may well provide a clue as to who Lumiansky thought would read the introduction and who he thought would skip it. Here Lumiansky unflinchingly clarifies the reasons for his refusal to translate "The Prioress's Tale." While he briefly explains that he has summarized three tales (Chaucer's "Tale of Melibee," "The Monk's Tale," and "The Parson's Tale") because they were "moralizing," Lumiansky offers a fuller exposition of the rationale behind his decision to omit the tale of the little clergeon:

One other story, the Prioress's, is presented in summary, but for another reason. Though anti-Semitism was a different thing in the fourteenth-century from what it is today, the present day reader has modern reactions in literature, no matter when it was written. From this point of view, the Prioress's story of the little choirboy who is murdered by the Jews possesses an unpleasantness which overshadows its other qualities. For most of us, "The Prioress's Tale" is ruined by the similarity between this sort of story and some of the anti-Semitic propaganda which was current in Nazi Germany, and which is still in operation, not only in numerous foreign countries but also here at home. (Lumiansky 1948, xxiii)

Fresh from his own military service, Lumiansky is quick to draw parallels between the bigotry of Chaucer's tale and that of Nazi Germany.[3] If that were his only point of reference perhaps he would not have struggled so with translating "The Prioress's Tale"—after all, the Nazis were defeated. But as a Jew who had lived in pre-war America, Lumiansky would also have had in mind other groups, groups like the German-American Bund, headed by Francis Kuhn, as well as a recently reinvigorated and surprisingly acceptable Ku Klux Klan, and mass media ideologues like Father Coughlin. These, of course, were not "defeated" in the war, and their legacy is one that remains in circulation with other forms of bigotry in American culture, albeit in a less brazen form.

Perhaps some critics might find his omission of the tale on these grounds to be an extremely personal response motivated by emotional and unscholarly concerns. Those who agree with, or at least sympathize with, Lumiansky's stance might counter that to behave otherwise would demand an almost ruthless separation between scholarly and human imperatives. Indeed, given his plan for a broad, non-academic audience, Lumiansky's decision to intervene (or at least attempt to) in the transmission of this particular bit of populist anti-Semitism speaks volumes about his own sense of professional responsibility. Why Lumiansky's decision to skip the tale represents the best traditions of professional ethics and not what some may be quick to call vulgar censorship (itself a seemingly unprofessional activity) becomes clearer if one accepts an evaluation of "The Prioress's Tale" from someone other than a medievalist. Folklorist Alan Dundes argues that anti-Semitic myths have flourished, in part, because they have found effective and oft repeated vehicles for their transmission. There can be, he contends,

> little doubt that the most famous literary articulation of Jewish ritual murder is Chaucer's "Prioress's Tale." . . . Inasmuch as Geoffrey Chaucer . . . is one of the acknowledged giants of English literature and his masterpiece is generally conceded to be his *Canterbury Tales*, of which "The Prioress's Tale" is one, Chaucer's version of the story is very much part of the history and dissemination of this anti-Semitic plot. (Dundes 1991, 91)

While Dundes is technically incorrect in calling "The Prioress's Tale" a ritual murder story, the essential element of Jews killing Christian children remains powerfully articulated in the tale. Audiences inclined to accept such fabrications are not likely to split such critical hairs. One need only recall Julius Streicher's infamous May 1934 edition of *Der Stürmer* devoted to the ritual murder libel to recognize that ritual murder accusations remained a myth with some currency in the twentieth-century, not only in small rural villages but also in major metropolitan centers like Nuremberg.[4]

I raise the issue of Lumiansky's dilemma here not to engage in a debate about whether his decision was right or wrong. As an example of an ethical judgment it cannot easily be measured in those moral terms. Rather, my interest in Lumiansky's edition stems from its demonstrative value. That is, his edition well illustrates that ethical conflicts do exist for modern readers of medieval texts. The case of concern here is Lumiansky's struggle with the problem of anti-Semitism immediately after the war, but other conflicts could surely present themselves to different readers. Such ethical conflicts don't emanate from the text itself but from the dual context of the historical past and the contemporary context of that reading. The obligation to account accurately for the past may not sit well against responsibilities issuing from contemporary sources. Lumiansky suggests such a dual context in his introduction: "Though anti-Semitism was a different thing in the fourteenth-century from what it is today, the present day reader has modern reactions in literature, no matter when it was written." Recognizing the potential impact of circulating the tale in a "freshly minted" form, Lumiansky was forced to judge between conflicting responsibilities. That Lumiansky found his initial judgment no longer satisfactory can be assumed from his subsequent decision to reinstate "The Prioress's Tale" in the 1954 edition of his translation.[5]

But what of these conflicting responsibilities? To whom is Lumiansky responsible? To what community? The community of general readers, including many high school and college readers? Exposing Chaucer to a wide range of audiences through modern prose seems to present Lumiansky with questions about how his text will be read and what types of responses it will evoke. There is something dangerous about the anti-Semitic art of "The Prioress's Tale" with which he does not trust some communities of this general reading audience. These communities might well range from active hate groups to the more likely and more prevalent religious and ethnic communities that harbor latent or passive-aggressive bias against the Jewish community. In either case, and recalling his sensitivity to anti-Semitism "here at home," he wants to fuel neither existing anti-Semitism nor foster new hatred. Alongside this general audience, though, are other communities as well, communities who knowing the tale's content might, for a variety of reasons, demand either the exposure or the erasure of the tale.

On the one hand, the community of medieval scholars emerges as significant for Lumiansky. His decision to restore "The Prioress's Tale" despite its anti-Semitism to the 1954 edition appears to indicate the recognition of responsibility to this community.[6] But what about the particular community to which Lumiansky undoubtedly felt some special responsibility? What about the larger community of Jews? His initial decision to try to "silence" this anti-Semitic legend clearly indicates an inclination to this particular community.

Again, trying to second-guess his judgments in both editions, trying to determine if he was right or wrong, would miss the central importance of Lumiansky's paradox: that the tale's anti-Semitism read among the ashes of the *Endlösung* forced him to make an ethical judgment, one that he himself ultimately found unsatisfactory. Like the Paradox of Abraham described by Jacques Derrida in *The Gift of Death*, Lumiansky is caught in an impossible situation (Derrida 1995, 53-81). To choose fidelity to one community is to refuse responsibility to another. Caught between the two, he must decide, but his decision to be responsible will invariably entail a sense of irresponsibility as well: honoring the dead of Auschwitz seemingly makes him an irresponsible medievalist engaged in the censorship of "great art"; being an honest medievalist who takes seriously the burden of comprehensiveness—despite the potential that this might entail the transmission of repugnant ideas—risks a refusal of what he seems to perceive as the ethical burden of the Shoah.

For Derrida this paradox is an inevitable part of the ethical because it marks the central component of the ethical that distinguishes it from the narrowly defined realm of morality: my relationship with the Other, and with others. The two do not occur separately. They remain condemned to operate in antithetical ways. The realm of the ethical is not, to be sure, a haven for the self-assured and the self-righteous; it is a palimpsest of contradiction, conflict, and ambiguity. One cannot engage in a relationship with a wholly singular Other without transgressing, to some degree, other relationships, in that this relationship supposes the denial—even if for an instant—of so many other others. Derrida explains:

> As soon as I enter into relation with the absolute other, my absolute singularity enters into relation with his on the level of obligation and duty. I am responsible to the other as other, I answer to him and for what I do before him. But of course, what binds me thus in my singularity to the absolute singularity of the other, immediately propels me into the space or risk of absolute sacrifice. There are also others, an infinite number of them, the innumerable generality of others to whom I should be bound by the same responsibility, a general and universal responsibility (what Kierkegaard calls the ethical order). I cannot respond to the call, the request, the obligation, or even the love of another without sacrificing the other other, the other others. Every other (one) is every (bit) other [tout autre est tout autre], every one else is completely or wholly other. As a result, the concepts of responsibility, of decision, or of duty, are condemned a priori to paradox, scandal, and aporia. (Derrida 1995, 68)

Whether debating the (in)justice of abortion, euthanasia, animal rights, absolute free speech or any other truly difficult ethical problem, many of us would be quick to recognize the difficulty of sustaining a definitive opinion that cannot in itself be undermined by contradictions and qualifications. In this sense, I think Derrida has hit upon the problematic aspect of any ethical dilemma: rather than being simple legal issues that allow one to see things as right or wrong and to which an external rule may be applied, they are defined by an essential paradox of conflicting responsibilities. Every time I am called into question by the other, every time I am called to judgment, I am confronted with this paradox and am condemned to be irresponsible even as I act at my most responsible. Without doubt, here we have Lumiansky's Paradox, caught between two communities—one indescribably private and another professional and public—to both of which he and I cannot remain equally responsible.

While Lumiansky's dilemma must remain a singular one, one that manifested itself within an immediate post-war context, his was not an isolated problem. Although no other editor has grappled so graphically with the ethical conflict of reading medieval anti-Semitic works after the Shoah, the critical history of "The Prioress's Tale" itself traces the very ethical conflict recognized by Lumiansky. Reviewing the history of the tale's reception prior to and after the *Endlösung*, one can see that the Shoah has posed a new imperative on reading the Prioress's anti-Semitic—but artfully crafted—legend. Alan T. Gaylord, Florence Ridley, and most recently Beverly Boyd have all provided critical surveys that recognize some shift in the reception of the tale after the Second World War.[7] However, while their surveys help to draw attention to this shift, none directly contends with the ethical dynamics revealed by it.

As Boyd (1987) rightly notes, commentary on the anti-Semitic nature of "The Prioress's Tale" pre-dates the Second World War. However, the criticism of the tale prior to the war does not focus on anti-Semitism as a central problem (whether aesthetic or ethical). Some of the earliest commentaries on the tale note its anti-Semitism. Thomas Percy (1765) and Thomas Tyrwhitt (1775) both look skeptically at the Prioress's representation of Jews, and William Wordsworth—in one of the best known pieces of commentary on the tale—notes that the "fierce bigotry of the Prioress forms a fine back ground [sic] for her tender-hearted sympathies with the Mother and Child; and the mode in which the story is told amply atones for the extravagance of the miracle" (1896, 240).

The critical history of "The Prioress's Tale" makes two things in particular quite clear. First, the anti-Semitic content of the tale has received some degree of notice since Percy and Tyrwhitt's comments in the late eighteenth century. Second, after the Shoah many critics have, like Lumiansky, found themselves confronted with a feeling that the stakes of reading "The Prioress's Tale" have shifted from literary to moral and ethical concerns. The responses to this feeling have been varied, some choosing to valorize Chaucer's enlightened humanism, others exonerating him through appeals to the historical ubiquity of medieval anti-Semitism.[8] More recently, others have found the best response to be one that directly addresses the moral and theoretical dimensions of anti-Semitism *per se*.[9] What these critics all indicate is that they—like Lumiansky—partake of the Paradox of Abraham in some degree. Like Lumiansky, critics after the war are apt to find themselves confronted by potentially conflicting obligations: fidelity to medieval history, responsibility for twentieth-century history, and concern for what it means to profess literature in the academy. As with any paradox, there can be no easy solution, if indeed one can continue to speak of solution in the face of paradox. However, while affording no solution, a paradox does provide an ample scene for thinking through the complexities of its components. That, I think, underlies the potency of Alfred David's rather disarmingly straightforward suggestion "that the issues are broader than the character of a nun or even conventional medieval anti-Semitism" (1982, 156). After Auschwitz, a name, a place, or better, an event that marks the ultimate path down which anti-Semitic art can lead, the stakes of reading and teaching "The Prioress's Tale" shifted and with them our responsibility for Chaucer's art.

Toward an Ethical Aesthetics

Wordsworth's contention that the "*mode* in which the story is told amply atones for the extravagances of the miracle" squarely sets the aesthetic category of form over and above ethical concerns, read here as vague "extravagances" (1896, 240). In stark contrast, Lumiansky reverses this hierarchy, arguing, "the Prioress's story of the little choirboy who is murdered by Jews possesses an unpleasantness which overshadows its other qualities" (1948, xxiii). Ethics trumps aesthetics in Lumiansky's recognition of social function over form. These two critical bookends encompass volumes of scholarly commentary (not only about "The Prioress's Tale" but also about other examples of bigoted art) and forefront the relationship between aesthetics and ethics for readers of Chaucer's Prioress. Medievalists have become unaccustomed in the past two decades to aesthetic criticism, as historicist modes of interpretation have dominated the field. But aesthetic criticism has been the subject of much discussion in other disciplines, and it has already made some small inroads into medieval studies.[10] The return of aesthetics to medieval studies holds much promise, but that promise will be short lived if the discussion does not move beyond the New Criticism's problematic mode of aesthetic commentary, especially when dealing with "The Prioress's Tale."

Commentary on the aesthetic quality of art faces two hurdles of special importance in medieval studies. First, aesthetics must confront the accusation that it tends to remove texts and objects from their historical context; as I'll argue, aesthetic commentary can usefully complicate the charge by demonstrating one way in which historicist criticism hasn't been sufficiently historical. Second, it must respond to the claim that aesthetic commentary is politically suspect. The latter charge is typically framed in one of two ways: either aesthetics ignores the political altogether by suggesting that art lacks any political content or that aesthetics functions as a sinister purveyor of objectionable political ideology. Terry Eagleton, for example, argues that the assessment of an object as beautiful has been an important element in the construction and theorization of community at the level of ideology (1990, 20-28). The claim that aesthetics quells difference is important for readers of "The Prioress's Tale," so I want to begin by better understanding it. Eagleton traces this development to the rise of the bourgeoisie after the collapse of absolutist polity. In an ideological environment lacking the top-down justification for all aspects of life, bourgeois society needed to provide its own seemingly egalitarian justifications for being together as a community (for the development of communal interest alongside of those of self interest). Kant's treatise on aesthetic and teleological judgment figures prominently in this justification. For Kant, judgment of the beautiful presupposes a communal assent to that judgment, which does not mean that all people do or will share that judgment, but that they ought to. More specifically, it offers the possibility of presupposing a critical audience unified as to the decision whether to read or not to read a poem, and it is this very possibility that places us—especially those interested in renewing the place of aesthetics in our field—within the ethical paradox so well exemplified in Lumiansky's initial decision to refuse to read "The Prioress's Tale." After the Shoah, aesthetic criteria continue to play a role in justifying the reading of this anti-Semitic tale, even though the tale's artistry serves to strengthen its ethical problems. Caught within such a paradox, critics are left with seemingly no way out: they must either read the tale (risking the transmission of its ideological fantasies about Jews) or remain silent (provoking any number of professional objections concerning censorship in the academy).

The poetry Chaucer places in the mouth of the Prioress is exactly the type of poem capable of evoking powerful aesthetic responses. Chaucer it seems was at his aesthetic best in composing both "The Prioress's Prologue" and her tale: one mainstay of commentary is the recognition of their artful construction. Descriptions of this poetic beauty come from a wide range of critics. In the nineteenth century Wordsworth deemed it worthy of translation and even submitted that translation for wider circulation; moreover, Matthew Arnold cited lines 649-655 as an example of Chaucer's finest verse (1891, xxxiii).[11] As the profession of English studies developed in the new century, the artistry of the work received accolades from such important scholars as John Livingston Lowes (1905) and R. K. Root (1906), who called it "as flawless work as Chaucer ever did" (1906, 197-98). More admiration was forthcoming in George Lyman Kittredge (1915), J. M. Manly (1926) and G. K. Chesterton (1932), who referred to it as "the beautiful legend of the child singing down the street on his way to the crown of martyrdom" (1932, 170). This praise continued after the Second World War: e.g., Brewer (1953), E. Talbot Donaldson (1958), R. O. Payne (1963), and G. H. Russell (1969). Marchette Chute (1946) described it as "a small, flawless jewel offered to the glory of Our Lady" (1958, 295-96); Brewer echoing Chute lauded it, "though brief it is perfectly proportioned—as much a gem of flawless artistry as 'The Miller's Tale'" (1953, 127); and Donaldson deemed her tale to be "in some ways as pretty as her own brooch," consisting of "a strange mixture of delicacy and horror" (1972, 934, 932). Even Lumiansky, who had struggled so much with the tale, found himself able to praise the artistry of the tale's prologue (1955, 81). More recently, comparing "The Prioress's Tale" to other Marian legends, Helen Cooper argues that through his skilled deployment of pathos and the quality of his rhyme royal stanzas Chaucer "rais[es] the genre to its highest level" (1983, 167-68); and Bruce Holsinger closes his ingenious mapping of the tale against the history of musical pedagogy with a reference to the "gem-like elegance and poetic precision of [its] rime-royal stanzas" (1997, 192).

That such accolades have accompanied a poem that at the same time often receives condemnations for the bigotry woven among its verses in itself raises a question: what is the relationship between the tale's anti-Semitism and its artistry? Can these two seemingly disparate realms be treated separately, especially in lieu of the connection between aesthetics and community so well articulated in Kant? Historicist critics answer in the affirmative, arguing that the tale's bigotry can only be treated within the confines of historical context. The text of the *Canterbury Tales*, however, provides a different answer. Following upon the heels of the Prioress's legend comes a notable moment of unity among the pilgrims. The sober silence that reigns immediately after the Prioress finishes her story confirms the unifying potency of her tale and magnifies the seriousness with which we as medievalists ought to treat the aesthetics of her tale.

Although this sober reaction has received some attention because it is out of place in relationship to the typical response of the pilgrims to the tales told by their companions, I think that the full weight of this silence has yet to be heard by the tale's commentators. Not only is the company's silence uncharacteristic of their usual banter, not only is the unified nature of the response in stark contrast to the typically dialogic nature of the text, but also—and perhaps most importantly—the unified silent sobriety of the pilgrims at this one moment marks the first time since the interruption of the tales' order by the Miller that the monologic impulse of the society of pilgrims has been restored. Upon completion of the tale, Chaucer the narrator observes:

> Whan seyd was al this miracle, every man
> As sobre was that wonder was to se,
> Til that oure Hooste japen tho bigan. . . .
>   (VII. 691-93)

Interestingly, the reader has no concept of how long this silent pause endures because silence defies the temporalizing impulse of narrative. The "Til" marks a moment of closure for this narrative: nothing seems to move; time literally stops. Only the warmth of the Host's japing heats up the spirit of the pilgrims, reintroducing an element of non-closure back into the narrative to destabilize the totalitarian impulse behind this unified moment.[12]

The real danger of this suspension of debate in favor of unified consent becomes more apparent when read in relation to the action of "The Prioress's Tale" itself. Set in an unspecified "greet citee" in "Asye," the tale presents a Christian community literally divided by a "Jewerye." This Jewry—"free and open at eyther ende"—stands as a supposed contaminant for the Christian community surrounding it. Less obviously, though, the ghetto also marks that community's own potential for internal discord. The little clergeon must fulfill his desire to learn the antiphon, *Alma redemptoris mater*, in secret because if he openly favored it over his primer, he would risk not only scolding but physical punishment as well:

> Now, certes, I wol do my diligence
> To konne it al er Cristemasse be went.
> Though that I for my prymer shal be shent
> And shal be beten thries in an houre,
> I wol it konne Our Lady for to honoure!
>   (VII. 539-43)

The only place for the clergeon at first to learn the song from his "felawe" and then practice and perform it is, ironically, in the Jewry itself (through which he walks daily to attend school):

> His felawe taughte hym homward prively,
> Fro day to day, til he koude it by rote,
> And thanne he song it wel and boldely,
> Fro word to word, acordynge with the note.
> Twies a day it passed thurgh his throte,
> To scoleward and homward whan he wente. . . .
>   (VII. 544-49)

Only in this *alien* enclave do he and his *conspirator* feel safe to practice such subversive and revolutionary readjustments of the catechism. Moreover, the means through which this dissent is articulated also flouts conventions: memorization of song "by rote" was not an accepted manner of training young students in song (Holsinger 1997, 171). The little clergeon's conscious thwarting of the Christian community's expectations of him indicates that within this (and implicitly any) Christian community dissent happens. But his fear of reprisal, his fear that "for his prymer he shal be shent/ And beten thries in an houre" provides clear indication that such dissent can expect to meet with physical retribution, particularly when that dissent is aimed squarely at the unhindered transfer of the community's doctrine through the "prymer."[13]

The anti-Semitic stage is thus set: the Jewish community—fantastically structured as allies with Satan—also harbors, or provides, a space in which the Christian community's alienation from itself is performed twice daily. Within this fictional space, the ensuing anti-Semitic violence becomes a unifying principle for the Christian community through which it purges the aliens in its midst. But, as the text itself demonstrates, this unification is spurious, a scapegoating facade that masks its own internal discord by symbolically sealing that discord away beneath the weight of a marble slab. Additionally, it is important to recognize that violence *per se* is not the motivation. The little clergeon's disappearance, an event that implies some physical violence and clearly visits psychic violence on the widow, seems to do little to bring the Christian community together. At first, the widow is left to wander the streets of this city by herself, alone with her panic and grief: "she gooth, as she were half out of hir mynde" (VII. 594). No one, no Christian that is, feels motivated to aid this single mother in her hour of need. Only when the little clergeon's miraculous singing—the mark of his dissent—pinpoints the violence as perpetrated by Jews does the Christian community act swiftly and of one accord.

Like the pilgrims traveling to visit Becket's martyred body, the Christian community of this tale swarms about this newly martyred body of the boy. *En masse* they arrive, and en masse they call for justice:

> The Cristene folk that thurgh the strete wente
> In coomen for to wondre upon this thyng,
> And hastily they for the provost sente;
> He cam anon withouten tariyng. . . .
> (VII. 614-17)

Their anti-Semitism violently purges the Jewish community living in their midst and sublates the differences internal to their own community through the sanctification of the little boy, dissenter but martyr. It is significant that the justice meted out to the entire Jewish community comes swiftly and with little elaboration.[14] The Jews are tried, convicted, and punished within the space of a stanza, in part because the goal of a unified Christian community requires their immediate disappearance. The remaining stanzas can then enact the far more complex unification of the Christian community with itself. "The Cristene folk" carry the body of the child to an abbey, placing him before the altar. After the removal of the "greyn" from the boy's throat, the abbot and his community fall prostrate and then rise in unison, acting as one body:

> And gruf he [the abbot] fil al plat upon the grounde,
> And stille he lay as he had ben ybounde.
> The convent eek lay on the pavement
> Wepynge, and herying Cristes mooder deere,
> And after that they ryse. . . .
>
> (VII. 675-79)

What began as a Christian community separated by a Jewry and divided internally by dissident youth is now left a unified whole: the Jews are hanged and the boy is safely enclosed in "a tombe of marbul stones cleere" (VII. 681). The tale's movement toward such a definitive closure ripples outward to its fictional audience, an audience who can only respond with universal silence.[15]

On the one hand, it is tempting to see the tale as a demonstration of the sociological explanation of the unifying power of what has become known as *othering* (a term often used to invoke a school of thought traceable to Émile Durkheim and powerfully articulated in medieval studies by R. I. Moore and others): the strategy whereby minority communities are stereotyped and held out as different in order to better define a sense of self. This alone might explain some of the potency of the effect of the Prioress's narrative on her fellow pilgrims. But this sociological rationale leaves some questions unaddressed, among them, why would anti-Semitism continue after the expulsion of the Jews from England in 1290, and why would it remain so prominent in literature in particular? Some critics who recognize the political utility of *othering* have argued that anti-Semitism after 1290 is just another trope, a means by which real political enemies (like the Lollards) are targeted.[16] Essentially, this maneuver makes anti-Semitism something other than what it is: a virulent hatred toward Jewish persons and culture. Such an approach leaves one scrambling for the real target of the Prioress's anti-Semitism; after all, she too speaks after 1290. Who are her real targets? The answer is difficult because no one objects; no one is left out in the open; no one is *othered*. Everyone is "sobre"; everyone is silent. They are all of one accord.

On the other hand, the unifying impact of the tale's artistry, the Prioress's deft combination of Marian prologue and Marian tale interwoven with hatred and cast in well-crafted stanzas, must also be better understood. If the tale's critical tradition is any guide, the Canterbury pilgrims (and Chaucer's real audiences) are likely to find the tale's art quite compelling. So much so that aesthetics, more than the socio-political explanation (*othering*), may provide a better explanation for the troubling silence of the entire Canterbury community, and of the potential ethical dilemmas presented to modern readers by this very artistry. In short, the sober silence of the community of pilgrims brings us face to face with the ethical dimensions of reading and teaching this artistic tale in a community setting like the classroom of a modern university. Classrooms are communities, albeit temporary ones, in which broader social and political realities are intentionally and unintentionally exposed, exercised, developed or diminished. They are also communities containing very clear lines of power. Whether in the front, in the middle or on the fringes of the classroom, the instructor (who wields the most power even—and perhaps especially—when s/he publicly disavows the mantle of authority) always risks annealing unpleasant ideas without being aware that it is happening. When teachers approach subjects like anti-Semitism they ought to look as broadly as possible for potential pitfalls. In the case of "The Prioress's Tale," the classroom's relationship to aesthetic discourses in general and as applied to the tale is one such pitfall.

While it is important to concede that Chaucer would not have thought about aesthetics in Kant's terms, Kant's work provides, as Eagleton notes, some useful insights into how art has functioned at an ideological level for those of us reared within the Western tradition of the individual and independent subject—the development of the English canon is an undeniable part of this history.[17] For Kant, to judge a landscape or poem beautiful is really a judgment of the state of thought upon itself and in no way founded upon objective qualities *per se*.[18] By arguing that aesthetic judgments are universally valid, Kant counters subjectivist views of aesthetics (beauty is palpably different for every person) and centers aesthetic judgment at the core of a community conceived as unitary. That is, when faced with what Lyotard calls the "occurrence of a form," the subject renders a judgment on his or her state of thought (1994, 19). Kant, moreover, contends that this judgment has a "general validity" (1952, 54). If I believe that X is beautiful, I can only do so with the understanding that everyone *ought* to agree with my judgment:

> The judgement of taste exacts agreement from everyone; and every person who describes something as beautiful insists that every one ought to give the object in question his approval and follow suit in describing it as beautiful. The *ought* in aesthetic judgements, therefore, despite an accordance with all the requisite data for passing judgement, is still only pronounced conditionally. (Kant 1952, 82)

To remark upon the beauty of a tulip, of a particular painting or landscape, or of "The Prioress's Tale" implies that this judgment of beauty ought to be shared by all, that it ought to be a universally held judgment. As such, aesthetic judgment of the beautiful holds out a certain promise of community, a community that, if nothing else, shares this particular judgment of the beautiful. However, this claim to universality must be qualified. It must be understood as always being indeterminate and subjective, and thus, it does not indicate that everyone shares a certain judgment of an object as beautiful, just that everyone *ought* to share in that judgment. In other words, the feeling of pleasure is viewed as universal, not the aesthetic object or the subject itself. In that sense, aesthetic judgments of the beautiful always gesture to a closure of debate and a desire for general consent, the type of consent manifest at the close of "The Prioress's Tale."

Recalling the survey of critical praise for "The Prioress's Tale's" beauty, it is evident that each of those critics is, initially at least, making a judgment in response to the art object. When Chesterton describes the tale as "the beautiful legend of the child singing down the street to the crown of martyrdom" or when Brewer deems it "as much a gem of flawless artistry as 'The Miller's Tale'" each offers a conditional *ought* to his critical community. Each gives voice (consciously or not) to some expectation that all readers of the tale share or should share this state of mind. Now certainly, their assessments of the tale are not in practice universally valid: they are not binding statements to which all readers must adhere. And indeed, not all readers have concurred with their judgments.[19]

Theoretically, then, such aesthetic judgments regarding the beauty of "The Prioress's Tale" itself (and even, to some extent, of the *Canterbury Tales* as a whole) have provided and may yet provide an authorizing and authoritative criterion for reading her tale. And while the reasons for reading any work by Chaucer are complex, part of the expectation underlying the general validity of these types of judgments of beauty is that other critics, other members of this academic community, will read the tale and will share that state of mind. However, in the face of bigotry so obviously untenable to readers of the poem after the Shoah, "The Prioress's Tale" continues to be read, and the aesthetic rationale for that reading exists on a continuum, at the far end of which sits the aestheticization of politics (i.e., the collapsing of the beautiful and the good into one) that played such a significant role in the rise of fascism in Nazi Germany.[20] This, in no way, means that commentators on "The Prioress's Tale" are fascists or bigots. Emphatically, they are not. Instead, I am contending that there is a similarity in the way that aesthetic rationales are treated in each instance: as a cornerstone of an idea of a unified community that seeks closure and consent rather than the non-closure of difference and debate. Eagleton writes tellingly of the real danger of the Kantian *sensus communis*:

Such solidarity is a kind of sensus communis, which Kant opposes in his work to the fragmentary, unreflective collection of prejudices and opinions which is doxa or common sense. Such doxa is what Kant himself . . . might have termed "ideology"; but sensus communis is ideology purified, universalized and rendered reflective, ideology raised to a second power, idealized beyond all mere sectarian prejudice or customary reflex to resemble the very ghostly shape of rationality itself. (Eagleton 1990, 96)

The moment of sober silence following "The Prioress's Tale" marks the emergence of Eagleton's "ghostly shape of rationality itself." The violence of the moment is difficult to read because it doesn't simply depend upon the utterance of "sectarian prejudice" by the members of the pilgrimage (or by the critics of the tale). That is, the sober silence of the pilgrims (or the potential *sensus communis* of the academy) does not result from the open assent to the bigoted message but from the silent closure of assent brought on by the aesthetics of the tale itself. The reflective nature of the judgment makes it harder to recognize as politically dangerous, as the Prioress's hatred can slip in under the moral radar, as it were. Nevertheless, it still "gets through"; it still gets aired in public. Even at a distance of several centuries, that medieval literature scholars have participated and in some ways continue to participate in a community constructed in part around a tale whose content is anti-Semitic should give us pause because the collaboration of aesthetics and anti-Semitism has had such devastating consequences in the past century.

But if reading the tale on account of its beauty is problematic, so too is the opposite: the refusal to read because of a lack of beauty. Given this uncomfortable realization of the dangerous concoction of art and anti-Semitism, critics might, following Lumiansky, condemn "The Prioress's Tale" as bad art, as ugly, and refuse to read and teach it. Lumiansky's initial decision to omit "The Prioress's Tale" from his modernized edition draws upon on aesthetics as a means of authorizing the refusal to read. In addition to the tale of the little clergeon, Lumiansky dropped three other tales: Chaucer's "Tale of Melibee," "The Monk's Tale," and "The Parson's Tale." The omission of these tales is unusual for they have little in common on the surface. Yet, as Lumiansky explains in the introduction to his text, he finds these tales to be overly didactic and moralizing: to him, a quality in art popular at the time but no longer appreciated by modern audiences. In other words, we no longer render the same aesthetic judgment concerning these tales: rather than being beautiful, they are—supposedly—deemed *poor* art by modern audiences. Within the context of Lumiansky's edition, the aesthetic judgment about these three tales bleeds over into "The Prioress's Tale" as well: it too makes for bad art. Indeed, John Archer directly connects the two with his condemnation of "The Prioress's

Tale" as bad art, "we cannot escape the virulent anti-Semitism of 'The Prioress's Tale,' even if Chaucer realized that diatribes against the Jews (or against anybody) make for bad art" (1984, 46-54). Given the offensive nature of its content, if anti-Semitic poetry is bad art, then why read it at all? Wouldn't this be a way of "respecting" (coming back to Art Spiegelman's phrase) the potential violence stored in such poems?

Accepting the question's complexity, I suggest the answer does not lie in a standing commitment to censorship because such a decision continues to enact a promise of a unified community constructed around the exclusion of a particular object. Critical silence based upon aesthetic judgment (even if that judgment is one of ugliness rather than beauty) remains as problematic as the conditional *ought* voiced in judgments of the beautiful (i.e., "this is beautiful; you ought to read it" is little different from "this is bad art [ugly]; you ought not read it"). Something akin to a photographic negative of the beautiful, the ugly, in Adorno's words, "preserves the moment of pleasure, if only as a distant echo" (1983, 22). Once again Lumiansky's paradox surfaces: silencing "The Prioress's Tale," even for the best of intentions, partakes of an ideological violence at a different, but still troubling, level.

If the nature of aesthetic judgments is such that those judgments risk reduplicating the universalizing impulses of a totalitarian community, then why not reject altogether, as some critics (especially materialist ones) have argued, the very concept of the aesthetic as ideologically dangerous? "The Prioress's Tale" could be read, so this argument goes, with the protective gloves of historical knowledge. This view challenges the legitimacy of the burgeoning work on aesthetics even before it can establish itself. The presumption is that silence about aesthetic matters resolves the problem of the aesthetic. I would argue, however, that the real danger lies in ignoring the aesthetic precisely because there is no way of eliminating our engagement with it. By this I mean not only that there will always be paintings, poems, landscapes, etc. that provoke responses of a certain type from us, but also that the idea of the aesthetic is too deeply ingrained in the history of the West for us to have done with it.[21]

If a critical aesthetic discourse remains not only valuable but, perhaps, even inevitable, then closer attention must be paid to how it affects our discourse. Terry Eagleton's work provides one possible means of respecting the full dimension of the aesthetic; by returning aesthetics to its roots he provides a path that even the most materially minded critics might follow. Not only does Eagleton demonstrate that the aesthetic should be the subject of materialist critique, but he also values it because the aesthetic marks a space where the body intersects with the realms of ideas and of spirit. Reminding us of its Greek root, *aisthesis*, Eagleton argues that aesthetics can, from a materialist perspective, help initiate inquiries into how the ideological forces of art objects act upon material bodies.[22] One need not be an avowed Marxist to appreciate Eagleton's re-inscription of the corporeal into a field often situated only at the level of ideas. He reminds us of what formalist criticism forgot: that the beautiful ultimately operates at the level of feelings (which for Kant were signals of reflective judgment), a level that demands the analysis of the context of the body that senses and the conditions under which it feels pleasure and or pain.

If aesthetics is an inevitable part of what we as readers experience, then it behooves us to think its presence more critically than we have over the past few decades dominated by historicist thinking. In addition to exploring its dangers, we should reexamine its potential as a critical and pedagogical tool. Doing so provides a space within which to approach aesthetics ethically. Eagleton's *aesthesis* is one such way of proceeding, a way that ought not prove difficult for materialist critics to accept. Examining the context of aesthetic feeling, feelings of pleasure and anxiety, enable an aesthetic attentive to its ethical and political consequences. Such an analysis can be as much a part of our evaluation of *ourselves* as readers as it is for our analysis of the reception of culturally central texts like the *Canterbury Tales*.

From the outset of this article I have been suggesting that, like Lumiansky, many readers of "The Prioress's Tale" after the Shoah are apt to try to think two temporalities at once, an instant of thought that lies at the heart of their aesthetic and ethical encounter with the poem. That is, when presented with the occurrence of this anti-Semitic poem through the act of reading the mind struggles with two distinct temporal absolutes: one that places it comfortably within an accepted medieval context and one that gathers around that reading the much more modern context of the Shoah. For me, at least, this moment has been signaled by quite visceral feelings of unease, and I suspect I haven't been alone in this. Trying to think or inhabit both contexts at once is irrational, and any effort to do so is bound to fail. This irrational materiality (irrational because it cannot be encompassed by logic or reason) stems from the recognition that "The Prioress's Tale" belongs to two worlds. Those of us who read the tale after Auschwitz may find it difficult to read this medieval tale without darker images of concentration camps arising as part of its horizon—even if distant, the presence of these images remains troubling. Unlike most other medieval texts, "The Prioress's Tale" calls into question the very idea of a stable medieval context. Whenever critics speak of these texts after the Shoah, the modern readerly context refuses to be set aside in favor of the medieval one. The resulting contextual heterogeneity is *unheimlich* [uncanny]—a term which for Freud was as much aesthetic as analytical—and may aptly name the feelings I've experienced. For Lumiansky, at least, the unexpected return of the Shoah as a context for reading a supposedly medieval text is signaled by his editorial struggle to decide whether or not to reproduce the anti-Semitic art of the single most important English artist of the Middle Ages. Lumiansky's paradox bespeaks the co-incidental (in the sense of a happening side by side in one event) awareness of an unrepresentable context for "The Prioress's Tale": we can sense the irrationality of this context as much, if not more than, we can understand it.

If matter-of-factly praising "The Prioress's Tale's" beauty has become not just reprehensible, but also virtually impossible for most readers finding themselves grappling with two impossible contexts, then recognizing the critical potential of this moment opens a space for considering more than formal or historical issues. "Respecting" (to use Spiegelman's phrase) "The Prioress's Tale," demands that we as readers inhabit the decentered subjective space created by the uncanny context and magnified by the aesthetic potency of the poem. The aesthetic cannot provide a safe haven for readers; rather, it is revealed as entailing an important ethical encounter precisely because the aesthetic cannot be abstracted from material conditions.

The feelings of pleasure and of anxiety produced in modern readers of "The Prioress's Tale"—the ruptured and decentered sense of self resulting from the uncanniness of its context—is *like* the subject of ethics elaborated by the recent work of Derrida. The analogy is crucial: ethics is not reducible to aesthetics; art (neither as a general category nor as a specific work) does not contain *a priori* the key to an ethical life as New Critical methodology supposed. The feelings signaled by *aisthesis* do, however, provide the opportunity to link the phrases of an aesthetic genre of discourse to those of an ethical genre, and it is the ethical genre that orients us to the future and to the other.[23] Dwelling on the unpleasantness of the aesthetic affect of the poem is, I believe, vital for such linkage to happen. What results from a reading of "The Prioress's Tale" (as Lumiansky's paradox shows) is never permanent, never a rigid model for how to proceed. The feelings of pleasure and anxiety provoked by reading "The Prioress's Tale"—feelings that are not likely to disappear—encourage us to see this text as ours, not theirs, as belonging to us, or at least of haunting our presence: a gift of history that we cannot repay or return (for surely it is an unwanted gift), one that exceeds even the discourse of repayment or satisfaction.

This essay contends "The Prioress's Tale" involves us in questions as fundamental as whether we ought to introduce bigoted texts into instructional environments and if so, how we as educators ought to proceed. If religious totalitarianism can be a breeding ground for hatred and if political totalitarianism can provide a means for the prosecution of existing hatreds in the form of physical violence, then, as I have argued, one characteristic of our approach to bigoted texts might be to expose ourselves and our students to the power of non-closure as a bulwark to totalitarian impulses. After the Shoah, one can never be *satisfied* with a reading of "The Prioress's Tale." In fact, our post-Shoah world demands that we continue to ask whether it ought to be read, *now*; more often than not, the answer will be, yes, but sometimes—as Lumiansky discovered—the answer may be no. Respecting the tale's implication in past traumas and its potential to be part of future traumas, means one can never be done with the responsibility entailed by its continual return, its (re)arrival, always singular in its happening, always demanding of us yet another response.

From *College Literature* 32, no. 4 (Fall 2005): 1-28. Copyright © 2005 by *College Literature*. Reprinted by permission of *College Literature*.

Notes

1. Art Spiegelman uses the term when describing our cultural responsibility for racist Warner Brothers cartoons: "We're prone to cartoon stereotyping because that's how we think, how we hold images in our heads. . . . It's preliterate thinking. They scare us because they cut deep, through all our layers of verbiage. It makes them seem charged and dangerous, and they are. But that just means you have to treat them with respect" (Leland 2001, 4.3). All quotations from Chaucer are taken from *The Riverside Chaucer.*

2. The physical nature of the book reinforces its populist ambitions. Colorful endpapers depicting many of the pilgrims encase a text block containing 21 full or near-full page illustrations.

3. A graduate of the Citadel, Lumiansky served as an officer in the French Second Armored Division in North Africa. He was awarded both the Bronze Star and the French *Crois de Guerre.* A brief biography is available in *R. M. Lumiansky: Scholar, Teacher, Spokesman for the Humanities*, 1988, ACLS Occasional Papers, no. 3 (1-5).

4. Just as deplorable is the English translation and release of this and other issues of *Der Stürmer* by the white-supremacist Christian Vanguard in the 1970s. Randall L. Bytwerk translates a portion of this issue as well as a reproduction of the front page of the Christian Vanguard reprinting in *Julius Streicher* (1983, 198-201). The cover art reproduced from the 1934 issue depicts Aryan youth strung upside down with their throats cut. A copy of the 1934 issue is on display at the Imperial War Museum in London. Muriel Bowden is to my knowledge the only commentator to connect "The Prioress's Tale" with this distant Nazi cousin (1987, 42-45).

5. Beverly Boyd states that Lumiansky restored "The Prioress's Tale" "for reasons of comprehensiveness" (1987, 44). By comprehensiveness I take it that Boyd has a literary professional category in mind. Lumiansky's second edition not only restores the tale but the introduction has also undergone significant revision. These revisions omit any discussion of the moral or ethical implications for modern readers of the *Tales* in favor of a more professional discussion of the life of Chaucer, a chronology of his work, and a brief reading of "The General Prologue" to illustrate Chaucer's poetic art. In short, gone are those probing questions about the relationship of contemporary audiences to past works when those works raise not just enlightening but also contemptible issues (1954, xiii-xxix).

6. Lumiansky's lifetime of commitment to the advancement of scholarship in the humanities (e.g., his role in establishing the National Humanities Center and the National Endowment for the Humanities as well as his presidency of the American Council of Learned Societies and the Medi-

eval Academy of America) amply demonstrates the seriousness with which he saw this responsibility. For a telling witness to his importance for humanistic scholarship in the United States see the collection of memorial tributes offered by friends and colleagues at the New York Public Library on September 21, 1987 (*R. M. Lumiansky: Scholar, Teacher, Spokesman for the Humanities*, 1988, ACLS Occasional Papers, no. 3 [1-5]).

7. For such a relatively brief text, "The Prioress's Tale" has been the subject of much critical ink. While I will highlight some key critical texts in the following pages, readers unfamiliar with this critical history are encouraged to turn to Beverly Boyd's thorough review (1987).

8. For examples of Chaucer the humanist, see Schoeck (1956) and Archer (1984); for examples of historical apologetics, see Brewer (1953), Ridley (1965), and Frank (1982).

9. See for example, David (1982), Fradenburg (1989), and Zitter (1991).

10. The biennial New Chaucer Society meetings in 2000 and 2002 both had panel discussions on aesthetics, and a forthcoming issue of *The Chaucer Review* is devoted to aesthetic questions.

11. Wordsworth initially published his modernization of the tale in *Selections from Chaucer, Modernized* (1820, 1827) but later submitted and subsequently withdrew it from Thomas Powell and Richard H. Horne's *The Poems of Geoffrey Chaucer Modernized* (1840) (Bowden 1987, 42-45).

12. Lawrence Besserman takes issue with scholars who read this moment as one of common assent. He bases his objection in part on his assertion that "sober" characters in Chaucer feel differently on the inside than they show on the outside (2001, 66). While interesting, Besserman doesn't provide the type of evidence needed to reject the accepted reading of the line.

13. Fradenburg reads this threat of violence as a tool to deflect a fear of change as well as a fear of the inability to change (1989, 105-6). Holsinger usefully reminds us of the ubiquity of violence in pedagogical practice and lore (1997, 176 and passim).

14. Frank argues that the justice meted out in this tale is "just" in that only those culpable of the crime are killed: "that of this mordre wiste" (1982, 187). Yet, throughout the entire tale the members of the Jewish community are treated monolithically. It is the Jews as an entity who conspire to kill the boy (although they hire one person in particular to do the deed). "Fro thennes forth the Jues han conspired/ This innocent out of this world to chace" (VII. 565-566). And the boy winds up in a privy wherein "thise Jewes purgen hire entraille" (VII. 573). It is unlikely, then, that the Prioress would suddenly shift registers to focus on only "guilty" persons. Rather, her anti-Semitism, like all anti-Semitism, remains directed at a mythic sense of Jews as a whole, even though this hatred invariably manifests itself in acts of physical, verbal, and psychic violence directed at singular human beings. For an overview of the mythic element of anti-Semitism see, Katz (1994) and Langmuir (1990). For a more detailed examination, see, especially, Trachtenberg (1943) and Cohen (1982).

15. The impact of this unifying exemplum on the Canterbury pilgrims is perhaps intensified in the Prioress's final stanza, wherein she connects this distant city of "Asye" with the more familiar town of Lincoln and an incident that happened "but a litel while ago" (VII. 686). The Prioress's reference is to the disappearance of Hugh of Lincoln in 1255. For more on this incident and the anti-Semitic accusation that followed see Jacobs (1972), Hill (1948), and Langmuir (1972). The first blood libel accusation has traditionally been placed in Norwich, 1144, see Langmuir (1984, 1985). McCulloh (1997) has challenged the certainty of Norwich as the original locus of blood libel.

16. See for example, Scherb (1991) and van Court (1995). Susan Schibanoff (1996) has offered a reading of "The Man of Law's Tale" that stresses this type of "*othering*"—what she calls the "rhetoric of proximity"—which well demonstrates this approach's strengths and weaknesses. For more general discussions of this sociological principle see Moore (1987) and Girard (1987).

17. On the relationship between the canon and the Western Tradition see Guillory (1993, especially chapter one).

---

18. Kant's third *Critique* describes two types of judgment: determinant and indeterminate (also known as reflective). Determinant judgment uses a universal concept to determine a particular case. The traditional conception of genre exemplifies this type of judgment. Working from a general definition of generic expectations, critics might examine a specific literary work and judge whether or not it belongs to a specific genre. Indeterminate or reflective judgment begins with only a particular from which the universal must be established; it cannot work from any a priori concepts, laws, or rules. Kant explains as follows:

> The reflective judgement which is compelled to ascend from the particular in nature to the universal, stands, therefore, in need of a principle. This principle it cannot borrow from experience, because what it has to do is to establish just the unity of all empirical principles under higher, though likewise empirical principles, and thence the possibility of the systematic subordination of higher and lower. Such a transcendental principle, therefore, the reflective judgement can only give as a law from and to itself. It cannot be derived from any other quarter. . . . (Kant 1952, 18-19)

19. See for example, Stephen Knight, who, after acknowledging the craft of the tale, calls the poetry "not so much religious as *religiose*, Christianity made melodramatic and over-emotional" (1973, 143). To this one would have to add the possibility of critical silence being read as itself a negative evaluation of the tale's artistry—I doubt Knight is alone in his assessment. Contrary to belief, Kant does not presume that the entire community will consent. The general validity postulated by the *ought* remains only conditional, only a promise of universality. The community that seems on the verge of actuality in aesthetic judgment does not pass beyond the state of being an *idea* of community:

> we may perceive that nothing is postulated in the judgment of taste but such a universal voice in respect of delight that is not mediated by concepts; consequently only the possibility of an aesthetic judgment capable of being at the same time deemed valid for every one. The judgment of taste itself does not postulate the agreement of every one (for it is only competent for a logically universal judgment to do this, in that it is able to bring forward reasons); it only imputes this agreement to every one, as an instance of the rule in respect of which it looks for confirmation, not from concepts, but from the concurrence of others. The universal voice is, therefore, only an idea. . . . (Kant 1952, 56)

20. For the aestheticization of politics see Benjamin (1969) and Jay's concise review of the development of this concept (1993, 71-83).
21. In *Paraesthetics*, David Carroll (1987) provides an illuminating review of the dependence of contemporary critical thought (both materialist and non-materialist) on aesthetic discourse.
22. It may be objected that Eagleton deals only with the modern sense of the aesthetic, but to the extent that the aesthetic steps into the vacuum of absolutist polity, it strikes me as a potentially fruitful avenue for scholars working in the field of late medieval English culture. For the growing contest between absolutist and associational polity see Wallace (1997). Although Eagleton and Lyotard are quite different in their aims, that appeals to the continuing importance of Kant's writing on aesthetics come from two such disparate thinkers provides a sufficient riposte to crude dismissals of his work as merely important for formalist criticism. See in particular Lyotard (1994). Consider as well John Guillory's suggestion that aesthetic pleasure (and the aesthetic judgment from which it is derived) be analyzed as taking place within a "mixed" realm of politics and culture (1993, 336).
23. For genres of discourse see Lyotard (1988). Calabrese (2002) recently forwarded a com-

plaint against an academic discourse he sees as dominated by affective commentary on the Prioress—a claim I find difficult to accept. My approach will certainly not satisfy his call for a rationalist criticism stripped of personal contact with the literature we study, a call that raises serious questions about the reasons for teaching literature in the university. Nor do I agree with his assessment that "affective criticism" furthers the Machiavellian interests of global capital. Calabrese's attempt to connect affective criticism with the operations of global capital founders on at least two levels. First, he regularly blurs the target of his attack, sometimes calling it new historicism, sometimes ethical criticism, and sometimes affective criticism. The straw man resulting from his shifting labels and critical examples doesn't actually exist. Second, while his understanding of the role of corporations in higher education is based primarily (with good reason) on Bill Readings's *The University in Ruins* (1996), that reading is very much at odds with the book's thesis. Readings argues that the content or methodology of research is always susceptible to manipulation by the managerial pressures of the University of Excellence. More rationality in our critical discourse (Calabrese's thesis) will do nothing to avoid this central problem.

Works Cited

Adorno, Theodor W. 1983. *Aesthetic Theory*. Trans. C. Lenhardt. London: Routledge.

Archer, John. 1984. "The Structure of Anti-Semitism in the Prioress's Tale." *Chaucer Review* 19: 46-54.

Arnold, Matthew. 1891. *The English Poets*. Ed. T. H. Ward. Vol. 1. London: Macmillan.

Benjamin, Walter, 1969. "The Work of Art in the Age of Mechanical Reproduction." In *Illuminations*, trans. H. Zohn. New York: Schocken.

Benson, Larry, ed. 1993. *A Glossarial Concordance to the Riverside Chaucer*. Vol. 1. New York: Garland Press.

Besserman, Lawrence. 2001. "Ideology, Antisemitism, and Chaucer's Prioress's Tale." *Chaucer Review* 36: 48-72.

Bowden, Betsy. 1987. *Chaucer Aloud: The Varieties of Textual Interpretation*. Philadelphia: University of Pennsylvania Press.

Boyd, Beverly, ed. 1987. "The Prioress's Tale." A Variorum Edition of the Works of Geoffrey Chaucer. Vol. 2: *The Canterbury Tales*. Norman: University of Oklahoma Press.

Brewer, Derek S. 1953. *Chaucer*. London: Longman.

Bytwerk, Randall L. 1983. *Julius Streicher*. New York: Stein and Day.

Calabrese, Michael A. 2002. "Performing the Prioress: 'Conscience' and Responsibility in Studies of Chaucer's Prioress's Tale." *Texas Studies in Language and Literature* 44 (Spring): 66-91.

Carroll, David. 1987. *Paraesthetics: Foucault, Derrida, and Lyotard*. New York: Methuen.

Chaucer, Geoffrey. 1931. *The Canterbury Tales: The Prologue and Four Tales with the Book of the Duchess and Six Lyrics*. Trans. Frank Earnest Hill. Illus. Herman Rosse. London: Longmans, Green, and Co.

_____. 1934. *The Canterbury Tales*. Trans. J. U. Nicolson. Illus. Rockwell Kent. Garden City, NY: Garden City Publishing Company, Inc.

_____. 1987. *The Riverside Chaucer*. Gen. Ed. Larry D. Benson. Boston: Houghton Mifflin.

Chesterton, G. K. 1932. *Chaucer*. New York: Farrar and Rinehart.

Chute, Marchette. 1958. *Geoffrey Chaucer of England.* 1946. Reprint. New York: Dutton.

Cohen, Jeremy. 1982. *The Friars and the Jews: the Evolution of Medieval Anti-Semitism.* Ithaca: Cornell University Press.

Cooper, Helen. 1983. *The Structure of the* Canterbury Tales. London: Gerald Duckworth and Co.

David, Alfred. 1976. *The Strumpet Muse: Art and Morals in Chaucer's Poetry.* Bloomington: Indiana University Press.

_____. 1982. "An A B C to the Prioress's Tale." In *Acts of Interpretation: The Text in its Context 700-1600: Essays on Medieval and Renaissance Literature in Honor of E. Talbot Donaldson,* ed. Mary J. Carruthers and Elizabeth D. Kirk. Norman, OK: Pilgrim Books.

Derrida, Jacques. 1995. *The Gift of Death.* Trans. David Wills. Chicago: University of Chicago Press.

Donaldson, E. Talbot. 1972. *Chaucer's Poetry: An Anthology for the Modern Reader.* 2nd ed. 1958. New York: Ronald.

Dundes, Alan. 1991. *The Blood Libel Legend: A Casebook in Anti-Semitic Folklore.* Madison: University of Wisconsin Press.

Eagleton, Terry. 1990. *Ideology of the Aesthetic.* Oxford: Basil Blackwell.

Ferster, Judith. 1990. "'Your Praise Is Performed by Men and Children': Language and Gender in the Prioress's Prologue and Tale." *Exemplaria* 2 (Spring): 149-68.

Fradenburg, Louise. 1985. "The Manciple's Servant Tongue: Politics and Poetry in the *Canterbury Tales.*" *English Literary History* 52 (Spring): 85-118.

_____. 1989. "Criticism, Anti-Semitism, and 'The Prioress's Tale.'" *Exemplaria* 1 (Spring): 69-115.

Frank, Hardy Long. 1991. "Seeing the Prioress Whole." *Chaucer Review* 25: 229-37.

Frank, R. W., Jr. 1982. "Miracles of the Virgin, Medieval Anti-Semitism, and the 'Prioress's Tale.'" In *The Wisdom of Poetry: Essays in Early English Literature in Honor of Morton W. Bloomfield.* Kalamazoo: Medieval Institute.

Gaylord, Alan T. 1962. "The Unconquered Tale of the Prioress." *Papers of the Michigan Academy of Science, Arts, and Letters* 47: 613-36.

Girard, René. 1987. "Generative Scapegoating." In *Violent Origins,* ed. Robert G. Hamerton-Kelly. Stanford: Stanford University Press.

Guillory, John. 1993. *Cultural Capital: The Problem of Literary Canon Formation.* Chicago: University of Chicago Press.

Hahn, Thomas. 1992. "The Performance of Gender in the Prioress." *Chaucer Yearbook* 1: 111-34.

Hill, J. W. F. 1948. *Medieval Lincoln.* Cambridge: Cambridge University Press.

Holsinger, Bruce. 1997. "Pedagogy, Violence and the Subject of Music: Chaucer's Prioress's Tale and the Ideologies of 'Song.'" In *New Medieval Literatures,* ed. Rita Copeland, David Lawton and Wendy Scase. New Medieval Literatures. Vol. 1. Oxford: Clarendon.

Howard, Donald R. 1976. *The Idea of* The Canterbury Tales. Berkeley: University of California Press.

_____. 1987. *Chaucer and the Medieval World.* London: Weidenfeld and Nicolson.

Jacobs, J. 1972. "Little St. Hugh of Lincoln." In *Jewish Ideals and Other Essays.* 1896. Reprint. Freeport, NY: Books for Libraries Press.

Jay, Martin. 1993. *Force Fields: Between Intellectual History and Cultural Critique.* New York: Routledge.

Kant, Immanuel. 1952. *The Critique of Judgment.* Trans. James Creed Meredith. Oxford: Clarendon Press.

Katz, Jacob. 1980. *From Prejudice to Destruction: Anti-Semitism, 1700-1933.* Cambridge: Harvard University Press.

Katz, Stephen. 1994. *The Holocaust in Historical Context.* Oxford: Oxford University Press.

Kittredge, George Lyman. 1960. *Chaucer and His Poetry.* 1915. Reprint. Cambridge: Harvard University Press.

Knight, Stephen. 1973. *The Poetry of the* Canterbury Tales. Sydney: Angus and Robertson.

Langmuir, Gavin. 1972. "The Knight's Tale of Young Hugh of Lincoln." *Speculum* 47 (July): 459-82.

_____. 1984. "Thomas of Monmouth: Detector of Ritual Murder." *Speculum* 59 (October): 820-46.

_____. 1985. "Historiographic Crucifixion." In *Les Juifs au regard de l'histoire: mélanges en l'honneur de Bernhard Blumenkranz.* Paris: Picard.

_____. 1990. *Toward a Definition of Antisemitism.* Berkeley: University of California Press.

Leicester, H. Marshall Jr. 1990a. *The Disenchanted Self: Representing the Subject in the* Canterbury Tales. Berkeley: University of California Press.

_____. 1990b. "Structure as Deconstruction: 'Chaucer and Estates Satire' in the General Prologue, or Reading Chaucer as a Prologue to the History of Disenchantment." *Exemplaria* 2 (Spring): 241-61.

Leland, John. 2001. "Rascal or Racist? Censoring a Rabbit." *The New York Times.* 3 June 2001. Section 4, page 3.

Lounsbury, Thomas R. 1962. *Studies in Chaucer.* Vol. 2. 1892. Reprint. New York: Russell.

Lumiansky, R. M., ed. and trans. 1948. *The* Canterbury Tales *of Geoffrey Chaucer.* New York: Simon and Schuster.

_____, ed. and trans. 1954. *The* Canterbury Tales, *by Geoffrey Chaucer.* 2nd ed. New York: Holt, Rinehart and Winston.

_____. 1955. *Of Sondry Folk: The Dramatic Principle in the* Canterbury Tales. Austin: University of Texas Press.

Lyotard, Jean-François. 1988. *The Differend: Phrases in Dispute.* Trans. Georges Van Den Abbeele. Minneapolis: University of Minnesota Press.

_____. 1988. *Peregrinations: Law, Form, Event.* New York: Columbia University Press.

_____. 1994. *Lessons on the Analytic of the Sublime.* Trans. Elizabeth Rottenberg. Stanford: Stanford University Press.

McCulloh, John M. 1997. "Jewish Ritual Murder: William of Norwich, Thomas of Monmouth, and the Early Dissemination of the Myth." *Speculum* 72 (July): 698-740.

Madeleva, M., C. C. C. 1925. "Chaucer's Nun's." In *Chaucer's Nuns and Other Essays.* New York: Appleton.

Moore, R. I. 1987. *The Formation of a Persecuting Society: Power and Deviance in Western Europe, 950-1250.* Oxford: Blackwell.

Payne, Robert O. 1973. *The Key of Remembrance: A Study of Chaucer's Poetry.* 1963. Reprint. Westport, CT: Greenwood Press.

R. M. Lumiansky: Scholar, Teacher, Spokesman for the Humanities. 1988. ACLS Occasional Papers, no. 3. American Council of Learned Societies.

Readings, Bill. 1996. *The University in Ruins.* Cambridge: Harvard University Press.

Rex, Richard. 1984. "Chaucer and the Jews." *Modern Language Quarterly* 45 (June): 107-22.

_____. 1995. *"The Sins of Madame Eglentyne" and Other Essays on Chaucer.* Newark: University of Delaware Press.

Ridley, Florence H. 1965. *The Prioress and the Critics.* University of California Publications, English Studies. Vol. 30. Berkeley: University of California Press.

Root, R. K. 1906. *The Poetry of Chaucer.* Boston: Houghton Mifflin.

Rudat, Wolfgang. 1994. "Gender-Crossing in 'The Prioress's Tale': Chaucer's Satire on Theological Anti-Semitism?" *Cithara* 33.2 (May): 11-17.

Russell, G. H. 1969. "Chaucer: 'The Prioress's Tale.'" In *Medieval Literature and Civilization: Studies in Memory of G. N. Garmonsway.* London: Athlone Press.

Scherb, Victor I. 1991. "Violence and the Social Body in the Croxton Play of the Sacrament." In *Violence in Drama.* Ed. James Redmond. Cambridge: Cambridge University Press.

Schibanoff, Susan. 1996. "Worlds Apart: Orientalism, Antifeminism, and Heresy in Chaucer's *Man of Law's Tale.*" *Exemplaria* 8 (Spring): 59-96.

Schoeck, R. J. 1956. "Chaucer's Prioress: Mercy and Tender Heart." *The Bridge: A Yearbook of Judaeo-Christian Studies* 2: 239-55.

Trachtenberg, Joshua, 1943. *The Devil and the Jews: The Medieval Conception of the Jew and its Relation to Modern Antisemitism.* New Haven: Yale University Press.

van Court, Elisa Narin. 1995. "The Siege of Jerusalem and Augustinian Historians: Writing About Jews in Fourteenth Century England." *Chaucer Review* 29: 227-48.

Wallace, David. 1997. *Chaucerian Polity: Absolutist Lineages and Associational Forms in England and Italy.* Stanford: Stanford University Press.

Wordsworth, William. 1896. *The Poetical Works of William Wordsworth.* Ed. W. Knight. Vol. 2. London: Macmillan.

Zitter, Emmy Stark. 1991. "Anti-Semitism in Chaucer's *Prioress's Tale.*" *Chaucer Review* 25: 277-84.

The Bodies of Jews in the Late Middle Ages_____

Steven F. Kruger

The miracle of Chaucer's Prioress's Tale is manifestly physical, involving as its central fact the dead-but-not-dead body of the tale's "litel clergeon" (VII.503).[1] That body, subjected to violence and degradation—cut open and thrown into "a wardrobe . . . Where as thise Jewes purgen hire entraille" (572-73)—remains, through the miraculous intervention of the Virgin Mary, undefiled and functionally whole. In the filthy "pit" (571, 606) "Ther he with throte ykorven lay upright" (611), the "innocent" (566, 608) is described by images not of defilement and injury but of purity and intactness. The boy becomes not a butchered child but "This gemme of chastite, this emeraude,/ And eek of martirdom the ruby bright" (609-10).[2] Indeed, the mutilated body is finally translated from its place of violent degradation to one of honor and safety: "And in a tombe of marbul stones cleere/ Enclosen they his litel body sweete" (681-82).

Bodily injury and intactness are among the tale's central concerns. As Chaucer repeatedly emphasizes, despite the nature of his injury, the slit throat that should make speech physically impossible, the boy sings out loud and clear, in a voice powerful enough to make his surroundings respond with their own sound: "Ther he with throte ykorven lay upright,/ He Alma *redemptoris* gan to synge/ So loude that al the place gan to rynge" (611-13). The abbot of the tale explicitly recognizes the paradoxical relation between the boy's singing and the injury that makes singing impossible: "Tel me what is thy cause for to synge,/ Sith that thy throte is kut to my semynge?" (647-48). And the boy responds (in a speech whose very existence is miraculous) by recognizing both the real, radical nature of his injury—"My throte is kut unto my nekke boon,/ . . . and as by wey of kynde/ I sholde have dyed, ye, longe tyme agon" (649-51)—and the physical capacity that miraculously survives that injury— "Yet may I synge O *Alma* loude and cleere" (655). The miracle of the boy's singing of course involves an intrusion of the supernatural into the world, but that intrusion, Mary's intercession, itself takes place in the realm of the physical:

> And whan that I my lyf sholde forlete,
> To me she cam, and bad me for to synge
> This anthem verraily in my deyynge,
> As ye han herd, and what that I hadde songe,
> Me thoughte she leyde a greyn upon my tonge.
>
> (658-62)

The "me thoughte" here may leave room for doubt about the actual physical quality of Mary's intervention, but when the abbot pulls out the boy's tongue and takes "awey the greyn" (671), all such doubt must vanish.

The emphasis on the physical in The Prioress's Tale is not unusual in late-medieval religious writing. Indeed, as Caroline Bynum has forcefully argued, late-medieval spirituality, especially women's spirituality, is intimately tied up with the physical, with food and with flesh; the body often serves as a locus for the immanent workings of divinity.[3] While such a valuation of body might seem to contradict the truisms with which, in shorthand, we tend to define medieval Christian attitudes toward body—body is the prison of soul; the flesh battles the spirit and the spirit the flesh[4]—it should not surprise us. Christianity is, after all, grounded in the marriage of flesh and spirit, the incarnation of a bodiless divinity and the concomitant spiritualization of his flesh. The Incarnation, the Virgin Birth, the Immaculate Conception, transubstantiation, resurrection, all involve body as much as spirit.

The miracles of the later Middle Ages often parallel the originary mysteries of Christianity; the divine often shows itself in the physical—for instance, in the workings of relics, pieces of body in which saintliness somehow inheres. In late-medieval literature, saints' lives and related genres (such as the "miracle of the Virgin" of which The Prioress's Tale is an example) are especially apt to focus attention on bodies dedicated and sacrificed to religious ends and on bodies miraculously preserved. Thus, Chaucer's own life of St. Cecilia, The Second Nun's Tale, is a story of voluntary, wedded chastity that includes two beheadings (398), a fatal flagellation (405-6), and a scene of extended torment. St. Cecilia is boiled "in a bath of flambes rede" (515), yet remains "al coold," feeling "no wo" (521). Smitten three times in the neck, "half deed, with hir nekke ycorven there" (533), she, like the Prioress's "litel clergeon," yet lives on, "And nevere cessed hem the feith to teche/ That she hadde fostred . . ." (538-39). Here, as in The Prioress's Tale, the story's central miracle allows an intactness of body despite violent attempts to destroy that intactness.

A recognition of the intimate involvement of body in late-medieval spirituality need not, however, negate our sense that medieval Christianity also deeply distrusts body, often indeed depicting body as a prison, as rebel to reason and spirit, as a force that must be controlled, denied, even sometimes destroyed. Bynum is, I believe, right "that medieval asceticism should not be understood as rooted in dualism, in a radical sense of spirit opposed to or entrapped by body": "late medieval asceticism was an effort to plumb and to realize all the possibilities of the flesh. . . . They were not rebelling against or torturing their flesh out of guilt over its capabilities so much as using the possibilities of its full sensual and affective range to soar ever closer to God." But medieval attitudes toward body are not revealed only in the ascetical practices that "arose in a religious world whose central ritual was the coming of God into food as macerated flesh."[5] Indeed, strikingly opposed to a theology centered in the positive valuation of suffering body are the frequent late-medieval attempts to repudiate *certain* human bodies as animal-like, disgusting, contaminating. Women's bodies, which might be intimately involved in the approach to God, were also treated as possessing abhorrent flesh:

> A woman is an imperfect creature excited by a thousand foul passions, abominable even to remember, let alone to speak of. . . . No other creature is less clean than woman: the pig, even when he is most wallowed in mud, is not as foul as they. If perhaps someone would deny this, let him consider their childbearing; let him search the secret places where they in shame hide the horrible instruments they employ to take away their superfluous humors.[6]

Leprous bodies, though they might also become part of spiritual practices,[7] were nonetheless segregated from society, treated as already dead.[8] Lepers were seen "as the most repellent, the most dangerous and most desolate of creatures, representing the last degree of human degradation."[9] Less ambivalently treated (because never incorporated into Christian spirituality) were the bodies of male homosexuals and of Jews. Late-medieval law sometimes classed homosexual intercourse alongside intercourse with animals (and with Jews) and sentenced those guilty to live burial;[10] Aquinas "compared homosexual acts . . . with violent or disgusting acts of the most shocking type, like cannibalism, bestiality, or eating dirt."[11] And Jews were often seen as the possessors of diseased and debased bodies:

> . . . the Jew suffered . . . from certain peculiar and secret afflictions that were especially characteristic of him, and which did not normally trouble Christians. . . . Most often mentioned among these ailments was that of menstruation, which the men as well as the women among the Jews were supposed to experience;[12] close seconds, in point of frequency of mention, were copious hemorrhages and hemorrhoids (all involving loss of blood). Among the great variety of these maladies were included quincy, scrofula, a marked pallor, various mysterious skin diseases, and sores that gave forth a malodorous flux.[13]

Even more disturbingly, Jews were depicted as destroying other (Christian) bodies and using body parts (especially blood) to heal their own diseases and to perform magical acts.[14] Partially in consequence of such myths, Jewish bodies were often themselves seen as the appropriate targets of violence.[15]

Bodies marginal to, and persecuted by, late-medieval society and Christianity deserve our close attention in the larger reassessment of medieval attitudes toward body that is currently in progress.[16] Here, as part of that reassessment, I would like to concentrate attention especially on the bodies of Jews, and in particular on the treatment of those bodies in two late-medieval English literary texts—Chaucer's Prioress's Tale[17] and the Croxton *Play of the Sacrament*—that closely link the corruptions of Jewish body to Christian bodily miracles. In doing so, I hope to clarify the relation between the positive valuation of body in late-medieval spirituality and the attack on body often present in the treatment of Jews.

I. Tortured and Torturing

In The Second Nun's Tale, violence works in only one direction, against the persecuted Christian minority. All the tale's victims are Christians; the pagan oppressors, so long as they remain pagan, are never subjected to physical torment.[18] Indeed, the tale dramatizes the opposition between Christian victim and pagan tormentor by showing us several violent pagans who convert to Christianity and who, as a result, become themselves the victims of torment. Valerian at first threatens violence against his wife Cecilia if, as he suspects, she loves "another man" (167)—"Right with this swerd thanne wol I sle yow bothe" (168). When, however, he is convinced of Cecilia's faithfulness and holiness, he takes on her religion and with that religion "the palm of martirdom" (240): he is beheaded for his faith (393-99). In a similar way, Maximus, an officer of the Roman prefect Almachius, and the often Roman "tormentoures" (373, 376) are converted by Christian "prechyng" (375): "They [the Christians] gonnen fro the tormentours to reve,/ And fro Maxime, and fro his folk echone,/ The false feith, to trowe in God allone" (376-78). Maximus, in his turn, becomes a Christian preacher, and as a result himself suffers an excruciating death: "And with his word [he] converted many a wight;/ For which Almachius dide hym so bete/ With whippe of leed till he his lif gan lete" (404-6). On the other hand, the tale's central villain, Almachius, remains a pagan, and (although his power erodes) he never himself becomes a victim of violence.

The Second Nun's Tale depicts a "former age" of primitive Christianity in which all Christians, even the pope ("Men sholde hym brennen in a fyr so reed/ If he were founde" [313-14]), are potentially Christlike victims of torment that brings with itself clear rewards—salvation ("Hir soules wenten to the Kyng of grace" [399]) and the demonstration of divine immanence (in the miracle of Cecilia's supernatural survival). The death and survival of the "clergeon" in The Prioress's Tale similarly make manifest divine care for the

Christian martyr; Mary directly promises the boy's salvation: "My litel child, now wol I fecche thee,/ Whan that the greyn is fro thy yonge ytake./ Be nat agast; I wol thee nat forsake" (667-69).

But the Christianity of The Prioress's Tale is less pristine than that of The Second Nun's Tale and the workings of violence in its world less clear-cut. Whereas, in The Second Nun's Tale, the whole Christian community is directly endangered by its oppressors and the solidarity of that community in Christian suffering is shown by a series of martyrdoms, the Church in The Prioress's Tale is powerful and its identity with the little boy's suffering is demonstrated not by direct physical endangerment but in a more symbolic mode. The leader of the Christian community, the abbot, seeing the "wonder" of the boy's death (673), in a vicarious experience of physical disability, "fil al plat upon the grounde,/ And stille he lay as he had been ybounde" (675-76). The abbot's community follows suit: "The covent eek lay on the pavement/ Wepynge, and herying Christes mooder deere" (677-78). In this physical and emotional reaction, the larger Christian community shows itself to be in sympathetic unity with the suffering martyr, a unity that the narrator, in part through her invocation of the English martyr Hugh,[19] wishfully extends to include both herself and her audience: "Ther he [the clergeon] is now, God leve us for to meete!" (683); "O yonge Hugh of Lyncoln . . . Preye eek for us, we synful folk unstable" (684, 687). Indeed outside the tale proper, we see the miracle's effect upon a Christian community of listeners (Chaucer's pilgrims), an effect less severe than but similar to that felt by the "covent" within the tale: "Whan seyd was al this miracle, every man/ As sobre was that wonder was to se" (691-92).

The powerful Church thus escapes a relentless reiteration of real bodily suffering even as it identifies with and soberly celebrates that suffering. Furthermore, its power allows the Christian community to move actively (and violently) against its "oppressors." Here, physical torment does not work, as in The Second Nun's Tale, in only one direction. The Jewish "persecutors" are (like the Christians persecuted in The Second Nun's Tale) in the minority. The "Jewerye" exists "*Amonges* Cristene folk" (489; emphasis mine), surrounded by Christianity, and it survives only through the patronage of a non-Jew: "Sustened by a lord of that contree/ For foule usure and lucre of vileynye" (490-91). The Jewish crime against the "clergeon" is punished and punished with a physical violence designed as direct retribution for the injuries to which the Christian body has been subjected:

With torment and with shameful deeth echon,
This provost dooth thise Jewes for to sterve
That of this mordre wiste, and that anon.
He nolde no swich cursednesse observe.
"Yvele shal have that yvele wol deserve";
Therfore with whie hors he dide hem drawe,
And after that he heng hem by the lawe.
(628-34)

"Torment" and "shameful deeth" clearly compensate here for the tale's earlier murder and defilement.

The suffering of the "litel clergeon" thus provides not only an occasion for the miraculous incursion of divinity into the realm of body and not only a demonstration of how the suffering Christian body may serve as a focal point for the feelings of the larger community. It also provides the opportunity for a Christian attack on bodies perceived and treated as radically different from the "innocent" body of the little boy. At the heart of The Prioress's Tale is an opposition between the Christian body, attacked but preserved, and the Jewish body, foul (purging its "entraille" [573]), attacking innocence, justly destroyed. And this opposition occurs not just at the level of the individual body. The punishment of the Jews is more than simply "just compensation" for a discrete crime, more than the old law "yvele" for "yvele" (632): not only the one "homycide" (567) directly responsible for the boy's death, nor only those Jews who "conspired/ This innocent out of this world to chace" (565-66), but all "this Jewes . . . That of this mordre wiste" (629-30) suffer painful and shameful execution. The action of the one "cursed Jew" (570) who commits the murder is presented not as an individual act but as part of a conspiracy that bears communal responsibility. While, when the crime is first described, we see the singular "homycide" killing the boy and casting his body into a pit (570-71), immediately afterward the description of the action is broadened to suggest communal guilt—"I seye that in a wardrobe *they* hym threwe" (572; emphasis mine). And the conclusion of the tale broadens Jewish culpability even further, leaving the particular crime and its exotic, Asian setting behind to find "cursed Jewes" closer to home:[20] "O yonge Hugh of Lyncoln, slayn also/ With cursed Jewes, as it is notable,/ For it is but a litel while ago" (684-86). The crime against one Christian body takes on wide implications, is seen as part of a larger Jewish threat, and, as a consequence, the corporate punishment imposed is "shown" to be justified. After all, Jews are communally "cursed": "Oure firste foo, the serpent Sathanas . . . hath in Jues herte his waspes nest" (558-59).

Ultimately, then, in Chaucer's tale, both individual suffering and individual guilt become corporate. Christians take on the suffering of the martyred child (and concomitantly they hope for a salvation like his); "cursed Jewes" suffer the punishment earned by the singular "cursed" "homycide" (570, 567). But while the relation between "clergeon" and "homycide" is clear—it is the archetypal relation between strong and weak, oppressor and victim[21]—the extension of that relation into the larger Jewish and Christian communities complicates matters. As we have seen, the Christian community does not simply suffer but also inflicts suffering.[22] The Jewish community not only makes the little boy a martyr but is itself victimized. Each community acts as both persecutor and persecuted, and, interestingly, both are, at least at one point, described in similar terms. The Jews, as they approach their "torment and . . . shameful deeth" (628), are bound (". . . the Jewes leet he bynde" [620]); similarly, the abbot, suffering along with the young Christian martyr and with his larger community, "lay as he had ben ybounde" (676).

I do not want to suggest that our sympathies, when we read The Prioress's Tale, are meant to be divided between Christians and Jews (though the modern reader, recognizing the tale's anti-Semitism, often does have a divided reaction). At least in the Prioress's presentation of events, the Jews are clear villains. However, even as it makes strong distinctions between "cursed," Satanic Jews and Christians who are "hooly" (642), "or elles oghte be" (643), the tale brings together the two opposed religions—by showing both to be tormentors of bodies as well as the possessors of tormented bodies and by (linguistically) binding together the "bound" bodies of Christians and Jews. As a result, the final picture of body in The Prioress's Tale is a complex one in which the role of both tormented and tormentor are simultaneously validated (as these roles are played by Christians) and repudiated (as they are represented by Jews). If the primary function of the Christian body is to suffer humbly and patiently in unity with the suffering, crucified Christ (a role Bynum identifies as central to late-medieval spirituality), that body, at least as it shows itself in the powerful, corporate body of the Church, also refuses to suffer, identifying its enemies and moving to inflict suffering on them. If the Jewish body is primarily a menace to Christian innocence, it is a menace easily contained, tormented, destroyed.

The introduction of Jewish bodies into a tale like the Prioress's thus allows for the enactment of a complex and deeply ambivalent Christian valuation of body. On the one hand, the weakness and vulnerability of the human body is placed center stage; in its very capacity for being wounded, body makes possible union with the humanity-divinity of the suffering Christ who stands at the origin of Christianity. But Christianity, at least as it is depicted in Chaucer's tale, is unwilling to embrace wholeheartedly the suffering body. Vulnerability is not in itself to be valued; indeed, as it shows itself in Jewish bodies, it is to be taken advantage of, and body itself is to be extirpated. Christianity moves—even as it celebrates the miracle of the little boy's martyrdom and shows itself in solidarity with his suffering—to assert its own power, the *invulnerability* of its corporate body, and to prove that power by victimizing the bodies of "cursed Jewes." It follows a path not taken by the crucified Christ and not accessible to the early Christian martyrs, availing itself of worldly power to impose punishment on criminal (Jewish) bodies. Thus, the Prioress's Tale presents us with bodies that are, as they suffer, both to be embraced and cast aside, and, as they cause suffering, both to be praised and anathematized.

II. Holy and Corrupt Body

In The Prioress's Tale, the miraculous mutilated body, preserved and celebrated as "This gemme of chastite, this emeraude" (609), lies starkly beside those "cursed" bodies that must "purgen hire entraille" (573), bodies drawn and hung (633-34), bodies thankfully destroyed. Hallowed and corrupted bodies stand together and work upon each other: Jews kill and defile the Christian "innocent," ironically making possible the miracle that preserves him and that binds the Christian community with the primal, redemptive suffering of Christ; Christians, even as they suffer vicariously with the martyred boy and praise the miracle that attends his suffering, bind, debase, and eliminate the Jewish bodies ultimately "responsible" for the miraculous events.

The complex relation between Christian and Jewish, corrupt and holy, bodies that we thus see in Chaucer's Prioress's Tale appears often in late-medieval literature and reveals, I believe, crucial elements of medieval attitudes toward both Jews and body. The late fifteenth-century Croxton *Play of the Sacrament*[23] is especially interesting as an expression of those attitudes in that it explicitly connects the holy body at the heart of Christian worship—Christ as he is made ever-immanent in the Eucharist—to those bodies that stand outside Christianity and attack it.

In this play, the immediate didactic purpose of which is to argue the truth of Christian doctrine concerning the Eucharist and transubstantiation,[24] Christian body is represented by the consecrated host, illicitly purchased and then tortured by Jews. Here, as in The Prioress's Tale, the Jews are cast in the role of tormentors and the torment they inflict is again visited back upon their own bodies. In some ways, the treatment of Jews in the play is more subtle and less violent than in Chaucer's tale: though punished, the Jews are not finally destroyed, and Jewish perfidy is less absolutely opposed to Christian purity than it might be.[25] The Jews do not act alone in their defilement of the host: Christian sin aids them. The Christian merchant Aristorye, after offering some weak resistance, agrees to steal the consecrated wafer and sell it to the Jewish merchant Jonathas (274-335). Indeed, even before the Jewish plot to torment the host is introduced, the play establishes an affinity between Aristorye and Jonathas: in a long, boastful speech (81-124),[26] Aristorye claims repeatedly to be "[a] merchaunte mighty" (90), "most mighty of silver and of gold" (87), "a merchante most [of] might . . . In Eraclea is non[e] suche" (85-86), and Jonathas introduces himself with similar boasts (149-204)—"I am chefe merchaunte of Jewes, I tell yow, by right" (196), "In Eraclea is noon so moche of might" (194).

These opening speeches, however, also serve to differentiate the two characters, and thus they begin to delineate Jewish and Christian roles in the play. Although, as soon as Aristorye begins speaking, he shows himself to be proud and avaricious, he also reveals his awareness of the Christian deity: "Now Crist, that is our Creatour, from shame he cure us" (81); "All I thank God of his grace, for he it me sent" (118). On the other hand, Jonathas worships not Christ but "almighty Machomet" (149), and he quickly institutes the play's central action by issuing a direct challenge to Christianity:

> The beleve of thes[e] Cristen men is false, as I wene,
> For the[y] beleve on a cake—me think it is onkind—
> And all they sew how the prest dothe it bind,
> And by the might of his word make it flessh and blode—
> And thus by a conceite the[y] wolde make us blind—
> And how that it shuld be He that deyed upon the rode.
>
> (199-204)

Christians may behave badly; as he himself is aware, Aristorye, in selling "Christ's body" to the Jews, commits a grave sin analogous to Judas's betrayal of Christ:

> For, and I unto the chirche yede,
> And preste or clerke might me aspye,
> To the bisshope they wolde go tell that dede,
> And apeche me of [h]eresye.
>
> (299-302)

Still, the Christian merchant remains a believer. He is finally not the instigator of "heresy," nor is he fully privy to the evil intentions of the Jews. In persuading Aristorye to procure the host, Jonathas whitewashes his "entent" (291), making no mention of the plan to torment Christ's body:

The Bodies of Jews in the Late Middle Ages

> Sir, the entent is, if I might knowe or undertake
> If that he were God all-might;
> Of all my mis I woll amende make
> And doon him wourshepe bothe day and night.
>
> (291-94)

Aristorye remains innocent of the most heinous part of the Jewish plot; Christians, though implicated through Aristorye in the crime at the play's center, remain finally peripheral to that crime, remote from the actual scene of torment.

On the other hand, Jonathas and the four Jews who serve him are from the very beginning intent on violence, prepared to torment the host. Jonathas is not, as Bevington argues, "*simply* a type of skeptic who considers the Christian dogma of the mass to be rationally indefensible,"[27] though skepticism indeed provides one of the two explicitly stated motivations for Jewish procurement of the host:

> Yea, I dare sey feythfully that ther feyth [is fals]:
> That was never He that on Calvery was kild!
> Or in bred for to be blode, it is ontrewe als.
> But yet with ther wiles they wold we were wild.
>
> (213-16)

But even as they state their disbelief in the host's sentience, the Jews of the Croxton *Play* express the desire to cause it physical and emotional distress:

> I swer by my grete god, and ellis mote I nat cheve,
> But wightly the[r]on wold I be wreke!
>
> (211-12)

> Yea, I am mighty Malchus,[28] that boldly am bild.
> That brede for to bete biggly am I bent!
> Onys out of ther handys and it might be exiled,
> To helpe castyn it in care wold I consent.
>
> (217-20)

The play does not seem concerned that the two motivations the Jews thus provide for their actions are contradictory (in the Middle Ages, Jewish attitudes toward Christian doctrine were often believed in fact to be self-contradictory—Jews knew the truth of Christianity even though they perversely insisted on denying it).[29] The Jews of the Croxton *Play* both boldly deny transubstantiation and act as though they believe in its truth: when Jonathas finally has the host in his possession, he refers to it skeptically as "this bred that make us thus blind" (388),[30] but he also addresses the host as if it were indeed a person: "Now in this clothe I shall the[e] covere,/ That no wight shall the[e] see" (383-84).

The Jews' double reasons for stealing the host continue to motivate their actions once they have it in their possession. Their skepticism shows itself in a careful consideration of the "mervelows" (394) claims of Christian doctrine. Jonathas describes the establishment of the Eucharistic meal at the Last Supper (397-408), and his four Jewish companions discuss other aspects of the Christian "heresy" (415, 424): the Annunciation and Virgin Birth (409-16), Christ's Resurrection and Ascension (417-24), the descent of the Holy Ghost on Pentecost (425-32), and finally the Last Judgement (433-40). Throughout this extended summary of Christian doctrine, the Jewish expositors remain deeply skeptical, concluding that the "entent" of these teachings is "To turne us from owr beleve" (439), and reiterating the desire to test the host (442-43).

The Jews do, however, accept one bit of Christian doctrine:

> There [in Bosra] stainyd were his clothys—this may we belefe,
> This may we know—there had he grefe,
> For owr old bookys verify thus:
> Thereon he was jugett to be hangyd as a thefe—
> *"Tinctis [de] Bosra vestibus."*[31]
>
> (444-48)

This evocation of the historical violence against Christ serves as a bridge between the Jews' skeptical review of doctrine and the expression of their other, more malicious, intentions for the host. Jason proposes "a conceit good" (450)—"Iff that this be he that on Calvery was mad[e] red . . . Surely with owr daggars we shall ses on this bredde,/ And so with clowtys we shall know if he have eny blood" (449-52)—and his companions respond to this suggestion with enthusiastic violence:

> *Jasdon.* . . . with owr strokys we shall fray him as he was on the rood,
> That he was on-don[e] with grett repreve.
> *Masphat.* Yea, I pray yow, smite ye in the middys of the cake,
> And so shall we smite theron wounds five!
> We will not spare to wirke it wrake
> To prove in this brede if ther be eny life.
>
> (455-60)

While the Jews are still concerned with disposing doctrinal claims ("if he have eny blood," "if ther be eny life"), they also express their belief in the host's sentience, in its capacity to suffer "wrake."

With these Jewish threats of violence begins the play's central action, the reenactment of the historical torment of Christ on the body of the host. The Jews' first actions economically evoke the buffeting and scourging of Christ (see lines 468 and 476) along with the five wounds of the Crucifixion:

> *Malchus.* Yea, goo we to, than, and take owr space,
> And looke owr daggarys be sharpe and kene!
> And when eche man a stroke smitte base,
> In the midyll part thereof owr mastere shall bene.
> *Jonathas.* When ye have all smityn, my stroke shal be sene:
> With this same daggere that is so stif and strong
> In the middys of this print I thinke for to prene!
> On[e] lashe I shall him lende or it be long.
> > *Here shall the four Jews prik ther daggerys in four*
> > *quarters, thus say[i]ng:*
>
> *Jason.* Have at it! Have at it, with all my might!
> This side I hope for to sese!
> *Jasdon.* And I shall with this blade so bright
> This othere side freshely afeze!
> *Masphat.* And I yow plight I shall him not please,
> For with this punche I shall him prike!
> *Malchus.* And with this augur I shall him not ease:
> Anothere buffett shall he likke!
>
> *Jonathas.* Now am I bold with bataile him to bleyke,
> This midle part all for to prene,
> A stowte stroke also for to strike:
> In the middys it shal be sene!
>
> (461-80)

Like the "homycide" of The Prioress's Tale, the Jews here act in an attempt to destroy the physical integrity of an innocent, holy body. But, as also in Chaucer's tale, the Christian body resists disintegration, and Jewish violence is finally visited back upon the Jews themselves, demonstrating simultaneously the corruptibility of their unholy bodies and the miraculous vitality of the sanctified body of Christ.

As soon as Jonathas delivers the fifth wound to the center of the host, it, to the Jews' horror, begins to bleed:

> Ah, owt, owt, harrow! What devill is this?
> Of this wick I am on were!
> It bledith as it were woode, iwis!
> But if ye helpe, I shall dispaire!
>
> (481-84)

Bleeding, for any normal body a sign of the loss of physical wholeness, here paradoxically proves the host's life—a life that the remainder of the play's action will demonstrate to be ultimately inviolate. Like the blood shed in Christ's crucifixion, the blood of the host is both a sign of wounding and token of life—both a result of Jewish violence and a proof of the fundamental impotence of that violence, which succeeds in its goal of wounding only to prove what it wants to suppress, the truth of Christianity.

Indeed, from this point on, the Jews' skepticism about the Eucharist is no longer an issue in the play: Jonathas and his companions now know with certainty "if he have eny blood" (452). But while the Jews can no longer rationally challenge Christian dogma, their violent attack on the host does not end so easily. Indeed, in an attempt to stop the disturbing Eucharistic bleeding, they intensify their violence. Jason calls for fire and a cauldron of oil (485-86), and Jasdon promises to "helpe it were in cast,/ All the three howrys for to boile" (487-88);[32] Masphat and Malchus set up a furnace and cauldron (489-96). But when Jonathas tries to "bring that ilke cak[e]/ And throwe it in" (497-98), violence begins to turn back upon itself. Masphat earlier promised to "wirke [the host] wrake" (459), but now, as Jonathas announces, "it werketh me wrake" (499). The violated host clings stubbornly to Jonathas's hand:

> I may not avoid it owt of my hond!
> I wille goo drenche me in a lake.
> And in woodnesse I ginne to wake!
> I renne, I lepe over this lond!
> *Her[e] he renneth wood, with the [h]ost in his hond.*
>
> (500-503)

Jewish violence here begins to destroy Jewish minds and threaten Jewish bodies. The proposed boiling of the host leads instead to Jonathas's proposed drowning.

That the torment of Christian body results instead in the destruction of Jews is made absolutely clear and literal in the play's next scene. The crazed

Jonathas is physically restrained by his companions (504-7), and, in the play's second reenactment of the Crucifixion, the clinging host is nailed to a post:

> Here is an hamer and nailys thre, I s[e]ye.
> Liffte up his armys, felawe[s], on hey,
> Whill I drive thes[e] nailys, I yow praye,
> With strong strokys fast.
>
> (508-11)

Of course, since Jonathas's hand is attached to the host, it too is nailed to the post. Here, the tortured and torturer are almost merged with each other; the Jews, in crucifying Christ, guarantee for themselves a kind of crucifixion.

Jonathas's fellows now try to free him by pulling him away from the host; they succeed, however, only in pulling him away from his own hand:

> *Masphat.* Now set on, felouse, with maine and might,
> And pluke his armes awey in fight!
> [*They try to pull Jonathas from the host.*]
> W[h]at? I se he twicche, felouse, aright!
> Alas, balys breweth right badde!
> *Here shall thay pluke the arme, and the hand shall*
> *hang still with the sacrament.*
> *Malchus.* Alas, alas, what devill is this?
> Now hat[h] he but oon hand, iwis!
>
> (512-17)

The dismembered Jewish "mayster" (518) and his companions, routed by their victim, now retreat for a time from the scene of torture and of their own humiliation.

At this point, the play moves briefly away from its concentration on the Eucharist to introduce two new characters, the physician "Mayster Brendiche of Braban" (533) and his servant Colle. The scene that follows is often treated as a comic interpolation having little to do with the main action, but, in its emphasis on the body and bodily rebellions, it clearly has thematic connections to the remainder of the play:[33]

All manar of men that have any siknes,
To Master Brentberecly loke that yow redresse!
What disease or siknesse that ever ye have,
He will never leve yow till ye be in yow[r] grave.
Who hat[h] the canker, the collike, or the laxe,
The tercian, the quartan, or the brynni[n]g axs;
For wormys, for gnawing, grindi[n]g in the wombe or in the boldyro;
All maner red eyn, bleryd eyn, and the miegrim also;
For hedache, bonache, and therto the tothache;
The colt-evill, and the brostyn men he will undertak[e],
All tho that [have] the poose, the sneke, or the tyseke.
Thow[g]h a man w[e]re right heyle, he cowd soone make him sek[e]!
Inquire to the colkote, for ther is his logging . . .

(608-20)

Colle and Master Brendiche thus comically bring to our attention all the ills to which flesh is heir and all the ways in which the physician of the flesh can intensify those ills. As the scene draws to its close, Jonathas's wound is explicitly associated with all the "hurtys" and "hermes" (637) that receive medical attention. Colle suggests that the good doctor make him a patient: "Here is a Jewe, hight Jonathas,/ Hath lost his right hond" (628-29).

Jonathas, however, concerned to keep his dismemberment under wraps (see lines 520-24 and 638-45), violently refuses the physician's advances:

Avoide, fealows; I love not yowr bable! [*To his servants.*]
Brushe them hens bothe, and that anon!
Giff them there reward that they were gone!
*Here shall the four Jewys bett away the leche and his
man.*

(649-51)

Having, in the physician episode, kept body prominently in the foreground, the play now returns to its central problem—the Jewish treatment of the host and the host's effect on Jewish body—with a vengeance. In action that parodies the deposition of Christ's crucified body, the Jews "pluck owt the nailys" (658, 662) and cover the host "in a clothe" (659).

But, instead of burial, the crucified body and attached hand now receive more torment. The cauldron, prepared earlier, is finally put to use:

> *Jason.* . . . . into the cawdron I will it cast.
> *Jasdon.* And I shall with this daggere so stowte
> Putt it down that it might plawe,
> And steare the clothe rounde abowte
> That nothing thereof shal be rawe.
> *Masphat.* And I shall manly, with all my might,
> Make the fire to blase and brenne,
> And sett thereundere suche a light
> That it shall make it right thinne.
>
> (664-72)

The torture of the host now necessarily also entails Jewish self-torture. And despite the new trial to which it is subjected, the host remains miraculously intact, continuing to prove its vitality by means of copious bleeding:

> Owt and harow, what devill is herein?
> All this oile waxith redde as blood,
> And owt of the cawdron it beginnith to rin!
> I am so aferd I am nere woode.
>
> (673-76)

On the other hand, Jewish flesh is destroyed—"The hand is soden, the fleshe from the bonys" (706)—finally becoming separable from the host, but not before it is has lost its own substance.

Confounded, the Jews nonetheless do not halt their violent attacks on the integrity of the host. To "stanche his bleeding chere" (687), they prepare a redhot oven (683-84), and, handling the host with self-protective care, they cast it into the oven:

> I shall with thes[e] pinsonys, withowt dowt,
> Shake this cake owt of this clothe,
> And to the ovyn I shall it rowte
> And stoppe him thow[gh] he be loth.
>
> (701-4)

In a final attempt to overcome the wafer, the Jews enclose it in a sealed structure (reminiscent of Christ's tomb) and try to bake the life out of it:

I stoppe this ovyn, withowtyn dowte;
With clay I clome it uppe right fast,
That non[e] heat shall cum owtte.
I trow there shall he hete and drye in hast!
(709-12)

This last-ditch attempt of course also fails. In the most "mervelows case" (716) yet, "This ovyn b[l]edith owt on every side" (714) and finally "ginnith to rive asundre" (715). The prison/tomb constructed to contain the host (like Hell faced by the power of the crucified Christ) loses its own physical integrity. And now not only does the host maintain its wholeness and ability to bleed, it is miraculously transformed into "an image" of Christ himself, "with woundys bleding" (712, 716).

The Jews are now confronted by incontrovertible proof of the host's identity with Christ, and (as if the bleeding image itself were not enough) Christ addresses the Jews directly, interrogating their motives in what is a condemnation of all Jewish disbelief:

Why blaspheme yow me? Why do ye thus?
Why put yow me to a newe tormentry,
And I died for yow on the crosse?
Why considere not yow what I did crye?
While that I was with yow, ye ded me velanye.
Why remembere ye nott my bittere chaunce,
How yowr kinne did me avance
For claiming of min[e] enheritaunce?
I shew yow the streitnesse of my grevaunce,
And all to meve yow to my mercy.
(731-40)

Faced directly by the body of Christ that they have been tormenting, the Jews suddenly convert, begging forgiveness for their misdeeds (741-61). They recognize finally that their violence presents a true danger not to Christ but to themselves: "Lord, I have offendyd the[e] in many a sundry wise./ That stickith at my hart as hard as a core" (758-59). As Christ himself makes explicit to Jonathas, Jewish pain and dismemberment result from the Jews' own attempts to inflict pain:

Ser Jonathas, on thin[e] hand thow art but lame,
And this thorow[gh] thin[e] own cruelnesse.
For thin[e] hurt thou mayest thyselfe blame:
Thow woldist preve thy powre me to oppresse.
                                                    (770-73)

Now, however, that Jonathas has given up the will "to oppresse" and "mekely" begs for "mercy" (745), his body can be restored. Christ recognizes the Jew's "grete contricion" (775) and miraculously heals him:

Go to the cawdron—thy care shal be the lesse—
And towche thin[e] hand, to thy salvacion.
*Here shall ser Jonathas put his hand into the
cawdron, and it shal be [w]hole again . . .*
                                                    (776-77)

This final bodily miracle dramatizes what is the central point of much of the play's action. Corruption of body attends disbelief, attacking those who presume to attack the fabric of Christianity; wholeness of body, on the other hand, comes with true belief. No matter how battered or wounded, the body of Christ, the host of the Eucharist, and those who partake of that body (even the newly converted Jonathas), can never lose their essential integrity and life.

Appropriately enough, the Croxton *Play* ends with a long communal ritual in which the chastened Jews are accepted into the body of the Christian community and that community reaffirms its intimate connection to the suffering but living body of Christ. The bishop, informed by Jonathas about what has happened, leads his people to "*the Jewys howse*" (813), where Christ's image, "A child appering with wondys blody" (804), remains. There, as in The Prioress's Tale, the martyr's suffering is felt vicariously in the body of the Church:

O Jhesu, fili Dei,
How this painfull Passion rancheth mine[e] hart!
Lord, I crye to the[e], *miserere mei,*
From this rufull sight thou wilt reverte!
Lord, we all, with sorowys smert,
For this unlefull work we live in langowr.
                                                    (814-19)

In response to the bishop's prayer for "grace," "marcy," and "peté," "the im[a]ge change[s] again into brede" (820-25), and the bishop now leads a community wholly unified in its dedication to the Eucharistic ritual:

Now will I take this holy sacrament
With humble hart and gret devocion,
And all we will gon with on[e] consent
And beare it to chirche with sole[m]pne procession.
Now folow me all and summe!
And all tho that bene here, both more and lesse,
This holy song, *O sacrum convivium*,
Lett us sing all with grett swetnesse.

(834-41)

"All" are finally united in "devocion" to the Eucharist. Aristorye repents and confesses that he "sold our Lordys body for lucre of mony" (902); he receives an appropriate penance, "nevermore for to bye nore sell" (915). The bishop bids him, in recompense for what he has helped do to Christ's body: "Chastis[e] thy body as I shall the[e] tell,/ With fasting and pray[i]ng and othere good wirk" (916-17). The Jews, who have already received their bodily penance, recapitulate, in a confessional mode, their crimes against the host (932-47) and pray for "a generall absolucion" (930) and "to be christenyd" (950). The bishop complies; Jonathas promises "Owr wickyd living for to restore . . . Never to offend as we have don before" (965-67); and the play ends with praise of Christ.

III. Conclusion

In the Croxton *Play of the Sacrament*, body thus shows itself to be, at one and the same time, wonderfully invulnerable and horribly corruptible. The body of the host and of Christ—passive, wounded, bloodied—is finally shown to be inviolate, uncontainable, capable of a miraculous healing. Jewish body, powerfully violent, succeeds ultimately in attacking only itself; it disintegrates and can only become whole by ceasing to be Jewish. These two kinds of body exist, as in The Prioress's Tale, in intimate connection to each other. The violence of Jewish body makes possible the miraculous suffering and survival of the host; the miracles of Christian body lead inexorably to Jewish dismemberment and disintegration. The images of hand and host crucified as one, of "bread" and "bone" boiled together, vividly depict the inseparability of the two kinds of body—one holy, tortured, yet vital; the other corrupt and violent, powerful, yet falling to pieces.

The intimate linking of Christian bodily miracles to the violence of Jews and to the dismemberment and disintegration of their bodies betrays an intense ambivalence in the late Middle Ages about body itself. On the one hand, as Bynum has shown, body—attacked, stabbed, boiled, baked, yet miraculously intact, alive, and enlivening—stands at the center of Christian ritual. This is the body of the crucified Christ, of the Eucharist, of the Christian martyrs and their relics, of the devout ascetic. But late-medieval Christianity does not simply embrace the bodies that link it to the archetypal body of Christ. Even as it celebrates the miraculous virtues of its own beleaguered bodies, it finds bodies to attack—the strange bodies of Jews, bodies suffering from "peculiar and secret afflictions,"[34] bodies broken but in no way to be identified with the broken body of Christ.

The relation of Jewish bodies to the bodies of Christian ritual is complex, as the complicated interactions between them in both The Prioress's Tale and the Croxton *Play of the Sacrament* show. Any attempt fully to explain that relation must take into account a broader range of historical, cultural, and literary material than I can here. I will only present one tentative suggestion. It is as though the deep involvement of medieval Christianity in body—the consumption of blood and flesh in the mass; the faith in the power of relics; the focusing of attention on food and on bodily exudings[35]—creates a correspondingly deep *nervousness* about body. Are these rituals and beliefs primitive, magical, even cannibalistic? Of course, such a question cannot be directly asked by Christians about the central ritual of Christianity. But anxiety can be projected outward, onto foreign bodies. Jews who needed to drink the blood of Christian innocents to be made whole; Jews who destroyed bodies for their own primitive, magical rituals and who were, in turn, dismembered—these could be imagined, created, and controlled.

Notes

1. Chaucer quotations are from *The Riverside Chaucer*, 3rd ed., gen. ed. Larry D. Benson (Boston: Houghton Mifflin, 1987).

2. As we see in a poem like *Pearl*, gemstones are often in the Middle Ages emblems of purity and completeness.

3. See Caroline Walker Bynum's recent work, especially *Jesus as Mother: Studies in the Spirituality of the High Middle Ages* (Berkeley and Los Angeles: Univ. of California Press, 1982), pp. 110-265; "Women Mystics and Eucharistic Devotion in the Thirteenth Century," *Women's Studies* 11 (1984): 179-214; "'. . . And Women His Humanity': Female Imagery in the Religious Writing of the Later Middle Ages," in *Gender and Religion: On the Complexity of Symbols*, ed. Caroline Walker Bynum, Stevan Harrell, and Paula Richman (Boston: Beacon Press, 1986), pp. 257-88; and *Holy Feast and Holy Fast: The Religious Significance of Food to Medieval Women* (Berkeley and Los Angeles: Univ. of California Press, 1987).

4. Contributing importantly to such negative evaluations of the worth of body are Neopla-

tonic and Biblical (especially Pauline) traditions. See, for instance, Macrobius, *Commentary on the Dream of Scipio*, trans. William Harris Stahl (New York: Columbia Univ. Press, 1952), 1.11.3 and Galatians 5.17.

5. Bynum, *Holy Feast and Holy Fast*, pp. 294-95.

6. Giovanni Boccaccio, *The Corbaccio*, trans. Anthony K. Cassell (Urbana: Univ. of Illinois Press, 1975), p. 24. The misogyny of Boccaccio's *Corbaccio* even goes so far as to deny the Virgin Mary a real female body: ". . . that only Bride of the Holy Spirit was such an undefiled, virtuous being, so pure and full of grace, and so completely remote from every corporeal and spiritual uncleanness, that in respect to the others, it is as if She were not composed of natural elements but were formed of a quintessence fit to be the dwelling place and hostelry for the Son of God, Who, wishing to become flesh for our salvation, prepared Her for Himself *ab eterno* as a worthy abode for such and so great a King, in order not to come and inhabit the pigsty of modern womanhood" (pp. 32-33). Such a view, of course, is related to the controversial doctrine of the Immaculate Conception.

7. Bynum, *Holy Feast and Holy Fast*, p. 209.

8. R. I. Moore, *The Formation of a Persecuting Society: Power and Deviance in Western Europe 950-1250* (Oxford: Basil Blackwell, 1987), pp. 58-59.

9. Moore, *The Formation of a Persecuting Society*, p. 60. It is, of course, the very repellent, degraded quality of the leper's body that allows it to play a part in Christian spirituality, in the embracing of suffering flesh that is Christ. Still, leprosy is not only embraced but vigorously pushed away. For more on medieval ambivalence about leprosy, see Moore, *The Formation of a Persecuting Society*, pp. 60-61. For a full treatment of medieval attitudes toward leprosy, see Saul N. Brody, *The Disease of the Soul: Leprosy in Medieval Literature* (Ithaca: Cornell Univ. Press, 1974).

10. John Boswell, *Christianity, Social Tolerance, and Homosexuality: Gay People in Western Europe from the Beginning of the Christian Era to the Fourteenth Century* (Chicago and London: Univ. of Chicago Press, 1980), p. 292.

11. Boswell, *Christianity, Social Tolerance, and Homosexuality*, p. 329. See further Boswell's treatment of the late-medieval "rise of intolerance," pp. 269-334; and see Moore's brief discussion, *The Formation of a Persecuting Society*, pp. 91-94.

12. For more on the myth of male menstruation among Jews, see Joshua Trachtenberg, *The Devil and the Jews: The Medieval Conception of the Jew and its Relation to Modern Anti-Semitism* (Philadelphia: The Jewish Publication Society of America, 1983), pp. 149 and 228 n.27; Léon Poliakov, *Histoire d l'antisemitisme: Du Christ aux juifs de tour*, vol. I (Paris: Calmann-Lévy, 1955), p. 160; and Sander L. Gilman, *Jewish Self-Hatred: Anti-Semitism and the Hidden Language of the Jews* (Baltimore and London: The Johns Hopkins Univ. Press, 1986), pp. 74-75 and 403 n.13.

13. Trachtenberg, *The Devil and the Jews*, p. 50.

14. Ibid., pp. 50-51, 140-55. Also see Poliakov, *Histoire de l'antisemitisme*, p. 160; and Gilman, *Jewish Self-Hatred*, p. 75.

15. See, for instance, Guibert of Nogent's description of a massacre of Jews associated with the First Crusade, *Self and Society in Medieval France: The Memoirs of Abbot Guibert of Nogent (1064?-c. 1125)*, ed. by John R. Benton, trans. C. C. Swinton Bland [revised by Benton] (New York: Harper & Row, 1970), pp. 134-35; and see Cecil Roth, *A History of the Jews in England*, 3rd ed. (Oxford: Clarendon Press, 1964), for descriptions of anti-Jewish violence at London in 1189, 1215, and 1263 (pp. 19-20, 36, 61-62) and at York in 1190 (pp. 22-24, 272).

We could, of course, multiply the instances of marginalized groups treated, in the late Middle Ages, as in possession of degraded bodies. See, for instance, Moore's discussion of heretics, *The Formation of a Persecuting Society*, esp. pp. 60-65, for the suggestion that heretics, Jews, and lepers all resemble each other "in being associated with flesh, stench and putrefaction, in exceptional sexual voracity and endowment, and in the menace which they presented in consequence to the wives and children of honest Christians" (p. 64); and see Moore's brief discussion of female prostitutes, pp. 94-98.

16. Bynum's work has been especially important in bringing body to our renewed attention; see the references in note 3 above. Recent work on medieval medicine also reflects a deep interest in the treatment of body; see, for instance, Danielle Jacquart and Claude Thomasset, *Sexuality and Medicine in the Middle Ages*, trans. Matthew Adamson (Princeton: Princeton Univ. Press, 1988); and Mary R. Wack, *Lovesickness in the Middle Ages* (Philadelphia: Univ. of Pennsylvania Press, 1990). All this work takes its place in a more general renewal of interest in the body's historical and literary importance. See, for instance, Peter Brown, *The Body and Society: Men, Women and Sexual Renunciation in Early Christianity* (New York: Columbia Univ. Press, 1988) and see Elaine Starry, *The Body in Pain: The Making and Unmaking of the World* (New York and Oxford: Oxford Univ. Press, 1985).

17. For an overview of the critical issues involved in reading the *Prioress's Tale*, see Florence H. Ridley, *The Prioress and the Critics*, University of California Publications: English Studies 30 (Berkeley and Los Angeles: Univ. of California Press, 1965). For various treatments of the tale's anti-Semitism, see R. J. Schoeck, "Chaucer's Prioress: Mercy and Tender Heart," *The Bridge: A Yearbook of Judaeo-Christian Studies* 2 (1956): 239-55 (reprinted in *Chaucer Criticism*, ed. Richard J. Schoeck and Jerome Taylor, vol. I [Notre Dame, Ind.: Univ. of Notre Dame Press, 1960], pp. 245-58); Sherman Hawkins, "Chaucer's Prioress and the Sacrifice of Praise," *JEGP* 63 (1964): 599-624; Ridley, *The Prioress*; Edward H. Kelly, "By Mouth of Innocentz: The Prioress Vindicated," *PLL* 5 (1969): 362-74; Albert B. Friedman, "The *Prioress's Tale* and Chaucer's Anti-Semitism," *ChauR* 9 (1974): 118-29; John C. Hirsch, "Reopening the *Prioress's Tale*," *ChauR* 10 (1975): 30-45; Hardy Long Frank, "Chaucer's Prioress and the Blessed Virgin," *ChauR* 13 (1979): 346-62; and John Archer, "The Structure of Anti-Semitism in the *Prioress's Tale*," *ChauR* 19 (1984): 46-54. Friedman suggests that anti-Semitism is largely "incidental" to the tale (p. 127), as does Frank (p. 358). Hawkins claims that "Anti-Semitism in the usual sense is quite beside the point" (p. 604); see Archer's brief reply (p. 46). I believe that the tale displays a deep anti-Semitism, manifested largely on the ground of the body.

18. Interestingly, toward the tale's beginning, Cecilia warns her new husband, Valerian, that the angel who guards her will execute him if he insists on having sex with her: "And if that he may feelen, out of drede,/ That ye me touche, or love in vileynye,/ He right anon wol sle yow with the dede,/ And in youre yowthe thus ye shullen dye . . ." (155-58). However, at no point in the tale do divine powers actually move to save Christians from martyrdom.

19. On Hugh of Lincoln, see Gavin I. Langmuir, "The Knight's Tale of Young Hugh of Lincoln," *Speculum* 47 (1972): 459-82.

20. This move is especially interesting in light of the absence of Jews from fourteenth-century England. The threat that is thus made present to Chaucer's audience is immediately (indeed, preemptively) contained or negated (by the expulsion of 1290), just as the Jewish threat within the tale is eliminated as soon as it is revealed.

21. In the statement, "The blood out crieth on youre cursed dede" (VII.578), Chaucer invokes the archetypal biblical account of victimization, Cain's murder of Abel. Compare Genesis 4.10: "dixitque ad eum: quid fecisti? vox sanguinis fratris tui clamat ad me de terra" [And He [God] said to him: "What have you done? The voice of your brother's blood cries out to me from the earth"] (my translation). See Archer, "The Structure of Anti-Semitism" (p. 48). The line also perhaps calls to mind the (Jewish) crowd's response to Pilate, Matthew 27.25: "et respondens universus populus dixit: sanguis eius super nos et super filios nostros" [and the whole people responding said: "Let his blood be on us and on our children"] (my translation).

Critical Insights

22. Perhaps the problem of a suffering Christianity that nonetheless holds power and itself inflicts suffering is meant to be minimized in the tale by the separation of the roles of abbot (sufferer) and provost (punisher). See Kelly's suggestion that the provost is, in fact, a non-Christian, "gentile" authority ("By Mouth of Innocentz," p. 368). However, any separation between religious and secular authority is mitigated by the provost's explicit association with Christian piety at the very moment he moves to punish the Jews: "He cam anon withouten tariyng,/ And herieth Crist that is of hevene kyng,/ And eek his mooder, honour of mankynde,/ And after that the Jewes leet he bynde" (VII.617-20). See Howard's comments on the "Chaucerian irony" of this passage—"which underscores the travesty of justice that takes place" (Donald R. Howard, *The Idea of the Canterbury Tales* [Berkeley and Los Angeles: Univ. of California Press, 1976], p. 277.)

23. In *Medieval Drama*, ed. David Bevington (Boston: Houghton Mifflin Company, 1975), pp. 754-88.

24. Cecilia Cutts, in "The Croxton Play: An Anti-Lollard Piece," *MLQ* 5 (1944): 45-60, argues that "the play was a deliberate piece of anti-Lollard propaganda composed and presented for the purpose of strengthening the faith of the people in the face of heretic teachings and influences" (p. 45). Sister Nicholas Maltman, in "Meaning and Art in the Croxton *Play of the Sacrament*," *ELH* 41 (1974): 149-64, sees the play's "purpose [as] the clear, accurate, vivid statement of the meaning of the Blessed Sacrament" (p. 149): "The impulse behind the play was undoubtedly pastoral and didactic; the message of the play is doctrinal, its matrix liturgical, and its tone serious" (p. 162). Richard L. Homan, in "Devotional Themes in the Violence and Humor of the *Play of the Sacrament*," *Comparative Drama* 20 (1986-87): 327-40, suggests that the play, concerned with "man's sinfulness, the Passion, the Eucharist, and Christ as child and as conqueror," is written "in the manner of serious devotional art" (p. 339). Indeed, G. R. Owst, in *Literature and Pulpit in Medieval England* (Cambridge: Cambridge University Press, 1933), proposes that "the Croxton drama of *The Sacrament* suffices . . . to show how a favourite pulpit story setting forth the miraculous virtues of the Host could be dramatized . . . direct from the preacher's notebook" (p. 490).

25. Indeed, critics have consistently denied the anti-Semitism of the *Play of the Sacrament*. See Cutts "The Croxton Play"; Maltman "Meaning and Art"; and David Bevington, *Tudor Drama and Politics: A Critical Approach to Topical Meaning* (Cambridge: Harvard Univ. Press, 1968), pp. 38-39. Homan, "Devotional Themes," concludes, more nervously, that, while it "derives from two especially odious articles of anti-Semitism," the play finally "addresses concerns important to the Christian community of fifteenth-century England . . . not in the manner of anti-Semitic ridicule but in the manner of serious devotional art" (339). While I would not want to deny the play's "serious devotional" intent, neither should we ignore what is manifestly anti-Semitic in it. To assume, as the play does, that human beings can be redeemed only through Christianity is in itself anti-Semitic. Further, as the following discussion will show, the depiction of the Jews, although milder than it might be, remains deeply troubling, particularly in its treatment of Jewish body.

26. "The Banns" occupy the first eighty lines of text.

27. Bevington, *Tudor Drama and Politics*, p. 38 (emphasis mine).

28. It is perhaps significant that one of the Jewish captors and tormentors of the host is named Malchus (the play's other Jews are Jonathas, Jason, Jasdon, and Masphat). Malchus is, in John's gospel account of the betrayal of Jesus, the high priest's servant whose right ear is cut off by Simon Peter (John 18.10). The association of bodily dismemberment with the betrayal of Christ, thus present in the brief account of the Biblical Malchus, is, as I will show, a central theme of the Croxton *Play*.

29. See Trachtenberg, *The Devil and the Jews*, pp. 15 and 17.

30. Compare line 203: "And thus by a conceite the[y] woude make us blind."

31. See Isaiah 63.1, typically read as a prophecy of Christ's Crucifixion: "quis est iste qui venit de Edom tinctis vestibus de Bosra" [who is this who comes from Edom, in dyed garments

from Bosra] (my translation). The Jews here adopt a Christian reading of the Old Testament, and their own words thus challenge their skepticism about Christian doctrine.

32. The "three howrys" here (and the "thre galons of oile clere" later in the passage [493]) call to mind the three days between Christ's Crucifixion and Resurrection, during which time Christ harrows the "furnace" and "cauldron" of Hell. The Harrowing and Resurrection are evoked again later in the play.

33. See also the readings of Maltman, "Meaning and Art," pp. 153-54, and Homan, "Devotional Themes," pp. 332-35. Maltman's proposal that Brendiche—"the quack, who gives ointment and potions that bring the patient not to life but to the grave"—stands here in opposition to "Christ the true physician" (p. 153), is especially attractive, given Christ's role in the following sections of the play.

34. Trachtenberg, *The Devil and the Jews*, p. 50.

35. See Bynum, *Holy Feast and Holy Fast.*

Critical Insights

Naturalism and Its Discontents in the *Miller's Tale*

Mark Miller

One of the most striking moments in the *Miller's Tale* is the one in which Absolon, waiting in the dark at Alisoun's window for a long-anticipated kiss, finds himself savoring the taste not of her mouth but of the "hole" she has so unceremoniously proffered:

> This Absolon gan wype his mouth ful drie.
> Derk was the nyght as pich, or as the cole,
> And at the window out she putte hir hole,
> And Absolon, hym fil no bet ne wers,
> But with his mouth he kiste hir naked ers
> Ful savourly, er he were war of this.
> Abak he stirte, and thoughte it was amys,
> For wel he wiste a womman hath no berd.
> He felte a thyng al rough and long yherd,
> And seyde, "Fy! allas! what have I do?"[1]

This moment has long been seen as central to the Miller's aim of "quiting" the *Knight's Tale* by deflating that tale's romantic and philosophical ambitions, baring the most basic natural facts of human animality, bodiliness, and desire which the Knight and his characters, and their surrogates in the *Miller's Tale*, seem so intent on sublimating.[2] On this account Absolon, who throughout the tale has seemed more interested in adopting a theatrical posture of love-longing than in attaining any erotic payoff, is finally brought into intimate and unmistakable contact with "the real nature of what he sought"; and with this unveiling of the real object of human, or at least masculine, desire, the perverse displacements of desire operating in the lyrical complaints and philosophical speeches of the *Knight's Tale* are supposed to become compellingly clear.[3] Recently, however, the intelligibility of this account of the moment and the coherence of the views that surround it have begun to come into question. The action has centered on questions about what it means for Alisoun, who throughout the tale has functioned as the ultimate object of desire, to present her "hole" to be kissed, and so at this fateful moment to become not merely an object but an agent; about the fact that there are after all several holes conflated here, and what it means for this hole, nominally an ass, to have lips and hair, or at the very least to seem to; and on how we are to interpret the fact that there are questions and conflations here at all, given the Miller's apparent insistence that there should not be any, since what this moment is supposed to reveal is a determinate, compelling, and naturally given object of desire.[4] I think these are good questions to be asking, as far as they go; but, as I will suggest, I do not think we can return accurate or full answers to them if we focus too exclusively on the most immediate issues they raise.

These issues, obviously enough I take it, concern gender identity and erotic desire, both of which, under the pressure of the questions posed, begin to look considerably less "natural" than we have usually taken them to be here—or, for that matter, than the Miller seems to take them to be. This seems right enough: as I will suggest, one thing the weird sexiness of this moment expresses is an unsettling mobility of desire and a porousness of gender identification the very possibility of which naturalism must deny. This is part of what I mean in referring to "naturalism and its discontents," and understood properly I think it brings with it significant consequences not only for a reading of the *Miller's Tale* but for an understanding of Chaucer's project in the *Canterbury Tales* as a whole. For if the edifice of the Miller's naturalism begins to crumble, then the relationship between the Knight's and Miller's tales cannot be adequately formulated in the terms in which it mostly has been, as the opposition of one distinct mode of consciousness or view of human nature by another; and as a result Chaucer's aim in leading off the *Canterbury Tales* with the sequence we find in Fragment I needs reformulating as well.[5] But a hasty focus on the surprising constructions of gender and eros in the *Miller's Tale* brings with it risks of its own, not the least of which is a tendency to discount far too quickly the force of the naturalistic views at work in the tale, trivializing their sources as merely ideological and self-serving, worthy of exposure and little more.[6] If an older generation of critics bypassed the problems raised by naturalism by imagining for it the coherence of a perfect formal structure, a more recent one has bypassed those problems just as effectively by imagining that those problems are all-too-easily identifiable, and that a constructivist account of gender and desire provides a kind of prophylactic against naturalistic false consciousness, a privileged position from which its errors can be seen for what they are and so avoided. As I will suggest, each of these critical attitudes participates in naturalistic fantasy no less thoroughly than does the Miller.

But my argument in this essay does not primarily concern critical methodology. It is rather an argument about what naturalism is in the first place, and how it is related to the phenomena it figures as normal and those it figures as perverse. What interests Chaucer here, I think, is not so much the sheer error in the Miller's views as the fact that those views are so compelling: they fit together into a picture of the human creature that, however problematic, has a deep claim. Part of the source of this claim, in turn, stems from the way naturalism links a set of normative intuitions about gender and desire to a broader theory of normativity as such, a theory of what it means for the human creature, to adapt Paul's famous phrase, to "be a law to itself."[7] As I will suggest, it is not easy to bring into clear view the claim this broader naturalistic picture exerts. But it is only by investigating the depth of this claim that we can begin to account for the pressures the Miller's conceptions of gender and desire, and his broader conception of the human animal, are under; and it is only by pursuing an account of those pressures that we can understand how the ideological regime of the normal expressed in this tale gets constructed and inhabited. I will begin, then, with an attempt to identify what could be meant by the most commonplace of critical notions, the "naturalism of exceptional force and vitality" that, however problematic, seems nevertheless to inform the entire tale.[8] If this at first takes us far away from the spectacular strangeness of Absolon's ill-fated kiss, I hope that by doing so it will enable us to return to that moment, and others that are perhaps less spectacular but just as interesting, and see in them a strangeness that is both more unsettling and more familiar than we otherwise might imagine.

I

As Muscatine, Kolve, and others have suggested, everything in the *Miller's Tale*, from narrative structure to characterization to tone to descriptive detail, suggests a picture of the human creature as a happy animal inhabiting a world in which it is perfectly at home.[9] Unlike the *Knight's Tale*, which takes place against a barren landscape in which all human projects seem to need elaborate management and are constrained by loss, absence, and ultimately death—so that, as Theseus says at the end of the tale, it seems that our true home must be somewhere else—the *Miller's Tale* represents a world of wonderful plenitude and freedom, alive with sensual experience and youthful energy, a place in which immersion in the pleasures of the here and now is all anyone could want. The central figure in this world is Alisoun, the object of desire that sets the plot and all of the male characters in motion; and, as the portrait of her that introduces her into the tale suggests, she functions both as the single most compelling instance of a desirable natural object and as a synecdoche for the plenitude of pleasures that the rest of nature offers: "She was ful moore blisful on to see/ Than is the newe pere-jonette tree,/ And softer than the wolle is of a wether" (I.3247-49); "Hir mouth was sweete as bragot or the meeth,/ Or hoord of apples leyd in hey or heeth" (I.3261-62). Alisoun's centrality to the plot's and characters' energies, the perfect natural sensuousness of her portrait, and her status as a readily available object of desire, "For any lord to leggen in his bedde,/ Or yet for any good yeman to wedde" (I.3269-70), all go to suggest two of the main ways in which the tale represents a world perfectly fitted to its human inhabitants, a world that is "the plaything of one's projects."[10] First, this is a place in which everything you could want seems to be ready to hand, present for the immediate gratification of desire. Second, it is one in which what you want is compellingly clear, and is made so just by the natural disposition of the world: unless you are a pervert or a fool, and an even bigger pervert or fool than even Absolon, what you want is Alisoun.

For now I want to pass over the obvious masculine, antifeminist, and heteronormative bias in this picture; the Miller pretty clearly has such a bias, and how and why it matters—and, in particular, what makes it more interesting than a mere occasion for critical exposure—will, I hope, become clear later. What needs clarifying first is just what it means to describe this picture as a species of naturalism.[11] Kolve puts the point well, if a bit too quickly, in saying that the tale represents "an animal world in which instinct takes the place that reason holds for man, a world in which instinct and necessity are one."[12] As Kolve's appeals to instinct and necessity suggest, his point is about the practical normativity of "the natural" here, the way it is supposed to settle questions of what to do, and so to take the place, at least initially, not of reason as a whole but of practical reason specifically. The tale presents a picture of human life according to which desire and its objects are determined by a set of naturally given facts: the fact that such a creature as Alisoun exists, for instance, is supposed to be enough to settle the matter when it comes to erotic desire, which is the Miller's central case. That much says, in effect, that nature determines both human ends, the goals towards which human action aims, and the human disposition towards those ends, the motivational structure by which they appear as goals for us. If instinct takes the place of reason in the tale, then, it does so first of all because according to the Miller's picture there is no role for reason to play either in deciding what our ends are or in giving those ends a normative claim on us, in making them count for us.

The Miller's project of "quiting" the Knight's Tale is to a large extent dependent on the success with which he can make the practical normativity of "the natural" seem both self-evident and exhaustive of any human needs that reason might address. The Knight's narrative centers on moments like Palamon and Arcite's paralyzed love for the inaccessible Emily, the destruction of individual and civil concord to which that love drives them, and the transfixion of nearly everyone in the tale by their grief over Arcite's death. These are moments in which the world is anything but the plaything of our projects, moments in which the objects of our desires seem to call to us as though from behind some barrier or from infinitely far away. Such moments of privation seem to the Knight and his characters to demand lyrical complaint or publicly edifying spectacle or efforts at philosophy, in each case as though the failure of desire to reach through to its object awakened a genuine need for several kinds of reflection: practical reasoning about what we really want or what we ought to do, and about how to make our beliefs about what to do effective at motivating us; but also speculative reasoning about who and what we are, about the nature of the world we inhabit, and about what it means that we suffer in the ways we do. But as far as the Miller is concerned there can be no genuine needs here of any kind. If our desires and their objects are transparent to us in just the way he thinks they are, then everything that counts about who we are and the world we live in must be transparent too; the reflective efforts of the Knight and his characters are not, as the Knight would have it, responses to privation, but ways of perversely generating a sense of privation where there is no genuine lack. The Miller must, then, make both practical and speculative reasoning seem perversely excessive from a practical point of view, willful acts of self-mystification by a creature for whom nature has already provided all that happiness could require. Only then will the impulse to reflection shown in the *Knight's Tale* become what it appears as in the *Miller's Tale*: the love Nicholas shows for his own cleverness in deferring sex with Alisoun in order to concoct an elaborate plan to fool John; the ridiculous and self-regarding posturing of Absolon as he sings silly love songs and plays Herod on a high scaffold; and John's gullible, worried concern with an end of the world that anyone can see is not about to come, a concern that diverts him from the cuckolding taking place nearly under his nose.

To achieve this further defeat of reason the Miller must do more than insist on the natural determination of human ends and their motivational transparency. For a world in which human desires and their objects were naturally determined could still leave plenty of room for the frustration of human happiness, even a world as rich and alive with desirable things as that of the *Miller's Tale*. We could face conditions in which it was not immediately obvious how to get what we want; then there would still, at the very least, be a practical role for reason to play in determining the means to our ends. Lyrical and philosophical reflection might not immediately be called for, but calculation would, and in the right (or wrong) circumstances the calculation required could be quite elaborate, and could still result in frustration. In the extreme case we could find ourselves with no means at all, and the objects of our desires would then remain tantalizingly out of reach, as Emily in her garden is for the imprisoned Palamon and Arcite. Such a condition would hardly allow for the glad animal spirits of the Miller's tale; a creature determined by instinct in just this way might just as well be nature's victim as nature's favored child. And what is worse, such a creature might easily form the *thought* of itself as nature's victim; then the door would be open wide to the complaint and speculation the Miller finds so nonsensical. For the creature that formed this thought would no longer merely suffer its frustrations as it were in animal fashion, just by coming up short in its reach for whatever it happens to want at the moment. It would have a conception of itself as a suffering creature, and this conception would add to its suffering in a myriad of ways, allowing for anticipation and fear of future suffering, despair of relief, and so on; such a creature might even, like Palamon in the *Knight's Tale*, come to envy the animals instead of identifying with them.[13] For the Miller's project to get off the ground, then, he must suggest not only that nature determines our ends and provides for their motivational transparency, but also that nature determines and provides the means to our ends; then the connection between desire and its objects will look completely seamless, and there will be no gaps left for practical reason to fill and speculative reason to reflect on.

The Miller manages this further suggestion partly through a wealth of descriptive detail that lays the circumstantial groundwork for the most central and the most trivial acts in the tale, so that the question of means can never so much as arise. Absolon may be reduced to courting Alisoun through her window, but the window is conveniently placed at a height that allows a kneeling lover to offer himself for a kiss; when Alisoun wants to chase Absolon off, there is a stone lying about in her bedroom, ready to be thrown; when Absolon wants to play Herod, there's a scaffold handy for his dramatic posturing, and when he wants revenge, there's a nearby blacksmith to lend a hot blade; when John's servant Robin wants to know what is happening behind Nicholas's locked door, he can peek through the hole the cat uses to creep in and out; and so on.[14] This descriptive density has the effect of suggesting a world so full of means to our ends that it is ready-made for human action. That is what drives the Miller's polemic against the Knight home, for in a world with the plenitude of utterly compelling pleasures that this one offers, and one so dense with all imaginable means to our ends, instinct can do all the work of mapping out a course of action, and there is no practical function left for reason to play. The proper thing to do in such a world is just to reach out and take what you want, as "hende" Nicholas does early in the tale with Alisoun when "prively he caughte hir by the queynte" (I.3276), and as he seems to forget in concocting his elaborate ruse.[15] And given the extent to which nature has prepared the way for human happiness, fitting the world so perfectly to human desire that there is no space even for the question of means to come up, there is no space either for the sense of privation and suffering that gives rise to speculative reasoning in the *Knight's Tale*. The direct target of the Miller's polemic is practical reason, then, because he thinks that by defeating the need for practical reason in the way he does he will provide all the argument he needs to insure the defeat of speculative reason as well. If there is any role left for reason to play in human life, it would seem to be restricted to the happy contemplation of our good fortune as creatures blessed by nature. This, in effect, is what the *Miller's*

Tale is supposed to be: a celebration of the blessed natural state of the human animal, a narrative expression of the particular pleasure we can take, as reflective creatures, in contemplating our inhabitation of a world that gives us everything we could want and ample opportunity to get it, a place in which there could never be a question for us about who we are or what we should do.[16]

I have meant the above account of the Miller's naturalism to be a way of spelling out the underlying conceptual commitments of what has been the almost universally accepted view of the tale and of Chaucer's interest in it. I think this view is right as far as it goes. It is right, that is, as an initial description of the Miller's project in the tale, of the work he wants the tale to do: he means it as an expression of these naturalistic attitudes, and as an invitation to his audience to recognize themselves in these attitudes as well. It is also right in suggesting the philosophical seriousness of the tale, the depth to which it engages the normative problems raised in the *Knight's Tale* rather than merely evading them with a joke: Chaucer means the tale as more than an occasion for laughs, and as more than the expression of a churlish man who simply fails to see what the Knight's concerns are.[17] But an articulation of these underlying views does not exhaust the Miller's investment in them or Chaucer's interest in them.[18] This further territory of interest begins to emerge when we attend, not just to the Miller's views themselves as a set of propositions about the world, but to the way he inhabits them, the range of claims they make on him, and the ways he disposes himself towards those claims.

The character of the Miller's investment here begins to look a bit more complex than one of simple belief if we notice a peculiar paradox that attends a project of the kind he pursues. The various features of the tale that support a normative naturalism are targeted against what the Miller takes to be the enemy, a perverse refusal to live in the world like the happy animals he thinks we are; and his polemical strategy is to hold the enemy up to a withering public laughter, first at the sheer folly of such a refusal, and second at the satisfying justice of the enemy's appropriate punishment, brought about by a series of narrative coincidences that seem to be less the effects of chance than signs of the natural order of things asserting themselves. What is peculiar about this, however, is that if anything like the Miller's naturalism were right, then there could not be such an enemy in the first place. If human desire and its objects were determined by a set of naturally given facts in such a way that instinct alone picked out our ends and made them transparent to us, then there would be no room for the perverse displacements of desire that the Miller is so interested in exposing. Anything anyone did would be neither more nor less than the sign of instinct's operative power; the possibilities for human action represented by the Knight, his characters, and their surrogates in the Miller's tale would either simply be impossible, and no one would do anything like them, or they would not be perverse, since if they did exist they would just be another set of ways for naturally determined desire to operate. This, then, is the problem: the point of the Miller's naturalism seems to be its recommendation of an ethos, a way of life suited to the human animal; but a naturalistic view of human action—at least one as thoroughgoing as that expressed in this tale—cannot have the normative force the Miller wants of it. It cannot recommend one way of life over another, since on such a view there can be no such thing as going wrong.[19]

The point is of course abstract, and it will take some time to suggest its upshot for an understanding of the tale; but it is, I think, the crucial step for understanding the discontents to which my title refers. The initial force of the paradox can perhaps best be seen if we notice a related problem about the motivation for telling a tale such as this. The Miller is clearly committed to a naturalistic repudiation of what he takes to be folly, paradox notwithstanding; that, on nearly everyone's account of the tale, is his main reason for telling it. His point seems to be that if there is such a thing as perversion, at least it can have no claim on him or those who think like him. But if we grant the thought, strictly unformulable in the Miller's terms, that the errors and perversions he parodies and punishes somehow do exist; and if we accept the supposed normative transparency of the natural, the plain fact as the Miller would have it that human desires and their objects are just there to be seen, perspicuous and inherently compelling; then those who suffer from such errors would hardly be enemies to be argued with. They would be more like pathetic madmen, inexplicably blocked from the world that is before their eyes, worthy perhaps of pity or of a quick mocking dismissal, but not of the sustained effort of a polemic. If the Miller's victory can be so easily won, and if what counts about ourselves and the world we inhabit is the joy we can take in our naturally blessed condition, then large portions of his narrative project look like a waste of time. He ought just to have left behind the aspects of his tale that mock the misguided and punish them for their foolishness, and have concentrated instead on straight appreciation of the world's bounty of the kind expressed in Alisoun's portrait. In this respect, then, the Miller's polemical project in the tale, with its elaborate dovetailing plot that functions like an intricate narrative machine to bring his point home, looks disturbingly like Nicholas's plan to cuckold John, an excessively clever construction designed to crush an enemy that needs no defeating, a perverse deferral of animal pleasure by a creature whose rational capacities have interposed themselves where they do not belong. In telling a tale that means to make normative claims of a naturalistic kind, the Miller locates himself both as the kind of creature for whom his own ethos cannot be right, and as the kind of creature who, in the terms of that ethos, is perverse.

The depth of the problem of perversity here begins to emerge if we imagine an alternative version of the tale that, unlike the Miller's, does concentrate on straight naturalistic appreciation.[20] Such a tale could still in a rather restricted sense have normative force: in its pure expression of glad animal spirits it could be taken to recommend itself as a model for human life. But it would not be able to give any expression to the normative problems to which it would be a response, the questions of what to do and how to live to which it would purport to give an answer: any such expression would be strictly ruled out from the beginning, since it would fall like a shadow across the tale's celebratory spirit, giving the lie to the views of human action and human motivation to which it must everywhere give voice. Such a tale would then be something more like a case of pure ideological posturing than the expression of an ethos, since its possibility would require a wholesale denial of the very problems that bring it into being. The *Miller's Tale* shares with this imagined case something of the quality of ideological posturing, since it too cannot squarely face the questions it purports to answer. But far from engaging in a wholesale denial of normative problems, the tale gives them loud expression in its polemical purpose. The Miller wants to recommend a way of life that the Knight and Absolon and their like are missing, and he wants to do so by exploring and exposing the error that leads them astray from their proper path. That motivation contaminates the Miller's naturalistic project from the ground up, as if in order to bring our condition as happy animals into view the Miller needed to cast it against an unaccountable perversion, an impossible possibility that, despite his apparent self-assurance, still does have a claim on him. What in the imagined case of pure naturalistic appreciation appeared only as a shadow slanting in from outside the narrative's scope appears here already on the inside, at the base of what sets the narrative in motion, at the heart of its deepest concerns. This shadow in the Miller's heart makes the relationship between the official naturalistic story and the inadmissible normative questions that motivate it more complex and unsettled than in the imagined case, and so makes of the *Miller's Tale* something considerably more interesting than a case of pure ideological bad faith.

What that something is might be put as follows. It is the most evident thing in the world to the Miller that humans can go wrong: he thinks that the Knight is wrong, that his whole romantic aristocratic ethos is wrong, that the social order that supports him and would squelch the Miller's voice in favor of a more suitable one is wrong. The Miller cares about this; it is what motivates his speech from the beginning. The problem of normativity, then—the problem humans face of trying to find a right way, and of wanting to say what such a way might be, what makes it right, and how we can follow it—is the problem he wants to address, just as the Knight does. But the Miller's way of addressing this problem is to wish that it would go away, or more precisely to wish that it could never have arisen, that we were the kind of creatures for whom it could not arise, like animals who really are just moved by instinct's operative power, or perhaps like small children who do not yet have the responsibility of owning up to a course of action and having reasons for it: it is the voice of a nostalgic longing for a condition of human animality that never was and never could have been.[21] Chaucer's project in the *Miller's Tale*, I would suggest, is one of exploring this response to the problem of normativity, of representing its expression in a way that opens up spaces for thought both about what makes such a response compelling and about some potential consequences of the attempt to think this way.

II

One such space can be found in a moment that unites the Miller's views of gender and desire with his larger normative concerns in a very general way—a way, in fact, that quite directly recalls the normative paradox I have just articulated. The moment I have in mind is the Miller's confrontation with the Reeve in the tale's Prologue. The Reeve has been angered by the Miller's announcement of a tale about the cuckolding of a carpenter, as though fears of his own wife's infidelity inclined him to take the coming story as a personal attack. The Miller replies by recommending to the Reeve his own attitude about such fears:

> I have a wyf, pardee, as wel as thow;
> Yet nolde I, for the oxen in my plogh,
> Take upon me moore than ynogh,
> As demen of myself that I were oon;
> I wol bileve wel that I am noon.
> An housbonde shal nat been inquisityf
> Of Goddes pryvetee, nor of his wyf.
> So he may fynde Goddes foyson there,
> Of the remenant nedeth nat enquere.
>   (I.3158-66)

The Miller wants this little piece of advice to communicate his sense of himself as a practical-minded purveyor of sound common sense, and up to a point this is just what the passage does. To judge yourself to be a cuckold, especially in the absence of convicting evidence, would reflect a pointless and excessive anxiety; the Reeve, like anyone else, would be much better off just believing that he is not one. The world, as we all can see, is full of God's plenty and we are free to taste of it. As long as we can do so we should be happy, and there should be no need to worry about "the remenant." This is advice straight from the heart of the naturalism that informs the tale. As in the tale, the world's plenitude is supposed to exempt us from the need to look beyond present satisfaction. Whatever is left over when a man is satisfied is God's concern, or his wife's, but not his, and any inquiry into it is supposed to be unnecessary, as excessive as a Reevish marital suspiciousness; to inquire into this "remenant" is just another way of erecting a barrier between oneself and the objects of one's desires, which are there for the taking. This advice is also clearly antifeminist. While antifeminism has more virulent strains—the Miller's attitude towards his wife, as towards Alisoun, is certainly a species of appreciation—"woman" as an object of appreciation here is fundamentally a means to an egocentric end, little more than a place for a man to find his own pleasure, as is suggested most starkly in the thought that the "there" in which he finds God's plenty is his wife's "pryvetee," that is her genitals, rather than her. That egocentric pleasure-seeking, in turn, is what constitutes his desire for her, as indeed it constitutes desire more broadly speaking throughout the tale. While a respect for his wife's "pryvetee," in the sense of her privacy, may seem to evade this identification of the masculine with the free activity of pleasure-seeking and the feminine with passive objectification, it is really part of the same attitude, a facile way of seeming to grant his wife her freedom while allowing himself to ignore her: what he cares about is getting his, that is what constitutes her value for him, and what she does in her spare time is of no consequence.[22]

The attitude this passage articulates is a familiar one, and finds frequent expression in the tale that follows. But however easily this passage can be recognized as the voice of a brand of patriarchal common sense, there is a duplicity in the Miller's rejoinder to the Reeve that calls into question just what we think we recognize here. The Miller says that he does not care about his wife beyond her role as a source of his pleasure, and more than that, that husbands need not care about their wives in any other way. This is what licenses his decision to believe that he is not a cuckold: his belief, even if false, is supposed to give nothing away, and adopting it saves him from the perverse self-frustrations of those who, like the Reeve, do not simply follow nature's course. If that is the case, however, the Miller should not need to believe that he is not a cuckold, especially if such belief amounts, as he says it does, to an act of will. As long as it does not interfere with his wife's erotic availability to him, her function as the ready-to-hand locus of his satisfactions, it just should not concern him whether or not he is a cuckold, and he should need no particular beliefs about the matter at all: he should, in effect, be even more careless than he manages to be.[23] The Miller's decision to adopt a belief in this regard suggests, then, that no matter how unconcerned he claims to be with his wife's private affairs, he is not content simply to take God's plenty where he finds it. Even if he were receiving all the "foyson" he could handle, he cannot cast his wife's private activities as a superabundance of plenty that does not concern him; the fact that she might have secrets, and the question of what those secrets might be, matters to him.

My point is not that the Miller is "really" afraid he is a cuckold. To locate the causal source of this passage's duplicities in some imagined antecedent psychological fact like a fear of cuckoldry would be to miss the scope of the problem the Miller faces: it is not merely personal, the sign of a bad marriage or a nervous character, and it is not restricted to the erotic context that provides its occasion.[24] The Miller's posture of carelessness towards his wife is part of a more general posture of carelessness towards "the remenant," towards whatever remains of the world's pleasures when he is done with them; and here as well the Miller does not manage to be as careless as his own views require. For it is one thing to say that we need not inquire into an innocent remainder, and quite another to say, as the Miller also does, that we should not be inquisitive. If we ought simply not to care about "the remenant" as long as the world's plenitude is available to us, then a prohibition of inquiry seems as oddly excessive as a decision to believe in one's wife's fidelity: "the remenant" should just be the sum of pleasures we do not find the occasion to enjoy, something that could never make a claim on us, something we would never need to confront or deny. But apparently God has his secrets too, secrets that, like a wife's, one may not want to know: the entire constitution of the world, or some coming fate—another flood perhaps—may make of the Miller's carelessness nothing more than a willful blindness, and he knows it. Under the pressure of the Miller's prohibition, then, another "remenant" seems to come into existence behind or beneath the "remenant" that is just the innocent remainder of untasted pleasures, a shadow-remainder that functions as a receptacle for things best kept out of sight.

This shadow-remainder haunts the Miller's picture of a world of plenty perfectly fitted to human desire in much the same way that the category of the perverse does. In each case, the Miller declares himself to be unimplicated in whatever possibilities shimmer into existence there: they are simply external to him, occupants of the empty spaces beyond the proper life of the human animal. And in each case, the declaration of non-implication is partly motivated by a claim that these empty spaces continue to exert. Further, in the face of this ongoing claim, the Miller's commitment to drawing a firm line between the natural and the perverse, between the all-encompassing space of God's plenty and the remainder where secrets go to hide, seems to leave him on both sides of the line at once, as a happy creature of nature and a secret pervert. God and his wife may be harboring damaging secrets, but the most damaging secrets seem to be the ones the Miller is harboring from himself, the inner companions to the metaphysical and erotic secrets that may be out in the world waiting for him.

A moment ago I said that my point is not that the Miller is really afraid he is a cuckold, and I want to be clear here that my point is not that he is really, secretly, a pervert. I do not mean to suggest that there just is some secret there, waiting to be exposed, but rather that a worry about secrecy, however muted by the Miller's loud avowals of carelessness, is the inevitable product of the way he responds to the normative problem. According to the Miller's naturalism, questions of what to do or how to live are settled by two fundamental relationships we have to the contents of our inner lives. The first is one of observation. Those contents, paradigmatically our desires, are introspectively available; all we need do to determine what they are is look and see the plain facts of nature in us. The second is one of passivity. Once we have seen what our desires are there is nothing further for us to do to make them effective at moving us; it is just of their essence that they reach through us, commanding us the way a desire for Alisoun or for one of those succulent ripe fruits on the "pere-jonette tree" is supposed to do. These two features together are what yield the motivational transparency of the natural on such a view. One of the problems with this, as I suggested earlier, is that in a sense it leaves no room for being wrong. Anything anyone does becomes the sign of a naturally determined desire's operative power, and thus if the reason an action counts as right is that it is natural, then any action will be right. But we might also say here that if the Miller wants to hold on to the notion of error and the category of perversity, as he clearly does, then if someone acts in a way the Miller deems to be perverse, then this too must be the sign of a naturally determined desire in operation: on this view it would just be a natural fact that some desires are perverse and the people who have them are perverts.[25] And this thought helps to specify the character of the problem the Miller faces in being the kind of creature who, in terms of his own ethos, is perverse. For if his way of conducting himself in the tale or elsewhere shows signs of motives that his naturalism does not endorse—signs, such as I have suggested are there in spades, of the ongoing claim of the perverse and of whatever constitutes that "remenant" no one is supposed to care about—then such motives on the Miller's own account can only be present in him as facts of his nature, the signs of a secret perverse self he never knew he was. The Miller's posture of carefree animality is supposed to insure that such secrets cannot exist. But the naturalism by means of which he seeks to justify this posture has the effect not of dispelling the possibility of such secrets but of reifying them into mysterious presences that then become the objects of a prohibition, an imperative not to look: what he means to be a way of dispelling any worries about metaphysical and erotic secrecy, the kinds of worries that seem to him to drive the Knight and the Reeve, only reinforces those worries by closeting them. One powerful form that the Miller's longing for a state of carefree animality takes, then, is something like a phenomenology of the closet, a relationship to a territory of secrecy which he is committed to saying does not exist and cannot matter, and which has the hold it does on him precisely by virtue of the way he seeks to deny it.[26] This is not to say that there are some naturally given facts in the Miller's closet, waiting to be known: the whole conception of a person's inner life as composed of determinate inner objects, available to introspection and compelling merely by virtue of one's knowledge of them, is part of the massive self-deception involved in the Miller's naturalism. The phenomenology of the closet at issue here is rather one in which a restless, unlocalizable worry appears not as the opposite of a careless self-gratification but as its hidden other face, the same thought in different form.[27]

III

I have suggested that the Miller responds to the problem of normativity in part by dispersing its claims into the various perversions represented in the tale, and that in doing so he locates them as the sites of an interior secrecy he does not want to examine. To understand the specific contours of those sites we need to look more closely at the perversions and the various fates they meet. The place to start, however, is not with the perversions themselves, but with what very nearly amounts to their opposite, the figure of Alisoun. For while she is the cornerstone of the normative views by which perversion is judged in the tale and by which eros and gender are brought within the orbit of the Miller's preferred version of the natural, this very function produces perverse effects that will help us understand what happens to Nicholas, Absolon, and John.

As the description of Alisoun as synecdoche for nature's plenitude and her function in the tale as the unmoved mover of male desire suggest, the narrative proceeds as though to be human is to be a man desiring a woman, and to be a woman is little more than to be the thing men desire—that is, as though the contrast between male and female straightforwardly tracked a contrast between activity and passivity, or more precisely between being a human agent and being a place, object, or locus of human activity; and further, as though a possessive masculine heterosexual desire were the only form desire could take.[28] What makes each of the male characters perverse from this perspective is the particular way each fails to respond properly to Alisoun, and so fails to participate adequately in the surrounding ideology of gender and desire. But there is an aspect of Alisoun's representation—and an absolutely fundamental one to her function in the tale—that cannot be accommodated to the set of oppositions on which these views of gender and desire are based. For the Miller means his picture of the human to have quite a general scope, to describe not just how it is for him, or even how it is for men, but how it is for everyone; and if any of his characters manages to exemplify this picture in its ideal form rather than a perversion or deformation of it, it is Alisoun.[29] She alone never acts in such a way as to erect an artificial barrier between herself and her own pleasure; she alone consistently lets instinct settle questions of what to do, or rather lets it prevent those questions from even arising; and as a result she alone remains unpunished by the crushing inevitability of cause and effect at the tale's end. The Miller, then, seems oddly to identify with Alisoun as the perfect exemplar of the human on his own account, the embodiment of the ethos he lays claim to and recommends, even as she also serves as a purely passive object of desire, the thing outside the all-male world of human action that sets it in motion.

If it is puzzling that Alisoun seems to serve mutually exclusive functions in the tale, as passive object and as perfect exemplar of human action, there is a sense in which this is just what we should expect from a figure of fully realized naturalism. Human action on such an account is, oddly, at its base a species of passivity, a way of being moved by forces to which we make no contribution: the only thing we do with respect to those forces is observe them, like objects in a kind of inner theater. Or alternatively, insofar as this view is supposed to be normative rather than descriptive—insofar as it is supposed to tell us what to do rather than just describing what it is we do—then when we act rightly, we do not make a contribution to these forces; the only contribution we can make, it seems, is the perverse one of turning our desires from their proper path. To say that the Miller identifies with Alisoun, then, is in part to say that she serves as the best figure for these two basic features of his view of human action, an underlying passivity on the one hand, and a spectatorial relationship to objects of desire on the other. That is why she never violates the tale's ethos, and is never violated by the operations of its plot. The fact that this also means that she is excluded from the territory of action into the status of an object, then, can help us clarify the sense in which the Miller suffers from a kind of nostalgic longing. For Alisoun's double function amounts to the recognition, however dim, that his view of human action is in fact a wish for escape from the conditions of human agency, a wish to be passive with respect to his own motivations, and so to become a pure and perfect object—a wish that is already foregone by the time it finds expression, since it arises, as I have said, precisely in response to the need to find a right way of acting.

This suggests that the problem with Alisoun's representation has an inwardly directed version as well: we might say that, as manly a man as the

Miller is, his own preferred version of himself looks like a woman, or at least like what he takes a woman to be. One occupant of the Miller's "remenant," then, is a wish to be, or be like, a woman, a wish that is quite directly the product of his most prevalent attitudes, even as it must be an embarrassment to them, a secret shame that can never be acknowledged. And more: if to be the perfect human is to be, or be like, a woman, we might just as well say what the narrative trajectory of the tale also suggests, that to be a man is to be perverse, and to deserve punishment. And here, too, we find support from the Miller's naturalistic views, for according to them to be a man—to be the active one, the doer, rather than the site, locus, or object of the action—is to make a contribution to the forces that move you, to interpose yourself between desire and its issuance in action: this is what the Miller and all his male characters do in failing to remain transparent to the motive force of natural desire. What emerges from the intersection of the Miller's naturalistic ethos with the gender views that seem so tightly bound to it, then, is a wish for a kind of effeminacy which takes the form of a desire to castigate whatever in him is masculine. This, in effect, is the gender-inflected form that his broader wish to escape his condition as an agent takes.

While the punishments visited on Nicholas, Absolon, and John are nominally directed towards external enemies, then, they are first of all directed on the Miller himself, ways of imagining a self-castigation that need never reveal itself as such. I will begin with Nicholas, for his case is the most straightforward, and remains most fully accommodated to the terms generated by the Miller's ethos. As I have already suggested, this "handy" man nearly remains faithful to the vision of a world provided for his own practical use, and his reward is a night "in bisynesse of myrthe and of solas" (I.3654) with Alisoun; and while his plan for cuckolding John exceeds the pure goal of appreciative immersion in the world's plenitude, it does so in much the same way as the Miller's tale does, and the Miller seems to regard it with gleeful enjoyment as much as suspicion. The punishment for Nicholas's tendency to defer animal satisfaction—the punishment the Miller brings on his own masculinity—is the humiliation and pain of anal penetration by Absolon's hot borrowed blade. The thought here seems to be, initially, that Nicholas, having displaced his erotic impulse into the more intellectual pleasure of a carefully orchestrated trickery, needs to be brought back to the material fact of his body by way of pain. Pain, then, is supposed to do what eros was initially supposed to do but could not, for the Miller any more than for Nicholas: provide a territory of sheer animal sensation incapable of being gotten wrong, incapable of being rerouted or reinterpreted, a sensation that can just be seen for what it is, and that, being seen, presents an agent with a transparent motive, in this case a motive to cry out and seek relief. Part of what counts about Nicholas's pain, then,

Critical Insights

is that it is overwhelming; it makes him passive with respect to its motive force; in the face of it, we might say, the body takes over. But part of what counts about it is also that it is humiliating, and humiliating precisely because of the way it makes him passive. The clever man who thought he could become a little prime mover in the world is reduced to his animality; his rationality is humiliated, and so is *he*—there is, in this moment, nothing of him that he *could* interpose between affect and action. The function of anal penetration as the mechanism of humiliation and pain here is that of returning this underlying passivity to the realms of eros and gender identity from which it had been displaced. For what needs humiliating is just as much his manliness, his existence as the doer of erotic life: he must be broken down, made forcibly into the female man that alone can be in possession of an agency with a passivity at its base, and so can live according to naturalistic norms. And since the Miller wants to live according to those norms—since he wants to be the passive agent, and wants this punishment visited on himself as much as he wants it visited on Nicholas—another occupant of the Miller's "remenant" is a desire for the scourging humiliation of anal penetration. This is one paradigmatic form of what he imagines the desire to be passive, to be acted upon rather than to act, to involve.

In the interpenetration of a desirable effeminacy with a wish for humiliation, we begin to touch on the territory opened by the figure of Absolon, in whom the Miller explores a humiliating effeminacy and its appropriate punishment with a thoroughness that borders on delectation. Absolon, more than any other character in the tale, suffers from an inability to live the life of a happy animal. He is deeply taken with the postures of love-longing—lyrical and dramatic expressions of passion, vows of servitude, wakeful nights—all of which take such ridiculous forms that they seem designed to keep the possibility of an erotic payoff at bay, and so to prolong the time of a theatrical self-regard as much as possible. Absolon's displacement of the erotic impulse suggests a certain aversion towards what ought to be its proper object; and in the context of his squeamishness about farting, his fastidious speech, and his obsession with fresh breath, this aversion begins to look like it has its source in a more general aversion towards the human body and its orifices, the places where inside and outside meet. As far as the Miller is concerned this is all quite unmanly, as he makes clear through repeated suggestions that Absolon is infantile and effeminate, most notably in the moment when Absolon tries to woo Alisoun through self-infantilization and self-effeminization: "I moorne as dooth a lamb after the tete" (I.3704); "I may nat ete na moore than a mayde" (I.3707). We can unpack Kolve's notion that the hole-kissing brings Absolon into contact with "the real nature of what he sought," then, as follows. Being a man, Absolon wants *this*: a creature with holes and hair, with a body, just like him, a piece of the natural world, a hard chunk of physical reality; and the disgust and humiliation he shows afterwards, as he rubs his lips with sand and straw and chips and weeps like a beaten child, while it shows him cured of the extravagances of love *paramours*, confirms him in the foolish aversion to reality and bodiliness that led to those extravagances in the first place, and so underlines the justice of the moment that exposes and punishes him.

The thought that the Miller's punishment of Absolon is also a self-punishment may seem more deeply counterintuitive than the same thought in the case of Nicholas, for while the fondness in the Miller's representation of Nicholas makes an identification between the two relatively straightforward, the representation of Absolon is all mockery and disdain. But it should not be surprising that an unacknowledged wish for what looks to the Miller like effeminacy should be packaged with disdain for a figure that embodies that wish directly. Further, there is a deeper sense in which Absolon embodies the Miller's ideal, or rather a peculiar kind of literalization of it that reveals its consequences more thoroughly even than Alisoun does. For Absolon seems to have nothing but a spectatorial relationship to objects of desire; he seems to want to do nothing with respect to his desires but observe their display; in Absolon, the reduction of human action to observation and passivity has become complete. The figure of Absolon, then, gives expression to the thought that the very views by which the Miller supports his sense of carefree manliness have as their upshot something he finds disgustingly unmanly, an aversion to the body and to the female, which he otherwise wishes to figure as the ultimate object of male desire. This aversion is yet another occupant of the Miller's closet; as is its companion here, the desire to punish himself for it by way of a humiliating confrontation with the body that simultaneously arouses and disgusts him.

This mingling of arousal and disgust helps to account for another feature of the scene, the conflation of Alisoun's sexual and excretory orifices into one "hole" that must do two apparently incompatible jobs for the Miller's joke on Absolon to work.[30] On the one hand, the narrative states that Absolon "kiste hir naked ers," and he must be thought to do so for the moment to produce the monumental disgust in him that makes his punishment so fitting. On the other hand, for the scene to achieve its purpose of exposing the real object of masculine desire, Alisoun's genitals must be thought to be at issue when she puts her "hole" out the window, as indeed they must when Absolon confronts that long-haired thing that seems in the dark to be a bearded face, unless Alisoun has an extraordinarily hairy ass. But doing both jobs at once with Alisoun's "hole" requires the Miller to gloss over the distinction between what, on his view, is desirable and what is disgusting—as again he must, and even more directly, in the punning punch-line that follows the scene, "his hoote love was coold and al yqueynte" (I.3754)—as though at this central moment in the

Miller's gesture of comic exposure he could no longer tell the difference between what arouses desire and what quenches it, or could not make the difference stick. The effect of this conflation, like that of Nicholas's anal penetration, is to keep the self-humiliation the Miller figures in the scene squarely in the territory of erotic desire, in the form of an erotics of disgust and self-degradation. But the Miller hardly has a settled, univalent relationship to such an erotics. That the most readily apparent aim of self-punishment here is the opposite of that imagined in Nicholas's fate—that it is the aim of mortifying the passive agent or female man rather than forcibly producing him—suggests just how deeply unsettled the Miller is with respect to his ideal, and so how deeply his pictures of the desirable and the aversible overlap and how readily they collapse into each other.

The unsettlement generated by the Miller's diagnostic and punitive impulses becomes even more evident when we turn to John; for John's perversity and punishment, unlike those of Nicholas and Absolon, never even provisionally comes into focus in the terms provided by a normative naturalism. In the Miller's initial portrait of John we hear that "Jalous he was, and heeld [Alisoun] narwe in cage,/ For she was wylde and yong, and he was old/ And demed hymself been lyk a cokewold" (I.3224-26). This description makes John look like a figure for a self-defeating Reevish worry that provokes the very situation it fears: it would seem that John's problem is a refusal of the carelessness the Miller avows, a refusal to be happy with what he can get from Alisoun without asking too many questions. But we never see John as the jealously restrictive husband, despite the opportunities the Miller has to cast him in such a light.[31] Instead John seems completely unpossessive of Alisoun, leaving her unguarded on his many business trips and remaining sublimely unconcerned on an obvious occasion for jealousy, when Absolon awakens him in the night singing love songs to Alisoun at his window. The Miller wants, of course, to cast this as folly in itself; it is what leaves John vulnerable to Nicholas's machinations and Alisoun's betrayal. But charging John with an incompatible jealousy and unguardedness hardly helps in diagnosing his error; and worse, the only apparent space afforded in the Miller's view to an unpossessive desire for another of the kind John seems to have for Alisoun is that of the very carelessness the Miller says John violates. In fact John becomes very nearly a mouthpiece for another feature of the Miller's avowed carelessness, a general commitment not to know secrets, when he echoes the Miller's comment in the tale's prologue: "Men sholde nat knowe of Goddes pryvetee" (I.3454). In this sense John begins, as Nicholas and Absolon do, to become a figure for an aspect of the Miller's naturalism, and the Miller seems to be setting up his own willful unknowing for punishment. But on closer inspection John cannot even be described in these terms. The first thing we learn about him is that "he lovede [Alisoun] moore than his lyf" (I.3222), and the strength of his love for her is borne out by his immediate reaction to Nicholas's news of the impending flood: "'Allas, my wyf!/ And shal she drenche? Allas, myn Alisoun!'/ For sorwe of this he fil almoost adoun,/ And seyde, 'Is ther no remedie in this cas?'" (I.3522-25). The fact that John loves Alisoun more than he does his own life, that the end of the world for him means first of all her death, provides the wedge in his psyche that opens him to Nicholas's plot. It also provides the clearest case for his perversity on the Miller's account; for the Miller's carelessness, and his entire view of human motivation, is predicated on nothing mattering more than one's own life. More pointedly, no *one* can matter that much. Other people are at most the objects or instruments of self-gratification: in the genesis of human motivation, self-interest always comes first.[32] This is something even Nicholas and Absolon, perverse as they are, seem to realize. Their problem is that in seeking self-gratification they transfer their attention from their ends to the means of achieving them, and so displace the properly gratifying object from view; but for all that they are still after self-gratification, and with a little chastising their knowledge that Alisoun is the properly gratifying object can be brought back into focus for them. But this saving knowledge is not available to John; he is too far gone, gone outside the realm of a fundamental self-interest altogether, into a territory of motivation the Miller has no easy way of imagining, even as its foreignness to a naturalistic view is palpable to him.

The extent of that foreignness will become clearer if we notice another feature of John's character, a general willingness to be moved by altruistic motives, as shown by his fears for Nicholas's health and life when Nicholas has locked himself in his room as the first step in his trick. John is the only character in the poem for whom altruism is even raised as a possibility. The closest anyone else comes is Gerveys's indifferent willingness to lend Absolon his kultour, but unlike the blacksmith John is actively concerned to attend to others' needs, even when doing so serves no apparent self-interest. This is a big mistake according to the Miller's theory, a point he underlines by making John's altruistic inquiry the first step by which he enters into Nicholas's plot. But for all that John's altruism is considerably easier to accommodate to naturalistic intuitions than is his love for Alisoun; for altruism can be sorted with a thought that motivates and underlies the Miller's view of human motive, namely that there is a clean split to be made between a concern for oneself and a concern for others.[33] This split is what allows for the thought that a concern for oneself always comes first, preceding any concern for another; and it can be preserved even when the possibility of altruism is admitted. The thought would then be that there is a clean distinction to be made between altruism and egoism: in a given instance, one is moved by one or the other, and the Miller's point would be that being moved by anything but egoistic concerns is foolish. Love, however, is a harder case, for it cannot be sorted so easily. John's reaction to the thought of a flood is clearly not motivated by a fundamental self-interest of the kind the Miller's other characters display. What moves him is the thought that Alisoun will die, not the thought that he will lose a major source of self-gratification; and further, an egoistic concern would certainly express itself here in what is notably lacking, a fear of his own death. But if love is not the expression of a fundamental egoism, neither is it a form of pure other-directedness. John is not moved by sheer impersonal concern for another, as though, for instance, he recognized an impartial duty to save Alisoun. It never occurs to him to worry about the rest of mankind perishing; and it is hardly the expression of a sense of duty when the sorrowful thought of Alisoun's death almost brings him to the ground, or when, imagining the flood drowning her, he quakes with fear and breaks into uncontrollable weeping and wailing. The disaster he faces is deeply personal; it goes to the heart of him, to what matters most to the particular person he is; only his heart cannot be figured in egoistic terms, or in any other terms that derive their significance from the underlying thought that a concern for oneself can be neatly distinguished from a concern for others.

In a sense, then, it is clear enough what John wants that makes him perverse on the Miller's account, and so what the Miller means to castigate in himself by way of John's punishment: he wants to be a lover, and to be loved; he wants intimacy of a kind that makes a concern for the desired other a constitutive feature of his concern for himself, and that makes her something without which he has no life he can recognize as his own. But since the Miller's naturalism offers no way of understanding such desires, all of the terms it provides misdescribe John, and in doing so create the need for further descriptions, even if they are incompatible with the ones that came before. So even as the Miller wants to say that John is a fool for love, he tries to cast this folly as jealousy and possessiveness, as though caring for someone as much as John does could only be a kind of hyper-possessiveness, an instance of the impulse to possession which has lost touch with the carelessness that is supposed to go along with it. But the Miller knows this cannot be right; he knows that John and the Reeve are worlds apart. This is the reason, I think, for the odd formulation by which the Miller tries to cast John's attitude as a version of Reevish suspiciousness, saying that he "demed hymself been lik a cokewold" (I.3226). Nothing John does suggests he thinks himself likely to be a cuckold; but from a naturalistic perspective, he is in a certain sense *like* a cuckold, for he has already been "betrayed" in the integrity of his narrow self-interest by the claim on him of another, who is free to return his love or not. Since John obviously does consider himself to be subject to that claim, he can in this sense be said to judge himself to be like what the Miller takes a cuckold to be, someone who lacks a relation of perfect possession to the object of his desire. The fact that he lacks this relation for a reason practically the opposite of the Reeve's—because the trope of perfect possession does not apply to his attitude rather than because it does apply but he fears it has been violated—only serves to underline the Miller's problem in bringing John into clear view. Nicholas and Absolon can be at least provisionally identified from a naturalistic point of view, and thus can be punished with a precision designed to set them back on the right path; but there is no setting John right, for from the point of view from which he appears to be perverse there is no way to say even what he is.[34] Instead the Miller does the only thing he can, bringing John in for as heavy a punishment as possible, having him suffer a broken arm, betrayal by his wife, and a resounding public humiliation in which his folly is made into a huge joke, he is held by everyone to be mad, and any explanation he tries to offer is drowned in the ensuing laughter. If John cannot be set right because he cannot be identified, he will simply be broken, and broken in such a way that everyone sees there is no identifying him: he is outside the space of intelligible discourse altogether, simply insane.

The problem posed by the figure of John, then—the problem the Miller poses for himself through the figure of John—is the problem of the lover, the problem of intimacy. This problem is so deep because the Miller knows that it cannot be what his picture says it must be, simply a matter of coming close to some desired object by possessing it; and if that is so, then the problem of intimacy cannot be figured in terms of a contrast between masculine and feminine that tracks contrasts between activity and passivity, agent and place; and someone who desires intimacy cannot be figured as having the kind of relations to himself that naturalism imagines, namely relations of observation and passivity between him and the objects that make up his inner life. I will explore each of these features of the problem at greater length; they are perhaps only implicit in what I have said so far. But first I want to be clear about what I think the bare fact of the Miller's interest in intimacy suggests. With an acknowledgement of the problem of intimacy the Miller's entire naturalistic posture is made more deeply porous and problematic than it is by any of the perverse phenomena we have examined so far, for those phenomena have each in their own way participated in the commanding tropes by which the Miller's picture finds expression. That something should exceed the representational capacity of these tropes is just what we should expect, however, since as I have argued from the beginning the phenomenon of naturalistic convictions cannot provide the terms for its own understanding. In the problem of intimacy, then, we find the specification within the Miller's preferred arena of erotic life of the more general problem posed by his views as a whole: just as the only way to see what is at issue in the Miller's denial of the normative problem is to see how that denial is a response to the normative problem, so here the only way to see what is at issue in the denial of the problem of intimacy is to see how that denial is a response to the problem of intimacy.[35] Nor is this a difficulty posed only by John. In him the pressures exerted by the Miller's concern with intimacy are perhaps most immediately evident, but similar pressures appear in the figures of Alisoun, Nicholas, and Absolon. The attempt to imagine them in the Miller's preferred terms, after all, produces the paradoxical figures of the passive agent and the female man, figures that the narrative simultaneously valorizes and repudiates; and the conflict of intuitions and impulses here suggests the restlessness that becomes most insistent with John. To explore fully the form taken in the narrative by a desire for intimacy and its denial, then, we need to return to the figures in whom the Miller manages that denial more successfully, to suggest how, in spite of this, the problem of intimacy does arise, as the very motivation for its denial.

IV

It will be helpful to begin again with Alisoun; for if intimacy is at issue in the tale, she is the embodiment of what the Miller imagines a (male) agent wanting to be near to, and a desire for that nearness is his paradigm for what moves an agent to act. As I have suggested, the Miller thinks of this nearness as a kind of touching, the kind expressed so gleefully by Nicholas when he teases John with a joke John is in no position to understand: "And after wol I speke in pryvetee/ Of certeyn thyng that toucheth me and thee" (I.3494). The laugh here comes from the thought that the matter which pertains to Nicholas and John is actually a *thing* that *touches* them, or rather, that they touch; and the Miller allows Nicholas this joke because while John is supposed to think that this thing is just his, in touching John's thing—that is, in touching Alisoun's—Nicholas gets possession of the object of John's desire.[36] I have already suggested that Alisoun's status as an exemplar of action presents a problem for such a reifying account of what she essentially is; but it also presents a problem for such an account of what it would mean to want to be near her. For the Miller knows that in wanting to touch her, one wants to touch not just a thing, but an agent; not just an object, but a subject of desire. Here we should remember the Miller's warnings about inquisitiveness in the tale's prologue. On the reading of "wyf" as an abbreviated possessive, one thing he is saying there is that husbands should not be inquisitive about their wives' genitals; and while one thing he means by that is that you might find out they have been busy with someone else, another thing his warning suggests is that in order to keep thinking of your wife's genitals as just a "thing," you have to try not to know too much about them, which requires not knowing too much about what you want in wanting them. The hole-kissing scene provides an example of this problem of knowing too much, for under the pressure of exhibiting the ultimate object of desire the Miller's whole notion of coming near to a desirable object begins to fall apart. But the problem is not local to any particular moment in the plot. From the very start, Alisoun is represented as having her own life of desire, a "likerous ye" (I.3244) that is essential to her sexiness both in the portrait and afterwards.[37] Her desiring eye, to be sure, is presented as one more object of consumption for the masculine gaze that wanders over her soft wooliness, sweet mouth, and supple, thin body; it is part of what makes her the perfect object of desire, and we are not invited to imagine it as much more than that. But that is already enough to disturb her ideological function; for it means that for her to be the satisfying object of an eroticized masculine look she must be able to look back, to have a desiring gaze of her own. The scopophilic thrill her portrait is supposed to provide could not exist if she were seen simply as an object, or again simply as an animal: there is no such thrill in looking at the pear tree or the sheep to which she is compared.[38] Nor could it exist if she were the kind of human creature the Miller imagines us to be, or imagines that we ought to be. For the thrill of looking at her would again be dampened if she were merely passive with respect to a desire that, as it were, looked out through her eye; the masculine looker does not want to imagine that her desire is, in effect, helpless, but that it is hers to bestow where she will, and that it might be pointed *here*. The thrill the portrait offers is not even that of a male observer imagining having his way with a woman, reducing her as a practical rather than a theoretical matter to a state of passivity, for then too the desire in her eye would be extinguished, or at least forcefully set to the side. The thrill is more like that of imagining a seamless return of desire, a perfect interaction between two agents who want exactly the same thing in exactly the same way. It is a thrill that depends on the desire for intimacy.

It must be said right away that the passage averts the possibility of intimacy on which it depends. If this scopophilic portrait of a woman with desire in her eye imagines an erotic interaction in which two agents want exactly the same thing in exactly the same way, the most immediate way they can be said to want it is with the desire of the man; Alisoun is, after all, the Miller's creation, and the thrills she provides are the ones he wants her to. In this sense the portrait provides the Miller with a way of imagining a desiring eye, like that of Pygmalion's statue come to life, that cannot help but be trained on him, since that is the way he made it. It is the erotic charge, that is, of a narcissistic wish for the other's desire to be an echo or reflection of one's own, even as it somehow, impossibly, maintains its status as other.[39] If we return to the tale's dominant gender ideology, this is the desire for a woman, the erotic locus or place, to be like a man, the erotic agent, and not just any man, but the very man who desires her. The narcissism of the Miller's desire then opens onto a narcissized homoeroticism that is very nearly adjacent to it, and that is part of what it means for the Miller to want to be a female man and to imagine the self-castigations of anal penetration and of a humiliating confrontation with the disgustingly desirable female body. This narcissized homoeroticism is another occupant of the Miller's "remenant," and suggests a further sense in which his tale pictures a world perfectly matched to human desire; in effect the tale's dominant trope of a perfect match is here figured as the desire of a man who reaches out to possess his own image.

It is worth pausing for a moment over the topic of the Miller's homo-eroticism; for while I have meant it to be implied for some time now in a way that makes its overt appearance seemingly inevitable, and while it is taken by many to be the first and most obvious consequence of attending to the problems of gender and desire in the tale, the bare fact of a homoerotic desire here tells us very little, and it is easy to make the wrong thing of it. We can take our cue from a line I have already cited from the Miller's description of Alisoun's animal sexiness, that she is "softer than the wolle is of a wether." Leicester reminds us that "a wether is a male sheep that has been castrated before it reaches maturity," and remarks that as a consequence "the thought of touching Alisoun has its scary side."[40] The comment is suggestive, but as it stands condensed and misleading. What exactly would be scary about touching an Alisoun figured in this way? The question has to do with the tropological value of castration rather than the explanatory value of an anatomically anchored anxiety related to some presumedly universal psychic event—as indeed it should for a reading of the Freudian thinking which informs Leicester's comment. The first thing to notice is that Alisoun—not, as Leicester implies, the one who desires her—is being imagined as a castrated male, and a sexy one at that. Evidently we are supposed to find the thought of touching a wether-like softness arousing. If Alisoun-as-sexy-male is being figured here as castrated—as lacking power, cut off from mature development, perhaps as passive—then the desire for such a one is what a desire for her is imagined as being. This is what I mean by calling the homoeroticism at issue here narcissized: it imagines the object of a homoerotic desire as figuratively castrated, and so imagines that the desiring, uncastrated male is the sole locus of power and activity in the erotic scene. But the point needs to be put more broadly, since the Miller clearly wants us to think of Alisoun's sexy softness as womanly, and since the narcissistic figuring of the object of desire as passive is hardly restricted to homoeroticism in this text. The trope of Alisoun-as-wether is a kind of gloss on the general impulse in the poem to figure erotic life in terms of a clean split between activity and passivity: it imagines that to be an object of desire is to be castrated, powerless, passive; that one cannot be both desired and active; that to be an object of desire is to be no more than an object, to be objectified. The scary side of the thought of touching Alisoun would then be the thought that she might be aroused by the touching, that she might desire you, so make of you an object, a castrate. This is a way of putting a fairly familiar thought, that part of what is involved in narcissism is an aversion to being desired. But it is crucial to remember that even the thought of being the object of a castrating masculine desire, fearful as it is, is not merely aversive. Like the fantasies expressed in Nicholas's anal penetration and Absolon's kiss, what is being imagined here is an erotics, and one not fundamentally powered by narcissism. For what is being imagined in each of these cases is the *desirability* of the other's agency, the fact that what makes the other appear in the Miller's gender ideology as "male" is essential to what constitutes the possibility of another's sexiness.[41]

Given the Miller's obvious investment in a heteronormative self-conception, this is a high price to pay for keeping the desire for intimacy out of sight. And as I have suggested it cannot even do that, since the impossibility of a purely objectifying desire is central to the emergence of a homoerotic desire here; and, to return to Alisoun, the erotics of her portrait is itself already predicated on the centrality of her desiring look, of her being the kind of creature that looks back at you. This means that part of what one wants in desiring her is to be desired by her, and so to be close not just to her body or her "thing" or anything else that can be imagined as simply a touchable or possessable object, but to be close to *her.* But to want this is to recognize that she might look back at you, not with desire, but with aversion; or she might not look back at all. This is knowledge that scopophilia, in its imagining of a seamless interaction between agents, wishes to avoid. The scopophilic eroticism of Alisoun's portrait, together with her representation as a touchable thing, means then to guarantee a kind of intimacy, a condition in which a desired nearness could never be lost because the ultimate object of desire is always close by, ready to hand like the rest of God's plenty, and always looking back at you with desire, never averting her gaze. But in representing the object of desire as necessarily close by the Miller also distances himself from it, banishing the desired other from the scene of intimacy; or at least he tries to do so, substituting a simulacrum of the other, perhaps her body, in any case a projection of her into the erotic scene as an object that can never really satisfy the desire for intimacy whose satisfaction it is supposed to guarantee. This structure of desire is one that first of all sends its object away, so that it then can be brought back in another form: a form consistent with the Miller's naturalistic picture, in which a concern for oneself precedes and underlies any concern for others, and other people are just one kind of thing the possession of which is what it means to bask in nature's plenitude; and a form consistent also with the nostalgia of his natural-ism, in which he freezes himself in longing for a condition that is necessarily already lost, and lost precisely because of the way he imagines that it has been guaranteed.

A structure of desire in which one pushes the desired object away in order to bring it back in another form: here the Miller is beginning to sound again like Nicholas, who bypasses the opportunity for immediate sex with Alisoun in order to have her in another form, as the sign that his will can fill the scene of an action in which others become little more than his instruments. Even in the figure of Nicholas, however, the Miller cannot imagine this sort of desire through to a moment of completion. There is a moment of completion, of course, to which the Miller refers with a rather vague description of Nicho-las's activity with Alisoun in bed: "Ther was the revel and the melodye;/ And thus lith Alison and Nicholas,/ In bisynesse of myrthe and of solas" (I.3652-54). But after all the queynte-grabbing and talk of touching people's things that has come before, this quadruple euphemism for the tale's sole moment of erotic satisfaction is a bit surprising, and more so since erotic satisfaction is the tale's prime example of the gratification of human desire. It would not take much to say, as the Merchant for one is quite willing to say, just what is in-volved in this "solas" in a way that would drive home the Miller's point about desire. If however the Miller were more specific in just the way he has been specific all along, one thing he would certainly lose would be the thought that Alisoun and Nicholas were doing something *together* there in bed. If Nicholas were not just doing something to Alisoun, the most the Miller could show while remaining consistent with his picture would be them doing something to each other, or more properly to the objects each took the other to be. This could be sexy in its own way, but it is evidently not the kind of sexiness the Miller wants of the moment: it would come too close to what he elsewhere imagines either as mere buildup, a reach and a grab that might produce a star-tled jerk back as much as a return of desire, or as punishment or victimization, the reception of a violating thrust. The result of this is that the central moment of satisfaction in the tale, what ought to provide the best case for a picture of the world as a place of plenitude, must be left blank, pointed to with multiple euphemism but not represented. This silence is the sign of another version of what happens there in bed, a version essential to the Miller's sense of the mo-ment as one of the ultimate happiness, the moment towards which all of the more tangible arousals he does represent are aimed, but a moment for which, it seems, he has no words.

If in Nicholas's case the problem that a desire for intimacy poses for the Miller is expressed in a moment in which something is not shown, in the case of Absolon it gets expressed in a far more spectacular moment in which something is shown. I am of course referring to the moment in which Absolon finally does draw near enough to Alisoun to touch her, the moment of that ill-fated kiss, which the Miller imagines with a sensual precision and slow-motion relish unmatched by anything in the tale outside of Alisoun's portrait. Here we are taken inside the phenomenal scene of the perceiving and desiring agent, the scene whose supposed specular passivity plays such a crucial role in the view of human action that the Miller offers. Absolon wipes his mouth "ful drie" with anticipation; he kisses Alisoun's "naked ers" "with his mouth," "ful savourly." During the moment of anticipation what is waiting for Absolon is the face of his beloved, in particular her beautiful, succulent lips crying out to be kissed. What impales Absolon on the Miller's joke is that those lips are still phenomenally there for him in his savoring the kiss of her ass, and their residual image and the savoring associated with it even lingers after Absolon starts to realize that something has gone wrong. What he does first is just to register error and jump back. What is there for him is still a face, only not any longer a woman's, for he knows that a woman does not have a beard. But the face is not exactly a man's either, since the sensation of beardedness only registers strongly enough to call into question the image of a woman. There is even a moment in which the object as it is for Absolon—the object, that is, of his perceptions and affects—loses its facedness entirely, becoming a bare unrecognizable thing with unreadable features. When Absolon feels "a thyng al rough and long yherd," that thing is no longer a bearded face of indeterminate gender, and not yet an ass; and when he cries out "what have I done?" he does so because he does not yet know what he has done, he only knows it was awful.

What makes the phenomenally rich features of this scene problematic for the Miller is that, while he must make them accessible to impale Absolon on the joke, neither the perversity they represent nor the punishment they provide can finally be cast in naturalistic terms. Absolon's problem as he is humiliated by kissing Alisoun's ass is not that he has the wrong object of desire present to his consciousness, leading him astray, as Nicholas might be said to have when he too cleverly presents Absolon with a target for his borrowed blade. Nor does the scene serve to reveal some normatively transparent object of perception and desire, something that, like Nicholas's pain, cannot be gotten wrong. What the scene does instead is to explore how what is phenomenally present can suddenly change faces, and change us with it. The humiliation in the moment for Absolon, and what makes the joke on him so biting, is that by the end of it he has become an ass-kisser: that may not have been his intention, but it is a fact about him, at the moment the only fact that counts. And if the shifting character of the object's identity is humiliating, the course of its transformation is even worse. The change, both in Absolon and in what he encounters, is not a matter of a switch from one determinate identity to another. When the object of his perception and desire becomes a mere "thyng al rough and long yherd," Absolon not only does not know what he has done, he does not know what he has become; the sheer attractiveness of a world of plenty perfectly matched to human desire, and the definitive human identity that goes with it, has been replaced by the sheer aversiveness of a world with nothing in particular in it, a world of disgusting thinginess that leaves him with nothing to want and no one to be.

Compared to this, being an ass-kisser—or being any of the various kinds of creature constructed in the Miller's relationship to his closeted "remenant"— would be a positive relief. Consider one such possibility produced in this scene. The appearance of that bearded face is partly meant as a reprimand to Absolon: it suggests that the passive lover or female man deserves to be confronted with the disgusting manliness of the love-object he has in effect been wishing for. This is what the Miller has Nicholas understand to be the force of the joke on Absolon when, in a remarkable act of something like telepathy, he exclaims "A berd! A berd!" (I.3742); so the Miller clearly has a lot invested in enforcing the sense that this is what is so humiliating here. If we follow through on the thought that in punishing these representatives of a perversion internal to him the Miller is expressing a wish for self-punishment, we can easily take this as further confirmation of a closeted homoeroticism that may now even seem to be the basic feature of the psychology the tale explores. In the joke on Absolon we have one more expression of the Miller's disgust towards his own ideal of the female man, where his disgust serves to keep the scene's identification of a homoerotic desire internal to him out of sight, and helps to define some of the contours of that desire's sexiness. I do not exactly want to deny this sense of the moment. But everything turns on what we would mean by taking this to be basic to the Miller's psychology. In particular we cannot mean by this that a homoerotic desire is what's really in there, in the depths of the Miller's soul which some theory we have gives us the technology to lay bare. That way of figuring the core attitudes the *Miller's Tale* expresses, after all, derives from thoughts that the tale's naturalism is meant to support: that human desires are inner objects that define us simply by their presence, and that our relationship to them is fundamentally one of observation, of seeing them for what they are or of covering them up and denying their existence. As I have been arguing all along, this is the crucial step in the Miller's self-deception; if a closeted homoeroticism structures his psychology in this way, or indeed if any of the various occupants of the shadow-remenant do so, they do so to the extent that this self-deception is successful, *not* as some secret fact about him that only we are in a position to see. It would be better, then, to describe this moment as expressive of a longing for the homoerotic, produced by the Miller's more obvious longing for the heteronormative, and in exactly the same naturalizing terms. For what the Miller gains in bringing Nicholas in on this version of the joke—and what would be perpetuated in any critical account that stopped here—is the preservation of a naturalistic account of human action and human identity, the preservation of the thought that inner life consists of a set of facts that just are what they are, and that, if known, would tell us what to do, by pointing us to the objects of our desires that are out there in the world waiting for us.[42]

But the scene of Absolon's kiss does not stop here, and in fact it never really started here at all. As I have suggested, the joke on Absolon works because his perceptions and attitudes help to constitute the object that is phenomenally there for him, and that object, in turn, helps to constitute him, in the particular way that we are constituted in and by our relations with objects that are also subjects and agents—that is, other people. The kind of humiliation Absolon suffers, then, is one of a family of reciprocal relations between agents, of which intimacy is another. Part of what binds this family together is that such reciprocal relations are not grounded in some primary relation each agent has to himself; on the contrary, the relations any agent has with himself are in part determined by the reciprocal relations he has with others. This is one reason why there is no set of inner objects in a person that just are what they are first, and that tell him what to do; and therefore why there is not the kind of basis the Miller imagines for generating human motive out of an antecedent self-interest. More to the point, *within* the conduct of reciprocal relations who and what each person is, what each person wants, and who and what each takes the other to be depends on any number of things, including what each person does, what they do together, and even just what happens between them and to them. However well Absolon's punishment fits his perversity, he is humiliated by that kiss not because he is a pervert or a fool, but because he is in the condition the Miller knows we all are in: the condition of creatures for whom the normative problem cannot be answered by recourse to some set of determinate interior facts, creatures whose identities outrun anything internal to them but who are bound by those identities nonetheless, partly because they are essentially determined by the fact that they live in a world with others who matter to them not just as objects but as agents.

One powerful motivation for holding to the Miller's picture of the human animal, then—and a motive that is neither peculiar to him nor dependent on the force of a suspect ideology—is that we are vulnerable in just the way Absolon is, to being made and unmade in relation to others who may have nothing more than our humiliation in mind. They may have something much better in mind, of course; but even in the best case of mutual good will, there is no way to say beforehand what the endpoint of reciprocal self-constitution will be, or even if there will be an identifiable end. This in itself can be a fearful thing. To the extent that we want to be able just to look and see who we are and what we want, and want to be able to look at another and see a determinate thing whose normative claim on us is transparent, it can seem that reciprocal relations require us to act blindly—or worse, to live in a world in which nothing is definitively identifiable at all, including ourselves. A particularly heightened version of this fear—heightened in a way determined by the Miller's conceptual commitments—finds expression in the progression of Absolon's kiss to a point at which his relationship to the world is one of sheer aversion to its thinginess. For given the way Alisoun's desiring eye is essential to her sexiness from the start, given the way she always looks back at her male observer, making a claim of reciprocity on him even from her "nether eye," the closest she comes to being the purely animal, purely bodily object that makes no agentlike claim is in the moment when she becomes that bare unrecognizable "thyng al rough and long yherd," terrifying in its failure to take part in any sense of what Absolon has done to or with it. Here the Miller's picture of the normative power of the object of erotic desire—his picture of the other's body as what is tangibly real, and of this reality as the source of motive—becomes a picture of the other as utterly alien, something you can have no identifiable relation to, something disgusting. This is yet another of the discontents that a Millerish naturalism brings in its wake, in which his fantasy of a seamless connection to the world opens onto an abyss of disgust and the sadness of a radical isolation from everything that was supposed to fill his world with value.

The character whom the Miller has the most trouble imagining as alone in this way, and who therefore figures most directly both the Miller's knowledge that he is not alone in this way and his sense of what this entails, is John. For John's entire way of thinking and acting is predicated on an acknowledgement of the others in his world. More than that, he has one particular other who *is* his world; for him the loss of her and the end of the world amount to the same thing, which is why Nicholas's gag about a second flood has the power it does over him. And now it should be somewhat clearer what it means for the Miller to punish John in the way he does. Breaking John's arm is the least appropriate of the punishments, for nothing that is at issue in the possibility John represents has to do centrally with the body. A broken arm hurts, but it does not hurt John where he lives; at most it is a kind of rearguard action on the Miller's part, an attempt to pull John's case back within a naturalistic orbit after the fact. The public and mocking denial of John's rationality is more interesting, in part because it just misses its mark. For it is not so much John's rationality that gets denied, despite the crowd's solidarity in declaring his madness; his fate is not that of having no reasons, but that of having no one listen to the reasons he so evidently has: "no man his reson herde" (I.3844). John's punishment, then, is less a denial of the rationality of intimacy than an attempt to destroy the possibility that the desire for intimacy might have reasons for it, born of the fearful fact that the reasons you have might be ones that no one else is willing or able to hear. This is also the reason for John's other, and worst, punishment, his betrayal by Alisoun: as it turns out, even the person he wants intimacy with does not care to hear him, and does not share his reasons. The fact that this fearful isolation is behind both of the latter two punishments suggests that part of the purpose of the tale's final moment is to take something of intimate concern and make it the occasion for a public scene, as though to deny its intimate scale, and by sidestepping intimacy to make of John's isolation an instance of the radical isolation the Miller fears, one that can presumably be avoided by participation in the solidarity of the crowd.

But John's isolation, fearful as it is, is quite unlike that entailed by the Miller's picture, for nothing says that John is in principle alone or unhearable; it just turns out that way. This suggests that here as elsewhere the Miller's nightmares are part and parcel of the wishes his naturalism embraces; for both his fantasy of seamless connection to the world and his nightmare of radical isolation participate in the wishful attempt to deny that it can just turn out that way, that who you are and the happiness you seek can rest on such contingencies. And here as elsewhere the Miller reveals his further sense that he cannot fully identify himself with the wishes that power his narrative, in either their idyllic or demonic form. For just as John is an object of greater hostility than either Nicholas or Absolon and so receives the heaviest punishment, there is a pathos in John's situation that goes deeper than that attending the other male characters, and that brings with it a sympathy lacking in their cases.[43] And this pathos is just what the Miller has said it is all along, the intimate pathos of staking your heart on someone only to find somewhere along the way that they have no such stake in you. The Miller depends on this pathos in making John out to be a fool; but once it is admitted, mere carelessness is no longer a viable option, for nothing in the world of God's plenty could replace what has been taken away.

From *English Literary History* 67, no. 1 (Spring 2000): 1-44. Copyright © 2000 by The Johns Hopkins University Press. Reprinted with permission from The Johns Hopkins University Press.

Notes

Among the interlocutors who have helped to form this essay, I must single out Jay Schleusener, to whom I owe the pleasure of deep intellectual debt and an ongoing conversation that continues to take surprising and interesting turns. Many thanks are also due to Eva Fernandez, Elizabeth Fowler, Anne Middleton, Janel Mueller, Debbie Nelson, Lee Patterson, Katherine Rowe, and

Christina von Nolcken, each of whom has helped clarify my understanding of the topics of the essay through conversations, reading drafts, or both. Much of the essay was written with the support of a Morse Fellowship from Yale University.

1. Geoffrey Chaucer, *The Miller's Tale*, in *The Riverside Chaucer*, ed. Larry D. Benson, 3d ed. (Boston: Houghton Mifflin, 1987), I.2730-39. Hereafter cited parenthetically in the text by fragment and line number.

2. As early as 1948 Paul Beichner noted the importance of the scene's baring of "the natural" for an understanding of the functions Alisoun and Absolon play in the tale: see "Characterization in the *Miller's Tale*," in *Chaucer Criticism, Volume 1: The Canterbury Tales*, ed. Richard J. Schoeck and Jerome Taylor (Notre Dame: Univ. of Notre Dame Press, 1960), 117-29. Charles Muscatine, in an account that was to set the terms for almost all subsequent discussion of the tale, placed the scene in relation to a more fully elaborated sense of the tale's naturalism and its "quiting" of the *Knight's Tale*: see *Chaucer and the French Tradition* (Berkeley: Univ. of California Press, 1957), 222-30. By the 1970s the terms of Muscatine's account had become quite widely accepted, and critics could make such offhand remarks as Alfred E. David's that Absolon's punishment is to "discover reality by kissing his lady's ass" with confidence that they were invoking a widely-held sense of the Miller's conceptual commitments: see *The Strumpet Muse: Art and Morals in Chaucer's Poetry* (Bloomington: Indiana Univ. Press, 1976), 98. V. A. Kolve has offered perhaps the richest account of the scene's and the tale's naturalism in *Chaucer and the Imagery of Narrative* (Stanford: Stanford Univ. Press, 1984), 158-216, esp. 193-97. Even the patristic critical tradition, with its concern for a moralizing Christian interpretation that would seem to have little in common with a Muscatinian humanism, shares a basic sense of the scene's function and conceptual structure: see for instance D. W. Robertson's claim that Absolon's kiss cures a misguided love that is essentially the same in Absolon, Nicholas, Palamon, and Arcite by showing the true nature of that love's object (*A Preface to Chaucer* [Princeton: Princeton Univ. Press, 1962], 469).

3. Kolve, 197 ("the real nature").

4. See Elaine Tuttle Hansen, *Chaucer and the Fictions of Gender* (Berkeley: Univ. of California Press, 1992), 223-36; H. Marshall Leicester, Jr., "Newer Currents in Psychoanalytic Criticism, and the Difference 'It' Makes: Gender and Desire in the *Miller's Tale*," *ELH* 61 (1994): 473-99, esp. 486-90; Karma Lochrie, "Women's 'Pryvetees' and Fabliau Politics in the *Miller's Tale*," *Exemplaria* 6 (1994): 287-304, esp. 299-301. I have cast the questions in a way meant to be neutral with respect to the rather different formulations of them, and the quite different senses of their import, in each of these critics.

5. Critics who have put the relationship in something like this way include Muscatine, David, and Kolve, for all of whom a sense of the distinctness and coherence of the Miller's naturalistic views—what we might call their commitment to a conceptual formalism—is a corollary of their sense of the distinctness and coherence of the tale's naturalism considered as a formal literary structure. Lee Patterson's politically-inflected account of the *Miller's Tale* explores a species of discomfort or anxiety concerning the Miller's naturalism which helpfully challenges such commitments but which is rather different from the problems I discuss here; see *Chaucer and the Subject of History* (Madison: Univ. of Wisconsin Press, 1991), 244-79. In some brief comments throughout the essay I will suggest further how an account of Chaucer's interest in the Miller's naturalism and an account of his project in Fragment I are related, although treating the issue substantively would require a fuller discussion of the rest of the fragment than I can offer here.

6. The best current work on the identificatory lability of desire suggests that this kind of condescension towards naturalism is a mistake. Both Eve Kosofsky Sedgwick and Leo Bersani have voiced their suspicion of the too-easy "antinaturalism" in which many cultural and literary critics indulge, and their sense of the unhelpfulness of the naturalist/constructivist binary which helps to

license that condescension. See Sedgwick, *Epistemology of the Closet* (Berkeley: Univ. of California Press, 1990), esp. 41; Sedgwick and Adam Frank, "Shame in the Cybernetic Fold: Reading Sylvan Tomkins," in *Critical Inquiry* 21 (1995), 496-522; and Bersani, *Homos* (Cambridge: Harvard Univ. Press, 1995), esp. 57. I will have more to say about the problem of thinking in terms of the trope of exposure as the essay progresses. A reliance on the gesture of critical exposure is particularly marked in the accounts of Hansen and Lochrie. Leicester depends on the gesture as well, as when he relies on a distinction between "the official" and "the transgressive" that is supposed to track quite neatly the distinction between understanding gender and desire in naturalistic, anti-feminist, and heteronormative ways and being open to a fluidity of gender and desire that "the sex cops" would proscribe. But he clearly has reservations about this schema as well, and at times seems more interested in the way our engagements with problems of gender and desire lend themselves to an impulse to exposure that misreads, or at least under-reads, the phenomena it means to describe. This makes Leicester's essay the closest of the three to my own. Still, as will become clear, I think Leicester quite precisely misses the mark in a number of crucial ways that suggest he has underappreciated the force of his own reservations.

7. The phrase is from Romans 2:14. One not inconsiderable advantage in considering the broader normative picture of the *Miller's Tale* is that it allows us to think of Chaucer's project here as part of a long cultural tradition in which sex and gender are particularly charged territories for investigating the problem of human autonomy—or, to borrow an Augustinian locution with important resonances for this essay, the problem of the inherent perversity of the human will. Alain de Lille's *De Planctu Naturae* and Jean de Meun's continuation of the *Roman de la Rose* are two texts in this tradition which were well known to Chaucer, and for which the problem of normative naturalism was particularly crucial. But the tradition is of course a vast one, both in temporal sweep and in the range of texts and cultural forms which participate in it. Two studies which have been particularly valuable for my thinking about this tradition, and have helped influence the ways in which I cast some of the issues of this essay, are Peter Brown's *The Body and Society: Men, Women, and Sexual Renunciation in Early Christianity* (New York: Columbia Univ. Press, 1988), and Caroline Walker Bynum's *Fragmentation and Redemption: Essays on Gender and the Human Body in Medieval Religion* (New York: Zone Books, 1992). The kinds of historical understanding that Brown and Bynum provide can help us to avoid the tempting but bogus thrill of thinking that in speaking of the lability of desire and the porousness of gender boundaries we are somehow discovering phenomena with which our benighted ancestors were unfamiliar, and the equally tempting and no less bogus worry that in speaking of these things we are indulging in the anachronistic projection of modern concerns into a culture in which they have no place.

8. Muscatine, 223 ("naturalism of exceptional").

9. See the discussions by Muscatine, Kolve, and Patterson. I owe a debt to each of these critics for my understanding of the conceptual structure of the Miller's views.

10. Leicester, 489. It is important to a sense of Leicester's account that this is part of what he takes to be inappropriate to the Miller's preferred views, a sign of repressed identifications coming to the surface. The reason for this, as I will suggest, is that Leicester has missed the full force of the underlying naturalism that drives the Miller's views of gender and desire.

11. I do not mean to suggest in what follows that anything going by the name of "naturalism" involves the conceptual commitments and compromises I explore here. There is some sense in which a naturalistic account of the human creature is surely correct: minimally, it is just a fact that humans are animals, and parts of the natural world. The problem lies in saying what this means, and in particular what consequences it has for an understanding of the various features of human life for which normativity is an issue. Since normative practices are in some sense a product of human natural history it would be a mistake to think it has no consequences; and in fact it is at times salutary to remind ourselves that this is so, as for instance Nietzsche so often does in resisting the

temptation to attribute our normative capacities to the presence in us of some mysterious metaphysical power or object. Still, while the *Miller's Tale* suggests a particular way of imagining what the fact of human animality entails for our lives as normative creatures, this way of imagining those entailments is perfectly common, and in many of its contours quite widely goes by the name of naturalism. For this reason I use the broader term interchangeably with more specific references to and descriptions of the Miller's picture.

12. Kolve, 185.

13. For Palamon's envy of the animals, see I.1303-33.

14. The descriptive density of the tale, and its purpose in supporting a naturalistic view, is particularly central to the accounts of Muscatine and Kolve.

15. For an early account of the importance of the term "hende" in the tale, as meaning clever, skillful, handy, and ready-to-hand, see E. Talbot Donaldson, "The Idiom of Popular Poetry in the *Miller's Tale*," in his *Speaking of Chaucer* (London: The Athlone Press, 1970), 13-29, esp. 17-19.

16. This one remaining function for reason to play on a naturalistic view—the function of allowing the human creature a sense of gratitude and the capacity to articulate it—helps account for Kolve's sense of the tale's sweetness and childlike innocence. That I do not entirely share this sense should be clear, and will become more so.

17. See Muscatine's claim that in the *Miller's Tale* "fabliau . . . is virtually made philosophical" (224). A way of putting my disagreement with Muscatine is that we have different senses of what it means to think that Chaucer's project in the *Miller's Tale* is no less philosophical than it is, say, in the *Knight's*.

18. Of course no one exactly thinks that an abstract view of the kind I have outlined exhausts Chaucer's interest in the tale. But the best accounts of the Miller's naturalism tend to identify the Miller much too strongly with such a view, and to describe Chaucer's interest much too strongly in terms of that identification. So Muscatine, in unpacking his notion that Chaucer makes fabliau nearly philosophical, outlines what he takes to be the tale's "assertions": "an assertion of the binding, practical sequentiality of all events"; "physical action becomes an ethical imperative"; and "the purest fabliau doctrine, the sovereignty of animal nature" (224). Kolve, in turn, says that the tale "presents a contrary view of human experience" to that of the Knight, and so "required of Chaucer the invention of a counter-art: nonhierarchic, nonhieratic, addressing no truth beyond itself" (160), as though the internal structure of the Miller's view were an essentially subjective and self-contained truth that Chaucer's art serves to represent. This is what I referred to earlier as the combination of conceptual and literary formalism. The result of this thought is that the question of what sense the Miller's naturalism has *for him* has mostly seemed an empty one, answered just by repeating the central tenets of the view itself; so all that has seemed left to say is that the Miller's view opposes the Knight's, or subverts its ideology, or lacks its greater wisdom. Of course the Miller's *view* does oppose the Knight's; my point here is that this tells us little about what it means to have such a view, or what it means to take an interest in someone's having it.

19. For a fuller discussion of the problems normative naturalism has in cashing out its own claims to normativity, see Christine M. Korsgaard, *The Sources of Normativity* (Cambridge: Cambridge Univ. Press, 1996), esp. 29-30, 145-46, and 160-61. Korsgaard's work has helped shape my overall sense of the normative problem as well.

20. What follows is in effect an attempt to imagine a tale for which Kolve's account would be right, a tale, that is, which really was just "a contrary view of human experience" to the Knight's.

21. Kolve's interest in the tropological function of animals and children in the tale is then precisely correct: they figure a condition of something like human action, minus the burden of the normative problem in its adult form, to which, among other things, our notions of accountability and responsibility belong (see 167, 215). Such a condition never was and never could have been the condition of human animality, however—and never could be coherently *thought* to be so,

---

even by the Miller—since as I have suggested what is imagined in the tale is a condition in which the normative problem would never have arisen, but in which the supposed fact of this condition plays the part precisely of providing an answer to as-yet-unasked, and indeed unaskable, normative questions.

22. This helps explain the oddness of the formulation "An housbonde shal nat been inquisityf/ Of Goddes pryvetee, nor of his wyf." "Wyf" here is commonly read as an abbreviated possessive parallel to "Goddes," rendering the sense of the passage as "husbands should not be inquisitive of their wives' secrets." But the passage also says just that husbands should not be inquisitive about their *wives*. My argument above is that there is no decision to be made between the two readings: in the view the Miller is avowing here they amount to the same thing. This is one of many places in Chaucer's poetry in which he takes advantage of semantic ambiguity to indicate the underlying conceptual structure of an attitude. I mention above a further thought expressed in the passage, that the "there" in which the Miller imagines husbands finding God's plenty is their wives' "pryvetee," that is their genitals. This suggests, however, that the Miller is also saying that husbands should not be inquisitive about their wives' genitals. One might well wonder here why not. This is a point to which I will return.

23. This is so even if we think of the danger of cuckoldry as being primarily its threat to a sense of manly mastery and pride rather than to the character of one's marital relations. That one's wife's activities, in the absence of any diminished erotic availability of her, could pose such a threat at all already suggests that she is more than just a locus of present satisfactions.

24. The account of the tale I am offering is not in this rather narrow sense psychological, which unfortunately is the sense that "the psychological" is usually taken to have in Chaucer criticism, both by those who have an interest in it and by those who want to exclude it on methodological grounds. The old debate between the "dramatic theory" or character-based study of Chaucer and any of the candidates that were supposed to replace it takes this form, as though, for instance, the *General Prologue* were supposed to provide a key to some basic psychological elements that produce what amount to secondary effects in the tales. That we have not come very far from the terms of this debate is suggested by the way they are replicated in much of the recent debate on the place of psychoanalysis in medieval studies, in which both proponents and opponents of psychoanalysis seem to take phenomena such as the Oedipus complex as providing the same kind of explanatory and causal foundation. Leicester is rightly worried about this tendency in psychoanalytic criticism, and rightly suggests that Freud himself exhibits it only at his most programmatic. For an account of Freud that emphasizes the tension in his work between a programmatic impulse to establish an institutionalized and clinically viable practice and a speculative impulse that restlessly problematizes the terms of its own understanding, see Bersani, *The Freudian Body: Psychoanalysis and Art* (New York: Columbia Univ. Press, 1986).

25. This is a familiar duplicity in naturalistic discourse, which often makes out "the natural" to be a justifying category while having no recourse to explain the existence of what it takes to be unjustified actions or desires other than their natural existence as perversions.

26. I am adapting a phrase from Eve Sedgwick, and pursuing a line of thinking about secrecy, interiority, prohibition, and knowledge suggested by Sedgwick and Michel Foucault; see Sedgwick, *Epistemology of the Closet*, and Foucault, *The History of Sexuality, Volume 1*, trans. Robert Hurley (New York: Vintage Books, 1978). My understanding of the issues for which "the closet" has become such a commanding trope—particularly my sense of what it means to be caught in the grip of a reifying picture of what interiority or subjectivity is, together with the thought that "epistemology" quite precisely fails to capture what is fundamentally at issue in our relations to our inner lives—also owes a great deal to Ludwig Wittgenstein's *Philosophical Investigations*, trans. G. E. M. Anscombe, 3d ed. (New York: Macmillan, 1958), and to Stanley Cavell's *The Claim of Reason: Wittgenstein, Skepticism, Morality, and Tragedy* (New York: Oxford Univ. Press, 1979).

My use of the trope of the closet does not imply that I take the Miller's situation to be simply a version of the problems Foucault and Sedgwick discuss concerning the interiority of erotic life in the nineteenth and twentieth centuries. The thought of a closet in the *Miller's Tale* is part of a very different set of cultural practices and authoritative discourses; sex and sexuality play different roles, and in particular while as I will suggest homoerotic desire is at issue here, it is not at issue in the same way as it is in the cases Foucault and Sedgwick discuss. In particular it is not linked to the existence of, or worries over the existence of, a distinct type of human creature known as "the homosexual."

27. In linking longing, the normative problem, and a naturalistic worry about hidden determining motives, I mean in part to be suggesting a further line of thinking about Chaucer's project in Fragment I. For now a few telegraphic remarks will have to do. The *Knight's Tale* expresses a powerful longing for a condition of self-command that it figures as already foregone, lost to the vicissitudes of history, desire, perhaps even materiality, and swallowed up in conspiracies of which we know nothing and which, even if we knew, we would be powerless to affect. While this nostalgia is quite directly turned towards a concern with the problem of reason's normative power rather than away from it, the restless character of the Knight's attempted resolutions suggests that a Millerish repudiation of reason is perhaps closer to the heartland of the Knight's struggles than most critics are inclined to think. On the other side, the Reeve's clear commitment to a naturalistic view of human motive, as reflected in his figuring of human desire as a territory of animality that inevitably carries us away, suggests that his predominant attitudes of vengefulness, morbidity, and moralizing suspicion are a kind of hardening of the worries I here locate as the "hidden other face" of the Miller's carelessness. The difference between the Miller and the Reeve, we might say, is primarily one of good luck and confidence, and we might describe the *Reeve's Tale* as an extended exploration of the thought, already part of the naturalism at issue here, that there is nothing to stop us from being nature's victims, and nothing to distinguish our victimization by nature from victimization by ourselves. If anything like this line of thinking seems right, then Fragment I begins to look like an investigation of a closely related family of problems and attitudes rather than a portrayal of clearly delineated and distinct characters, subjectivities, or ideologies; or, to put the point another way, an understanding of how such a family is related is crucial to an understanding of what Chaucer takes character, subjectivity, and ideology to be.

28. Muscatine and Kolve faithfully capture this aspect of the representation of Alisoun in referring to her respectively as a "delectable little animal" (230) and as "the object of all desires" (162). Despite the differences among the accounts of Patterson, Hansen, Leicester, and Lochrie, each is concerned, as I am here, to register both this function of the figure of Alisoun and its incoherence.

29. Although the consequences of Alisoun's function as the embodiment of the Miller's ideal have not been registered in the way I mean to here, many critics have recognized it. Muscatine refers to her as "the one precious illusion in the poem" (229); Kolve says that "the way in which [Alisoun] moves . . . decisively establishes [the tale's] underlying ethos" (162); and Patterson calls her "the norm by which we are invited to understand her world" (286). Patterson further registers the fact that this ought to be a surprise given the tale's presiding gender ideology, and that this surprise is related to the limitations internal to the tale's normative views; but he does not elaborate on what this might mean for a further understanding of those views.

30. Hansen has done the most to bring out this feature of the scene, although she ends up missing the depth of the conflation, reading the scene as though Alisoun's ass were the rock-bottom term, and nearly dropping eros out of the picture, as though the ass were not itself an erotic object. What the scene finally presents on Hansen's account is the Miller in retreat from a disgusting femaleness that cannot effectively be distinguished from what men have down there too (227-30). While this leads Hansen to the topic of homoeroticism—something that is certainly at issue in that

bearded kiss—it does so too bluntly: homoeroticism becomes simply an object of aversion, hardly the locus of an eroticism at all, and at the same time the Miller's aversion to it becomes the stopping-point in the analysis, as though in noticing it we both knew what we were dealing with and had already dealt with it. Partly because I do not want simply to elide the homoeroticism of this scene, and for that matter of the entire tale, with what I describe here as its expression of an erotics of disgust and self-degradation—something Hansen's account unfortunately does—I defer an explicit treatment of homoeroticism until later in the essay, when the terms for a fuller understanding of it will be available.

31. Both Kolve (188) and Leicester (484) note this.

32. This, I take it, is the thought behind Muscatine's somewhat hyperbolic claim that "the ethic of the poem" is one of "assault" (227). Kolve puts the point more precisely in saying that fabliau "admits no goals beyond self-gratification, revenge, or social laughter" (160), although just how social such laughter can be is a question, since on the Miller's theory each person's participation in laughter, as in anything else, ought to be fundamentally egoistic.

33. I do not mean to suggest that a full and satisfying account of altruism could be given in these terms; just that, given the thought that there is a clean distinction to be made between a concern for oneself and a concern for others, altruism will easily appear as motivated only by a concern for others. The best account of altruism I know argues that altruism cannot be understood in these terms: see Thomas Nagel, *The Possibility of Altruism* (Princeton: Princeton Univ. Press, 1970). Much classical and medieval discussion of friendship makes it clear that, at least in the case of such intimate relations with others, there is no clean split of the kind to be made: see for instance Cicero's *De Amicitia* for a discussion which would certainly have been familiar to Chaucer.

34. The depth of the Miller's inability in this respect is responsible, I think, for what Leicester rightly describes as the "[extraordinary] amount of slandering against John in the criticism" (484): the Miller's lack of focus makes it hard even to notice that John is a problem, so we have mostly just taken the Miller's characterizations of him at face value. This "slandering," like the basic terms of the "exposure" reading of the hole-kissing scene, is shared by critics who otherwise have little common ground; so Robertson, for instance, joins with critics who have what he considers a misplaced interest in "character" in describing John's desire for Alisoun as though it were only a desire for possession (385). But noticing the problem of misdescribing John is not enough. Leicester obviously notices it, yet he describes John's attitude towards Alisoun as one "not of desire but of *care*, of a parental, nonsexual attraction" (484). It is true enough that John's attitude is one of care, and not fundamentally one of desire: nothing suggests that eros is the basic motive in his attraction for and interest in Alisoun. But nothing suggests his attraction and interest is fundamentally nonsexual either; Leicester just assumes that it is. And this assumption is itself of a Millerish sort—and, in slightly different terms, of a Robertsonian sort—as though the mere presence of a caring for someone which cannot be reduced to an epiphenomenon were enough to take eros out of the picture, or as though eros just were always and only a desire for possession that makes of others objects of egoistic gratification. I do not think Leicester believes this description of erotic desire. But it does partake of the impulse to exposure he occasionally indulges, and if he does not believe it he ought to say something rather different about John than he does.

35. A failure to register these necessities and their relation to each other is behind most of what I take to be the distortions in criticism concerning the construction of gender and desire in the *Miller's Tale*. This leads on the one hand to a lack of interest in the Miller's naturalism, a mistaken belief that the issues it raises are already settled by invoking the term "construction"; and on the other hand it leads to a lack of interest in the problem of intimacy, or perhaps to the thought that the Miller lacks an interest in it. For Hansen and Lochrie, the issue of intimacy never comes up: they seem to think that the only desires at work in the tale are objectifying and possessive. For Leicester, the alternative imagined in the tale to an objectifying and possessive desire is a pure

boundary-destroying *jouissance* that looks backward to the infant's seamless connection to its mother and a world that is "the plaything of one's projects" (489), and forward to a world of desire "beyond the phallus" (489). Leicester rightly describes this as a nostalgic and utopian fantasy (490). But, as my earlier citation of Leicester's line about the world-as-plaything is meant to suggest, this very description makes it odd to think of such *jouissance* as an *alternative* to the Miller's picture: it looks more like a peculiar instance of it, since it sidesteps the problem of needing to act in a world that is not such a plaything, and since as an image of adult erotic life it also sidesteps the problem of intimacy, of what is involved in being close to another who is not a mere plaything, or who is not from the start an undifferentiated and surrounding maternal presence. The difficulty here, then, is related to Leicester's misdescription of John, and provides another indication that a lack of clarity about the problem of intimacy and a lack of clarity about the motivations and depth of normative naturalism are quite closely related.

36. John Ganim notes the pun on "touching" here, as well as the further thought, implied by the line's "thingifying" language, that what John and Nicholas are imagined as touching is in the first place Alisoun's body; see *Chaucerian Theatricality* (Princeton: Princeton Univ. Press, 1990), 118. Ganim does not however note any difficulties with ascribing such a reifying view of Alisoun to the Miller.

37. The point is noted by Leicester (485, 494).

38. There could be some such thrill in looking at the sheep, but it would be parasitic on the thrill of looking at a human; it would involve imagining the sheep as looking back at you, or enjoying the proximity of the sheep to the capacity to do so, and finding excitement in that capacity being as it were narrowly averted. This may seem to take us ridiculously far from anything imagined in the *Miller's Tale*—thus its relegation to a footnote—but a scopophilic eroticism directed straight at animals might be seen as a kind of allegorization of the eroticism directed towards the figure of Alisoun in the text, or as the expression of a naturalism turned even more squarely away from the human conditions that give rise to it than the Miller's is.

39. In linking Narcissus and Pygmalion in this way, as figures who express a masculine desire for woman to be simultaneously a perfect object and an agent, I am following Jean de Meun, and suggesting that the *Miller's Tale* is one of many places in which Chaucer takes up and pursues further what he finds interesting and expressive in the *Roman de la Rose*. In this context, another bit of Alisoun's portrait—the Miller's enthusiastically self-promoting claim that "In al this world, to seken up and doun,/ Ther nys no man so wys that koude thenche/ So gay a popelote or swiche a wenche" (I.3252-54)—reads like a claim to having out-Pygmalioned Pygmalion.

40. Leicester, 486.

41. My casting of the Miller's homoeroticism requires some specific reformulations of that topic as it has been broached by other critics. In particular, it has been easy to think that homoeroticism involves the utter disappearance of "woman" from the scene of desire (Lochrie, 299-300); or that it appears fundamentally in relation to "the possibilities of homosexuality and castration" (Hansen, 229); or, a bit more technically, that it is the sign and product of Oedipal anxieties, or of the simultaneous presence of such anxieties and a more positive valuation of bisexuality and gender fluidity (Leicester, 486-91). I have already suggested my reasons for rejecting Lochrie's claim: homoeroticism is not here involved in a mutually exclusive binary relation with hetero-eroticism; and we can hardly understand the objectification of Alisoun—which, on Lochrie's account, is what allows for a reading of homoeroticism in the tale—independently of understanding the way she becomes an object of desire, and not just of an objectifying desire. Hansen's formulation raises three closely related issues. One lies in her use of the term "homosexuality," which raises methodological problems, familiar from Foucault, concerning an unavoidable terminological ambiguity in the term "homosexuality." As a technical term it is clear that its use here is anachronistic: homosexuality in this sense is restricted to a range of historical constructions of

---

homoeroticism which are not yet fully operative in the fourteenth century. On a more copious definition of the term, of the kind favored for instance by John Boswell, homosexuality might be taken to refer to any form of homoeroticism which is bound to same-sex object-choice, however that binding happens in the life of the subject and whatever its cultural value and meaning (see Boswell, *Christianity, Social Tolerance, and Homosexuality* [Chicago: Univ. of Chicago Press, 1980]). For this more copious definition to avoid the Foucaultian critique it would need squarely to resist any definition of "the homosexual" which relies for its identification of a sexuality on a reifying psychology. But—and this is the second problem—this is just what Hansen does, despite her many protestations to the contrary, in locating a particular pair of aversions (to the feminine and to castration) as the motivational bedrock whose identification settles the matter. Finally, in choosing aversions as the bedrock it in effect banishes desire, homoerotic or otherwise, from the scene; but if this scene is to do any of the work anyone thinks it does, one thing it must centrally be is a scene of desire. Leicester's view is closest to my own, since it works against the localization of the Miller's motive in a single univalent set of attitudes; but it has the unfortunate consequence of making it seem as though a specific technical account of gender and desire is needed to understand the phenomena under discussion, and so of raising worries about anachronism in talking this way at all. In developing my account out of the inner logic of normative naturalism and of a set of antifeminist and heteronormative attitudes which are common coin in the middle ages as today, I mean in part to be suggesting that we do not need a Freudian or post-Freudian story about the origins of a desiring gendered subject to bring the Miller's range of attitudes into focus. That is not to say, as so many want to say these days, that Freud, or some revisionary version of Freud, is wrong. It is just to say that an account of what something is and an account of where it comes from, however much each may illuminate the other, are two different things. One thing I mean this essay to suggest is that it can help us understand our stories of origins to try to understand on independent grounds what they are stories of.

42. This is what I referred to early in the essay as the first, seemingly innocent step by which a naturalistic view of human identity and action gains its hold on us, and does so even when what we centrally have in mind is the repudiation of such a view.

43. Patterson notes the Miller's surprising sympathy towards John and the problem of reconciling it with his more obvious hostility towards the character (270-73). Here as elsewhere Patterson's account differs from mine in focusing on the way this local representational incoherence reflects problems in fourteenth-century English social structure and class-based ideology.

The Pardoner's Body and the Disciplining of Rhetoric

Rita Copeland

The term 'disciplining' in my title has a double value: it stands for the construction of rhetoric as an academic discipline, and it also suggests the way that rhetoric's disciplinary power has always been subject to the most severe kinds of institutional regulation, or 'discipline'. This double sense of discipline is dramatised in the figure of Chaucer's Pardoner, in the homologous relation of his rhetoric, with its ambiguous content and transgressive morality, and his sexuality, with its bodily ambiguity and its transgression of gender boundaries. The Pardoner's claims for the disciplinary autonomy of rhetoric are suppressed in the same way that his sexuality is subject to public correction through the Host's virtual threat of (re)castration. The linkage that I want to explore here between sexuality, disciplining of the body, and the discipline of rhetoric is not something that I have manufactured for the sake of (rhetorical) argument; it is a linkage that is already there in the history of rhetoric itself.

Just as there is no historically transcendent category of the body, so there is also no unitary discursive category of bodiliness. As a symbolic domain the body is the expressive language through which many cultural discourses, including intellectual relations, aesthetics and science, define themselves.[1] In this essay I will examine how scientific or disciplinary classification in antiquity and the Middle Ages constitutes one domain or category of the body, and how notions of violent physical correction or 'discipline' to be enacted on the human body are transferred metaphorically to the realm of intellectual disciplines. This has particular implications for the institutional history of rhetoric; I want to give the disciplinary body of rhetoric a history.[2] In locating this historical inquiry at the literary site of Chaucer's Pardoner I do not pretend here to advance on the innovative and important insights that recent work in feminist and gay theory have brought to Chaucerian texts, especially new readings of the *Pardoner's Tale* as a site for the discursive conflicts of gender.[3] Rather, what I offer is an attempt to understand how gender and sexuality are part of the political text of rhetoric's institutional history.

As a science, rhetoric—from antiquity onwards—has been suspect, subject to regulation and control by dominant institutional interests. Ancient and medieval (as well as modern) practitioners and theorists of rhetoric have always to answer to question, first posed by Socrates to Gorgias: 'does rhetoric constitute a legitimate study of its own?' I want to recast this question in the terms of its most radical implications: 'does rhetoric have a body?' This is the question to which the disciplinary legitimacy of rhetoric was (and indeed still is) linked; judgement of rhetoric's disciplinary status is articulated through a discourse about its bodily status.

To begin we can turn for illustration to two modern perspectives on medieval rhetoric, one which denies rhetoric any disciplinary autonomy in the Middle Ages by denying it a body, and one which denies medieval rhetoric a disciplinary legitimacy by giving it a transgressive, fragmented body. The first of these, which denies rhetoric any disciplinary status in history by denying it a body, is well exemplified through a recently published account of an extraordinary professional exchange. James J. Murphy, the foremost modern historian of medieval rhetoric, recounts how in 1960 he sent an article on medieval rhetoric to the journal *PMLA*. The article was rejected with this response from the reader: 'rhetoric is not a subject; and if it were, there would be no history of it'. Fifteen years later, after the appearance of Murphy's *Rhetoric in the Middle Ages*,[4] the reviewer was moved to apologise to Murphy and retract that opinion.[5] The view that the reviewer first expressed, that rhetoric is no subject itself and has no history of its own, is in metaphorical terms a denial of rhetoric's body, of its location in space or time; the reviewer's later admission of ignorance or shortsightedness was itself predicated on the 'embodiment' of rhetoric's disciplinary history in Murphy's substantial volume, a physical codex that the reviewer and others could see and touch as evidence of a body of historical facticity. One other notable example of the model of denying the disciplinary 'body' of rhetoric is Richard McKeon's influential article 'Rhetoric in the Middle Ages',[6] which also argues that medieval rhetoric has no history of its own, but can be known to us as the imprint of the many other intellectual (and specifically philosophical) practices with which it was associated. McKeon proposes to write a history of rhetoric that accounts for its multiple, shifting, and ephemeral nature:

> Such a history would not treat an art determined to a fixed subject matter (so conceived rhetoric is usually found to have little or no history, despite much talk about rhetoric and even more use of it, during the Middle Ages) nor on the other hand would it treat an art determined arbitrarily and variously by its place in classifications of the sciences (so conceived the whole scheme and philosophy of the sciences would be uncontrolled in their alterations and therefore empty). . . . Yet if rhetoric is defined in terms of a single subject matter—such as style, or literature, or discourse—it has no history during the Middle Ages.[7]

Very possibly the reviewer of Murphy's article (who was not, incidentally, McKeon himself) derived a point of view (as well as wording) from the *auctoritas* of McKeon's study. McKeon's language is virtually that of the body or bodily physics; rhetoric has no 'fixed' subject matter, nor does it have a 'place' in classifications of the sciences. Interestingly McKeon's language also betrays some anxiety about what would happen to the regulation of the sciences under classificatory schemes—a regulation that represents a coercive 'discipline' or control imposed on the sciences—if rhetoric were to be understood solely through its metamorphic and irregular appearances in those schemes; the entire system would be 'emptied' of its content and meaning and would no longer yield to our managerial control of its many and various parts. In other words, rhetoric shifts its position so often in medieval classifications of the sciences that it threatens to reduce the whole system to a meaningless jumble; rhetoric is so disruptive a force that it can only be historically and discursively managed, according to McKeon, by denying it a veritable scientific body of its own and treating its appearances in scientific classifications as merely suggestive illusions. The assumption behind this theoretical model that denies rhetoric a body is that rhetoric by its very nature defies the principles of solidity and stability attributed to the body; rhetoric is not substantive, it is not about or of anything, but is only a tool (in the Aristotelian sense of *organon*) that comes into being through application to other things.

The second modern perspective also challenges rhetoric's claims to disciplinary legitimacy, but in this case by giving it a body: an unruly, fragmented body that confirms rhetoric's illegitimacy. This is the view propounded quite explicitly by Brian Vickers in his recent book *In Defence of Rhetoric*,[8] which is argued through an unabashed bias of classical humanism. Vickers's chapter on the Middle Ages is entitled 'Medieval Fragmentation': the Middle Ages represent a falling away from rhetoric's integrity of purpose in antiquity, and are characterised by atrophy, reduction to mere tropology, a loss of the whole aesthetic picture, and a decline of function in favour of an endless pursuit of form. The Middle Ages fragment rhetoric into the repetitive mechanics of abbreviation and amplification. Medieval rhetoric is externally fragmented in that the classical rhetorical texts survive 'in a damaged and haphazard state'; it is internally fragmented in that 'readers atomized what had been transmitted to fit their own needs' (p. 220). The emergence in the Middle Ages of three specialised arts of rhetoric (*poetria*, *dictamen*, and the *ars praedicandi*) represents a 'dismemberment' (p. 236) of what had once been (in Vickers's humanist view) a coherent and homogeneous lore. This view (which Vickers also extends to poststructuralist criticism as a twentieth-century fragmentation of rhetoric) can be seen as a consequence of the logic of the 'bodiless' model exemplified by McKeon and the *PMLA* reviewer. Rhetoric's transmutative heterogeneity makes it incapable of possessing a stable or healthy body; but those institutional interests that abhor a vacuum and that would manage that instability can nevertheless assign rhetoric a body, a body that symbolically confirms and justifies that imposition of coercive management. In the interests of institutional discipline rhetoric is given a body, a transgressive, atrophied or fragmented, illegitimate body that by its very nature invites corrective regulation. In the limited case of Vickers's book, the long-range project of institutional management of rhetoric is the moralised chronology that he aims to produce; here, operating in the same symbolic sphere of language that (as we will see) Quintilian also uses, Vickers invents a bodily image for rhetoric in order to discriminate between his ideal models of rhetoric (classical and Renaissance) and its fallen forms (medieval and modern). Thus the real purpose of giving rhetoric a body is to identify the transgressive tendencies of rhetoric when it is unguarded or unregulated (as Vickers believes it was during the Middle Ages), and to enclose it within a managerial paradigm of organic stability which can monitor its propensity for resistance.

These two modern perspectives on medieval rhetoric are very close to views of rhetoric that were propounded in antiquity and especially in the Middle Ages. In their views of medieval rhetoric, Vickers and McKeon actually voice the terms of censure that were used in the Middle Ages to vilify and marginalise rhetoric; indeed, their view of the Middle Ages is produced by the Middle Ages themselves, and through the institutional power of their voices is continually reproduced. In the metaphorical language about rhetoric from antiquity to the Middle Ages we see an opposition between a bodiless and an embodied rhetoric. These contradictory models reveal the enormous ideological stakes in this metaphorical discourse. Rhetoric by its very nature defies the principles that attached to ideas of the integrated body and, by extension, to ideas of a disciplinary body of knowledge. As I will argue here, rhetoric for this very reason had to come under some institutional and discursive regulation, and so a 'body' had to be invented for rhetoric to allow it to be 'disciplined'. The body invented for rhetoric was a transgressive, unlicensed body that would justify the severest regulation or discipline.

The relationship between scientific disciplinarity and the body as an object of punishment or discipline emerges in the history of the Latin word *disciplina*, which constitutes the larger framework for my investigation here. The extraordinary history of this word has been documented by Henri Marrou, to whose philological research my account here is indebted.[9] *Disciplina* is related to *discere*, 'to learn', although in classical usage it can also mean 'teaching', as in the teachings of a master. In classical antiquity, the broadest meaning of *disciplina* (in the plural) is intellectual culture or scientific knowledge. These meanings passed into patristic and early medieval use. Here we find the application of the word still familiar to moderns; *disciplina* designates a particular science, such as rhetoric, dialectic, astronomy, geometry, or music.[10] In the plural it designates all the various sciences together as a group.[11] Other words that are used synonymously with *disciplina* in this sense, sometimes with slightly different emphases, are *doctrina* (for which Marrou finds a more general and abstract connotation, the broader sense of study, intellectual work, or knowledge), *ars* (which early on was the preferred term for the elements of the trivium), and *scientia*.[12]

Thus in this application, *disciplina* is a particular body of knowledge. In signifying an individual branch of knowledge, it is a term for differentiating between kinds of scientific discourse and for delimiting and containing each branch of knowledge according to the rules that pertain to (or inhere within) a given discipline.[13] What *disciplina* really signifies is a set of rules which impose order. Here the rich semantic field of the word *disciplina* comes into play, for it has a much wider range of meaning than its synonyms, including *doctrina*. In classical use, *disciplina* is the Latin equivalent of the Greek *paideia*, acquiring the sense of rules imposed by a master on a student, especially moral rules aimed at the conduct of one's life. In this respect ancient usage is very informative. In classical Latin, *disciplina* is applied to military life, to designate the rules and principles that are used to maintain order, in other words, military discipline.[14] From this we need not look far to find the word used to designate the imposition of rules or order in the civil domain. Cicero speaks of '*disciplina civitatis*', and Tacitus speaks of the 'most severe discipline and laws' of Sparta and Crete.[15]

These various senses of *disciplina* were carried over into early Christian use. The practical, moral orientation of *disciplina* finds expression in the idea of a rule of Christian life: for Augustine, Christian discipline is the 'law of God', the wisdom and knowledge that constitute a rule of Christian living.[16] *Disciplina* is also the rule imposed by the Church on believers, and later by ecclesiastical authority on clergy. Along these lines we arrive at the notion of monastic discipline, the order and submission to authority that are required by observance of the rule within the monastic community.[17] Thus the discipline of civil law becomes the self-regulation of an enclosed religious community.

Finally, there is one meaning of *disciplina* unknown in classical usage, a meaning introduced in the language of the Septuagint and the New Testament: punishment, correction, pain inflicted for a transgression. Of course, ancient pedagogical practice involved corporal punishment, but the terms *paideia* in Greek and *disciplina* in Latin were not used to signify this aspect of instructive correction (even though corporal punishment would be understood as part of the educative system denoted by these terms).[18] In the Greek and Latin scriptures, however, the terms were extended to include this sense, taking on, moreover, the idea of the punishment that God reserves for correction of the sinner.[19] In the language of the Church Fathers, the punitive connotation of *disciplina* is associated with an educative function, corporal punishment as deterrent or correction. Here the term *disciplina* becomes linked with *verber-*

are, 'to flog', and with *vapulare*, 'to get a beating'.[20] The term inevitably acquires civil and legal dimensions: physical punishment by secular authority; the power to inflict punishment; and punitive law itself.[21] Out of its association with flogging and beating it also takes on the specialised meaning of flagellation, both in the sense of punishment under law and of self-inflicted scourging.[22] Thus by the early Middle Ages the idea of intellectual regulation, of observing a rule or scientific order, is identified semantically with the idea of physical punishment, *disciplina corporis*, disciplining of the body to correct or guard against vice, whether imposed by parent, teacher, monastic rule, civil law, or self.

From *disciplina* as a metaphorical body of knowledge we have arrived at *disciplina* as physical regulation and correction of the body. The implications of this semantic association for the discourse of scientific classification are readily apparent. To call a form or body of knowledge a discipline is to mark off its boundaries from another form of knowledge, and through this process of division to constitute that knowledge as an object. But it is not simply that disciplines create knowledge as a discursive object; as Foucault reminds us, the disciplinary order itself also becomes the object to be surveyed and regulated.[23] From antiquity onwards we see that discussions of the disciplinary relations between the sciences often carry corrective and restrictive overtones. In the *Institutio orataria*, for example, Quintilian places firm restrictions on the territory of the grammarians, lest their work overlap with, or trespass into, the territory of the rhetoricians (1.9.6; 2.1.4-5).[24] Even Quintilian's attempts to promote a broad-based 'liberal' education for the orator are predicated on precise taxonomies and hierarchical differentiations between the domains of the various arts (1.10.1-12.7). We find similarly deterrent boundaries placed around the individual disciplines in Martianus Capella's *De nuptiis Philologue et Mercurii*. Grammar's discourse is interrupted at the moment when she is about to discuss figures and tropes and introduce the question of metre (§ 326), subjects which are within the competence of grammatical teaching but which are normally governed by the disciplines of rhetoric and music respectively. Minerva also stops Dialectic from proceeding to the discussion of sophistic arguments, asserting that such a subject will dishonour the discipline of dialectic (§ 423). As these examples suggest, disciplinary structures function to contain and regulate bodies of knowledge, just as the human body is often subject to corrective discipline as a guard against moral or physical transgression. But disciplinary formations in turn are also subject to such corrective measures, so that it is not simply raw knowledge that is embodied as an object of control, but the construction of the discipline itself. The discourse of intellectual taxonomy, classification of the sciences, carries a clearly restrictive imperative that can be understood both in terms of the interests of territoriality,

---

to mark off one intellectual property or domain from another, and of subjuga-
tion, to ensure the manageability of individual scientific systems.

The obvious link between *disciplina* as a science and *disciplina* as punishment is correction. But metaphorically the link is the body. It is this deep and
secure metaphorical linkage that rhetoric, with its particular claims to disciplinary legitimacy, seems always to unfix. We see this in the important statements of Plato and Aristotle on rhetoric. In Plato's *Gorgias*, the sophist Gorgias argues that rhetoric's disciplinary power lies in its open borders; the art of
persuasive speech comprises or overlaps all other arts. For Socrates the permeability of rhetoric makes it no science at all, but a mere knack gained from
experience, a counterfeit of true science that panders (like cookery and cosmetics) to gratification and pleasure.[25] In identifying rhetoric with the temporal contingencies of experience and the arts of the pleasure-seeking body,
Plato's text suggests that rhetoric is a kind of incontinent body that does not
know its own boundaries. The discipline that Socrates imposes on the transgressive, permeable body of rhetoric is to condemn it to the realm of bodily
provisionality from which it can make no claim to scientific integrity. Aristotle's rigorous programme of scientific classification recasts the Platonic hierarchy of knowledge in more pragmatic institutional terms. In the *Rhetoric*
Aristotle says that rhetoric, like dialectic, is a tool (*organon*) of inquiry, not a
science; rhetoric and dialectic 'are concerned with such things as are, to a certain extent, within the knowledge of all people and belong to no separately defined science'.[26] But for Aristotle, the permeability of rhetoric positions it, not
only outside any disciplinary category, but in *opposition* to the body. Rhetoric
is a system of artifice, of construction or invention of the modes of persuasion;
the body is a *natural* site of truth which furnishes preexisting ('inartificial' or
'extrinsic') proof in the form of evidence extracted from slaves under torture.[27] In Athenian judicial discourse, as Page duBois argues, the slave represents a primordial form of bodiliness, and the slave body is a secret repository
of truth to be yielded up (and possessed by free men) through the application
of torture.[28] In this context Aristotle uses the body to describe a coherent
realm of truth in counterdistinction to the artificial system of representation
that is rhetoric.[29]

In neither of these models is the body represented *within* the discipline of
rhetoric. For Plato rhetoric is only body and thus a counterfeit discipline; for
Aristotle, rhetoric is outside disciplinary order and in opposition to the body. It
is Roman teaching on the art that places the body securely within the disciplinary order of rhetoric and judges rhetoric through its bodily manifestations.
The political and pedagogical institutions of Roman culture confer on rhetoric
a privileged status as the highest of the arts because of its application to the
pragmatic interests of civic oratory. But because rhetoric holds so crucial a

cultural position it is the more subject to severe containment, monitoring, or scrutiny. It is here that rhetoric is truly invented as a discipline; it becomes a body capable of yielding up valid knowledge provided that it is successfully managed. Most importantly, to regulate rhetoric is to control its artificial excesses; in this context artifice, and especially ornamentation, is identified with mere bodily form, comparable to Plato's notion of counterfeit gratification. Whereas for Aristotle artifice is bodiless, in Roman theory artifice is inscribed on the body, as the possibility of monstrous or corrupt disfigurement; it is only by subjecting rhetoric's body to a disciplinary regime that its transgressive potential can be channelled into the production of truth. Significantly rhetoric here registers its own unrestrained artifice and permeability in terms of the disfigured body and the sexually ambiguous body. The *Rhetorica ad Herennium*, which was to become the main authority on style in the Middle Ages, represents style that has gone out of control in terms of the tumorous or disjointed body:

> Nam ita ut corporis bonam habitudinem tumor imitatur saepe, item gravis oratio saepe inperitis videtur ca quae turget et inflata est, cum aut novis aut priscis verbis aut duriter aliunde translatis aut gravioribus quam res postulat aliquid dicitur. . . . Qui in mediocre genus orationis profecti sunt, si pervenire eo non potuerunt, errantes perveniunt ad confine genus eius generis, quod appellamus dissolutum, quod est sine nervis et articulis; ut hoc modo appellem fluctuans, eo quod fluctuat huc et illuc nec potest confirmate neque viriliter sese expedire.

> For just as a swelling often resembles a healthy condition of the body, so, to those who are inexperienced, turgid and inflated language often seems majestic—when a thought is expressed either in new or in archaic words, or in clumsy metaphors, or in diction more impressive than the theme demands. . . . Those setting out to attain the Middle style, if unsuccessful, stray from the course and arrive at an adjacent type, which we call the Slack because it is without sinews and joints; accordingly I may call it the Drifting, since it drifts to and fro, and cannot get under way with resolution and virility.[30]

As this example suggests, rhetoric can legitimise itself as a true discipline if it can expose—and thus subject to severe disciplinary scrutiny—its own capacity for distortion. In other words, rhetoric needs its own potential for transgression in order to demonstrate its capacity for self-discipline.

Quintilian's *Institutio orataria* is even more explicit on this point, registering the threat of an unlicensed artifice in terms of the *sexually* permeable body, the body that has crossed the acceptable bounds of gender identity into a kind of monstrous spectacle:

Corpora sana et integri sanguinis et exercitatione firmata ex iisdem his speciem accipiunt ex quibus vires, namque et colorata et adstricta et lacertis expressa sunt; at eadem si quis volsa atque fucata muliebriter comat, foedissima sint ipso formae labore. Et cultus concessus atque magnificus addit hominibus, ut Graeco versu testatum est, auctoritatem; at muliebris et luxuriosus non corpus exornat, sed detegit mentem. Similiter illa translucida et versicolor quorundam elocutio res ipsas effeminat, quae illo verborum volo esse sollicitudinem. . . . Maiore animo aggredienda eloquentia est, quae si toto corpore valet, ungues polire et capillum reponere non existimabit ad curam suam pertinere.

Healthy bodies, enjoying a good circulation and strengthened by exercise, acquire grace from the same source that gives them strength, for they have a healthy complexion, firm flesh and shapely thews. But, on the other hand, the man who attempts to enhance these physical graces by the effeminate use of depilatories and cosmetics, succeeds merely in defacing them by the very care which he bestows on them. Again, a tasteful and magnificent dress, as the Greek poet tells us, lends added dignity to its wearer; but effeminate and luxurious apparel fails to adorn the body and merely reveals the foulness of the mind. Similarly, a translucent and iridescent style merely serves to emasculate [translating *effeminat*] the subject which it arrays with such pomp of words. . . . It is with a more virile spirit [translating *maiore animo*] that we should pursue eloquence, who, if only her [for *eloquentia*, feminine noun] whole body be sound, will never think it her duty to polish her nails and tire her hair.[31]

This remarkable passage, from Quintilian's prologue to his lengthy discussion of style, gives expression to what was always implicit in the condemnation of rhetoric; that the undisciplined body is a sexually wayward body, that pandering and gratification are tantamount to a weakening of sexual identity, and that the disciplinary permeability of rhetoric is nothing less than ambiguity of gender. Stylistic excrescence allows the well-trained, masculine body to sink into effeminacy (not femininity), counterfeiting its proper virility. It is interesting that rhetoric's anxiety about its corporeality is given the most striking expression in relation to style, that rhetoric admits its own propensity for unruly excess when it turns to consider its most visible aspect, *elocutio*. Style is the part of rhetoric that can be seen, and as such is always in danger of being considered merely deceptive surface, whether as dress on the body or as the bodily exterior itself. It thus also threatens to be taken for the body as a whole, to reduce by perverse metonymy the art of *eloquentia* to pandering style, the body to its appearance. But style is not an external excrescence that can be surgically removed and expelled from the realm of rhetoric. It is a function inherent to rhetoric. Rhetoric cannot deny or suppress the force of body as appearance, for it operates through the persuasive appeal of appearance. Thus to constitute itself as a proper discipline, rhetoric repeatedly—almost ritually—re-enacts and enforces its self-discipline by exposing its continual struggle with its wayward body.[32] It invents itself as a discipline by inventing a corrupt bodily image over which it can always be seen to be triumphing by determined self-discipline. And part of its self-discipline is to punish that counter-image of its body by exposing it to public condemnation as a kind of trophy of its agonistic victory over its own unruliness. This is borne out at wearisome length in nearly all rhetorical manuals from antiquity to the Middle Ages (and beyond), which illustrate precept through sharp castigation of defective practice.

Thus on the terms of its own construction, rhetoric, like the body, must be subjected to a healthy regimen, disciplined lest it lapse into license, disease, or disfigurement.[33] The most familiar image of rhetoric is female excess. Martianus Capella's allegorical depiction of Rhetoric as a garish, physically imposing woman in martial attire whose swollen speech threatens to overrun the time allotted to it is not far removed from representations of rhetoric as a richly arrayed mistress or even a female courtesan.[34] But the other common trope, which we have already seen in Quintilian, uses the male body to identify an undisciplined rhetoric with transgressive sexuality. In the Middle Ages, images of masculine licence are tied to the enforcement of social constraints on male clerical sexual behaviour.[35] The most familiar medieval example of this is Alan of Lille's *De planctu Naturae*, which describes the corruption of the language arts of the *trivium* in terms of proscribed sexual practice, representing the effect of rhetorical figuration in terms of bodily disfigurement:

> sic methonomicas rethorum positiones . . . Cypridis artificiis interdixi, ne si nimis dure translationis excursu a suo reclamante subiecto predicatum alienet in aliud, in facinus facetia, in rusticitatem urbanitas, tropus in uicium, in decolorationem color nimius conuertatur.

> so too I banned from the Cyprian's [i.e. Venus'] workshop the use of words by the rhetors in metonymy . . . lest, if she embark on too harsh a trope and transfer the predicate from its loudly protesting subject to something else, cleverness would turn into a blemish, refinement into boorishness, a figure of speech into a defect and excessive embellishment into disfigurement.[36]

The governing image of Alan's text (announced in metre 1) suggests that the vice of tropes, departing from the governance of grammar, has turned man into hermaphrodite.[37] In the passage above, the perversion of rhetoric results in the defilement of appearance. Here, as in the *Rhetorica ad Herennium* and Quintilian, rhetoric displays the effects of perverse figuration.

Alan's text represents an indictment of rhetoric from outside the borders of the discipline. But as we see elsewhere, the figural relationship of rhetoric to the transgressive body is so ingrained in discourse about the art that rhetoric even teaches its own precepts through this trope. In the *Ars versificatoria* of Matthew of Vendôme, one of the models of rhetorical *descriptio* takes as its subject the depravities of Davus (a stock figure of ancient comedy). Here the pedagogical occasion of exemplifying rhetorical *descriptio* through the attributes of the person becomes the vehicle for exposing the vices of rhetoric:[38]

> Ne per se patiatur idem consordeat [*or* cum sordeat] intus
> Et foris, in Davo methonomia parit . . .
> Vergit ad incestum, Venus excitat aegra bilibres
> Fratres, membra tepent cetera, cauda riget.
> Metri dactilici prior intrat syllaba, crebro
> Impulsu quatiunt moenia foeda breves.
> Nequitia rabiem servilern praedicat, actu
> Enucleat servae conditionis onus.
> Urget blanda, furit in libera terga, rebellis
> Naturae vetito limite carpit iter.[39]

Since he is foul both inside and out in Davus metonymy falls flat [literally: 'metonymy is made equal'].[40] . . . He inclines to lewdness; his sickly libido (*Venus aegra*) excites the Brothers Testicles (they weigh two pounds), the related members warm up and he gets a hard on. The first syllable of the dactyl enters; with repeated batterings, the foul short syllables shake the ramparts. His baseness foretells his slavish frenzy and the act declares the work of a slave. He presses hard upon alluring backs and rages against the backs of freeborn men. A rebel to nature, he goes the route to forbidden borders.[41]

In this extraordinary and explicit passage, the body that knows no boundaries is one with a debilitated rhetoric; impossible metonymy is the attribute of Davus, and Davus embodies impossible metonymy. The ostensible subject here is not the nature of rhetoric, but the nature of Davus. The real subject, however, is the technique of rhetorical *descriptio* which this passage teaches through exemplification. But the vehicle of this particular pedagogy is the image of the incontinent sexual body, where the breaking of (hetero)sexual correctness is the sign of unlicensed permeability and of lawless metonymy (Davus is 'foul' outside and within, so that there are no borders between container and contained). Here the transgressive body is used to teach rhetorical *descriptio*, and within that corrective teaching is identified with an 'incorrect' rhetoric.

As these examples suggest, rhetoric is invented through constructions of sexual transgression. As a sexual body, rhetoric can be disciplined from within its own system through a kind of enforced purity, in which it is compelled to expose, and therefore be purged of, its excesses. This is the model that we see in Quintilian and Matthew of Vendôme, who teach rhetoric through the proscription of sexual-rhetorical vice. Or, as we see in Alan of Lille, rhetoric can be disciplined from outside its own system, through subordination to external governance, such as the balanced structure of the *trivium*, which maintains the 'body' of science in a 'normative' or prescriptive (sexual) order.[42] In both cases we see the operation of what Jonathan Dollimore has called, after Foucault, a 'politics of containment'.[43] Giving rhetoric a sexual body establishes a discursive construct through which institutional power can work. Rather than simply eliding the sexual body, the institutional powers of pedagogy, literature, and intellectual tradition continually stage their repression of the body, and it is in this drama of its own correction that rhetoric willingly participates.

This is the nexus of ideas that lies behind Chaucer's Pardoner. As Robert Payne has acutely recognised, the Pardoner is more than a figure of corrupt preaching in the particular context of late-medieval anti-fraternalism; in the form of corrupt preacher he is a figure out of long traditions of theoretical contest about rhetoric as a science, of debate going back to the *Gorgias* about rhetoric's appeal to appearances, contingency, appetite, will, and belief.[44] But it is the Pardoner's bodily presence, the sexual ambiguity of his bodily appearance, that most clearly associates him with the representation of rhetoric in the tradition that leads from Quintilian to the medieval language arts. The narrator's description of him in the *General Prologue* as either 'a geldyng or a mare' (1.691),[45] pointing either to a disfiguring absence or a transgression of gender boundaries, can be taken as a realisation, a making literal, of the figuring of rhetoric as an emasculated or effeminate male body. In this, of course, Chaucer's Pardoner has his most direct literary forebear in Faus Semblant of the *Roman de la Rose*, whose incarnation of false preaching takes the form of indeterminate gendering; as Carolyn Dinshaw points out, Faus Semblant is both man and woman.[46] Both Faus Semblant and the Pardoner are products of the metaphorical tradition of rhetoric as unregulated sexuality. But with the Pardoner's embodiment of rhetoric, the metaphors of rhetoric as body achieve a crucial and complex articulation. The social politics of sexuality and the institutional politics of rhetoric meet with renewed force in the performance of the Pardoner and the claims that he makes for the disciplinary autonomy of rhetoric.

The Pardoner's performance is realised through images of the disabled, fragmented body and unruly appetite. As recent readers of the text have pointed out, the Pardoner professionally associates himself with the purveying of false relics, which are merely fragments of animal bodies cut off from reference to any symbolic unity beyond themselves; he even submits his own body to a figurative dismemberment when he describes his physical gestures during his preaching in terms of a grotesque choreography of nodding neck and busy tongue and hands (6.395-9).[47] His own body, of course, is fragmented or dismembered, and the text continually plays with the linguistic and symbolic substitution of relics and other objects, such as the bag of pardons in his lap (*General Prologue*, 686-7), for the 'coillons' or testicles that the Pardoner apparently lacks.[48] But beyond the force of these visual emblems of fragmentation, the Pardoner's discourse is linked with and follows from the *Physician's Tale*, a story which offers the choice of a defiled maidenhead or a decapitation.[49] The *Physician's Tale* leaves us with the headless body of Virginia, the patriarchal vindication of Virginius, and the punishment of the lascivious judge Appius whose violent and wayward bodily appetites have moved him to violate the girl's virginity and the family honour that places so much emphasis on her intact virtue. There is not much left intact at the end of this story, save a rigid social code predicated on male power over the female body; the transgressive will of the prospective rapist and the violent defence of the girl's bodily integrity. Such a story scarcely brooks interpretative intervention from its listeners; their response is that of powerlessness. Indeed, the tale told by the Physician makes the audience sick. Harry Bailly says that the story so grieves him that he thinks it will almost give him cardiac arrest: 'But wel I woot thou doost myn heare to erme/ That I almoost have caught a cardynacle' (6.312-13). Unless he has a drink or hears a merry tale, he tells us, 'myn heare is lost for pitee of this mayde' (6.317). Harry's threatened heart attack is as vivid a rhetorical response as we could want; both inside and outside the *Physician's Tale* there are bodies fragmented, dead, or dying, from the decapitated Virginia to Harry's 'cardynacle' or chest pains.

The Host's call to the Pardoner to supply a pleasant diversion, 'som myrthe or japes', and the protesting call from the 'gentils' of the company for 'som moral thyng' (6.319, 325), move us from the power, in the *Physician's Tale*, of an arbitrary and rigid law which requires obedience without interpretation, to the affective power of rhetoric, which requires only belief. Indeed, it is one of the powers traditionally ascribed to rhetoric to be able to fulfil the opposing demands of mirth and morality, to offer something that is moral and edifying but at the same time pleasant and entertaining. The Pardoner's brief here is to offer something curative for the Host's disabled body, and by extension for the whole company, in this sense the social body constituting the audience and judge of a rhetorical performance. The Pardoner achieves his curative effects, however, not through his tale, but through his very presence as an embodiment—literally a bodying forth—of the danger of rhetoric. If the horrible rigidity of the *Physician's Tale* strips the audience of its interpretative power and ethical leverage, of its capacity to make sense of an uncompromising law that permits (in Virginia's words), 'no grace . . . no remedye' (6.236), it seems that the community can regain its ethical and interpretative bearings when it learns how to govern and contain the force of rhetoric. The Pardoner's disquisition on rhetoric, his lecture on his own *techne* in his Prologue, teaches not just a body of rhetorical theory, but the means of controlling this body, how to make the body of rhetoric yield up its dangerous truths about itself so that it can be regulated from outside. The Pardoner's 'medicine' is to deliver up his professional secrets into the company's disciplinary control. As we know, it is in the act of threatening the Pardoner with corrective violence at the end of his tale that Harry Bailly springs back to life, miraculously cured.

My discussion here focuses on the Pardoner's Prologue. The Prologue dramatises in a very concentrated way something that I have described earlier in this essay as one of the key characteristics of rhetoric's discourse about itself: its compulsion to perform its disciplinary instabilities by performing the exposure of its own vices, thereby inviting (or establishing the need for) disciplinary correction. The Pardoner's Prologue is a consummate performance of rhetoric's self-exposure of its transgression and counterfeit. There are, of course, a number of ways in which the Pardoner's text differs in its dynamics from traditional rhetorical texts. Most obviously, the Pardoner does not himself demonstrate the self-governance of rhetoric from within its own text; unlike Quintilian, who stages rhetoric's vices in order to show how rhetoric can redeem itself by monitoring its own transgressions, the Pardoner simply stages the incontinence of his rhetoric, and leaves it to the dramatic response of his audience (in the person of Harry Bailly) to complete the work of punishing and containing his waywardness. Along more complex lines, the Pardoner's discourse does not need to make explicit the identification of a transgressive rhetoric with 'distortion' of the sexual body; this has already been accomplished dramatically through the person of the Pardoner, who embodies the sexual (dis)figuring of rhetoric. Thus while the Pardoner's discourse is yielding up the 'truth' about rhetoric's persuasive appeal to mere appearances, his bodily appearance and attributes—his high voice, his beardlessness, his playing at male fashion ('hym thoughte he rood al of the newe jet', *GP* 682), as well as his excessive 'stylistic' display of both hetero- and homosexual roles[50]—are yielding up or pointing to the 'truth' about his body, that is, his alienation from the masculine, heterosexual norm of patriarchal cultural power. One way of reading the truth about his body, as Dinshaw notes, is that we cannot know; the Pardoner may or may not be a eunuch, his exterior may or may not be consistent with his interior.[51] All we have is the narrator's judgment or belief, based on his appearance: 'I *trowe* he were a geldyng or a mare' (*GP* 691). The appearance of the Pardoner's body produces, not conviction of truth, but mere belief. This is also the very mechanism by which the Pardoner, as a latter-day Gorgias, describes the efficacy of his rhetoric; as the sophist must admit to Socrates, oratory produces only belief based on provisional appearances, not conviction based on knowledge of truth.[52] But another way of reading the question of his 'truth' is that his body, in conjunction with his rhetoric, becomes a locus of truth for others to know and possess, that his body and rhetoric together confess or yield up the truth about themselves into the corrective possession of his audience. The 'truth' is that his body is permeable, without definable gender identity, just as his permeable and ambiguous rhetoric defies proper disciplinary identity; because he cannot be known, he must be contained the more severely. Thus at the end of his *Tale*, when the Pardoner singles out the Host as the one 'moost envoluped in synne' (6.942) and tries to purvey to Harry the very relics that he has just finished describing as false, the Host's threat of violent (re)castration, 'I wolde I hadde thy coillons in myn hon . . . Lat kutte hem of' (6.952-4), directs itself *at* the incontinence of the Pardoner's rhetoric *through* the ambiguity of the Pardoner's sexual body.

In his Prologue, the Pardoner describes how he gains the trust of gullible crowds by preying on their fears and displaying false relics, and he asserts the alienation of his own moral condition from the moral effect of his preaching:

> For though myself be a ful vicious man,
> A moral tale yet I yow telle kan
> Which I am wont to preche for to wynne.
>
> (6.459-61)

From a technical point of view, the Pardoner's speech is a careful manifesto on *ethos* or ethical proof, the Aristotelian principle of a speaker's representation of his own character as part of his material for persuasion.[53] Aristotle's model of ethical proof survives in the Middle Ages in some attenuated forms in the *artes praedicandi* which recommend persuasive appeal to audiences.[54] But Robert Payne's crucial insight into the Pardoner's discourse is that it represents, within the terms of Chaucerian poetics, a forceful new articulation of the theory of character as a form of persuasion.[55] The Pardoner speaks *de arte*, that is, about the mechanics of his rhetoric, and describes in some detail how he invents an authoritative character for himself when he preaches, how he constructs a credible persona through his techniques of delivery and through his personal and professional display. When preaching in churches, he says, 'I peyne me to ban an hauteyn speche/ And rynge it out as round as gooth a belle' (6.330-1); he always announces from where he has come, shows his papal bulls along with the authorising seal on his letter patent (in order, he says, 'my body to warente' [6.338]), and then proceeds to display the paraphernalia of his trade (indulgences and relics), all the while sprinkling his speech with a few words of Latin to impress the crowds and 'stire hem to devocioun' (6.346). The construction of character for the purpose of persuasion is certainly efficacious, even on the terms of his vicious mockery of the enterprise: 'Thus spitte I out my venym under *hewe*/ Of hoolynesse, to *semen* hooly and trewe' (6.422-3; my emphasis).

Through his articulation of appeal to *ethos* or character as a means of persuasion, the Pardoner makes a strong claim for the disciplinary autonomy of rhetoric. According to the Pardoner, the efficacy of rhetoric should depend on nothing except its own art; its success need be tied to no moral system, no verification of truth beyond the belief that it produces. The most immediate contexts for the Pardoner's pronouncement that 'many a predicacioun/ Comth ofte tyme of yvel entencioun' (6.407-8) are scholastic debates about the efficacy of immoral preachers and the proper fulfilment of the office of preaching.[56] But his question, the relation of a speaker's character to his speech, has a much longer history in rhetorical theory, in the anxiety of rhetoricians such as Quintilian to differentiate a 'responsible'—that is, institutionally validated—rhetoric from the 'debased' or institutionally discredited theory of the sophists.[57] I would like to read the Pardoner's pronouncements about the autonomy of rhetorical *techne* as a kind of staging—however historically unlikely it may be—of the momentary possibility of a sophistic rhetoric. The Pardoner gives a view of rhetoric that is very much like that of the sophists, a view of a world to be negotiated through language and skilful argument rather than through a priori truth value, and in which there need be no coherence between the moral content of the message and the moral character of the speaker.[58] This is the epistemology of an autonomous rhetoric which emerged the loser in ancient debate, which Plato's institution of philosophy discredited, and the history of which came to be written by its adversaries.[59]

Whether or not Chaucer knew anything directly or indirectly about the sophists is not important here; the *mechanics of suppression*, Socrates (Plato) of Gorgias, the Host (or even Chaucer) of the Pardoner, are almost the same. Just as Socrates condemns Gorgias' rhetoric to the realm of mere bodily fragmentation from which it can make no claims to disciplinary integrity, so the Pardoner is condemned to make his claims for rhetoric in the person, in the body, of an unwhole man. It is here that his manifesto on *ethos* is subsumed by the dramatic *manifestatio* of the 'truth' about rhetoric that he is compelled to perform. More than a system of ethical proof, the Pardoner's Prologue is an exercise in rhetorical *descriptio* designed to manifest character, such as Matthew of Vendôme exemplifies in his description of Davus.[60] The corruption or moral vacuity of character that the Pardoner manifests—his pronouncements on his bald avarice, his indifference to the 'correccioun of synne' (6.404)—is metonymic for the deficiency or permeability of his sexual body and the incontinence of his rhetoric. The Pardoner's performance or *manifestatio* of his character is nothing less than a ritual exposure of the vices and transgressions of the body of rhetoric. Any claims for the disciplinary autonomy of rhetoric that the Pardoner may make through his exposition of *ethos* will be immediately invalidated by the self-admitted transgressiveness of the character that makes the claims.

Yet it is through his confessional exposure of his vices that the Pardoner's discourse stages the invention of rhetoric as a discipline. As a figure of rhetoric the Pardoner differs from Gorgias in one significant way: where the fragmentary body of rhetoric in the *Gorgias* consigns it to the sphere of nonscience, of mere knack like cooking, the Pardoner represents the tradition of rhetoric that I have traced here from later antiquity to the Middle Ages, in which rhetoric comes into being as a discipline by offering up its corrupt or counterfeit body to be disciplined. The production of scientific truth here about the body and about rhetoric is enabled through the ritual of confession;[61] and the Pardoner's confession differs only in dramatic degree, not in kind, from the compulsive self-exposure that we have seen rhetoric undertake in its various pedagogical and technical appeals, from Quintilian to Matthew of Vendôme. At the end of his *Tale*, where the Pardoner turns to his audience and, as if mechanically compelled to complete his whole routine, invites the Host to kiss the relics that he has just proclaimed to be false, it is not that he has forgotten his audience; rather, it is that the dynamic of rhetoric is to confess and perform itself continually, to display and stage its wilful excess.

The Pardoner's manifesto on *ethos* and his larger *manifestatio* of rhetoric have already given the pilgrims the key to his *techne* by showing them how the art of persuasion works. Now that they understand how rhetoric works as a professional system they are in a position of power to regulate it. The Pardoner has theorised and performed a powerful rhetoric that threatens to exceed its proper limits; what is important is that the necessity to contain and thereby discipline rhetoric is expressed by the Host as a threat of violence against the Pardoner's body. The Host enacts the disciplining of rhetoric by naming the Pardoner's bodily deficiency. The Host, rebounding from his 'cardynacle', wishfully threatens to castrate the Pardoner, swearing in the optative mood that he would like to cut off the Pardoner's coillons:

I wolde I hadde thy coillons in myn hond
In stide of relikes or of seintuarie.
Lat kutte hem of, I wol thee helpe hem carie;
They shul be shryned in an hogges toord!
(6.952-5)

The denunciation and threatened assault is a public humiliation tantamount to
public punishment. It is a punishment directed at the Pardoner's rhetoric
through the Pardoner's body, for his body, ambiguous, transgressive, probably
already emasculated, reproduces the nature of his crime, rhetoric. Foucault's
observations about the value of public torture and execution are strikingly (if
anachronistically) relevant here: through those public procedures of criminal
discipline,

> the body . . . [produces] and [reproduces] the truth of the crime—or rather it consti-
> tutes the element which, through a whole set of rituals and trials, confesses that the
> crime took place, admits that the accused did indeed commit it, shows that he bore
> it inscribed in himself and on himself, supports the operation of punishment and
> manifests its effects in the most striking way.[62]

It is through this kind of public display at the end of the *Pardoner's Tale* that
the containment of rhetoric, and thus its induction into disciplinary order,
takes place. Just as the Pardoner has exposed the capacity of rhetoric for distortion, the Host now exposes the Pardoner's bodily disfigurement. For the
Host to want to castrate a man who is already a eunuch is to want to punish
him for the crime of monstrous distortion that his body has already committed, to reinscribe that crime in a public, ritual way. On the logic of its own tradition of self-representation, rhetoric does become a genuine discipline here;
even the kiss that Harry gives to the Pardoner to mend their rupture inscribes
the Pardoner and his rhetoric in a system of discursive control. Under this regime, rhetoric will produce the truth about itself.

Rhetoric and its disciplinary formation may be apprehended through intellectual history and textual analysis; but we cannot forget that rhetoric is a discourse of the real world, of temporality, circumstance, shifting interests and
fragmented experience; in other words, a discourse of the body itself. The Pardoner and his sophistic forebears hold out the possibility of a critically detached knowledge 'in the subjunctive mode', as Nancy Struever has described
rhetoric's shaping of language as contingent experience, feeling and desire.[63]
But its very capacity for such a contingent detachment inevitably places rhetoric in conflict with hierarchical disciplinary interests that would seek to con-
strain its epistemological permeability. Thus in the Middle Ages, rhetoric's

techne is channelled or pressed into the service of dominant interests; it is accessory to grammar in primary education, to logic in the cathedral schools and universities, or it is 'redeemed' through its harnessing to scriptural study and homiletics, as we see from Augustine to Bede and Aquinas. Even with its magnification, in the civic ideologies of Brunetto Latini and Dante, to the highest order of statecraft, it is still contained and delimited, its capacity for artifice and manufacturing of belief firmly regulated by the reigning institutional science of politics. The subjunctive autonomy that rhetoric would claim for itself, even today, to be a kind of metadiscipline, would also constitute a kind of science of the body in history, a science of provisionality, contingency, and even fragmentation. The legitimisation and 'disciplining' of rhetoric is inevitably its repression, a process in which rhetoric participates by naming its own bodiliness.

From *Framing Medieval Bodies*, edited by Sarah Kay and Miri Rubin (1994), pp. 138-159. Copyright © 1994 by the New Chaucer Society. Reprinted by permission of the New Chaucer Society.

Notes

1. See Peter Stallybrass and Allon White, *The Politics and Poetics of Transgression*, Ithaca, NY, 1986, which offers a materialist examination of the relationship between the 'cultural categories of high and low, social and aesthetic. . . . the physical body and geographical space' (p. 2).

2. My concern here is with the construction of rhetoric as a discipline in relation to external discourses of knowledge, not with the internal features of rhetorical theory. In this my project differs from the work of some recent critics who deal with the question of rhetoric and the body in terms of the elements and practices of rhetorical figuration as language use and as a form of cultural representation; see Patricia Parker, *Literary Fat Ladies: Rhetoric, Gender, Property*, London and New York, 1987; R. Howard Bloch, 'Medieval misogyny', *Representations*, XX, 1987, pp. 1-24 (the arguments of which are recast in larger terms in his book, *Medieval Misogyny and the Invention of Western Romantic Love*, Chicago and London, 1991); and Tzvetan Todorov, *Theories of the Symbol* trans. Catherine Porter, Ithaca, NY, 1982.

3. See most importantly Carolyn Dinshaw, *Chaucer's Sexual Poetics*, Madison, Wisc., 1989. Other significant recent work includes Steven F. Kruger, 'Claiming the Pardoner: towards a gay reading of Chaucer's *Pardoner's Tale*', *Exemplaria*, VI, 1994, pp. 115-39, Glenn Burger, 'Kissing the Pardoner', *PMLA*, CVII, 1992, pp. 1143-56, and the ground-breaking article by Monica McAlpine, 'The Pardoner's homosexuality and how it matters', *PMLA*, XCV, 1980, pp. 8-22. I have also benefited from hearing presentations of new work on gay theory and the Pardoner that had not reached publication at the time that this essay was written; in particular I want to cite papers by Carolyn Dinshaw (New Chaucer Society, Seattle, 1992) and Allen J. Frantzen (International Congress on Medieval Studies, Kalamazoo, Michigan, 1991).

4. James J. Murphy, *Rhetoric in the Middle Ages*, Berkeley and Los Angeles, 1974.

5. This exchange is recounted by Murphy in the published transcript of a conference panel, James Berlin *et al.*, 'The politics of historiography', *Rhetoric Review*, VII, 1988, p. 33.

6. Richard McKeon, 'Rhetoric in the Middle Ages', *Speculum*, XVII, 1942, pp. 3-32.

7. McKeon, 'Rhetoric in the Middle Ages', pp. 3, 32.

8. Brian Vickers, *In Defence of Rhetoric*, Oxford, 1988.

9. H.-I. Marrou, '"Doctrina" et "disciplina" dans la langue des Pères de l'Èglise', *Bulletin du Cange*, IX, 1934, pp. 5-25.

10. See, e.g., Martianus Capella, *De nuptiis Philologiae et Mercurii*, ed. A. Dick, Leipzig, 1925, § 362.

11. Marrou, '"Doctrina" et "disciplina"', p. 7.

12. Marrou, '"Doctrina" et "disciplina"', pp. 7-8.

13. See, e.g., Cassiodorus, *Institutiones*, ed. R. A. B. Mynors, Oxford, 1937, book 2, section 21, on the division of mathematics into four disciplines (arithmetic, music, geometry, astronomy).

14. Vegetius, *De re militari*, ed. C. Lang, Leipzig, 1885, 2.3; 2.9; 3.1; 3.10; cited by Marrou, '"Doctrina" et "disciplina"', p. 11.

15. Cicero, *Tusculan Disputations*, ed. M. Pohlenz, Leipzig, 1918, 4.1; Tacitus, *Dialogus de oratoribus*, ed. A. Baehrens, Leipzig, 1881, 40; citations from Marrou, '"Doctrina" et "disciplina"', p. 11.

16. Augustine, *De ordine*, ed. W. M. Green, Turnhout, 1970, 3.8.25; cited in Marrou, '"Doctrina" et "disciplina"', p. 18.

17. *Ibid.*, pp. 19-21.

18. *Ibid.*, pp. 21-2.

19. *Ibid.*, p. 23.

20. *Ibid.*, p. 24, and citation of Augustine, *Sermones* 83.7.8, *Patrologiae latinae* cursus completus (hence PL), XXXVIII, col. 518: 'Jam ergo obsecrant pueri indisciplinati, et nolunt vapulare, qui sic praescribunt nobis, quando volumus dare disciplinam: Peccavi, ignosce mihi.'

21. J. F. Niermeyer, *Mediae latinitatis lexicon minus*, Leiden, 1984, s.v. 'disciplina', 8, 10, 11.

22. Niermeyer, *s.v.* 'disciplina', 9 (citing, for example, 'disciplina corporis' in Merovingian law). On the term 'discipline' in relation to flagellation see also Giles Constable, *Attitudes Toward Self-Inflicted Suffering in the Middle Ages*, The Ninth Stephen J. Brademas Sr Lecture, Brookline, Mass., 1982.

23. Michel Foucault, *The Archaeology of Knowledge*, trans. A. M. Sheridan Smith, New York, 1972, pp. 40-9.

24. Quintilian, *Institutio oratorio*, text with translation by H. E. Butler, 4 vols, Loeb Classical Library, Cambridge, Mass. and London, 1921, repr. 1976.

25. *Gorgias*, trans. B. Jowett, *The Dialogues of Plato*, II, Oxford, 1953, pp. 544-54. On the disciplinary permeability of sophistic rhetoric before the constraints imposed on sciences by Platonic and Aristotelian epistemology, see Susan C. Jarratt, *Rereading the Sophists: Classical Rhetoric Reconfigured*, Carbondale and Edwardsville, 1991, p. 13.

26. *Rhetoric*, trans. George A. Kennedy, *Aristotle on Rhetoric; a Theory of Civic Discourse*, New York and Oxford, 1991, pp. 28-9.

27. Aristotle distinguishes between artificial proofs, which are provided by the rhetorician's art or *techne* and take the form of appeals to ethical, logical, or pathetic argument (*Rhetoric*, trans. Kennedy, pp. 36-47), and inartificial (extrinsic or 'nonartistic') proofs, which are furnished at the outset of the judicial case, not constructed by the speaker's *techne*; under inartificial proofs, Aristotle considers laws, the testimony of witnesses, contracts, oaths, and evidence or testimony extracted from slaves under torture (*Rhetoric*, pp. 109-18).

28. Page duBois, *Torture and Truth*, New York and London, 1991, especially pp. 63-8.

29. As duBois recognises, Aristotle also questions the reliability of evidence extracted under torture; see the *Rhetoric*, pp. 115-16, and duBois, *Torture and Truth*, p. 68. Jody Enders, in a forthcoming article entitled 'Rhetoric and Drama, Torture and Truth' (which posits and explores a striking relationship between judicial torture in classical rhetorical theory and the spectacle of torture in medieval drama), further suggests that the distinctions rhetorical theory preserves between

torture as extrinsic proof and the intrinsic proofs supplied by the speaker's invention are not so firm; both *inventio* and torture are described in terms of verisimilitude and the appearance of plausibility. In other words, evidence derived from the body can also be 'fashioned' by the speaker's artifice to appear the more plausible to a case. I am grateful to Professor Enders for showing me the typescript of her important essay.

30. (Pseudo-Cicero), *Ad Herennium*, 4.10.15-16, text with translation by Harry Caplan, Loeb Classical Library, Cambridge, Mass. and London, 1954 (repr. 1977).

31. Text and translation from Butler, 8. Pr. 19-22. In reproducing Butler's translation of this passage I have indicated where the choice of English words develops the sexual metaphors that are implicit or at least more ambiguous in Quintilian's Latin.

32. Todorov has remarked that rhetoric, faced with the contradiction of presiding over stylistic art but having to prefer discourse without the appearance of stylisation, practises its art with a guilty conscience (*Theories of the Symbol*, pp. 72-3). I would say instead that rhetoric confesses its anxieties about its *techne* so publicly, submits itself to such critical scrutiny, that it can hardly keep any secrets of which to be guilty.

33. The idea that within the text of rhetoric the disciplining of the body and of discourse 'configure' each other is treated at length by Susan E. Shapiro, 'Rhetoric as ideology critique: the Gadamer-Habermas debate reinvented', *Journal of the American Academy of Religion* (forthcoming).

34. See, for example, Patricia Parker, 'Literary Fat Ladies and the Generation of the Text', in Parker, *Literary Fat Ladies*, pp. 8-35. John Alford has recently shown how these feminine figures of rhetoric, ranging from the garrulous to the promiscuous, find their way into the portrait of the Wife of Bath as an image of rhetoric in opposition to the Clerk's embodiment of dialectic. See 'The Wife of Bath versus the Clerk of Oxford: what their rivalry means', *The Chaucer Review*, XXI, 1986, pp. 108-32. Alford cites Lucian's *The Double Indictment* (second century AD) for an example of rhetoric depicted as a female courtesan. The image of rhetoric as a charming mistress is well exemplified in Dante's *Convivio*, book 2, where rhetoric as love poetry is identified with Venus. The more generalised image of rhetoric as a richly-adorned, beautiful (but not promiscuous) woman is also a medieval commonplace, from Alan of Lille's *Anti-Claudianus* to Stephen Hawes's *Pastime of Pleasure*. The medieval iconography of the Liberal Arts typically shows the influence of Martianus Capella's allegorical representation of Rhetoric in martial attire; see Philippe Verdier, 'L'Iconographie des arts libéraux dans l'art du moyen âge jusqu'à la fin du quinzième siècle', *Arts libéraux et philosophie au moyen âge*, Actes du quatrième congrès international de philosophie médiévale, Montreal and Paris, 1969, pp. 305-55.

35. See John Boswell, *Christianity, Social Tolerance, and Homosexuality: Gay People in Western Europe from the Beginning of the Christian Era to the Fourteenth Century*, Chicago, 1980, pp. 310-12 (with specific reference to Alan of Lille).

36. Text from Nikolaus M. Häring, ed., 'Alan of Lille, "De planctu Naturae"', *Studi medievali*, 3rd series, XIX, 1978, p. 848 (prose 5). Translation from James J. Sheridan, *Alan of Lille: The Plaint of Nature*, Toronto, 1980, p. 162 (section 10).

37. On grammar and its complex curricular relations in this text, see Jan Ziolkowski, *Alan of Lille's Grammar of Sex: The Meaning of Grammar to a Twelfth-Century Intellectual*, Cambridge, Mass., 1985.

38. In Ciceronian theory, the attributes of the person and the act supply the information that supports propositions in argument. These furnish topics for argumentation. Under attributes of persons Cicero considers name, nature, manner of life, fortune, disposition, feeling, interests, purposes, achievements, accidents, and speeches made. See *De inventione*, ed. and trans. H. M. Hubbell, Loeb Classical Library, Cambridge, Mass. and London, 1949 (repr. 1976), 1.24.34-36.

39. Text in Edmond Faral, ed., *Les Arts poétiques du XIIe et du XIIIe siècle*, Paris, 1962, p. 126, lines 53-4, 77-84. In line 53, Faral offers alternative readings: consordeat/ cum sordeat.

---

40. The text is corrupt here, and I offer some alternatives for translation of this difficult but crucial passage: 'since he submits of himself just as he partners in filth (or: "even as he is befouled") both inside and out.'

41. Translation from Ernest Gallo, 'Matthew of Vendôme: Introductory Treatise on the Art of Poetry', *Proceedings of the American Philosophical Society*, CXVIII, 1974, p. 69.

42. Cf. John of Salisbury's defence of rhetoric within the structured relations of the trivium: *Metalogicon*, ed. C. C. I. Webb, Oxford, 1929, 1.7, pp. 21-3 and 1.12, pp. 30-1.

43. Jonathan Dollimore, *Sexual Dissidence: Augustine to Wilde, Freud to Foucault*, Oxford, 1991, pp. 82-3.

44. Robert O. Payne, 'Chaucer's realization of himself as rhetor', in James J. Murphy, ed., *Medieval Eloquence: Studies in the Theory and Practice of Medieval Rhetoric*, Berkeley and Los Angeles, 1978, pp. 270-87.

45. All quotations of Chaucer's text are from *The Riverside Chaucer*, 3rd edn, ed. Larry D. Benson, Boston, 1987.

46. Dinshaw, *Chaucer's Sexual Poetics*, p. 175; *Roman de la Rose*, ed. Felix Lecoy, Paris, 1970-82, lines 11177-81. For a mythographical view of indeterminacy of form, see Jane Chance, '"Disfigured is thy face": Chaucer's Pardoner and the Protean Shape-shifter Fals-Semblant (a response to Britton Harwood)', *Philological Quarterly*, LXVII, 1988, pp. 423-37.

47. On these lines and the Pardoner's identification with relics, see Dinshaw, *Chaucer's Sexual Poetics*, pp. 162-8; see also Eugene Vance, 'Chaucer's Pardoner: relics, discourse, and frames of propriety', *New Literary History*, XX, 1989, pp. 723-45.

48. Dinshaw's chapter on the Pardoner presents comprehensive arguments about the problem of substitution and fetish, including the symbol and word 'relike' for 'coillon'. See also Dolores Warwick Frese, *An 'Ars Legendi' for Chaucer's 'Canterbury Tales': Reconstructive Reading*, Gainesville, Fla, 1991, pp. 23-57.

49. Lee Patterson has also argued, along very different lines, for the necessity of taking seriously the link between the *Physician's Tale* and the *Pardoner's Tale*. See *Chaucer and the Subject of History*, Madison, Wisc., 1991, pp. 368-74.

50. The Pardoner identifies himself with those 'yonge men' who would learn about wives and marriage from the Wife of Bath (3.163-87) and in his own Prologue claims to enjoy 'a joly wenche in every toun' (6.453); in the *General Prologue* he plays at a 'love duet' with the Summoner (*GP* 672-3).

51. Dinshaw, *Chaucer's Sexual Poetics*, pp. 157-8, especially on the significance of the Pardoner's identification within the terms of heterosexual, androcentric patriarchy.

52. *Gorgias*, trans. Jowett, pp. 542-3.

53. Aristotle, *Rhetoric*, trans. Kennedy, p. 38: '[There is persuasion] through character whenever the speech is spoken in such a way as to make the speaker worthy of credence ... character is almost, so to speak, the controlling factor in persuasion'. Cf. the survival of this concept in Quintilian, *Institutio oratoria* 6.2.8-19; here the speaker can appeal to *ethos* as a quality of emotional moderation to characterise the persons of whom he speaks, and for such appeals to work the speaker must also embody the virtue of moderation. For Aristotle, the speaker need only project a credible character; for Quintilian the speaker must possess a good character.

54. See, for example, Margaret Jennings, CSJ, 'The *Ars componendi sermones* of Ranulph Higden', in Murphy, ed., *Medieval Eloquence*, pp. 112-26.

55. Payne, 'Chaucer's realization of himself as rhetor', especially pp. 274, 278-83.

56. See most recently Alastair Minnis, 'Chaucer's Pardoner and the "office of preacher"', in Piero Boitani and Anna Torti, eds, *Intellectuals and Writers in Fourteenth-Century Europe*, The J. A. W. Bennett Memorial Lectures, Perugia, 1984 (Tübingen and Cambridge, 1986), pp. 88-119.

57. See, for example, *Institutio oratoria* 12.1.32 (ed. and trans. Butler): 'Hoc certe procul

eximatur animo, rerum pulcherrimam eloquentiam cum vitiis mentis posse misceri. Facultas dicendi, si in malos incidit, et ipsa iudicanda est malum; peiores enim illos facit, quibus contigit' ('At any rate let us banish from our hearts the delusion that eloquence, the fairest of all things, can be combined with vice. The power of speaking is even to be accounted an evil when it is found in evil men; for it makes its possessors yet worse than they were before').

58. On sophistic epistemology see Richard Leo Enos, 'The epistemology of Gorgias' rhetoric: a re-examination', *Southern Speech Communications Journal*, XLII, 1976, pp. 35-51. On Gorgias' examination of the relation between truth and language see John Poulakos, 'Gorgias' *Encomium to Helen* and the defense of rhetoric', *Rhetorica*, I, 1983, pp. 1-16. See also Jarratt, *Rereading the Sophists*, pp. 49-61.

59. See Jarratt, *Rereading the Sophists*, pp. 1-29, and John Poulakos, 'Towards a sophistic definition of rhetoric', *Philosophy and Rhetoric*, XVI, 1983, pp. 35-48.

60. On the Pardoner's Prologue as an example of the rhetorical technique of *manifestatio* see Gallo's introduction to his 'Matthew of Vendôme', pp. 57-8.

61. Cf. Michel Foucault, *The History of Sexuality I: An Introduction*, trans. Robert Hurley, New York, 1980, pp. 58-9.

62. Michel Foucault, *Discipline and Punish: the Birth of the Prison*, trans. Alan Sheridan, New York, 1979, p. 47.

63. Nancy S. Struever, *The Language of History in the Renaissance: Rhetoric and Historical Consciousness in Florentine Humanism*, Princeton, 1970, pp. 145, 155; cf. Jarratt, *Rereading the Sophists*, pp. 11-12, who uses Struever's idea of rhetoric as a subjunctive mental mode to define a new historiography of rhetoric.

Adventurous Custance:
St. Thomas of Acre and Chaucer's
*Man of Law's Tale*_____

Lawrence Warner

> From the new triumph of the new martyr himself, the Church now gives new thanks.
>
> —Bosham 1412: sermon on Becket's feast day, 1180s

> Read all the lives and passions of the holy martyrs and you will not find any martyr who wished to kill his persecutor. It is a new kind of martyr who wishes to kill another.
>
> –*Liber de poenitentia* 213: 893

The last decades of the twelfth century in Western Christendom witnessed a fundamentally new conception of the act of sacrifice that was at the heart of their faith, according to which Christ's passion established the model of martyrdom by which future saints could achieve their bliss. Herbert de Bosham's celebration of his mentor St. Thomas of Canterbury's new martyrdom appears as nothing more than an identification of Becket's actions as ritualistic in nature, new in history but ancient in signification. But the spread of the archbishop's legends in the decades following his martyrdom in 1170 and canonization in 1173 was attended by the development of another new form of martyrdom for the cause, of which his example was quickly appropriated. This is the creation of the "crusade martyr," who no longer passively suffers for the faith but goes down fighting, and killing, and about whom the Benedictine author of the second epigraph above, writing in about 1190, is so dismayed.[1]

At precisely this moment, the "newness" of Thomas's martyrdom dovetailed with the "new kind of martyrdom" lamented by the Benedictine moralist, for Becket was called into the service of the Third Crusade in the Far East, most prominently in the form of the Order of St. Thomas of Acre. Chroniclers attributed the founding of this crusading order to either Henry II, who took the cross as part of his penance for the murder of Becket, or Richard I, who was saved, by an apparition of St. Thomas, from shipwreck as he arrived in the Holy Land for the crusade of 1190 (Forey; Watney 1-9). Knowledge of this is crucial to our understanding of the cult of Becket in Chaucer's London, the focus of this chapter, for in 1227 Becket's sister granted the order the site of his birthplace on the Cheap, which remained the Church of St. Thomas of Acre (or Acon) and "one of the most celebrated religious institutions in London"

(Robertson 139) until the Reformation. The military aspects of the Order of St. Thomas of Acre had by then long since been abandoned—it now followed the rule of St. Augustine—and its headquarters in the East had relocated to this London site, whose master was calling himself head of the whole enterprise in 1379 (Forey 502). In 1383, its founding was commemorated by a visitation of Robert, bishop of London, at which the grant of 1227 was displayed (Watney 9), and that same year the rebuilding and enlargement of the church commenced (Robertson 39).

The Christian transformation of holy passion into violent aggression in the later Middle Ages was accompanied by another, similar shift, which would have even broader consequences for Chaucerian historical consciousness, and in which St. Thomas of Acre again plays a major role. This shift concerns the idea of the "adventurer," in the classical concept of which "an individual can be nothing other than completely *passive*, completely *unchanging*," as Bakhtin noted (105). But a "new conception of the adventurer" arose in the Middle Ages, one with an "essential hallmark that distinguishes it from the classical conception," according to Michael Nerlich: "that adventures are undertaken on a *voluntary* basis, they are *sought out* (*la quête de l'aventure*, 'the quest for adventure'), and this quest and hence the adventurer himself are glorified" (5). The most vibrant "adventurers" of the fourteenth century were no longer knights on a quest, but, rather, the merchants whom Chaucer knew so well throughout his lifetime. What attracted merchants to this ideology of adventure was not only the traditional appeal of romance on the high seas, which they could appropriate in figuring their own voyages, but also the fact that the term *aventure* connoted "risk" or "chance," which they so fervently sought out. Thus Chaucer's friend Gower asserts that the law allows "that he who can lose in a venture (*en aventure*) should also be allowed to gain from it when his fortune brings it about"; therefore we should not blame that honest merchant who wants to risk his money, "son argent *aventurer*" (25,202-7).[2] An alchemist in Chaucer's *Canon's Yeoman's Tale* claims that his peers, like the merchants, "moste putte oure good in aventure" (VIII [G] 946; cited by Carus-Wilson xii);[3] perhaps it is no surprise that Chaucer's own Merchant shows an interest in such risk, having Damian burn so hotly with desire for May that "he putte his lyf in aventure" (IV [E] 1877).

The tensions between passion and action, legendary and new, martyrdom, unchanging adventure and nautical risk, are the forces that generate Chaucer's *Man of Law's Tale*. This pious collection of stanzas dramatizes the adventures of both one of his most passive heroines, Custance in her rudderless boat, and the merchants and crusaders who sail the Mediterranean. Its careful rhyme royal form evokes a sense of timelessness, to be sure; but the *Man of Law's Tale* refracts such large-scale military and mercantile movements by means of local and material connections with the Church of St. Thomas of Acre. I suggest that in this tale Chaucer sought to produce a narrative form of *aventure* in which the mercantile and the military are inextricably fused. Through the tale's associations with the church on the Cheap, our poet seeks to identify his own storytelling as a participant, as the martyrdom of Becket had become; in the redemption of the Holy Sepulcher.

While no records associate Chaucer directly with the church, we can confidently place a number of his associates there. At least two of them remain (unless the burial grounds were dug up when the Mercers' Hall was built on the site), for those whose final resting places were in St. Thomas of Acre included (see Watney 174) Richard Goodchild (d. 1390), citizen and cutler, Chaucer's agent in settling the Cecily Champain affair (*Chaucer Life-Records* 346-47), who had made a bequest to the church (*Calendar of Wills* 281; Watney 32), and Thomas Gernon, sheriff, who, together with our poet, was among those granted livery of mourning for Joan of Kent (*Chaucer Life-Records* 104). Among the most illustrious supporters of the church were the Cavendishes, under whose powerful influence Chaucer might well have fallen: the will of Thomas Cavendish, one of many of the family buried there, leaves a bequest to a brother named John, perhaps the chief justice who heard the case of trespass brought against Chaucer by Thomas Stondon in 1379—and who was beheaded by rebels in Bury St. Edmunds during the Rising of 1381.[4]

These were not the only figures in Chaucer's milieu whom we can definitely locate in St. Thomas of Acre. The Man of Law is another. In identifying him as "A Sergeant of the Lawe, war and wys" (I [A] 309), Chaucer signals that Custance's narrator was a member of the Order of the Coif, as it came to be known, the highest order of his profession, from which the justices of the King's Bench, including the ill-fated John Cavendish, were selected. In Richard II's reign (1377-99), a total of twenty-two new sergeants of the law were "created": eight in January 1383, another by Michaelmas 1387, eight at Michaelmas 1388, and five in October 1396 (Baker 158-59). The prestige and cost of the creation ceremonies were enormous. In 1396, the king himself helped procure the provisions for the feast; Sir John Fortescue, in his mid-fifteenth-century treatise "In Praise of the Laws of England," remarks that on the day of their creation, the sergeants "are to hold, among other solemnities, a feast and entertainment such as are held at the coronation of a king, which lasts for seven days" (71; see Baker 99). After the feast, the sergeants processed to St. Paul's, where Becket's parents were buried, stopping en route to make an offering at the shrine at St. Thomas of Acre (Baker 101, 309).

The new sergeants' procession to St. Thomas of Acre was but one example of the church's service as a focal point of civic London. On major feast days throughout the year, the mayor and aldermen met after dinner at the chapel on the Cheap for devotional services, usually proceeding from there to St. Paul's. John Carpenter's *Liber Albus* (1419) gives a detailed account of the most elaborate such procession, which took place annually when the mayor was inaugurated. After he hosted a banquet,

> it was custom for the new Mayor to proceed from his house to the church of Saint Thomas de Aeon, those of his livery preceding him; and after the Aldermen had there assembled, they then proceeded together to the church of Saint Paul. . . . They then moved on to the churchyard, where lie the bodies of the parents of Thomas, late Archbishop of Canterbury; and there they also repeated the *De profundis*, etc., in behalf of all the faithful of God departed, near the grave of his parents before mentioned. After this, they returned through the market of Chepe (sometimes with lighted torches, if it was late) to the said church of Saint Thomas, and there the Mayor and Aldermen made an offering of one penny each. . . . (Carpenter 23-24)

Of the victualler Perkyn Revelour, Chaucer's Cook remarks, "whan ther any ridyng was in Chepe,/ Out of the shoppe thider wolde he lepe" (IV [E] 4377-78), so delectable a sight were these ceremonies (see Wallace 183). Langland, too, as James Simpson has suggested, might have inscribed such processions into his portrayal of the Paraclete's descent upon Piers and his fellows (109-10).[5]

In the civic imagination, as in the city's geography, then, St. Thomas of Acre had a place parallel, if not equal, to that of St. Paul's Cathedral. While their physical proximity certainly made the association convenient, "the strong emphasis placed on the memory of St. Thomas Becket, London's chief citizen, is especially significant" to these processions (Robertson 77). A sixteenth-century reformist document describes the sergeants' creation ceremonies as an "old popyshe pylgremage or offringe to St Thomas of Acon in the nether ende of Chepesyde," which, its author attests, by his own day had been replaced by simple prayers (Baker 309). The reference to pilgrimage is not far off the mark. Indeed, if we are to see the journey from Southwerk to Canterbury as a figure "Of thilke parfit glorious pilgrymage/ That highte Jerusalem celestial" (X [I] 50-51), so too can we see in these civic processions to St. Thomas of Acre a means of ceremonially identifying London with the Holy Land, over which St. Thomas kept watch by means of his English crusade order.

Because they were located on or near the Cheap, St. Paul's and St. Thomas of Acre had ties to London's mercantile communities that were even closer than were their connections to the politicians and lawyers. If our Benedictine commentator was unsure about the status of the new kind of martyr that arose with the crusade, Chaucer's Sergeant of Law is unabashed in his celebration of the new "adventurers" that appeared in the same era. Through him and his tale Chaucer explores the material and intellectual connections between the taking of the cross and the adventuring of merchants. The Sergeant himself has close ties with the mercantile communities that aligned themselves with the Becket cult: as Chaucer tells us, he "often hadde been at the Parvys" (I [A] 310), a reference to the pillars inside St. Paul's Cathedral, where he conducted business dealings (Baker 101-4; Wallace 197-98). On the Cheap near St. Thomas, an even larger variety of trade took place, for chandlers, cutlers, and spicers sold their wares alongside the more prominent groupings of the drapers and the mercers (Keene 8-9). The church itself served as a site where debts were settled, as in a certain Thomas's agreement to pay two hundred pounds to William of Holbeche at St. Thomas in 1361 (Forey 302). Moreover, many crafts and guilds—the city's carpenters from as early as the 1330s (Wright 131), its bakers by 1382, and the mercers by 1391 (Sutton, *Mercery* 73-74)—held their meetings on its grounds.

This latter association came to dominate the identity of Thomas of Acre, for the annual elections of the mercers' wardens took place there, where the Company, chartered as such by Richard II in 1394, had a hall, a chapel, and a chest for keeping records (Keene 13; Watney 36). And those records, as Linne Mooney has discovered, were written by none other than Chaucer's scribe, Adam Pinkhurst (Mooney 106-12). Moreover, for eight days in April 1385, Pinkhurst was co-owner of a property adjoining St. Thomas of Acre, which was sold back to its previous owners and "later accorded to the Mercers for their sole use within the hospital" (Mooney 110; see also 101 n. 15, 109). Mooney remarks that "it seems possible that Pinkhurst had a foothold at the hospital as well and conducted his scribal work out of it" (111). The earliest records of the fifteenth-century Company of Merchant Adventurers would become wholly mixed with Pinkhurst's records in that chest; indeed, that company's material origins in the church were so widely known that they would be commemorated in the name by which its branch in the Netherlands was often called, the Fraternity of St. Thomas beyond the Sea (Carus-Wilson 150; Sutton, "Merchant" 28-32).

It is appropriate, then, that the Man of Law's subsequent tale of adventurous Custance follows upon a prologue in which he fantasizes that fortune always smiles on the "riche marchauntz" he apostrophizes: "Youre bagges been nat fild with ambes as,/ But with sys cynk; that renneth for youre chaunce;/ At Cristemasse myrie may ye daunce!" (II [B1] 122, 124-26). Indeed, the Sergeant's fascination with merchant adventuring explains his own luck in having a tale at all. Merchants, he claims, "been fadres of tidynges/ And tales, bothe of pees and of debaat"; "many a yeere" ago one brought him tidings of Custance (II [B1] 129-30, 132). The Sergeant's tale thus issues from, and is

---

aimed at, those who would come to be known as the Fraternity of St. Thomas beyond the Sea, those merchants centered on the Cheap at the church devoted to the martyr, most prominent among whom were the mercers.[6] Our narrator further tips his hat to this powerful guild by opening the tale with an account much more elaborate than that in his sources:[7]

> In Surrye whilom dwelte a compaignye
> Of chapmen riche, and therto sadde and trewe,
> That wyde—where senten hir spicerye,
> Clothes of gold, and satyns riche of hewe.
> Hir chaffare was so thrifty and so newe
> That every wight hath deyntee to chaff are
> With hem, and eek to sellen hem hire ware.
>   (II [B1] 134-40)

In identifying this company as mercers via the reference to "spicerye,/ Clothes of gold, and satyns riche of hewe," this stanza offers information not in the parallel passages of Chaucer's sources.[8] Trevet's Anglo-Norman *Chronicle* refers simply to "heathen merchants from the great Saracen land carrying much diverse and rich merchandise" ("marchaunz paens hors de la grant Sarizine, aportauntz trop diverses et riches marchaundises" [18-20]). Gower's tale in the *Confessio Amantis* subordinates, both grammatically and thematically, the merchants and their wares: Constance is so full of faith that she has converted "the greteste of Barbarie,/ Of hem whiche usen marchandie" (599-600). Chaucer thus goes out of his way to inscribe mercery into the opening stanzas of the *Man of Law's Tale*, in part surely to celebrate the "adventuring" of the rising merchant class of London.[9] More important, though, this reference serves to call forth to Chaucer's Ricardian audience the crusading force of the cult of Becket, most obviously represented by the name and history of the mercers' home, St. Thomas of Acre.

Before we turn to this violent aspect of the Becket legendary, it is worth noting the clear, if often overlooked, point that crusading is a governing force of the Constance legend, which compels much of the approach of our poet, in particular, toward the Muslims. While Chaucerians have expended much energy demonstrating the ways in which the *Man of Law's Tale* is what the narrator says it is not—one of the "cursed stories . . ./ Of swiche unkynde abhomynacions" (II [B1] 80, 88) as those of Canacee or Apollonius of Tyre (e.g., Dinshaw 88-112)—few have treated the fact that, as Joerg Fichte has recently noted, the "Constance story which Trevet included in his Anglo-Norman *Chronicles* bears all the marks of a crusading tale" (239). And merchant adventuring plays a central role in the crusading ethos of the tale. Both

---

Trevet and Chaucer discarded the motif of the incestuous father from the "ca-lumniated queen" tale (Schlauch, *Chaucer's Constance* 62-70), relating in-stead the conversion of the Sultan via the merchants' tidings of Constance. The account in the Anglo-Norman history, much fuller than those in the tales of his Ricardian followers, firmly establishes the crusading impulse of the marriage negotiations: the Sultan signs a treaty that grants the Romans "free passage to travel freely for trade"; moreover, "he surrendered the city of Jeru-salem to the lordship of the Christians to live in" ("fraunch passage do aler fraunchement e marchaunder" [55-56]; "la cité de Jerusalem abandona a la seignurie des Cristiens pur enhabiter" [59-60]). A number of crusading texts with similar episodes could have inspired Trevet to include this account of Muslim-Christian negotiations: the early-thirteenth-century romance the *King of Tars*, William of Tyre's narration of one "Constance" in his *History of Deeds Done beyond the Sea*, or the 1229 treaty between the Holy Roman Em-peror Frederick II and the sultan of Egypt, in which, "without striking a blow, the excommunicate Emperor won back the Holy Places of Christendom" (Runciman 187).[10]

The identification of the company's trade as mercery is not the only differ-ence between Chaucer's account and those of Trevet and Gower. The *Man of Law's Tale* also underscores, in an innovative manner, the crusading spirit that his early source had first put forth. These mercers, unlike their literary fore-bears, remain wholly separate from the Christianity embodied in our heroine, leaving in their wake a violence that issues in the tale's particular crusading energy, directed against all who embrace what the Sultan's advisers call "oure lawe sweete/ That us was taught by Mahoun, oure prophete" (I [B1] 223-24). Both Trevet and Gower have Constance convert the merchants, but in the *Man of Law's Tale*, "the commune voys of every man" (II [B1] 155) that expresses Custance's goodness and beauty has no effect on their spiritual lives:

> And al this voys was sooth, as God is trewe.
> But now to purpos lat us turne agayn.
> Thise marchantz han doon fraught hir shippes newe,
> And whan they han this blisful mayden sayn,
> Hoom to Surrye been they went ful fayn,
> And doon hir nedes as they han doon yoore,
> And lyven in wele; I kan sey yow namoore.
>
> (II [B1] 169-75)

Here it remains for the Sultan alone to convert; the "other," embodied in the exotic and sensual merchants, remains intact, venturing off to other lands. Never to be seen or heard from again, these Syrian mercers are constant in a way that threatens the unity endorsed by Trevet and Gower, who make all who accept Constance convert to her faith, and all who reject her die painful deaths.

The Syrian merchants' non-assimilation into Christendom contradicts Chaucer's original source in a way that brings the crusading ethos directly to bear on the Mediterranean journeys of the *Man of Law's Tale*. In Trevet's version of the story, the Christianized merchants are the agents for the Sultan's own conversion, leading to his ensuing treaty with the Romans as part of his marriage negotiations. This treaty, as mentioned earlier, granted Christian merchants full trading rights in the East (as well as access to tourist attractions like Bethlehem and Nazareth) and put Jerusalem in Christian hands. If Trevet invokes the crusading ethos in order to dispel it immediately, Gower refuses even to acknowledge its existence.

Chaucer's approach differs from both of his models. Unlike Trevet, he refuses to indulge fantasies of the recapture of the Holy Land, and by attending so carefully to the Syrian mercers and refusing to have them convert, he aligns his tale with crusading and mercantile energies wholly absent from Gower's tale in the *Confessio Amantis*. Indeed, the hostilities upon which the crusade ethos was founded generate crucial elements of his tale's plot. Thanks to the Sultan's mother, all the Christian wedding guests and the would-be groom himself "Been al tohewe and stiked at the bord" (II [B1] 430), Custance being sent forth to venture (passively, unchangingly) alongside the active merchants at large. In response, her father, having learned about "The slaughtre of cristen folk, and dishonour/ Doon to his dogther by a fals traytour" (II [B1] 956-57), launches a full-scale attack on the Syrians:

> For which this Emperour hath sent anon
> His senatour, with roial ordinance,
> And othere lordes, God woot, many oon,
> On Surryens to taken heigh vengeance.
> They brennen, sleen, and brynge hem to meschance
> Ful many a day; but shortly—this is th'ende—
> Homward to Rome they shapen hem to wende.
> (II [B1] 960-66)

Here again, Chaucer here draws much greater attention than do his sources to the Emperor's revenge, putting it into the declarative voice of the narrator rather than having the senator relate the episode to Custance, as in Trevet (460-72) and Gower (1178-86). He thus presents crusading as a form of Christian *aventure* that answers the risks undertaken by the Syrian mercers, the "merchant adventurers" who live or die by the role of the dice. Their "tidings" of Custance turn out to be much more adventurous, much riskier, for the Sultan and indeed all the Syrians than for themselves: while the Syrian mercers wander the seas in search of more tales and winnings, the Emperor's senator extends the *meschance* to the entire Muslim people of Syria—no "sys cynk" for them.

Chaucer thus portrays this proto-crusade, as do the chronicles of the First Crusade, as an endeavor guided by divine providence, not subject to the vicissitudes of chance. The wanderings of Custance proceed under the watchful eye of the lord of Fortune: "No Wight but God" kept her from death (II [B1] 476), "No Wight but Crist" fed her (II [B1] 501), for "The wyl of Crist was that she sholde abyde" (II [B1] 511).[11] She is, as V. A. Kolve so beautifully shows (297-358), the embodiment of the Ship of Church, cast about by *aventure* (II [B1] 465) yet finally having "scaped al hire aventure" (II [B1] 1151). David Wallace, pointing to the Syrian merchants, remarks that "this dominant image is not an uncontested one; there are other ships at sea" (184); his corrective applies equally to our understanding of Custance's own ship as well. For even as a figure for the Ship of Church, Custance need not be reduced to allegory: insofar as she traverses the Mediterranean from Northumberland to Syria, she also embodies the Ship of the Church Militant—now literalized, and no longer merely a reference to the spiritual battles in which Christians engage in this world—that will prepare the way for the Church Triumphant. At the end of the tale, Custance reluctantly acknowledges as much, begging her father, "Sende me namoore unto noon hethenesse" (II [B1] 1112). Chaucer's only other use of this last term, in his portrait of the Knight, indicates that the Man of Law's heroine seeks to disavow a region that occupies a specifically crusading register: "And therto hadde he riden, no man ferre,/ As wel in cristendom as in hethenesse" (I [A] 48-49; see Fichte 238-39 on this appearance of the term).

Merchant ships were as crucial to the material history of crusading campaigns as they would be to the tidings of Custance. The commercial fleets of Genoa, Venice, and Pisa "played a vital role in transporting men and supplies to the Holy Land, and also in capturing the seaports which ensured the future preservation of communications with western Europe," notes J. R. S. Phillips. "Most of the major ports, . . . and many of the lesser ones . . . were taken with the assistance of the ships of one or other of the Italian cities" (44; see also Atiya 169-73). The West's crusading and mercantile impulses were crystallized in the original home of the Order of St. Thomas of Acre: for the century in which it was under Christian control, Acre had been the "command centre of the Latin trade network in the Middle East" (Abulafia 8). This status is commemorated in day two, story nine of the *Decameron*, in which a wife falsely accused of adultery begins her reentry into Italian society at a trade fair at Acre.[12]

Furthermore, this inextricable relationship between the crusade and mercantilism was promulgated in the Becket legendary, in large part due to the presence on the Cheap of St. Thomas of Acre. Both merchant adventurers and crusading leaders, as we have seen, accepted Becket as their patron; these connections were put into powerful narrative form in the popular legend of his birth to a Saracen princess and a London crusader and merchant, Gilbert Becket. Indeed, it might have come into being as a form of etiology, intended to explain to Londoners why the site of the martyr's birth on the Cheap was called St. Thomas of Acre.[13] While Chaucer had no need to rely on this popular story for the bulk of his own tale, it was certainly circulating among those "riche marchauntz" who sold their wares on the Cheap and ventured overseas under St. Thomas's protection. From its appearance in mid-thirteenth-century *Vitae* of the martyr, the legend proliferated in many genres and media: Chaucer would have encountered it in the *South English Legendary* and would certainly have heard it as well from the pulpit, if not also from the mercers on the Cheap.[14]

The tale has crusading overtones from its first words: Gilbert Becket, a good man of London, "took the cross" (*crucem . . . arripuit*) to the Holy Land (29). Although he does so because of a vow of penance and not ostensibly to fight Muslims, this action powerfully suggests a crusading context for his actions, for the term "crusader" derives from *crucesignatus*, man signed with the cross, which the candidate receives via a liturgical rite (Brundage). Subsequent events confirm that Christian-Muslim relations, not just pious pilgrimage, are at stake. Upon the emergence of Gilbert and his serving man Richard from prayer at holy places in Jerusalem, they are taken prisoner by Muslims, remaining in bondage to a certain Prince Amiraud. After a year and a half, Amiraud, having noticed the worthiness of the London merchant, invites him (in chains) to his table for conversation about the customs of the world. The prince's daughter, like Desdemona, is enraptured by the foreigner's tales, and one day in private she asks Gilbert about his religion. Impressed by the passion of his exposition, the Muslim princess declares that she will convert to Christianity if he will marry her, yet before she can ever get a commitment from Gilbert, his companions and he escape and return to London.

At this point the princess takes on the role of Custance alone in her ship, albeit willingly, and in a manner that distances her from the unchanging classical concept of the adventurer: she does not hesitate "to face the innumerable perils of a vast extent of country and of a stormy sea, so long as she might seek for one man, far away and ignorant of her love" (30). Her overriding erotic passion is helped by other adventurers, for she joins "certain pilgrims and merchants who knew her language" (30) who are en route to England, with whom she survives the dangers at sea. Able to say only "London! London!"

she makes her way to that city, where "she chanced to pass in front of the house of Gilbert, which was situated in one of the better known and more frequented sections of the city, where now a hospital has been erected in honor of St. Thomas" (30), that is, our Church of St. Thomas of Acre. Richard recognizes her and runs to report this wonder to Gilbert, who gives Richard charge over her. Gilbert proceeds to St. Paul's, where he confers with six bishops, there for important business, about the matter. The bishop of Chichester proclaims that this is the work of God, and that this woman "would be the mother of a son whose sanctity and labors would elevate the Church, to the glory of Christ. The others agree with the bishop in this opinion, and advise that Gilbert should marry her, provided she be baptized" (31). These sacraments are conferred the next day, and that night the former Muslim conceives the future St. Thomas. "On the next day," however, "Gilbert was filled with a great desire to return to the Holy Land"; with his wife's encouragement, "he set out for Jerusalem, where he remained for three and a half years. Afterward he returned and found his son Thomas, a beautiful child, and held in high esteem in the eyes of all" (31-32).

Readers who, like Chaucer (VII 899), are familiar with the Middle English romance *Bevis of Hampton* will recognize its numerous parallels with the legend of the Muslim princess (Brown 57-58). But the *Man of Law's Tale* shares with the Becket legend a number of crucial elements that are lacking even in *Bevis*. First, its startling end: Gilbert's alacrity in leaving his bride the day after their wedding will remind us of the Man of Law's Alla, who, upon begetting a child with Custance, leaves to seek his foes in Scotland, and takes her for safekeeping "to a bisshop, and his constable eke" (II [B1] 716). This romance motif is rare, appearing elsewhere, according to Paul Alonzo Brown, only in *Guy of Warwick* and the later (c. 1400) *Emaré*, another contribution to the fourteenth century's passion for "Constance-sagas."[15] Second is the motif at the core of what Kolve identifies as the poem's dominant image, "The Rudderless Ship and the Sea" (297-358), for in *Bevis of Hampton*, Josian's wanderings in search of Bevis are neither solitary (she is with Saber and the twelve knights) nor nautical (3893-98; see Brown 58). Although the Muslim princess, unlike Custance, achieves a desired destination, their journeys in the Mediterranean have much in common: both rely on merchants as conduits of the respective maidens and both enable a constancy lavishly praised by their narrators. The Latin version of the legend exclaims, "O wonderful beyond measure both the courage and the love of this woman in undertaking such difficulties and hardships!" (30) ("O mirandam nimis hujus mulieris tam audaciam duam amorem tanta difficilia et ardua praesumentis!" [col. 347]). Likewise, the Man of Law praises his heroine's travels: "O my Custance, ful of benignytee,/ O Emperoures yonge doghter deere,/ He that is lord of Fortune be thy steere!" (II [B1] 446-48). Such use of apostrophe is typical of saints' legends (Paull); in these instances, although neither the princess nor Custance is a saint, both still represent womanly virtue via their constancy and birthing of marvelous sons.

The third similarity is even more compelling than these motifs, for it pertains to a passage unique to Chaucer's version of the tale of Constance. Both the Becket legend and the *Man of Law's Tale* treat the matter of marriage between faiths by similarly dramatizing a bishops' consultation, a figure absent from Trevet, Gower, or *Bevis of Hampton*.[16] In the Becket legend, Gilbert proceeds to St. Paul's, even before the maiden has encountered him in London, to confer with the six bishops. The Man of Law relates a similar circumstance from the Muslim perspective: having "caught so greet plesance/ To han hir figure in his remembrance" from the merchants' tidings of Custance (II [B1] 186-87), "This Sowdan for his privee conseil sente" to learn how he might achieve his goal (II [B1] 204):

> Diverse men diverse thynges seyden;
> They argumenten, casten up and doun;
> Many a subtil resoun forth they leyden;
> They speken of magyk and abusioun.
> But finally, as in conclusioun,
> They kan nat seen in that noon avantage,
> Ne in noon oother wey, save mariage.
>
> Thanne sawe they therinne swich difficultee
> By wey of reson, for to speke al playn,
> By cause that ther was swich diversitee
> Bitwene hir bothe lawes, that they sayn
> They trowe that no "Cristen prince wolde fayn
> Wedden his child under oure lawe sweete
> That us was taught by Mahoun, oure prophete."
> (II [B1] 211-24)

Paul Beichner is certainly correct to call attention to the juridical terminology of *disparitas cultus*, disparity of worship, in the phrase "swich diversitee/ Bitwene hir bothe lawes," whose uniqueness to the Man of Law's version of the Constance story "reveals the interest in his own legal mind" (70; cf. Fowler 62-63). But as we have seen, our narrator is interested in much more than the law. He directs his tale specifically toward a body of mercantile listeners centered on one church on the Cheap, a maneuver that prompts him to send his heroine along the routes of merchant adventurers and crusaders, both, from England to the Holy Land. Chaucer, to be sure, does not tell the legend of the Saracen princess. But his focus on merchant adventurers, and his appropriation of the legend's central and distinctive motifs, enable him to imbue adventurous Custance with the holiness of St. Thomas himself, patron saint of mercers and crusaders.

By issuing in opposite conclusions, these two counsels about *disparitas cultus* highlight the tense balance between chance and fate so prominent in both narratives. The Sultan charges the members of his counsel "To shapen for his lyf som remedye" (II [B1] 210), but his efforts at shaping fortune are useless, for the death of every man is written "in the sterres, clerer than is glas" (II [B1] 194-96). Nor do the Christians' attempts to "shape" their destinies (II [B1] 249, 253) succeed: "is noon oother ende" (II [B1] 266) but violence and death for all but Custance. Yet in the early version of the legend of Gilbert, "it chanced," *incedens* (30), that the Muslim princess was standing in front of Gilbert's home on the Cheap when Gilbert's serving man walked by and recognized her, leading to the bishops' declaration that divine providence has guided her for the sake of the church. Despite their differences, however, both instances give rise to expressions of crusading ideology, which so many propagandists understood to be written "in the sterres" (see Warner, "Sign"). Gilbert, having conquered at least one Muslim (the former princess, who has now been wife and Christian for one day), is able to repeat his journey to Jerusalem, from which he returns to the future site of St. Thomas of Acre to find the future protector of Richard the Lion-Hearted being admired by London; and in the *Man of Law's Tale*, the Emperor's inability to shape the Christians' destiny upon his daughter's wedding leads to his vengeful crusade against the Syrians.

This ongoing Chaucerian tension between chance and fate can be directly correlated to the tension in the *Man of Law's Tale* between the two modes of *aventure*, Custance's classical passivity and the medieval willfulness of the Sultan and the Emperor.[17] For the former mode serves not so much to distance the Man of Law's protagonist from knights and merchants as to suggest that the mercantile-chivalric "adventures" against Muslims are actually the work of the lord of Fortune, of the God "That kepte peple Ebrayk from hir drenchynge,/ With drye feet thurghout the see passynge" (II [B1] 489-90)— the God, that is, who had led the mercantile and chivalric campaigns against the Muslims in the Holy Land from 1095 to Chaucer's own day.[18]

Chaucer's Sergeant of Law might have enjoyed a sumptuous celebration upon his creation, but his subsequent career would have been (and still remains) fraught with anxiety (Askins). The Man of Law's reputation today is little better than it was among his contemporary enemies, for critics have been quick to indict, among his other errors, his desire for land: "So greet a purchasour was nowhere noon:/ Al was fee symple to hym in effect;/ His purchasyng myghte nat been infect" (I [A] 318-20).[19] To be sure, the Sergeant's methods are suspect, but his quest for land accords very well with the tale he chooses to tell and the context in which he tells it. Trevet's Sultan, we will remember, offered Jerusalem itself to the Christians in return for Constance's hand. Because such events occurred so rarely in the Crusades, those signed with the cross had to rely on force in their attempts to take what they saw as their "patrimony." This term already implies a legal framework for much crusading ideology; it is central, for instance, in the consolidation of crusading thought offered by Innocent III, source for so many of the Man of Law's verses (Lewis), in the bull *Quia Maior* (1213) and in the decree *Ad Liberandam* (1215) of the Fourth Lateran Council (Tyerman 35-41).

While the Canterbury pilgrims are not on a mission to free Jerusalem, their "patrimony," from the Muslims, their ultimate destination is "Jerusalem celestial," the city to which, crusading propagandists never tired of asserting, the terrestrial city points (e.g., Mézières 71). Their storytelling contest opens with one told by the sole pilgrim to have campaigned "in hethenesse," the Knight, and in the Ellesmere manuscript at least their first grouping of stories culminates in the tale of a journeyer "in hethenesse" told by a Sergeant (Kolve 364-71), himself deemed *miles* for legal purposes (Baker 17-20). Real-life pilgrims to the martyr's shrine, like Erasmus in the early 1500s, saw among his relics "a certayn leden table hauynge grauyd in hym a tytle of saynte Thomas of Acrese,"[20] an appellation that recalled London-based pilgrims both to the markets on the Cheap and to the Holy Land under siege. The Man of Law, in other words, is not alone in seeking to "purchase," for the *Canterbury Tales*, as many have recognized, is driven in large part by a mercantile impulse (Eberle, Georgianna). The converse, we might imagine, obtains as well: while selling their wares on the Cheap, those among the merchants who maintained a pious idealism could hope that their enterprise constituted a form of pilgrimage. They could even hope that, insofar as mercantilism entailed the stewardship of God's bounty (Thrupp 174-80), it participated in the impulse that sought to redeem the Holy Land.

A desire for healing, both physical and spiritual, drives Chaucer's individual pilgrims to Becket's shrine at Canterbury. On a communal level, such a desire attracted the mercers and men of law to the Church of St. Thomas of Acre, an institution that fuelled their vision of the crusade as written in the stars, so natural an undertaking that it need not be spoken, even if it is a fundamental justification for the journey. Thomas Hoccleve, in a stanza from his rhyme royal "Learn to Die," made explicit some of the paradigms that underlie the *Man of Law's Tale*, the legend of the Saracen Princess, and the journeys to St. Thomas of Acre and Canterbury:

Right as a Marchant stongynge in a port,
His ship þat charged is with marchandyse
To go to fer parties / for confort
Of him self / lookeþ / þat it in sauf wyse
Passe out / Right so, if thou wirke as the wyse,
See to thy soule so / or throw hens weende,
Þat it may han the lyf þat haath noon eende.
(Hoccleve 212; see Kolve 349)

This bold simile leaves unspoken the fact that, like the pilgrims seeing to their souls en route to Canterbury, merchants tell tales—and that their tidings can effect a single woman's voyage that makes her so lonely that she begs "Sende me namoore unto noon hethenesse," a region as yet unconquered by those who take the cross.

From *Place, Space, and Landscape in Medieval Narrative*, edited by Laura L. Howes (2007), pp. 43-59. Copyright © 2007 by the University of Tennessee Press. Reprinted by permission of the University of Tennessee Press.

Notes

1. On crusade martyrdom, see, for example, Riley-Smith, "Death on the First Crusade" (he cites this Benedictine treatise at p. 29).

2. Citations of Chaucer, Trevet, Gower, and *Bevis of Hampton* are by line number. This chapter focuses on the Man of Law and his tale as they are presented in the Ellesmere manuscript, accepting that the appearance of *MLPro* and *MLT* after fragment I, and their link with each other, are authorial (see Blake 84-85 for other opinions). Nolan offers a nuanced reading of this performance that takes account of the textual difficulties presented in this portion of the *Tales*.

3. On Chaucerian *aventure* in relation to commerce, see Wallace 205.

4. On the possibility that the Chief Justice is the "John" in Thomas's will, and Thomas's interment at St. Thomas of Acre, see Bickley 2-3; on the will, see *Calendar of Wills* 149 and Watney 35, 173. The documents relating to the action brought against Chaucer are in *Chaucer Life-Records* 340-42. On John Cavendish's beheading during the Rising of 1381, see Maddicott 61-65.

5. Simpson cites *Piers Plowman* B.19.202-12. The Pentecost procession Simpson adduces does not involve St. Thomas of Acre, but most of the others do: see *Liber Albus* 23-27.

6. Beidler even suggests that these stanzas constitute a Chaucerian request, apart from the Man of Law's performance, for funds from merchants, perhaps read aloud at a guild meeting.

7. Most scholars (e.g., Block) have assumed that Chaucer's most direct source was the passage on Constance in Trevet's *Chronicle*. Yet Nicholson has made a strong case that "in the most significant respects, it is fair to say not only that Gower provided Chaucer's most important model, but that it was Gower's tale rather than Trevet's that Chaucer chose to retell" (171).

8. Gower's mercer hawks "silks, satins, imported cloths" (*Mirour de l'Omme* 1.25,292). The term "spicerye" was a catch-all term for many types of wares, not just spices (*Medieval Trade in the Mediterranean World* 108-14), and mercery in earlier centuries had dealt extensively in "spices" proper as well (Sutton, *Mercery* 3, 3n19, 23).

9. See Thrupp, especially 53-60, 234-87, on merchants' political and social prestige.

10. On the possible reliance of Trevet's Constance story upon the *King of Tars*, see Hornstein's two essays: upon William of Tyre, Schlauch, "Historical Precursors," and upon the 1229 Treaty, Wynn.

11. See Kaske 25-32 on this theme in the *Man of Law's Tale*.

12. On these trade fairs, see Atiya 177-82.

13. See Brown 65-67 on the legend's possible connection with St. Thomas of Acre.

14. Brown 28-37 surveys many of its appearances (though not in drama or sermons). On its appearance as late as the sixteenth century in drama, see Davidson 58-59. My essay "Becket and the Hopping Bishops" discusses medieval English preachers' interest in this legend and Langland's allusion to it, and Kelly has now discussed it as part of his survey of materials relevant to the contextualization of the treatment of non-Christians in works like the *Prioress's Tale*. I cite the legend by page number from the translation of the earliest four of the legend, the *Later Quadrilogus*, in Brown; the Latin is from *Vita et Passio Sancti Thomae*.

15. The sole manuscript containing *Emaré*, BL Cotton Caligula A.ii, dates from the early fifteenth century, and the poem's dialect features "indicate a late fourteenth-century Northeast Midlands or East Anglian dialect" (Laskaya and Salisbury). Hanks argues that *Emaré* influenced the *Man of Law's Tale*.

16. In *Bevis of Hampton*, the hero does seek counsel from the patriarch of Jerusalem (Brown 58; see 2582-84), but her Christening is brought about without any clerical consultation about how to proceed concerning the two faiths, which issue is already decided.

17. On his tale's affinities with the genre of the Greek romance, see Schlauch, *Chaucer's Constance* 75n.

18. On the use of the exodus in crusading rhetoric, see D. H. Green 228-71, especially 258-71.

19. See R. F. Green for one such reading. Spearing (101-36) has mounted a comprehensive and convincing assault on the critical tendency to take such readings to the extreme, according to which Chaucer wrote the *Man of Law's Tale* for the purpose of satirizing its teller: "He was truly interested in the possibility of connections between stories and their tellers, and voiced narratives and unreliable narrators are the ultimate outcome of the process he set going; but we must not suppose that Chaucer in the late fourteenth century could make an immediate transition into the world of the dramatic monologue (or would have wished to do so)" (120-21).

20. This is from the "Pilgrimage of Pure Devotion" of 1513, in Erasmus 169. "The inscribed slip of lead seen by Erasmus was evidently such as it was usual to deposit in coffins, in order to identify the corpse in case it should be disturbed" (Nichols 120-21).

Works Cited

Abulafia, David. "The Role of Trade in Muslim-Christian Contact during the Middle Ages." *The Arab Influence in Medieval Europe*. Ed. Dionisius A. Agius and Richard Hitchcock. Reading: Ithaca, 1994. 1-24.

Askins, William. "The Anxiety of Affluence: Chaucer's Man of Law and His Colleagues in Late Fourteenth-Century England." Congress of the New Chaucer Society. Dublin, Ireland. 25 July 1994.

Atiya, Aziz S. *Crusade, Commerce, and Culture*. Bloomington: Indiana UP, 1962.

Baker, J. H. *The Order of Serjeants at Law*. London: Seldon Society, 1984.

Bakhtin, Mikhail. "Forms of Time and of the Chronotope in the Novel." *The Dialogic Imagination: Four Essays*. Ed. Michael Holquist. Trans. Caryl Emerson and Michael Holquist. Austin: U of Texas P. 1981.

Beichner, Paul E. "Chaucer's Man of Law and Disparitas Cultus." *Speculum* 23 (1948): 70-75.

Beidler, Peter G. "Chaucer's Request for Money in the Man of Law's Prologue." *Chaucer Yearbook* 2 (1995): 1-15.

Bevis of Hampton. Ed. E. Kölbing. Early English Text Society, e.s. 46, 48, 65. London, 1885-94.

Bickley, Francis. *The Cavendish Family.* Boston: Houghton, 1911.

Blake, N. F. *The Textual Tradition of the Canterbury Tales.* London: Edward Arnold, 1985.

Block, Edward A. "Originality, Controlling Purpose, and Craftsmanship in Chaucer's *Man of Law's Tale.*" *PMLA* 68 (1953): 572-616.

Bosham, Herbert de. *De natalitio martyris die.* Patrologia Latina 190: cols. 1403-14.

Brown, Paul Alonzo. *The Development of the Legend of Thomas Becket.* Philadelphia: n.p., 1930.

Brundage, James A. "Cruce Signari: The Rite for Taking the Cross in England." *Traditio* 22 (1966): 289-310.

Calendar of Wills Proved and Enrolled in the Court of Husting, London, a.d. 1258-a.d. 1688. Vol. 2. Ed. R. R. Sharpe. London, 1890.

Carpenter, John. *Liber Albus.* Trans. Henry Thomas Riley. London, 1861.

Carus-Wilson, E. M. *Medieval Merchant Venturers: Collected Studies.* London: Methuen, 1954.

Chaucer, Geoffrey *The Riverside Chaucer.* Gen ed. Larry D. Benson. 3rd ed. Boston: Houghton, 1987.

Chaucer Life-Records. Ed. Martin M. Crow and Clair C. Olson. Oxford: Clarendon, 1966.

Correale, Robert, with Mary Hamel, eds. *Sources and Analogues of The Canterbury Tales.* Vol. 2. Cambridge: D. S. Brewer, 2005.

Davidson, Clifford. "The Middle English Saint Play and Its Iconography." *The Saint Play in Medieval Europe.* Ed. Clifford Davidson. Kalamazoo: Medieval Institute, 1986. 31-122.

Dinshaw, Carolyn. *Chaucer's Sexual Poetics.* Madison: U of Wisconsin P, 1989.

Eberle, Patricia. "Commercial Language and the Commercial Outlook in the *General Prologue.*" *Chaucer Review* 18 (1983-84): 161-74.

Erasmus, Desiderius. *The Earliest English Translations of Erasmus' Colloquia, 1536-1566.* Ed. Henry de Vocht. Louvain: Uystpruyst, 1928.

Fichte, Joerg O. "Rome and Its Anti-Pole in the *Man of Law's* and the *Second Nun's Tale*: Cristendom and Hethenesse." *Anglia* 122 (2004): 225-49.

Forey, A. J. "The Military Order of St Thomas of Acre." *English Historical Review* 364 (1977): 481-503.

Fortescue, John. "In Praise of the Laws of England." Trans. S. B. Chrimes. *On the Laws and Governance of England.* Ed. Shelley Lockwood, Cambridge: Cambridge UP, 1997. 1-80.

Fowler, Elizabeth. "The Empire and the Waif: Consent and Conflict in the Laws in the *Man of Law's Tale.*" *Medieval Literature and Historical Inquiry: Essays in Honour of Derek Pearsall.* Ed. David Aers. Cambridge: D. S. Brewer, 2000. 55-67.

Georgianna, Linda. "Love So Dearly Bought: The Terms of Redemption in *The Canterbury Tales.*" *Studies in the Age of Chaucer* 12 (1990): 85-116.

Gower, John. *Mirour de l'Omme. The Complete Works of John Gower.* Ed. G. C. Macaulay. Vol. 1. Oxford, 1899, 1-334.

_____. *Mirour de l'Omme* [The Mirror of Mankind]. Trans. William Burton Wilson. Rev. Nancy Wilson Van Baak. East Lansing: Colleagues, 1992.

_____. "Tale of Constance." Ed. G. C. Macauley. Correale with Hamel, 330-50.

Green, D. H. *The Millstätter Exodus: A Crusading Epic.* Cambridge: Cambridge UP, 1966.

Green, R. F. "Chaucer's Man of Law and Collusive Recovery." *Notes & Queries* n.s. 40 (1993): 303-5.

Hanks, D. Thomas, Jr. "Emaré: An Influence on the *Man of Law's Tale.*" *Chaucer Review* 19 (1983): 182-86.

Hoccleve, Thomas. *The Minor Poems.* Ed. Frederick J. Furnivall and I. Gollancz. Rev. J. Mitchell and A. I. Doyle, Early English Text Society, e.s. 61, 73. London: Oxford UP, 1970.

Hornstein, Lillian Herlands. "The Historical Background to The King of Tars." *Speculum* 16 (1941): 404-14.

_____. "Trivet's Constance and the King of Tars." *Modern Language Notes* 55 (1940): 354-57.

Kaske, R. E. "Causality and Miracle: Philosophical Perspectives in the *Knight's Tale* and the *Man of Law's Tale.*" *Traditions and Innovations: Essays on British Literature of the Middle Ages and the Renaissance.* Ed. David G. Allen and Robert A. White. Newark: U of Delaware P, 1990. 1-34.

Keene, Derek. "The Mercers and Their Hall before the Great Fire." Introduction. *The Mercers' Hall.* By Jean Imray. Ed. Ann Saunders. London Topographical Society Publication No. 143. London, 1991. 1-20.

Kelly, Henry Ansgar. "'The Prioress's Tale' in Context: Good and Bad Reports of Non-Christians in Fourteenth-Century England." *Studies in Medieval and Renaissance History* 3rd ser. 3 (2006): 73-132.

Kolve, V. A. *Chaucer and the Imagery of Narrative: The First Five Canterbury Tales.* Stanford: Stanford UP, 1984.

Laskaya, Anne, and Eve Salisbury, eds. *The Middle English Breton Lays.* Kalamazoo: Medieval Institute Publications, 1995. "Introduction to Emaré" consulted online. July 4, 2006. http://www.lib.rochester.edu/camelot/teams/emint.htm.

Lewis, Robert E. "Chaucer's Artistic Use of Pope Innocent III's *De miseria humane conditionis* in *The Man of Law's Prologue and Tale.*" *PMLA* 81 (1966): 485-92.

Liber de poenitentia et tentationibus religiosorum. Patrologia Latina 213: cols. 863-904.

Maddicott, J. R. *Law and Lordship: Royal Justices as Retainers in Thirteenth- and Fourteenth-Century England.* Oxford: Past and Present Society, 1978.

Medieval Trade in the Mediterranean World. Ed. Robert S. Lopez and Irving W. Raymond. New York: Columbia UP, 1955.

Mézières, Philippe de. *Letter to King Richard.* Ed. and trans. G. W. Coopland. Liverpool: Liverpool UP, 1974.

Mooney, Linne R. "Chaucer's Scribe." *Speculum* 81 (2006): 97-138.

Nerlich, Michael. *Ideology of Adventure: Studies in Modern Consciousness, 1100-1750.* Trans. Ruth Crowley. Vol. 1. Minneapolis: U of Minnesota P, 1987.

Nichols, John Gough, ed. and trans. *Pilgrimages to Saint Mary of Walsingham and Saint Thomas of Canterbury by Desiderius Erasmus.* Westminster, 1849.

Nicholson, Peter. "*The Man of Law's Tale*: What Chaucer Really Owed to Gower." *Chaucer Review* 26 (1991): 153-74.

Nolan, Maura. "'Acquiteth yow now': Textual Contradiction and Legal Discourse in the Man of Law's Introduction." *The Letter of the Law: Legal Practice and Literary Production in Medieval England*. Ed. Emily Steiner and Candace Barrington. Ithaca: Cornell UP, 2002. 136-53.

Paull, Michael R. "The Influence of the Saint's Legend Genre in the *Man of Law's Tale*." *Chaucer Review* 5 (1971): 179-94.

Phillips, J. R. S. *The Medieval Expansion of Europe*. 2nd ed. Oxford: Clarendon, 1998.

Piers Plowman: The B Version. Ed. George Kane and E. Talbot Donaldson. Rev. Ed. London: Athlone, 1988.

Riley-Smith, Jonathan. "Death on the First Crusade." *The End of Strife*. Ed. David Loades. Edinburgh: T. & T. Clark, 1984. 14-31.

Robertson, D. W., Jr. *Chaucer's London*. New York: Wiley, 1968.

Runciman, Steven. *History of the Crusades*. Vol. 3. Cambridge: Cambridge UP, 1954.

Schlauch, Margaret. *Chaucer's Constance and Accused Queens*. New York: New York UP, 1927.

_____. "Historical Precursors of Chaucer's Constance." *Philological Quarterly* 28 (1950): 402-12.

Simpson, James. "'After Craftes Conseil clotheth yow and fede': Langland and London City Politics." *England in the Fourteenth Century: Proceedings of the 1991 Harlaxton Symposium*. Ed. Nicholas Rogers. Stamford: P. Watkins, 1993. 109-27.

Spearing, A. C. *Textual Subjectivity: The Encoding of Subjectivity in Medieval Narratives and Lyrics*. Oxford: Oxford UP, 2005.

Sutton, Anne F. *The Mercery of London: Trade, Goods, and People, 1130-1578*. Burlington, VT: Ashgate, 2005.

_____. "The Merchant Adventurers of England. Their Origins and the Mercers' Company of London." *Historical Research* 75 (2002): 25-46.

Thrupp, Sylvia. *The Merchant Class of Medieval London*. Ann Arbor: U of Michigan P, 1948.

Trevet, Nicholas. "Of the Noble Lady Constance." Ed. and Trans. R. M. Correale. Correale and Hamel, 296-329.

Tyerman, Christopher. *The Invention of the Crusades*. Toronto: U of Toronto P, 1998.

Vita et Passio Sancti Thomae. Ch. 2. Patrologia Latina 190: cols. 346-49.

Wallace, David. *Chaucerian Polity: Absolutist Lineages and Associational Forms in England and Italy*. Stanford: Stanford UP, 1997.

Warner, Lawrence. "Becket and the Hopping Bishops." *Yearbook of Langland Studies* 17 (2003). 107-34.

_____. "The Sign of the Son: Crusading Imagery in the Cacciaguida Episode." *Electronic Bulletin of the Dante Society of America*. 16 Sept. 2002. "Paradiso." http://www.princeton.edu/-dante/ebdsa.

Watney, John. *Some Account of the Hospital of St. Thomas of Acon, in the Cheap, London, and of the Plate of the Mercers' Company*. London, 1892.

Wright, Laura. "The London Middle English Guild Certificates of 1388-89, ii: The Texts." *Nottingham Medieval Studies* 39 (1995): 119-45.

Wynn, Phillip. "The Conversion Story in Nicholas Trevet's 'Tale of Constance.'" *Viator* 13 (1982): 259-74.

Chaucer and the Absent City_____

David Wallace

Chaucer's *Canterbury Tales* does not begin in London: it begins south of the Thames in Southwark and moves us steadily away from the city walls. Chaucer's solitary attempt at pure London fiction comes to an abrupt end after just fifty-eight lines: "Of this cokes tale," writes the Hengwrt scribe, "maked Chaucer na moore."[1] The projected return journey from Canterbury is never made. In Chaucerian fiction, then, the City of London is chiefly remarkable for its absence. This essay attempts to read that absence. I begin by establishing the relationship of London to Southwark; I then consider texts from fourteenth-century London and Trecento Florence that offer precedents for the kinds of urban narrative that Chaucer might have written. Having shown how Boccaccio's story of Cisti the baker (*Decameron* VI. 2) succeeds in generating a unifying ideology of associational form, I proceed to a detailed reading of Chaucer's *Cook's Tale* as a London narrative. I end by observing how, as a plurality of discourses, Chaucer's London continues to defy poetic and political representation as a single, unified site.

London and Southwark

The absence of London from *The Canterbury Tales* is rendered more striking when Chaucer's text is read against its Italian twin, Boccaccio's *Decameron*. Boccaccio's text begins and ends in Florence. The form of governance that orders its storytelling is established in the church of Santa Maria Novella, a key site in both the religious and political history of the city. The rhetorical skills that the ten young Florentines take to the countryside will prove indispensable for the governance of the city once the plague has abated and civic life can be reestablished. Their tales feature dozens of historical Florentine protagonists and Florentine locales; the Sixth Day is entirely devoted to stories set in Florence. The only figures in Chaucer's text that may be paired with historical personages are Chaucer himself and "Herry Bailey" (I.4358), who is presumably to be associated with the "Henri Bayliff ostlyer" recorded by the Southwark Subsidy Rolls in 1380-81. The "Cook of London" (I.4325), who names Harry Bailey, identifies himself as "Hogge of Ware" (I.4336). The Cook is himself addressed with facetious reverence by the Host as "gentil Roger" (I.4353); he may be associated with the "Roger of Ware of London, Cook," a convicted nightwalker who figures twice in pleas of debt.[2]

The choice of a Southwark tavern as the gathering place for Chaucer's pilgrimage is at once realistically plausible and arrestingly eccentric. Pilgrims

---

from London to Canterbury often spent the night in Southwark so that they could begin their journey before the city gates were opened for the day: Chaucer's pilgrims, we should note, "made forward erly for to rise" (I.33). But there was nothing to prevent Chaucer from assembling his pilgrimage at a familiar London landmark, the cross at St. Paul's, for example. The effect of assembling at Southwark is to emphasize the randomness of this encounter between Chaucer and the "compaignie" (which is itself a random grouping, "by aventure yfalle, In felaweshipe," I.26). And the business of establishing a form of governance in Southwark under the tutelage of an innkeeper must have seemed (to a London readership) comically misguided. Southwark functioned as a dumping ground and exclusion zone for early modern London: messy or marginal trades such as lime burning, tanning, dying, brewing, innkeeping, and prostitution flourished there; criminals fleeing London courts and aliens working around London trade regulations found a home. Southwark was a suburb of London but also an independent parliamentary borough (albeit a borough lacking a charter of incorporation). The "tangled and disharmonious snarl of jurisdictions"[3] overlapping in Southwark is a historian's nightmare. Southwark recognized no single authority but was divided between five manorial jurisdictions (four in ecclesiastical hands; one owned first by the Crown and later by the City); each had its own set of courts. Southwark's parishes were only partially coterminous with these manorial jurisdictions, and the boundaries of the aggregate term "Southwark" vary from document to document. The Crown controlled the courts and prisons of the Marshalsea and King's Bench and exercised its authority through permanent county officers such as sheriffs, escheators, coroners, and justices. The City of London struggled tirelessly to swallow up (sometimes by legal tactics, sometimes by simple encroachment) the unchartered community on its south bank that continually undermined the monopolies and privileges of its trade and craft guilds: the charter of 1444 confirming the City's rights in the Guildable manor speaks of the "diverse doubts, opinions, differences, ambiguities, controversies, and dissensions"[4] that had characterized relations between London and Southwark since time immemorial. This is the site at which Chaucer's pilgrim body recognizes Harry Bailey as "oure governour" (I.813).

Chaucer's relationship to London at the opening of his *Canterbury Tales* is thus markedly different from the *Decameron*'s relationship to Florence. Boccaccio establishes a form of associational governance within the city that is then carried to the countryside. Chaucer establishes no form of governance until his pilgrimage has left the city; his order of storytelling is then established at a place experienced by fourteenth-century London as a challenge to its own integrity, as "a perpetual jurisdictional affront."[5] Southwark defined itself against London politically but, economically, found London indispensable. The name of Southwark, in short, identifies governance as a problematic issue, takes this issue out of the city, and yet cannot quite leave the city behind.

Having emphasized the centrifugal impulse of Chaucer's Canterbury pilgrimage—its rapid distantiation from London as a point of origin—we should also recognize that there was much movement in the opposite direction in late-fourteenth-century England. Religious and secular magnates continued to maintain residences in the capital and to buy up and rent out properties. The royal household moved in a tighter circle around London and more of its administrative apparatus was permanently housed at Westminster.[6] Foreigners, *uplondish* and *outlandish* men, sought out the royal court, the law courts, the Inns of Court, and the international markets; young men and women from every part of Britain came to serve their time as apprentices, to find work, or to contract marriages. Both modern historians and medieval Londoners tend to speak of London as a fluid entity, a place to which people come and go, rather than as a permanent, sharply delimited site.[7] And yet, at the same time, London authorities were keen to represent London as "the capital city and the watchtower of the whole realm," and to insist "that from the government thereof other cities and places do take example."[8]

Narrative and Governance in Fourteenth-Century London

Chaucer's London was, by postpandemic standards, a metropolis: the poll tax returns of 1377 indicate a population more than three times greater than that of York or Bristol, its nearest English rivals. And although Chaucer wrote little of the city he lived and worked in, there are many contemporary texts that give us a detailed sense of the specifically *urban* character of London life. Many of them feature the kind of tricksters and impersonators that flourish as the urban division of labor grows ever more complex. One such character, a Welshman called John Haslewode (alias John Harehull), goes on a tour of London breweries with a white staff in his hand, purporting to be "a taker of ale for our Lord the King."[9] Another, Roger Clerk of Wandlesworth (Wandsworth), offers to exercise his skill as a physician to cure the bodily infirmities of Johanna, wife of Roger atte Hacche. Having received a down payment of 12*d.*, Roger Clerk hangs a scroll (*cedulam*) around Johanna's neck upon which, he says, "was written a good charm for fevers." Later, on being asked what the words of this charm of his were, Roger replies:

"Anima Christi, sanctifica me; corpus Christi, salva me; in isanguis Christi, nebria me; cum bonus Christus tu, lava me." And the parchment being then examined, not one of those words was found written thereon. And he was then further told by the Court, that a straw beneath his foot would be of just as much avail for fevers, as this charm of his was; whereupon, he fully granted that it would be so.[10]

The court in question is that composed of the mayor and aldermen who sat in the Chamber of the London Guildhall. The Letter Books that record their proceedings usually employ Latin, but often switch to Anglo-Norman or Middle English when noting proclamations and ordinances. Their narratives of crimes and misdemeanors often detail some quite spectacular examples of native wit and inventiveness. In 1380, for example, John Warde and Richard Lyneham, two men considered "stout enough to work for their food and raiment," came before the court accused of impersonating mutes through an elaborate pantomime employing pincers, an iron hook, two ell measures,

and a piece of leather, in shape like part of a tongue, edged with silver, and with writing around it, to this effect,—"This *is the tongue of John Warde*"; with which instruments, and by means of diverse signs, they gave many persons to understand that they were traders, in token whereof they carried the said ell measures; and that they had been plundered by robbers of their goods; and that their tongues had been drawn out with the said hook, and then cut off with the pincers; they making a horrible noise, like unto a roaring, and opening their mouths; where it seemed to all who examined the same, that their tongues had been cut off: to the defrauding of other poor and infirm persons, and in manifest deceit of the whole of the people, etc.[11]

This piece of street theater, which seems no great crime by modern standards, evidently shocked and scandalized the mayoral court. The "evil intent and falsity" of the malefactors are denounced at some length and the punishment meted out to them is exceptionally severe: on the Monday, Wednesday, and Friday before the Feast of St. Simon and St. Jude they are to be placed upon the pillory, with their pincers, hook, leather tongue, and ell measures hanging around their necks; they are then to be jailed in Newgate until further notice. The Guildhall was evidently determined to stage some theater of its own (a one-week run) "to the end that other persons might beware of such and the like evil intent, falsity, and deceit." What accounts for this severe reaction by the London authorities? The reference to "other poor and infirm persons" offers one line of explanation: both secular and religious authorities in this period showed a new and determined resolve to discriminate between "genuine" paupers (who had a right to beg because of physical infirmity) and sturdy beggars (who could work but were too idle to do so).[12] A second explanation, a complementary rather than alternative one, concerns the false signifier of the text-inscribed severed tongue. City authorities needed to enforce a respect for the integrity of symbolic representation within the city, since the limits and partialities of their own power could only be disguised through the persuasive power of symbolic forms. When the tongue is isolated as the object of attention, the listener is invited to disassociate the tongue from what the tongue speaks of. Chaucer's Pardoner issues one such invitation in modeling his false preaching: "Myne handes and my tonge goon so yerne/ That it is joye to se my bisynesse" (VI.398-99).

The City authorities could not allow the populace to see its tongue wagging as it spoke its judgments, sentences, and ordinances. And yet, at times, the limitations of the symbolic acts performed by and within the mayoral court were readily apparent. One such high point of symbolic drama came in 1387, when the right hand of William Hughlot was laid upon the block in the Guildhall Court, ready to be chopped off by an axe held by one of the sheriff's officers.[13] The right hand that Hughlot was about to lose had earlier stabbed a barber in his house in Fleet Street, assaulted an alderman, and wounded one of the Fleet Street constables. But Hughlot's hand was never amputated because at the last minute John Rote, the alderman he had attacked, asked "that execution of the judgment aforesaid might be remitted unto him." Hughlot was then sentenced to imprisonment for a year and a day and "condemned to suffer the disgraceful punishment of the pillory." But he never went to the pillory and was released from prison just nine days later. Such leniency is soon explained: it is exercised, the Letter Book tells us, "in reverence for our said Lord the King, whose servant the said William then was." The mayor and aldermen are at pains to emphasize, throughout the document, that they too are officers of the king. But even as officers of the king they were not bold enough to strike off the right hand of someone in royal service: they settled for a lesser drama, in which Hughlot was obliged, on the day of his release from prison, to carry a lighted wax candle from the Guildhall to the Church of St. Dunstan, the parish in which he had committed his crime.

The light sentencing of William Hughlot is in sharp contrast to the fate of two men convicted of breaking into the house of a "citizen and mercer of London" in 1390.[14] The brief entry devoted to their trial concludes as follows: "The said John Prentys and John Markyngtone are guilty of the felony aforesaid. Therefore they are to be hanged. Chattels of the same felons there are none etc." The fact that the two men have no possessions, that they are men of no substance, means that they have nothing with which to pay for their crimes except their miserable lives. This ideal of commutative justice is dramatized in the punishment of the pillory (which is generally reserved for people of lower degree): the malefactor is reunited with his crime as he stands with the symbols or instruments of his transgression around his neck. John Haslewode, the would-be ale-taker, stood with his white wand at his side; Roger Clerk, the quack physician, having been led through the City with trumpets and pipes on a saddleless horse, stood with his magic spell and a whetstone around his neck and urinals hanging before and behind him.[15] Such imaging of justice, which freezes malefactors in time at the moment of their crime, is most perfectly represented by Dante's *Inferno*: we think, for example, of the Florentine usurers sitting in the seventh circle with their purses hanging around their necks (each one decorated by their family coat of arms).[16] The lower reaches of the *Inferno* are encompassed by the walls of a city; Dante's Hell is a subterranean version of Dante's Florence.

But although the narratives in the London Letter Books terminate with a Dantean imaging of justice—an hour in the pillory warns of, prefigures, an eternity of punishment—the narrative energy that precedes such closure is more strongly reminiscent of Boccaccio. These texts do, after all, issue from a group of merchant capitalists that compares with the *Decameron*'s first audience and matches Boccaccio's mercantile origins. And they reflect a comparably detailed understanding of the urban milieu that they seek to control and regulate. In unraveling a fraud case in 1391, for example, *Letter Book H* takes us on a journey through the streets and suburbs of London almost as complicated as that of Andreuccio of Perugia through Naples: we follow a cloth merchant's servant through various wards, parishes, and hostelries inside and outside the city walls until he is finally locked into a room at "'Le Walssheman sur le Hoope,' in Fletestret, in the Parish of St. Martin without Ludgate, in the suburb of London": here he is finally parted from his master's merchandise by a con artist posing as a nobleman's servant.[17]

Such a detailed concern with the regulation and division of time and space in the city is a constant feature of the Letter Books; when we read their narratives in sequence we begin to see how the lines of power in the city run. On folio cxiii of *Letter Book H*, for example, we find the names of eleven women who have paid the sum of 13s. 4d. each for the privilege of maintaining market stalls at specific points around the High Cross of Cheapside for one year.[18] On the reverse side of the same folio (two pages later in Riley, who breaks up the sequence of the manuscript), we find that these fees are to be diverted to one John Charney by virtue of his office as *venator communitatis London*, "Common Hunt for the Commonalty of London." Common Hunt is responsible for overseeing the stables and kennels maintained for the use of the citizens of London. The art of city government here, then, consists in a masculine oligarchy selling city space to women traders so that London citizens can pursue their aristocratic pretensions outside the city walls through the art of hunting. Such models of expropriation were not, of course, made visible to the general public: the *Letter Book* keeps to Latin here and only turns to the vernacular when it wishes the citizens, foreigns, and aliens of London to take notice of its ordinances and proclamations.

I am not suggesting that Chaucer spent his evenings leafing through record books at the Guildhall.[19] But it is important to recognize that these records attest to a sophisticated understanding of the functioning and governance of urban space; they suggest, in short, an urban consciousness.[20]

Urban Narrative: Italian Precedents for Chaucer

So far we have simply established that Chaucer had ample opportunity to develop the kind of urban narrative we associate with the Italian Trecento. Why, then, does he refuse this possibility? We might begin our attempt at an answer by noting that the urban scenes of both Dante and Boccaccio are set within all-inclusive (hence all-explanatory) ideological frameworks. Dante deploys the greatest framework imaginable: his sunken city is reached only by the path that leads us beneath the Trinitarian inscription of *Inferno* III, which begins: "PER ME SI VA NE LA CITTÀ DOLENTE" (THROUGH ME YOU ENTER THE WOEFUL CITY). Here, beyond this inscription, the familiar mechanisms of urban justice are regulated with superhuman impartiality. Boccaccio, however, operates above ground within an ideological space that may be read in conjunction with, or as part of, a Florentine tradition of mercantile historiography.[21] This begins with Giovanni Villani, who assigns the moment of inspiration for his *Chronicle* to 1300, the year of Dante's imaginary journey through the afterlife, and makes a Dante-like attempt to square events in Florence with an all-encompassing, God-guided scheme of historical explanation. Matteo, who took up the *Chronicle* on Giovanni's death, is interested more in the city-state of Florence and less in any putative universal history it might form part of. By the time we get to Goro Dati at the turn of the next century, the Florentine state has become the transcendent subject of history: "the commune," says Dati, "cannot die."[22] The *Decameron* situates itself, in time of composition, revision, and ideological positioning, somewhere near the midpoint of this Trecento tradition of merchant-class chroniclers. The imaginative power of the afterlife makes itself felt, but the compelling confidence of Boccaccio's text is invested not in the interpretive power of religion, but rather in the city-state's ability to regulate itself through its own urban mechanisms and to identify and expel those who threaten its internal equilibrium.[23]

Chaucer, like Boccaccio, explicitly rejects the Dantean option of writing a text with pretensions to omniscience: "ther is noon dwellynge in this contree," he writes in opening his *Legend of Good Women*, "that eyther hath in hevene or belle ybe" (F, 5-6).[24] And yet he is also denied the Boccaccian option of associating with a vernacular tradition that is gradually adapting the religious universalism of monastic chronicling to the market-driven exigencies of urban society. London was the center of chronicle writing in Chaucer's time, but was not the *subject* of it; there was no tradition of merchant-class chronicling in fourteenth-century England.[25] We might make an exception here for *Letter Book H*, which suddenly turns into a chronicle of sorts in June 1381. On the same folio that records Ralph Strode's prosecution of a poulterer who had attempted to sell eighteen pigeons, "putrid and stinking, and an abomination to mankind," we hear of "the most wondrous and hitherto unheard-of prodigies that have ever happened in the City of London."[26] The hero of this narrative is Sir William Walworth, the then mayor; the climactic scene is played out at Smithfield, where Mayor Walworth rides at Watt Tyler with peasants to the one side of him and king, lords, knights, esquires, and citizens on the other. The narrative concludes, after the jousting mayor has unseated and slain the rebel captain, with the mayor and his accomplices being knighted in the field beneath the royal banner. When the Letter Book scribe turns historian, then, he sounds more like a chivalric chronicler than a mercantile one. The rebels are not analyzed as a class, as part of the social equation calculated so carefully elsewhere in the Letter Book, but are reported as a prodigy, a natural disaster. This strategy is shared by clerical authors in 1381 and by the poet who, meditating upon the earthquake of 21 May 1382, remembers the rebels only to fold them back into clerical discourse:

> The rysyng of the comuynes in londe,
> The pestilens, and the eorthe-qwake,
> Theose threo thinges, I understonde,
> Beoth tokenes the grete vengaunce and wrake
> That schulde falle for synnes sake,
> As this clerkes conne declare.[27]

This sense of being obliged to record every egregious act of nature and to interpret it as a message from the Almighty is shared by Giovanni Villani. But once Giovanni's *Chronicle* has been abruptly silenced by the plague of 1340, the most egregious act of all, the floods, fires, and falling chimney pots begin to fade from Florentine historiography; attention is now concentrated upon the inner workings of the city itself. But the later chroniclers never cut the cord that attaches them to the religious universalism of earlier generations; they tend, rather, to identify the workings of Providence more closely with the exigencies of Florentine polity. By the 1370s the citizenry has enough faith in its defining civic virtue of *libertas* to set it against the hierocratic authority of Rome: Florence goes to war against the papacy. In Boccaccio, too, we see a powerful commitment to what might be termed an ideology of associational form. In the next few pages we will consider how this ideology of association within a self-sufficient, self-regulating city is developed in one short novella. We will then move straight to a reading of the *Cook's Tale* and see how associational form plays in Chaucer.

The first thing to say about this ideology of associational form is that it is an ideology, not an ontology.[28] The Florentine Republican regime of 1343-78 certainly started out as one of the broadest-based regimes in the history of early modern Europe: shopkeepers, artisans, and tradesmen shared in the business of government with patrician merchants, bankers, and rentiers. But powerful class antagonisms did, of course, remain. The greater guilds controlling the major industries did not think that the principle of *libertas* should extend to include lower guildsmen; the shopkeepers and craftsmen of the lower guilds were keen to accentuate their own privileged status by keeping the lower classes out of office and by preventing them from forming guilds of their own. No single group was trusted to hold office for very long (the priors of the Signoria served two-month terms), and no citizens were trusted with the administration of justice: outsiders were hired on short, fixed-termed contracts to serve as *podestà* or *capitano del popolo*. This, then, was the fragile and intricate political structure that prevailed in Florence as Boccaccio wrote his *Decameron*. Republican regimes were keen to celebrate Ciceronian *aequitas*, an ideal that puts all members of a specific social group on level terms with one another.[29] But although this might be achieved within (or across) the lowest and highest political forms of a commune—from the parish guild to the Signoria—the space between such constituent forms was itself, of course, hierarchized. There was a need, then, for some form of cultural production that would both challenge ideologies that were hostile to associative polity and conceal the divisions within such polity by reconciling hierarchized relations along a single plane of *aequitas*, of *unitas civium*. Such complex ideological maneuvers, which defeat the strict logic of political theory, are most adeptly performed by imaginative texts that conceal their own ideological character through the techniques of novelistic realism. Let us consider just one such narrative: the second novella of the *Decameron*'s Sixth Day.

Cisti the Baker and the Ideology of Associational Form

The novella begins with the narrator, Pampinea, questioning the logic of Fortune and Nature (and hence of class-structured society): why do they sometimes assign a noble spirit to an inferior body or social calling? Pampinea insists that these powers show great wisdom in "burying their most precious possessions in the least imposing (and therefore least suspect) part of their houses, whence they bring them forth in the hour of greatest need" (p. 485; VI.2.5).[30] Here, then, is an attempt to develop the notion of an intelligence buried deep within the lower reaches of Florentine society that will make itself heard at times of danger. In Pampinea's novella this intelligence is embodied by the unlikely figure of "Cisti fornaio," Cisti the baker.

The novella is set in 1300, the year in which a papal delegation visited Florence to make peace between two feuding factions, the Black and White Guelfs. Pope Boniface's representatives, who assumed the role of peacemakers, were in fact working to bring the pro-papal Blacks to power by exterminating the Whites. This is precisely what was to happen in November 1301, when Boniface turned to Charles de Valois and his army: the Whites were massacred or (like Dante) exiled and the Blacks came to power. By beginning her novella with this papal delegation of 1300, then, Pampinea is indeed setting it at an "hour . . . of greatest need" for the citizenry of Florence.

According to Pampinea, the papal delegation was lodged during its visit to Florence under the roof of Messer Geri Spina, a prominent Florentine merchant and friend of the pope. Most mornings they would walk with their host past the Church of Santa Maria Ughi, beside which Cisti had his bakery. Cisti realizes that it would show "gran cortesia" (2.10) to offer Messer Geri and the papal envoys some of his delicious wine, but, being conscious of the difference in rank between himself and Messer Geri, he considered it would be presumptuous of him to issue an invitation (p. 486). So he resorts to the stratagem of sitting outside his door each day, dressed in a freshly laundered apron, with white wine cooled in a bucket and spotless wineglasses. He drinks his wine just as Messer Geri is passing with the ambassadors:

> e a seder postosi, come essi passavano, e egli, poi che una volta o due spurgato s'era, cominciava a ber si saporitamente questo suo vino, che egli n'avrebbe fatta venir voglia a' morti. (VI.2.12)

> [He then seated himself in the doorway, and just as they were passing, he cleared his throat a couple of times and began to drink this wine of his with so much relish that he would have brought a thirst to the lips of a corpse. (p. 486)]

Cisti dares not speak across the difference in social rank that divides him from Messer Geri and the papal envoys, but in clearing his throat to drink he both draws attention to his lowly status (plebeians customarily spat and freed their throats from catarrh before drinking) and inscribes his social superiors within this common human desire to drink cool wine in hot weather. By the second day, Messer Geri has been seduced: Cisti fetches a bench from his bak-

---

ery and serves his guests from a small flagon of his best wine. This becomes a regular occurrence. When the diplomatic mission is concluded, Messer Geri holds a magnificent banquet, to which he invites some of the most distinguished citizens of Florence; he also invites Cisti, who cannot be persuaded to attend the "magnifico convito" (2.18). Messer Geri then orders one of his servants to take a flask to Cisti, so that each of his guests may be served with half a glass of the exquisite wine during the first course. The servant replaces the small flask with a huge one and presents it to Cisti. When Cisti sees this, he says: "Figliuolo, messer Geri non ti manda a me" (My son, Messer Geri has not sent you to me, VI.2.20).

Cisti, a man of noble qualities, can read this huge flask as a counterfeit sign; Messer Geri would not have sent it to him. The servant returns to Messer Geri, and reports Cisti's words. Messer Geri sends the servant back to Cisti, briefed to repeat that he is sending the servant to *him*; and if Cisti should give the same answer, he is to ask "to whom I am sending you" (p. 487). The servant, returning with the huge flask, does as he is told and asks the question he was sent with: "'Adunque,' disse il famigliare 'a cui mi manda?' Rispuose Cisti: 'A Arno'" ("So then," said the servant, "to whom is he sending me?" Cisti replied: "To the Arno," VI.2.23-24).

When these words are reported back to him, Messer Geri demands to see the flask that his servant had presented to Cisti. On seeing the huge flask, he immediately understands the force of Cisti's comment. Having scolded the servant, he sends him back to Cisti with the small flask. Cisti now acknowledges that the flask has been sent to him; he fills it up and sends it back. A few days later, he fills a small cask with wine of the same vintage and sends that along, too. He then, finally, visits Messer Geri and explains the rationale for his actions. His visit is not, strictly speaking, necessary: the only thing he now needs to explain is the significance of sending Messer Geri his wine. In an extraordinary closing sentence, Cisti takes the opportunity to inscribe himself in what can only be described as a relationship of feudal vassalage: "Ora, per ciò che io non intendo d'esservene più guardiano, tutto ve l'ho fatto venire: fatene per innanzi come vi piace" (Now, since I do not intend to be the guardian of the wine any longer, I have let it all be sent to you: do with it henceforth as you please, 2.29).

Cisti suggests that as *guardiano* he has enjoyed *possessio* of the wine, and *usus fructi*: but now he returns it to the *dominium* of Messer Geri. Messer Geri, for his part, prizes Cisti's gift and thanks him "as profusely as the occasion seemed to warrant" (p. 488: he cannot, of course, appear to be in Cisti's debt, since this would disturb the dialectical mutuality of the feudal bond. But the bond can be acknowledged as a permanent one: "e sempre poi per da molto l'ebbe e per amico" (and from then on he held him as a man of worth and as a friend for life, 2.30).

Boccaccio is not suggesting that Florence should resolve its political difficulties through a revival of the vassalic bond. There is, however, a kind of *eros* that grows between the two men as they come to recognize one another, one that is best expressed through the suggestive power of feudal relations. The language and structure of courtly love is, after all, deeply indebted to the founding metaphors of feudalism. The metaphors of postfeudal society, in which we speak not of bonds but of contracts, do not have the ideological force of feudal mutualities. But although he defers to the vertical plane of feudal hierarchizing, Boccaccio also insists upon the lateral, associative aspects of social relations: his novella sees a ceaseless movement back and forth across city space. It falls to Cisti, the Florentine baker, to alert Messer Geri to the importance of this lateral dimension. He initiates this process while Messer Geri is moving across Florence, in the company of papal envoys, between the headquarters of the White and Black Guelfs, the factions that have torn Florence apart for generations. Once these envoys have left the city, a new diplomatic mission is conducted across the face of Florentine society as the *famigliare* moves back and forth between the baker and the Black Guelf. Through this transfer of tokens and messages, which owes as much to the devices of courtly love as to the protocols of Florentine politics, Boccaccio suggests an ideal unity of the Florentine body politic in the face of external treachery.

Chaucer's Cook and the Limits of Associational Ideology

In moving from Florence to London, from Cisti the baker to Perkyn the apprentice, we should note that the teller of each tale is a representative figure; representative, that is, of the city they speak of. Pampinea, the oldest of Boccaccio's women, is the guiding intelligence of Boccaccio's *brigata*: she conceives of the plan for an organized flight from Florence, works out the ground rules for the *brigata*'s governance, and rules as queen for the first day. Chaucer's Cook, who speaks twice of "oure citee" (I.4343, 4365), is the only pilgrim to associate the pilgrimage collectively with London. He is also the only pilgrim to be explicitly identified as a Londoner: the five guildsmen he serves as cook are assumed to be from London only on the basis of their association with him. But although he is twice identified as a "Cook of London" and is said to be a connoisseur of "Londonn ale" (I.382), the Cook identifies himself as originating not from London but from Ware, a town in Hertfordshire thirty miles due north of the city. Ware had been a notorious trouble spot since the 1350s, when attempts to enforce the Statute of Laborers had led to rioting; the vicar of Ware and a local hermit were indicted for preaching that the statute was wicked. In 1381 a subsequent vicar of Ware led a good cross section of his townsmen on an attack against John of Gaunt's castle in Hertford; they then marched on to London and took a prominent part in sacking Gaunt's palace at the Savoy.[31]

The name of Ware, then, comes freighted with suggestions of unruliness or violence imported to the city from the provinces. And some of the details with which Chaucer's Cook is credentialized as a Londoner have disquieting or unsavory connotations. The Host's suggestion that many of the Cook's pastries have been doctored recalls an ordinance of 1379: no pastry maker in the City of London shall bake in pastries "rabbits, geese, and garbage, not befitting, and sometimes stinking, in deceit of the people"; no one shall purchase such garbage from the cooks of Bread Street or from the cooks of great lords.[32] And the Cook's familiarity with the language of Flemings—"'sooth pley, quaad pley,' as the Flemyng seith"—reminds us of the wholesale slaughter of Flemings that went on in London in 1381. The Cook's incorporation of a Flemish proverb into his own discourse seems, on the face of it, benign, if not impressively cosmopolitan. But in 1381, according to one chronicle, such an awareness of linguistic difference became the mechanism that led to murder: on being asked to say "Breede and Chese" by the London mob, the Flemings would say "Case and Brode" (*kaas en brood*) and so seal their own fate.[33] The fact that the Cook knows some Flemish, then, does not mean that he is a friend of Flemings. He might, of course, have learned the language in a brothel, since many London prostitutes were of Flemish origin.[34]

The opening couplet of the *Cook's Tale* brings us directly to an intricate structure of social and political relationships set within "oure citee," the unifying term: "A prentys whilom dwelled in oure citee,/ And of a craft of vitaillers was he" (I.4365-66). Two sets of political relationship are suggested here, one defined internally and the other externally. The first, that of the apprentice to his master (there can be no apprentices without masters) is one of strict subordination with some overtones of feudal mutuality. An apprentice is enjoined to respect his master as his lord, his "seigneur"; one young man, apprenticed to his uncle, is directed to hold the stirrup while his master mounts his horse as a mark of respect and obedience.[35] The apprentice, who is by definition a "foreign" or noncitizen, elects to work for his master for a specified number of years in the hope of learning his master's craft and of eventually being sponsored for citizenship by his master's guild. But this ideal of an orderly hierarchy within the guild structure is immediately brought up against the political hostility that sets one guild against the next: "And of a craft of *vitaillers* was he." It would hardly be possible, for a contemporary audience, to think of the London victualers without thinking of their binary pairing, the non-victualers, and of the affrays, riots, and disputes between these rival parties that fill the

London Letter Books in the 1380s. But our attention is soon distracted from such matters by some vigorous lines of physical description:

> Gaillard he was as goldfynch in the shawe,
> Broun as a berye, a propre shorte felawe,
> With lokkes blake, ykemb ful fetisly.
> (I.4367-69)

Such fruit, animal, and grooming imagery puts the *Riverside* annotator in mind of both Alison and Absolon from the *Miller's Tale*.[36] Interestingly, though, we are not invited to make comparisons between the apprentice and the *General Prologue*'s Squire, although certain points of description clearly overlap:

> So hot he loved, that by nyghtertale
> He sleep namoore than dooth a nyghtyngale.
> (I.98-99)

> He was as ful of love and paramour
> As is the hyve ful of hony sweete.
> (I.4372-73)

The squire and the apprentice are young men of comparable age and of comparable sexual energy living in the shadow of a powerful master. But whereas the squire's sexuality is seen as charming and innocuous (and is not associated with the energy of a professional killer),[37] that of the apprentice is at once ridiculous and dangerous. It is ridiculous in that any attempts to regulate it through the elegant, *fetys* decorums of courtly behavior only serve to remind us that the apprentice is a churl: he is dark in complexion; he is short in stature. And yet if this energy is left uncultivated it poses an immediate threat to civil society—or, more specifically, to "the shoppe":

> At every bridale worde he synge and hoppe;
> He loved bet the taverne than the shoppe.
> For whan ther any ridyng was in Chepe,
> Out of the shoppe thider worde he lepe—
> Til that he hadde al the sighte yseyn,
> And daunced wel, he wolde nat come ayeyn.
> (I.4375-80)

The chief threat to the sober world of commerce here would seem to be a restless personal energy that cuts across the threshold of "the shoppe." But as the passage continues, this reckless individualism suddenly shows associative tendencies and a capacity for planning and organization:

> And gadered hym a meynee of his sort
> To hoppe and synge and maken swich disport;
> And ther they setten stevene for to meete,
> To pleyen at the dys in swich a streete.
>
> (I.4381-84)

The term *meynee*, used over thirty times by Chaucer, is a slippery but indispensable term occupying that liminal space between the shop and the street: its primary meaning is "family, household"; its second, "a body of retainers, attendants, dependents, or followers; a retinue, suite, train"; its third, "a company of persons employed together or having a common object of association; an army, ship's crew, congregation, assembly, or the like."[38] *Meynee* is itself a neutral term, "deriving ultimately from the Latin *mansionem*," that is rarely employed in neutral contexts: specific *meynees* are generally figured as a force for good or evil, as constructive or destructive of social and moral order. Chaucer speaks in one place of "the ryght ordene hous of so mochel a fadir and an ordeynour of meyne"; at another of "he Jakke Strawe and his meynee": the same term covers both God Almighty and the leader of the *Peasants' Revolt*.[39] The occasion of its deployment in the *Cook's Tale* is particularly complex: it is applied to a group of young men who come together to agree on a time and place in the city so that they can reconstitute themselves as an organized body; they will then engage in the random business of dice playing.[40] This, according to the Cook, poses a direct and immediate threat to the master's business, his "chaffare" (I.4389): the rolling dice soon lead to the "box ful bare" (I.4390), a diminution of the master's capital. But we should note that it is not so much the vice of gaming that the tale insists upon as the root of social evil, but rather the act of association that makes such evil possible. This emphasis predominates again once the master has given the apprentice his walking papers:

> And for ther is no theef withoute a lowke,
> That helpeth hym to wasten and to sowke
> Of that he brybe kan or borwe may,
> Anon he sente his bed and his array
> Unto a compeer of his owene sort.
>
> (I.4415-19)

This new association of wasters makes capital from its own excesses: as the tale breaks off a new shop arises to challenge that of the master; the dangerous sexuality of Perkyn returns as the energy that spins the wheels of commerce:

> . . . That lovede dys, and revel, and disport,
> And hadde a wyf that heeld for contenance
> A shoppe, and swyved for hir sustenance.
>
> (I.4420-22)

We have still not moved far from the world of the London Letter Books. Many of the themes from Chaucer's tale are developed in a case heard before Mayor Brembre in 1385. This concerns a woman called Elizabeth, wife of Henry Moring, who, "under colour of the craft of embroidery," retained various female apprentices and ran a prostitution ring. Things went well until one of the apprentices, under pressure from her mistress, stole a breviary from a chaplain she was sleeping with.[41] The comic potential of this story was entirely lost on the mayoral court: Elizabeth is to be put upon the *thewe*, the pillory for women, and then taken to "some Gate of the City, and there be made to forswear the City, and the liberty thereof, to the effect that she would never again enter the same." Through such dramas of punishment and expulsion the City authorities were able to suggest that their political interventions were motivated by a concern for the City's moral welfare. And by associating prostitution with unruly gatherings they are able both to discredit such gatherings and to find a pretext for breaking them up:

> Also,—whereas many and divers affrays, broils, and dissensions, have arisen in times past, and many men have been slain and murdered, by reason of the frequent resort of, and consorting with, common harlots, at taverns, brewhouses of *huksters*, and other places of ill-fame, within the said city, and the suburbs thereof; and more especially through Flemish women, who profess and follow such shameful and dolorous life.[42]

This proclamation of 1393 goes on to restrict prostitutes to two sites outside the City walls, namely Cock Lane (Smithfield) and the Stews in Southwark. It also empowers City officers to remove the upper garment and hood of any prostitute they see outside these areas: if they bring these items of clothing to the Guildhall they "shall have the half thereof for their trouble." This drama of unveiling is, of course, consistent with what goes on in the final couplet of the *Cook's Tale*: the wife of the compeer of Perkyn, the riotous apprentice, pretends ("or contenance") to be a respectable businesswoman, but as the couplet completes itself she is revealed to be a whore. Her whoredom, of course, further delegitimizes the association of apprentice Perkyn with "his owene sort."

It seems that the more we attempt to contextualize Chaucer's *Cook's Tale*, the more strikingly it differentiates itself from the Boccaccian tale of Cisti the baker. In the Italian novella two men of differing class and culture meet, albeit fleetingly, at a common level of understanding. In the English tale, the differences between master and apprentice prove so intractable that the master cuts the cord that binds them together. Whereas Boccaccio's narrative generates an associational ideology that will unite the city against external dangers, the social divisions within Chaucer's city widen dramatically as the tale runs on. And two of the proverbs that frame and inform the Cook's narrative reflect an ideology not of association, but of its opposite. The first, spoken by the Cook himself, borrows the wisdom of Solomon: "'Ne brynge nat every man into thyn hous,'/ For herberwynge by nyghte is perilous" (I.4331-32). The text from Ecclesiasticus with which the Cook glosses the *Reeve's Tale* itself forms an excellent introduction to the fragmented and mistrustful London milieu he is out to evoke: "Bring not every man into thine house, for many are the plots of the deceitful man" (11.29). And the nugget of popular wisdom that comes "mysteriously" to the master as he contemplates his wayward apprentice also counsels the wisdom of putting limits on forms of association: "nat every man"; not every apple "Wel bet is roten appul out of hoord/ Than that it rotie al the remenaunt" (I.4406-7).

This antiassociational rhetoric is remarkably consonant with that which informs a mayoral proclamation of 1383. This proclamation, the earliest Middle English entry in the London Letter Books, begins by situating king, mayor, sheriffs, and aldermen on a single vertical axis of power; it then goes to extraordinary lengths by way of defining, or finding names for, the kind of political association that threatens this hierarchy:

The Mair, Shirreues, and Aldermen, and alle othere wyse wyth hem, that habbeth the gouernaille of the Citee, under oure lige Lord the Kyng, by vertue of the Chartre of oure franchise, comaundeth on the Kynges bihalf, and on hire owene also, that noman make none congregaciouns, conuenticules, ne assembles of poeple, in priue nen apert, ne no more than other men, with oute leue of the Mair; ne ouer more in none manere ne make alliances, confederacies, conspiracies, ne obligaciouns, forto bynde men to gidre, forto susteyne eny quereles in lyuingge and deyengge to gidre; upon peyne of enpresonement.[43]

The proclamation goes on to give "euery fre man of the Citee" powers to arrest any such gathering "he may aspie": everything, in theory, at least, from a parish guild meeting to the dice game in the *Cook's Tale*. London and Crown authorities had good reason to be nervous of "swich congregaciouns or covynes"[44] in this period, of course. The proclamation above dates from the turbulent period of Northampton's mayoralty.[45] The experience of 1381, when laborers had employed the associational mechanism of the "commissions of array" to organize themselves for their march on London,[46] was still a recent memory. And in 1388 Richard II was to issue writs at the Cambridge parliament requiring all guilds, fraternities, mysteries, and crafts to give an account of themselves to the Royal Chancery.[47] Some London guilds, it seems, avoided making any kind of return; some London craft fraternities apparently tried to pass themselves off as parish guilds.[48] The parish guild of St. Bridget, Fleet Street, was anxious to point out that although it was called a fraternity, it was really not a fraternity, and that "theirs is no malicious gathering" even though they wear hoods on the Feast of St. Bridget's Translation. Besides, they have no money and no rents; some of the members named in the return are dead, others have moved away, and the rest, "since they heard the decision of the last parliament, have refused to pay anything towards keeping the premises made."[49] As the return runs on, this fraternity or guild of St. Bridget seems to evaporate before our eyes.

The mayors and aldermen of London, we have noted, were quick to claim that their authority descended directly from the king, especially when that authority was challenged or their dignity offended. A man who tells an alderman to kiss his arse (*culum*) is extending the same invitation to his mayor and his monarchs.[50] A butcher who objects to aldermen who ride on the pavement is speaking "in disparagement of our Lord the King" and is hence obliged to walk barefoot through the Shambles (a horrible fate) with a candle to the Guildhall Chapel.[51] But in borrowing authority from the king, the City oligarchy was, of course, making itself vulnerable to it. In 1377 rumors spread that the City was about to be taken into the king's hands and the mayor replaced with a royally appointed captain. In 1392 Richard committed the mayor and sheriffs to prison and appointed his own warden. On 20 February 1388 Nicholas Brembre, mayor of London from 1383 to 1386, was hanged by the Lords Appellant.[52] Such episodes remind us that although the London Letter Books evoke an orderly, hierarchical vision of society, the class of merchant capitalists they (usually) represent was continuously engaged in political struggles with Crown, magnates, small masters, foreigns, aliens, and peasants. The signs of such struggles are visible not only in major political events of the kind noted above, but in the business of everyday life:

> Whereas the foreign drapers bringing woollen cloths to the City of London for sale, do sell the same in divers hostelries in secret, where they make many disorderly and deceitful bargains, as well between foreigner and foreigner, as between foreigner and freeman, to the great scandal and damage of all the City.[53]

The city is figured in this ordinance as an all-encompassing entity ("all the City") that is sensitive to acts of moral outrage; and yet this notion of a city is clearly predicated on acts of exclusion and disenfranchisement. Noncitizens were habitually referred to as "foreigns"; although a foreign might live in London he was not, in any meaningful political sense, a Londoner. So when foreigns got together within the walls of London this could only be interpreted, by the City authorities, as a threat to the City. In 1387, for example, an attempt by journeymen cordwainers to form a fraternity was taken as "a deed which notoriously redounds to the weakening of the liberties of the . . . city."[54] At such moments the mayoral oligarchy reveals itself as just one more associational form that is anxious to discourage attempts at association lower down the political scale. At other moments it acts to preserve one form of association by banning another. In 1396, for example, the mayoral court heard that "there had arisen no small dissension and strife between the masters of the trade of Saddlers, of London, and the serving men, called *yomen*, of that trade." This dispute centered on the right of the *yomen* to dress themselves in livery and meet as a fraternity. The *yomen* insist that they have been meeting like this since "time out of mind," and that their objects are religious. Their masters argue that this tradition is no more than thirteen years old,

> and that under a certain feigned colour of sanctity, many of the serving-men (*servientes*) in the trade had influenced the journeymen among them, and had formed covins thereon, with the object of raising their wages greatly in excess; to such an extent, namely, that whereas a master in the said trade could before have had a serving man or journeyman for 40 shillings or 5 marks yearly, and his board, now such a man would not agree with his master for less than 10 or 12 marks, or even 10 pounds, yearly; to the great deterioration of the trade.[55]

Here, once again, the decisive rhetorical gesture consists of ripping away a veil of apparent respectability, or piety, to reveal corruption and rascality beneath. This time, however, the unveiling process is credentialized not by a moral vocabulary or by the language of the church, but by the language of the shop: an unadorned economic language that, in the mayoral court, carries the force of moral argument. This whole dispute, of course, is pitched very close to the ideological terrain of the *Cook's Tale*; further correspondences suggest themselves as the case progresses. Whereas apprentice Perkyn would leave

---

the shop for street processions and weddings, these journeymen leave for funerals:

> And further . . . the serving-men aforesaid, according to an ordinance made among themselves, would oftentimes cause the journeymen of the said masters to be summoned by a bedel, thereunto appointed, to attend at Vigils of the dead, who were members of the said fraternity . . . whereby the said masters were very greatly aggrieved, and were injured through such absenting of themselves by the journeymen, so leaving their labours and duties, against their wish.

It is no great surprise to learn that the mayor and aldermen side with the masters in this dispute, determining that in future the *yomen* "should have no fraternity, meetings, or covins." It is evident that the masters would wish their *yomen* and workers to have no social life at all beyond the confines of the shop: every conversation could spell trouble for business. And yet the pleasures and privileges of political association and of fraternity life are what every alderman, master, and master's wife lives for:

> It is ful fair to been ycleped "madame,"
> And goon to vigilies al bifore,
> And have a mantel roialliche ybore.
> (I.376-78)

Chaucer here momentarily adopts the viewpoint of the women who are married to the five guildsmen in the *General Prologue*. Moments before he had set out the ambitions of the guildsmen themselves; their qualifications for civic office are chiefly a matter of capital, property, and (to venture a term that seems both anachronistic and apposite) image:

> Wel semed ech of hem a fair burgeys
> To sitten in a yeldehalle on a deys.
> Everich, for the wisdom that he kan,
> Was shaply for to be an alderman.
> For catel hadde they ynogh and rente.
> (I.369-73)

We have here not one associational form, but two: the "solempne and . . . greet fraternitee" that employs the Cook and the corporation of mayor and aldermen that this group dreams of becoming.[56] What, then, is the relationship of the Cook to these associational forms, real and imaginary? The Cook as described in the *General Prologue* is absorbed by his office: all lines but two are given over to boiling, tasting, roasting, simmering, baking, and blancmange making—except, of course, for that couplet devoted to the "mormal" (I.386; "a species of dry scabbed ulcer, gangrenous rather than cancerous")[57] he bears on his shin. This single sign of danger[58] alerts us to further unsettling suggestions about the Cook's provenance and personal habits in his own Prologue.[59] And yet, once he has launched into his tale, we find him speaking lines worthy of a knight, alderman, or mayor:[60] "Revel and trouthe, as in a lowe degree,/ They been ful wrothe al day, as men may see" (I.4397-98).

The lower classes are viewed here from the elevated perspective of the *General Prologue's* guildhall dais (I.370). The argument is that the privileges and pleasures of association (i.s. *revel*) can only be entrusted to those of proven virtue (dedicatees of *trouthe*, such as masters, aldermen, and their wives). This is, of course, a circular argument, since if *trouthe* is to have any social meaning it must be exercised as a public virtue; those forbidden any form of public association cannot, therefore, practice or embody *trouthe*. Since the lower classes cannot aspire to *trouthe*, what need do they have of *revel*, or of any other form of association? Such logic (like *trouthe* itself) pretends to impartiality, universality, and verifiability ("as men may see"), but the state of angry enmity ("they been ful wrothe") between the lower orders and social order is there only because the City authorities say it is so. Hostility to public virtue is legislated into the lower orders so that those of "lowe degree" can be legislated out of political existence.

Many critics have noted that the high-principled Cook of Fragment I sorts ill with the Cook who, at the beginning of Fragment IX, has reached the far side of revel and (the Host notes) is about to tumble:

> "Is ther no man, for preyere ne for hyre,
> That wole awake oure felawe al bihynde?
> A theef myghte hym ful lightly robbe and bynde.
> See how he nappeth! See how, for cokkes bones,
> That he wol falle fro his hors atones!
> Is that a cook of Londoun, with meschaunce?"
>
> (IX.6-11)

The fall of the Cook, when it finally comes, is strongly identified with the end of language. This end is presaged by the Cook's huge yawn that runs for six lines as the Manciple heaps abuse on him: the mouth is open, but emits no sound (35-40). The act of falling occupies the same narrative moment as the act of falling silent:

And with this speche the Cook wax wrooth and wraw,
And on the Manciple he gan nodde faste
For lakke of speche, and doun the hors hym caste,
Wher as he lay, til that men hym up took.

(IX.46-48)

It is interesting that the notion of *wrothe* reappears at the moment of the Cook's falling: he too, it would seem, reveals himself to be a figure of "lowe degree" who, having revelled to excess, finds himself "ful wrothe" with *trouthe* (and also with language, the ground of *trouthe* as a social virtue). And the image of the drunken, voiceless Cook lying inert on the ground (thereby bringing the entire pilgrimage to a halt) seems to validate all the Letter Book arguments about the inability of the lower orders to function within an associative framework.

How, then, are we to reconcile this Cook of Fragment IX with the Cook of Fragment I? The first Fragment Cook seems, in retrospect, a dummy of a character through which his masters ventriloquize the mores of craft masters and would-be aldermen. This makes him little better than the Summoner, who parrots terms learned from his masters in the law courts ("*Questio quid iuris*") without understanding them (I.637-46). But it is important to note that the Cook of Fragment IX does not remain on the ground; his fellow pilgrims pick him up and set him back on his horse. Nor does he remain in a state of enmity with the Manciple. He falls through drink, but through drink he rises or rides again: in taking the gourd from the Manciple and returning it to him, and in thanking him "in swich wise as he koude" (90-93), the Cook returns to some form of social consciousness. The Manciple's gesture of reconciliation is figured as an explicit rejection of *wrothe*: "I wol nat wratthen hym, also moot I thryve" (IX.80). The Host, having laughed "wonder loud" at this rapprochement, observes:

> . . . "I se wel it is necessarie,
> Where that we goon, good drynke with us carie;
> For that wol turne rancour and disese
> T'acord and love, and many a wrong apese."

(IX.95-98)

This reference to "good drynke" might appear to suggest some reference to sacramental wine. But "good drynke" was also commonly associated with (employed as a facilitator of) "acord and love" in the meetings of craft and parish guilds:

Also ordeynd it is, yat eueriche nyth qwil drynkynd lastetʒ at ye general time, yei shul haue ye preyeers for ye pees and ye state of holy chirche, and for ye pes and ya state of ye lond.[61]

The association of communal drinking with the feast day of a guild's patron was sufficiently strong for this meeting to be referred to as the *potatio* or "ye drynkyng" or the "tyme of drynk."[62] Drinking on these occasions amounted to more than a symbolic gesture. The guild of Holy Cross, Hultoft, reckoned to get through thirty gallons of ale at its guild feast (the residue being given to the poor).[63] The alderman of the Guild of St. James, Lynn, was entitled to two gallons; every steward got a gallon, and "ye Clerk, a potel." Brothers or sisters of this guild who were absent through sickness "in tyme of drynkyng" were likewise entitled to "a potel."[64] Sick brothers and sisters of the guild of the Holy Cross, Bishop's Lynn, were entitled to a full gallon, as were "ony brother or sister . . . in pelgrimage."[65] Some guilds moved from the church to an inn for their guild-day meeting; some held their drynkyng at the house of a brother or sister.[66]

This emphasis on drinking no doubt accounts, in part, for the considerable space dedicated to group discipline in these guild regulations. No guild member shall call one of his brethren thief or "scurra"; nobody shall be "rebel of his tounge," or fall asleep "in tyme of drynke," or refuse to pass the cup.[67] There should be no "noyse or janglinge" at the meeting; any brother who resorts to physical violence at the *drynkyng* will be fined four pounds of wax.[68] One London guild states that "eny riotour, oþer contekour," shall be expelled from the guild until he amends his ways; all members "shul be helpynge aʒeins þe rebelle and unboxum." Brothers and sisters "ne schal noght debat with oþer." Those who do fall "in debat" shall reconcile their differences within the guild structure "and make bytwene hem a good acord": for the "fraternitee" was founded "for amendment of her lyues and of her soules, and to noriche more loue bytwene þe bretheren and sustren of þe bretherhede."[69] Another London guild specifies that every new brother and sister shall kiss each member of the fraternity "in tokenynge of loue, charite, and pes."[70] Conversation at such "dayes of spekyngges tokedere" shall be dedicated "to here comune profyte."[71]

The lexicon of misbehavior found in the 1389 guild returns is familiar enough to readers of *The Canterbury Tales*; so, too, is their concern to promise collective order and well-being. The associative ideal that the guild regulations record in such concrete detail is of particular importance for Chaucer's *compagnye*, a group that brings together a wide (not all-inclusive) range of backgrounds and professions. How, after all, could such a group hope to govern itself unless its members recognized some common parameters of collective behavior? Such behavior, I am suggesting, was learned in the guilds. The difference between a rich guild and its poor neighbor could, of course, be immense: the poor men's guild of St. Austin, Norwich, could hardly compete with the fraternity of Lincoln Cathedral that Philippa Chaucer joined in 1386 with Henry, earl of Derby, and other Lancastrian luminaries.[72] But within each guild, a comparable associative ethic was taught. Such is the schooling that has prepared each pilgrim for the associative project of Chaucer's *Canterbury Tales*.

Cooks and Canons: Chaucer's Londons

It is particularly interesting that Chaucer should choose the Cook and the Manciple to play out a reconciliation scene reminiscent of a guild-sponsored *drynkyng*, for both are men of "lowe degree," and both are Londoners (or "of Londoun"). Both men serve corporate organizations above their own station: Roger cooks for "a solempne and a greet fraternitee," and the Manciple purchases provisions for one of the London Inns of Court (I.567-86). The *Cook's Tale* and the mayoral Letter Books, we have noted, operate on the assumption that lower-class Londoners are incapable of peaceable association. The "acord and love" that breaks out between the Cook and Manciple (the last such reconciliation in *The Canterbury Tales*) would seem to discredit this assumption. Are we to conclude, then, that Chaucer begins his opus by endorsing the political outlook of London merchant capitalists and ends by celebrating the political capacities of the common man?

If Chaucer's opus were an organic and completed whole, like the *Commedia* or the *Decameron*, we might be tempted to look for an orderly progression in its politics. But *The Canterbury Tales* is an uncertain sequence of fragments, and the fragments featuring the Cook are plainly at odds with one another. The tale of Fragment I develops a strain of London discourse that we can associate with that of the Guildhall, but it comes to no conclusion, it breaks off incomplete. Fragment IX starts up as if the Cook had never spoken, or told a tale: perhaps, as Larry Benson suggests, this indicates that Chaucer intended to cancel the Cook's appearance in Fragment I.[73] Fragment I is itself, of course, ambivalent about the Cook: at one moment he suggests an ulcerated, low-life image and the next a figure who should sit at the Guildhall dais rather than wait on it. Each image found its illustrator: the Ellesmere Cook, with "his fleshhook, soiled apron, torn slippers, and bandaged shin" suggests—in V. A. Kolve's arresting phrase—"the livery . . . of labor and poverty and disease."[74] The Cambridge Cook (University Library MS Gg. iv. 27, fol. 193v) is a prosperous, fur-trimmed citizen holding a large, elaborate whip; his legs are covered.

These images might be reconciled by arguing that whereas the Ellesmere artist is guided by the *General Prologue* portrait of the Cook, the Cambridge illustrator is responding to the discursive level of the *Cook's Tale*. But the difficulty of sustaining such an argument might also suggest that the impulse to reconcile diverse aspects and embodiments of London on a single imaginative plane is altogether misguided: perhaps London can only be imagined as a discourse of fragments, discontinuities, and contradictions. But before committing ourselves to this conclusion we should consider, albeit briefly, one last narrative of London that suddenly and unexpectedly overtakes the pilgrimage in Fragment VIII. I am speaking, of course, of the *Canon's Yeoman's Tale* and specifically of its *pars secunda* in which a canon-alchemist swindles a London chantry priest to the tune of £40.

The key motif of this tale, and particularly its second part, is betrayal. The Canon is obviously intent on betraying the trust the London chantry priest puts in him as an alchemist. But the Canon, the Yeoman argues, is also betraying his own kind, canons; such a man is a Judas to his community (III.1007-9). And the narrator is himself, of course, engaged in a narrative of bad faith: he is betraying the professional secrets of the Canon he has served for seven years, the man he acknowledged at the outset as "my lord and my soverayn" (590). He may also be betraying the pilgrimage and the readership: the suspicion that the Canon of the first half of his tale is the Canon of the second is so strong that the Yeoman plucks it from the air—to deny it:

> This chanon was my lord, ye wolden weene?
> Sir hoost, in feith, and by the hevenes queene,
> It was another chanoun, and nat hee.
>
> (VIII.1088-90)

Earlier, as the duplicity of the first canon had begun to emerge, the Host was moved to ask a key question:

> "Where dwelle ye, if it to telle be?"
> "In the suburbes of a toun," quod he,
> "Lurkynge in hernes and in lanes blynde,
> Whereas thise robbours and thise theves by kynde
> Holden hir pryvee fereful residence,
> As they that dar nat shewen hir presence;
> So faren we, if I shal seye the sothe."
>
> (III.656-62)

By the beginning of *pars secunda* the disease that infects the canon-alchemist has been carried from the blind alleys of the suburbs, the criminalized margins of civic life, to the city itself:

> Ther is a chanoun of religioun
> Amonges us, worde infecte al a toun,
> Thogh it as greet were as was Nynyvee,
> Rome, Alisaundre, Troye, and othere three.
> (VIII.972-75)

Nineveh was threatened with destruction; Troy was betrayed from within. What hope does London, New Troy, have of surviving this new threat in its midst?[75] The argument is made that the city may escape betrayal through language by more language: the Yeoman's alerts "us" (his word) to the second canon's duplicity so that "men may be war therby."[76] The discourse that saves us is, of course, the discourse of a *yoman* betraying his master. The form of the discourse adheres remarkably closely to depositions heard in the London Guildhall, and its tale of deception through magic or false science is no more fantastic than that of many Letter Book narratives. But the notion of a *yoman* proposing to save a city, or a pilgrim body, by betraying his master's secrets ("Thou . . . discoverest that thou sholdest hide," 695-96) turns the operative assumptions of the Guildhall on its head. It also raises the possibility that Chaucer's Yeoman may be a Sinon, a foreigner who betrays a community by joining it belatedly and pretending to save it from ruin. It is worth recalling that in the last *bolgia* of Dante's Hell we first encounter two Tuscan alchemists and then (after a passage lamenting the ruin of Thebes and Troy) two arch-deceivers: "false Sinon, the Greek of Troy" and Master Adam, falsifier of the gold florin.[77] London, as New Troy, knew that the threat of economic disaster posed by alchemy and false coinage was every bit as serious as the threat of political betrayal.

The discourses of London in Chaucer's *Canterbury Tales*, then, are freighted with suggestions of duplicity and bad faith: we have a Cook who sounds like two Cooks, one Yeoman, and two (perhaps one) canon-alchemists. Perhaps it is just an irony of history that the two most authoritative texts in *The Canterbury Tales'* manuscript tradition perpetuate and define such ambiguities: Ellesmere contains the *Canon's Yeoman's Tale*, and Hengwrt does not.[78]

The conclusion this essay seems bound for differs markedly from that offered (in advance, one might note) by D. W. Robertson's celebrated *Preface to Chaucer*. "To conclude, the medieval world was innocent of our profound concern for tension. . . . We project dynamic polarities on history as class struggles, balances of power, or as conflicts between economic realities and traditional ideals. . . . But the medieval world with its quiet hierarchies knew nothing of these things."[79] The most cursory reading of London history or of London legal documents makes such statements seem unintelligible: how on earth, one wonders, did Robertson manage to research and write a whole book on Chaucer's London without revising such opinions? The fact that Robertson did write such a book, prefaced by the strictures that preface *A Preface to Chaucer*,[80] only testifies to the determinant power of a certain mode of formalist reading and the nostalgic desire for a bygone epoch of "quiet hierarchies." David Aers, in his *Community, Gender, and Individual Identity*, suggests that in this passage Robertson is seeking to authorize his own critical agenda (and disguise its partiality) by presenting it as "seemingly . . . congruent with social models propagated by the medieval clerisy."[81] Aers is surely right here. At the same time we must concede that the notion of "community" (singular rather than plural) that figures so prominently in Aers's own agenda sometimes seems partial and archaic as it participates in the quest for "knowable community" associated with British socialists such as Raymond Williams. There is a nostalgia of the left as well as the right.[82]

My own reading of Chaucer and of London history is, of course, a partial one; an essay that sets out to read an absence cannot claim to be innocent of poststructuralist presuppositions. My account of the absence of a single, unified discourse that could be taken to represent the city as an organic and knowable entity seems suspiciously consonant with Gabrielle M. Spiegel's account of what happens to New Critical reading under deconstruction: "A text's coherent statement . . . is fractured into a series of discontinuous, heterogeneous, and contradictory codes which defy interpretive unification except at the level of allegorical recodification, itself suspect as the ideological imposition of a false coherence where none in truth exists."[83] I cannot claim to be thinking outside the terms of current critical thought. But I do claim that this essay does not deconstruct a "coherent statement" of city consciousness in Chaucer or in the archives for the simple reason that no such statement has been found. There is no idea of a city for all the inhabitants of a space called London to pay allegiance to; there are only conflicts of associational, hierarchical, and antiassociational discourses, acted out within and across the boundaries of a city wall or the fragments of a text called *The Canterbury Tales*.

The singularity of all this becomes more fully evident when we compare the absence of the city in Chaucer to the representation of Florence in Boccaccio. Boccaccio's tale of the friendship of a lowly baker and a powerful merchant-politician may well be read as "the ideological imposition of a false coherence." But it is important to note that such an ideological imposition, which romances the inhabitants of the city with the notion of *unitas civium*, is at least thought to be possible in Boccaccio's Florence.

No such attempt is made in Chaucer or in Chaucer's London because (as the *Cook's Tale* demonstrates so clearly) any discourse which begins with pretensions to all-inclusiveness soon reveals specific allegiances and hostilities. Not only is the city absent in Chaucer, then; the conditions for the possibility of a credible ideology of the city do not yet exist. One last trip to the Guildhall archive, specifically to an Anglo-Norman proclamation of 1391, makes this abundantly and painfully clear. Brembre, hanged for treason by the Lords Appellant, has been dead for three years; Northampton has not held political office since 1383. The chief threat to city independence in the 1390s is, of course, the king himself, the master mayor Adam Bamme must be seen to serve:

> Whereas many dissensions, quarrels, and false reports have prevailed in the City of London, as between trade and trade, person and person, because of diverse controversies lately moved between Nicholas Brembre, Knight, and John Northamptone, of late Mayors of the said city, who were men of great power and estate, and had many friendships and friends within the same; to the great peril of the same city, and, maybe, of all the realm. . . .[84]

Here again, as in the *Cook's Tale*, we see that personal association of any kind is (to borrow an apposite Chaucerian term) *suspect*: no good can come of it; "destruction and annihilation to the said city may readily ensue."[85] In addressing the inhabitants of London the proclamation must find some associative terms suggestive of a common interest. But even as it deploys these unifying terms ("common profit"; "of one accord in good love") the Guildhall text once again points to divisions in the working world and so divides itself from the body politic it presumes to serve and govern. Its contradictory call for civic unity visualizes political association (beneath its own level of association) as a revel that leads to Newgate; its end, like that of the *Cook's Tale* in Fragment I and the Cook in Fragment IX, is silence:

> [D]esiring to maintain the peace of our Lord the King . . . for the common profit, they [the mayor and the aldermen] have ordained and established, that no man, great or small, of whatsoever estate or condition he be, shall speak from henceforth, or agitate upon any of the opinions, as to either of them, the said Nicholas and John, or shall by sign, or in any other manner, shew that such person is of the one opinion or the other. But let the folks of the same city be of one accord in good love, without speaking, any person to another, on the said matter, in manner of reproof or of hatred; on pain, if any one shall speak or do against any of the points aforesaid, of imprisonment in Neugate for a year and a day, without redemption.[86]

Notes

1. See Larry D. Benson, ed., *The Riverside Chaucer,* 3rd ed. (Boston, 1987), note to line 4422, p. 853. All references are to the Riverside edition. I argue later in the chapter that the *Canon's Yeoman's Tale, pars secunda,* may be read as a London fiction.

2. See V. A. Kolve, *Chaucer and the Imagery of Narrative: The First Five Canterbury Tales* (Stanford, Calif., 1984), p. 259; and Muriel A. Bowden, *A Commentary on the General Prologue to the Canterbury Tales* (New York, 1948), pp. 187-88. The first plea of debt is entered in 1377.

3. Martha Carlin, *The Urban Development of Southwark, c. 1200-1550* (Ph.D. diss., University of Toronto, 1983), p. 439.

4. Quoted in Carlin, *Southwark,* p. 467.

5. Ibid., p. 7.

6. See Chris Given-Wilson, *The Royal Household and the King's Affinity: Service, Politics, and Finance in England, 1360-1413* (New Haven, Conn., and London 1986), pp. 15, 22-23, 28-29, 34-35.

7. See Carlin, *Southwark,* pp. 550-53; Sylvia L. Thrupp, *The Merchant Class of Medieval London (1300-1500)* (Chicago and London, 1948), pp. 1-3; and H. T. Riley, ed. *Memorials of London and London Life in the XIIIth, XIVth and XVth Centuries, A.D. 1276-1419* (London, 1868), p. 492. Riley translates from the Latin of *Letter Book H,* fol. ccx, which records pleas held at the London Guildhall before Mayor Nicholas Extone in January 1387. The need for "good governance" in London is of paramount importance since "there is a greater resort, as well of lords and nobles, as of common people, to that city, than to any other places in the realm, as well on account of the Courts there of our said Lord the King, as for transacting business there" (p. 492).

8. *Letter Book H,* fol. ccx (1387), in *Memorials,* ed. Riley, p. 492.

9. Riley, ed., *Memorials,* p. 536.

10. Ibid., p. 465; *Letter Book H,* p. 184.

11. Riley, ed., *Memorials,* p. 444. Should this performance be counted as a dramatic record? On the problematics of such questions, see Teresa Coletti, "Reading REED: History and the Records of Early English Drama," in *Literary Practice and Social Change in Britain, 1380-1530,* ed. Lee Patterson (Berkeley, Calif., 1990), pp. 248-84, especially p. 268.

12. See David Aers, *Community, Gender, and Individual Identity: English Writing, 1360-1430* (London, 1988), pp. 20-35; and Miri Rubin, *Charity and Community in Medieval Cambridge* (Cambridge, Eng., 1987), pp. 291-93. Such discriminations were formulated and enforced as part of the reaction to the labor shortages occasioned by the Black Death. They mark the decline of a long-lived tradition of uncalculating almsgiving and the rise of a new work-oriented ethic.

13. Riley, ed., *Memorials,* pp. 490-94; *Letter Books,* pp. 295-96.

14. Riley, ed., *Memorials,* p. 520.

15. See ibid., pp. 536, 466.

16. See *Inferno* XVII.52-78, in *Dante Alighieri: The Divine Comedy,* ed. and trans. C. S. Singleton, 6 vols. (Princeton, N.J., 1970-75). All references are to this edition. On the representation of commutative justice in Dante, see Anthony K. Cassell, *Dante's Fearful Art of Justice* (Toronto, 1984).

17. See *Decameron* II. 5, in *Tutte le opere di Giovanni Boccaccio,* ed. Vittore Branca, vol. 4

(Milan, 1976); David Wallace, *Giovanni Boccaccio: The Decameron* (Cambridge, Eng., 1991), pp. 39-41; and Riley, ed., *Memorials*, pp. 522-25.

18. See Riley, ed., *Memorials*, p. 435; *Letter Books*, pp. 132-33; the year is 1379. The same entry records the names of seven women who paid either 10s. or 6s. 8d. for the right to sell their wares near "Le Brokenecros" by the north door of St. Paul's. On the office of Common Hunt, see Thrupp, *Merchant Class*, pp. 241-42.

19. It is worth noting, however, that a good number of cases in the *Letter Books* record the participation of Ralph Strode as prosecutor or spokesman. Strode was an acquaintance of Chaucer's who was common serjeant of the City of London from 1373 to 1385. He is probably to be identified with the "philosophical Strode" to whom Chaucer commends his *Troilus and Criseyde*; see Stephen A. Barney's note to V.1856-59 in *Riverside Chaucer*, ed. Benson, p. 1058. Chaucer himself appears in *Letter Book G*, fol. cccxxi, on the occasion of his lease of the house above Aldgate in 1374 (see Riley, ed., *Memorials*, pp. 377-78; *CLR*, pp. 144-47).

20. This suggestion is scrutinized more closely later in the chapter. For now it is important to note the indefinite article: "*an* urban consciousness"; one, perhaps, of several.

21. See Louis Green, *Chronicle into History: An Essay on the Interpretation of History in Florentine Fourteenth-Century Chronicles* (Cambridge, Eng., 1972); Christian Bec, "Il mito di Firenze da Dante al Ghiberti," in *Lorenzo Ghiberti nel suo tempo. Atti del Convegno Internazionale di Studi (Firenze, 18-21 Ottobre 1978)*, 2 vols. (Florence, 1980), 1:3-26; Donald Weinstein, "The Myth of Florence," in *Florentine Studies: Politics and Society in Renaissance Florence*, ed. Nicholai Rubenstein (London, 1968), pp. 15-44; and Charles T. Davis, "Il Buon Tempo Antico," in *Florentine Studies*, ed. Rubenstein, pp. 45-69.

22. See Luigi Pratesi, ed., *L'"Istoria di Firenze" di Gregorio Dati: Dal 1380 al 1405* (Norcia, 1902), p. 74. Dati records that the citizens of Florence, in facing Gian Galeazzo Visconti in 1402, "sempre si confortavano con una speranza che pareva avere loro la cosa sicura in mano, cioé che il Comune non può morire e il Duca era uno solo uomo mortale, ché finito lui, finito lo stato suo" (cap. 97).

23. For a detailed discussion of this process, see my *Decameron*, pp. 39, 92-94; and David Wallace, "Chaucer's Body Politic: Social and Narrative Self-Regulation," *Exemplaria* 2.1 (1990), 221-40.

24. See Piero Boitani, "What Dante Meant to Chaucer," in *Chaucer and the Italian Trecento*, ed. Piero Boitani (Cambridge, Eng., 1983), pp. 115-39, especially p. 125.

25. See Antonia Gransden, *Historical Writing in England, 77, c. 1307 to the Early Sixteenth Century* (Ithaca, N.Y., 1982), p. 61; and John Taylor, *English Historical Literature in the Fourteenth Century* (Oxford, 1987), pp. 14-16.

26. See Riley, ed., *Memorials*, pp. 448-51; and *Letter Books*, pp. 165-66.

27. These are the first six lines from the eighth stanza of a poem found in two MSS and printed in *Political Poems and Songs Composed during the Period from the Accession of Edward III to That of Richard III*, ed. Thomas Wright, 2 vols. (London, 1859-61), 1:250-52. The poem consists of eleven stanzas rhyming *ababbcbc*.

28. The first definition of *ideology* offered by Webster's Ninth *New Collegiate Dictionary* (Springfield, Mass., 1984) seems particularly apt for the novella we are about to consider: "visionary theorizing."

29. For a precise imaging of this process in Ambrogio Lorinzetti's famous Sienese fresco cycle (1337-40), see Quentin Skinner, "Ambrogio Lorinzetti: The Artist as Political Philosopher," *Proceedings of the British Academy* 72 (1986), 1-56, especially p. 34.

30. Translations follow Giovanni Boccaccio, *The Decameron*, trans. G. H. McWilliam (Harmondsworth, 1972). Quotations from the Italian text follow *Boccaccio*, ed. Branca, vol. 4 (Milan, 1976).

31. See Andrew Prescott, "London in the Peasants' Revolt: A Portrait Gallery," *London Journal* 7 (1981), 125-43, especially pp. 128-29. Trespass actions of John of Gaunt and John Butterwick list rebels from five counties. The group from Ware Hertfordshire is by far the largest (forty-three rebels); the next largest group is from Manningtree, Essex (seventeen).

32. Riley, ed., *Memorials*, p. 438; *Letter Books*, p. 139. This entry is in Anglo-Norman.

33. See Cotton Julius B II (in Kingsford): "And many fflemmynges loste hir heedes at that tyme, and namely they that koude nat say Breede and Chese, but Case and Brode" (p. 15). This chronicle covers the years 1189-1432 and concludes with Lydgate's verses on the reception of Henry VI in London in 1432. Kingsford dates the manuscript 1435 (pp. viii-ix).

34. See E. J. Burford, *Bawds and Lodgings: A History of the London Bankside Brothels, c. 100-1675* (London, 1976), p. 78.

35. See Thrupp, *Merchant Class*, p. 17.

36. See Douglas Gray's note to I.4367 in *Riverside Chaucer*, ed. Benson, p. 853.

37. It is always worth reminding ourselves that the Knight, the Squire's father, is credited with having killed at least eighteen men (see I.43-78). It is interesting to note, too, that Chaucer makes the relationship of Knight to Squire a natural one (father to son), whereas the master-apprentice relationship exists only on paper.

38. See *The Oxford English Dictionary*, ed. James A. H. Murray et al. (Oxford, 1933), s.v. *menie*. The other fourteenth-century meaning noted is "4. The collection of pieces or 'men' used in a game of chess." *MED* records a comparable range of meaning under *meine*.

39. See *Boece IV, prosa* 1.41-42; *Nun's Priest's Tale*, VII.3394.

40. Apprentice contracts specify that an apprentice must not waste his master's goods on dice, dress, riot, etc.: see, for example, George Clune, *The Medieval Guild System* (Dublin, 1943, pp. 90-91.

41. See Riley, ed., *Memorials*, pp. 484-86; and *Letter Books*, pp. 271-72. For a more legitimate example of female apprenticeship, see *Letter Books*, pp. 185-86, where the daughter of a deceased "wolmongere" is first made a ward of John Munstede, draper, and then apprenticed as a "thredwomman" to John Appleby and his wife Johanna.

42. Riley, ed., *Memorials*, pp. 534-35.

43. Ibid., p. 480.

44. Ibid., p. 481 (same document).

45. See *Letter Books*, p. 226; and Ruth Bird, *The Turbulent London of Richard II* (London, 1949), pp. 63-85.

46. See A. F. Butcher, "English Urban Society and the Revolt of 1381," in *The English Rising of 1381*, ed. R. H. Hilton and T. H. Ashton (Cambridge, Eng., 1984), pp. 84-111, especially p. 101.

47. See *English Guilds*, ed. Toulmin Smith, EETS, OS 40 (London, 1870), pp. xxiv-xxv; and H. F. Westlake, *The Parish Gilds of Mediæval England* (New York, 1919), pp. 36-37.

48. See Caroline M. Barron, "The Parish Fraternities of Medieval London," in *Essays in Honour of F. R. H. Du Boulay*, ed. C. M. Barron and Christopher Harper-Bill (Woodbridge, 1985), pp. 13-37, especially pp. 20-21.

49. Westlake, *Parish Gilds*, p. 182.

50. See Riley, ed., *Memorials*, pp. 500-502; and *Letter Books*, p. 323.

51. See Riley, ed., *Memorials*, pp. 502-3.

52. For details of these episodes, see Given-Wilson, *Royal Household*, p. 52; Bird, *Turbulent London*, pp. 24-25, 86-101; and Caroline M. Barron, "The Quarrel of Richard II with London, 1392-7," in *The Reign of Richard II; Essays in Honour of May McKisack*, ed. F. R. H. Du Boulay and C. M. Barron (London, 1971), pp. 173-201.

53. Riley, ed., *Memorials*, p. 551; *Letter Books*, pp. 449-50. This Anglo-Norman document (fol. cccxxvii, 1399) apparently records an ordinance made during the mayoralty of Richard

Whityngton (1398). This is the last numbered folio in *Letter Book H*, with the exception of fol. cccxxxi. Two of the three folios immediately preceding cccxxxi have been cut out; one half of the other, cut vertically, has been removed.

54. Riley, ed., *Memorials*, p. 496; *Letter Books*, pp. 311-12.

55. Riley, ed., *Memorials*, pp. 542-44 (especially p. 543); *Letter Books*, p. 431.

56. Britton J. Harwood rightly observes that these five guildsmen stood little chance of becoming aldermen of London: of the 260 aldermen elected in fourteenth-century London, only nine were from the lesser companies these guildsmen represent. See "The 'Fraternitee' of Chaucer's Guildsmen," *Review of English Studies*, n.s. 39 (1988), 413-17.

57. Gray, note to I.386, in *Riverside Chaucer*, ed. Benson, p. 814.

58. Mormals were attributed, by some authorities, to generally intemperate or unclean habits. One critic argues that they were runny rather than dry; they were said to smell strongly (Gray in *Riverside Chaucer*, ed. Benson, p. 814). On the notion of "danger" as employed here, see Mary Douglas, *Purity and Danger: An Analysis of Concepts of Pollution and Taboo* (New York, 1966). The sign of danger confirms, of course, the need for social regulation and cleansing.

59. See pp. 70-71.

60. A good number of mayors and aldermen in Chaucer's London were, of course, knights; others refused to be knighted since they did not wish to be moved into a higher tax bracket.

61. *English Guilds*, ed. Toulmin Smith, pp. 71-72 (Guild of the Nativity of St. John the Baptist, Bishop's Lynn).

62. See, respectively, Westlake, *Parish Gilds*, p. 168 (Guild of St. Anne, St. Peter's Parish in the Skin Market, Lincoln); *English Guilds*, ed. Toulmin Smith, p. 69 (Guild of St. James, Lynn); and *English Guilds*, ed. Toulmin Smith, p. 79 (Guild of St. John the Baptist, Bishop's Lynn).

63. Westlake, *Parish Gilds*, p. 166.

64. *English Guilds*, ed. Toulmin Smith, p. 70.

65. Ibid., p. 84.

66. See *English Guilds*, ed. Toulmin Smith, p. 30 (Guild of the Pelterers, Norwich); and Westlake, *Parish Gilds*, p. 166 (Corpus Christi, Hultoft).

67. See Westlake, *Parish Gilds*, p. 220 (Holy Trinity and Holy Cross, Daventry); and *English Guilds*, ed. Toulmin Smith, p. 84 (Guild of the Holy Cross, Bishop's Lynn). Barbara Hanawalt has pointed out to me that a payment or gift of drink was often employed to seal an arbitration or as a price for peace (see, for example, A. H. Thomas, ed., *Calendar of Early Mayor's Court Rolls Preserved among the Archives of the Corporation of the City of London at the Guildhall, A.D. 1298-1307* [Cambridge, Eng., 1924], pp. 16, 34).

68. *English Guilds*, ed. Toulmin Smith, p. 84 (Guild of the Holy Cross, Bishop's Lynn).

69. Ibid., pp. 3-5 (Guild of Garlickhith, London).

70. Ibid., p. 6 (Guild of St. Katherine, Aldersgate).

71. Ibid., p. 67 (Guild of St. Katherine, Lynn).

72. See *CLR*, pp. 91-93; Westlake, *Parish Gilds*, p. 202.

73. See *Riverside Chaucer*, ed. Benson, pp. 951-52.

74. Kolve, *Imagery of Narrative*, p. 264.

75. According to the Benedictine chronicler Walsingham, Nicholas Brembre, sometime mayor of London, had intended to massacre thousands of his fellow citizens, rename London "New Troy," and proclaim himself duke of the city. See Thomas Walsingham, *Historia Anglicana*, ed. Henry T. Riley, 2 vols., Rolls Series (London, 1863-64), 2:173-74.

76. "And," he adds as a curious afterthought, "for noon oother cause, trewely" (VIII.1306-7).

77. See *Inferno* XXIX-XXX.

78. Norman Blake argues that the *Canon Yeoman's Prologue and Tale* are spurious and does not include them in his Hengwrt-based edition (see *The Canterbury Tales by Geoffrey Chaucer.*

Edited from the Hengwrt Manuscript [London, 1980], pp. 6, 9). Critics generally agree that they were written late in the Canterbury period (see John Reidy's note in *Riverside Chaucer,* ed. Benson, p. 946). Their case is supported by Riley's observation that "this title [*yoman*] first appears in the City Books about this period"; Riley is commenting on an entry for 1396 (*Memorials,* p. 542). Riley speculates that the term may be "an abbreviation of the words 'yong man'" (*Memorials,* p. 542). But it seems clear that the term refers to rank rather than age: a *yoman* is a non-liveried member of a company or trade.

79. D. W. Robertson, Jr., *Preface to Chaucer* (Princeton, N.J., 1962), p. 51.

80. D. W. Robertson, Jr., *Chaucer's London* (New York, 1968): "We should expect, then, to find in medieval London an hierarchical classless society" (p. 5).

81. Aers, *Community, Gender, and Individual Identity,* p. 7.

82. This point is well made, in a mean-spirited sort of way, by R. W. Johnson, "Moooovement," *London Review of Books* 12.3 (8 February 1990), 5-6.

83. "History, Historicism, and the Social Logic of the Text in the Middle Ages," *Speculum* 65 (1990), 59-86, especially p. 62. The phrase "in truth" is anomalous here since it is borrowed from the language of epistemological coherence that is itself the subject of suspicion.

84. *Letter Book H,* fol. cclix, in *Memorials,* ed. Riley, pp. 526-27, especially p. 526.

85. Riley, ed., *Memorials,* p. 526. For Chaucer's most intensive usage of the terms *suspect* and *suspecious,* see *Clerk's Tale,* IV.540-42.

86. Riley, ed., *Memorials,* pp. 526-27.

The Illustrated Eighteenth-Century Chaucer_____

Alice Miskimin

No reader of Blake's illuminated books can ignore the synthetic design of every page: images and words are reciprocal. But when eighteenth-century illustrated books attract critical attention, one or another element is often minimized. Because several hands are involved, the texts are separated from their design and illustration. Thus, Marcia Pointon's study of the history of *Milton and English Art* passes over the evolution of Milton's text, while in the only recent discussion of the Augustan Chaucer, Alderson and Henderson make no mention at all of the thirty copperplate engravings in their principal text, the Urry edition of 1721.[1] *Bell's Chaucer* of 1782, also fully illustrated, has never to my knowledge been taken into account by critics of Romantic medievalism.[2] Like those made for new editions of *Paradise Lost* and Shakespeare, the forgotten illustrations of the *Canterbury Tales* are striking elements of the 1721 and 1782 *Works*, indicative of Chaucer's impact on the eighteenth-century reader and important as visual models or types, to be set against the later Romantic Chaucer pictures of Stothard and Blake at the turn of the century. Examined in context, not dismissed as a minor idiom in the history of art, such illustrations provide evidence of contemporary interpretations of Chaucer's poetry and a cumulative record of revision, in both the artistic styles and themes chosen to portray Chaucer's world.

Describing the extraordinary influence of Thomson's *Seasons* and its pictorial analogs, Ralph Cohen observes, "There exist different criteria for the illustration as interpretation and . . . as independent work of art; a 'bad' engraving may still be a valuable commentary upon artistic tradition. [But] the inspiration of one art by another must not be confused with the interpretation of one art by another."[3] Contemporary styles of illustration, typography, and format in eighteenth-century editions of Chaucer's poems reveal several kinds of historical change and afford us a view of incipient Gothic romanticism. The evidence suggests significant shifts: in attitudes toward medieval Chaucer, in the role of the reading public qua buyer—to be attracted as well as instructed—and in the historicism of literary painting, when poetic illustration was becoming increasingly independent of its text. After 1700 there was no one clearly dominant version of Chaucer in print, as had been the case with Thynne's and Speght's editions in the sixteenth and seventeenth centuries. By the end of the eighteenth century, the Romantics inherited a wealth of "Chaucerian" excerpts (like Dryden's) in translation, imitations (by Pope, Gay, Smart, and many others), annotated *Works* in modern print, the old Renaissance Black letter folios, and various illustrated versions of the *Canterbury Tales* and the Pilgrims, based on both medieval and modern models. The *Chaucer*s of Urry (1721) and Bell (1782-83) represent two typically "bad" editions of the *Works*; their textual corruption and neo-Gothic engravings are their most interesting features. In spite of their obvious defects, however, the Urry and Bell editions altered the eighteenth-century and early Romantic reader's perception of Chaucer in Middle English. Further, these texts cast light on Blake's radical reading of the *Tales* and on the context of his painting of the Pilgrims (begun in 1805). At another level, commercial motives for speculation on "Gothic" are to be found—partly hidden among aesthetic and historical interests, hence rarely noticed by recent critics.

The eighteenth-century Chaucer was the source of three successive reinterpretations of "Gothic" poetry in English art, commissioned in turn by publishers who recognized a growing market for medieval English poems: George Vertue's copperplate cuts for Urry (1721), Thomas Stothard's designs for Bell (1782-83), and, finally, Stothard's large "cabinet picture," *The Procession of Chaucer's Pilgrims* (exhibited 1807, later engraved for popular sale). Stothard's 1807 Chaucer painting was commissioned by the entrepreneur-engraver Cromek, who had seen Blake working on his Canterbury Pilgrims "fresco" in 1805. Cromek deviously suggested that Stothard also attempt the theme, which he did (unbeknown to Blake), thus ruining the friendship of the two artists and forestalling Blake's prospective exhibition of the Chaucer picture as his own "Original . . . Poetical and Historical Invention."[4] Finally shown in 1809 after Stothard's had become famous and its engraving a commercial triumph, Blake's version failed to find an audience, and his engravings of it (1810-12) went almost unnoticed.

The gradual growth of eighteenth-century medievalism—that is, of enthusiasm for virtually anything symbolic of English culture before the reign of James I, whether authentic or imitation—runs parallel with the growth in economic power of the book trade and the mass reading public, steadily increasing after the Copyright Act of 1709 "For the Encouragement of Learning" until the end of the century.[5] At every stage in the emergent neo-Gothic revival in literature and the arts, socioeconomic factors were at work and were recognized early by contemporaries. So Blake bitterly commented with a pun on Stothard's Chaucer picture, "He has done all by chance, or perhaps his Fortune, money, money."[6] Alderson and Henderson record in detail the maneuvers of Atterbury in 1711-13 to bring Bernard Lintot into the projected Christ Church, Oxford, Chaucer. The contract was signed in 1715 when the publisher sensed a climate favorable to investment in such a work and agreed to go in for a third.[7] The terms gave Urry's edition sole right to Chaucer until 1728, or 1742 if renewed. In this context, comparison of the new *Chaucers* (Urry's and Bell's, and Blake's version with Stothard's) must entail not only

---

the sequence of texts and pictures but also the physical realities—conditions of publication, supply and demand, and competitive pressure—in which they were conceived to be sold. An extended perspective reveals more of the meaning of publishers' gambles on Chaucer and Gavin Douglas in the early decades of the century, and Blake's furious responses to the marketplace in art and poetry expressed a century later in the *Descriptive Catalogue*:

> The painter [of *Blake's Chaucer*] courts comparison with his competitors who, having received 1400 guineas and more from the profits of his designs . . . have left him to shift for himself, while others, more obedient to an employer's opinions and directions, are employed, at a great expense, to produce works in succession to his, by which they acquired public patronage. This has hitherto been his lot—to get patronage for others and then to be left and neglected, and his work, which gained that patronage, cried down as eccentricity and madness.[8]

Blake's hyperbole on "the artist's violent temper" concludes with a protest that he had composed his picture of Chaucer's Pilgrims "in self-defence against . . . insolent and envious attacks" on his sanity and artistic skill, which had in turn become economic, hence doubly destructive. The evidence shows that the chance of possible profit to be made on medieval Chaucer was increasingly taken throughout the eighteenth century, with cumulative effects on Gothic Romanticism and its audience after 1800.

Urry's Edition

Originally, the Augustan Chaucer known as Urry's edition was planned by Francis Atterbury (ca. 1710) as a scholarly project to enhance the intellectual prestige of his college, Christ Church, Oxford. Still rightly considered the worst edition of Chaucer ever published, the work was plagued by disruption almost as soon as it was begun. Atterbury left the deanship of the college for the see of Rochester in 1713; John Urry, the Scots antiquarian he had chosen as editor, died in 1715, leaving no clear outline for the completion of the unfinished work, and Urry's assistant, Ainsworth, died shortly thereafter. Under the uncertain supervision of Timothy and William Thomas, the edition was salvaged for its three sponsors, the college, Urry's executor William Brome, and the publisher Lintot. Lintot paid for the paper, printing, and engraving of 1,250 copies (250 on Royal paper, 1,000 on small) to sell for £2.10 and £1.10, respectively. The text itself was in print by August 1719, but the glossary, John Dart's new Life of Chaucer, and the preface took two years more. Before his death Urry had lost a battle with Lintot, who insisted that the new Chaucer should not be set in the old Black letter. The result was that financial and artistic control remained in Lintot's hands, while Urry's editorial principles were only partly understood and applied by his successors.

Urry's *Chaucer* finally appeared in 1721, in clear modern roman and italic print. Its modernity strikes the eye, in contrast to the last edition of Speght's Black letter *Works* published in 1687. To contemporaries, the visual archaism of Speght's edition seemed consistent with the archaism of Chaucer's language, but Urry's partly normalized text looked incongruous in the mixed classical-Gothic setting newly designed for it. The 1721 edition was both a financial and critical failure. Ten years later, Urry's friend Hearne commented with regret, "Curious men begin to esteem the old editions more than the new one, partly on account of the letter [i.e., roman type] and partly on account of the change . . . [Urry emended] without giving the lections, which would have been of great satisfaction to critical men."[9] The new *Works* provided marginal line numbering for the first time, but no critical apparatus, no brackets for emendations, or a satisfactory key to Urry's radical respelling of Chaucer's text as it had previously been known. The legibility of the new edition increased the visibility of its flaws.

The 1721 *Works* was not the first Chaucer printed in roman: Tonson's first edition of Dryden's *Fables* (1700) included Middle English texts of the *Knight's*, *Wife of Bath's* and *Nun's Priest's Tales* and *The Flower and the Leaf*, printed in "white letter" in an appendix (Sig. Dddd^v-Ooool^v) dropped in later issues. But the appendix to the *Fables* is an early sign of the new practice of discarding Black letter in revivals of medieval books, followed thereafter in Ruddiman's edition of Gavin Douglas's *Eneados* (1710) and Alan Ramsay's popular Middle Scots lyric anthology *Ever-green* (1724). The Augustan reader of Chaucer in Dryden's *Fables*, Pope's imitations, or the Urry *Works* became used to seeing Middle English in instantly legible form; as a result, Black letter all the more obviously now symbolized the obsolete.[10] In Urry's edition, only four lines at the end of *Sir Thopas* and the rediscovered *Retraction* at the end of the *Parson's Tale* (reprinted for the first time since 1526) appear in Black letter. The *Retraction* is thus set off from the rest of the *Tales* and given conspicuous status as "the poet's last words" (so described by Timothy Thomas). The quatrain in the *Thopas* endlink looks to be merely interpolated; elsewhere, quoted fragments appear in italic. Further, where Urry had found marginal pointing hands highlighting *sententiae* in Speght or in manuscripts, he printed the line in italics but omitted any explanation for the italicized lines—Elizabethan printers' and scribal convention. Thus passages appeared with added emphasis given them not by the poet but by anonymous consensus, as if a marginal gloss were silently incorporated into the text. Chaucer's *Works* did not appear again in Black letter until William Morris's great Kelmscott edition of 1896 with its high Victorian Gothic illustrations by Burne-

Jones. The precedent for the modern "reading text" thus was set by Lintot in 1721: old-spelling text but new-style design, to compete with contemporary "Chaucer Modernis'd" and poetic imitations.

The overall design of the Urry *Chaucer* reflects its sponsors' intention to honor medieval English poetry with the kind of treatment given Greek and Latin classics in comparable modern editions. Lintot's folio is very tall (the page measures 16¼ by 12¼ inches), in the text set in double columns and decorated throughout with classical *bas de page* ornament and border decorations: garlands, busts, putti, rosettes, urns, and masks. The volume opens with two full-page portrait engravings—first Urry, engraved by Pigné, then Chaucer, engraved by George Vertue after the Hoccleve sketch in the *Regement of Princes* (Harl. MS 4866 fol. 88). The title page has a cut of Chaucer's tomb in the Abbey (like the Renaissance editions'), and the *Tales* are illustrated with twenty-eight large copperplate engravings, unsigned but also by Vertue. These cuts are modern descendants of two Chaucerian traditions, long lapsed and now revived in consciously anachronistic style. Vertue's designs are based on two closely related models: first, the miniature portraits of the Pilgrims in manuscript marginalia (Ellesmere and others); second, the formulaic woodcuts in the early printed editions of Caxton, de Worde, Pynson, and Thynne.[11] The fifteenth- and sixteenth-century pictures of the Pilgrims gradually faded from view, and had disappeared after the second issue (STC 5076) of the Stow folio, which dropped the cuts still contained in the first issue (STC 5075), both dated 1561.[12] None of the subsequent Speght folios (1598, 1602, 1687) has Pilgrim portraits; their neo-Gothic imitations first reappear in the engravings set prominently at the *Prologue* of each *Tale* in the 1721 *Works*.

The most important new picture is the one for the *General Prologue* (fig. 1), a group portrait of the Pilgrims riding in procession across a vaguely Tudor London backdrop, with the sign of the Tabard visible in the foreground. Close inspection reveals that the small mounted figures lined up in single file in this cut are in fact miniature copies of the large individual portraits of each Pilgrim found at the opening of the separate *Tales*. Detailed correspondences of pose, costume, and gesture among large and small versions of the same figures make it possible to attribute all of the 1721 Chaucer pictures (except for Pigné's Urry portrait) to Vertue, who signed only the portrait of Chaucer the poet. It has not hitherto been noticed that Walpole cataloged (without title) this "Departure from the Tabard" among Vertue's works in his expanded *Life* of the artist (1786), not naming its source: "Class 17. Frontispieces. . . . A procession, with the sign of the tabard; for one of Chaucer's tales."[13] Walpole's failure to recognize the famous scene is explained by his preference for reading the Chaucer modernized in Dryden's *Fables*, which of course omits the *Prologue*. In a letter to Mason (November 13, 1781), Walpole had turned

FIG. 1.—The procession of Chaucer's Pilgrims, from *The Works of Jeoffrey Chaucer*, ed. John Urry

down an offer of "a Black letter Chaucer for one guinea," commenting "I am too, though a Goth, so modern a Goth that I hate the Black letter and I love Chaucer better in Dryden and Baskerville than in his own language and dress." The somber engravings of the Pilgrims commissioned by Lintot for the richly decorated Urry edition reinterpret their crude medieval and sixteenth-century antecedents in a new idiom. The results are anomalous: Vertue's are unlike any previous Chaucerian illustrations yet faithful to the archaism of their prototypes.

Technical changes in medium in these texts—from painted miniatures and woodcut blocks to Vertue's engraved copperplates of the Pilgrims—comprise a short history of English popular book illustration from medieval to modern technique. At the same time, the 1721 *Chaucer* sums up an iconographical tradition. Vertue's neo-Gothic portraits still focus on the tellers of the *Canterbury Tales* as an array of moral, social, and psychological types, much as Dryden describes them in the Preface to the *Fables*. However, later eighteenth-century artists turned from the tellers to illustrate the *Tales*, reflecting a shift of interest toward Chaucerian narrative. In the 1770s and 1780s, illustrations of *Troilus* and the dream visions reappear for the first time since Pynson's editions of 1526, and the individual Pilgrims are shown only as a company banded together on the road, no longer in separate portraits. Vertue was apparently the last to portray the Pilgrims one by one, and the first to make the simple juxtaposition that creates the composite *Prologue* vignette (although in his research he might have seen an illuminated manuscript of Lydgate's *Siege of Thebes* such as Royal MS 18 D ii, which shows the poet among the Pilgrims on the return trip from Canterbury). Urry's edition contains both conceptions, the individual and the group, and marks a point of transition not heretofore observed.

If the large separate portraits (each 5¾ by 4¼ inches) of Vertue's Pilgrims differ from their medieval and Renaissance models more in technique and style than in conception, their visual impact is unmistakably Augustan. Each figure is enclosed in a narrow oval frame and provided with a stylized setting in deep perspective—an Oxford tower for the Clerk, the sea with ships for the Merchant—in contrast to the flat plane of the marginalia and the woodcuts (their horizons defined by a single line or a tuft of grass), and the woodcuts' heavy rectangular borders (cut off in Thynne's 1532 folio only). Vertue's skill with the burin produced smoothly modeled features and fine details of costume; he used chiaroscuro with obvious care to heighten the realism and balance the shapes in each vignette. Horses, gestures, and symbolic attributes (the Wife's whip, the Knight's sword) are clearly outlined, given symmetry and a sense of enclosure. The cosmetic effect of highly finished engraving technique results in an elegant stage image of each Pilgrim, much larger and more graceful than any previous version. The antiquarian ideal of historicity sent Vertue to the earliest texts in search of authentic formulas. His technical finesse, however, did not produce fair copies, but modern "restorations," closer to the conventions of classical equestrian portraiture than to any medieval model.

The nearest analog to Vertue's attempt to improve on Chaucerian tradition is Urry's effort to normalize the language of Chaucer's poems according to philological assumptions his successors only dimly understood and failed to follow. The inconsistencies of Chaucer's language are in effect multiplied line by line by editorial errors and silent emendation. The result was memorably described in 1778 by Tyrwhitt, the best eighteenth-century editor of Chaucer, who put a summary comment in the headnote to his own glossary for the *Tales*: "This Glossary . . . will be found to be almost equally well adapted to every edition of these *Works* except Mr. Urry's. Mr. Urry's edition should never be opened by anyone for the purpose of reading Chaucer."[14] Vertue's sophisticated engravings of the Pilgrims curiously complement Urry's "restored" texts in bold modern print. As a whole, the 1721 edition combines neo-Gothic nostalgia with high Augustan elegance, the utmost seriousness of purpose, and unprecedented anachronism of effect. The Augustan Chaucer's importance has been overlooked by scholars and critics, after Tyrwhitt condemned Urry for not only meddling with Chaucer's words but for including so much non-Chaucerian poetry—all the Renaissance apocrypha and more, which Tyrwhitt was virtually the first to recognize. But it is the conspicuous defects of the Urry *Works* which are of most value to our assessment of Augustan and Romantic readings of Chaucer. The modernized Gothic illustrations of the *Tales* reveal another more subtle kind of contemporary interpretation.

Eighteenth-Century Gothic and Chaucer

The long rise in Gothic enthusiasm after 1700 has been described as a phenomenon in the history of taste by B. Sprague Allen, Kenneth Clark, and others.[15] The evidence suggests that scholarly literary antiquarianism was a relatively small factor among the links that connect Augustan Chaucer with the later eighteenth-century. On the other hand, the most interesting differences between Urry's *Chaucer* and the various editions of the *Works*, the *Tales*, and the modernizations printed after 1775 are immediately apparent to the eye and suggest critical questions as important as the continuities Allen and Clark have stressed. Further comment on the substance and style of the later texts and pictures will follow a short synopsis of their origins in the world of eighteenth-century publishing. It is evident that commercial interests and developments in English common law directly determined whose books were published and at what price.

It is difficult to analyze the indirect effect of decisions made by booksellers and artists (like Lintot's and Vertue's on Chaucer) which influenced the fate of poems offered in the market. Where ancient, medieval, and modern works meet in constant competition, aesthetic and commercial considerations seem to converge and overlap. The more elusive aspects of impact are probably not traceable, but there are suggestive clues to be noticed. For example, in spite of the stipulation that every entering student of Christ Church must buy a copy of the Urry *Chaucer*, the elite intellectual audience envisioned by its backers responded negatively to the new edition's mixture of Augustan clarity and medieval disorder. The pompous format and design were not thought wrong for the revival of an English ancient: only the "white letter" and Urry's editorial faults were noted. However, the sheer weight and size of the 1721 Chaucer become significant in retrospect when compared with the text's reappearance in *Bell's Chaucer* of 1782, the first of the new cheap editions intended for a mass audience. Bell's edition reprinted both Tyrwhitt's excellent text of the *Tales*, and all the rest of the canon published in Urry with notes, commentary, and new illustrations, in fourteen small (16mo) inexpensive volumes. These "sixpenny poets" are probably irrelevant to textual and critical history, but such books are primary evidence in the study of changing popular culture, particularly that branch concerned with the continuous revision of the Gothic past which Chaucer represented. The huge 1721 folio weighs almost 11½ pounds, the little Bell volumes about 3½ ounces each; the engraved plates of the Pilgrims in Urry are larger than Bell's whole page (ca. 3 by 5 inches unbound). At even cruder levels of perception, the reader's expectations and experience are subliminally modified by the physical object of the book in his hands. As I have suggested, the replacement of the silent signal of Black letter revised the reading of Chaucer after 1721, by shifting the sense of verbal archaism visible to the eye from the shapes of the words to their linguistic difficulty alone. Other changes in format and new illustrations for new audiences after mid-century give further witness to the mingling of artistic and commercial elements in the revival of Gothic Chaucer.

The social context in which eighteenth-century medievalism grew has been well described from the perspectives of art history and the sociology of taste; the literary evidence is also well known. In sum, the term "Gothic," as Walpole and his friends used it among themselves, was becoming increasingly loose and flexible in the 1760s and after. It could be applied as easily to a merchant's castle as to a medieval ruin, a garden dovecote or a supernatural horror novel, a modern or an ancient poem.[16] In the atmosphere that welcomed Percy's *Reliques* (1765), Warton's *History* (1775), Chatterton's "Rowley" poems, and "Ossian," and among those who sought to copy the eclectic medievalia exhibited at Strawberry Hill, the ironic, witty Chaucer of Pope and

Gay was becoming a vaguely picturesque antique. The incongruous Urry *Chaucer* was discarded before 1750, and the need for a better version was frequently expressed.[17] When the new Chaucers arrived, they reflected and simultaneously reinforced newly popular meanings of "Gothic" in art and poetry, already broad enough to include the confused archaisms of Macpherson and Chatterton—counterfeits still taken seriously even after 1800. On pictorial evidence alone, the later eighteenth-century editions of the *Canterbury Tales* could be easily mistaken for either Spenser or Sir Walter Scott: the same kinds of illustration served all three, in the similar formats of widely sold editions. The single element of medieval Chaucer that resisted assimilation was his language. But in modern print, both original and imitation "medieval" poetic diction had come to look much alike—more or less remote, but not quite unintelligible. After about 1750 it had become difficult to distinguish among poems preserved, restored, or invented in authentic English Gothic styles. At the same time, the task of separating out the imitations and apocrypha in the Chaucer tradition was begun by Tyrwhitt, whose role in unmasking Chatterton's "Rowley" (1778) brought him more fame than his edition of the *Canterbury Tales* (1775-78). The perception of Chaucer was also obliquely affected by the pseudo-Gaelic fantasies Macpherson published in the 1760s. The "Ossian" affair aroused great curiosity in both England and Europe about native history and myth, and publicized the idea of early oral tradition. If the new *Chaucers* benefited from the public interest in the middle ages at mid-century, that revival itself received impetus from the struggle over copyright and the London publishers' monopoly.

The Booksellers' War and *Bell's Chaucer* of 1782

In contrast to the single Black letter Speght *Works* available at the end of the seventeenth-century, after 1800 readers could choose among three eighteenth-century versions of Chaucer as a result of the success of Bell's edition. Now one could buy old-spelling texts, either with or without illustrations, and modernized (usually expurgated) collections of "specimens" by various hands. There were also some fifteen editions of Dryden's *Fables* before 1800, three of the Chaucer tales only, and two more in 1806 of the Chaucer and Boccaccio, a number of them also illustrated. At first the new pictorial Chaucer paralleled the text, but soon the illustration itself became autonomous as a free-standing Gothic history painting—the antecedent of Ford Madox Brown's huge "Chaucer at the Court of Edward III" (1851) and Burne-Jones's "Dorigen of Bretaigne."[18] Sold as engravings, Blake's and Stothard's rival pictures of the Canterbury Pilgrims of 1807 and after reached an even wider audience than Chaucer's *Tales* (figs. 2*a* and 2*b*). Describing Stothard's and Blake's estrangement over the idea of the Pilgrimage design, Anthony Blunt expressed the majority view of modern scholars that Blake indeed had been robbed of his "composition on the subject—one never treated before that time."[19] While the two paintings will be discussed briefly later, here Blake's claim of precedence can be set in a wider context. First, it is unlikely that the design of the Pilgrims in procession was unprecedented; both Stothard and Blake knew Urry's *Chaucer*, and were thus aware of Vertue's *General Prologue* plate (fig. 1). Blake's right to his own image of the Pilgrims is not invalidated by recognition of a prior source, but the issue of Stothard's equal access to the idea is at least moot. Second, while Blake saw it mainly as a moral and artistic issue, the quarrel over the design of the Pilgrimage picture also belongs to the financial and legal struggle fought in the later eighteenth-century among writers, artists, and publishers, known afterward as the Booksellers' War. John Bell (one of Stothard's first employers when Blake was still engraving his designs) was a hero on the winning side, which finally broke the London booksellers' monopoly in the 1770s.[20] The early eighteenth-century revival of medieval poetry and Urry's *Chaucer* can be directly linked to the debates in parliament which led to the Act of 1709 and its clarification of authors' and publishers' rights in common law.[21] The copyright act also inspired another prolonged and complicated redefinition of free commerce, turning on the questions of originality, priority, and the property of ideas. From the outset, the "Act for the Encouragement of Learning" provided a stimulus and suggested immediate motives for printing old books in new forms for a growing audience.

As the great power of the patron in the first half of the century gradually gave way to city booksellers, the London publishers' attempts to gain control of an increasingly profitable trade became ultimately self-defeating. Their attempts to exclude Dublin and Edinburgh from competition at mid-century led to the collapse of the London trade barriers in 1774 and full recognition of the value of a greatly enlarged mass reading public. The advantage of free trade in books immediately benefited living English writers, and indirectly, among the ancients, Chaucer—who came first in the Enlightenment's systematic classification of all aspects of its culture, past and present.

In the 1740s and 1750s, the London dealers attempted to achieve for themselves the perpetual copyright protection not provided in Queen Anne's Act of 1709. They used both physical intimidation and legal injunctions against the Scots and Irish booksellers, who undersold London by 30 to 50 percent. The conflict came to a crisis in the 1770s. The House of Lords resolved it in 1774 by granting the appeal of the Edinburgh firm of Alexander Donaldson to print Thomson's *Seasons* after the fourteen-year copyright interval had elapsed. Parliament thus finally established that there is no perpetual copyright, and the monopoly power the London booksellers tried to maintain was broken.

FIG. 2a.—*The Canterbury Pilgrims*, Thomas Stothard (1807)

FIG. 2b.—*The Canterbury Pilgrims*, William Blake (1809). Municipal Museum, Glasgow

After 1774, Irish and Scottish editions of the *Dramatists, Poets, Novelists*, and *Essayists* poured into the London shops, evoking new cheap editions from the English trade in reply. The London establishment turned to Samuel Johnson in 1777, asking his support on their behalf. The famous request of Strahan, Cadell, and Davies (representing about forty London booksellers) resulted in the publication of Johnson's *Prefaces, Biographical and Critical, to the Most Eminent English Poets . . .* , the first four volumes in 1779, the last six in 1781. While he "recommended" Blackmore "on the Creation" and Watts, Johnson's *Poets* were selected mainly by those Boswell called "[holders of] the honorary copyright . . . still preserved among them by mutual compact."[22] The Johnson series' chief competition was John Bell's *The Poets of Great Britain Complete from Chaucer to Churchill* (London, 1777-83). *Bell's Chaucer* appeared in 1782-83, to complete the set announced on the fronts of each of Bell's 108 volumes. *Bell's Milton* (1777), the first to appear, contained the major works, the Latin poems, Addison's critique of *Paradise Lost*, and a glossary in four books. The older poets required more apparatus: *Bell's Spencer* (*sic*) occupies eight and his *Chaucer* fourteen volumes. In consequence, these two large sets are more fully illustrated than all the rest, with one and sometimes two engravings per volume of text.

Since neither Chaucer nor Spenser were included in Johnson's "elegant and accurate edition of all the English poets of reputation" (from Cowley to Lyttelton), Bell's editions were now the best and cheapest texts of the early modern poets in print. In spite of their very small size ("fillagree"), the 1782 *Chaucers* are remarkably clear and readable. The quality of the Edinburgh series' design and typography—"meant to command superlative admiration [and] calculated for a lady's pocket"—set a high standard for the London publishers to meet. Appealing to Johnson for help in putting down "the trifling [Bell] edition of the *Poets*," Dilly cited "their inconveniently small size and conspicuous inaccuracy" as well as the question of piracy, but none of the charges bear examination.[23] The London response was caused by commercial threat, expressed as moral and aesthetic disapproval.

In Bell's series the poets are distributed to achieve approximately uniform size among the volumes; the number per poet thus suggests a crude critical measure of the "ancients" and the moderns reduced to a common format. Each poet's volumes were numbered separately as they were issued, in a virtually continuous stream after November 1777. Since some twenty-two editions of *Paradise Lost* appeared in the last two decades of the century, it is not surprising that the first of *Bell's Poets* was *Milton* (illustrated by J. B. Mortimer); the series' *terminus ad quem*, *Churchill's Poems*, came out in the summer of 1779. *Chaucer's Works*, first in historical order, were the last of *Bell's Poets* to appear. They consisted of Tyrwhitt's good text of the *Tales* and the balance of the canon from Urry. Shortly after Bell's Chaucer series was completed in June 1783, Tyrwhitt wrote the *Gentleman's Magazine* a bitter letter of complaint, disavowal, and self-defense to explain his failure to copyright his *Tales*, which left him no recourse to law to prevent republication.[24] He deeply regretted the reprinting of his own errors, but even more so the revival of Urry's. "As you very well know, there is scarce a line [in Urry] as the author wrote it." Nevertheless, Bell's edition was highly successful and continuously reprinted until 1807, when it was reissued in seven double volumes with a new critique taken from Warton's *History*, evidently in response to the great popularity of Johnson's *Lives* for the London *Poets*. The frontispiece of Bell's final volume (xiv, Glossary) is entitled "The Pilgrimage to Canterbury" (dated May 29, 1783). It shows four mounted figures, floating in a cloud of horses, capes, and plumes with the Wife of Bath leaning toward the Squire across the enigmatic gaze of the poet at the center. If Stothard's plate bears little resemblance to his and Blake's large paintings of the Pilgrimage of 1807-9, nevertheless it interprets the archetypal scene some twenty-five years before Cromek saw Blake's design and commissioned Stothard to undertake it without Blake's knowledge. The 1783 Glossary also reprints Tyrwhitt's warning to the reader never to open the Urry *Chaucer*, republished almost intact in Bell's edition. The only alternative to the 1721 text for all the works save the *Tales* was still the Black letter Speght of 1687.

When the London dealers engaged Johnson to write the "Little Lives, and Little Prefaces, to a little Edition" (as he put it to Boswell), the committee appointed to engage "the best engravers, viz. Bartolozzi, Sherwin, Hall, etc." failed to do so; thus the text volumes of the *English Poets* (small 8vo) were issued with "The lives . . ." without illustration. In 1810, Alexander Chalmers published a supplementary *English Poets* from Chaucer to Cowper (unillustrated) to accompany Johnson's "Prefaces, biographical and critical." For the first time, Urry's Chaucer texts were discarded to return to the Black letter editions, which Chalmers said, "with all their faults, are more to be depended upon." As will be seen, Blake did the same, rejecting both Tyrwhitt and Urry to go back to the 1687 Speght for the quotations in the *Descriptive Catalogue* and *Advertisements* to the engravings of his Pilgrimage picture in 1809-12.

The new, composite Chaucer for which Bell's edition was the prototype was published again in the cheap editions of Cooke and Robert Anderson.[25] The latter was Wordsworth's Chaucer, from which he worked on his translations of the *Prioress's* and *Manciple's Tales*, the *Cuckoo and the Nightingale*, and *Troilus*, in 1801, and which Dorothy records (in her *Journals* for 1801-3) she read aloud at tea—the *Knight's*, *Man of Law's*, and *Miller's Tales*. Bell's miniature edition thus produced a greater impact than either of its base texts could have had. By arousing competitive publication, Bell demonstrably increased public awareness of Chaucer, Spenser, and other early modern poets. Anderson filled out his first volume of Chaucer with Wyatt, Surrey, and Sackville; other editors put together small anthologies—the *Specimens*, *Reliques*, *Delights*, etc., that became fashionable in the 1790s. In Charles Cowden Clarke's copy of volume 12 of *Bell's British Poets*, Keats found the Chaucerian *Flower and the Leaf* in March 1817—the source of his epigraph to *Sleep and Poetry*, the allusions in *Endymion*, and the self-conscious sonnets on Chaucer and inspiration.[26]

Stothard's Designs in *Bell's Chaucer*

Tyrwhitt's acerbic letter of 1783 remarks that the new *Chaucer* was meant "for young people"—"Having given them a Picture at the beginning of the volume, [Bell] seems to have thought they would be perfectly unconcerned about everything else."[27] The comment singles out a strong shift of emphasis in Bell's new illustrations, compared with all earlier editions (including Tyrwhitt's own). But as we have seen, the first signs of reinterpretation of Gothic Chaucer had appeared in the Urry *Works* of 1721, whose design compromised between postmedieval archaism and the modern kinds of poetic illustration introduced by J. B. Medina's and Aldritch's plates for *Paradise Lost* in 1688, and van der Gucht's and François Boitard's for the Rowe *Shakespeare* of 1709. While the 1721 Chaucer was neither confidently modern nor convincingly medieval, the influence of its text and pictures lasted to the end of the century.

The fourteen designs Stothard made for *Bell's Chaucer* typify the "poetical painting" of the 1770s and 1780s. They are important as precedents—the first pictorial interpretations of Chaucerian narrative, *Troilus*, and the visionary poems—if not for their artistic worth. Set next to the fiery contemporary Miltonic illustrations of Fuseli or any of Blake's, Stothard's Chaucer pictures look lifeless, reductive, and tame. However, these engravings clearly reveal the half-conscious Romantic recreation of the middle ages in its own image, mingled with the literary historicism of the antiquaries the painters consulted. Stothard's Gothic images are gratifying, easy-to-read illustrations that belong to a new level of discourse: popular best-selling fiction and its narrative trade art.[28]

The new *Chaucer* in late eighteenth-century art depicts not the Pilgrims, but their *Tales*, and Chaucer's other long poems. In the rise of narrative and anecdotal painting and graphic art after 1700, book illustration played an increasingly strong role, as Pointon's study of the impact of *Paradise Lost* and Paulson's of Hogarth and his followers have shown: Milton was "a storehouse of themes for painters for a century," during which literary painting proliferated in illustrated novels, plays, and poems for all classes of readers.[29] Chaucer's storytelling now became the central subject, and interest in the Pilgrims as individual characters declined. Simultaneously, the illustration became a full-page visual analog of the text, no longer a decorative miniature addendum. The antecedents of Stothard's Chaucer pictures include not only Vertue's engravings and the old woodcuts, but recent works like William Kent's thirty-two illustrations for *The Faerie Queene* of 1751 and Samuel Wale's design for the modernized *Merchant's Tale* (Pope's "January and May") in Warburton's edition of Pope's *Works* (1751). Wale set the Gothic romance in "an Italianate garden with balustrades, pilasters, ordered cypresses and a paved, rectangular pool."[30]

Stothard's first commission, four plates for Macpherson's "Ossian" in 1779, was engraved by Blake. From the start of his career until his death in 1834, R.A. and "the most distinguished mural painter of his age," the somberly genteel imagery of Stothard's early illustrations for medieval poems remained almost unchanged.[31] His 1805 plate for "The Flower and the Leaf" in Dryden's *Fables* and the 1782 plate he made for the same text (figs. 3 and 4) differ only in subject, not in style or mood. Each evokes another view of the dream vision of the middle ages he first designed in the 1780s and repainted to the end of his life. Of the forty-two frontispieces he made for *Bell's British Poets*, only the Chaucers illustrate a major poet and present an artistic challenge. Since this set is the largest for any poet in the series, Stothard's work provides a survey of changes in "Gothic Chaucer" since 1721. The sharp, bawdy satirist prized by Pope and Gay has become almost invisible, and a tender, melancholy poet has been discovered. Stothard chose to portray incidents from the *Tales* and minor poems that stress their dramatic and sentimental appeal. The Chaucerian range of genres is still perceptible in Stothard's "picturesque moments," but the *Tales*' comic sexuality and moral ironies are suppressed. As a reader, Stothard expurgated Chaucer, finding the recognizable commonplace and the familiar scene—safe for general audiences. His Gothic is sweet, soft, and civilized. Several nonliterary factors also influenced his work; the scale, format, and number of his plates were given, since as a commercial undertaking *Bell's Poets* was to achieve "the highest excellence," and pulled its various components toward an unstated norm—four centuries, twenty-one poets, presented uniformly to be marketed as a set. The unity imposed by the series' format is strong, and the reader must get beyond the similarities of size, shape, and illustration in Bell's volumes in order to see the differences among the poets they contain. Only the language of the poemsremains distinctive and relatively unretouched.

The division of the Chaucer canon into fourteen parts determined the range of Stothard's imagery. He made six designs for the *Tales* (plus the "Pilgrim-

(continued on page 430)

Fig. 3.—*The Flower and the Leaf*, T. Stothard, frontispiece for *Bell's Chaucer*, vol. 12 (J. Heath, sc., May 1, 1783).

FIG. 4.—*The Flower and the Leaf*, T. Stothard, for *Dryden's Fables from Boccaccio and Chaucer*, ed. J. Aitken (London, 1805) (R. Cromick, sc.), facing p.173.

age" for the Glossary): two for *Troilus*, and one each for the *Romaunt of the Rose*, the *Legend of Good Women*, and two apocryphal poems, "The Flower and the Leaf" and "The Praise of Women." Stothard also illustrated the *Tale of Gamelyn*, published for the first time in Urry, although its non-Chaucerian diction was already recognized. Its ancestral relation to *As You Like It* probably outweighed its uncertain status. Mortimer's frontispieces for the 1777 Bell *Milton* set the pattern for the whole series. The plate is divided into three parts: a rectangular series title at the top, a smaller lozenge with volume title and quotation keyed to the text below, and a rondel containing the vignette in the center. In the finished engraving, the illustration is compressed to a circle $2\frac{5}{8}$ inches in diameter. Stothard followed the examples provided by Mortimer's Milton and Spenser plates. His freedom as an interpreter, tied to the lines of the text it was his task to make explicit, was constrained as well by other models: Bell employed Hayman, until his death, and Angelica Kauffmann, then reaching the top of her fame.

In 1738, John Bancks addressed a poem "To Mr. HOGARTH," glancing at the clichés that link poet and painter with an allusion to Chaucer meant to flatter the latter by association: "Perhaps in Chaucer's antient Page/ We view the Hogarth of his age." But the Stothard Chaucer of the 1780s rarely suggests Hogarth, and only in the first of his plates are there signs of "antient" Gothic authenticity (fig. 5). The first plate for volume 1 (*General Prologue* [*GP*], lines 768-80) shows a scene at the table in the Tabard with Harry Bailly standing to address the seated Pilgrims (six of whom are shown), while a boy lifts a loaded tray in the background. In the center foreground stands a curious-footed pitcher, and on the table knives and plates are scattered; the Host reaches out with his right arm, while his left cradles a flask. The costumes are vaguely Elizabethan (ruffs, a Tudor pointed hat) as are the paneled wall and carved chair. Nevertheless, this scene (not described in Chaucer's *Prologue*) seems to look back to an image in the earliest printed editions of the *Tales*, the Caxton woodcut of 1484 (fig. 6) which de Worde inherited and used for his later edition of Chaucer and again for Lydgate's *Assemble of Goddes*. Finally the cut appeared in Robert Redman's and John Skot's edition of Lydgate's *Interpretacioun of the Names of Goddes* (after 1529). The cut shows the twenty-nine Pilgrims and the Host sitting at a round table on which are scattered knives and plates, and the same curious-footed pitcher; the Host gestures with his right arm. This is the only one of Stothard's designs for Bell which seems to quote a medieval prototype. For the rest, he takes his cues from the *Tales* and poems where the story suggests an emotionally appealing scene.

Stothard's postmedieval Emily bending over her roses under Palamon's jail window (*Knight's Tale*, vol. 2) resembles Mortimer's romantic Eve among

FIG. 5.—*Prologue of the Canterbury Tales, 1.768*, T. Stothard, frontispiece of *Bell's Chaucer*, vol. 1 (Grignion, sc., August 1, 1782).

The Illustrated Eighteenth-Century Chaucer

Fig. 6.—The Canterbury Pilgrims, unknown. First printed in Caxton's 2d ed. of the *Tales* (London, 1484).

her flowers (*Milton*, vol. 11). In vols. 4 and 5, there are a few obvious Gothic motifs: for the *Second Nun's Tale* an angel flies in the window with a crown for St. Cecilia;[32] for the *Shipman's Tale*, the lecherous Monk and the Wife walk in a garden set against a fragment of ancient architecture. But the Gothic walled garden of the *Romaunt of the Rose* (vol. 7) conflicts with the foreground figures, the Lover and Idleness in Elizabethan dress. Some forty lines in Chaucer's *Romaunt* describe the Lady's symbols of Venus, but here her allegorical rose garland, mirror, and gloves are gone, replaced by a fashionable hat, decolletage, and long tight sleeves. Mixtures of vaguely Renaissance details with timeless landscapes elsewhere blur the pastoral scenes Stothard set for the *Wife of Bath's Tale, Gamelyn*, and the *Book of the Duchess* (vols. 3, 6, 9). In each we see a confrontation under a large, overarching tree between the principal figures in the story as it raises its central question: who is the OldHag talking to the Knight, the father figure addressing the young men, the sad nobleman about to be disturbed? The native folk and fairy-tale motifs evoke from Stothard stylized pictorial clichés, minimally medievalized and almost anonymous. They seem neither distinctly Chaucerian nor non-Chaucerian, simply "poetic" narrative, escapist fiction. Their historicity raises no problems; they exist in a limbo of stage convention where anachronism is taken for granted and is seemingly self-justified. The "real" Chaucer is beside the point.

Stothard's strongest designs are those for classical Chaucerian themes: the Ovidian Ariadne on the rocks (*Legend of Good Women*, vol. 10), Samson in Delilah's lap ("Praise of Women," vol. 13), and the engravings for *Troilus*. Stothard combines Chaucer's two most vivid moments of romance with the more authentic Trojan world of Shakespeare's version. He shows (figs. 7, 8) Troilus riding beneath Criseyde's window in Greek battle dress (vol. 9), and the climax of Book 3, Criseyde's embrace of him, naked and unconscious, while a young Pandar watches over the bed (vol. 8).[33] The intense light and shadow in these plates deepen the play of emotion that Stothard at his best could portray. His stagy "Theseus Joining Palamon and Emily" (for Dryden's *Fables*, 1805, engraved by Cromek) reflects an automatic response to Dryden's Chaucer, as well as increased facility with the conventions of literary painting. The idiom was already becoming a genre in its own right, and Stothard had become one of its popular masters.

If Stothard's Chaucerian illustrations share one common quality, it is humorlessness. The "Hogarthian" wit of the Augustans' Chaucer does not emerge in these serious, sentiment-laden scenes. Instead, Stothard has picked up and made concrete Chaucer's *gentilesse*, his poignance, and supernatural mysteriousness-romance elements that can be formulated at a relatively shallow level of perception. However, a wider range of attitudes toward the *Tales* and English medievalia was also appearing in art in the last decades of the century, which I shall note only briefly here. About 1780 James Jeffreys made a portfolio (unpublished) of twenty-four sepia and wash drawings of the Pilgrims with quotations from Chaucer; another set of nine drawings for the *Tales* was made ca. 1776 by Mortimer, later engraved and published in a quarto edition of Tyrwhitt.[34] Unlike Stothard's, Mortimer's plates stress the fabliaux and the supernatural: the *Miller's* and *Reeve's Tales*, the Cook and Perkin Warbeck, the *Friar's*, *Summoner's*, and *Merchant's Tales*, the Pardoner's Three Gamblers and Time, and Palamon and Arcite fighting. *Gualterius and Griselda, or Happiness Properly Estimated, a Tale* appeared in 1794 in *Angelica's Ladies' Library*, a small quarto of Ogle's 1741 translation of the *Clerk's Tale* with eight plates by Angelica Kauffmann. The title is highly suggestive of her style.

At the end of the century there is evidence of increasing demand, in high culture as in commercial publishing, for a visible Gothic past in combined artistic forms: paintings are accompanied by stanzas of verse, poems are illustrated, murals and "frescoes" exhibit their texts. Anthony Blunt's survey of

(continued on page 436)

Fig. 7.—*Troilus and Criseyde*, T. Stothard, frontispiece of *Bell's Chaucer*, vol. 8 (Grignion, sc., December 19, 1782).

Fig. 8.—*Troilus and Criseyde*, T. Stothard, frontispiece of *Bell's Chaucer*, vol. 9 (Grignion, sc., March 18, 1783).

paintings shown at the Royal Academy for 1769-76 lists works by seven artists (Boydell, Kauffmann, Mortimer, Penny, Wade, and West) illustrating high medieval historical subjects, paralleling the projects of antiquarian art history undertaken in the 1770s, 80s, and 90s, like Gough's *Sepulchral Monuments in Great Britain* (1786, 1796) which Blake worked on for Basire, Strutt's *History* of costume (1796-99), James Bentham's monograph on Ely cathedral (1771), and Milner's on Winchester (1798).[35] The huge scheme of Macklin's *British Poets* (begun in 1788) aimed at the upper level of the audience Bell's and Johnson's *Poets* had sought and found. Similar attempts to fuse the arts of painting and poetry inspired Boydell's Shakespeare Gallery (1798) and Fuseli's Milton Gallery (1799), but Macklin's was the biggest in scope. His prospectus announced a series of "100 Pictures of the most interesting Subjects from the Poets of Great Britain"; after display, they were to be issued twice a year in sets of four engravings, each with a single page of letterpress, their "poetic source."[36] Macklin commissioned paintings from Gainsborough, Hamilton, Reynolds, Fuseli, and Stothard, to be engraved by Bartolozzi and his pupil Tomkins. Stothard's "Solomon Rejected" (for Prior's *Solomon*) was shown, but not published. Three plates of new Chaucer paintings were published in 1790—Rigaud's neo-classical "Constantia" (for the *Man of Law's Tale*) and two scenes for the *Knight's Tale* by Hamilton, "The Departure for the Combat" and "The Death of Arcite." Six numbers (twenty-four pictures) of *Macklin's Poets* were published in the decade 1788-99, but all three galleries of "poetical painting" failed by 1804 for economic reasons. Such attempts to achieve the ideal union of the arts proclaimed in Reynolds's *Discourse Eight* left behind catalogs filled with quotations from the poets, sufficient for the ideal reader of the paintings. But outside the academy, the new audience for the old poetry was being created by the mass-produced volumes of Johnson and Bell.

Bell's British Poets' fourteen plates offer a visual interpretation of Chaucer which suggests to the reader that he is little more remote than Spenser or Shakespeare, as accessible perhaps as Dryden or Pope. The easy readability of the pictures is belied, however, by the difficulty of understanding the poems in Chaucer's language. Chaucer the poet remained archaic and probably unintelligible except to scholars and poets, as is witnessed by the continuous effort to translate and explain him. A three-volume modernized *Canterbury Tales* (Ogle's 1741 versions) edited and expurgated by Rev. William Lipscomb came out in 1795; Dryden's *Fables* (with Stothard's plates) was re-edited by Aiken in 1805 (omitting Ovid and Homer as "too familiar to the modern reader"). Contradicting his own opinion in the 1800 Preface to the *Lyrical Ballads* that "the affecting parts of Chaucer are almost always expressed in language pure and universally intelligible to this day," Wordsworth undertook to translate him for the common reader in 1801.[37] It is probably true that of the enormous audience who welcomed Stothard's "Canterbury Pilgrimage" painting in 1807 and bought its engraving throughout the nineteenth century, most regarded it with respect and affection but very little idea of who the Pilgrims were or what they were talking about.

Stothard's and Blake's Pilgrims

The two cabinet pictures of the Pilgrimage by Stothard and Blake climaxed the new illustration of Chaucer that began in the eighteenth century. However, I shall discuss them only briefly here. After the great popular success of Stothard's picture in the nineteenth century, his art has gradually faded into a status in cultural history like Scott's and Dickens's in literary history—between learned and popular culture—until their relatively recent rehabilitation. Blake's time has come, as he foresaw: "Posterity will *know.*" But Stothard's vast output of some 5,000 illustrations, the mural designs for Buckingham Palace, and the fresco dome of the Edinburgh Advocates' Library now belong to the detritus of commercial bourgeois art of the Romantic period. Stothard's later works are worth examining insofar as they illuminate Blake and the contemporary Chaucer after 1800.

Since he made no public reply to Blake's attacks on his Chaucer painting ("All is misconceived, and its mis-execution is equal to its misconception"), the best evidence for Stothard's idea of his "Procession of the Canterbury Pilgrims" is the companion piece he made for it years later, just as Blake made a parallel tempera "fresco" for his Pilgrims. All four paintings are roughly the same size and shape (3 feet, 1 inch by 1 foot) and in each pair the later picture more clearly establishes the generic differences between the two rival versions of the Pilgrims. The later Stothard, "The Flitch of Bacon" (1832), is a lyrical, Romantic narrative painting which tells the story remembered in the *Wife of Bath's Prologue* about the Dunmowe rites honoring marital peace still celebrated in nineteenth-century Essex. The theme offered Stothard a "real" event he could invest with the Gothic associations and romantic sentiment of English history painting. The later Blake, in contrast, is a complex iconographical vision of "The Characters in Spenser's *Faerie Queene*" (1825?). Blake presents a crowded company in equestrian procession, enigmatically analogical to the Pilgrims in his Chaucer picture.[38] Blake interprets Spenser's allegory in his own symbolic language, again making a myth that demands a reading of its own beyond the literary text. As always, where Stothard's allusions are transparent, Blake's are elliptical and deliberately ironic.

Chaucer's *Prologue* provided Stothard with a rich, realistic narrative of poetic verisimilitude, and it gave Blake a series of allegorical personifications for symbolic reading. The titles of the paintings make explicit the two modes and relations of the artists to the text. Stothard's title is "The Procession of Chaucer's Pilgrims . . ."; Blake's is always called "Blake's Chaucer," followed by a subtitle, for example, the *Notebook*'s "being a Complete Index of Human Characters as they appear, Age after Age."[39] The question of the stolen design, Stothard's ignorance, bad drawing, and Rubensian color and chiaroscuro were for Blake only the beginning of the alienation between them. Blake saw Stothard's Chaucer painting as a betrayal, not of himself or of the poet, but of the artistic imagination—the visionary power of the painter to see through Nature, which Stothard's art intentionally falsified.[40] The misreading of Chaucer for which Blake also chastises Stothard and his admirers was in fact derived from early eighteenth-century criticism, to which Stothard might have appealed in self-defense. Dryden's critique of Chaucerian "realism" in the Preface to the *Fables* was echoed in John Dart's "Life" in Urry's *Works* (reprinted in Bell) and his *Poem on Chaucer* (1772).[41] Dart compares Chaucer's morning landscapes with Titian's: "He stript off every disguise with which the Gothick writers had cloathed [Nature]. There is a wild beauty in his *Works* which comes nearer . . . Homer than any other that followed him. . . ."[42] Dart's *Poem* opens with a series of similes, a gallery for "Titian's Day or Tintoretto's Night/ Rubens' bold Stroakes, or Raphael's awful Grace/ or Kneller's just similitude of Face." These formulas introduce Chaucer's "deathless Page/ Filled with as various and as just Designs/ In Deeper Colours laid, and drawn in stronger Lines. . . ." Dart's theme is a variant on Dryden's idea of Chaucerian pictorial realism—"as if some ancient painter had drawn [the Pilgrims]." The critical analogies that infuriated Blake in 1809 were the latest versions of Dryden, such as William Carey's "Appreciation" of Stothard, written for Cromek's campaign to sell the engraving. Carey's pedantry enraged Blake. Confusing Dürer's linear exactness with Venetian coloring, Carey describes Chaucer's Knight with Dart's terms: "It cannot be denied that Chaucer's description of the Knight is very marked in all its details. It unites the minute accuracy of Albert Dürer's St. Hubert with the fine colouring and dignity of Holbein in his most Titianesque portraits."[43] Carey praises the realism of Chaucer's own portrait of the Knight: "his intimacy with the Courtiers of Edward III probably furnished him with the most prominent features of the original." In Blake's eyes, Stothard's "realist" Chaucer was debased historicism, "that [blur] which is fabricated to destroy art."

But Stothard's picture was approved by his contemporaries because it presents the Pilgrims in the proper order and decorum ("in which we may suppose Chaucer himself to have seen them") and "it bears no mark of the period in which it was painted, but might well pass for the work of some able artist of the time of Chaucer." Stothard sought his realism in the British Museum, where he copied from Hoccleve's "portrait" and Gothic sculpture. He also borrowed from the Vertue engravings. Several of his Pilgrims strike familiar poses, still recognizable in the glow of romantic morning light and color. The Squire, barely in control of his rearing white horse in the foreground, is Stothard's Rubensian version of the traditional type of the Knight in the Renaissance woodcuts and the 1721 plate of the Squire, which Stothard's most nearly resembles. To Blake, as every reader of the *Descriptive Catalogue* knows, Stothard's painting reduced Chaucer's archetypal figures to illusory realism, sacrificing their eternal truth for seductive credibility.

In 1851 Stothard's daughter Anna Bray published her *Life* of her father in three Royal folio volumes, fully illustrated.[44] Her book provides forgotten evidence of contemporary critical opinion and Bray's knowledge of Stothard's habits as a painter. She recalls his love of opera and of Watteau, his devotion to details of setting and costume, and his "sympathy with early poets and writers," especially Froissart and Cervantes. Remarkably, she thinks Stothard the only painter of his day fully equal to Hogarth in the telling of a continued story; while Hogarth invented his own fictions, "Stothard embodied those . . . written for him."[45] On the Chaucer picture, Bray is circumspect: Blake's name is never mentioned, but the financial fleecing Stothard also suffered from Cromek and the artist's generosity are recorded. She quotes Douce's praise of the Chaucer picture in his *Illustrations of Shakespeare* (1807) and Hoppner's letter on its historicity,[46] and describes the great difficulty the Pilgrims first presented: so many figures, so much alike, such risk of monotony—"Who could ever make anything of it? was always the cry." She recalls Stubbs's visit and his comment on Stothard's horses, whose beauty "resembles Rubens."[47] Bray eulogizes the painting as her father's humane and literal rendering of Chaucer's text, explaining his subservience to the meaning of the *Prologue* at great length:

> In the Pilgrims, Stothard has discriminated the characters with the utmost judgment and delicacy of tact, never masquerading or grotesqueing his creations. . . . The [Wife of Bath is] represented to the life; she has all the joyance and hearty good will of a blithe and bold spirit, unclouded by any delicacy or . . . courtly reserve of manner. [She] is speaking to the Pardoner, who . . . seems to be cracking some joke. . . . The painter himself used jocosely to say that he liked . . . to take his stand near the Wife of Bath, listening to . . . her pleasant and witty sayings. "You will find me," he said, "resting by the bridle of her steed."

Here Bray adds her own opinion: "It shows great judgement in Stothard that he has not represented the Wife as a gross or disgusting woman. She is to Chaucer's party what Ninon de l'Enclos was, four centuries after, to the court of Louis XIV—a refined voluptuary, delicate in appearance, not in mind or manners. She rides, like the Muse of Comedy, light and gaily along."[48] In Blake's *Descriptive Catalogue*, the Wife is demonic, "a scourge and a blight," and unspeakable. Point for point, Stothard's and Blake's Pilgrims depict two unreconcilable readings of the same text. That Blake's were too difficult for his contemporaries need not be argued here.

Blake's repeated attempts to find an audience for his engraving of *Blake's Chaucer* resulted in the series of smaller plates (with the 1687 *Prologue* text and Ogle's modern English version) issued as *The Prologue and Characters of Chaucer's Pilgrims*, the last in 1812. After a slow start, Stothard's engraving received a puff from Jeffrey in the *Edinburgh Review* and thereafter (in Bray's words) had "the most extensive sale of anything of the kind published in the last 100 years." Stothard's sentimental neo-Gothic nostalgia and easy readability made no demands on the spectator; Blake's symbolic allegory still does. *Blake's Chaucer* does not translate back into the language of the *Prologue* but—like *Blake's Spenser*—needs a full exegesis of its own.[49] One of the few among Blake's contemporaries who sensed what his second sight meant was Charles Lamb. Everyone knows Stothard's Chaucer, he wrote to Bernard Barton (May 15, 1824), and nobody knows Blake's, but "it is far above Stothard's. . . . His Catalogue is a most spirited criticism of Chaucer, but mystical and full of vision."[50] In the library at Abbotsford, "the chief ornament of Scott's study was the print of Stothard's 'Canterbury Pilgrims,' which hung over the chimney piece and . . . must have been in great favor."[51] The inventory of Scott's books lists the Chaucers in his possession before 1832: the Black letter Stow (1561) and Speght (1602), Urry's 1721 *Works*, Chalmer's *English Poets* (1810), Tyrwhitt's *Tales* (1798), Ogle's 1741 modernizations, and Godwin's *Life of Chaucer* (1803). Virtually the whole range of Renaissance, Augustan, and Romantic Chaucers were there, except for Blake's. If in his own eyes the Pilgrims were *Blake's Chaucer*, for the time being the Romantics' Chaucer was Stothard's.

From *Modern Philology* 77, no. 1 (August 1979): 26-55. Copyright © 1979 by The University of Chicago Press. Reprinted by permission of The University of Chicago Press.

Notes

1. *The Works of Jeoffrey Chaucer*, ed. John Urry (London, 1721); William A. Alderson and Arnold C. Henderson, *Chaucer and Augustan Scholarship*, University of California Publications in English 35 (Los Angeles, 1970); Marcia Pointon, *Milton and English Art* (Manchester, 1970); Joseph A. Wittreich, "Milton's First Illustrator," *Seventeenth Century News* 32 (1974): 70-71; T. S. R. Boase, "Illustrations of Shakespeare's Plays in the 17th and 18th Centuries," *Journal of the Warburg and Courtauld Institutes* 10 (1947): 83-108.

2. *Bell's Poets of Great Britain from Chaucer to Churchill*, 108 vols. (London, 1777-82); 109 vols. (London, 1777-87, 1777-96); 50 double vols. (London, 1782); 61 double vols. (London, 1807).

3. Ralph Cohen, *The Unfolding of "The Seasons": A Study of James Thomson's Poem* (Baltimore, 1970), pp. 251, 259.

4. Sir Geoffrey Keynes, *Blake Studies*, 2d ed. (Oxford, 1971), pp. 25-27; A. M. Coxhead, *Thomas Stothard, R.A.* (London, 1906), pp. 21-31. Blake engraved Stothard's designs for Hoole's edition of *Orlando Furioso* (1783) and his *Tasso* (1798-99) (cf. Robert M. Essick, "Blake and the Traditions of Reproductive Engraving," *Blake Studies* 5 [1972]: 59-103; Robert M. Essick and R. R. Eassen, *William Blake, Book Illustrator* [Normal, Ill., 1972]).

5. Under the terms of the act (which took effect April 10, 1710), Shakespeare, Milton, and Dryden passed into the public domain in 1731, twenty-one years after the date relevant for "old Books."

6. *Descriptive Catalogue of Pictures III*, in *The Poetry and Prose of William Blake*, ed. David V. Erdman (1965; reprint ed., New York, 1970), p. 529.

7. Alderson and Henderson, pp. 81-96. Political elements in Atterbury's and Urry's relationship are noted by Michael Shugrue, "The Urry Chaucer and a London Uprising of 1384," *Journal of English and Germanic Philology* 65 (1966): 229-37. Among favorable factors were the recent successes of Pope's "January and May," "Wife of Bath's Tale," and "Temple of Fame"; and Ruddiman's edition of Douglas's *Aeneid* (1710), Hughes's *Faerie Queene* (1715), and Dryden's *Fables* (1700, 1713). But Gower, Malory, Langland, and Lydgate were not re-edited until after 1800.

8. Erdman, p. 528.

9. Hearne to Richard Rawlinson, March 13, 1734, quoted in Alderson and Henderson, p. 82.

10. Charles Mish, "Black Letter as a Social Discriminant in the 17th Century," *PMLA* 68 (1953): 621-30; Bertrand Bronson, *Printing as an Index of Taste in Eighteenth-Century England* (New York, 1963); Alice Miskimin, "Counterfeiting Chaucer," *Studies in Medieval Culture* 10 (1977): 133-45. Black letter had no artistic value, but was considered vulgar; in 1770, Philip Luckombe commented, "Black letter is so far abolished . . . it is seldom used in any work than what belongs to law . . ." (see Bronson, p. 32).

11. The manuscripts are described in John M. Manly and Edith Rickert, *The Text of the Canterbury Tales* (Chicago, 1940), 1:561-606; Margaret Rickert, *Painting in Britain: The Middle Ages* (Baltimore, 1954), p. 176 and pl. 178; Margaret Galway, "The *Troilus* Frontispiece," *Modern Language Review* 44 (1949): 161-77. The Chaucer portraits are discussed in George Lam and Warren Smith, "George Vertue's Contributions to Chaucerian Iconography," *Modern Language Quarterly* 5 (1944): 303-22. The woodcuts are described in Arthur M. Hind, A *History of the Woodcut in the Fifteenth Century* (London, 1935), vol. 2, chap. 9; Edward Hodnett, *English Woodcuts, 1480-1535*, Illustrated Monographs 22 (London, 1935), passim.

12. The cuts are scattered through the *Prologue* in STC 5075, which thus has four more leaves before the *Knight's Tale* than STC 5076. See Derek Brewer, ed., *Geoffrey Chaucer, The Works, 1532* . . . (facsimile) (1969; reprint ed., London, 1976).

13. *A Catalogue of Engravers Who Have Been Born or Resided in England Digested by Mr. Horace Walpole from the MSS of Mr. George Vertue, to which Is Added an Account of the Life and Works of the Latter* (London, 1765, 2d ed. 1786), p. 303.

14. Thomas Tyrwhitt, ed., *The Canterbury Tales of Chaucer*, 5 vols. (London, 1775-78), vol. 5, *Glossary*, "Advertisement," p. ii; reprinted in *Bell's Chaucer*, 14:8.

15. B. Sprague Allen, *Tides in English Taste, 2* vols. (Cambridge, Mass., 1937), vol. 2, chap. 14; Sir Kenneth Clark, *The Gothic Revival*, rev. ed. (New York, 1962); Evelyn S. de Beer, "Gothic: Origin and Diffusion of the Term," *Journal of the Warburg and Courtauld Institutes*,

vol. 11 (1948); George Germann, *Gothic Revival*, trans. G. Onn (Cambridge, Mass., 1973), pp. 59-63.

16. John Carter (architect, engraver, and antiquarian) published the *Builder's Magazine* (1774-78), a "Monthly Companion for Architects . . . Masons, etc. as well as for Every Gentleman . . . consisting of designs for every Style and Taste," which included plans for a Gothic observatory, pulpit, mansion, pavilion, market cross, and municipal charnel house.

17. Alderson and Henderson, chap. 6; Entick's *Proposals* (1736) and Morrell's *Canterbury Tales* (London, 1737-40) combine texts and translations "by several Eminent Hands." George Ogle's *Canterbury Tales . . . Modernis'd by Several Hands*, 3 vols. (1741,1742; reprint ed., Dublin, 1795) and Andrew Jackson's *Matrimonial Scenes . . . from Chaucer* (London, 1750) both contain modernizations only.

18. The larger version of Brown's painting is in the Municipal Gallery, Sydney, Australia; a second version is in the Tate Gallery, London. Burne-Jones's watercolor is in the Victoria and Albert Museum collection, London.

19. Anthony Blunt, *The Art of William Blake* (New York, 1959), p. 77.

20. Stanley Morison, *John Bell, 1745-1831* (Cambridge, 1930); Stothard's earliest works were fashion plates for Harrison's *Magazines*; for *Beauties of British Poetry* (1782) he illustrated Goldsmith, Young, Shenstone, Prior, Parnell, Pope's "Temple of Fame," and *Lycidas*.

21. A. W. Pollard, "Some Notes on the History of Copyright in England, 1667-1774," *Library*, 4th ser. 3 (1922): 97-114; A. C. Collins, "Some Aspects of Copyright, 1700-1780," *Library*, 4th ser. 7 (1926): 67-81; idem, *Authorship in the Days of Johnson, 1726-80* (London, 1927); idem, *The Profession of Letters, 1780-1832* (London, 1928); F. A. Mumby and Ian Norri, *Publishing and Bookselling* (London, 1930, rev. 5th ed. 1974).

22. R. W. Chapman, ed., *Boswell's Life of Johnson* (Oxford, 1957), pp. 1008-9. Boswell represented Donaldson in successful litigation in 1773. In an exchange of letters, April 24-May 3, 1777 (*Boswell's Life*, pp. 799-801), he asked Johnson, "is not the charm of this publication chiefly owing to the *magnum nomen* in the front of it?"

23. Edward Dilly to Boswell, September 26, 1777, quoted in *Boswell's Life*, pp. 801-3.

24. *Gentleman's Magazine* 53 (June 12, 1783): 461-62. Tyrwhitt had in fact received no royalties, nor was Bell obliged to pay any.

25. Cooke (London, 1798); Anderson (1793, 1795; reprint ed., London, 1814).

26. The Bell volume containing Keats's holograph "Sonnet on Chaucer" is now BL Add. 33516; the poem was published in the *Examiner* (March 16, 1817) and evoked from Reynolds a sonnet to Keats "On Reading His Sonnet Written on Chaucer" (see W. J. Bate, *John Keats* [Cambridge, Mass., 1963], pp. 144-46; F. E. L. Priestley, "Keats and Chaucer," *Modern Language Quarterly* 5 [1944]: 439-47).

27. See above, n. 24.

28. David Bland, *A History of Book Illustration* (New York, 2d ed. 1958); idem, *The Illustration of Books* (London, 1962); Iola A. Williams, "English Book Illustration, 1700-35," *Library*, 4th ser. 17 (1937): 1-21; Hans Hammelman and T. S. R. Boase, *Book Illustrators in Eighteenth-Century England* (New Haven, Conn., 1976).

29. Pointon (n. I above), p. 93.

30. Bronson (n. 10 above), p. 37.

31. Stothard's murals are discussed in E. Croft-Murray, *Decorative Painting in England, 1537-1837* (London, 1962), vol. 1; he made illustrations for the six volumes of Spenser's *Faerie Queene* (Upton's text) in the 1802 Aiken edition of *Johnson's Works of the English Poets*; in 1810, for Sharpe's edition of Spenser (6 12mo vols.) he provided portraits of Sidney and Raleigh and four cuts, variants on the 1802 *Spensers* (see Coxhead [n. 4 above], pp. 92-93, for both sets of Spenser designs). For Bell, he did fronts for eighteen poets; Mortimer (d. 1779) did twenty-five;

Angelica Kauffmann, Mauritius Lowe, and E. Edwards made small contributions. The engravers for Stothard were Grignion, de Lattre, Heath, and Sharp.

32. Leigh Hunt is reported to have thought "the girl's figure worthy of Raphael" (cited in Coxhead, p. 85).

33. Errors in Grignion's engraving of the captions for the *Troilus* plates resulted in their misplacement. The cut for Book 2 was switched from vol. 8 to vol. 9, so it follows rather than precedes the consummation scene. Stothard's quotations are accurate, but the plot appears confused in the pictures.

34. (1787; reprint ed., London, 1798). Jeffreys was an Academy gold medalist at 17; see Caroline Spurgeon, *500 Years of Chaucer Criticism and Allusion, 1357-1900*, 3 vols. (1925; reprint ed., New York, 1960), 1:458-59. F. J. Furnivall described his copy of Tyrwhitt with these cuts in *Notes and Queries* 6th ser. ii (1880): 325-26; the engravers were J. Hogg, Sharp, E. Williams, and J. K. Sherwin. The nine original drawings (1776?) are in the Victoria and Albert Museum collections, London.

35. Blunt, pp. 5-7; James Bentham, *The History and Antiquities . . . of . . . the Cathedral Church of Ely . . . from AD 673 to the Year 1771* (Cambridge, 1771); Joseph Strutt, *A Complete View of the Dress and Habits of the People of England*, 3 vols. (London, 1796-99).

36. T. S. R. Boase, "Macklin and Bowyer," *Journal of the Warburg and Courtauld Institutes* 26 (1963): 148-55.

37. Wordsworth's *Prioress's Tale* appeared in *Poems, 1815-20*, his *Cuckoo and the Nightingale* and stanzas from *Troilus* in Horne's *Geoffrey Chaucer Modernis'd* (1841), but his version of the *Manciple's Tale* remained unpublished in his lifetime.

38. Blake's *Faerie Queene* is in the Egremont Collection, Petworth, Sussex. It has been reproduced with commentary by John Grant and Robert Brown in *Blake Newsletter*, vol. 31 (1974-75).

39. *Sic* in Cromek's Prospectus for Stothard, printed in *Blair's Grave* (1808), a book designed by Blake. Douce's *Illustrations of Shakespeare* (1808), Hoppner's "Letter to Richard Cumberland" (1807), and William Carey's seventy-seven-page "Critical Description" (1808) (the two latter published by Cromek) describe Stothard's Chaucer in glowing terms. Blake's drafts for his prospectus and the published texts (1809-10, 1812), his *Notebook* entries, and the *Descriptive Catalogue* all refer to *Blake's Chaucer/The Canterbury Pilgrims/The Fresco Picture/Representing Chaucer's Characters Painted by/William Blake; Blake's Chaucer/An Original Engraving by William Blake*. The 1812 *Advertisement* is titled "The Prologue and Characters of Chaucer's Pilgrims, Intended to represent a particular design of Mr. Blake's . . . ," making explicit the shift of emphasis from poem to painter. Blake's design reorganizes the order of the Pilgrims according to his idea of their moral and social hierarchy of types: "The Franklin is . . . the Bacchus, as the Doctor is the Escalapius, the Host is the Silenus, the Squire is the Apollo, the Miller is the Hercules . . ." (Erdman [n. 6 above], p. 527). Blake's Pilgrimage begins with the Knight and the Squire, as in Chaucer's *Prologue*; Stothard starts with the Miller, the order in Chaucer's action and the 1721 Vertue frontispiece.

40. *Descriptive Catalogue* (Erdman, pp. 529-31); *Notebook*, "Public Address" (Blake, pp. 560-71).

41. "Chaucer followed Nature everywhere, but never was so bold to go beyond her. . . . He has taken into the compass of his . . . Tales the various manners and humours of the whole English nation in his age" (Preface to *Fables*). Cf. Blake: "Every age is a Canterbury Pilgrimage; we all pass on, each sustaining one or another of these characters; nor could a child be born, who is not one of these characters" (Erdman, p. 523). Dryden's medieval "types" are Blake's eternal universals.

42. Urry's *Works*, sig. eii^v; John Dart, *Poem on Chaucer and His Writings . . . to the Lord Bishop of Rochester* (London, 1722), lines 6-10.

43. Critical *Description/of the Procession/of/Chaucers/Pilgrims/to/Canterbury/Painted by/ Thomas Stothard, Esq., R.A./to John Leigh Philips, Esq.* (London, 1808), p. 26.

44. Anna E. Bray, *Reminiscences of Thomas Stothard, R.A.* (London, 1851).

45. Ibid., 2:131.

46. Hoppner wrote to Richard Cumberland, May 30, 1807, "The effect is not . . . the result of any association of ideas connected with the costume, but it appears in a primitive simplicity and the total absence of all affectation, either of colour or pencilling"; the letter was printed in Cromek's *Prospectus* and quoted in Bray, 2:137.

47. "Stubbs exclaimed, 'I am astonished at [your horses]. Where did you get your horses?' 'From everyday observation,' replied Stothard. Stubbs departed, [saying] he could do nothing in comparison with such work. His wonder would have been much greater still had he known that the Canterbury Pilgrims was . . . painted by candlelight" (Bray, 2: 138). Cf. 2:134 on Stothard's sketching trips to the Old Kent Road to observe the morning light on the Surrey hills.

48. Bray, 2:131.

49. K. Kiralis ("William Blake as an Intellectual and Spiritual Guide to Chaucer's Canterbury Pilgrims," *Blake Studies* 1 [1969]: 130-90) offers a modern Blakean's explication, as yet unanswered by Chaucer critics.

50. Spurgeon, 2:151.

51. *J. G. Lockhart's Memoirs of Sir Walter Scott (Edinburgh, 1838)*, ed. A. W. Pollard, 5 vols. (London, 1900), 5:130.

RESOURCES

c. 1343	Geoffrey Chaucer is born in London to John Chaucer, a wealthy winemaker, and his wife, Agnes.
c. 1357	Chaucer begins serving as a page in the household of Elizabeth de Burgh, countess of Ulster.
1359	When the countess's husband, Lionel of Antwerp, first duke of Clarence, joins the English army to fight in the Hundred Years' War, Chaucer travels with him to France, where he is taken prisoner during the attempted siege of Reims.
1360	Chaucer is ransomed by King Edward III for the sum of sixteen pounds. Peace is declared, and Chaucer travels between England and Calais as an emissary for Lionel.
1366	Chaucer marries Philippa Roet, a lady-in-waiting to Philippa of Hainault, Edward III's queen consort, and the sister of Katherine Swynford, who would become the third wife of Edward III's son, John of Gaunt, first duke of Lancaster and duke of Aquitaine. Chaucer travels to Spain. His father dies, and his mother remarries, wedding Bartholomew Chappel.
1367	Chaucer becomes a valet to Edward III. His son Thomas is born.
1369-1370	Chaucer serves in the army in France under John of Gaunt.
c. 1370	*Book of the Duchess* and *Romaunt of the Rose* are composed.
1372-1373	Under orders from the king, Chaucer travels to Genoa to establish an English trading port. He visits Florence.
1372-1380	*Tragedies of Fortune*, *House of Fame*, and *The Legend of St. Cecilia* are composed.
1374	Chaucer becomes a controller of customs and subsidy for the Port of London.
1377	Chaucer travels to France and Flanders as an emissary to negotiate peace and Richard II's marriage.

1378	Chaucer travels to Lombardy, Italy.
1380	*Boece, Anelida and Arcite*, and *Parlement of Foules* are composed. Chaucer's son Lewis is born.
1380-1386	*The Legend of Good Women* and *Palamon and Ersyte* are composed.
1381	Agnes Chaucer dies. Chaucer's daughter Elizabeth becomes a nun at Barking Abbey in London.
1382	*Troilus and Criseyde* is composed.
1385	Chaucer becomes a justice of the peace in Kent.
1386	Chaucer serves as member of Parliament for Kent.
1387-1392	*A Treatise on the Astrolabe* is composed.
1387-1400	*The Canterbury Tales* is composed.
1389	Chaucer leaves his position as justice of the peace to become clerk of the King's Works in London.
1391	Chaucer is appointed deputy forester of the Royal Forest of North Petherton in Somerset.
1400	Chaucer dies in London and is buried in Westminster Abbey, in what is today known as the Poets' Corner.

Poetry

Book of the Duchess, c. 1370
Romaunt of the Rose, c. 1370 (translation, possibly not by Chaucer)
House of Fame, 1372-1380
The Legend of St. Cecilia, 1372-1380 (later used as *The Second Nun's Tale*)
Tragedies of Fortune, 1372-1380 (later used as *The Monk's Tale*)
Anelida and Arcite, c. 1380
Parlement of Foules, 1380
The Legend of Good Women, 1380-1386
Palamon and Ersyte, 1380-1386 (later used as *The Knight's Tale*)
Troilus and Criseyde, 1382
The Canterbury Tales, 1387-1400

Nonfiction

Boece, c. 1380 (translation of Boethius's *The Consolation of Philosophy*)
A Treatise on the Astrolabe, 1387-1392

Bibliography

Aers, David. *Chaucer*. Brighton: Harvester Press, 1986.

_____. *Chaucer, Langland, and the Creative Imagination*. Boston: Routledge & Kegan Paul, 1980.

Allen, Judson Boyce, and Theresa Anne Moritz. *A Distinction of Stories: The Medieval Unity of Chaucer's Fair Chain of Narratives for Canterbury*. Columbus: Ohio State University Press, 1981.

Arrathoon, Leigh A., ed. *Chaucer and the Craft of Fiction*. Rochester, MI: Solaris Press, 1986.

Ashton, Gail. *Chaucer: "The Canterbury Tales."* New York: St. Martin's Press, 1998.

Baldwin, Ralph. *The Unity of "The Canterbury Tales."* Copenhagen: Rosenkilde and Bagger, 1955.

Benson, C. David. *Chaucer's Drama of Style: Poetic Variety and Contrast in "The Canterbury Tales."* Chapel Hill: University of North Carolina Press, 1986.

Blamires, Alcuin. *Chaucer, Ethics, and Gender*. New York: Oxford University Press, 2006.

_____. "Chaucer the Reactionary: Ideology and the General Prologue to *The Canterbury Tales*." *Review of English Studies* 51.204 (2000): 523-39.

_____. "The Wife of Bath and Lollardy." *Medium Ævum* 58.2 (1989): 224-42.

Boitani, Piero, and Jill Mann, eds. *The Cambridge Companion to Chaucer*. New York: Cambridge University Press, 2003.

Borroff, Marie. *Traditions and Renewals: Chaucer, the Gawain-Poet, and Beyond*. New Haven, CT: Yale University Press, 2003.

Bowden, Muriel. *A Commentary on the General Prologue to "The Canterbury Tales."* 2nd ed. New York: Macmillan, 1967.

Bowers, John M. "'Dronkenesse Is Ful of Stryvyng': Alcoholism and Ritual Violence in Chaucer's Pardoner's Tale." *ELH* 57.4 (1990): 757-84.

Brewer, Derek. *Chaucer*. 3rd ed. London: Longman, 1977.

_____. *An Introduction to Chaucer*. London: Longman, 1984.

_____. *The World of Chaucer*. Rochester, NY: D. S. Brewer, 2000.

_____, ed. *Chaucer: The Critical Heritage*. 2 vols. Boston: Routledge & Kegan Paul, 1978.

Bronson, Bertrand H. *In Search of Chaucer*. Toronto: University of Toronto Press, 1960.

Brown, Peter, ed. *A Companion to Chaucer*. Malden, MA: Blackwell, 2000.

Burger, Glenn. *Chaucer's Queer Nation*. Minneapolis: University of Minnesota Press, 2003.

Carlson, David R. *Chaucer's Jobs*. New York: Palgrave Macmillan, 2004.

Carruthers, Mary. "The Wife of Bath and the Painting of Lions." *PMLA* 94.2 (1979): 209-22.

Chaucer, Geoffrey. *The Canterbury Tales: Fifteenth-Century Continuations and Additions*. Ed. John M. Bowers. Kalamazoo, MI: Medieval Institute Publications, 1992.

Chute, Marchette Gaylord. *Geoffrey Chaucer of England*. Rev. ed. New York: E. P. Dutton, 1962.

Coghill, Nevill. *The Poet Chaucer*. 2nd ed. New York: Oxford University Press, 1967.

Condren, Edward I. *Chaucer and the Energy of Creation: The Design and the Organization of "The Canterbury Tales."* Gainesville: University Press of Florida, 1999.

Cooper, Helen. *The Canterbury Tales*. Oxford Guides to Chaucer. 2nd ed. New York: Oxford University Press, 1996.

_____. *The Structure of "The Canterbury Tales."* London: Duckworth, 1983.

Crow, Martin M., and Clair C. Olson, eds. *Chaucer Life-Records*. Austin: University of Texas Press, 1966.

Curry, Walter Clyde. *Chaucer and the Mediæval Sciences*. 2nd ed. New York: Barnes & Noble, 1960.

Dinshaw, Carolyn. *Chaucer's Sexual Poetics*. Madison: University of Wisconsin Press, 1989.

Evans, Ruth, and Lesley Johnson, eds. *Feminist Readings in Middle English Literature: The Wife of Bath and All Her Sect*. New York: Routledge, 1994.

Gittes, Katherine S. *Framing "The Canterbury Tales": Chaucer and the Medieval Frame Narrative Tradition*. Westport, CT: Greenwood Press, 1991.

Gust, Geoffrey W. "Reevaluating 'Chaucer the Pilgrim' and Donaldson's Enduring Persona." *Chaucer Review* 41.3 (2007): 311-22.

Hansen, Elaine Tuttle. *Chaucer and the Fictions of Gender*. Berkeley: University of California Press, 1992.

Harding, Wendy, ed. *Drama, Narrative, and Poetry in "The Canterbury Tales."* Toulouse: Presses Universitaires du Mirail, 2003.

Hirsh, John C. *Chaucer and "The Canterbury Tales": A Short Introduction*. Malden, MA: Blackwell, 2003.

Horobin, Simon. *The Language of the Chaucer Tradition*. Rochester, NY: D. S. Brewer, 2003.

Howard, Donald R. *Chaucer: His Life, His Works, His World*. New York: E. P. Dutton, 1987.

_____. "The Conclusion of the Marriage Group." *Modern Philology* 57.4 (1960): 223-32.

_____. *The Idea of "The Canterbury Tales."* Berkeley: University of California Press, 1976.

Joost, Jean E. *Chaucer's Humor: Critical Essays*. New York: Garland, 1994.

Jordan, Robert M. *Chaucer and the Shape of Creation: The Aesthetic Possibilities of Inorganic Structure*. Cambridge, MA: Harvard University Press, 1967.

Kittredge, George Lyman. *Chaucer and His Poetry*. Cambridge, MA: Harvard University Press, 1915.

_____. "Chaucer's Discussion of Marriage." *Modern Philology* 9.4 (1912): 435-67.

_____. "Chaucer's Pardoner." *Atlantic Monthly* 72 (1893): 829-33.

Knapp, Peggy A. *Chaucer and the Social Contest*. New York: Routledge, 1990.

_____. "The Work of Alchemy." *Journal of Medieval and Early Modern Studies* 30.3 (2000): 575-99.

Knight, Stephen. *Geoffrey Chaucer*. New York: Blackwell, 1986.

Lambdin, Laura C., and Robert T. Lambdin, eds. *Chaucer's Pilgrims: An Historical Guide to the Pilgrims in "The Canterbury Tales."* Wesport, CT: Greenwood Press, 1996.

Lawrence, William Witherle. *Chaucer and "The Canterbury Tales."* New York: Columbia University Press, 1959.

_____. "The Marriage Group in the *Canterbury Tales*." *Modern Philology* 11.2 (1913): 247-58.

Leicester, H. Marshall, Jr. *The Disenchanted Self: Representing the Subject in "The Canterbury Tales."* Berkeley: University of California Press, 1990.

Lumiansky, R. M. *Of Sondry Folk: The Dramatic Principle in "The Canterbury Tales."* Austin: University of Texas Press, 1955.

Mann, Jill. *Chaucer and Medieval Estates Satire: The Literature of Social Classes and the General Prologue to "The Canterbury Tales."* New York: Cambridge University Press, 1973.

_____. *Feminizing Chaucer*. Rochester, NY: D. S. Brewer, 2002.

Muscatine, Charles. *Chaucer and the French Tradition*. Berkeley: University of California Press, 1957.

Neuse, Richard. *Chaucer's Dante: Allegory and Epic Theater in "The Canterbury Tales."* Berkeley: University of California Press, 1991.

O'Brien, Timothy D. "'Ars-Metrik': Science, Satire, and Chaucer's Summoner." *Mosaic* 23 (1990): 1-22.

Patterson, Lee. *Chaucer and the Subject of History*. Madison: University of Wisconsin Press, 1991.

_____. *Temporal Circumstances: Form and History in "The Canterbury Tales."* New York: Palgrave Macmillan, 2006.

Payne, Robert O. *Geoffrey Chaucer*. 2nd ed. Boston: Twayne, 1986.

Pearsall, Derek. *The Canterbury Tales*. Boston: Allen & Unwin, 1985.

_____. *The Life of Geoffrey Chaucer: A Critical Biography*. Malden, MA: Blackwell, 1992.

Percival, Florence. *Chaucer's Legendary Good Women*. New York: Cambridge University Press, 1998.

Robertson, D. W., Jr. *A Preface to Chaucer: Studies in Medieval Perspectives*. Princeton, NJ: Princeton University Press, 1962.

Rogers, William E. *Upon the Ways: The Structure of "The Canterbury Tales."* Victoria, BC: University of Victoria, 1986.

Rooney, Anne. *Geoffrey Chaucer: A Guide Through the Critical Maze*. Bristol: Bristol Press, 1989.

Rossignol, Rosalyn. *Chaucer A to Z: The Essential Reference to His Life and Works*. New York: Facts On File, 1999.

Rowland, Beryl, ed. *Companion to Chaucer Studies*. Rev. ed. New York: Oxford University Press, 1979.

Ruggiers, Paul G. *The Art of "The Canterbury Tales."* Madison: University of Wisconsin Press, 1965.

Schoeck, Richard, and Jerome Taylor, eds. *Chaucer Criticism*. 2 vols. Notre Dame, IN: University of Notre Dame Press, 1960-61.

Stillwell, Gardiner. "The Political Meaning of Chaucer's *Tale of Melibee*." *Speculum* 19 (1944): 433-44.

Sturges, Robert S. *Chaucer's Pardoner and Gender Theory: Bodies of Discourse.* New York: St. Martin's Press, 1999.

West, Richard. *Chaucer, 1340-1400: The Life and Times of the First English Poet.* New York: Carroll & Graf, 2000.

CRITICAL
INSIGHTS

About the Editor

Jack Lynch is Associate Professor of English at Rutgers University in Newark, New Jersey. He has published both scholarly and popular books and essays, mostly on British and American culture in the long eighteenth century. He is the author of *The Age of Elizabeth in the Age of Johnson* (2003), *Becoming Shakespeare: The Unlikely Afterlife That Turned a Provincial Playwright into the Bard* (2007), *Deception and Detection in Eighteenth-Century Britain* (2008), and *The Lexicographer's Dilemma: The Evolution of "Proper" English, from Shakespeare to South Park* (2009). He is also the editor of *The Age of Johnson: A Scholarly Annual* and coeditor of *Anniversary Essays on Johnson's Dictionary* (2005). His essays and reviews have appeared in scholarly forums such as *Eighteenth-Century Life*, *The Review of English Studies*, and *Studies in Philology*, as well as in *The American Scholar*, *The New York Times*, and the *Los Angeles Times*.

About *The Paris Review*

The Paris Review is America's preeminent literary quarterly, dedicated to discovering and publishing the best new voices in fiction, nonfiction, and poetry. The magazine was founded in Paris in 1953 by the young American writers Peter Matthiessen and Doc Humes, and edited there and in New York for its first fifty years by George Plimpton. Over the decades, the *Review* has introduced readers to the earliest writings of Jack Kerouac, Philip Roth, T. C. Boyle, V. S. Naipaul, Ha Jin, Ann Patchett, Jay McInerney, Mona Simpson, and Edward P. Jones, and published numerous now classic works, including Roth's *Goodbye, Columbus*, Donald Barthelme's *Alice*, Jim Carroll's *Basketball Diaries*, and selections from Samuel Beckett's *Molloy* (his first publication in English). The first chapter of Jeffrey Eugenides's *The Virgin Suicides* appeared in the *Review*'s pages, as well as stories by Rick Moody, David Foster Wallace, Denis Johnson, Jim Crace, Lorrie Moore, and Jeanette Winterson.

The Paris Review's renowned Writers at Work series of interviews, whose early installments include legendary conversations with E. M. Forster, William Faulkner, and Ernest Hemingway, is one of the landmarks of world literature. The interviews received a George Polk Award and were nominated for a Pulitzer Prize. Among the more than three hundred interviewees are Robert Frost, Marianne Moore, W. H. Auden, Elizabeth Bishop, Susan Sontag, and Toni Morrison. Recent issues feature conversations with Salman Rushdie, Joan Didion, Norman Mailer, Kazuo Ishiguro, Marilynne Robinson, Umberto Eco, Annie Proulx, and Gay Talese. In November 2009, Picador published the final volume of a four-volume series of anthologies of *Paris Review* interviews. *The New York Times* called the Writers at Work series "the most remarkable and extensive interviewing project we possess."

The Paris Review is edited by Philip Gourevitch, who was named to the post in 2005, following the death of George Plimpton two years earlier. A new editorial team has published fiction by André Aciman, Colum McCann, Damon Galgut, Mohsin Hamid, Uzodinma Iweala, Gish Jen, Stephen King, James Lasdun, Padgett Powell, Richard Price, and Sam Shepard. Poetry editors Charles Simic, Meghan O'Rourke, and Dan Chiasson have selected works by John Ashbery, Kay Ryan, Billy Collins, Tomaž Šalamun, Mary Jo Bang, Sharon Olds, Charles Wright, and Mary Karr. Writing published in the magazine has been anthologized in *Best American Short Stories* (2006, 2007, and 2008), *Best American Poetry, Best Creative Non-Fiction*, the Pushcart Prize anthology, and *O. Henry Prize Stories*.

The magazine presents two annual awards. The Hadada Award for lifelong contribution to literature has recently been given to Joan Didion, Norman Mailer, Peter Matthiessen, and, in 2009, John Ashbery. The Plimpton Prize for Fiction, awarded to a debut or emerging writer brought to national attention in the pages of *The Paris Review*, was presented in 2007 to Benjamin Percy, to Jesse Ball in 2008, and to Alistair Morgan in 2009.

The Paris Review was a finalist for the 2008 and 2009 National Magazine Awards in fiction, and it won the 2007 National Magazine Award in photojournalism. The *Los Angeles Times* recently called *The Paris Review* "an American treasure with true international reach."

Since 1999 *The Paris Review* has been published by The Paris Review Foundation, Inc., a not-for-profit 501(c)(3) organization.

The Paris Review is available in digital form to libraries worldwide in selected academic databases exclusively from EBSCO Publishing. Libraries can contact EBSCO at 1-800-653-2726 for details. For more information on *The Paris Review* or to subscribe, please visit: www.theparisreview.org.

Contributors

Jack Lynch is Associate Professor of English at Rutgers University in Newark, New Jersey. He is the author of *The Age of Elizabeth in the Age of Johnson* (2003), *Becoming Shakespeare: The Unlikely Afterlife That Turned a Provincial Playwright into the Bard* (2007), *Deception and Detection in Eighteenth-Century Britain* (2008), and *The Lexicographer's Dilemma: The Evolution of "Proper" English, from Shakespeare to South Park* (2009). He is also the editor of *The Age of Johnson: A Scholarly Annual*.

Judith Laird taught English at Southwestern Texas State University, San Marcos, and has served as Artistic Director of the Wimberley Players in Wimberley, Texas.

Benjamin Lytal teaches at the Pratt Institute. His criticism has appeared in *The Nation*, *The Believer*, and other publications.

Dominick Grace is Associate Professor of English and Chair of the Arts and Humanities Division of Brescia University College. His research interests are eclectic, and his publications range from work on Chaucer and Shakespeare to work on contemporary literature and popular culture.

Matthew J. Bolton is Professor of English at Loyola School in New York City, where he also serves as the Dean of Students. He received his doctor of philosophy degree in English from the Graduate Center of the City University of New York in 2005. His dissertation at the university was titled "Transcending the Self in Robert Browning and T. S. Eliot." Prior to attaining his Ph.D., he also earned a master of philosophy degree in English (2004) and a master of science degree in English education (2001). His undergraduate work was done at the State University of New York at Binghamton, where he studied English literature.

Rosemary M. Canfield Reisman was Professor of English and Department Chair at Troy University and is now Adjunct Professor at Charleston Southern University. She is the coauthor of *Contemporary Southern Women Fiction Writers* (1994) and *Contemporary Southern Men Fiction Writers* (1998) and has published numerous essays. She has presented lectures on British and American literature at the University of Hanover, Germany, at the American University in Cairo, and throughout the southeastern United States.

Lewis Walker teaches English at the University of North Carolina, Wilmington, where he focuses on the late medieval and early modern periods and occasionally offers a course on cartoons and comic strips. He has published articles on the influence of Chaucer on Shakespeare (*The Nun's Priest's Tale* on *Troilus and Cressida* and *The Franklin's Tale* on *The Tempest*). His bibliography *Shakespeare and the Classical Tradition* appeared in 2002. He has twice received the UNCW English Department's award for excellence in teaching.

E. Talbot Donaldson was Distinguished Professor of English Emeritus at Indiana University. He is the author of *Piers Plowman: The C-Text and Its Poets* (1966) and *Chaucer's Poetry: An Anthology for the Modern Reader* (1958) and coauthor of *Piers Plowman: The B Version* (1996). He is also the founding editor of *The Norton Anthology of English Literature*.

Donald R. Howard was Professor of English and Olive H. Palmer Professor in the

Humanities at Stanford University, where he taught for ten years. A renowned Chaucerian scholar, he is the author of *The Idea of the Canterbury Tales* (1976) and *The Three Temptations: Medieval Man in Search of the World* (1966), contributor to *Incipits of Latin Works on the Virtues and Vices, 1100-1500 A.D.* (1970), and producer of *Troilus and Criseyde and Selected Short Poems* (1976) and *The Canterbury Tales: A Selection* (1969).

H. Marshall Leicester, Jr., is Professor of English Literature at the University of California, Santa Cruz. He is the author of *The Disenchanted Self: Representing the Subject in "The Canterbury Tales"* (1990) and several articles on Geoffrey Chaucer.

Barbara Nolan was Professor Emeritus of English and Medieval Literature at the University of Virginia. Her interests spanned the literature and culture of the Middle Ages and the influence of classical Latin writers on medieval authors. She is the author of *Chaucer and the Tradition of the "Roman Antique"* (2008) and *The Gothic Visionary Perspective* (1977).

Glending Olson is Professor Emeritus of English and former Chair of the Department of English at Cleveland State University. His publications include *Literature as Recreation in the Later Middle Ages* (1982) and *The Canterbury Tales: Nine Tales and the General Prologue* (1989), which he coedited. He is also the author of "The Cultural Context of Chaucer's Fabliaux," published in 1968 by Stanford University.

Douglas Brooks was Associate Professor of English at Texas A&M University and General Editor of *Shakespeare Yearbook*. His books include *Printing and Parenting in Early Modern England* (2005) and *From Playhouse to Printing House: Drama and Authorship in Early Modern England* (2000).

Alastair Fowler is Regius Professor Emeritus of Rhetoric and English Literature at the University of Edinburgh. His publications include *How to Write* (2006), *Renaissance Realism: Narrative Images in Literature and Art* (2003), and *Time's Purpled Masquers: Stars and the Afterlife in Renaissance English Literature* (1996).

Martin Stevens served as Distinguished Professor of English at City University of New York and as Dean of Liberal Arts and Sciences at Baruch College before moving to San Francisco. His research interests are varied, but they often focus on linguistics, Old English, medieval Latin, Chaucer, and the Middle English drama. He is coeditor of *A Glossary for College English* (1966), *The Performance of Middle English Culture: Essays on Chaucer and the Drama* (1998), and *Old English Literature: Twenty-two Analytical Essays* (1976).

Katharina M. Wilson is Professor of Comparative Literature at the University of Georgia. She is the author of *European Women Writers* (1997), *Encyclopedia of Continental Women Writers* (1991), and *Women Writers of the Renaissance and Reformation* (1987).

Susan Crane is Professor of English and Comparative Literature at Columbia University, where her work focuses on English and French medieval literature and culture. Her publications include *The Performance of Self: Ritual, Clothing, and Identity During the Hundred Years War* (2002), *Gender and Romance in Chaucer's "Canterbury Tales"* (1992), and *Insular Romance: Politics, Faith, and Culture in Anglo-Norman and Middle English Literature* (1986).

Cathy Hume is Leverhulme Early Career Research Fellow in the Department of English at the University of Bristol. Her publications include "'The Name of Soveraynetee': The Private and Public Faces of Marriage in *The Franklin's Tale*" (2008) and "Domestic Opportunities: The Social Comedy of *The Shipman's Tale*" (2006). She is currently working on her first book, a revision of her Ph.D. thesis, which covers Chaucer's treatment of love, relationships, and marriage.

Greg Wilsbacher is a teacher of English and Director of the Newsfilm Library at the University of South Carolina, an archive of unique and rare film. He is the author of "Something Queer Is Going On: Sex and Methodology in the Middle Ages," which appeared in the spring 2003 issue of *College Literature*.

Steven F. Kruger is Associate Professor of English at Queens College and a member of the faculty in the Certificate Program in Medieval Studies at the City University of New York Graduate School. He has published articles focusing on the Middle Ages, Chaucer, and issues of sexuality in medieval literature. He is the author of *Dreaming in the Middle Ages* (1992).

Mark Miller is Associate Professor of English and Codirector of the Master of Arts Program in the Humanities at the University of Chicago. His focus is in the field of late-medieval literature, and he is the author of *Philosophical Chaucer: Love, Sex, and Agency in "The Canterbury Tales"* (2004). He is currently working on his upcoming book, *Handling Sin: Conditions of the Ethical in Fourteenth-Century English Literature*.

Rita Copeland is Professor of Classical Studies and English and Chair of Comparative Literature and Literary Theory at the University of Pennsylvania. Her publications span a range of literary fields and periods, including literary theory, history of rhetoric, and the Middle Ages. She is coeditor and cofounder of the Medieval Cultures Series published by the University of Minnesota Press and the annual *New Medieval Literatures*. She is the author of *Pedagogy, Intellectuals, and Dissent in the Later Middle Ages: Lollardy and Ideas of Learning* (2001).

Lawrence Warner is Senior Lecturer of English at the University of Sydney. He specializes in medieval literature and cross-cultural contact in medieval Europe and has published articles on subjects such as Chaucer's works, *Piers Plowman*, and other medieval texts. His book *The Lost History of "Piers Plowman": The Earliest Transmission of Langland's Work* is forthcoming.

David Wallace is Judith Rodin Professor of English at the University of Pennsylvania. He served as President of the New Chaucer Society from 2004 to 2006. His recent publications include *Premodern Places: Calais to Surinam, Chaucer to Aphra Behn* (2004), *The Cambridge Companion to Medieval Writing* (2003), and *The Cambridge History of Medieval English Literature* (1999).

Alice Miskimin is a Chaucer scholar and expert in Renaissance literature. She is the author of *The Renaissance Chaucer* (1975).

Acknowledgments_____

"Geoffrey Chaucer" by Judith Laird. From *Cyclopedia of World Authors, Fourth Revised Edition*. Copyright © 2004 by Salem Press, Inc. Reprinted by permission of Salem Press.

"The *Paris Review* Perspective" by Benjamin Lytal. Copyright © 2011 by Benjamin Lytal. Special appreciation goes to Christopher Cox, Nathaniel Rich, and David Wallace-Wells, editors at *The Paris Review*.

"Chaucer the Pilgrim" by E. Talbot Donaldson. From *PMLA: Publications of the Modern Language Association of America* 69, no. 4 (September 1954): 928-936. Copyright © 1954 by the Modern Language Association of America. Reprinted by permission of the Modern Language Association of America.

"Chaucer the Man" by Donald R. Howard. From *PMLA: Publications of the Modern Language Association of America* 80, no. 4 (September 1965): 337-343. Copyright © 1965 by the Modern Language Association of America. Reprinted by permission of the Modern Language Association of America.

"The Art of Impersonation: A General Prologue to *The Canterbury Tales*" by H. Marshall Leicester, Jr. From *PMLA: Publications of the Modern Language Association of America* 95, no. 2 (March 1980): 213-224. Copyright © 1980 by the Modern Language Association of America. Reprinted by permission of the Modern Language Association of America.

"'A Poet Ther Was': Chaucer's Voices in the General Prologue to *The Canterbury Tales*" by Barbara Nolan. From *PMLA: Publications of the Modern Language Association of America* 101, no. 2 (March 1986): 154-169. Copyright © 1986 by the Modern Language Association of America. Reprinted by permission of the Modern Language Association of America.

"Chaucer's Idea of a Canterbury Game" by Glending Olson. From *The Idea of Medieval Literature: New Essays on Chaucer and Medieval Culture in Honor of Donald R. Howard*, edited by James M. Dean and Christian K. Zacher (1992), pp. 72-90. Copyright © 1992 by Associated University Presses. Reprinted by permission of Associated University Presses.

"The Meaning of Chaucer's *Knight's Tale*" by Douglas Brooks and Alastair Fowler. From *Medium Ævum* 39, no. 2 (1970): 123-146. Copyright © 1970 by The Society for the Study of Mediæval Languages and Literature. Reprinted by permission of The Society for the Study of Mediæval Languages and Literature.

"'And Venus Laugheth': An Interpretation of the *Merchant's Tale*" by Martin Stevens. From *The Chaucer Review* 7, no. 2 (Fall 1972): 118-131. Copyright © 1972 by The Pennsylvania State University. Reprinted by permission of Penn State Press.

"*Figmenta* vs. *Veritas*: Dame Alice and the Medieval Literary Depiction of Women by Women" by Katharina M. Wilson. From *Tulsa Studies in Women's Literature* 4, no. 1 (Spring 1985): 17-32. Copyright © 1985 by the University of Tulsa. Reprinted by permission of the University of Tulsa.

"Alison's Incapacity and Poetic Instability in the Wife of Bath's Tale" by Susan Crane. From *PMLA: Publications of the Modern Language Association of America*

102, no. 1 (January 1987): 20-28. Copyright © 1987 by the Modern Language Association of America. Reprinted by permission of the Modern Language Association of America.

"'The Name of Soveraynetee': The Private and Public Faces of Marriage in *The Franklin's Tale*" by Cathy Hume. From *Studies in Philology* 105, no. 3 (2008): 284-303. Copyright © 2008 by the University of North Carolina Press. Used by permission of the publisher. www.uncpress.unc.edu.

"Lumiansky's Paradox: Ethics, Aesthetics, and Chaucer's 'Prioress's Tale'" by Greg Wilsbacher. From *College Literature* 32, no. 4 (Fall 2005): 1-28. Copyright © 2005 by *College Literature*. Reprinted by permission of *College Literature*.

"The Bodies of Jews in the Late Middle Ages" by Steven F. Kruger. From *The Idea of Medieval Literature: New Essays on Chaucer and Medieval Culture in Honor of Donald R. Howard*, edited by James M. Dean and Christian K. Zacher (1992), pp. 301-323. Copyright © 1992 by Associated University Presses. Reprinted by permission of Associated University Presses.

"Naturalism and Its Discontents in the *Miller's Tale*" by Mark Miller. From *English Literary History* 67, no. 1 (Spring 2000): 1-44. Copyright © 2000 by The Johns Hopkins University Press. Reprinted with permission from The Johns Hopkins University Press.

"The Pardoner's Body and the Disciplining of Rhetoric" by Rita Copeland. From *Framing Medieval Bodies*, edited by Sarah Kay and Miri Rubin (1994), pp. 138-159. Copyright © 1994 by the New Chaucer Society. Reprinted by permission of the New Chaucer Society.

"Adventurous Custance: St. Thomas of Acre and Chaucer's *Man of Law's Tale*" by Lawrence Warner. From *Place, Space, and Landscape in Medieval Narrative*, edited by Laura L. Howes (2007), pp. 43-59. Copyright © 2007 by the University of Tennessee Press. Reprinted by permission of the University of Tennessee Press.

"Chaucer and the Absent City" by David Wallace. From *Chaucer's England: Literature in Historical Context*, edited by Barbara A. Hanawalt (1992), pp. 59-90. Copyright © 1992 by the Regents of the University of Minnesota Press. All rights reserved. Reprinted by permission of the University of Minnesota Press.

"The Illustrated Eighteenth-Century Chaucer" by Alice Miskimin. From *Modern Philology* 77, no. 1 (August 1979): 26-55. Copyright © 1979 by The University of Chicago Press. Reprinted by permission of The University of Chicago Press.

Index

Clark, Kenneth, 419

Class issues. *See* Social class issues

Clergy, 7, 21, 23, 38, 80, 197, 206, 213, 341, 403

Clerk's Tale, The (Chaucer), 48, 68, 188-189, 217, 433

Coghill, Nevill, 27, 193

Coleridge, Samuel Taylor, 3

Collette, Carolyn, 231

Condren, Edward I., 24

Confessio Amantis (Gower), 4, 81, 141, 365

Consolation of Philosophy, The (Boethius), 57, 119, 128, 133

Constable, Giles, 244

Convivio (Dante), 143, 357

Cook's Tale, The (Chaucer), 150, 391

Cooper, Helen, 18, 70, 256

Coss, Peter, 245

Courtly love, 40, 46, 53, 68, 90-91, 390

Craik, T. W., 185

Croxton *Play of the Sacrament*, 280

Cruttwell, Patrick, 86

Culler, Jonathan, 113

Curry, Walter Clyde, 22, 159, 164, 166, 183

Cutts, Cecilia, 295

Daniell, David, 65

Dante, 6, 31, 67, 81-82, 125, 200, 357, 384

David, Alfred, 229, 254, 329

Davis, Craig R., 238, 242

Decameron, The (Boccaccio), 4, 32, 141, 156, 229, 379

Derrida, Jacques, 113, 252

Deschamps, Eustache, 71

Dillon, Bert, 69

Dinshaw, Carolyn, 24, 348, 350, 358, 365

Dollimore, Jonathan, 348

Donaldson, E. Talbot, 20, 85, 106, 113, 116, 185-186, 194, 256

Dor, Juliette, 231

DuBois, Page, 343

Duby, Georges, 206, 219

Dundes, Alan, 250

Eagleton, Terry, 255, 261, 263, 268

Edwards, Robert R., 229

Enders, Jody, 356

Evans, Ruth, 45

Fairchild, H. N., 160

Fehrenbacher, Richard W., 61

Feichtinger, Barbara, 46

Female characters, 24, 45, 51, 198, 213, 216

Feminist literary theory, 24, 45, 337

Fichte, Joerg O., 365

Filostrato, Il (Boccaccio), 6

Foucault, Michel, 332, 335, 342, 354

Fradenburg, Louise O., 24, 267

Frame narratives, 12, 31, 110, 114, 141, 156

Franklin's Tale, The (Chaucer), 53, 228

Friar's Tale, The (Chaucer), 38, 131

Friedman, Albert B., 294

Frost, William, 100

Furnivall, F. J., 17, 443

Fyler, John M., 242

Ganim, John, 335

Gaylord, Alan T., 137, 253

Gender identity, 25, 216, 222, 298, 313, 321, 335, 337, 344, 348, 350

General Prologue (*The Canterbury Tales*), 17, 27, 56, 62, 69-70, 101, 107, 111, 115, 147, 186, 416, 422, 430

Gentilesse, 50, 229, 241, 433